MW00649447

Exploring Choices

The Psychology of Adjustment

Donald Meichenbaum
University of Waterloo

Richard Price
University of Michigan

E. Jerry Phares
Kansas State University

Naomi McCormick
SUNY College at Plattsburgh

Janet Hyde
University of Wisconsin

Scott, Foresman and Company
Glenview, Illinois   Boston   London

Library of Congress Cataloging-in-Publication Data

Meichenbaum, Donald
  Exploring choices.

  Bibliography: p.
  Includes index.
  1. Adjustment (Psychology)
I. Meichenbaum, Donald.
BF335.E96   1988   158   88-18582
ISBN 0-673-18695-4

Acknowledgments are listed at the back of the book on pages
465 and 466, which constitutes a legal extension of the copyright page.

PREFACE

We live in a world that continually presents new and demanding choices. At the same time, the field of psychology is providing new insights and techniques for coping and making choices, even when those choices are stressful or difficult. These observations shaped our goals in writing *Exploring Choices: The Psychology of Adjustment.* We wanted to show that psychology can help people make more effective choices in coping with the problems of everyday life. We wanted to write a book that provides insight into the stresses of life and into the coping processes used on the job and in personal relationships. Finally, we wanted to write a book that discusses sex roles and committed relationships and illuminates the difficult choices they present.

The content and organization of *Exploring Choices* reflect these goals. The first section of the text focuses on the person and the processes of choice and challenge throughout the life span. It emphasizes theories of personal adjustment and the development of self-concept, motivation, and personal values. The chapters in this first section provide a broad overview of theories of personal development and show how psychology can help students learn strategies for more effective coping.

The second section of the text focuses on stress and coping processes. The chapters in this section help students understand not only stress and coping but also strategies to improve coping ability in the future. This section also helps students to learn about the range of professional resources available to them if they wish to seek psychological help.

The third section of the text considers personal relationships and sexuality in a frank, straightforward fashion. Both unconventional and conventional personal and sexual relationships are considered with sensitivity and thoughtfulness. The chapters in this section reflect an appreciation of the challenges in sex-role orientation and sexual relationships that confront adults of all ages today.

The final section of the text considers work in today's world and the issues of individual choice in a society that presents a range of challenges. These include technological change, sexual harassment, career choices, work stress, racial prejudice, and pressures for conformity.

Two special features in this text help students to experience the issues discussed in each chapter as directly as possible. A feature called "Exploring Choices" gives students an opportunity to examine concrete examples of the choices they may have to confront in their own lives. This special section can be used by instructors for homework or to stimulate class discussion. A second major feature, called "On the Research Frontier," shows how new developments in psychological research actually apply to the lives of students in such areas as making career choices or making decisions about intimate relationships.

To make the text even more useful to students, glossaries in the margin define important psychological concepts where they are first encountered in the text. Chapter summaries highlight key ideas and provide an additional study aid.

To further aid students in the use of the book, a Study Guide has been prepared by Deborah Weber and Velma Pomrenke of the University of Akron. John Lyke of Metropolitan State College developed the Instructor's Manual, which also contains test items.

In writing *Exploring Choices: The Psychology of Adjustment*, we have had the help of a number of able professionals. At Scott, Foresman, we would like to thank Scott Hardy, Paula Fitzpatrick, Kay Bartolo, and Sue Baugh. In addition, we would like to thank the following reviewers for their insightful suggestions and commentary on various drafts of the manuscript:

- Paul Aschenbrenner, Hartnell College
- Leslie Caplan, Ball State University
- James Davis, Southwest Missouri State University
- Lynn Godat, Portland Community College
- Margaret P. Isaac, Central State University
- Christin H. Lewis
- John Lyke, Metropolitan State College
- Velma Pomrenke, University of Akron
- Jay B. Pozner, Jackson Community College
- James Riley, Southeastern Massachusetts University
- Fred Robbins, Daytona Beach Community College
- Robert Tomlinson, University of Wisconsin—Eau Claire
- Deborah Weber, University of Akron
- David Weight, Brigham Young University

They have helped make *Exploring Choices* a text that students can use to make more effective choices in a rapidly changing world.

Donald Meichenbaum
Richard Price
E. Jerry Phares
Naomi McCormick
Janet Hyde

CONTENTS

EXPLORING CHOICES

ON THE RESEARCH FRONTIER

Exploring Choices

The Psychology of Adjustment

Chapter 1

Introduction: Choices in a Changing World

The following people are talking about choices and challenges in their own lives or the lives of people they know. They are dealing with both external demands and inner feelings. While the people speaking are college students, some of them will face even greater challenges after they graduate from college and begin careers and independent lives.

- "I never had much competition in high school, but it sure is different in college. I wasn't prepared for the difference. It's pretty scary. . . ." —Emily
- "Stan drinks because he's frightened of girls, or at least that's how it got started. Things seem to go better for him if he has a few drinks before he goes out, and he just keeps going during the evening."—Sally
- "I had an erection but was afraid to make love with her. I was afraid that I might go soft in the middle of it and that she would think I was gay."—Bill
- "I'm not sure whether I should play an aggressive male role or a more passive one. Neither one really feels right."—John
- "Every time I think I'm ready for the exam, but then I seem to go blank. What are my parents going to say when they see my grades?"—Don
- "Now that I've become really close to Neil, I don't know what is going to happen to our relationship after college. He wants to have a family, but I have my heart set on law school."—Bev
- "I have always wanted to major in English, but everyone tells me that I should go into computer programming."—Charles
- "My roommate is pretty depressed and hasn't gone to class in a week. I think maybe I ought to tell the dorm counselor, but I'm not sure what to do."—Barb
- "Almost flunking out was the best thing that ever happened to me. For the first time, I realized that it was up to me—no one else was going to do it for me."—Richard

In this chapter, we hear from people like these and learn a good deal about how they cope with the challenges that confront them.

CHALLENGES IN A CHANGING WORLD

You have already faced many challenges, and you will face many more as your life unfolds. Some are predictable because they are more likely to happen at a particular stage of life, as when young adults enter the world of work for the first time. Other challenges, such as the loss of a loved one, may be quite unpredictable and call on your deepest reserves. Still other challenges await those who have chosen to chart a completely new course in life. For example, more people with families and jobs are going back to school for personal growth and to increase career options.

Many challenges arise because we are living in a rapidly changing world. Technology is transforming the worlds of work and leisure in unexpected ways. A larger proportion of our population is elderly, and these people are seeking new sources of community and life satisfaction. Expectations about the roles of women and men in our society are also altering rapidly. The changes create new demands on both sexes at work and in family life. Today, more couples find themselves wrestling with two careers and a marriage when job opportunities and geography do not seem to match.

Table 1–1 shows some of the major changes in our society that create challenges and choices now and will in the years ahead. Your developing sense of yourself as a person, worker, parent, and friend to others will be shaped to a great extent by these changes. Whether you work at home or outside the home, whether you decide to have children, and even the way in which you care for your aging parents will be affected by current social changes.

But you do have choices. How you decide to handle these challenges will have an important effect on you and on those who are part of your life. Your choices and how you cope with change are what this book is about.

Changes in society create new demands on both sexes.

TABLE 1–1   Changes and Challenges in Today's World
_____

We are becoming an information society.
- Scientific and technical information now doubles every five years.
- Having more information available makes choices a necessity.

Technology will dominate work and home life.
- Computers now allow large companies to write unique contracts for each employee.
- Real estate firms are using videotapes to show customers properties.

Self-help is replacing institutional help.
- More couples are delivering their babies at home.
- Hospices allow terminally ill people to die with dignity.

We are becoming more ethnically diverse.
- There are now over one hundred ethnic groups in the United States.
- Advertising firms are specializing in different ethnic markets.

The family is being redefined.
- Only 7 percent of today's society fits the traditional family profile of male breadwinner, house-wife, and two children.
- Single parents, co-habitation, two career couples, and blended families from previous marriages are on the rise.

Women have more options than ever before.
- Women are choosing to have children later in life.
- By 1990 the number of women earning business BA's will be eight times that of the 1960s.
- More choices for women mean more choices for men as well.

Traditional work organizations are changing.
- Workers may have several bosses.
- Quality circles give workers new control over how they do their jobs.

_____
Source: Adapted from J. Naisbett (1984). *Megatrends: Ten new directions transforming our lives.* New York: Warner Books.

ADJUSTMENT: COPING AND CHOICE

In writing this book we have adopted a particular approach to human adjust-ment. Our view reflects our own assumptions about how people think and behave, and about the relationship between behavior and well-being. We be-lieve it is important to talk about these ideas at the outset, since they form our underlying philosophy about adjustment. To begin, we define **adjustment** as the active process of coping and making choices that affects an individual's well-being and personal growth. In the following section, we consider each aspect of our definition in more detail.

adjustment the active process of coping and making choices that affects an individual's well-being and personal growth

Adjustment Is Active

Adjustment is not a passive acceptance of the status quo or conformity with social conditions as they currently exist. On the contrary, humans are active, striving seekers and problem solvers. We are all social cooperators and compet-itors who shape the environment as well as being shaped by it. Even Helen

Keller as a child without sight, hearing, or speech was an active, striving person, struggling to make her needs known to the world around her. Despite her handicaps, she grew up to inspire generations of people with her courage.

Adjustment Is a Process

Adjustment is a continuous, evolving interaction between the individual and the environment of things, ideas, and people. Adjustment is a dynamic process, and in that sense, it is continuously changing. We all have good and bad days, and daily hassles. We all face major challenges in our lives—crises, failures, and achievements—that upset our equilibrium for extended periods of time. Yet, because adjustment is dynamic, we work to regain our balances and go on with our lives.

Adjustment Involves Coping

coping action or thought that responds to the demands of the environment

Coping is how we respond to the demands of the environment in terms of solving problems or overcoming difficulties. Our coping responses can be routine and simple, such as dressing according to the weather. Or they can be complex and long-term, such as deciding on a major that will help us meet our life goals.

It is important to recognize that not all coping responses produce positive outcomes or are necessarily adaptive in the long run. In one of the examples at the beginning of this chapter, Sally's friend used drinking as a way of dealing with his discomfort in the company of girls. While drinking may have reduced his social anxiety in the short term, the long-term impact of this form of coping could be a dependence on alcohol that is difficult to overcome.

Adjustment Involves Choice

Our methods of coping with demands from the environment are not aimless or random. Adjustment involves making choices among alternative courses of action. It follows that the more we know about the choices available to us and the likely consequences of those choices, the better able we will be to choose the best outcomes for our adjustment.

psychological well-being a subjective sense of happiness, optimism, or control that is a result of effective coping

This does not mean, of course, that all of our choices are rational; far from it. We constantly make decisions with less than perfect information about the choices available to us or their consequences. Nevertheless, as the philosopher Jean-Paul Sartre observed, choice is unavoidable. In fact, *not* choosing, by withdrawing from a situation, for example, is choosing, too.

Adjustment Affects Well-Being and Personal Growth

physical health a state of physical well-being and absence of illness

The way we cope and the choices we make have important consequences for our **psychological well-being** and **physical health**. Because coping and making

personal growth increasing personal capacities in terms of skill, insight, or wisdom

psychology the scientific study of behavior, the goal of which is to predict, understand, and control behavior

psychoanalytic theory school of psychology based on the work of Sigmund Freud that looks beyond conscious awareness to unconscious desires and impulses

choices are active psychological processes, they place demands that produce a certain amount of psychological strain. When you study for examinations in this course, you will experience some tension and expend a certain amount of effort to learn the material. Normally, challenges like exams are well within your capacity to handle.

Severe and prolonged challenges, however, can have more serious effects on well-being. Some survivors of war, natural disasters, and concentration camps, for example, show more permanent signs of psychological strain, such as prolonged anxiety or depression.

At the same time, coping and making choices can provide learning experiences that contribute to **personal growth**. Successfully mastering a new job or a difficult course can provide new confidence and skills to meet new challenges in the future. As a result, coping with life's challenges is not something to do only when things get tough. Coping and choosing are the very processes by which individuals become better able to meet future challenges.

WHAT PSYCHOLOGY CAN TEACH ABOUT ADJUSTMENT

social learning theory learning theory of personality that describes the two-way interaction between the individual and the environment

humanistic-existential theory a theory that views each person as an integrated whole and that takes an optimistic view of the human potential for growth and choice

research systematic collection of observations to test their consistency with a hypothesis or theory

determinists people who believe that all events have causes, even if the causes are not yet known

Psychology is the scientific study of behavior. Like biology, chemistry, and physics, psychology seeks to establish general principles about behavior. Psychologists use the tools of theory and research to uncover and verify those general principles. The following section examines three basic theories of adjustment, each of which provides complementary and sometimes competing views of human behavior. These theories—psychoanalytic, social learning, and humanistic-existential—give powerful insights about the nature of human behavior from very different vantage points.

Psychoanalytic theory focuses on our aggressive and sexual impulses and how we deal with them. On the other hand, the **social learning theory** concentrates on how we learn social behavior through reward, punishment, and observation of others. **Humanistic-existential theory** emphasizes choice and personal growth. While no single theory has emerged to explain all human behavior, the perspectives provided by these three approaches have deepened and enriched understanding of what might cause certain behaviors.

Psychologists know that theories by themselves cannot provide proven general principles about behavior. Theories must be tested through **research**. Throughout the text we offer numerous examples of the ways psychologists have used research to test theoretical propositions and to examine the range of circumstances under which a theoretical proposition may be true.

As Price and Lynn (1986) observe, scientific researchers are a lot like detectives. Both scientists and detectives are basically **determinists**. That is, they are both primarily concerned with the causes of events. For a detective, the causal agent may be a criminal; for a scientist it may be a chemical in the blood. In each case, the search is for causes. In addition, both detectives and scientists must reconstruct past events. A detective may have only the victim and the scene of the crime. A scientist may have only a pattern of behaviors and a sketchy life history with which to work.

Both scientists and detectives rely heavily on observation to gather evidence in their searches for truth, and both are concerned about the dependability of their observations. Some detectives take photographs, search for fingerprints, and question witnesses independently. Some psychological researchers use standardized interviews and tests. Both gather evidence to increase the **reliability** of their observations.

Based on their theories, detectives and scientists construct **hypotheses** about the causes of events. During their investigations, they try to rule out the less plausible hypotheses. To do so, each draws on a body of knowledge. For the detective, this may include information about the chemical composition of cigar ashes. For the scientist, it may include understanding how people's problem-solving strategies change with age. Both use prior knowledge to test their hunches (theories).

reliability the extent to which a test or observation method is consistent in measuring

hypotheses propositions tested in an experiment and denied or supported by empirical results but never proved conclusively

Scientists rely heavily on observation.

Finally, both scientists and detectives search for the truth but tend to be extremely cautious about the conclusions they draw—and for similar reasons. Their conclusions must withstand rigorous scrutiny from a jury of critical peers. In one case, it is the jury in the courtroom; in the other, it is scientists throughout the world.

The analogy between detectives and scientists, however, should not be carried too far. One important difference is that scientists are concerned with arriving at general statements that make it possible to group apparently dissimilar events under a single rule or generalization. Detectives, on the other hand, wish to narrow the search to the most likely suspects. They are usually less interested in the generalizations that might be produced from their work (Price & Lynn, 1986).

Both theory and research, then, are tools that psychologists use to pursue the scientific and practical goals of psychology, but what are those goals, and how are they related to human adjustment? In general, psychology has three goals: predicting, understanding, and controlling behavior.

prediction the foretelling of future events or behaviors based on current knowledge

understanding the ability to see the relationships between behaviors and events in terms of some larger scheme or idea

control the ability to influence events or behaviors

1. **Prediction.** Psychologists might ask, Under what circumstances is a bystander willing to help someone in distress, and when might the bystander ignore the person? Understanding those circumstances can help us predict future helping behavior because we learn under what conditions it is likely to occur.

2. **Understanding.** Psychologists are often concerned with understanding the relationships between our needs and values and how we behave in different social situations. They might ask, Why does one person see a situation as competitive while another sees it as an opportunity for cooperation?

3. **Control.** Psychology also seeks to discover how we can control behavior, including our own. Why do some people overeat? Why does smoking seem to be such a difficult habit to break? Knowledge about controlling behavior can help us learn to be more effective in anxiety-provoking situations, such as important examinations or job interviews.

Because of its goals of predicting, understanding, and controlling behavior, psychology can be particularly useful when it comes to learning about the nature of adjustment. For example, psychology can help us understand the processes of coping and making choices in our own lives. Why do some people persist at difficult tasks while others give up? We can also learn how our choices are related to our own well-being and personal growth. For example, Janis (1983) has found that people who carefully consider both the positive and negative consequences of a course of action are more likely to persist in seeking their goals and are usually much happier about the outcomes. They not only realize the rewards of achievement but also recognize some of the sacrifices required to succeed.

LOOKING AHEAD

The chapters that follow cover a great deal of territory. They explore what psychologists have learned about personal adjustment, about stress and coping, about the choices in intimate relationships, and about the challenges presented by work and the larger society.

The Person: Choice and Challenge Through the Life Span

What are we really like? Are we boiling with sexual and aggressive impulses striving for expression? Or as some psychologists suggest, is our personality really a product of conditioning, heavily determined by previous experiences, rewards, and punishments? Are we all free to choose who we will become?

What are we really like?

Chapter 2, "Theories of Personal Adjustment," begins by discussing psychological theories of personality development and tells about adjustment. Many people never stop asking the question, Who am I? Is the self consistent from situation to situation, or are we all like actors who play out different roles as the circumstances seem to require? To understand our motivations and who we are, we must know our own values. How do we clarify our values? Are values something that should be taught, and if so, who should do the teaching?

Chapter 3, "The Person: Self, Motivation, and Values," explores these questions and some of the connections between values, motivation, and adjustment. For example, shortly after Ben arrived at college he began to feel homesick. It seemed as if everyone else was confidently exploring the possibilities of a new life away from home. Ben sorely missed the reassuring feeling that his parents were there to help him take on difficult decisions and to support him when the going got tough. In fact, Ben was coping with one of the major tasks of late adolescence, developing a sense of autonomy in the move away from childhood and into adult roles.

Chapter 4, "Patterns of Adjustment Through the Life Span," examines how the tasks and challenges of adjustment change throughout a person's life. Even in middle and old age, there are critical periods when people face new choices and life circumstances essential to personal adjustment.

Stress, Coping, and Getting Help

Close your eyes for a moment and think back to the last time you took a major exam. If you are like most people, you experienced considerable stress. You felt butterflies in your stomach. Your hands may have been sweaty, and you may have had a hard time getting to sleep the night before. Stress is an inevitable part of living, and you will experience it many times throughout your life. But how are people who cope effectively with stress different from those who do not?

Chapter 5, "The Nature of Stress and Coping," looks at the relationship between stress and adjustment. Is it possible to predict adjustment by adding up the life changes to which someone has been exposed, such as moving to a new city, taking a new job, or losing an important relationship? Can a certain amount of stress be good?

People do not passively experience major life changes; they actively strive to cope with them. Chapter 6, "Ways of Coping with Stress," explores what psychologists have learned about effective strategies for coping with stress. Does relaxation help? What problem-solving steps can you take to cope more effectively with life's stresses? This chapter discusses strategies that psychologists have recently developed for actually inoculating people against some of the future stresses they may experience. How does that inoculation work? Can we inoculate people to make major surgery less stressful or a final exam easier to take?

Stress is an inevitable part of living.

While many of our strategies for coping are adaptive and help us meet life's challenges, some strategies are not healthy either physically or emotionally. Chapter 7, "Maladaptive Behavior," examines the impact of negative coping patterns on physical and mental health. Perhaps you know someone who deals with setbacks in life by eating compulsively, or someone who wants to quit smoking but has been unable to do so. Chapter 7 examines how people develop behaviors that harm health. It also outlines strategies that can help eliminate maladaptive health behaviors. It examines a variety of abnormal emotional responses to stress, including severe anxiety, deep depression, and suicidal tendencies that can result from overwhelming life challenges.

Despite our efforts to cope, life's demands sometimes can become temporarily overwhelming. When and where should one seek professional help? What kinds of help are available? How does one choose the right one? Chapter 8, "Getting Help," discusses various types of psychotherapy and counseling to help you understand what is available and whether getting professional help is appropriate for you.

Relationships and Sexuality

Perhaps nothing is so important to adjustment as the kind and quality of personal relationships with others. These relationships are influenced by our assumptions of what it means to be male or female. Chapter 9 is "Sex Roles and Relationships." Is certain work really "women's work"? Is someone with a strong male or female sex-role identification better or less adjusted than someone with a more flexible idea of what it means to be a man or a woman?

The most involving, and ultimately the most satisfying, relationships are the intimate ones. Intimacy implies choices. Should sex be part of an intimate relationship? How do you decide? How do you communicate your needs to others? Chapter 10, "Intimate Relationships," discusses the differences between liking and loving, how people select others for intimate relationships, and how to build an intimate relationship.

Almost thirty years ago, a national survey (Gurin, Veroff, & Feld, 1960) indicated that most people in America believed there was something wrong with a woman who remained single throughout her life. Today, a repeat of the survey reveals that Americans no longer believe this. Must everyone get married? Chapter 11, "Marriage and Other Committed Relationships," reveals that marriage is only one of several kinds of committed relationships and that no single model is ideal. However, any committed relationship, including living together, involves choices regarding the division of labor, the nature of power, and decisions about parenthood.

During the Victorian era at the end of the nineteenth century, people—especially women—were not supposed to enjoy their sexuality. Today, many feel something is wrong if they do not enjoy it. Chapter 12, "Sexuality," examines the role of sexuality in adjustment. What are the choices for contraception, and what are their costs and risks? What are the choices about premarital

Perhaps nothing is so important to adjustment as personal relationships.

sex? What parts do values play in making those choices? What about homo-sexuality and adjustment?

Work and Social Influences

Work is more than a job. It can become a source of psychological strength and adjustment or a major cause of distress. Chapter 13, "Work in Today's World," looks at the technological and social changes occurring in the world of work. Women are entering the workplace in unprecedented numbers and changing traditional ideas about careers for men and women. Choosing a career is more complicated than ever before. Is there a relationship between personality and career? Do women executives experience special stresses? How is the relation-ship between family and work changing? What does all of this have to do with you?

Humans are intensely social, trying to figure out ways to become success-fully interdependent. We influence and are influenced by one another. Every day, we are confronted with choices about helping someone else in need or ignoring that need. In many ways our own personal adjustment is related to the ability of our larger society to care and to cooperate. Chapter 14, "Social Influence and Individual Choice," discusses what psychologists tell us about social influence and choice. Under what circumstances can prejudice be over-come? Are there times when it is necessary to choose between the well-being of the group and that of the individual? Can you really make a difference in your own social world?

SPECIAL FEATURES OF THE BOOK

We have designed two features of the book—"Exploring Choices" and "On the Research Frontier"—to make your learning experience more effective and interesting. We have also included a number of learning aids.

Exploring Choices

Our goal in writing this book is to help you better evaluate the choices you will face in life. Knowing your options and evaluating them thoughtfully are central to meeting the challenges of adjustment. Because we think that making choices is so critical to successful adjustment, we have included a special feature, "Exploring Choices," in each chapter. We highlight a critical issue in each case and show how your choices can make an important difference in adjustment. We think exploring those choices in terms of your unique circumstances is valuable in self-exploration.

On the Research Frontier

Psychology is also a field of scientific research. We believe firmly that new psychological knowledge can contribute to personal adjustment. Consequently, we have included a second feature in each chapter, called "On the Research Frontier." Our goal is to show you how research can deepen your understanding of yourself and your social world. Sometimes scientific findings may challenge your previously held beliefs. In other cases, they may provide deeper insight into your values and behavior. Understanding what is on the research frontier can help you to be a critical consumer of psychological knowledge.

Learning Aids

We have included several learning aids to help you master the psychological principles and concepts central to understanding the psychology of adjustment:

1. A *running glossary* of important concepts and terms is presented in the margins of the text. The same terms and definitions are repeated alphabetically in the back of the book.
2. *Chapter outlines* are presented at the beginning of each chapter to give an overview of the contents.
3. *Chapter summaries* review each of the important ideas discussed in the chapter.

SUMMARY

1. Rapid changes are occurring in the world of work, the nature of the family, technology, and sex roles. Such changes require you to choose and cope effectively.

2. Adjustment is the active process of coping and making choices. It affects your psychological well-being, physical health, and personal growth.

3. Psychology is the scientific study of behavior. Its findings can provide knowledge to improve your adjustment and personal effectiveness.

4. Psychology draws upon a number of theories to explain behavior, including psychoanalytic, social learning, and humanistic-existential theories.

5. Psychology tests theories and improves our knowledge of adjustment through systematic observation of events or behavior to eliminate less plausible hypotheses.

6. The goals of psychology are to predict, understand, and control behavior. Each of these goals is important in developing your knowledge of adjustment, coping, and choosing and in applying that knowledge to your own well-being and personal growth.

7. In the rest of the book, we discuss theories of personal adjustment, the nature of stress and coping, personal relationships, and work and social influences. Our discussions are aimed at you as an actively coping, choosing, and developing person.

8. To make this book more interesting and more relevant to your own life, we include special features: "Exploring Choices" and "On the Research Frontier." Other learning aids are designed to make you a more effective student.

Part 1

THE PERSON: CHOICE AND CHALLENGE THROUGH THE LIFE SPAN

Chapter 2

THEORIES OF PERSONAL ADJUSTMENT

personality pattern of
characteristic thoughts,
feelings, and behaviors
that persists over time
and situations and dis-
tinguishes one person
from another

Nearly everyone is fascinated by personality. Why? For one thing, if we believe we are good judges of people or know something about what makes them tick, we feel we have some control over our complex, ever changing world. Phares (1988) defines **personality** as "the pattern of characteristic thoughts, feelings, and behaviors that persists over time and situations and distinguishes one person from another" (p. 592). If we can make sense of this pattern in ourselves and others, we are better able to make informed decisions and rational choices in our lives. This ability to make decisions and choices can pave the way for better adjustment to life.

Understanding people is not easy, however. Human beings are among the most complicated creatures on earth. In addition, the ways they think, feel, or act reflect the particular circumstances in which they find themselves. A shy person faced with a life-and-death situation may suddenly discover the strength to act like a leader. Even though we think we understand someone's personality, we cannot possibly know everything that lies hidden under the surface. We can never completely predict the kinds of situations the person will have to confront.

You can begin by attempting to understand the one person who is always available for study—yourself! Are your sexual and aggressive impulses striving for expression? Have you been programmed by your genetic structure or your childhood upbringing to think, feel, and act in certain ways? Or do you freely choose who and what you are and the life you lead? What you believe about human personality depends on how you view it.

THE MANY VIEWS OF PERSONALITY

Three of the most notable students of human nature have been Sigmund Freud, Carl Rogers, and B. F. Skinner. Each is recognized as an authority in his own right, but it would be difficult to find three more radically different views of human nature.

Freud worked in the sexually repressed Victorian age. He was educated in a scientific world that emphasized the role of instincts in guiding behavior. He saw people as driven by sexual and aggressive impulses struggling for expression. Rogers grew up in a religious family, attended theological school, and worked with young college students. He viewed humanity as striving for growth and self-enhancement. Skinner was drawn to behavioral psychology. He worked with animals confined in a laboratory environment. He came to regard human personality as shaped by a system of rewards and punishments, much as animals are trained.

Each of these men—and other researchers after them—looked at the complex human personality and saw one or two facets. It may be more accurate to describe a human being as a gem with a multitude of facets, each reflecting slightly differently as it catches a different source of light. Perhaps no one can comprehend the enormous complexity of human personality, but each advance in knowledge brings us a little closer. Different theories of personality can help us along the road to that comprehension.

THE IMPORTANCE OF THEORIES

Although most people believe that theories are for scientists or philosophers, everyone is a theorist of sorts. Each time you speculate about why people act the way they do or what characteristics make people attractive or unattractive, you are developing theories about personality.

implicit personality theory theory used by laypersons to account for the way another person's traits are seen as fitting together to form the personality

Bruner and Tagiuri (1954) called this kind of speculation **implicit personality theory**. The term refers to the fact that everyone develops a set of ideas (theory) to explain how other people's personality characteristics fit together. For example, some people believe that good-looking men or women are vain or that people with close-set eyes are untrustworthy. Still others may be convinced that brilliant people are always emotionally unstable. Right or wrong, complex or simple, such ideas help us make sense of the world. They can make us feel that we have some aspects of life under control.

Theories serve much the same purpose in the work of psychologists. For example, clinical psychologists use theories to develop different strategies to help their clients. Psychologists who believe that people are afraid of their sexual and aggressive urges might try to help clients understand these urges and become less afraid of them. Those who believe that human problems can be traced to faulty learning might provide new learning experiences to help their clients overcome the previous ones.

There is a difference, however, between ordinary people's implicit theories and the more formal psychological theories. Implicit theories are often haphazard, based on vague feelings or prejudices about others, and difficult to explain. Formal theories, based on research and careful observations of human nature, allow us to communicate about personality in a more exact manner. They also provide a framework that helps organize what we know about people and predict and understand human behavior better. That framework also can help us be more consistent in how we view people. It can even help us search for new insights about personality and adjustment.

UNDERSTANDING HUMAN PERSONALITY

This section explores three formal theories or approaches to understanding human personality. These approaches are the psychoanalytic, behavioral and social learning, and humanistic-existential.

The Psychoanalytic Approach

The psychoanalytic approach refers to theories that view behavior as a surface reflection of forces that are largely unconscious and that determine our every thought, feeling, and action. This approach has its origins in the work of Sigmund Freud (1933/1964). His pioneering work in psychoanalysis began in the late 1800s and continued until his death in 1939. Since Freud's theory of personality and adjustment has been enormously influential, it is fitting that we begin our survey of theoretical approaches with an outline of his ideas.

Sigmund Freud did the pioneering work in psychoanalysis.

psychic determinism
psychoanalytic notion that a person's every behavior, thought, and emotion have meaning and purpose

unconscious motivation term describing the notion that much of what people do, think, and feel is motivated by unconscious forces

Two key elements. Freud believed that two key factors—psychic determinism and unconscious motivation—must be considered to understand people. **Psychic determinism** is the idea that everything we do, think, and feel has meaning and purpose. Slips of the tongue, career choices, and even some food preferences have a cause and a function; they are not accidents or unrelated events. The causes of these incidents may be buried in early childhood, but they can be uncovered.

The second major element, **unconscious motivation**, was used to explain that much of what we think, feel, and do is motivated by unconscious forces within. Our conscious mind remains unaware of them. Freud thought of the mind as a map containing the conscious, preconscious, and unconscious (see Figure 2–1). The *conscious* region is the smallest. It contains everything that we are aware of at any given moment.

The *preconscious* region consists of the memories, feelings, and perceptions that are accessible to us. This does not mean that we can recall a specific memory or perception right away, but with a little effort and prompting, we can retrieve it. Everyone has had the experience of having to search his or her mind for a name or telephone number and eventually finding it.

The *unconscious* is by far the largest region. It contains all our urges, drives, and impulses. Sexuality and aggression reside here, and they continually strive for expression and gratification. We are not aware of their full impact, but according to Freud, we are influenced strongly by them.

FIGURE   2-1   Freud's Psychic Map of the Mind

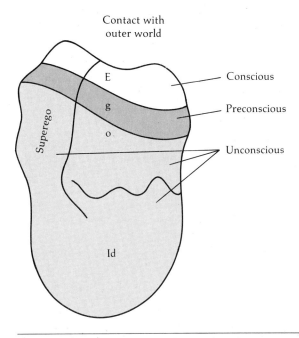

Source: Redrawn from *The Structure and Meaning of Psychoanalysis* by W. Healy, A. F. Bronner, and A. M. Bowers (New York: Knopf), 1930. Copyright 1930 by Alfred A. Knopf, Inc. Used with permission

life instincts in psychoanalytic theory, the instincts responsible for the positive, constructive aspects of behavior (referred to as Eros by Freud)

death instincts in psychoanalytic theory, the instincts responsible for the destructive aspects of human behavior (referred to as Thanatos by Freud)

id in psycholanalytic theory, the deep, unconscious part of the personality composed of the biological, instinctual drives, which seek immediate gratification

Instincts. Freud regarded all human behavior as the interplay of two powerful sets of instincts or drives. **Life instincts** (called Eros) account for the positive, constructive side of human actions. Urges such as hunger or thirst and the higher forms of activity (such as love, creativity, and spiritual aspiration) are products of the life instincts. On the other hand, the capacities to hurt people, to wage war, and to be self-destructive are outgrowths of the **death instincts** (called Thanatos). Life instincts are more prominent in people who are reasonably happy and well adjusted. When the death instincts dominate, people become maladjusted to the point where they may attempt suicide or even harm other people. While an important part of Freud's theory at the time, the concepts of life and death instincts no longer play such a prominent role in current psychoanalytic thinking.

Personality structure. Freud believed that the psychic map is dominated by three structures that fight to control our behavior. These structures, which come to make up the personality, are the id, ego, and superego (see Figure 2–1).

The **id** is the deep, inaccessible portion of the personality. It is in direct contact with our unconscious, our biological processes, and everything fixed or inherited in our personal constitutions. Freud believed the id represents a form of primitive reality and that its contents are accessible only through dreams or clues from our more neurotic behaviors.

All instinctual urges reside in the id, which has no contact with everyday reality and is without morals, ethics, or logic. It demands complete gratification of desires and operates on the **pleasure principle**; that is, it seeks to avoid pain and to obtain pleasure. The id will even try to imagine or hallucinate the satisfaction of its needs for food, water, or pleasurable sensations if they are not gratified in reality. Of course, such a strategy doesn't work well for long, and out of such failures another structure—the ego—arises. The id never ceases to make its demands, however.

The **ego** can be described as the executive of the personality. It is the organized, rational part of us that operates on the **reality principle**. It defers immediate satisfaction or pleasure until the proper time and enables us to sacrifice short-term gains to acquire long-term goals. The ego uses learning, perception, and memory to satisfy the demands of the id in ways that will not put the organism in danger. The ego works hard to gratify the id, but it must also satisfy an equally hard taskmaster, the superego or conscience.

The **superego** is a kind of moral director that represents the ideals, values, and standards of society as they are interpreted by parents or parent figures. The superego develops as a result of the rewards and punishments given by parents and other authority figures. The jobs of the superego are to block socially unacceptable impulses from the id, to pressure the ego to do the right thing rather than the merely convenient or practical thing, and to encourage the person to strive for perfection.

Freud saw the ego as balancing the demands of the id and the superego. If the superego is weak, more of the id's demands are met, and the person may appear impulsive, selfish, childish, or amoral. If the superego is too strong, the person may appear overly controlled, inhibited, and excessively judgmental. A person with a weak ego may be torn between satisfying primitive urges and trying to live a rigidly controlled life. These three structures must find some way to coexist in a healthy balance. As Geiwitz and Moursund (1979) noted:

> Imagine a sex-starved hedonist, a black-frock-coated Puritan minister, and a totally humorless computer scientist chained together and turned loose in the world and you have a good approximation of what Freud was trying to show us about the personality.
>
> Because they are chained together, the id, ego, and superego cannot decide to go their separate ways. They have no alternative but to adjust to one another. And the result, for better or for worse, is the adult human personality. (p. 27)

How personality develops. With this psychic map, Freud was confronted with the puzzle of how human personality develops from infancy through adolescence. His work with his patients began to supply what Freud considered an answer. Many of his patients told him that in childhood they had experienced sexual encounters with their parents. They found these experiences deeply disturbing, and several of his patients had developed various emotional and mental illnesses as a result.

pleasure principle in psychoanalytic theory, the operational principle by which the id seeks to avoid pain and obtain pleasure

ego in psychoanalytic theory, the reality-oriented portion of the personality, which utilizes learning and reasoning to satisfy id impulses in the light of real-world constraints

reality principle in psychoanalytic theory, the operational ego principle whereby gratification is postponed until an appropriate situation is identified

superego in psychoanalytic theory, the conscience, representing the ideals, values, and standards of society as acquired from the parents or parent figures

Freud at first believed them and wrote a paper proposing that sexual abuse in childhood is the origin of many neuroses. Over time, however, he was unable to accept that the sexual abuse of children by parents or relatives was as widespread as his patients' stories indicated (Masson, 1984). As a result, he developed the concept of infantile sexuality—that is, it is the *child* who sexually desires the parent, not the parent who desires the child. This concept has dominated psychoanalytic thinking for over eighty years. It is only now gradually being altered, as we learn that sexual abuse of children by parents and relatives is more common than once thought.

In any case, Freud constructed a theory of personality development that emphasized psychosexual matters. He described five stages of personality development associated with different parts of the body: (1) the oral stage, (2) the anal stage, (3) the phallic stage, (4) the latency period, and (5) the genital stage.

The *oral stage* is a period of total dependency for the child. It lasts about eighteen months. Mouth, lips, and tongue are the areas from which the infant receives gratification, and sucking and swallowing reduce tension. When the teeth erupt—at about eight months or so—the child can bite in response to frustration. According to Freud, this is the beginning of the child's knowledge of separateness from the mother.

The *anal stage* covers the period from about one to two years of age. The chief modes of pleasure seeking shift to those of expelling and retaining feces. The child may have to deal with weaning, the birth of a sibling, and toilet training during this time. As a result, a battle of wills often develops between parents and child. The parents' demands that the child forgo immediate gratification and learn the ways of society set the stage for the crude beginnings of superego development.

From the age of two or so until five or six, the child is in the *phallic stage*. The genital region becomes the major pleasure-seeking area. This period may be marked in boys by such events as urination contests or in girls by the desire to play nurse. The child also starts to develop a growing awareness of sexuality—a primitive realization that babies are not made in heaven, but in the bedroom.

According to Freud, this period marks the beginning of the "family romance," when boys cling to their mothers and girls to their fathers. In a childish way, the little boy has made a sexual choice—his mother—and perceives his father as a rival. Perhaps at this time, the boy has been caught masturbating, which may lead some parents to go so far as to threaten castration to stop the practice. The threats may be explicit ("If you don't quit, we will cut that thing off"), but they are more often subtle and indirect. This family triangle involving boys is referred to as the **Oedipus complex**, after the character from Greek mythology (Oedipus unknowingly killed his father and married his mother). The boy becomes increasingly anxious because of the conflict of wanting his mother while fearing retaliation from the father.

The child unconsciously resolves this dilemma by identifying with the father and repressing his dangerous sexual feelings for his mother. He adopts the father's values, goals, and sometimes even his mannerisms and transforms his sexual impulses toward his mother into affection for her. This resolution of the Oedipal conflict is a big step toward the full development of the superego.

Oedipus complex in psychoanalytic theory, sexual longing by a boy for the mother, which occurs during the phallic stage

Electra complex in psychoanalytic theory, the counterpart in girls of the Oedipus complex in boys

In girls, the conflict is different and more complex. It is referred to as the **Electra complex**, after a Greek legend in which a daughter (Electra) pursues her father. In Freud's theory, a girl becomes aware of her lack of a penis at this stage and blames her mother for the loss. Whereas the boy's fear of castration leads him out of the Oedipus complex, the girl's belief that she has been castrated leads her into the Electra complex. She makes her father the object of her sexuality in the hopes of sharing his penis and overcoming her loss. This may push the girl into a lifelong search for power and envy of the male role—what Freud termed *penis envy*. Gradually the Electra complex wanes, as the girl realizes she cannot possess the father, and she turns her attention to other males. She begins to lose her anger toward her mother and begins to identify with her and her roles as wife and mother.

Freudian explanations of the development of females are male-centered. Many psychoanalysts are realizing that socially defined roles for women assign them far less power than men are permitted. What women seek is not the penis but an equal opportunity to exercise their own abilities.

With the resolution of the Oedipus and Electra complexes, Freud stated, the child enters the *latency period*, which lasts until age twelve or thirteen. The child's sexual interests recede, and he or she seeks out friends of the same sex. Boys generally want nothing to do with displays of kissing or affection. For girls, the latency period is usually shorter, with a less stringent avoidance of sex.

neurotic anxiety in psychoanalytic theory, a fear that unconscious id impulses will find expression

The onset of puberty and the hormone changes that accompany it bring about the genital stage. Sexual interests intensify once more. The ultimate development in this stage is establishing a mature interest in relationships with the opposite sex, with the object of marriage and starting a family.

moral anxiety in psychoanalytic theory, an emotional state experienced as guilt, stemming from the threat of punishment by the superego

In Freud's view, the mature, well-adjusted person successfully negotiates all these psychosexual changes. But things do not always go so smoothly. If we receive too little gratification at a given stage, we may seek to regain those lost pleasures throughout our lives. Too much gratification can prevent us from outgrowing a particular stage. Thus, our psychosexual experiences help shape the adults we become. Those who undergo severe psychosexual stages may develop various types of neurotic problems as defenses against anxiety.

ego defenses methods employed by the ego that distort experience to protect the person against threats from the id

Anxiety. Anxiety in Freud's theory is a painful emotional state that ranges from mildly uncomfortable to crippling. **Neurotic anxiety** is especially threatening, since it is an apprehension or dread that some terrible unconscious impulse is about to break through into the conscious mind. **Moral anxiety**, can occur as a threat of punishment from the superego when an impulse from the id begins to surface. Anxiety serves as a signal to the ego that steps must be taken to change the conditions that created it. The ego employs a variety of defenses to protect the individual from the effects of anxiety.

repression in psychoanalytic theory, an unconscious ego defense in which threatening impulses or thoughts are involuntarily banished to the unconscious

Ego defenses. Everyone uses **ego defenses** from time to time. They become symptoms of poor mental health only when an individual relies on them excessively to deal with everyday life. The most basic defense is **repression**, in which we involuntarily banish to the unconscious impulses or events that truly threaten the way we view ourselves. Repression does not destroy an impulse, but it removes it from the conscious mind and relieves anxiety about it. However, repression is a rather primitive technique. When the task of ego defense becomes more difficult, we may turn to such other techniques as projection, reaction formation, displacement, and denial, as shown in "Exploring Choices: Conflict and Ego Defenses" on pages 30 and 31.

Modifications of psychoanalysis. Not all psychoanalysts have agreed entirely with Freud. For example, such subsequent Freudians as Alfred Adler, Karen Horney, Erich Fromm, Harry Stack Sullivan, and Erik Erikson (Hall et al., 1985) believed that Freud overemphasized sexual urges at the expense of family relationships and other social factors. Erikson, in particular, has been a major figure in developing a psychosocial version of psychoanalysis. In his view, the crises and threats people encounter in life give them chances to triumph over adversity and master their own lives. His optimism contrasts sharply with the Freudian themes of conflict and warfare among the id, ego, and superego. Erikson (1963) describes a series of eight developmental stages from birth to death, each representing a crisis to be overcome. His emphasis on development throughout life gives his work broader relevancy to human existence than does Freud's, which focuses mainly on childhood.

The nature of adjustment. In the psychoanalytic view, healthy individuals have made peace with the unconscious and do not need to resort to repression and other ego defenses outlined in "Exploring Choices: Conflict and Ego Defenses." They take pleasure in love and work. However, many of their adult traits can be traced to psychosexual stages of childhood. For example, in Freudian theory, the lawyer who likes to paint as a hobby may be expressing traces of a childish interest in feces. That such traits originate in the psychosexual stages does not make them problems. They become problems only when they are excessive, bring unhappiness, or otherwise interfere with one's life.

Adjusted people can accept their inner needs, understand them, and learn to direct them rather than be directed by them. The choices one makes, although colored by childhood experiences, are not compulsions driven by fears that the id or superego will dominate. Rather, choices become reasoned responses to reality, made with the awareness that instinctual energies can be recognized and harnessed and the superego can be modified.

The Behavioral and Social Learning Approaches

Not everyone views human nature as do the Freudians, who look inside people to check on the battles among id, ego, and superego. Others believe that the environment is the critical element in shaping the ways people behave. Never mind about instinctual urges or demands from a mythical superego. Outside forces can override them all. In the 1930s, John Watson (1930), a major exponent of the behavioral approach, boasted:

EXPLORING CHOICES

CONFLICT AND EGO DEFENSES

Many people are beset by conflicts. They have strong desires but are bothered by anxieties as they contemplate trying to fulfill those desires. These anxieties are unpleasant, but at the same time, they can be insistent. How, then, can an individual ward off the anxiety and yet achieve at least some gratification of the desires in the process? Freud had some answers. He felt that the conflict is between the id and reality or the superego. The job of the ego is to either satisfy or thwart the desires of the id and still protect the person from punishment from the superego or the environment. To do all this, the ego employs a variety of defenses. The defense most often used depends on the person's earlier experiences and psychosexual development. The choice of defense seems to be unconsciously determined. An example shows how this works.

Desire 1:   I would love to have sexual intercourse with that person.

Anxiety: This feeling is bad; it goes against everything I have been taught. I will surely be punished by my conscience if I go through with it.

Conflict: Between the id and superego.

Ego defenses that may help one cope with the conflict follow:

Ego Defense	Behavioral Outcome
Projection—one's unacceptable thoughts or desires are attributed to others.	The feeling "I want to have sex with you" is changed into "you want to have sex with me."
Reaction formation—one's conscious thoughts or desires become the opposite of the unconscious ones.	The feeling "I want to have sex with you" is changed into "you are very unattractive to me."

Give me a dozen healthy infants, well-formed, and my own specified world to bring them up in, and I'll guarantee to take any one at random and train him to become any type of specialist I might select—doctor, lawyer, artist, merchant-chief, and, yes, even beggarman and thief, regardless of his talents, penchants, tendencies, activities, vocations, and race of his ancestors. (p. 65)

While this boast is an exaggeration, it is in tune with the Western tradition, which sees people as changeable and adaptable. These notions are in keeping with the ideals of equality, democracy, and upward mobility, particularly in the United States.

In short, behavioral and social learning approaches emphasize learning in their attempts to understand personality. Whereas Freud had to infer what his patients were thinking, psychologists such as Watson relied on objective ob-

Ego Defense	Behavioral Outcome
Repression—one's sexual desires are prevented from reaching consciousness.	All sexual impulses toward the person are denied access to awareness.

Another example of a desire and conflict follows.

Desire 2: I would really like to strike out at the people who make me feel bad about myself.

Anxiety: If I express my hostilty toward these people, they may retaliate and hurt me more or else not provide the support I would like.

Conflict: Between the id and reality.

Ego defenses that may help one cope with the conflict follow:

Ego Defense	Behavioral Outcome
Displacement—an id impulse is deflected from its true object to a less threatening one.	Angry at a friend for critical remarks, the person picks a fight with a younger brother.
Denial—protecting the self from an unpleasant reality by refusing to perceive it.	One's perception becomes "I never feel angry" or "I'm not afraid of anyone."

Of course, these are only a few of the ego defenses. In addition to these, Anna Freud (1946) has discussed fantasy, emotional insulation, intellectualization, undoing, regression, identification, and overcompensation.

servations of behavior and the conditions that made it change. In their search to understand this learning process, and thus know more about human personality, behavioral theorists rely heavily on two major forms of learning: classical conditioning and operant learning.

classical conditioning process in which a previously neutral stimulus repeatedly paired with another stimulus that normally produces a given response produces the latter response

Classical conditioning. **Classical conditioning** is a very basic form of learning. It was made famous by Pavlov and his experiments with dogs. Classical conditioning refers to a process by which a neutral stimulus, such as a ringing bell, is repeatedly linked with another stimulus, such as food, which normally produces a given response, such as salivation in a dog. After repeated trials, the neutral stimulus will produce that same response—the dog will salivate when it hears a bell ringing whether or not food appears.

STANLEY   By **MURRAY BALL**

Watson and Rayner (1920) wanted to prove that many emotional reactions are really learned and thus have no mysterious origins. They gave a little boy a white rat to play with. The child showed no fear of the animal and enjoyed their time together.

The researchers then began banging a steel bar with a hammer every time the child started to approach the rat. The child was frightened of the loud noise. Soon he associated the noise with the rat. In time, the mere presence of the white rat made the boy extremely fearful. Watson and Rayner had shown that a previously neutral or even positive stimulus (the rat) through repeated pairings with a negative stimulus (the loud noise) could produce the fear response. However, by modern research standards, Watson and Rayner's conclusions are considered highly tentative and subject to further testing (Samelson, 1980).

Figure 2–2 shows the basic elements of classical conditioning. Since nearly all children are instinctively afraid of loud noises, no conditioning is required to elicit their fear. Thus, the loud noise is termed an unconditioned stimulus (US). It provokes an unconditioned response (UR) of fear. Children do not instinctively fear such things as white rats, but they can be conditioned to do so. As a result, the white rat is termed a conditioned stimulus (CS), which when linked with the loud noise (US) elicits a conditioned response (CR) of fear. The conditioned response is similar to the unconditioned response but is generally not so strong or intense.

However, if the conditioned stimulus occasionally is not paired with the unconditioned stimulus, the conditioned response may eventually die out. This loss of the conditioned response is called *extinction*. For instance, if the rat had been repeatedly presented without the loud noise, the child would probably have lost his fear of the animal. In some cases, extinguished responses may recur on their own—a phenomenon known as *spontaneous recovery*. Even if the boy's fear response had been extinguished by failure to accompany appearance of the rat with a loud noise, the fear might have occasionally returned.

Classical conditioning can also result in *generalization*, in which, for example, a child learns to fear not only white rats but other animals or objects that

FIGURE 2-2   Diagram of Classical Conditioning Illustrating How the
                    Association Between Fear and a White Rat Is Developed

Before conditioning:

CS (white rat) ⟶ Neutral response, no fear

US (loud noise) ⟶ UR (fear)

During the conditioning process:

CS (white rat) ⟍

US (loud noise) ⟶ UR (fear)

After conditioning:

CS (white rat) ⟶ CR (fear)

resemble them. Likewise, a child who has a harsh parent may learn to see all adults in authority as harsh. In short, classical conditioning can sometimes result in people's responding in stereotypical ways. When they generalize too readily, their learning experiences have, in effect, robbed them of the ability to choose among responses. This fact can result in many adjustment problems. In contrast, *discrimination* is the ability to distinguish between the conditioned stimulus and other objects that resemble it. When we can discriminate among stimuli, we recapture the ability to make choices.

Operant conditioning. Not everything is learned through classical conditioning. In **operant conditioning**, we learn from the consequences of our own behavior and that of other people. For example, we learn to turn the key in the ignition because it starts the engine. We confide in a friend because we learn that person will not make fun of us.

operant conditioning process by which responses become more likely when followed by desirable consequences and less likely when followed by negative ones

Operant conditioning works on the basis of reinforcers, positive and negative reinforcement, and punishments and rewards. Responses become more likely when followed by desirable consequences and less likely when followed by undesirable ones. A *reinforcer* is anything that increases the likelihood that a certain response will occur. According to behaviorist B. F. Skinner (1938), *positive reinforcement* is an outcome or event that encourages one to maintain or increase certain behavior. For example, someone remarks that blue is a flattering color for you, so you buy more clothes in blue. A *negative reinforcement* also increases the likelihood of a response because it allows one to eliminate or avoid an unpleasant situation. For example, if an aspirin relieves your headache, you are likely to take an aspirin again when you get another headache. **Punishment**, in contrast, decreases the likelihood of a behavior's occurring again because of the negative consequences. For example, you fail to study and keep up your grades; as a result, you lose your scholarship. *Rewards* tend to strengthen responses. For example, you study hard, bring your grades up, and

punishment event that decreases the likelihood that behavior will occur, since the latter is seen as leading to an aversive outcome

win a scholarship the next year. These are relatively simple notions, but they can be very powerful in affecting behavior.

According to Skinner, it is not necessary to look inside people's complex psyches. If we observe how people behave in relation to various stimuli, we can tell whether those stimuli are reinforcing behavior or discouraging it. In Skinner's approach, **discriminative stimuli** allow us to know more precisely when to respond or to avoid responding. We learn through prior experience—known as antecedent conditions in behaviorist terms—to be more discriminating in our responses. If you want to go up in an elevator, for instance, you learn to enter it only when the up arrow is lit.

Skinner also believed that all human behavior is controlled by the outcomes or consequences that follow it; systematically scheduling the reinforcements that follow someone's behavior, it is possible to control that behavior. We can even mold, or shape, behavior if we work at it. For example, it is possible to teach a rat to dance by **shaping** its behavior, that is, by reinforcing the movements it makes that resemble dancing. Rewarding the rat with food or some other reinforcer for stepping to the right, then to the left, selectively reinforces the responses that lead to the final act of "dancing." Soon, the rat is dancing. As shown in "On the Research Frontier: Applications of Shaping in Humans," operant conditioning can be used to shape many aspects of human behavior as well.

Social learning. It may seem to you that classical and operant conditioning cast human learning and behavior in a somewhat mechanical light. If so, you are not alone. While social learning theorists agree that such theories explain a great deal of human behavior, they also take into account that human beings think, reason, and anticipate. When a reinforcement occurs, people are likely to evaluate it and assess its meaning (Mischel, 1986). We are not always the passive receivers of conditioning influences. We are active participants, who can affect our environment as much as we are affected or changed by it. Social learning theorists also point out that we learn with and from the other humans around us. We are not like isolated laboratory animals pecking at keys to get food. Human learning is truly **social learning**!

Julian Rotter (1954) was one of the first psychologists to build his work around the concept of social learning. He contends that our behavior is determined by not only rewards and punishments but also by our attitudes and expectations regarding those rewards and punishments. For example, people tend to study hard only if they think that by doing so they have a reasonably good chance of getting a passing grade. If they believe getting a passing grade is impossible, they are not likely to study. In other words, behavior is guided by the size and occurrence of rewards, as the behaviorists claim, and also by the extent to which we anticipate or expect our behavior to achieve that reward or avoid that punishment successfully.

Problem-solving expectancies. Social learning theorists have proposed that people learn to develop generalized **problem-solving expectancies** in pursuing

discriminative stimuli in operant conditioning, characteristic or specific stimuli that come to signal the proper occasion for a given response

shaping in operant conditioning, the gradual molding of behaviors into the final desired behavior through reward

social learning learning in a social context, which emphasizes the role of cognitive processes

problem-solving expectancies in Rotter's approach, beliefs about how best to categorize situations in order to solve the problems presented by them

ON THE RESEARCH FRONTIER

APPLICATIONS OF SHAPING IN HUMANS

There are many examples of the use of the operant principle of shaping in humans. Let us consider the following two possibilities.

1. Bourne and Ekstrand (1982) discussed how shaping can be applied to a child with a short attention span. This problem often leads to classroom disruptions and poor grades. First, the child is rewarded for paying attention to schoolwork for even very short periods. For example, if the child can concentrate on studying for only a minute, then the child is rewarded at the end of every minute of actual studying. After several days, when the habit is established, the stakes are raised a bit. Now a reward is given only after a two-minute period of studying. This is gradually increased until the child is studying for thirty minutes or more without interruption. From a modest beginning, the selective and systematic application of rewards can shape behavior to the desired product.

2. Isaacs, Thomas, and Goldiamond (1960) reported a dramatic illustration of shaping. A hospitalized schizophrenic had been mute for nineteen years. Accidentally, the therapist dropped some cigarettes and gum and noticed that the patient glanced at the gum. This became the response from which to begin the shaping. For two weeks, the therapist would hold up a stick of gum in front of the patient. When the patient clearly noticed the gum, it was given to him. For the next two weeks, the therapist demanded that the patient move his lips before being given the gum. After four weeks, the gum served to elicit eye and lip movements and a vocalization "resembling a croak." Two more weeks followed, in which the therapist required the patient to say "gum, gum" before receiving the reward. By six weeks, the patient would say spontaneously "gum, please." Still later, the patient began to reply to questions about his age and name. While this example of shaping is hardly a breakthrough in curing schizophrenia, it does illustrate its potential therapeutic role.

It should be added that analogous procedures have been used to help autistic children develop improved language skills. Likewise, similar shaping methods have been used to help overcome disabling fears.

their goals. That is, through prior experience people develop attitudes and ways of thinking that they apply to solve a variety of problems that arise in their lives. For instance, one person learns to trust others; another person learns to be suspicious of people. The first person, when trying to make a decision about buying a car, tends to believe what the salesperson says. The second person tends to assume the salesperson is lying. Both have learned to apply generalized expectancies to a new situation, in which they must make a decision partly on the basis of what someone else tells them. In "Exploring Choices: The Locus of Control," we see how people's beliefs regarding who has control over their lives can affect the choices they make.

Observational learning. We have just seen how social learning theorists supplement simple conditioning ideas with concepts that recognize people as thinking, planning organisms. It is also true, however, that people can learn a great deal by observing others. **Observational learning**, also called *modeling*, is learning without direct reinforcement. This simple yet powerful notion has been developed over recent years by Albert Bandura (1974). For example, teenagers do not learn the latest dances by repeated conditioning experiences that build up dancing movements one by one as with the dancing rat described earlier. They learn by watching each other or people on television and practicing at home. At the same time, we do not observe and slavishly imitate everything we see. We pick and choose what and who to imitate. Gradually, we build our own unique behavior. "On the Research Frontier: Observational Learning Cuts Both Ways" describes how observational learning relates to television viewing.

According to Bandura, observational learning involves several stages: attention, memory, imitation, motivation, and vicarious reinforcement. We start learning by observation through *paying attention* to those around us. We must also have the opportunity to pay attention. A child growing up in a home in which no one reads has little opportunity to observe reading behavior.

Second, we must *remember* the behavior we see. Usually, forming mental images and rehearsing the model's behavior helps us to remember. Third, we have to imitate, or *reproduce*, the behavior, practicing until we perfect it. This process requries *motivation*. To pay attention to appropriate models, remember what they do, and then reproduce their behavior means that we must want to do so.

Part of what motivates us may be the expectation of a reward when we have mastered the behavior. For example, your friends' admiration for your skill in playing an electric guitar may motivate you to practice more. So may winning a spot on the volleyball or baseball team. The idea of **vicarious reinforcement** can also boost motivation. That is, when we see our model rewarded for some action, we, too, may feel rewarded. If the singer you are modeling yourself after wins a Grammy, in some sense you share that reinforcement, and you may imagine yourself receiving a similar award someday.

The nature of adjustment. According to the behavioral theorists, mental health has nothing to do with repression or ego defenses, as the psychoanalysts assert. The maladjusted person is the product of faulty conditioning—learning inappropriate responses to stimuli. A child who is rewarded for developing an "upset stomach" in order to avoid school learns the value of such behavior and may continue it into adult life. The adjusted person, on the other hand, has been rewarded for making what society regards as appropriate responses to stimuli.

observational learning learning by means of observing a live or symbolic model (sometimes referred to as modeling)

vicarious reinforcement achievement of reinforcement by observing a model's being reinforced

EXPLORING CHOICES

THE LOCUS OF CONTROL

In order to solve problems or have an impact on our environment, we must believe that our efforts can make a difference. This expectancy about the relationship between our actions and their outcomes is called *locus of control* (Rotter, 1966). People who believe that outcomes are due to luck, fate, or powerful other forces are called externals. In contrast, internals believe their behaviors or personal qualities determine outcomes. Of course, internal and external beliefs vary somewhat, depending on the nature of the situation. Nevertheless, believing that the locus of control is internal rather than external can have a powerful influence on how one chooses to behave (Phares, 1978). As an example, much research in health-related behavior has shown that internals are more likely to pay attention to health messages, to try to improve their physical health, and even to be less susceptible to high blood pressure and heart attacks. Thus, internals choose behaviors that have a greater possibility of improving their health. Externals, however, are more likely to be passive in such matters, since they do not think behavior has an impact one way or the other.

Several scales measure locus of control. The following items are similar to ones that appear on some of those scales. They will give you an idea of how people are classified into the internal and external categories. However, note that while it is convenient to use the terms *internal* and *external*, locus of control is not a typology. Instead, it is a continuum. A person can fall anywhere along that continuum, from internal at one end to external at the other.

I more strongly believe that:

1. a. Many people can be described as victims of circumstance.
   b. What happens to other people is pretty much of their own doing.
2. a. Much of what happens to me is probably a matter of luck.
   b. For the most part, I control my own fate.
3. a. The world often seems so complicated that I just cannot figure things out.
   b. The world may be complicated, but I can usually work things out by effort and persistence.
4. a. It is silly to think one can really change another's basic attitudes.
   b. When I am right, I usually can convince others.
5. a. Most students would probably be amazed at how much grades are determined by lucky events.
   b. The marks I get in class are almost always a matter of my own responsibility.

Our beliefs about personal control are very important. They pervade many areas of our lives. The relationship between personal control and stress is further elaborated in Chapter 6.

ON THE RESEARCH FRONTIER

OBSERVATIONAL LEARNING CUTS BOTH WAYS

The television set in the average North American home is probably turned on for over seven hours per day. Children watch television an average of two to six hours every day (Liebert, Neale, & Davidson, 1973). Television is a powerful force in our society because it gives us the chance to see things we might not otherwise see. So far, so good. But what we really are saying is that television offers everyone the opportunity for observational learning and an opportunity to imitate what we observe. The problem is that people can imitate bad things as well as good ones. Stated another way, observational learning cuts both ways. Some research illustrates this quite well.

Some years ago, Gerbner (1972) estimated that 80 percent of television dramas contained some form of violence. By age sixteen, the average child has seen 13,000 murders on television (Waters & Malamud, 1975). Recently, a group of investigators studied the relationship between television violence and aggression in its viewers (Huesman, Lagerspetz, & Eron, 1984). They interviewed and tested 758 boys and girls in the United States and another 220 in Finland. All the children were in grades one to five.

It was a complicated study, but several findings stood out. First of all, for girls in the United States and for boys in both countries, seeing violence on television was related to aggressiveness. Both the kind of television violence they saw and the regu-larity with which they saw it were related to aggressive behavior in those children. For boys, the relationship was even stronger when they identified with aggressive television characters.

The investigators suggested that seeing violence on television leads to aggressiveness and also that behaving aggressively leads to more viewing of television violence. What kind of child is most likely to be aggressive? The investigators described an aggressive child as one who does the following:

1. Watches violent programs when they are on.
2. Thinks such shows faithfully portray life.
3. Identifies strongly with aggressive television characters.
4. Often has aggressive fantasies.
5. If a girl, likes boys' activities.
6. Has an aggressive mother.
7. Has parents with lesser education and social status.
8. Is doing poorly in school.
9. Is unpopular with peers.

The investigators conclude that observational learning and attitude changes are involved with television viewing. Justifications for violence and cues for solving problems violently also may be furnished by television.

While accepting behavioral concepts, social learning theorists such as Bandura and Rotter go beyond simple conditioning principles. They state that the expectancies and beliefs people have about themselves, their world, and their futures are equally important in shaping human personality and behavior. Some theorists add that adjusted people are those who have brought their needs and the expectations of satisfying them into harmony (Rotter, Chance, & Phares, 1972). People who set goals for themselves and are reasonably confident of attaining them are said to be well adjusted. On the other hand, people who routinely expect to fail or find ways to sabotage their efforts are considered to be maladjusted and to need to learn new behaviors. Social learning theorists have helped focus attention on the fact that people help create their environments and affect the ways other people react to them. For example, if you *think* that someone dislikes you, you may avoid the person, which may well result in that person's disliking you.

More and more, those who diagnose and treat emotional problems are adopting an approach that focuses on how people think about themselves, an approach known as **cognitive behaviorism**. Thoughts, learned in a variety of ways, help determine whether people choose adjusted or maladaptive behaviors (Meichenbaum, 1977). The assumptions people make about themselves, learned from those around them and from their interactions with the environment, directly affect their potentials for achieving happy, productive lives. Behavioral and social learning theories are used to help people correct their faulty learning and assumptions by incorporating new information and experiences, and thus to lead better lives.

The Humanistic-Existential Approach

In our efforts to understand human personality, what if we give up words like *motives*, *urges*, *instincts*, and *forces*? What if, instead, we adopt a completely new language to talk about people and human life, a language that includes such terms as the following:

- *Experience*—the totality of one's awareness of what occurs within one's body as well as what is happening in the external world.
- *Existential*—the idea that human beings have the freedom to choose.
- *Humanistic*—believing that human interests and values are of primary importance.
- *Phenomenology*—an approach emphasizing that our thoughts, emotions, and reactions are determined by how we view the world.

Taken together, these terms describe the **humanistic-existential approach** (also called the **phenomenological approach**). This approach paints a positive, optimistic picture of human personality, one that focuses on the ability to choose freely among the alternatives that life offers. Our reactions are not caused so much by the outside world as they are by our perceptions of that

cognitive behaviorism psychological approach that emphasizes that how people think about themselves is a powerful determinant of their behavior

humanistic-existential approach psychological approach that emphasizes the positive aspects of people and focuses on their abilities to freely choose among alternatives

phenomenological approach the humanistic-existential approach, which emphasizes the importance of one's perceptions

world. Someone else's view of reality may be quite different from ours, yet both can be true. Humanistic-existential concepts have far-reaching implications in explaining how human beings function and what constitutes adjusted behavior.

The world of experience. No one has done more than Carl Rogers (1980) to promote the idea that our individual perceptions and experiences are critical in determining who we are and how we live. He stated:

> The only reality I can possibly know is the world as I perceive and experience it at this moment. The only reality you can possibly know is the world as you perceive and experience it at this moment. And the only certainty is that those perceived realities are different. There are as many "real worlds" as there are people! (p. 102)

Rogers contended that each person's experiences result in the development of a *self,* the I or me we identify as ourselves. Our perceptions of the world gradually lead to the formation of self-concepts, which form reality as we know it. (We examine the concept of self more fully in Chapter 3.) Once the self is formed, the individual becomes concerned primarily with protecting, maintaining, and enhancing that self.

Rogers went even farther. He maintained that within us all, even in the most disturbed people, there is something that constantly strives to develop our capacities to the fullest, a quality termed **self-actualization**. Even in the person who has lived a barren existence, there remains an inner potential seeking release, a potential that awaits only the proper environment to assert itself.

Abraham Maslow (1970) was an especially fervent advocate of humanism. He believed that despite the dark side of human nature, we must focus on people's positive characteristics in order to enhance adjustment and prevent human problems. Maslow believed that two forces—psychoanalysis and behaviorism—had too long dominated psychology. He advocated a **third force**, whose key concepts were experience, choice, creativity, and self-actualization. Like Rogers, he felt that by trying to understand the inherent capacity for self-actualization, we can eventually achieve our potentials. The goals of this process are the dignity and enhancement of all people.

Maslow's hierarchy of needs. According to Maslow, people continuously grapple with their unsatisfied needs. As soon as one need is met, another starts clamoring for gratification. Maslow began to see, however, that needs are not random. He believed they are arranged in a hierarchy, much like the pyramid shown in Figure 2-3. Needs at the lower levels must be reasonably well satisfied before one begins to meet those at a higher level.

The needs nearest the bottom are physiological (such as hunger and thirst), and these must be taken care of before the next layer (involving safety needs, such as security and avoidance of pain) can be met. Our primitive ancestors may have been so busy satisfying their physiological and safety needs that they had little opportunity to deal with the higher-level needs. As society pro-

self-actualization tendency or desire to become all that one is capable of becoming

third force Maslow's emphasis on experience, choice, creativity, and self-actualization

FIGURE   2-3   Maslow's Need Hierarchy Represented as a Pyramid

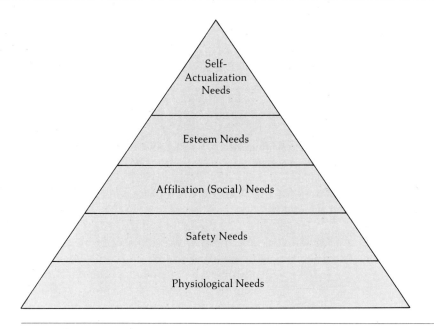

gressed, however, the higher needs began to gain attention. Such changes on the broad scale have their parallels in the lives of individuals. Once we have satisfied our needs to belong and be loved, for example, we can set about the pursuit of self-respect and esteem from others.

Maslow's hierarchy is not rigid, however. There are many exceptions, such as the artist, inventor, or spiritual leader, who may have a greater need to pursue aesthetic or mental activities than to belong to any particular group or to seek safety and security. Nor does the satisfaction of lower needs automatically guarantee that people will seek to satisfy higher needs. For the most part, however, Maslow's hierarchy proves a useful model for the humanistic viewpoint of human personality. It paints a picture of humanity striving toward ever higher goals.

The existential emphasis. Psychoanalytic and behavioral traditions seem to suggest that we are captives of early upbringing, biological heritage, environment, or all three. But according to *existentialism*, we all have freedom of choice. The present is not predetermined by the past, nor does it foretell the future. Human beings have within them the power to choose to be happy, unhappy, content, dissatisfied, or whatever they wish; individuals who make wise choices and take responsibility for their lives avoid the anxieties and maladjustment so common to many.

The existential view restores meaning to life. It proclaims that individuals—regardless of background or circumstances—can achieve a spiritual awakening, grow as human beings, and free themselves from the restrictions placed on them by their past, their families, society, or any other limiting factor. However, if we forsake our freedom of choice, refuse to face the world with courage, or fail to take responsibility for our own lives, we condemn ourselves to repeat the past.

The nature of adjustment. The humanistic-existential approach identifies several barriers to healthy adjustment. First, people who feel that life has no meaning experience *alienation* in their lives; that is, they feel separated or detached from themselves and others. They feel that their lives and experiences lack *authenticity*, or realness. They often describe themselves as spectators in their own lives or as living through false personalities instead of from their true selves.

People who feel alienated and inauthentic begin to regard personal identity as something that can be manipulated by themselves or others. What is more, they tend to be neither active nor committed participants in life, and their adjustment suffers. When people feel alienated and inauthentic, their lives are marked by feelings of anxiety, dread, and despair that may have no concrete causes. They may tend to view all human endeavor as absurd and the whole panorama of life as leading nowhere.

According to the humanistic-existential approach, people can recover from this sense of meaninglessness by realizing that they control their lives. As a result, adjusted individuals are able to accept themselves and their experiences. Reality need not be threatening. It can be incorporated without denying or distorting one's experience or self-image. Such people are open to new experiences and are able to live up to their potentials. While not many reach the peak of Maslow's pyramid (Figure 2–3), those who do can inspire countless others to strive for the goal. Table 2–1 summarizes the humanistic-existential portrait of a fully adjusted, self-actualized person, based on work done by researchers Jourard and Landsman (1980).

Further, the humanistic-existential approach states that this goal of healthy adjustment is not reserved for the few—it is the birthright of every human being. Psychologists trained in this approach help their clients realize their own powers of choice and the abilities within themselves to overcome their weaknesses and adversities.

EVALUATING THEORIES OF PERSONALITY

Each of the three theories we have examined—psychoanalytic, behavioral and social learning, and humanistic-existential—represents a different perspective regarding human personality and society. However, none represents reality faithfully. Even if we cannot decide which is absolutely the best theory, at least we can look at their respective strengths and weaknesses.

TABLE 2-1   Some Characteristics of Self-Actualizers

Self-actualizers tend to do the following:

1. Perceive reality accurately and fully.
2. Show greater acceptance of themselves, others, and things generally.
3. Be spontaneous and natural.
4. Focus on problems instead of themselves.
5. Prefer detachment and privacy.
6. Be autonomous and thus independent of the physical and social environments.
7. Have fresh outlooks and appreciate much of life.
8. Have mystical or peak experiences.
9. Enjoy a spirit of identity and unity with all people.
10. Reserve deep interpersonal relations for a few people, usually self-actualizers like themselves.
11. Possess a democratic character structure.
12. Be ethical people.
13. Be creative.
14. Have a sense of humor that is philosophical rather than hostile.
15. Resist excessive influence from the culture; they are not easily seduced by society.

Psychoanalytic Theory

Psychoanalysis has several important advantages. It is a broad theory, covering many aspects of human behavior. Its principles have been applied to everything from selling soap to treating severely disturbed patients. The concepts of psychic determinism and unconscious motivation have given us tools to understand ourselves in ways never before possible. The preeminent role Freud gave to human sexuality as the great motivator also clarified a great deal of human behavior that had seemed inexplicable. Freud was a truly amazing observer. His depth of approach enabled him to root out the long-buried causes behind many of his clients' emotional and mental illnesses.

Psychoanalytic theory has always had significant weaknesses, however. Psychoanalytic concepts are difficult to measure in an objective way. Exactly where in one's mind do the id, ego, and superego reside? How does one measure the strength of the death instincts in different people? Can the concept of death instinct be used as a predictor for those at risk of committing suicide? Also, some researchers say that evidence for the psychosexual stages of development is sparse at best. Many observers believe that Freud overemphasized the importance of childhood at the expense of events that occur in adulthood. In addition, Freud underestimated the *inter*personal, or social, aspects of human development. He focused almost exclusively on the *intra*personal factors. Psychoanalytic theory also may have badly misunderstood development in women—judging them by standards of a male norm. Modern psychoanalysts have modified Freud's views on sexuality to place more emphasis on interpersonal, social, and cultural factors in determining behavior.

With all its defects, many observers feel that psychoanalysis still represents the single most sweeping contribution to personality theory in the history of psychology. At the same time, it is wise to keep in mind that psychoanalysis does not have a multicultural view. It sprang from Western culture, and it reflects the values, traditions, and beliefs of that culture. As a result, psycho-analysis often seems to apply best to middle- and upper-class Europeans and North Americans.

Psychoanalysis does not have a multicultural view.

The Behavioral and Social Learning Approaches

The primary strength of behavioral and social learning theories is that they are grounded in the scientific tradition that began with animal and laboratory research. The more precise language of this background allows researchers and psychologists to measure various aspects of human behavior relatively objectively. Thus, arguments among "experts" are replaced by objective research to decide matters on the basis of facts instead of opinions. Behavioral and social learning theories emphasize the environmental or situational factors that determine behavior. We are not so much prisoners of our childhood as we are products of faulty learning experiences. Social learning theory, in particular, stresses the role of thinking or cognition, as well as conditioning and observational learning. Behavioral and social learning principles can apply to everyone, regardless of social, economic, or ethnic background. *What* is learned varies from individual to individual or from group to group, but *how* things are learned does not. Thus, these theories are truly multicultural in their approach.

Critics of behavioral and social learning theory, however, contend that it suffers from a certain narrowness and superficiality. They suggest that the principles and techniques developed in animal studies are applied too rigidly to human beings. What is true of animal behavior may not be true of human behavior. Behavioral and social learning theorists may also forget the role of inherited factors. Critics say that many of the differences among individuals can be traced to genetic factors, and thus they are not simply the result of different learning experiences. While such things as observational learning are important, developmental stages are ignored almost entirely in the theories. Since it is well known that children go through distinct stages, there may be something genetically structured within us that together with our environment programs us to become terrible two-year-olds and later lovestruck adolescents.

Other critics have suggested that even the objectivity of behavioral and social learning approaches is more apparent than real. For example, *reinforcement* is hardly a precise term—it can cover anything from a pat on the back to winning a trip around the world. How can the strength of a reinforcer be measured objectively when it can mean so many different things? Also, can an observer really explain precisely what is going on in observational learning? Exactly what parts of a model's behavior are reinforcing? To what degree are they reinforcing? Such approaches can seem narrow when compared with the breadth and sweep of psychoanalytic theory.

The Humanistic-Existential Approach

The primary strength of the humanistic-existential approach is its view that human beings have an infinite capacity to change. No instincts, unconscious urges, conditionings, or environmental manipulations are considered here. Individuals interpret their own experiences and make their own choices. Scientific rigor takes a backseat. The approach emphasizes our positive, creative capacities instead of our potential for self-destruction or our behavioral deficits. The future is not determined by the past or by even the present—it lies within ourselves if we are willing to take the responsibility for creating it day by day.

At times, the writings of many humanistic-existential theorists seem almost lyrical or poetic, which can make them difficult to understand. Also, translating their ideas into testable research questions can be an investigator's nightmare. How, for example, are we to verify the following: "An individual's pitch at a certain moment determines in advance the choice, brightness, and coloring of his relationships to the world" (Boss, 1963, p. 41)? In addition, the humanistic-existential approach has been criticized for sometimes taking an overly romantic view of human nature. So much emphasis is placed on growth, potential, optimism, and the inherent goodness of people that the darker, more destructive side is overlooked. An approach that puts such stock in self-awareness has to rely on self-reports, that is, on an individual's evaluation of his or her improvement or progress toward personal goals. As many psychoanalysts assert, people often do not know themselves as well as they think they do.

A Matter of Choices

Everyone wants to make choices that lead toward healthy adjustment. What, then, do these theories tell us about making such choices?

According to psychoanalysis, our choices are determined in large part by unconscious forces acting within us. Even though we are unaware of them, they influence nearly every aspect of behavior. The unconscious is shaped by our experiences in infancy and childhood, and the choices we make are directly linked to these early experiences. As a result, the freedom to choose is largely an illusion. Our actions are determined by forces of which we are at best only dimly aware and by childhood experiences that have left indelible marks upon us.

Psychoanalysts say we can regain some freedom of choice, however, by gaining insight into the nature of our unconscious and of our psychosexual histories. We can then begin to guide our lives. The adjusted person is not nearly so fearful of the unconscious. The person has either come to terms with it or been blessed with experiences that did not lead to fear, repression, or avoidance. For those not so blessed, the insights achieved through therapy can lead to better adjustment.

For behavioral and social learning theorists, everything is reduced to choices influenced by conditioning and learning situations. As a result of early learning experiences, each of us has a vast repertoire of behaviors from which to choose. We select a behavior on the basis of two criteria: (1) how strongly we expect it to achieve a particular goal and (2) the value of that goal. In a very real sense, then, our choices are determined by our expectations and the values we attach to particular rewards. Both of these are products of learning.

We can learn to alter our choices through understanding and new learning experiences. We can consciously analyze our expectations for the success or failure of certain behaviors to determine why we value certain goals so highly. In social learning terms, we can examine our cognitive processes to determine in what ways they may be faulty. Through this process, our expectations and reward values may change. The social learning theorist views human beings as adaptable and able to discriminate among choices. As Mischel (1977) states:

> *The image is one of the human being as an active, aware problem-solver, capable of profiting from an enormous range of experiences and cognitive capacities, possessing great potential for good or ill, actively constructing his or her psychological world, and influencing the environment but also being influenced by it in lawful ways—even if the laws are difficult to discover and hard to generalize. (p. 253)*

The humanistic-existential theorists talk at length about freedom to choose, contrary to the psychoanalysts, who see human beings as driven by the past. If we orient ourselves to the future by accepting full responsibility for our lives today and if we are authentic with ourselves and others, we can free ourselves from the domination of events or other people. *We* choose; we must not allow others to choose for us.

Good choices cannot be made in a threatening atmosphere, however. We must seek conditions and people who are accepting of us. In a nonjudgmental climate, we can admit to our deepest fears, destructive urges, and fantasies. By accepting ourselves, we can make choices based on our own inner natures. In the absence of threat, our perceptions of the world can be clarified. We can take charge of our lives by exercising the power of free choice. This process is not easy or quick, but it is possible.

Whatever differences these approaches have regarding how free or predetermined the ability to choose may be, they all agree on one point. People *can* change. Human beings trapped in fear and despair can be helped to live healthier, fuller lives.

SUMMARY

1. Understanding human personality can help people exert some control over themselves and their environments. Such understanding may be difficult to gain, since behavior is not simply the result of personality factors. Behavior is partly determined by circumstances.

2. All of us develop theories to explain others' behaviors. These explanations are called implicit personality theories.

3. Three major theories attempt to explain human personality. They are psychoanalysis, behavioral and social learning theories, and humanistic-existential theory.

4. Psychoanalysis is a theory that emphasizes psychic determinism and unconscious motivation. According to psychoanalytic theory, behavior is driven by the life instincts (Eros) and the death instincts (Thanatos).

5. The three structures of the personality—the id, ego, and superego—are developed as the individual goes through a series of psychosexual stages. The struggle among these three structures can create anxiety, which people try to control using ego defenses. Later modifications of psychoanalytic theory have taken into account the social aspects of development and have downplayed the psychosexual factors.

6. Psychoanalysts view adjusted individuals as those who have come to terms with their unconscious and have less need to employ ego defenses.

7. From a behavioral and social learning perspective, behavior is viewed as shaped by classical and operant conditioning and by observational learning. Over the years, a person builds up a large repertoire of behaviors. Social learning also takes into account the roles of thinking, planning, and anticipating in shaping human behavior.

8. Behavioral and social learning theorists view adjusted people as those who have learned to make appropriate responses to various situations. Adjusted individuals do not avoid life, and their expectations of satisfying their needs are in harmony with the strengths of those needs.

9. The humanistic-existential approach promotes a positive, optimistic picture of human personality, one that tries to restore meaning to life. This approach emphasizes the freedom of choose. Behavior is determined by people's perceptions of reality. Out of these perceptions grows a sense of individual identity. We then seek to maintain and enhance this identity and to achieve self-actualization.

10. Maslow believed that people's needs are arranged in a hierarchy with primitive needs at the bottom and self-actualization needs at the top. Each need must be satisfied before the next can be met.

11. From a humanistic-existential perspective, adjusted individuals accept themselves, take responsibility for their lives, and are authentic rather than alienated.

12. Each theoretical approach to understanding human personality has strengths and weaknesses. Psychoanalysis, while providing a broad explanation for human behavior, focuses too exclusively on childhood experiences and intrapersonal structures. Behavioral and social learning theories can be tested more readily, but they tend to disregard the influence of heredity and unconscious motivations. The humanistic-existential approach recognizes creativity and innate freedom in human beings but may overly romanticize human personality and not pay enough attention to the darker side.

13. Each of the three theoretical approaches also has something different to say about our abilities to make choices. Psychoanalysts see people as having little freedom to choose, since behavior and personality are determined by childhood experiences. In social learning theory, people are regarded as able to adapt and to discriminate among choices, provided they acquire correct learning experiences. From the humanistic-existential perspective, people have the power to choose how they will live if they are willing to take responsibility for their lives and if they seek conditions that encourage growth.

Chapter 3

The Person: Self, Motivation, and Values

People think, feel, and act in many different ways. In attempting to understand and explain human nature, psychologists over the years have developed various concepts about personality and behavior. Prominent among these concepts have been the *self*, *motivation*, and *values*. That is, the manner in which you see yourself, the motives that drive you, and the factors that influence your choice of goals contribute to who and what you are. This chapter discusses each of these three concepts to determine the roles they play in human personality.

THE SELF

A client in a counseling session some years ago made the following statements (Rogers, 1947):

> *I'm worried about myself.*
> *I haven't been acting like myself; it doesn't seem like me.*
> *I don't understand myself. (p. 359)*

Over 2,000 years ago, the Greek philosopher Socrates advised all seekers of wisdom, "Know Thyself." What Socrates realized, and what this client and countless others have discovered, is that the self is the most vibrant, compelling, and baffling reality we can know. For many of us, the most common word in our vocabularies is the pronoun *I*.

self perception of oneself and its associated values; the I or the me

Despite such intuitive knowledge, the concept of the **self** has provoked a mixed reaction among many psychologists. While they realize the importance of the self, they also know how difficult it can be to measure or investigate a concept that is largely private and subjective. Some behaviorists, such as Watson, have even gone so far as to reject the concept as unscientific precisely because it is so subjective.

Yet critics of the self have not been able to make the concept go away. Today, the self is very much with us. It is recognized as a major factor in determining how people adjust to life. Not every theory uses the exact term *self*. However, many of them contain such notions, as the ego in psychoanalysis or expectancies in social learning, which incorporate self-like ideas.

The Nature of the Self

Questions like "Who am I?" are not the inventions of modern people wrapped up in themselves. Deciding who and what we are is an indoor sport with a long history. In fact, William James (1890), known as the father of American psychology, set the tone for many of our present ideas about the self when he described one aspect of it as:

> [T]he total of all he can call his, not only his body and his psychic powers, but his clothes and his house, his spouse and his children, his ancestors and friends, his reputation and works, and his land and horses, and yacht and bank account. (p. 291)

Although written in the late 1800s and sexist in its language, James' description is not so very different from those of today.

Many ideas about the self have sprung from the humanistic-existential perspective described in Chapter 2. In particular, we owe a lot to Carl Rogers for helping to crystallize our ideas about the self. For Rogers (1959) the self has a number of important characteristics. These may be summerized as follows:

1. It is organized and consistent.
2. It includes one's perceptions of all that comprises I or me.
3. It also includes the relationships among the I or me and other people and features of life, as well as the value and importance of these relationships.
4. The self is available to consciousness (we can become aware of it) but it is not always conscious at any given moment.
5. The shape of the self is constantly changing yet always recognizable.

Another researcher, Ruth Wylie (1984), contends that the self has three major aspects—the personal self, social self-concepts, and self-ideals. Her ideas are especially appropriate to the study of adjustment.

personal self-concept part of the self containing physical, behavioral, and psychological characteristics

Personal self-concept. The **personal self-concept** is the part of the self that includes the physical, behavioral, and psychological characteristics that help establish uniqueness. For example, "My eyes are green," "I can run faster than anyone else in my class," "I love cheeseburgers," and "I'm not very good at math." Personal self also includes gender, racial or ethnic identity, and age status. It is not something that fluctuates wildly over time. It is generally stable. However, you do tend to qualify your self-concept from time to time. You may generally see yourself as confident, for example, but before an examination or when having to perform in public, you may become nervous and fearful.

---

cathy®   **by Cathy Guisewite**

social self-concepts
self as one believes
others view it

Social self-concepts. **Social self-concepts** are how you believe others see you. These concepts may vary with the person or group you find yourself among. An executive may believe that her employees see her as a slave driver. On the other hand, she may feel her children regard her as indulgent.

At times, personal and social self-concepts clash. Thus, others tell you that they regard you as warm and sympathetic (social self). You, however, see yourself as detached and uninvolved (personal self). The clash between these two selves indicates that there may be a distortion in the way you view yourself or that you have learned to imitate the behavior of a caring person while actually feeling remote. In either case, it may be wise to investigate the discrepancy and try to determine the cause of it.

self-ideals self as one
would like it to be

Self-ideals. **Self-ideals** are the idealized images of what you would like to be. Few people have attained their ideal selves. For most, the self-ideals and personal self often are at odds: "I would like to be tall, but I'm only slightly above average height," "I wish I were rich, but I'm far from it," or "If only I could be socially clever instead of such a klutz."

Interactions among the components of the self. Personal self, social self-concepts, and self-ideals are not static components of the self. These aspects interact with each other in a variety of ways that can result in healthy adjustment or in maladjustment. Interactions between the personal self and self-ideals focus on how you *feel* when your personal and idealized selves clash. For example, "I just die every time I get a C in class instead of the A that I really want." Clearly, adjustment suffers when your personal self falls short of your idealized self— especially when your ideal is important to you.

The interaction between social self-concepts and self-ideals involves how you would like others to see you. For example, "I wish my folks would believe in me more than they do," "If only my boss would believe I'm really dedicated to my job," "I want others to admire my abilities," and "I'm glad other people see me as smart, even if I'm not sure they're right." To the extent that others fail to see you in your self-idealized way, your self-regard or adjustment may suffer.

Consistency of the Self

Even with the constant interaction of these three aspects of the self, one of the most notable features of the self is its consistency over time. Of course, there are momentary changes. You feel depressed after a disappointment; you feel elated when someone compliments you. These momentary fluctuations, however, do not alter the overall sense of self any more than the play of light and shadow on a partly cloudy day alters the landscape beneath.

For Rogers (1959), the key to adjustment lies in the person's ability to maintain consistency of self and harmonize the self and experience. Rogers found consistency to be so essential that people would go to extreme lengths to maintain it. Failure to do so can lead to anxiety, so people rationalize incompatible aspects of their personalities to make them consistent with their self-concepts.

You often distort parts of your experience to maintain your self-image.

"WINSTON CHURCHILL ALSO STARTED OUT AS AN UNDERACHIEVER."

For example, someone may believe, "In important matters, I am an honest person," yet excuse falsifying an income tax return on the basis that such lies are "unimportant." After all, the person may tell himself or herself, the government takes too much money from people. If you view yourself as a kind person yet commit unkind acts, you may rationalize them by blaming other people: "They asked for what they got."

As a result, you often distort or deny parts of your experience to maintain your self-concept. The meaning you attach to experiences is highly colored by this need for consistency. The power of consistency is evident in the statements people make about themselves on self-report questionnaires. The statements tend to show a great deal of stability over time (Mischel, 1968). Current investigators are becoming more interested in people's desire to reduce inconsistency and simplify incoming information so they can cope with it more easily (Nisbett & Ross, 1980). "On the Research Frontier: Maintaining the Self via Social Contacts" presents a research example of how self-concepts can be maintained.

ON THE RESEARCH FRONTIER

MAINTAINING THE SELF VIA SOCIAL CONTACTS

Sometimes it seems as if self-concepts are like pillars of stone, which last forever. Other times it seems as if they shift like leaves blown about in a windstorm. So, then, which is it? While no single piece of research ever settles things once and for all, a recent study by Swann and Hill (1982) does seem to shed some light on the question.

These investigators reasoned that when people receive feedback about themselves that is consistent with their own views of self, they will accept the information. In contrast, when people are given feedback that does not coincide with their self-concepts they will strive to discredit the feedback. The result will be little change in self-concept. When people do not have the opportunity to discredit feedback, noticeable changes in the self will appear.

To test their reasoning, the investigators arranged an experiment. They selected forty-six female college students who perceived themselves as either dominant or submissive in their relationships with others. Each student played a game (Mastermind) with another person (in fact, this person was a confederate of the investigators). Just before the game started, half of the students were told they seemed to be the kind of dominant, forceful person who should serve as the leader in the game. The other half were told that they appeared to be hesitant and unsure of themselves and therefore the confederate would serve as leader. For half of the students, this feedback contradicted their self-

conceptions; for the other half, the information was consistent with their own views. Some of the students were allowed to respond to or protest the confederate's assessment of their dominance or submissiveness. The other students did not have the opportunity. Later, the students filled out questionnaires designed to measure their self-concepts regarding dominance-submission and also their perceptions of how the confederate would rate them.

In essence, the data confirmed the investigators' initial reasoning. Subjects who received discrepant information about themselves tried to discredit that information. As a result, their self-concepts underwent very little change. When changing the feedback is not possible or when the feedback is consistent with their self-concepts, little change occurs. Based upon their research, Swann and Hill conclude the following:

> [I]t may be erroneous to argue that the self is empty . . . and that people are Milquetoasts who knuckle under to any social feedback they happen to encounter. Instead, our findings suggest that it may be more accurate to regard people as active agents who carefully monitor the feedback they receive and take active behavioral steps to refute and undermine feedback that threatens their existing self-conceptions. Apparently, once they form their self-conceptions, people will go out of their way to sustain them—even if it means changing the very nature of social reality. (p. 66)

Self-consistency lives!

In more extremes cases, people may simply refuse to accept inconsistent information about themselves. Experience is categorized into what is consistent (and acceptable) and what is inconsistent (and rejected or denied). Such attitudes can have severe consequences for adjustment if information critical to a person's growth and development is continually rejected.

Self-Schemata and Consistency of the Self

self-schemata broad generalizations people make about themselves that then affect such things as information processing

Some psychologists and researchers have chosen to think of the preceding concepts of the self as **self-schemata** (Markus, 1977). These are broad generalizations you make about yourself, such as, "I am very shy," or "I am an easy-going person." Once these schemata are formed, they guide the manner in which you process new information about the self. Information pertinent to your self-schemata is assimilated and recalled better than is less relevant material.

You can see how this process works in research on the relationship between self-schemata and gender (Markus et al., 1982). Markus and his colleagues found that people with strong masculine self-schemata, those with strong feminine self-schemata, and those with androgynous (high in both masculine and feminine traits) self-schemata processed gender-related information differently. For example, men and women with strong masculine schemata could provide more examples of past masculine behavior than feminine behavior. People with feminine schemata showed the reverse pattern. Androgynous people, on the other hand, processed information on masculine and feminine behavior with equal skill. People who were low in both masculine and feminine traits (called aschematic individuals) were not able to provide many examples of behavior that could be clearly labeled masculine or feminine. Thus, you tend to be highly effective in processing information that is consistent with your self-schemata and to downplay or even disregard information that is inconsistent or irrelevant to it.

Uniqueness and the Self

Conformist behavior—the desire, for example, to dress, talk, and act like other people—often obscures the fact that individuals also pursue uniqueness (Snyder & Fromkin, 1980). Individuals strive to develop a self that is at the same time similar to and different from the self of others. This striving for uniqueness—and the conflicting feelings it can produce—is expressed charmingly in the following poem (Cohen, 1968):

> *I wonder if my fingerprints*
> *get lonely in the crowd*
> *There are no others like them*
> *& that should make them proud. (p. 212)*

There are both risk and reward in uniqueness—the loneliness and pride mentioned in the poem. Generally, you want to be recognized for the positive side of uniqueness (your achievements and abilities) and not the negative side (your failures and weaknesses).

Advertisers have long capitalized on the need to feel unique. They try to create the illusion that their products or services are designed exclusively for special individuals, who do not run with the crowd, as shown in Figure 3-1. Such claims may fit in well with your self-schemata and motivate you to buy the product.

Your sense of uniqueness has a basis in reality—no two individuals are exactly alike. Moreover, a healthy sense of the unique self is part of being well adjusted. However, some researchers have found that very often what you believe are personality attributes unique to yourself may be more illusion than reality, as the exercise in "On the Research Frontier: An Experiment in Uniqueness" demonstrates (see page 60).

Development of the Self

No one can say precisely when a child first acquires a sense of self. Gordon Allport (1961) argued that for the first year, a child is a primitive organism, totally concerned with food and comfort. Allport believed there is no sense of self at this stage and there are no lasting memories. In fact, Allport stated that the first year is the least important one for personality or growth of self (assuming, of course, no serious injuries to the child's health). After the first year, however, there is a clear evolution of the self from bodily self to propriate striving, as shown in Table 3-1. This description contrasts with Freud's psychosexual stages of personality formation, presented in Chapter 2.

There is some research to support Allport's ideas. Lewis and Brooks (1975) put a red mark on the noses of a group of babies ranging from under one year to eighteen months and older. If, after seeing themselves in a mirror, the babies touched their own noses, the action would seem to indicate a realization that the baby in the mirror is "me." Lewis and Brooks found that no babies under a year old touched their reddened noses. However, 75 percent of the babies over eighteen months did. Further, by twenty-one months, toddlers often recognized photographs of themselves even when the photos were mixed in with those of other babies of about the same sex and age.

As children mature, the concept of self also develops. Harter (1982) constructed a questionnaire to assess the level of children's self-concepts in such areas as schoolwork, friendships, and physical skills. She found that children in the third through sixth grades can rate themselves consistently and reliably, showing a good grasp of self. Their self-ratings also coincided with their teachers' ratings of them—a trend that became progressively stronger in the higher grades.

The development of a sense of self does not take place in a vacuum, however. It involves a complex interaction between the child and those intimately involved in caring for that child. Perhaps no one has described this interpersonal context better than Harry Stack Sullivan (1953).

FIGURE 3–1   Advertisements Often Cater to the Need to Feel Unique

ON THE RESEARCH FRONTIER

AN EXPERIMENT IN UNIQUENESS

Try to recruit a few friends to serve as subjects in this experiment described by Snyder and Fromkin (1980). Tell them you have learned something from psychology classes about how to assess personality from inkblots. Next, construct an inkblot by putting a drop of ink on a piece of paper and then folding it down the middle to make the blot symmetrical. Ask your subject to write down everything he or she is reminded of while looking at the blot. Indicate that you need about fifteen minutes to come up with the correct personality interpretation. In longhand, write out the following interpretation (from Snyder & Larson, 1972) and then present it to your subject for comment:

Some of your aspirations tend to be pretty unrealistic. At times you are extroverted, affable, and sociable, while at other times you are introverted, wary, and reserved. You have found it unwise to be too frank in revealing yourself to others. You pride yourself on being an independent thinker and do not accept others' opinions without satisfactory proof. You prefer a certain amount of change and variety and become dissatisfied when hemmed in by restrictions and limitations. At times you have serious doubts as to whether you have made the right decision or done the right thing. Disciplined and controlled on the outside,

you tend to be worrisome and insecure on the inside. Your sexual adjustment has presented some problems for you. While you have some personality weaknesses, you are generally able to compensate for them. You have a great deal of unused capacity which you have not turned to your advantage. You have a tendency to be critical of yourself. You have a strong need for other people to like you and for them to admire you. (p. 386)

After your subject has read this "specially developed interpretation," have him or her rate its accuracy on a five-point scale (5 = excellent, 4 = good, 3 = fair, 2 = poor, 1 = very poor). Finally, in an offhand fashion ask the subject (in terms of the same five-point scale) how well the interpretation would fit other people generally. After everything is done, you should "debrief" your subject. Explain that this was just a demonstration to illustrate the *illusion of uniqueness* and that you really did *not* derive the interpretation from his or her inkblot responses.

If everything went according to plan, your subjects probably rated the interpretations as more accurate for them than for other people generally. This outcome shows that while we work at feeling unique, we are like everyone else in doing so.

TABLE 3-1   Allport's Seven Aspects of the Developing Self

Stage or Aspect	Age of Emergence	Features
1. Sense of bodily self	15 months	Sense of the bodily me first emerges
2. Sense of self-identity	In the 2nd year	Recognition of oneself as separate and distinctive
3. Sense of self-esteem	About 24 months	Self-enhancement emerges, often in the form of negativism. By the age of four or five this desire to enhance the self turns negativism into competitiveness.
4. Extension of self	4 to 6 years	Period of self-centeredness and possessiveness. Focus is mainly on things that relate to the self.
5. The self-image	Around 6 years	Concern over how others regard one. Starting to school triggers incorporation of perceptions of others.
6. The self as rational coper	From 6 to 12	Realization that one can cope, solve problems, and think rationally. Period of close alliance with family, groups, peers, church, etc.—age of conformity.
7. Propriate striving	About 13 and beyond	Self-enhancement is fostered by choosing a life goal. Maturity is realized when realistic life plans are formulated.

Source: Table is based on G. H. Allport (1961). *Patterns and growth of personality.* New York: Harcourt, Brace & World.

self-system Sullivan's term to describe the self as consisting of the good-me, the bad-me, and the not-me.

According to Sullivan, the self-concept a child develops is largely determined by the responses of those around him or her. Sullivan was particularly fond of describing three parts of what he labeled as the developing **self-system**: the good-me, the bad-me, and the not-me. The good-me is comprised of experiences, thoughts, or behaviors that are rewarded and bring approval from parents and others. Children who are given a great deal of approval are likely to develop a strong sense of the good-me and high self-esteem.

The bad-me is associated with anxiety and the disapproval of parents or other caretakers. However, the disapproval is moderate instead of overwhelming, enabling the child to develop a conscience. The growth of the bad-me helps children learn to monitor their feelings, thoughts, and actions. It acts as a brake against undesirable behavior.

The not-me is an abnormal, often crippling element of selfhood. It develops when care and approval are deficient and disapproval is so harsh that the child is overcome with anxiety. The not-me splits apart from the rest of the self system, but it still exists with a vengeance. Whenever later events remind the person of these earlier, harsh experiences, the not-me surfaces. The result is likely to be severe anxiety, inability to think straight, and a general disruption of normal behavior and feelings.

Of course, not every instance of parental approval or disapproval has a permanent effect on the self-system. The overall pattern is important—the weight of many similar responses that accumulate as the child is developing. Likewise, other people in the child's environment (such as friends, grandparents, relatives, and teachers) can help modify parents' approval or disapproval.

Who are the primary caregivers in a child's life today? Traditionally, developmental researchers have focused almost exclusively on mother-child relationships. More recently, as single-parent households continue to increase and more women enter the work force, fathers have become more involved with infant and child care. However, as Zigler and Finn-Stevenson (1987) point out, research on the father's role is just beginning to accumulate, so it is far from conclusive. Although more active in child care, fathers as a rule spend less time with infants and do not care for or play with the infants as much as mothers do. Still, according to the research available, fathers appear as competent as mothers in caring for infants and equally sensitive to babies' cues (Zigler & Finn-Stevenson, 1987).

It would also be a mistake to assume that the parent-child relationship flows only one way—from parent to child. Quite often, the child also influences parental reactions. The nature of the child may trigger positive or negative reactions in parents who might react differently to a different child. The result is a different set of self-concepts, as "Exploring Choices: The Self-Concept as a Two-Way Street" illustrates.

Self-Esteem: Key to Adjustment

self-esteem one's overall level of self-evaluation, self-regard, or self-confidence

The term **self-esteem** refers to the overall evaluation of oneself—whether one likes or dislikes who one is, believes in or doubts oneself, and values or belittles one's worth. How you evaluate yourself is critical to your psychological adjustment. People with low self-esteem are not likely to be happy, to form healthy relationships with others, or to achieve their dreams. Those with high self-esteem have a good chance of achieving all of the above.

unconditional positive regard For Rogers, total and genuine love and respect for the individual

conditions of worth For Rogers, the bases upon which approval, attention, and rewards are given

Origins of self-esteem. Carl Rogers believes that the development of a healthy self-esteem comes about when individuals learn to value themselves. Such positive self-regard comes through approval from others, most commonly parents and other family members. Ideally, the child receives **unconditional positive regard**, that is, unconditional love and respect. This does not mean that the child's every whim is granted, but the child's worth and individuality are recognized and supported. In most families, the child must also learn the **conditions of worth**, or the bases upon which approval, attention, and rewards are given. When the child meets these conditions and receives the positive results, self-esteem probably will be enhanced.

EXPLORING CHOICES

THE SELF-CONCEPT AS A TWO-WAY STREET

Thomas and Chess (1977) have observed that some babies are cheerful and easy right from the start. They sleep regularly and adapt to new experiences and people easily. Other children are difficult right from the start. They begin as fussy babies and go on to be overactive and difficult to toilet train. These seem to be built-in tendencies. Consider the following example adapted from Babladelis (1984):

> A baby boy is born one fine day. From the very start he is active and energetic—perhaps even a bit hyperactive. But he is not cranky or irritable—just very active. He quickly learns to sit up, and in no time at all, he is crawling all over the place. He is into everything. No table, cupboard, or object within his reach is safe. He is delighted when he manages to take things apart, and so disorder is his constant companion.

Given this thumbnail sketch, how might the parents respond? Well, at least two broad possibilities come to mind. The choices made could certainly influence this little boy's developing sense of self.

1. The Smiths are parents who do not like messes. They like an orderly house. They also believe that children should show instant obedience. At the same time, they have definite ideas about what is proper behavior for boys. As a result, punishment seems to follow this little boy everywhere. He is constantly reminded that he is troublesome, clumsy, and disobedient.

2. The Martins are parents who can tolerate a mess. They do not especially like the disorder, but they learn to live with it as part of the parenting price. They do, however, like the curiosity they see in their son. They see this as a sign that he may develop an inquiring mind. Maybe he will grow up to become a physicist and make important discoveries. Their strategy becomes one of rewarding his curiosity and labeling him as good or smart even as they try to cut down a bit on the breakage.

What is likely to be the outcome in these cases? Although undoubtedly oversimplifications, the following are possibilities:

1. The Smiths could create a son who develops into a tense, maybe overcontrolled person who believes he must conceal or suppress his own wishes in order to gain approval from others.

2. The Martins could create a son who develops a feeling of competence, is open with others, and seeks approval by striving to achieve.

Had each set of parents been blessed with a child with a different temperament, things might have developed quite differently. So parent-child interactions are a two-way street. At the same time, however, had each set of parents been able to make different choices about how to react to the child, things might also have developed differently.

reflected appraisals
self-esteem as determined by one's views of how others evaluate or react to one

As a result, much of your self-esteem grows out of the **reflected appraisals** of others in society. Who you are and how you feel about yourself is the result of others' reactions to you. Many years ago, Cooley (1902) described this looking-glass self when he said:

> The kind of self-feeling one has is determined by the attitude . . . attributed to that other [person's] mind. A social self of this sort might be called the reflected or looking-glass self:
>
> > Each to each a looking glass
> > Reflects the other that doth pass.
>
> As we see our face, figure, and dress in the glass, and are interested in them because they are ours, and pleased or otherwise with them according as they do or do not answer to what we should like to be; so in imagination we perceive in another's mind some thought of our appearance, manners, aims, deeds, characters, friends, and so on, and are variously affected by it. (pp. 152–153)

Research by Coopersmith (1967) demonstrates the importance of reflected appraisals. Coopersmith developed a way of measuring self-esteem in children by having them rate themselves. He also asked these children about their perceptions of their parents. At the same time, the attitudes of the mothers of these children were rated by investigators during interviews, and the mothers were asked to describe their child-rearing practices and attitudes.

Coopersmith discovered that parental attitudes and the ways in which parents reacted to their children were more important in shaping children's self-esteem than family income or parents' education or occupation. For example, the children with high self-esteem were the ones whose mothers were more loving and who developed closer relationships with their children. This closeness seemed to mean to the children that they were important and merited the attention, concern, and time devoted to them. While parents of children with high self-esteem made firm demands on them and enforced these demands, they influenced the child's behavior primarily through rewards. When punishment was dealt out, it was usually designed to manage behavior. It did not threaten the child with a loss of love. These parents did not punish their children less, but they did it without harshness and in a way that took into account the child's feelings.

In contrast, parents of children with low self-esteem usually punished their children harshly and in ways that told them, "You are not all that important!" They did not make firm demands on their children, nor did they provide explicit rules. Such children grew up without clearly defined limits for behavior. They perceived their parents as authoritarian, rejecting, and uncompromising.

As children move out of the tight family circle, other people become sources of reflected appraisals. In general, children do not accept the appraisals of just anyone. They react more to those who seem knowledgeable about them, such as friends or teachers.

social comparison
comparing oneself to others, which in turn, affects one's level of self-esteem

At this stage, self-esteem can also be affected by **social comparison**, or the tendency to compare oneself with others. Depending on how you believe you

How you feel about
yourself depends on
others' reactions to
you.

measure up, your self-esteem is raised or lowered. The child who is constantly reminded of an older brother's or sister's achievements may feel a slow decline in self-esteem. The child may protect his or her self-esteem by finding ways to devalue the other person or group (remember people work to maintain a consistent self-image). Thus, "That boy isn't smarter than I am; his parents are friends with the teacher and he gets extra help." While some defensiveness is normal, one who relies too heavily on such a strategy may be headed for trouble.

On the other hand, when a whole category of people is the target of **social discrimination**, the effects on self-esteem can be devastating. Discrimination against people because of race, religion, sex, or ethnic background creates not only individual tragedies but major social problems as well. The targeted groups are excluded from equal housing, job opportunities, education, and so-

social discrimination
lesser treatment of
others based on their
race, religion, sex, or
ethnic background

cial services. They may end up crowded into ghettos or in neighborhoods going through rapid social change. Such factors are related to high risk of mental illness, to say nothing of lowered self-esteem. Children may compare a parent's honest but menial job with the greater material success of a drug pusher, prostitute, or thief and wonder if honesty is really the best policy (Pettigrew, 1964). Such conflicts can drive wedges between parents and children and negatively affect children's self-esteem.

Just as the concept of the self is consistent over time, so is self-esteem—for better or for worse. People tend to choose, consciously or unconsciously, the information and experiences consistent with their general feelings about themselves. If you believe you are ugly, you will tend to disbelieve someone who compliments your appearance. If you believe you can succeed, you will tend to disregard those who try to discourage you. You can see from these situations how important it is to develop a positive, healthy self-esteem and how crippling a negative, limiting sense of self can be.

Self-efficacy. Social learning theorists, notably Bandura (1982), recently have focused on an aspect of self-esteem—one's belief that one can successfully carry out the behaviors required by a given situation. This belief has been labeled **self-efficacy**. When you feel capable of doing what is required to achieve success or when you realize that your goals and accomplishments are fairly in line, your self-esteem is enhanced. To a great extent, the level of your self-efficacy determines whether you attempt new activities, take risks, or keep working toward your goals. People low in self-efficacy do not test or challenge themselves too often. As a result, they feel even less capable.

self-efficacy belief that one can successfully execute the behaviors required in a given situation

Consequences of high self-esteem. Epstein (1980) has described people blessed with high self-esteem as carrying within them a loving parent—someone who is proud of their successes and tolerant of their failures. These people are optimistic. They can tolerate stress without becoming very anxious. Even though they experience disappointments and problems, they tend to recover quickly. It is almost as if parental love has inoculated them against defeat.

Those who carry around a harsh or disapproving parent have a low tolerance for anxiety and experience defeat or failure as a severe blow. Even success leads to only brief interludes of self-esteem. Failure or rejection seems to stalk these individuals everywhere.

In children, high self-esteem can be seen to have positive effects on behavior. Such children are more active, expressive, and confident than their peers with low self-esteem. They do better in school and in social and athletic activities. They are more creative, and they are not so easily pressured by authority figures. Children with low self-esteem, in contrast, are more socially isolated and tentative or fearful in interpersonal relationships. They may even be physically weaker. As if they are aware of their difficulties, they are likely to be absorbed with their inner selves (Coopersmith, 1967).

Self-efficacy lets you
try new activities or
take risks.

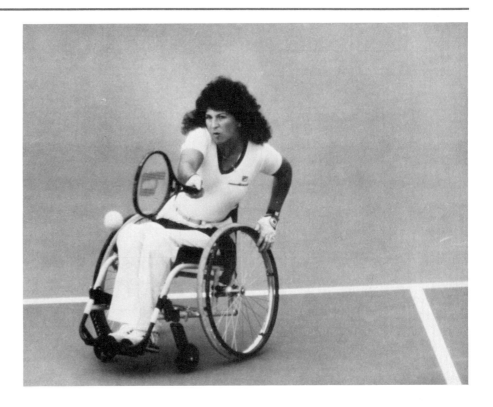

Improving self-esteem. Many people feel that their self-esteem is not what they would like it to be. When the personal self does not match up well with the self-ideal, regard for oneself is likely to suffer.

How can self-esteem be improved? It must be admitted that raising self-esteem is sometimes easier said than done. However, we offer a few general ideas here. Chapters 6 and 8 also discuss ways to resolve problems that stem from low self-esteem.

One way to raise self-esteem is to reduce the gap between your personal self and ideal self. First, examine carefully the goals and values that make up your ideal self. Do they all make sense? Are they really as important to you as you have always assumed? Perhaps some of those goals you have set for yourself are unrealistic or inappropriate. If so, you are punishing yourself by continuing to chase them. It is not easy to give up goals and values you have pursued for a long time. However, a thoughtful examination of how you came to adopt them may help you be more realistic.

Second, take careful stock of your strengths and weaknesses. Again, it can be difficult to be objective about yourself. A good inventory of assets and liabilities, however, can point up deficiencies in your knowledge and skills that are preventing you from attaining your goals. Once you have pinpointed these

deficiencies, you can set about remedying them. Not knowing how to be assertive or not having specific job skills, for example, are liabilities that can be
remedied through training and practice. If you discover that certain goals are
realistically out of reach, you can develop other goals that may prove more
rewarding.

The important point is to break the cycle of pessimism and avoidance that so
often characterizes people with low self-esteem. Calmly appraising past experiences and efforts, acquiring new information and behaviors, and achieving
successes along the way are steps that can significantly raise self-esteem.

Self Versus Selfism

selfism excessive
preoccupation with
oneself

Some have questioned whether the concern about self-image has, in some
instances, gone overboard. Cultural observers such as Peter Marin (1975) and
Christopher Lasch (1979) have suggested that for many the search for personal identity has crossed over into self-indulgence, or **selfism**. In fact, the
1970s were termed the era of the me-generation.

narcissism psychoana-
lytic term for extreme
absorption with oneself

Narcissism, the psychoanalytic term for extreme absorption with oneself,
was perceived as a kind of liberation. Where people once worried about community, neighbors, or family, they came to worry about themselves. Book-
stores prominently displayed such best-sellers as *The Art of Being Selfish* and
Looking Out for Number One. Even psychiatrists reported they were seeing a different breed of patients. Instead of neurotics with clearly defined symptoms,
the new patients complained of vague dissatisfactions and worry over their
aimless lives. Nothing seemed to be enough; people seemed unable to satisfy
their needs. Narcissism had replaced neurosis!

There has been enough observation to suggest that a sense of self-
preoccupation has continued into the 1980s. As yet, little scientific research
has been done on these trends. They are reported mainly by cultural historians
and psychoanalytic therapists. Some of the research beginning to appear is
shown in "On the Research Frontier: The Study of Selfism."

Origins of selfism. The roots of narcissism are complex. Many psychoanalytically oriented observers point to parent-child relationships as the cause. Parents may devalue their children by being cold and rejecting. The children may
respond by believing that only the self can be relied on or trusted—even loved.
The children fail to idealize the parents and instead idealize the self. In other
cases, parents may overvalue their children, giving them an unrealistic sense
of their importance. Such an illusion can never be sustained in the real world,
and the children may sacrifice reality to preserve the idealized self (Millon,
1981).

The roots of narcissism can also be found in society, particularly when that
society contains the threat of global nuclear warfare. Many people wonder if
the world has a future or if it will blow itself up in a senseless thermonuclear
explosion. Such a society gives rise to many people who do not worry much

ON THE RESEARCH FRONTIER

THE STUDY OF SELFISM

Many people certainly believe that narcissism and self-interest abound in our society. Believing is one thing, but providing objective measurements is another. To enable investigators to objectively quantify people's attitudes, Phares and Erskine (1984) developed a scale to measure selfism—a general self-preoccupation. To do this, they first devised a twenty-eight item scale. The person responded to each item on a five-point agree-disagree basis. Several items that appeared on early versions of the selfism scale follow:

- In the final analysis, the worth of an activity depends on whether it makes you feel good.
- Being true to yourself is more important than any ties to another person.
- I would be so excited if my child grew up to be just like me.
- Conversations that don't concern me personally really turn me off.

So far, several things suggest that this scale really does measure selfism. For example, when friends who know each other well are asked to fill out the selfism scale as the friend would, they can do so quite easily and correctly. In order for this to happen, selfism must somehow be reflected in overt behavior.

It has been found that people who are high in selfism tend to judge others in the light of their own selfism, and they see selfish motives in others just as they do in themselves. In addition, they are not very sympathetic to others who have gotten into difficulty through no fault of their own because they attribute cynical motives to those individuals. With scales such as this, it may be possible in the future to investigate selfism experimentally instead of just speculating about it.

about the needs of the next generation (Lasch, 1979). The tensions and anxieties of modern life, the weakening of traditional social ties, and the steady march of technology seem to foster a preoccupation with the self.

Psychology and selfism. Some observers feel that psychology also has contributed to this flight into self-absorption (Wallach & Wallach, 1983). Perhaps unintentionally, psychology encourages an emphasis on the self and personal desires. The Freudian movement, for example, asserts that maladjustment or neurosis results from insufficient satisfaction of the instinctual needs (sexual and aggressive). Psychoanalytic therapy sometimes involves weakening the superego so that instinctual gratifications can be pursued. Freud (1908/1959a) stated it thus: "All who wish to be more noble-minded than their constitution allows fall victim to neurosis; they would have been more healthy if it could have been possible for them to be less good" (p. 151).

Carl Rogers and Abraham Maslow are often cited to support the idea that individuals should be free of the restraints and demands of others and thus allowed spontaneity. Rogers and Maslow felt that encouraging people to act in accord with their true feelings and to develop their potentials would permit self-actualization, even if it meant at times going against the grain of society. Neither man regarded self-actualizers as selfish. Instead, they believed that only by being good to oneself can one be good to others. Self-acceptance must occur if one is to understand and accept others.

But is this always good? The Wallachs (1983) think not. As they put it:

> Far as it was from [Maslow's and Rogers'] intention, these psychologists inevitably promote selfishness by asking us to realize ourselves, to love ourselves, to view the environment as a means for our own self-actualizing ends, and to consider whether something will contribute to our own development as the only real criterion for what we should do. (p. 196)

While understanding and loving oneself is crucial to personal happiness and fulfillment, critics of selfism caution that one must also balance personal needs and desires against those of others.

Self-actualization, self-esteem, uniqueness, and the like are not just words. They are psychological states that, like needs, energize people. Thus, it seems that self and motivation are closely linked. The next section looks at the power of motivation and the factors that motivate us.

MOTIVATION

Theorists such as Maslow and Rogers treated self-actualization as a uniquely human energizer, but they also acknowledged the power of biological motives (for example hunger and thirst) and psychological ones (for example, achievement and power). Rogers (1963) felt that such urges as hunger are merely specific expressions of the more complex need to maintain the self.

Some Basics of Motivation

motivation forces or factors that energize behavior and give it direction

Motivation, or *motives*, refers to the forces that activate behavior and direct it toward one goal instead of another. When we ask, "Why is she doing that?" or "Why did he decide to go to college?" we are asking questions about motivation. Motives are often categorized as biological or learned.

Biological motives are rooted in the physiology and nervous system of the body. They relate directly to the physical survival of individuals and the species. Everyone needs food and drink to live, and while individuals can survive without sex, the species cannot. Biological motives are often fixed and unlearned. They include reflexes, instincts, and drives.

reflexes automatic, involuntary reactions

Reflexes are automatic reactions to stimuli that are not learned, and they are usually beyond conscious control. They include the response of the tendons at the knee and elbow when tapped and salivation when food enters the mouth.

Instincts are more complex. They involve innate behavior patterns specific to a particular species. Instincts are aroused by a narrow range of stimuli. An infant's suckling response, for example, is instinctive. It is necessary for the baby to take in nourishment and survive.

drives biological needs created by bodily deficits

Drives are tissue needs produced by deficits (lack of food, for example) that create physical disturbances. These drives, sometimes called **primary drives**, do not provoke automatic or fixed behavior patterns, however. In human beings, they stimulate behavior designed to reduce hunger or thirst. The *exact* way in which the reduction is accomplished, however, is influenced greatly by what one has learned.

primary drives basic, innate drives such as hunger and thirst

Learned motives are distinguished from biological motives in two important ways. First, the behaviors calculated to achieve a goal must be learned. Second, the *value of the goal itself* must be learned. Often termed **secondary drives**, these motives may push us toward goals that have been acquired earlier through association with biological motives. For example, a child develops a strong desire to be with its mother in part because she has become associated with the satisfaction of hunger and the reduction of various discomforts. However, the strength of that desire varies from person to person. Likewise, the strength of human needs for achievement, affiliation, and power (to name just a few motives) also varies from person to person. The value an individual places on such motives does not grow out of physiological deficits. The value comes from life experiences—especially those during childhood.

secondary drives learned drives, such as fear, guilt, and need for approval

For most people in industrialized countries, the biological motives, such as hunger, thirst, and avoidance of extreme temperatures, can be readily satisfied. These needs do not serve as major motivators, nor do they have significant effects on adjustment. This is not the case for the poor and homeless in American society, however, nor is it true for many people in Third World nations. In such instances, much of people's energy is devoted to getting enough to eat and drink and to finding adequate shelter. Once these needs can be satisfied easily, however, the learned motivations, such as achievement, power, and affiliation, are likely to become as prominent as they are in the lives of people in industrialized societies.

Achievement Motivation

Some people consistently strive for excellence, driven by internal motivation as well as by external pressures. Others feel little or no need to strive to improve. The **need for achievement**, then, is a learned, internalized desire to perform well and to strive for excellence in a variety of activities.

need for achievement learned desire to perform well and strive for excellence

Assessment. It may seem that the most direct way to identify individuals high in the need for achievement would be to catalog their accomplishments. However, too many factors can prevent people from achieving, including lack of education, opportunity, or resources. For these and other reasons, David McClelland, a leading researcher in this field, and his colleagues decided to use fantasy methods for measuring the strength of the need for achievement (McClelland et al., 1953). They presented pictures of people involved in somewhat ambiguous activities. In one picture a boy was seated before a violin and apparently daydreaming. In another, two men were standing before a machine. See Figure 3-2 for such an ambiguous picture.

Subjects were asked to make up stories about each picture, indicating who the people were, what they were doing and thinking, and how things would turn out for them. The idea was to give subjects a setting in which to create stories in line with their own achievement needs. Trained scorers graded the stories for the achievement themes present in them. They found that stories in which the main character accomplishes something important, expresses pride in achievement, or indicates a concern about standards of excellence were directly related to a high need for achievement.

Features. Over the years, enough research has been done on need for achievement that we know something about how people high in that motive behave and how those low in the motive behave (Byrne & Kelley, 1981). For example, individuals high in the need for achievement are more persistent, and they perform better on examinations. They seem more competitive and willing to take responsibility for the outcomes of their performances. They tend to challenge themselves in realistic ways, so that their aspirations are in line with their capacities.

Those low in need for achievement tend to be less realistic in their behavior. They often choose tasks that are either so easy it is impossible to fail or so difficult that failure is inevitable. For example, college students high in need for achievement may switch majors to areas within the range of their capabilities. Students low in need for achievement, in contrast, are likely to switch to extremely difficult majors or very easy ones. In either case, the change is usually outside their capabilities—too high or too low on the scale. In occupational choices, achievement-oriented people are more likely to select occupations that require initiative, such as business or selling. Those low in need for achievement more often choose structured jobs, such as clerical work.

Research has also shown that individuals with a high need for achievement are particularly likely to do well in business (McClelland, 1985). Success in business requires people to take moderate risks and to assume personal responsibility—characteristics of those with strong achievement motives. Such a finding seems to apply across cultures. It suggests that achievement motivation is closely linked to entrepreneurial success.

fear of failure fear that in combination with the desire for success determines achievement-oriented behavior

Fear of failure. In his research, Atkinson (1964) contends that two factors are involved in determining need for achievement—the strength of the desire for success and the **fear of failure.** Everyone wants to achieve success and at the same time avoid failure. At times, even a strong need for achievement does not bring success if the fear of failure is equally strong.

FIGURE   3-2   A Picture Similar to Those Used to Measure Need for Achievement

What makes one person able to persist even in the face of failure? How does one learn to control a fear of failure? Many factors are involved, but childhood experiences bear particular mention. Families in which standards of excellence are closely linked to the process of child rearing are more likely to produce children who become achieving adults. Families that encourage their children to be independent and that foster self-confidence tend to foster aspirations for achievement as well. The children may model themselves after successful parents, striving to be like the mother or father who has achieved a high level of skill and recognition in an occupation. In addition, the value one's culture places on achievement and the degree to which this value is reinforced by parental standards is certainly important.

All these factors may contribute to strengthening the desire for success and lessening the natural fear of failure. Individuals with such a background tend to persist in their efforts despite setbacks or temporary failures. However, keep in mind that people are enormously complex, and childhood influences from many different sources combine to produce a given outcome.

Women and achievement. As more and more women have entered the work force and become active in formerly all-male occupations, the subject of the need for achievement in women has received more attention. While some gender differences in achievement exist, differences between the *need* for achievement in men and women are inconsistent (Spence & Helmreich, 1978). It may be that women choose different goals to satisfy their achievement needs (Deaux, 1976a)—choices that are heavily influenced by their early learning experiences. Parents, the media, role models, and cultural expectations may all influence a woman's choices before she has even reached college age. For example, some women equate their own achievement with the level of their husbands' success. In some college-educated women, their earlier achievement needs may weaken as they become involved with marriage and children.

As with men, the origins of achievement behavior in women go back to childhood. Women may be somewhat more likely to blame themselves for failure and attribute success to external events, such as luck. Significant failures or setbacks may lead to an unwillingness to strive for achievement and a tendency to give up instead of trying harder. Licht and Dweck (1984) found that such a pattern is more likely to occur in girls than in boys, in part because of teachers' different problem-solving expectations for girls. Boys are expected to confront problems and overcome them; girls are expected to ask for help or have someone else solve problems for them.

Other women, however, particularly those who have had strong encouragement from their families, are able to set goals and achieve them as competently as their male counterparts. The evidence is available for all to see. Today, more women serve as corporate board members, top executives, entrepreneurs, professional people, and politicians than ever before.

Fear of success. Women who receive high achievement scores do not always behave in achievement-oriented ways. In 1969, Matina Horner offered the results of a study that seemed to explain the phenomenon. She claimed that women wanted the rewards that come from achievement but had learned early that successful women are not only disapproved of by society but also regarded as unfeminine. Thus, women came to feel that success leads to negative consequences. This feeling creates a motive to avoid success—referred to as **fear of success**! Such a motive also aplies to some men when they believe that success will lead to even further demands on their abilities.

fear of success fear said to occur in women who anticipate social disapproval or feel they will not be seen as feminine if they behave in achievement-oriented ways

Later research has called Horner's conclusions into question. Fear of success may actually be a woman's judgment about the negative outcomes that can occur when her behavior deviates from the traditional sex-role expectations established for women by society. Thus, a woman may be making a realistic assessment that in our society men reject women who threaten their sense of personal security and competency. The price of success may be more than some women are willing to pay, so they scale down their needs for achievement. As our society continues to change, however, the negative attitudes toward strongly achievement-oriented women will probably fade. Indeed, a high need for achievement in women is already valued in many professional areas.

Power Motivation

Power motivation is the desire of individuals to exert control over the events that affect their lives (McClelland, 1975). This motive has triggered wars, fueled political struggles, led to corporate takeovers, and prompted nearly every form of interpersonal, national, and international conflict imaginable. If anything characterizes the history of the world, it is the quest for power.

Assessment. Much of the recent work on power has been modeled on the achievement work of McClelland and his colleagues. They designed pictures to elicit stories that would reveal something about individuals' power motives. They asked people to make up stories about the pictures. Winter (1973) described the techniques for administering and scoring responses to these pictures.

Features. Winter and Stewart (1978) identified a number of features that distinguished those who scored high in the need for power from those who scored low. In a sense, the need for power involves the wish to make events and people do one's bidding. As a result, people high in the need for power tend to select careers that allow them to affect the behavior of others directly through rewards and punishments. Such careers include public office, business, teaching, religion, and journalism. It seems that the desire to use direct, legitimate power in influencing events guides people with strong power needs into these occupations.

The person motivated to achieve power usually comes equipped with certain tactics to attain power. One of these is visibility. For example, it has been found that students who write letters to the newspaper usually receive high need-for-power scores. Such students are also willing to take greater risks and to imagine themselves confronting prominent people. Another tactic is to build a power base of loyal supporters. Power-motivated students attract a circle of friends who are not well known on campus but are loyal. In discussion groups, power-oriented students are better able to define issues, to encourage others to participate, and to influence other members of the group. Their goals are not so much getting others to like them as to wield influence.

The road to power, then, is not necessarily through technical expertise, hard work, or popularity. As Winter and Stewart (1978) put it, "For wielding power, the rules seem to be: speak up, define the problem (but encourage others to offer solutions), participate, and do not neglect evaluations of others in an attempt to be liked" (p. 404).

Power can be the ability to get things done or the ability to exploit others for one's own ends. While most people probably have a little of both qualities, democratic cultures tend to believe that power should be used for the general good of society. Likewise in personal relationships, power can either be shared or be retained primarily in one person. Regardless, power should be used to the benefit of all, not to exploit others. Much of the emphasis on the inequalities between men and women focuses on correcting imbalances of power in relationships, the workplace, and society at large.

Affiliation Motivation

need for affiliation
desire to seek the company of others, to value being with others, and to care for others

Human beings differ in terms of not only the needs for achievement and power but also the need for the company of others—the **need for affiliation** (Mehrabian & Ksionzky, 1974). People who tend to seek out others, value being with them, and care about them are said to be exhibiting a need for affiliation. Such people have learned that others can offer comfort or aid. Others can provide information important to attaining goals and can act as models or spur one on to greater efforts.

Assessment. To measure the need for affiliation, many investigators have turned to the same technique described to assess the needs for achievement and power—the use of ambiguous pictures. One study using such a technique found that people high in need for achievement but low in need for affiliation tend to solve problems by working with experts rather than with friends. For those whose affiliation needs were higher than their achievement needs, the choice was to work with friends (French, 1956).

Features. Affiliation is an especially important motive because it can lessen the negative effects of the desire for power or achievement and can reduce stress. An incessant pursuit of power or achievement can often produce a variety of health problems, including high blood pressure, ulcers, and heart disease. Caring for others and being cared for by others can counteract some of the potential harm stemming from a high-powered life-style (McClelland, 1982).

For many people, stress can be reduced by being with others. In a classic study, Schachter (1959) put women students in an experiment where they believed they would receive painful electric shocks. While waiting for the procedure to begin, the students could wait either alone or in the presence of other students. Over 60 percent of the women who were very fearful chose to wait with others; only about 33 percent of those who were not especially fearful chose to wait with other people. Women who waited with others reported that their fears diminished. Clearly, these women experienced a reduction in stress. The relationship between social support and stress is explored further in Chapter 6.

For some people, of course, the presence of others can *increase* their stress level. Generally, such individuals distrust others. They do not relate well to a wide range of people. They prefer to work out fears and problems on their own or with experts instead of seeking comfort from those in the general environment. Men more often than women refrain from reaching out to others in times of emotional stress. The cultural emphasis on men's suppressing fear or pain sometimes works against them. As women become more free to express

Affiliation is an important motive.

their achievement needs, perhaps men will be more free to express their affiliation needs.

Achievement, power, and affiliation are just examples of the universe of human needs learned from and sustained by our interpersonal environment. These needs, along with those involving dependency, love, affection, physical comfort, and approval from others, motivate behavior in countless ways and help make up the complex nature of the self.

VALUES

So far, this chapter has focused on the self and motivation. It has described the importance of the sense of self and the biological and learned needs that act as motivators for so much of our behavior. Yet does it make sense to talk about self-concepts or satisfaction of needs without considering values? Surely one of the most human of all characteristics is the capacity to formulate a set of values.

The ideals of Western culture have been strongly influenced by the golden rule: Do unto others as you would have them do unto you. Even such homey sayings as "honesty is the best policy" transmit the value system of society to its members. People without values are known in the field of abnormal psychology as psychopaths, sociopaths, or antisocial personalities. A person with the intelligence of an adult yet the value system of a two-year-old can be a threat to society. Knowledge of right and wrong and the ability to abide by that knowledge are parts of the stitching that holds together the fabric of society.

Values, meaning, and hope are essential to human beings. Surprisingly, however, relatively little systematic research has been done on these topics. As shown in "Exploring Choices: The Search for Meaning," meaning is vital. **Logotherapy** is Frankl's (1963) existential approach to therapy, which is often referred to as therapy of meaning.

logotherapy Frankl's existential approach to therapy, which is often referred to as the therapy of meaning

Values Defined

values things regarded by a person as good, desirable, or preferred

Values are standards or ideals of thought and behavior that a particular society has deemed good, desirable, or preferred. A value system helps determine thoughts, actions, and feelings about people and the world. The choices one makes, the alternatives one considers, and the overall directions of one's life are heavily influenced by the values one learns growing up.

EXPLORING CHOICES

THE SEARCH FOR MEANING

Viktor Frankl (1963) developed a form of existential therapy called logotherapy. It is designed to encourage the client to find meaning in what seems to be a callous, uncaring, and meaningless world. Frankl's early orientation was Freudian. However, he shifted to an existential framework as he tried to come to grips with his experiences in Nazi concentration camps. He lost his mother, father, brother, and wife to the Nazi Holocaust and was himself driven to the brink of death. He decided that those who could not survive these camps had only the conventional meanings of life to sustain them. But conventional meanings could not absorb the horror of Nazi atrocities—a personal meaning for existence was required. Out of his wartime experiences and the existential insights that followed came the will to live.

Ultimately, Frankl developed logotherapy—the therapy of meaning. Through logotherapy, the therapist strives to inculcate a sense of the person's own responsibility and obligations to life once the meaning of life has been grasped and articulated.

Value systems often can be seen most clearly when they are called into question. The 1960s and 1970s, for example, were times when our traditional national values were challenged. Among other things, the nation was forced to confront the realities of racial discrimination, involvement in Vietnam, and the struggle of women to achieve equal rights. These events pointed up glaring discrepancies between what we said and what we did as a people.

conceived values
ideals as emphasized by the culture, religion, or philosophers

In scholarly terms, such a discrepancy is referred to as a difference between conceived values and operative values. **Conceived values** represent an ideal. They are the values emphasized by culture, religion, or philosophers. In contrast, **operative values** are those that influence behavior in immediate, concrete situations. Thus, a businessperson may truly believe in an abstract way that "honesty is the best policy." Yet in day-to-day dealings, the value "let the buyer beware!" is more likely to be followed. Likewise, people may become concerned over the starving children in other nations yet neglect their own children at home.

operative values
values that influence behavior in the immediate, concrete situation

Rokeach (1973) describes this conflict in terms of instrumental and terminal values. **Instrumental values** are the means of attaining goals. **Terminal values** are the goals or ends themselves. In some instances, people justify immediate behavior by the long-term good it is supposed to achieve. The question is always whether the end justifies the means or ultimately destroys the very goal one sought to attain. Asking such questions forces us to consider the values that guide our lives.

instrumental values
values that refer to the means by which goals are attained

terminal values
values that refer to ultimate goals or ends

Values, Personality, and Adjustment

Many years ago, Spranger (1928) suggested that people could be classified into six primary categories according to the values that shaped the conduct of their lives (although some people showed a mixture of characteristics). A summary of the categories follows:

1. *The theoretical person.* The basic value for this person is the discovery of truth through rational, critical, and scientific methods. This individual tends to become an intellectual, a philosopher, or a scientist.

2. *The economic person.* The basic value is usefulness. The person tends to become business oriented and involved in the production, selling, or consumption of goods and services. What one owns becomes a central value.

3. *The aesthetic person.* The basic values are form and harmony. Artistic and aesthetic experiences become most important.

4. *The social person.* The basic values are affiliation and love. These individuals orient their lives around others and tend to be sensitive to their needs.

5. *The political person.* The basic value is power. This category does not refer to politics in the narrow sense. It refers to the ability to control other people and events and to dominate personal relationships.

6. *The religious person.* The basic value in this category may be termed the quest for unity. Such individuals have a mystical side that compels them to seek meaning in higher forces and to be drawn to religious philosophy.

Allport, Vernon, and Lindzey (1960) published a scale still used widely today. Their scale is designed to assess the degree to which an individual emphasizes these six value categories in his or her life. Table 3–2 shows some sample items from this scale.

These six categories reflect a preoccupation with emphasizing the desirable, healthy, and good in the human personality. This preoccupation has been a prominent feature of various cultures since the dawn of recorded history. In ancient Greek civilization, the ideal person was committed to a life ruled by reason. Through the rational faculty, one could speculate, imagine, investigate, and enjoy all aspects of the environment and even begin to approach the level of the gods. Fifteenth- and sixteenth-century Europe gave us the concept of the Renaissance person—an individual who masters skills in a wide range of fields from science to commerce to diplomacy and the military to philosophy, art, music, and literature.

Various religious value systems have also influenced Western culture. Christian and Jewish values, rooted in their histories and sacred books, have contributed the concept that the proper life is moral, reflecting the will of God. Reason, emotions, and actions must be guided by God's commandments. Later, the Protestant ethic supported sacrificing one's impulses, urges, and desire for pleasure for calm, rational planning in accordance with God's will. The modern view of the Protestant ethic emphasizes work, savings, and sacrifice. The system supports economic values as well.

Values and Mental Health

When psychiatry began to assume importance in modern society, it brought with it the value of mental health, or adjustment. The goal of life was healthy adjustment rather than mere hard work, sacrifice, reason, or moral precepts. What, exactly, does psychiatry mean by mental health? For researchers such as White (1976), mental health has five important features:

1. *Psychological maturity (also termed emotional maturity).* Psychological maturity includes the following characteristics: (a) a shift from getting to giving; (b) independence; (c) freedom from inferiority feelings, egotism, and competitiveness; (d) appropriate socialization; (e) sexuality oriented less to self than to the other person; (f) a creative parental orientation rather than a destructive one; (g) a strong sense of reality; and (h) flexibility and adaptability.

2. *Ego strength.* This quality refers to strength of character, determination, and the ability to confront difficulties. The person who can endure frustration under stress, control emotional tension, and keep working toward his or her goals is showing ego strength.

3. *Liberation.* Liberation is a state in which the person is free to live life as he or she wishes while remaining aware of the demands made by reality.

4. *Self-actualization.* The self-actualized person is able to realize his or her fullest capabilities while living in conditions that are usually less than ideal.

TABLE 3-2   Sample Items from the Study of Values

From Part I (30 questions)

1. The main objective of scientific research should be the discovery of truth rather than its practical application.
   (a) Yes
   (b) No
4. Assuming that you have sufficient ability, would you prefer to be:
   (a) a banker?
   (b) a politician?
15. At an exposition, do you chiefly like to go to the buildings where you can see:
   (a) new manufacturing products?
   (b) scientific (e.g., chemical) apparatus?

From Part II (15 questions—rank-order preferences)

3. If you could influence the educational policies of the public schools of some city, would you undertake:
   ____a. to promote the study and participation in music and fine arts?
   ____b. to stimulate the study of social problems?
   ____c. to provide additional laboratory facilities?
   ____d. to increase the practical value of courses?
12. Should one guide one's conduct according to, or develop one's chief loyalties toward:
   ____a. one's religious faith?
   ____b. ideals of beauty?
   ____c. one's occupational organization and associates?
   ____d. ideals of charity?

Source: From G. W. Allport, P. E. Vernon, and G. Lindzey (1960). *A study of values.* Boston: Houghton Mifflin. Copyright 1960 by Houghton Mifflin Co. Reprinted by permission.

5. *Generativity.* This quality includes the ability to care for the next generation and for the institutions and traditions that will help foster the growth and development of that generation.

Clarification of Values

The current global situation of uneasy peace sometimes has been termed a crisis of values. Choices made today will affect not only the future of billions of human beings but even whether there is a future. Individuals must make choices no less momentous. Without a clear set of values, little guides us through the countless choices that confront us. These choices may include which major in college to select, how to handle sexuality, what career to pursue, whether to marry and have children, what political party to support, how to plan your financial future, and what long-range goals to set.

Clarifying your values can be more than a simple exercise. It can help you make decisions that build a satisfying and productive life. "Exploring Choices: Personal Characteristics Suggesting Value Problems," presents examples of common value problems. It may be wise to spend time in your college career examining what values are most important to you and whether you need to refine or change them.

EXPLORING CHOICES

PERSONAL CHARACTERISTICS SUGGESTING VALUE PROBLEMS

In drawing together several of the ideas in this section, note that Raths, Harmin, and Simon (1978) have identified several types of people who seem to be having difficulties leading integrated, value-directed lives:

1. Apathetic, uninterested people are energized by nothing. They are passive and uninvolved.

2. Flighty people are interested in many things but for only a moment. They go into projects with high spirits but quickly abandon them in favor of new ones.

3. People who are extremely uncertain have trouble making up their minds. They seem bewildered by the choices available to them.

4. People who are very inconsistent are involved in mutually contradictory, if not destructive, things. They are active one week and totally without energy the next. They are selfish one day and generous the next.

5. Drifters are without plans or enthusiasm. They are like ships without rudders.

6. Overconformers are without goals for their lives. They are attracted by each passing fad or trend.

7. Overdissenters are chronically nagging, complaining, and irrational in their dissent. They seemingly seek identity by opposing others.

8. Role players hide their fuzzy values by playing roles. They are like cardboard cutouts, without vitality or substance.

GARFIELD

Because of the contemporary problems with values, public schools have begun to offer programs in value clarification. These programs are often controversial. Many parents feel that teaching values is the job of parents, not schools. Others argue that the parents themselves have failed in the task of clarifying values for their children; therefore, if not the schools, who will do the job? School officials say that they are not trying to push a particular set of values; they are just trying to help children clarify their own values. More specifically, Raths, Harmin, and Simon (1978) claim that adults who would help children develop values should do the following:

1. Encourage children to make choices, and to make them freely.
2. Help them discover alternatives when faced with choices.
3. Help children weigh alternatives thoughtfully, reflecting on the consequences of each.
4. Encourage children to consider what it is that they prize and cherish.
5. Give them opportunities to affirm their choices.
6. Encourage them to act, behave, live in accordance with their choices.
7. Help them be aware of repeated behaviors and patterns in their life. (p. 38)

SUMMARY

1. The self is organized and consistent. It includes a sense of the I or me in a person. The importance of this concept has been recognized by laypeople and researchers alike.

2. The concept of self also includes the relationships between this I or me and other people and events. The self is usually conscious of its own existence and, though changing, is always recognizable.

3. The self includes a personal self-concept, social self-concepts, and self-ideals. The relationships among these various aspects of self can be harmonious or conflicting.

4. Once people have established a consistent sense of self, they tend to work at maintaining this self by engaging in various degrees of denial or distortion of reality. Self-schemata help preserve the consistency of one's self.

5. The development of the self is a complex, interpersonal process. Responses of parents and other caretakers to the developing child lead the child to create a self-system that includes a good-me, bad-me, and not-me.

6. Self-esteem is critical to healthy adjustment. It grows out of the reflected appraisals of the child by other people. Self-esteem is also influenced by social comparisons and social discrimination.

7. A more specific feature of self-esteem is self-efficacy—the belief that one can do what is required by a situation. Low self-esteem has a variety of negative effects on adjustment, while high self-esteem creates positive outcomes.

8. Improvements in self-esteem can be made by carefully examining one's assets and liabilities and by considering the values and goals that comprise one's ideal self.

9. Some observers believe that concern with the self has become a preoccupation, known as selfism or narcissism. Self-development is then used to justify avoiding commitment and responsibility to family, community, and others.

10. Motivation is closely linked to the self. A motive activates behavior and directs it toward one type of goal instead of another. Biological motives, reflexes, instincts, and drives are based on the physiology and nervous system of the organism.

11. In contrast, learned motives are acquired. Learned motivation includes such powerful motives as a need for achievement, for power, or for affiliation.

12. Values are standards or ideals of thought and behavior that a particular society has deemed good, desirable, or preferred. Once formed, values influence behavior, thoughts, and feelings in many ways and help determine the choices made.

13. Conceived values represent an ideal standard of behavior; operative values are those that actually guide actions in specific situations. Instrumental values refer to the means of attaining goals, while terminal values involve the goals or ends themselves.

14. Some researchers have argued that people can be categorized according to dominant value orientation as theoretical, economic, aesthetic, social, political, or religious persons.

15. Psychiatry has made adjustment, or mental health, an important value in modern society. Mental health has been defined to include the following personal characteristics: psychological maturity, ego strength, liberation, self-actualization, and generativity.

16. Clarifying one's values can help one make sound decisions and build a satisfying, productive life. Even public schools are beginning to deal with questions of values by introducing value clarification programs in the classroom.

Chapter 4

PATTERNS OF ADJUSTMENT THROUGH THE LIFE SPAN

THEORETICAL PERSPECTIVES

Psychoanalytic Perspectives
Behavioral-Social Learning Perspectives
Cognitive Developmental Perspectives
Issues in Development

THE COURSE OF DEVELOPMENT

Infancy
Childhood
Late Adolescence
   The task: leaving childhood
   The crisis: personal identity
Young Adulthood
   The tasks: marriage, children, and work
   The crisis: intimacy versus isolation
Middle Adulthood
   The tasks: guiding home, children, and career
   The crisis: generativity versus stagnation
   Midlife crisis: fact or fiction?
   Menopause
Later Adulthood
   The task: dealing with the aging process
   The crisis: integrity versus despair
Death and Dying

SUMMARY

Developmental psychologists are especially interested in the changes in thinking and behavior that occur throughout life. They are especially concerned with changes that signal substantial alterations in the individual's ability to cope with the world.

- Gail is a sophomore in high school. Her behavior has increasingly become a source of concern for her parents. Two years ago she was outgoing, almost always pleasant, and a real help around the house, but she has become surly toward her parents. She spends virtually every moment that she is home holed up in her room with the door closed. Her parents wonder, "Is Gail's behavior something we are responsible for, or is this some crisis or stage through which all adolescents go?"

- Tom, a 46-year-old dentist, had a loving, supportive wife; two children doing well in school; and a highly successful dental practice, but then he began to change. From three-piece suits he went to silk shirts open halfway down his chest. Next came expensive haircuts, an expensive sports car, and a torrid extramarital affair. After eighteen months of this, his wife divorced him. Friends and neighbors shook their heads sadly and decided it must be a midlife crisis.

- Harold worked for forty years as an accountant for a major trucking firm. He never got intrinsic satisfaction from his work and always wished he had chosen another career. He had no real hobbies. He did not enjoy socializing very much. For years, he looked forward to retirement. Then it happened—he retired. To the surprise of everyone, he has become a cheerful, actively involved senior citizen. Unlike some other older adults who retire, he seems to be enjoying life for the first time.

The three individuals just described underwent changes. Were these transitory changes, or were they fundamental shifts in their lives? Were these changes the result of the unfolding of some master blueprint hidden in the genetic fiber of all people? Are there critical periods in life that make one particularly vulnerable to certain experiences? Are these developmental changes the result of biological changes, products of experiences, or outgrowths of subtle interactions between biology and the environment? This chapter examines these questions as they relate to adjustment across the life span.

THEORETICAL PERSPECTIVES

As we saw in Chapter 2, human nature is elusive and subject to a variety of interpretations. This is no less true of development over the life span. In particular, there are three prominent developmental perspectives: (1) the psychoanalytic, (2) the behavioral-social learning, and (3) the cognitive developmental. We examine each in turn.

Psychoanalytic Perspectives

psychosexual stages
in Freudian theory, a universal course of sexual development with a different body area serving as a focus in each stage

Freudian psychoanalysis is viewed as developmental because it describes individuals as passing through sequential stages that are qualitatively different from one another. These were described in Chapter 2 as the **psychosexual stages**. As sexual energy is focused on succeeding parts of the body, the individual's behavior and orientation change accordingly. From this perspective, the individual is buffeted by biological urges that seek satisfaction. These begin with the oral stage, move on to the anal stage, thence to the phallic stage, and culminate in the genital stage. In each stage, the individual is thwarted by the demands of civilization—toilet training, threats of castration, and the like. In this sense, Freud was a stage theorist.

stage period in life in which a particular behavior or psychological characteristic asserts itself

A **stage** is a period in life in which a particular behavior or biological characteristic asserts itself. As a strict stage theorist would, Freud believed that the psychosexual stages are universal. More than that, he argued that how we weather each stage affects our later adjustment. Either too much or too little gratification in a given stage can mark the person for later difficulties.

Freud's was essentially a biologically determined stage theory. Each stage presented the individual with a different conflict or crisis over the gratification of instinctually determined urges. But one can be a psychoanalytic stage theorist without depending on biological urges so much. A case in point is the psychosocial theory developed by Erikson (1963). For Erikson, development was not so much defined in sexual terms as it was in terms of tasks that the individual must learn to master. Indeed, Erikson saw these tasks as crises to be overcome. Each stage presents the individual with a crisis—a point at which personality development can go one way or another. If the crisis is resolved poorly, future adjustment is impaired and the likelihood that the next crisis (stage) can be successfully resolved is diminished. A positive resolution has beneficial effects. Of course, most resolutions are neither all good nor all bad. The critical issue is the balance of the positive and the negative in each stage of development.

psychosocial stages
Erikson's term for development over the life span, which incorporates psychosexual factors but emphasizes interaction with the social environment and the resolution of crises at each stage

Erikson referred to his stages as **psychosocial stages** rather than psychosexual. This is no accident, since he saw stages as more than opportunities for sexual gratification of one sort or another. He saw them as encounters with other people and society. Especially important was Erikson's notion that these stages unfold in a predetermined sequence. The developing personality follows a ground plan that guides the individual toward broader and broader social interactions. While the details of this plan may vary somewhat from culture to culture, the basic elements of the psychosocial stages are universal.

Another special feature of the psychosocial stages is the fact that they occur over the entire life span of the individual. Erikson's willingness to address the crises of adulthood has made his work especially useful in the field of aging. We shall see Erikson's influence repeatedly as we deal later in this chapter with adjustment across the life span. For now, a brief description of his eight stages is presented in Table 4-1.

TABLE   4-1   Erikson's Eight Stages of Crises and Associated Emerging Traits

Stage	Age	Successful Resolution Leads To:	Unsuccessful Resolution Leads To:
1. Trust versus mistrust (oral)*	Birth– 1 year	Hope	Fear
2. Autonomy versus shame and doubt (anal)*	1–3	Willpower	Self-doubt
3. Initiative versus guilt (phallic)*	4–5	Purpose	Unworthiness
4. Industry vs. inferiority (latency)*	6–11	Competency	Incompetency
5. Ego-identity versus role confusion	12–20	Fidelity	Uncertainty
6. Intimacy versus isolation	20–24	Love	Promiscuity
7. Generativity versus stagnation	25–65	Fidelity	Selfishness
8. Ego identity versus despair	65–death	Wisdom	Meaninglessness and despair

*Roughly corresponding Freudian stage.
Source: E. J. Phares (1988). *Introduction to personality* (2nd ed.). Glenview, IL: Scott, Foresman, 123.

Sullivan (1953) was another psychoanalyst who moved away from the bio-logical determinism of Freud toward an interpersonal view of development. He saw development of the self as largely determined by interactions among the child, various family members, and others in the social environment. While holding to a stage conception of development, both Erikson and Sullivan did move psychoanalytic views a bit closer to the learning perspective. We now examine those views.

Behavioral-Social Learning Perspectives

Radical learning theorists have sometimes held that the human mind at birth is little more than a blank slate waiting to be written upon by the hand of expe-rience. The stages of development as well as the ultimate product of this devel-opment are dependent upon whatever is learned. This view was well repre-sented by Watson's remarks (quoted in Chapter 2) about molding children at will into doctors, lawyers, or even beggars and thieves.

Learning approaches rely heavily upon the principles of classical and oper-ant conditioning. For example, suppose a little boy shoves his smaller sister around, talks back to his parents, and generally becomes very negativistic. Conventional wisdom says that all little boys pass through such a stage be-tween, say, the ages of one and three years. It is to be expected and is pretty much inevitable. The learning theorist says that it is not. Whether the behav-ior becomes established is due to reinforcement. That is, the behavior is stamped in because it works for the boy; he gets what he wants more often than not. If the consequences are unpleasant, he will soon give up the negativism.

In addition, social learning theorists turn to such principles as observational learning. They see the cognitive processes of memory and perception as critical to understanding how we all acquire behaviors. Thus, the social learning perspective on development casts the individual in a more active role, interpreting experience instead of just reacting to it as the conditioning model would suggest.

Many learning theorists do not find stage approaches especially congenial. They tend to emphasize the differences among individuals of the same age rather than their similarities. In these differences, the learning theorist sees proof of the role of socioeconomic, ethnic, and cultural factors. Thus, the role of learning is more important than any internal blueprint that decrees that everyone will develop in exactly the same fashion. In fact, Bandura, the social learning theorist, asserts that people do not pass through well-defined stages at all (Bandura & Walters, 1963). Furthermore, he comments that rarely can stage theorists agree among themselves about the correct number of stages or the behaviors that occur within a given stage.

Cognitive Developmental Perspectives

These perspectives expand upon the cognitive elements within the social learning approach. In the cognitive developmental approach, the individual is said to construct an understanding of the world, which affects all corners of experience. Development becomes a process in which the person recasts ideas that do not work well. The individual's task becomes one of making sense out of the world. Some have referred to this as Piagetian theory, since the originator and prime proponent of the approach was Jean Piaget, the Swiss psychologist.

Piaget (1970) felt that children's thinking is quantitatively different from that of adults. This becomes clear as we examine the logic of children. For example, children learn to make generalizations about features of the world that they have not actually observed. Piaget was fascinated by the logical processes that enable children to get from the real, physical world to the world of concepts. He saw the growth of logic as a constant interaction between the present understandings of children and the reality successively encountered. Two cognitive processes, he felt, are especially important. **Assimilation** allows children to absorb and incorporate their environments in terms of their current understandings of the world. **Accommodation** is a process whereby these understandings are modified by new information from the environment. The existing **schema** (internal psychological structures or organizations) are thus affected by the processes of assimilation and accommodation.

Piaget (1977) described a sequence of stages through which the child passes. These stages transform the child's understanding of the world. Piaget was able to specify the principles and rules that determine how children think and reason. The four stages are the (1) **sensorimotor stage**—birth to two years, (2) **preoperational stage**—two to seven years, (3) **concrete operational stage**—seven to eleven years, and (4) **formal operational stage**—eleven years onward. All children go through these stages in the same order, although one child may develop faster than another. These stages begin with the primitive thought of

assimilation according to Piaget, a process by which a person's understandings of the world are modified by new information from the environment

accommodation according to Piaget, a process by which the person interprets elements of the environment in terms of his or her current understandings of the world

schema according to Piaget, internal psychological structures or organizations

sensorimotor stage Piagetian stage for the individual from birth to two years of age

preoperational stage first Piagetian stage of thinking

concrete operational stage second Piagetian stage of thinking

formal operational stage third Piagetian stage of thinking

the newborn, which consists of little more than automatic responding to stimuli, and end with the ability to respond to hypothetical questions, deal with abstractions, and design formal methods to test abstract ideas.

These stages differ from the psychoanalytic stages in at least two ways. First, they deal with changes in the child's cognitive processes rather than with sexual, emotional, or social agendas. Second, they result from the active exploration of the environment by the child, not from an inevitable unfolding of biological maturation. In contrast to social learning views, however, both the psychoanalytic and cognitive developmental perspectives describe fixed sequences of development, and they both see each stage as qualitatively different from all the others. According to the cognitive developmental perspective, children are not just miniature adults, following the same laws of behavior or thinking. When infants cannot see an object, that object does not exist! Only later does a child begin to realize that it is possible to think about objects not physically present. At first, the child learns slowly that a cause-effect relationship exists between behavior and environmental response. I scream, so someone comes running. Later, the child gets to the point of being able to mentally manipulate cause-effect sequences. If I *were* to scream, mother would come running but my brother Timmy would not. Children know the world differently from adults and they behave accordingly, but eventually their experiences enable them to think and perceive as adults.

A stage approach has also been applied to the development of moral reasoning. Kohlberg (1969), drawing upon Piaget's work, analyzed the thinking of thousands of children and adults from all walks of life, intellectual levels, and cultural backgrounds. Out of this mass of data, he determined three broad levels of moral development. He also believed that each of these levels, in turn, consists of two stages, as shown in Table 4–2. The stages are said to apply to everyone regardless of background.

At the same time, Kohlberg has his critics. Some have suggested that his scheme contains significant bias and that there is an almost cultish quality to his work. Others (such as Alston, 1971) claim that he placed too much emphasis on how people reason and too little on how they actually behave.

Issues in Development

A major issue in developmental psychology is that of learning versus maturation. Learning theorists see both the stages and the ultimate adult product of those stages as basically determined by learning experiences. Most parents, however, will tell you that this is more apparent than real. They will suggest that children pass through developmental stages on a predetermined schedule and even become one kind of person instead of another. Indeed, they say it is almost as if each child is walking along the path of life in step with a private drum—a path laid down by some hereditary force.

The hereditary force they are describing is usually referred to as **maturation**—developmental changes that are generally both regular and preprogramed as to when they occur. Thus, people crawl, walk, speak, and even

maturation
developmental changes that are regular, preprogrammed, and relatively unaffected by environmental conditions

TABLE 4-2   Kohlberg's Six Stages of Moral Reasoning

Level I—Preconventional morality (young children). Child is influenced by the consequences of a behavior and does not analyze society's standards.

- *Stage 1—Punishment-obedience orientation.* Actions are good or bad depending on whether one is punished or not punished.
- *Stage 2—Instrumental-relativist orientation.* Actions are geared toward satisfying one's own needs and wishes. Pragmatism is most important.

Level II—Conventional morality (middle childhood). Child is influenced by the ideals of maintaining the standards of the family, group, or country.

- *Stage 3—"Good or nice" child orientation.* Altruistic rather than selfish actions are desirable. Getting approval from others is paramount.
- *Stage 4—"Law and order" orientation.* One must act in accordance with authority and maintain social order.

Level III—Postconventional morality (adolescence and adulthood). One's sense of right and wrong becomes separate from identity with the group.

- *Stage 5—Social contract orientation.* General sense of rightness and wrongness, realization that there are different values, importance of consensus, awareness that intent is critical, and growth of empathy.
- *Stage 6—Universal orientation.* Evolution of one's own ethical position over the years. Principles are abstract and comprehensive.

Source: Adapted from "From Is to Ought: How to Commit the Naturalistic Fallacy and Get Away with It in the Study of Moral Development" by L. Kohlberg. In *Cognitive Psychology and Genetic Epistemology* by T. Mischel (Ed.). New York: Academic Press, 1971. Copyright by Academic Press. Used with permission.

pass through midlife crises on a roughly predetermined schedule. Of course, all such behaviors are subject to environmental influences.

The supporters of either of the above extreme views are surely few. Most developmentalists take a mainstream view, that both processes—learning *and* maturation—are critical. They argue that a true understanding of the developmental process most likely will come from studying how these two processes *interact* to create growth and change. Take the case of language. Although most children begin to use words and (later) sentences at about the same time, most little girls have more highly developed verbal skills than boys of the same age. This suggests the importance of maturation, but learning and experience are important as well. After all, children born and raised in New York City rarely say their first words with a southern accent. Even more extreme, some children develop stuttering speech patterns, in some cases because their parents put too much pressure on them as they struggle to master the new skill called speaking. In short, those who would account for everything as either learned or predetermined are likely to have difficulty understanding human growth and development.

Another reflection of the learning versus maturation issue is whether development is a continuous process (**continuous development**) or is best understood as occurring in stages (**discontinuous development**). In short, do people change gradually, a little bit each day, or is their behavior changed more abruptly as they enter and leave discrete stages? The answer is that continuity

continuous development
development that occurs gradually, without any clearly delineated stages

discontinuous development
development that occurs in discrete stages

and discontinuity operate side by side. Rarely does a person's behavior show radical changes from one day to the next, yet there are relatively abrupt changes. A child crawls for months and months and then suddenly, within the space of a week, is walking. The outlook on life of a 65-year-old is likely to be vastly different from that of a 35-year-old. Therefore, as one examines behavior on a day-to-day basis one will probably perceive little evidence of stages. But when one stands back and gazes with a longer perspective, the discontinuities seem to stand in sharp relief.

A final issue of importance is the manner in which developmental research is conducted. The answers to questions are always influenced by the methods employed to investigate them. Suppose you ask the question, How much does intellectual performance decline in later years? The answer depends upon whether you look at longitudinal or cross-sectional studies (Botwinick, 1984). **Longitudinal research** is research that follows the same persons over a period of years, usually taking repeated measures on the variable under study. In contrast, **cross-sectional research** is the study of different age groups at roughly the same point in time. Thus, researchers might test three groups of subjects, ages twenty, fifty, and seventy-five, all during the month of January 1988. In a longitudinal approach they would select a group of 20-year-olds, test them and then retest them when they are fifty and again at seventy-five.

In fact, longitudinal studies show less decline in intellectual performance than do cross-sectional studies. What is more, decline sets in later, as you can see when you examine data based on longitudinal rather than cross-sectional methods. One reason is that initially less able persons tend to drop out of longitudinal studies over the years. Thus, they are not available for later testing. Although there are other, more complex research designs, the point is that you must always interpret findings in the light of the methods of research used.

longitudinal research research in which subjects are tested and retested over intervals during their lives

cross-sectional research research in which subjects of different ages are tested at about the same time

THE COURSE OF DEVELOPMENT

The focus of this chapter is development through the life span. Therefore, we begin our journey through the developmental stages with a brief review of social development in infancy and childhood. A more extensive account of the specific stages of child development (including perception, intelligence, and language) may be found in Mussen et al. (1984).

Infancy

In infancy, the process of **socialization** begins. By this process, society, through the agency of the parents, attempts to make the individual like other members of society. At the same time, the complementary process of **differentiation** begins. This means the formation of a personal identity that is separate from the identity of others. Thus, while one must become like other members of the group, one must also achieve a measure of uniqueness. In a real sense,

socialization process by which a child comes to resemble the other members of the cultural group

differentiation process by which a child achieves an identity separate from the cultural group

Socialization and differentiation begin in infancy.

these complementary processes of socialization and differentiation continue throughout life.

The process of socialization begins with a pattern of behavior that allows the infant to achieve close, sustained contact with the parents. By a variety of behaviors, ranging from cooing to crying, the infant is able to attach itself physically and psychologically to its parents. This, of course, ensures the infant's survival through the parents' efforts to provide food, warmth, shelter, and the like. There is strong evidence that this **attachment process** is biologically determined (Harlow & Harlow, 1966). The attachment process has several interesting implications. For example, Ainsworth and Bell (1970) have studied in detail the behaviors shown by both secure and insecure infants as related to attachment. Securely attached infants seem more willing to explore their environments. They also tend to greet their mothers warmly after an absence.

Eventually, the attachment process gives way to an attempt to establish an identity separate from that of the parent. Asserting one's separateness can be seen, for example, in the so-called terrible twos, when the child seems to be little more than a package of negativism. While a two-year-old can be tough on parents, the individual is becoming a differentiated, or separate, person (Clarke-Stewart, Friedman, & Koch, 1985).

attachment process process by which the infant becomes bonded to the mother

Childhood

Childhood is a period of peer relationships. Especially between the ages of three and five years, a sense of cooperation and reciprocity begins. At earlier ages, children play together, but their play is likely to be either solitary (the child plays alone with toys in the presence of other children) or else parallel (the child plays independently with toys like those of nearby children). Later, play becomes interactive or cooperative (children play together and help each other in an activity involving both of them).

As children grow older, they begin to form more lasting friendships. Friends then are not just people to play with, but people in their own right, who share, listen, and help.

As in all early stages, parental influence is important. As an example, parents tend to evolve characteristic styles of child-rearing behavior. To illustrate, Baumrind (1968) has described three chief types. First, there is the **authoritarian style**. This is characterized by strictness and a demand for maturity coupled with what often amounts to poor communication and little warmth or support. The **authoritative style** is described as controlling and demanding but in a more democratic, nurturant context. In the **permissive style**, parents communicate a great deal with the child but provide little discipline, and they are not very demanding. Interestingly, Baumrind discovered that children of authoritative parents were the ones most likely to become socially responsible, achievement-oriented, and vigorous. This was especially true in the case of girls.

Another important task of childhood is the acquisition of sex roles and relationships. This, however, is a topic treated in detail in Chapter 9. Now, let us turn to a more detailed exposition of adolescence and the remainder of the life span.

Late Adolescence

For many observers, adolescence has always seemed to be a period of storm and stress (Keniston, 1975). One person, asked to recall her adolescence, described it this way:

> It was a blur of intensity. There were so many peaks and valleys that I could not keep track of them. I was happy, I was sad, I was confused. I wouldn't want to go through it again.

But another had this to say:

> I don't know, it was kind of pleasant, you know? I knew I had a lot ahead of me—college, marriage, and stuff. But I sort of relaxed and thought, hey, I better enjoy this while I can.

This seems to support observers such as Hill (1980), who question the storm and stress theory. Perhaps each stage of life has a different effect on each person. Even so, each stage is marked by a specific set of tasks to deal with, crises to resolve, and physical, behavioral, and emotional changes to understand.

In a sense, late adolescence is the period at which one is pulled away from childhood and into the adult role. In more primitive societies, the transition is

authoritarian style parenting style characterized by parental strictness, demands for maturity, and poor communication

authoritative style parenting style characterized by parental control carried out in a democratic, nurturant way

permissive style parenting style characterized by considerable communication on the part of the parents in the context of little discipline and few demands on the child

Parental influence is important to children.

celebrated with rituals and ceremonies. This makes the transition abrupt but clear. In modern Western societies the transition is more ambiguous and drawn out. As Newman and Newman (1984) put it, "In complex societies the end of adolescence is a psychological event rather than a social occasion" (p. 318). This reflects the fact that adolescence comes to a close only when the person finally makes a commitment to the adult role (marriage, a job, personal independence, and so forth). The critical factor is not one's age but one's state of mind. Some individuals forty years old and more are still psychologically and financially dependent on their parents. The commitment to an adult identity signals the passage into adulthood.

So, then, does one choose to be an adult or is one pushed by circumstances? Like most cases, the answer is both of the above. For one, circumstances may force the issue—pregnancy, death of a parent, and so on. In such cases, the person may not be well prepared for the transition. For another, a conscious, planned decision to become an adult may be the case—marriage, joining the military, or quitting school for a job. For most, however, choice and circumstance mingle to produce the outcome.

The task: leaving childhood. Although we often joke about it, homesickness can be excruciatingly painful. The college student or military recruit away from home for the first time may suffer in a way only one who has been through it can appreciate. It will pass, but it does not seem so at the time. Such a reaction suggests that the individual is for the first time facing one of the major tasks of late adolescence—achieving an identity separate from that of the parents (Erikson, 1963). For the first time perhaps, one must confront the end of one's own childhood. Sometimes the confrontation serves only to remind one of how nice it would be to return to that dependent state of childhood. The lonely college student lies awake in bed at night thinking of how great Mom's pies always tasted. The twinkling lights of town make the individual envious of the people who are safe and snug in their own homes while some "unfortunate" must endure a dormitory.

The tasks of late adolescence are moving away from childhood and developing a life separate from the parents (Erikson, 1963). In most cases this means the development of a sense of control separate from one's parents. Eventually, this will mean economic independence. It also may involve physical separation, holding a job in another city, or going to school away from home. Perhaps the sense of separateness first strikes adolescents when they begin to feel they are visitors in their parents' home.

None of this is usually sudden or dramatic, although it may sometimes seem so. Rather, there is a gradual evolution of independence over time. Initially, there is usually ambivalence toward independence. For example, eighteen-year-old college students do not want phone calls from home "just to see how you are doing." Visits from Mom and Dad may be completely taboo. Yet these same students may not be above dropping a few hints about extra money or sending home dirty laundry. Some students like to brag about their independence to other students or to make fun of their parents and their old-fashioned ideas. At times, the very intensity of these assertions of independence seems to suggest a hidden longing for a return to parental shelter.

Achieving independence, then, can be painful—painful for both the adolescent and the parents. In the quest for independence, the adolescent often reacts by seeming to reject all that the parents stand for. For some, even being pleasant to parents or crediting them with any positive qualities is equated with parental control and loss of independence. Fortunately, in most cases achievement of independence is gradual, which eventually allows the individual to realize that independence does not require rejection of the parents or even physical separation from them. Once independence is completed, the relationship between parent and adolescent can move to mutual acceptance. The truly independent person is no longer threatened by the parents. By the same token, independence need not be a threat to parents when they can see it for what it really is—the culmination of their own parental tasks. Successfully

Adolescents develop a
life separate from
parents.

completing the task of independence opens the way for the resolution of the major crisis of late adolescence—the attainment of a personal identity.

The crisis: personal identity. Whatever the content of adolescence may have been for a given individual (turmoil, struggle, contentment, or nonchalance), movement into adulthood is greatly facilitated by a sense of personal identity (Rogers, 1985). In late adolescence the individual has all the intellectual and physical tools of an adult, but in many areas of life, the person is still groping for a feeling of being oneself. In terms of social power, sexual values, and career goals, late adolescence is a period of transition.

Erikson (1963) attached great importance to the crisis of ego identity versus role confusion (see Table 4–1). He described this stage with great sensitivity, as the following remarks illustrate:

> Like a trapeze artist, the young person in the middle of vigorous motion must let go of his safe hold on childhood and reach out for a firm grasp on adulthood, depending for a breathless interval on a relatedness between the past and the future, and on the reliability of those he must let go of, and those who will "receive him." (p. 90)

identity crisis according to Erikson, a period in life in which the person struggles to define the "real me"

Erikson felt that so many conflicts arise out of this transition stage that he used the term **identity crisis** to describe them. This crisis reflects the struggles of the individual to define the "real me." Between the ages of sixteen and twenty or so, the person must begin to sort out the staggering array of life options available. This is truly a period of choices. From movies, television, magazines, peer interactions, and adult advice, the adolescent is literally bombarded with choices. Adults who are safe and secure in their roles and identities may have difficulty recalling their own adolescence. Thus, they may find it hard to sympathize with an adolescent, whose choices are both numerous and difficult—to study or drink beer; to take drugs or to say no; to be sexually active or not. Taken separately, each little choice on any given day may not mean much. Added up over time, however, the choices frame the adolescent's identity plight. Searching for an identity often means dealing with pressure, being exquisitely sensitive about the image peers have, and trying to match the self-image.

Finding yourself can be a period that is both difficult and lengthy. It often involves trying on for size a number of roles and aspirations. This search can include everything from idealism to vandalism, and falling in love to studying to having panic attacks. Role confusion often is the order of the day. Considering the turbulence of this period, we can begin to understand the attraction of rock groups, movie stars, and other charismatic figures. They provide a starlike quality to which the individual can relate and thereby take on some sense of personal identity.

An unresolved identity crisis can be discomforting and produce what appear to be pathological symptoms. One can lose a sense of time, self-consciousness may become acute, one may become unable to work, and sexuality may become confusing. Wagner, Lorion, and Shipley (1983), using questionnaires, found a greater incidence of insomnia in college students who had failed to resolve the crisis of identity. In most cases, this period is best regarded as one of developmentally induced stress; it is not usually a clinical disorder, since most individuals resolve the period without psychological treatment. The signs of successful resolution of an identity crisis include an acceptance of oneself and one's actions, a feeling of comfort and appropriateness associated with one's self-image, and a general sense of psychosocial well-being—a realization that "I am what I am" (Damon, 1983). "On the Research Frontier: The Crisis of Decision" discusses some research confirmation of these identity analyses.

Young Adulthood

For a long time, it seemed as if personality theorists were not very interested in anything beyond adolescence. After all, Freud taught us that our basic personalities are pretty firm by the age of six. But Erikson (1963) contended that development does not stop even with adolescence. Indeed, it could be argued that everything that has gone before young adulthood is but a prelude. At age twenty to twenty-two or so, young adulthood begins. The individual can look forward to another fifty years at least. In this period, the individual will learn to handle the several roles that define adulthood. The child is but a child—or maybe a student as well—but the young adult must edge into several roles at one time—worker, intimate partner, father or mother, and so on.

ON THE RESEARCH FRONTIER

THE CRISIS OF DECISION

Although Erikson described the stage of ego identity versus role confusion with great sensitivity, how do we know that he was right? Where, in other words, is the research evidence? Well, for one thing, Marcia (1980) has made a significant start in verifying some of Erikson's hypotheses. Marcia wanted to understand how people arrive at major decisions in their lives. Do they go through crises and conflicts? He concentrated on religious, occupational, and political decisions.

Marcia conducted extensive interviews with men and women to determine whether they had made commitments and, if so, whether there had been an associated crisis. From his interview data he concluded four levels of identity: (1) foreclosure, (2) identity achievement, (3) moratorium, and (4) identity diffusion. These levels may be described as follows:

- *Level 1: Foreclosure.* Firm commitment is made fairly early in life regarding occupation, ideology, and sexuality (in the case of women). Little sense of crisis is experienced. Parents play a big role in the early foreclosure of options. For example, the student who selects a premed major because his father is a doctor may make the decision before college.

- *Level 2: Identity achievement.* Commitment is achieved through trial and error, with resulting crisis and conflict. For example, the student who tries several majors before settling on one may fit this level. For females, this level can be quite stressful.

- *Level 3: Moratorium.* Crisis and conflict seem perpetual. The student is still experimenting with courses and majors but has no occupational goals. Anxiety is high for males here.

- *Level 4: Identity diffusion.* No identity has been achieved. Often there is really little conflict about it. The person may be a psychological drifter, who is not bothered by his or her lack of commitment.

This supports Erikson's theorizing about adolescence. The research also provides a framework for others to test Erikson's ideas. For example, Waterman, Geary, and Waterman (1974) found that first-year college students are more often at the moratorium level. As seniors, however, they have moved up to the identity achievement level. Of course, a person can be at one level in one sphere (say, religion) and at another level in another sphere (say, sexuality).

As an adult you must begin to gauge your behavior against standards of what is appropriate for your age. Your relatives may begin to worry if you remain unmarried at age thirty. If you are not promoted after five or six years on the job, you may begin to think others are wondering about you. Relationships with other people and the world of work begin to assume deeper dimensions. The time for childish dreams and superficial values is over.

The tasks: marriage, children, and work. In young adulthood the general frame-work of one's adult life begins to take shape; particularly in Western, indus-trialized societies. This framework reflects the choices one makes—to marry or to remain single; to have children or not; the kind of work or career to pursue; and general matters of life-style, including hobbies and the use of lei-sure time (Newman & Newman, 1984).

The overwhelming majority of men and women marry sometime during their lifetimes (Stevens-Long, 1984). As the rehearsal period of dating winds down and young adulthood proceeds, increasing pressure is placed upon the single person to marry. For those whose personal identity is still diffuse, there is often difficulty in establishing such intimate relationships (Orlofsky, Mar-cia, & Lesser, 1973).

Of course, marriage does not end all stresses in life, for it has its own pecu-liar conflicts. Two people must quickly get on the same wavelength regarding sexuality, money, food, friends, leisure activities, parents, in-laws, and much more. In successful marriages, a commitment emerges out of the stress and conflict and greater intimacy, trust, and mutuality develop. In some ways, mar-ital adjustment is even more difficult for women than it is for men (Bell, 1983). Women often have less work experience and are often financially dependent on their husbands. They may have anxieties about childbearing and child rear-ing. Then, too, men may have trouble coping with the intimacy and commit-ment desired by their wives. When the level of marital stress becomes exces-sive, the response is often divorce, which can represent another assault on one's sense of identity. Divorce continues to be a significant social phenom-enon in the United States. For example, the divorce rate in 1981 was 23 per 1,000 married women fifteen years of age and older (U.S. Department of Commerce, 1983). Somehow, the divorced person must forge a new identity.

The decision to have children is a complicated one. Once the decision is made, the presence of a child creates one of the most formidable tasks facing the young adult couple (Perlmutter & Hall, 1985). The physical demands of caring for a newborn can be draining. The marital relationship itself enters a new phase. There are issues about the division of labor in caring for the child, especially when both parents work outside the home. No longer can a spouse lay exclusive claim on the time, emotions, and attention of the partner. There is now a competitor in the family.

One must also grapple with the new role of a parent. Sometimes this can mean fighting through one's selfism. A new social attachment must be formed and given prominence. A sense of responsibility for a dependent, loving child can be one of life's greatest rewards, but it can also awaken a feeling of inade-quacy or fear. One must face up to what it really means to be an adult.

Work is still another critical area for both men and women in young adult-hood. Work, too, requires choices (Perlmutter & Hall, 1985), and these choices often span several years. Some jobs require a heavy investment of time and money (it takes ten or more years to become a physician); others require but a few months of training. The choices also require an inventory of personal skills, abilities, interests, motivation, and the like. For women, the choices are even more complicated, since women must weigh traditional female role expectations against career goals. The individual must learn how to deal with authority figures as well as peers in the workplace. The socialization can often be as important as the job skills themselves. The choices one makes largely determine the satisfactions down the road. "Exploring Choices: The World of Work" illustrates several of the choices facing males in the world of work across the span of early adulthood.

The crisis: intimacy versus isolation. The decade of the twenties is a period in which the establishment of a durable, intimate relationship with another person becomes paramount. One's newly found identity can be committed to

EXPLORING CHOICES

THE WORLD OF WORK

Levinson and colleagues (1978) carried out an extensive series of interviews. They interviewed forty males in four different occupations—a biologist, a novelist, an executive, and an hourly worker. They were able to divide the early adulthood period (ages seventeen to forty) into four stages. Each stage can be viewed as presenting the person with a series of choices. An outline of the four stages and the problems and choices they entail follows:

1. *Early adult transition (ages 17–22).* The major choice is between continued dependence or a move toward independence. For example, does the person leave home and join the military, go to college, or find a job, or does the person remain at home or otherwise fail to really begin to affiliate with an organization outside the family unit?

2. *Early adult period (ages 23–28).* The major choice is the selection of an occupation.

This is not necessarily a final choice; rather, the person is often engaged in exploring occupational options.

3. *Mid-thirties transition (ages 29–33).* The major choice is occupational commitment. The exploratory phase of the earlier periods is winding down. This is the time to change once and for all or else accept a commitment to the present occupation.

4. *Settling down (ages 34–40).* The choice has been made. It is time to consolidate one's position and move up the occupational ladder. An important choice is whether to be independent or remain in the shadow of others. The process of achieving an independent role often leads to conflict with others and the breaking of one's ties to them. For example, a junior executive finally must choose whether or not to sever ties with an older, more experienced corporate protector.

another person. An identity creates the opportunity for love, affiliation, intimacy, and commitment. For Erikson, the failure to build a stable identity prevents relationships from developing fully. Such a person is likely to withdraw into isolation or to create a false sense of intimacy through shallow, transitory relationships that fail the test of commitment. Keeping others at an emotional arm's length fosters isolation and leads to superficial human relationships. Intimacy requires that one give as well as take in a relationship. One must learn to find pleasure in the relationship. Identity must be bound up with others—spouse, children, coworkers—and not reflect just oneself any longer.

A sense of intimacy arises out of the ability of people to meet each other's needs. In addition, there must be the ability to accept the weaknesses and failures (or even, sometimes, the strengths) of the other. If adolescence is a period of fantasy and idealization, adulthood is a period of reality. Failure to deal with reality fosters isolation or regression to less mature stages of adjustment. Much of this discussion is reducible to an awareness of shared experiences. Sharing a house, a child, a promotion, or even tragedies binds people together. Sharing one's life with a spouse, a friend, or even (to some extent) a coworker can lead to mutual trust. This trust reflects the commitment of one person to another. Feelings of trust can move people to new plateaus of intimacy. Lack of trust will eventually shatter a relationship and propel a person toward isolation.

Middle Adulthood

This stage of life is commonly described as a lengthy period from an age as young as thirty to about age sixty. However, based on a review of several studies, Whitbourne and Weinstock (1979) divide middle adulthood into Phase I (ages 30–45) and Phase II (ages 45–60). Also, you saw in "Exploring Choices: The World of Work" that Levinson described early adulthood as lasting from age seventeen to age forty. Yet others (for example, Newman & Newman, 1984) describe it as ending at age thirty. Thus, you should not be surprised to find that investigators divide the stages in varying ways. It all depends upon the purposes, the particular subject populations, and the methods of study.

Because middle adulthood is often described as a lengthy period, it can sometimes seem as if development and change are slow. This is especially true when looking at the rate of physical and intellectual change that went on during infancy and childhood. But if you ask adults in middle adulthood how fast things are moving, the answer will likely be, "Very fast indeed!" During this time, events seem to race by so quickly that change seems continuous and universal. The point is that middle adulthood is a period of important changes and development. The changes and development are more likely to be social and psychological than physical or intellectual. Usually during this period, the wider vistas of life begin to open. A sense of perspective and generativity, (the desire to contribute to coming generations) begins to appear. The younger person may think that little is going on in middle adulthood. For the person in it, the period is busy indeed.

The tasks: guiding home, children, and career. Some observers have analyzed the management of a household in terms of administrative or executive skills (Newman & Newman, 1984). Successfully running such a unit often requires an ability to assess the needs and skills of all living in that unit. The family may include the married couple, children of varying ages, and sometimes an elderly parent. Each of these people is an individual, with different needs, aspirations, and abilities. Successfully managing a home demands the sensitive and continuing assessment of all such characteristics.

Guiding children is a task of middle adulthood.

Assessments help the decision-making process. Even the barest familiarity with what goes on in a household is enough to suggest the avalanche of decisions that must be made. Can we afford a new car, and if so, then what kind? What color paint should we use for the house? Should Billy be allowed to watch television when his homework is not done? Should Mary go to parochial school, or would she be better off in public school? Should I wash the clothes today or wait till tomorrow? Do I need to go to the store tonight? Should we go swimming at the lake or camping in the mountains? Is it time to pay back our friends with a party, or can it wait another month? Should toilet training be started right now or in another month? Do I spank the kids or cut off their allowances?

How these decisions are made, who makes them, and under what conditions help define the tasks of the middle years. Does one person in the family (mother or father) make most of the decisions? Are the children left out of the decision making while the adults in the family decide? Or does everyone in the family—children (to the extent they are intellectually able), parents, and grandparents alike—share in the responsibility?

Increasingly, however, people are delaying marriage for a variety of social, economic, and personal reasons. One especially salient reason is the declining prejudice against single persons (in particular, unmarried women). The career-oriented woman may even be admired by her female married friends these days. The changes in attitudes about marrying young do not, however, always extend to remaining single forever (Rice, 1986).

Raising children is another central task of middle adulthood for many people (Perlmutter & Hall, 1985). This can be a form of on-the-job training, since few are really prepared for it. With successive children, the job usually becomes easier and less influenced by feelings of inadequacy and anxiety.

Of course, the tasks of raising children vary with the age of the child. The period of pregnancy and the ensuing months of infancy present the tasks of forming an attachment to the child and providing it with intense care. Providing a safe, caring, and reassuring environment for the child dominates the parents' attention. But children grow. Infants turn into toddlers, who challenge parents in new ways. Methods for controlling the child through discipline must be found and limits to the child's attempts to overcome parental control and develop autonomy must be imposed. First, parents merely take care of the child. Next, training the child to become a real human being begins, with all the rules, rewards, and punishments. Children of even the most sainted parents are not always going to find the imposition of rules pleasant.

Then, there is the period of elementary school to the eighth grade. During this period, parents often become very involved in the school system and related acitivities. Their lives may seem to revolve around the parent-teacher association. When parents are not involved in some school activity, they are probably busy chauffeuring the kids and their friends around town somewhere. Parents move beyond simple care and imposition of rules; they actively help their children expand their horizons and broaden their competencies and interests.

Every stage of child development seems to tax parents' emotional resources, but adolescence seems to push many to the very brink. Adolescents are striving for independence. They have their own lives with peer groups, and they spend much time away from home. Parents often feel they are losing control. Earlier, the issues were controlling a high fever or making sure the child ate the right food. With adolescent children, the issues include sexual activity, drugs, and vandalism. How the parents handle the delicate balance between maintaining control over their children while giving them increased freedom and responsibility becomes crucial. Love, communication, and trust are the beacons that illuminate healthy parent-child relationships at this stage.

Later, children go to college, leave home for a job, or leave to establish their own homes. For parents with only one child, this is an abrupt transition, which can be trying. With several children in the family, the transition is usually more gradual, providing a better opportunity to adjust. How the parents handle the transition varies a great deal. For some parents, the empty nest syndrome is fraught with anxiety. Others find the new freedom to be exhilirating (Glenn, 1975). They can rejuvenate their own interests and even get to know each other again. But this, too, can be stressful; parents may find the only thing they have in common is the children, who now are gone.

Of course, the parent-child relationship still exists. The child often remains financially dependent on the parents for some years. The child still has the problems of career selection, marriage, and the like, about which the parents can offer advice and support. Psychologically, the parents often remain a safety net for their children, even though those children are young adults with their own responsibilities and stresses. Just knowing the parents are there in case of need can be extremely reassuring to young adults and gratifying as well to the parents.

A growing task of many middle-aged people, especially women (since the culture seems to expect this sort of thing from them) is that they look after their own aging parents or those of their spouses. It appears that the family cycle may include the care of aging parents shortly after the oldest child leaves home.

A particularly satisfying role develops for many as they become grandparents. Some grandparents have been known to remark that the great thing about being a grandparent is that you can have all the fun of being a parent without the responsibility. Aside from this, there is real pleasure in observing the continuity of life. For the first time, perhaps, a person gains a real sense of the life cycle. Seeing one's children function successfully as parents themselves can be a source of pride. It can also be a reminder of what one has contributed to the lives of others. Being a grandparent can also help revitalize one's experience. Once more, it is possible to see things through the eyes of a child. Ordinary events take on new meaning as you rediscover with the help of an open, curious child. Grandparents play a variety of roles (Kivnick, 1982). Some spoil the child, some reengage the past through the child, some sense a kind of immortality, some play the role of elder, and others combine several roles.

In addition to managing a home and children, middle adulthood presents the challenge of managing a career. One's personal growth can often be measured by the yardstick of career development. In an occupation, one must learn to both cooperate and compete with others. Out of such experiences the person grows or else falls back. In either case, development has occurred. Other facets of career or occupation are learning how to deal with authority figures and how to assume personal authority and responsibility. A major part of one's personal identity is developed out of the way in which one comes to grips with interpersonal and authority relationships in the workplace. This says nothing of the work or career competencies and skills developing at the same time.

To a significant extent, people are judged by the skills they display over the course of a life of work. In addition, the person must learn to balance the demands of work with the demands of marriage and family. The potential for conflicts among these three spheres is great. Sometimes they are so great that families or relationships come apart under the strain.

The stresses of marriage, career, and family have been complicated further by the growth in careers for women. Both husband and wife often work these days. Even though many males pay lip service to sharing household and child care chores, often the two responsibilities actually fall disproportionately on the working wife. For the woman who either must work or wants to work, this can be a heavy burden. Some in society object to mothers working outside the home. However, little evidence indicates any detrimental effects on the children of such mothers (Gold & Andres, 1978).

The crisis: generativity versus stagnation. It was Erikson's (1963) belief that during the period of middle adulthood the dominant motive that emerges is one of contributing to the next generation—**generativity**. This motive can be fulfilled by raising a family successfully or by being a productive, creative person in many other ways. The central concern is one of caring about those who will come next—future generations. When one fails to be guided by the aspirations of generativity, the outcome is likely to be personal stagnation, boredom, and shallowness—a kind of self-defeating focus.

generativity in Erikson's theory, the developing concern in middle age for the well-being of the next generation

By the end of middle adulthood, the motive of generativity is, ideally, firmly in place. Since no one lives forever, individuals cannot hope always to guide the lives of their children, friends, or fellow citizens. Therefore, individuals must learn to contribute to society in ways that ensure that things will be good for those who follow. Through this motive of generativity, society continues to grow and flourish despite the continual demise of the individuals in it.

The generativity motive is not reserved just for eminent people, such as Einstein, Lincoln, or Curie. There are also the people who, in lesser ways, give of themselves to their children, their work, or their community. Individually these contributions may not amount to much, but collectively they are the cement that holds together the bricks that are society so that future generations can continue. Adler (1939) referred to this as **social interest**—a predisposition nurtured by experience to contribute to society. More precisely, it is a desire to subordinate one's selfish motives in favor of the good of others. The person headed for stagnation has failed to learn this lesson.

social interest according to Adler, a predisposition nurtured by experience to contribute to society

midlife crisis popular term used to describe a stressful period of identity crisis thought to commonly occur in middle-aged males

Midlife crisis: fact or fiction? The idea that around age forty there is a midlife transition has been widely circulated in recent years. In the case of men, this is said to be a potentially stormy period, or a **midlife crisis**. The male begins to realize that he is not going to live forever; that youthful plans, hopes, and dreams are not working out. It becomes a phase of evaluation and reappraisal (Gould, 1972). The male finds himself asking such questions as, "Should I switch jobs?" Or "Is this marriage really a fulfilling one?" This is a period in which one's fundamental life values and goals are questioned. The stereotype here is of the 40-year-old male dentist described at the beginning of this chapter. Although midlife crises usually are attributed to men, there is some evidence that women, especially independent, career-oriented women, sometimes have similar experiences (Livson, 1976).

Others have suggested that the evidence for a special or inevitable midlife crisis is rather thin. For example, Vaillant (1977) reported that depression and

"I THOUGHT THEY'D HIT IT OFF. THEY'RE ALL GOING THROUGH THEIR MID-LIFE CRISES."

crisis at midlife are exceptions rather than the rule. What is more, every stage produces its share of crises and disharmony.

The concept of midlife crisis became prominent upon the publication of Levinson's research (noted earlier—"Exploring Choices: The World of Work"). This research was done in the late 1960s and early 1970s. During these years a lot of men were engaged in self-analysis. The times were heavy with self-doubt, uneasiness, and restlessness. Perhaps what Levinson and his colleagues thought was characteristic of many men in their forties was really culturally determined—a product of the times. Maybe when the economy is shaky men are too busy to wallow in their crises, but the idea of the pervasiveness of midlife crises in men persists. The idea is so common that one wonders whether men, expecting to have a midlife crisis, actually set about fulfilling those very expectations.

menopause in women who are in their late forties or early fifties, cessation of ovulation and menstruation sometimes accompanied by physical changes such as hot flashes and mood swings

Menopause. In the late forties or early fifties women cease ovulation and menstruation—a time known as **menopause**. Often, there are accompanying physical changes, including hot flashes and mood swings. All of this, coupled with a realization that having children is no longer possible, was once thought to cause inevitable neurotic reactions and sometimes major depressive episodes. Because "everyone" was sure, women's expectations for problems at this stage of life became self-fulfilling prophecies. Most investigators have come to the conclusion that both the attitudes and behaviors associated with menopause are determined more by learning than by the physical changes themselves. For example, Neugarten and her colleagues (1963) surveyed women's attitudes toward menopause. One of the striking findings was that women aged 45–55 felt that they became more confident after menopause and that the symptoms of menopause could be controlled. As women approached the age of menopause they became less worried about such matters as losing their husbands or experiencing mental problems. Younger women even expressed the belief that menopause brings with it an increased interest in sex. In a similar vein, research by Greene and Cooke (1980) indicates that psychological factors are more important than biological ones in explaining women's reactions to menopause. Still, old myths die hard.

Later Adulthood

This period is variously described as beginning at age sixty or sixty-five and lasting until death. Some prefer to use the categories of early old age (65–74) and advanced old age (75 or older), but defining old age as beginning at sixty-five is really arbitrary, based more on social custom and Social Security regulations than anything else. Whatever the exact definition, however, it is clear that the elderly are growing in number and are becoming an increasing subject for study. By the year 2025, it is estimated that 15 percent of the population of North America will be over sixty-five. Currently, about 11 percent of the population is over sixty-five. Some projected effects of changes in life expectancy are shown in Figure 4–1.

FIGURE   4-1   Population in the United States (by age and sex)
                      in 1978 and Projected to 2000 (in thousands)

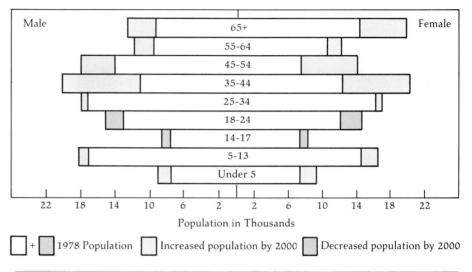

Source: U.S. Department of Commerce (1980). *Statistical abstract of the United States: 1979* (100th ed.). Washington, DC: U.S. Government Printing Office, 8–9.

From birth on, women survive at a higher rate than men. This means that a disproportionate number of the elderly are women. All too often, the elderly have very small incomes. Their lives become burdened with the problems of poverty, including poor health. Loneliness is also a compelling reality for many of them.

More than anything, aging is an individual process. It is not a state that begins for everyone at sixty-five. The actual reduction in ability between the ages of forty and seventy is very small (assuming that one's spouse has not died, that there has been no forced retirement, and that one's health is good). Of course, a slow decline in perceptual and cognitive abilities occurs, but too often the aged are defined by extreme cases, who are poor or sick. Most of the older adults are not like that at all, yet there is a tendency to stereotype groups. In fact, there are a lot of myths about aging, as Table 4–3 illustrates (p. 112).

The task: dealing with the aging process. As noted a moment ago, in general, there is little decline in competency from age forty to age seventy. Yet there is a gradual decline in resiliency. This decline is perhaps most apparent in sensory capabilities. Hearing, vision, taste, and smell suffer somewhat from the aging process (Kermis, 1984). Although each sense becomes less acute, or reactive to stimuli from the environment, adjustments and corrections are often possible. Lights can be turned up and sound levels can be raised a bit. Though there is loss in sensitivity, there are wide variations in these losses from person to

TABLE 4-3   Some Myths About Aging

There is a good deal of mythology about the aging individual, which often turns into a form of prejudice, called *ageism*—the tendency to make inaccurate prejudgments about the elderly. Neuhaus and Neuhaus (1982) have identified several of these myths.

1. Everyone steadily goes downhill after sixty-five.
2. Old people are all pretty much alike.
3. Old age is a form of disease.
4. The elderly really have it easy in so many ways.
5. Everybody should retire at sixty-five, since old people cannot work very well.
6. Old people just cannot learn new skills.
7. The elderly have little interest in sex and certainly not very much capacity for it.
8. Most of the elderly are bedridden and dependent.
9. Aging individuals are all quite conservative.

person. Some people at seventy can barely move; others are out jogging. Focusing on the competencies of the elderly, not on the limitations, is crucial.

There is also evidence that the elderly do not respond as rapidly to stimuli as they once did (Botwinick, 1984). This slowing can be seen in reaction time, speed of movement, problem solving, remembering, and so on, but many of the changes are products of situations or temporary states. For example, an unfamiliar task may lead to lowered motivation or to a heightened fear of making mistakes. Put the individual in a different setting and the outcome may be quite different.

In many tasks, decline is barely noticeable. In fact, on certain phases of intelligence tests (such as information and vocabulary), the older adults often do better than the young. Sometimes, the elderly perform more poorly on memory tasks than younger people. However, when the memory tasks are more relevant to the aging person's experience, performance is usually much better. Also, when the elderly are encouraged to use better strategies for processing and retrieving material to be recalled, their performance improves (Burke & Light, 1981).

In general, tasks that require speedy responses place the elderly at a disadvantage. Similarly, living a barren existence in an unstimulating environment hampers performance in most cases as much as the presence of physical limitations, such as heart problems or sensory deficits. Perhaps the most difficult obstacle to overcome is the person's perception of himself or herself as incompetent, obsolete, or unworthy. Beyond the age of eighty, however, a tangible decline is apparent for most individuals. In closing this section, we summarize Neugarten's (1976) views:

1. The elderly who remain physically and mentally active do better than those who become inactive.
2. Educational level is related to performance in the older years. The greater one's education, the higher the performance level is.

3. Those who are intellectually less competent tend to die younger than those whose intellectual level is higher.

4. Older men show a greater intellectual decline than do older women.

The bottom line is that virtually everyone is capable of learning. This applies to the elderly as well as the young. However, it may be that the techniques for teaching the elderly should be altered somewhat on occasion, as shown in "Exploring Choices: Instructing the Elderly."

Another major task of later adulthood is adapting to a change in one's life role. More specifically, there is often a loss of role. These years can be bittersweet. With advancing age comes the loss of friends and even spouse through death. For many in this period, the role of grandparent must also be mastered.

disengagement
process of mutual withdrawal of the person and society, often said to begin in late middle age but especially prominent as one retires from work

Retirement can be loaded with great pain or can lead to equally great satisfaction. Retirement often signals a kind of **disengagement** (that is, a phasing out from society) for some older people. It can bring with it a lowering of self-esteem and loss of satisfaction, almost as if one's purpose for being has been lost. For the first time, the person may realize just how much one's personal identity is tied to the work role.

It need not be this way, however. In a survey of nearly 2,000 retirees, Streib and Schneider (1971) found that few in their sample felt negative about their

EXPLORING CHOICES

INSTRUCTING THE ELDERLY

Aiken (1962) has suggested the following instructional techniques when teaching the elderly:

1. Provide ample time for students to master the lesson or task.

2. Repeat the material to be learned several times if necessary.

3. Employ a generous amount of positive reinforcement, providing for success experiences as needed.

4. Set short-term goals that students are capable of attaining within a reasonable period of time.

5. Use shorter practice periods than with younger students, because older people are more easily fatigued.

6. Verbalize what you are doing and have the learners do also, when demonstrating a physical skill.

7. Be aware of and make provisions for those students with visual or auditory defects (e.g., sufficient illumination, books with large print, tape recordings, louder than normal speech). (p. 91)

lives or that retirement was really unpleasant. As we have seen in other events, retirement is personal. It is dealt with differently by different people. Given preparation for retirement, good health, adequate financial resources, and the support of relatives or friends, retirement can be highly rewarding. Others have noted that retirees develop individual styles of life (Walker, Kimmel, & Price, 1980–81). For example, there are the *reorganizers* (usually volunteer workers), the *holders on* (those still doing paid work), the *rocking chair people* (those who do not do much of anything), and the *dissatisfied* (those having trouble keeping busy).

Often, adjusting to retirement is gradual. Atchley (1976) describes the retired individual as going through several stages. First, there is the *honeymoon* phase, a period of perceived freedom and satisfaction. Later, there is the period of *disenchantment*, when the person begins to realize that retirement is not all it was cracked up to be. Next comes the *rebuilding* phase, when both reality and fantasy are confronted and integrated. This period gives way to a *stable life* and, finally, to *death*. These descriptions are, of course, stereotypical. Many individuals are exceptions. Research will have to clarify how widely they apply.

Another major role change can be one of dealing with a decreasing ability to maintain independence and personal control. Age sometimes brings with it physical problems—one can no longer drive, shop alone, or do simple household chores. All too often, one's initial reaction of frustration in the face of these obstacles turns into depression and bitterness. The importance of allowing the elderly person to maintain at least some semblance of personal control is shown vividly in research by Langer and Rodin (1976). They studied groups of nursing home residents aged 65–90. One group was allowed to exert a relatively great deal of personal control. The individuals could arrange their rooms as they liked, meet visitors where they wished, and decide how to spend their time (read, watch television, and such). They were also urged to complain to the staff when problems arose. Each was also given a plant to care for personally. A comparison group was left with the impression that everything was a matter of staff responsibility and that the staff was eager to take care of every need—even to the point of caring for their plants!

Even though the residents in each group were matched in terms of health, clear differences emerged in the residents by the conclusion of the study. The group with personal control was more alert and happy. The individuals generally felt better than did those in the comparison group. Staff ratings of their behavior confirmed these self-ratings. The results were exceptional in themselves, but also suggestive were the results of a follow-up study eighteen months later (Rodin & Langer, 1977). Only half as many personal control residents (7 out of 47) had died as had residents in the comparison group (13 out of 44). This result was, however, only marginally significant statistically, but it certainly bears further investigation. In any case, the implications of this research for the importance of personal control in the aging are quite clear. As a side note, however, it is important to consider ethical issues in the quest for increased knowledge about the aging process (see "On the Research Frontier: When Research and Ethics Collide").

ON THE RESEARCH FRONTIER

WHEN RESEARCH AND ETHICS COLLIDE

Schulz (1976) believed that much of the depression that goes along with physical decline in the aged is due to a loss of personal control. To prove his point, he asked college students to visit residents (ages 67–96) of a retirement home. The visits took place under four conditions:

1. Residents completely controlled the length and frequency of the visits.
2. Residents knew when the visitor would come but could not control the timing or duration of the visits.
3. Residents received visitors in the same pattern as in Condition 1, but the visits appeared to be random.
4. Residents received no visits at all.

The results showed that when residents could either control or predict their visits by the students, their health status, psychological condition, and activity levels were better than those for residents who were visited randomly or not at all.

Later, Schulz and Hanusa (1978) conducted a follow-up study on the same residents to see whether the earlier results persisted for as long as forty-two months. What they found was both startling and dismaying. Not only did the positive effects of personal control not hold up, but the two groups that had most benefited from the visits showed a drastic decline in health and zest after the forty-two months.

These results raise important points. First of all, in trying to increase someone's sense of personal control, researchers should be careful not to use inherently unstable methods. That is, visits such as those used in this study cannot go on forever. Thus, personal control is tied to people (students) who in reality cannot be completely controlled or predicted by the resident. When the visits cease abruptly, the resident must find an explanation. The explanation may turn out to be that what was thought to be personal control was really an illusion. Facing an illusion may be so shattering that it not only wipes out the gains formerly achieved but pushes the individual even farther toward apathy and gloom.

If this is so, then the second point becomes an ethical one. Does such research actually harm the participants? In the present example, is it responsible to allow bonds of friendship between visitors and residents to develop only to be terminated in the name of research design? Is it responsible to build a sense of control only to remove it later? These are critical issues that each investigator must answer. Fortunately, Schulz and Hanusa had the presence of mind and the courage to raise these questions about their own work. By doing so, they have provided a service and reminder to us all.

The fact that Rodin and Langer (1977) did not encounter similar adverse long-term effects in their research is probably explained by the nature of the interventions they used. The sense of control they induced was probably less dependent on another figure (visitor) and more directly related to the residents' own efforts.

By and large, the image people have of the elderly is that of a group of hypochondriacs who like to sit around and recite their ailments or describe their latest surgery. Actually, even this stereotype is probably no worse than the one of adolescents endlessly examining their acne problems, hairstyles, and physical development. Recently, however, more and more observers are concluding that aging individuals are not excessively or unrealistically concerned with their health (Costa & McCrae, 1985). Contrary to myths, the enderly are not chronic complainers. In fact, given the burden of their real illnesses and disabilities, they are remarkably calm. Nor are most elderly confined to nursing homes or bedridden, as noted in Table 4–3.

Another myth, also noted in Table 4–3, is that the elderly display little in the way of sexual interest. The truth is that people's sexual habits and inclinations in later years are continuations of their earlier sexual habits. The person who was active early will continue to be active in later adulthood assuming health permits and the opportunity is there. Although there is a gradual decline in sexual activity for both sexes, the range in activity level is as great as for any other age group. Even the elderly contain their share of sexual athletes! The decline for women sets in noticeably in the late sixties, but this is most often due to the husband's death or illness or his lack of interest. For men, the biggest decline occurs in the late seventies, but men generally show greater interest and activity than women even up to the age of ninety. However, it is interesting to note that older men seem to talk more about their sexual activities and interests than their performance would warrant (an observation probably not exclusive to older males). Nevertheless, the stereotype that so many younger people have of the sexless aged is simply not true.

The crisis: integrity versus despair. From the age of sixty to sixty-five or so until death, the individual has the opportunity to consolidate the experiences of the previous stages into a final period of **integrity**. Ideally, this integrity represents a period of contentment resulting from the acceptance of the worth of one's life on earth. One cherishes the experiences, people, and events of life without wishing they could have been different. By recognizing the inevitability of so many things in life, one can come to value and accept them. The person can review life and find much that has been good. Of course, when integrity fails, despair takes its place. Fear of death, disappointment, resentment, and depression make reviewing one's life painful and an examination of the present unrewarding. However, the circle is complete, as Erikson notes, when mature adults who have obviously achieved a sense of integrity provide models that convince the young that life can be trusted and is truly worth living.

One process that can help one reach the integrity stage is *life review*, or **reminiscence**. This is a process by which recall of the past can often have highly therapeutic benefits. The popular image has always been that of elderly people who sit around and live endlessly in the past. Often, they betray a failing memory in the process—or so it is said. Butler (1961), however, countered this conventional wisdom by claiming that reminiscence is a normal, even vital, process of life review that can give meaning to life as one approaches death.

integrity for Erikson, a period of contentment resulting from the acceptance of the worth of one's life in the past as well as the value of the present

reminiscence process in which review and recall of the past can hasten the stage of integrity (sometimes referred to as life review)

Older adults are often unfairly stereotyped.

More recently, Butler and Lewis (1982) have said that this life review process grows out of the very awareness of approaching death. The process is marked by the progressive return to consciousness of past experiences and the resurgence of unresolved conflicts. Such conflicts can be examined once more and reintegrated. Successful reintegration can give new significance and meaning to one's life and prepare one for death by reducing fear and anxiety. Of course, not everyone has had a "good" life, but skilled assistance can help even the less fortunate ones attach new meanings to earlier experiences, thereby providing a more benevolent integration.

The evaluation and integration of one's experiences through reminiscence, or life review, are important. If Butler is correct, the topic is not just poignant; it strikes at the very heart of what it means to be human. The injection of final meaning into one's life as death approaches is as functional as it is sentimental.

Death and Dying

The most intimate companion of life is death. The reality of death, however, has become obscured for many. People now die in institutions or hospitals and less often in their homes. As a result, death has tended to become shrouded in mystery; we shield ourselves and our children from the reality of it. Furthermore, early in this century, people of all ages died for all sorts of reasons—childhood infectious diseases, tuberculosis, and so on. But as nutrition and sanitation have improved and medical intervention has become increasingly successful, death has come to be largely associated with old age. All this has made death seem less unpredictable, and we are freed from the necessity of thinking much about it these days (Marshall, 1980).

Despite this, however, it sometimes seems that we are less able to cope psychologically with the fact of death. Most of us feel that death comes too soon. Not nearly so many elderly feel this way; instead, they tend to react to death in a more practical fashion and seem to fear it less (Kalish & Reynolds, 1976). Their fear is more of pain, indignity, and loneliness.

How do individuals react as they face their own death? Kubler-Ross (1969) interviewed sick patients and identified five reactive stages along the way to death. When the person discovers that death is imminent, the first stage, *denial and shock*, sets in. In effect, the patient says, "No, it cannot be true!" In a short time, the second stage, *anger*, begins. The classic cry here is, "Why me?" The person may become envious of the healthy. The third stage is called *bargaining*. The patient may try to strike a deal with God or the attending physician. Shortly, the stage of *depression* occurs. Finally, if there is time, the stage of *acceptance* takes over. There is now neither anger nor depression; rather, quiet expectation. Of course, even in this stage there may be silent hope of remission or deliverance.

Despite Kubler-Ross's extensive observations, research does not seem to confirm the existence of these stages. For example, in a study by Kastenbaum and Weisman (1972), patients who were informed of their impending death seemed to react in either of two ways: (1) withdrawal and inactivity or (2) intensified activity. Also, most of Kubler-Ross's patients were young—how well her results can be generalized to the elderly is questionable. Furthermore, it is not clear whether her patients were aware of their terminal condition.

With a growing population of elderly persons, society must find solutions to many problems surrounding the process of dying. There are serious issues of personal control. How, for example, can we protect people from medical procedures that prolong life at the expense of human dignity? Do we allow the dying to choose when and how they will die? Do we permit **euthanasia**, whereby the incurable patient is painlessly put to death? What about suicide when

euthanasia painlessly putting to death someone who is suffering from an incurable illness

Society must find solutions for many problems of the elderly.

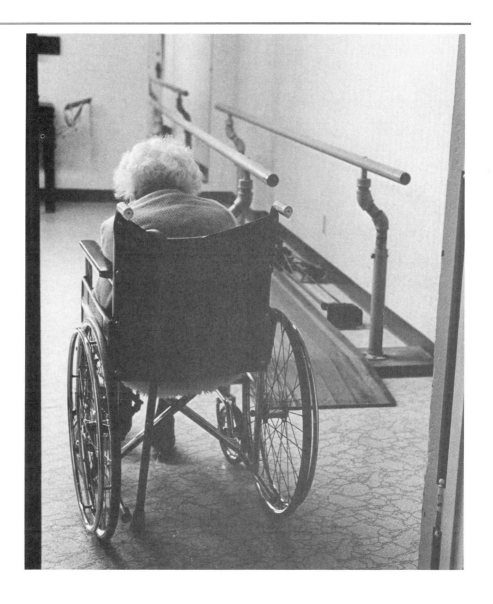

the person is undergoing extreme pain and suffering? Do we provide increased funds to support facilities for the dying? All of these are critical issues.

The solutions will tax the ingenuity and compassion of society (Kermis, 1984). A growing trend is the development of the hospice to care for the terminally ill. **Hospice care** is a community-based system of care (in either an institution or the home) for the dying individual. It is especially appropriate for the individual in extreme pain and the one whose condition is beyond the scope of modern medical technology. The patient is given attention and affection, but no technology is used to extend the life of the incurably afflicted patient.

hospice care system in which emotional and physical support as well as relief from pain are provided to the terminally ill

SUMMARY

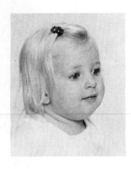

1. Developmental psychologists are concerned with the changes in thinking and behavior that occur throughout the life span.

2. The Freudian perspective of development is one of biologically determined psychosexual stages. In contrast, Erikson focused on the psychosocial and Sullivan on the interpersonal aspects of development.

3. The behavioral-social learning perspectives emphasize operant and classical conditioning along with observational learning. They tend to ignore the operation of stages as such.

4. The cognitive developmental approach goes even farther than social learning theory in viewing the individual as one who actively interprets experience. Piaget has described various stages of thinking in development. Kohlberg focused on the description of stages of moral reasoning.

5. One of the controversies in life-span development is the relative importance of learning versus maturation. The extreme learning view is that psychological development is dependent upon whatever we learn, while the maturational view is that developmental changes are both regular and predetermined. Most observers steer a middle course between these opposing views. Also important is the kind of research design employed to answer questions. The results are always influenced by the method used—examples are longitudinal and cross-sectional methods.

6. In infancy, attachment to the mother occurs and the processes of socialization and differentiation begin.

7. The period of childhood is characterized by the growth and development of peer relationships and the influence of parent-child relationships.

8. Late adolescence is thought by many to be a period of storm and stress. Adolescents must develop a sense of independence and a sense of personal control. The crisis comes over the establishment of an identity separate from parents or family.

9. By the age of twenty or so, the stage of young adultdhood begins, and one's focus shifts to deeper, more intimate relationships at home and work. The chief tasks of this period are marriage, children, and work, as adult life begins to take shape. The crisis in the decade of the twenties is intimacy versus isolation. Young adults face opportunities for love, affection, intimacy, and commitment. Poor choices may lead to withdrawal into an isolated, self-oriented existence.

10. Middle adulthood is a lengthy period said to last anywhere from age thirty up to sixty or sixty-five. The major tasks of the period are guiding a home, children, and a career. During this stage, one's need to contribute to the next generation begins to develop. One can either cultivate this motive of

generativity or sink into a state of stagnation, which represents a failure to substitute interest in others for a narcissistic preoccupation with oneself.

11. There is still controversy over the inevitability of midlife crisis (the stormy period of reappraisal of life as one reaches about age forty). Although thought to be primarily a male event, some evidence suggests that it can occur in career-oriented women as well. In fact, however, evidence for inevitable midlife crisis in either sex is rather thin. When a crisis occurs, it may be determined more by one's expectations than by any innate maturational process.

12. Women in the late forties and early fifties undergo menopause. How serious the physical and psychological changes of this stage turn out to be seems largely dependent on the woman's expectations about what she should experience.

13. Beginning at age sixty or sixty-five, the period of later adulthood begins. While aging is a highly individual process, there is a slow decline in perceptual and cognitive abilities as well as other physical functions. The chief tasks of this period are adjusting to these physical changes and coming to terms with the role changes that accompany aging and retirement. An especially critical task is maintaining a measure of personal control during this stage.

14. The crisis of later adulthood is one of integrity versus despair. When one can successfully consolidate the experiences of a lifetime, contentment and a sense of the value of life emerge. Failure to achieve consolidation can lead to disappointment, fear of death, and depression.

15. A helpful process in achieving this state of integrity is reminiscence, or life review. Through life review and reevaluation, the meaning and worth of one's life can make the approach of death less threatening.

16. As inevitable as death is, recent generations have become increasingly insulated from it. As a result, many people seem less able to cope psychologically with death.

17. Some observers believe that as death approaches, the dying person passes through detectable stages. These stages are (1) denial and shock, (2) anger, (3) bargaining, (4) depression, and (5) acceptance. Other observers question the existence of these stages or feel that other stages would be more descriptive.

18. A gradually aging population will create difficult issues involving personal control over one's life, euthanasia, suicide, and increased support of the hospice movement. These are just a few of the problems and challenges that will face us and our children in the years ahead.

Part 2

STRESS, COPING, AND GETTING HELP

Chapter 5

THE NATURE OF
STRESS AND COPING

The concepts of stress and coping are central to an understanding of psychological adjustment. Everyone must deal with such stressors of life as the death of a loved one, blocked goals, interpersonal conflict, natural or human-engineered disasters, illness, and eventually one's own death. How one copes with such stressors can greatly influence the quality of life. In this chapter, we consider what science knows (and doesn't know) about stress and coping and the relationships of stress and coping to physical and mental well-being. In Chapter 6, we examine some of the ways in which you can improve your ability to cope.

THE NATURE OF STRESS

What exactly is stress? Unfortunately, there is no simple answer to this question. While people often use the word *stress* to explain the cause behind someone's mental or physical disability, scientists have found it difficult to develop a precise definition. Part of the problem is that the term has been used in several ways.

Some people define stress as a condition of the environment, for example, the stress of examinations, work, or war. The concept of stress as a set of external forces affecting the individual comes from the engineering field. Engineers use the term to describe the action of outside forces on an object, which produces strain. Some students share this view of stress. As one student commented:

> I'll tell you what stress is. It's having too many assignments due in too short a time. . . . It's working your butt off in school and not knowing if there's a job available when you're done. . . . It's my in-laws. Should I go on?

Another view of stress emphasizes the individual's *response* when placed in a threatening or challenging environment. In this context, when one speaks of the individual as being under stress or stressed, one describes physiological or psychological reactions to outside stimuli. As one student noted:

> Stress is the knot in my stomach, sweaty hands, heavy breathing, feeling overwhelmed, at the end of my rope, not able to concentrate. How much time do you have? I can fill your afternoon.

Thus, stress may be viewed in terms of external events that can overwhelm the individual or in terms of internal events—one's physiological and psychological reactions. In psychological terms, stress is equated with the stimulus (input) as well as with the response (output).

However, something besides stimulus and response must define stress. Researchers have found that stress, like beauty, is largely in the eye of the beholder. What is stressful for one individual may not be for someone else. How individuals appraise and interpret events and appraise their resources to cope with such events will determine, in large part, whether they feel stressed by any particular situation.

Stress is in the eye of the beholder.

"I'D SAY THE SALES CHART IS THE ULCER, THE PHONE IS THE HYPERTENSION, THE PAPERWORK IS THE MIGRAINE..."

Picture the following scene: Two individuals, both possessing essentially the same speaking skills, are asked on separate occasions to give a speech in public. One individual has a high level of anxiety about public speaking, while the other has a low level of anxiety. During each speaker's presentation, some members of the audience walk out of the room. The action provokes entirely different thoughts and feelings from the two speakers. The person with the most anxiety is likely to think, "I must be boring. How much longer do I have to speak? I knew I could never give a good speech," and so on. Such thoughts reflect and increase anxiety and become self-fulfilling prophecies. The more one *thinks* one is a poor speaker, the more likely one will become so. On the other hand, the individual with less anxiety is more likely to regard people leaving as simply rude or as having other business elsewhere. This speaker may think, "Too bad they have to leave; they'll be missing a good talk."

A similar pattern may be found between those with high or low anxiety about taking tests. Consider an examination situation in which some students hand in their exams early. For an individual with a high level of anxiety, this action often elicits such thoughts and feelings as, "How can they be finished already? I'll never finish. I can't concentrate on what I have to do." The result is more anxiety and further self-defeating thoughts. In comparison, the student with low anxiety might readily dismiss the other students' performance by thinking, "People who hand in their papers early probably don't know as much. I hope they score this exam on a curve."

In both of these examples, the same event (in the first case people walking out in the middle of a speech; in the second case, students handing in their examinations early) elicits completely different appraisals, thoughts, feelings, and behaviors in high-anxiety and low-anxiety individuals. The same event may be viewed as threatening by some and as challenging or even growth-producing by others. Sometimes the same event may be threatening in one instance and challenging in another. As the Stoic philosopher, Epictetus, stated in the first century A.D., "We are disturbed not by things but by the views we take of them." This time-honored adage has been supported by recent psychological studies on the role of appraisal processes—or how people evaluate events—in stress and coping.

THE APPRAISAL PROCESS

When the concept of stress was first popularized by the Canadian physiologist Hans Selye in the 1930s and 1940s, he proposed that stressors have a direct physiological effect on organisms. He conceived of stress as the nonspecific, generalized response of the body to any demand. This conception grew out of a series of studies in which he demonstrated that laboratory animals show a common set of general physiological responses to stress no matter what the source (heat, cold, deprivation, injury, disease). What mattered to Selye was not the specific kind of response but only the intensity of the adjustment to stress called for in each instance.

general adaptation syndrome pattern of nonspecific physical reactions to a variety of stressors, as proposed by Selye

The General Adaptation Syndrome

Following from these studies, Selye proposed that when stressed, the organism goes through a pattern of physiological responses called the **general adaptation syndrome**, which includes three states: (1) an alarm reaction, (2) a stage

Some students
become anxious over
tests.

diseases of
adaptation illnesses
such as ulcers or
increased susceptibility
to infection that result
from chronic exposure
to stress

of resistance, and (3) a stage of exhaustion. The *alarm reaction* consists of the body's immediate reaction to some stressor. It represents a general mobilization of the body's defenses. This reaction is followed by a *stage of resistance*, in which heightened defensive responses—deeper breathing, faster heart rate, muscle tension, and so on—are evident. If the stressor is prolonged and severe, the organism's ability to resist eventually begins to fail, and the defenses are reduced during a *stage of exhaustion*. If this condition continues, **diseases of adaptation**, such as ulcers, infections, and heart attack, begin to develop. If exposure to the stressor does not stop and the stress reaction continues, the organism may die.

Until recently, Selye's model of the automatic impact of stressors on the body was widely accepted. However, in recent years a number of criticisms have been directed at Selye's (1978) theory. These criticisms have a direct bearing on understanding of what the term *stress* means. For instance, research on how organisms respond physiologically when challenged or taxed indicates that what happens in the stress response is not so straightforward as Selye stated. Instead, complex bodily processes are set into motion.

For example, **endocrinologist** John Mason (1975) reported that specific types of stressors trigger specific hormonal reactions. This means that somehow the body, at some level, must determine what type of challenge it is facing in order to respond. In short, individuals need to appraise—that is, screen or evaluate—events in order to react in the most effective and adaptive way. Even at the physiological level, there is an increasing recognition that some form of appraisal process is needed to understand the nature of stress.

Research has indicated that all organisms must somehow recognize a stressful situation before the physiological stress response can take place. Bodily assaults must be perceived as threatening before the various hormonal adjustments are set into motion. Mason found that if care is taken to reduce the uncertainty and novelty that accompany physical stressors, then the stress response is minimal.

This role of the appraisal process has been extensively studied by Richard Lazarus and his colleagues at the University of California in Berkeley (Lazarus & Folkman, 1984). In both laboratory and field studies, they found that how individuals appraise situations affects how they react and cope.

Primary and Secondary Appraisal

For Lazarus, the term **appraisal** refers to an individual's judgment of the demands and constraints of various situations and of the options and resources for resolving those situations. There are two main types of appraisal: primary and secondary.

Primary appraisal is an evaluation of the significance of an event—whether it is stressful, harmless, positive, or neutral. This form of appraisal answers the question, "Am I okay or in trouble?" It evaluates what is at stake. This judgment may be made at a conscious or unconscious level. Stress can arise in the absence of conscious evaluation when one's biological needs are not met. You may feel stress, for example, when you have not eaten for several hours. Whether primary appraisal operates at the conscious or unconscious level, it is influenced by one's beliefs, values, goals, and commitments.

Secondary appraisal is an evaluation of a person's coping resources and options. It answers the question, What can I do about the situation? The person evaluates coping strategies in terms of the cost (possible outcomes) and the probability of their success (likelihood of occurrence). The individual's past successes in similar situations, general level of self-confidence, and available resources (material, social, psychological) influence the secondary appraisal

endocrinologist
medical specialist of the endocrine system, which controls hormones and related bodily processes

appraisal one's judgment of the situational demands and one's assessment of the ability to meet them

primary appraisal
evaluation of the significance of an event as stressful, harmless, positive, or neutral

secondary appraisal
evaluation of a person's coping resources and options

process. Thus, the level of stress is affected by how people perceive events and by how they view their abilities to handle them.

Both primary and secondary appraisals may change continuously, a process that has been called **reappraisal**. Appraisal processes are dynamic over time, as individuals continually assess and reassess their abilities to meet life's demands.

To make the concepts of primary and secondary appraisal and reappraisal come alive, consider a stressful experience you may have had recently. How did you appraise the situation? What, if anything, did you do? As you reflect on the situation now, how do you feel you handled it? How do you feel about your responses at the time? Would the same situation be as stressful for you now, and would you handle it in the same way?

Often the complicated appraisal and response processes occur in an automatic, instantaneous fashion. Consider the way you drive your car. When you were first learning, your appraisal of each new situation on the road was intentional and deliberate. You noticed everything—road conditions, where other cars were behind and ahead of you, how the brakes felt, how you approached a stop sign. Your appraisal processes were working overtime deciding whether you were safe or in danger. As you became more skilled at driving, your appraisal processes became more automatic and you adjusted your responses accordingly. When the automatic nature of driving is interrupted (a police car begins to follow you, the driver in front stops without warning) the appraisal process becomes voluntary and intentional again.

Scientific Definition of Stress

Now that we have introduced the notion of appraisal processes, we offer a more formal scientific definition of stress. **Psychological stress** is a particular relationship between a person and the environment that is appraised by that person as taxing or exceeding his or her personal resources and endangering

reappraisal process by which one reevaluates one's primary and secondary appraisals

psychological stress dynamic concept that reflects the discrepancy between individuals' perceptions of the demands of the environment and their perceptions of their resources when they believe their well-being is endangered

his or her well-being (Lazarus & Folkman, 1984, p. 15). In other words, if you feel or notice that something important is at stake or that your well-being is challenged and you do *not* have the resources readily available to meet these demands, you experience stress. Since your evaluation of any particular challenge is likely to change over time, you should think of stress as a *process* rather than as a state or outcome.

This definition of stress highlights the fact that stress is influenced by what you feel the situation demands of you and whether you can mobilize and use the necessary resources to overcome the situation. Thus, the definition and experience of stress are reflections of the changing relationships between you and your environment, relationships influenced by cognitive, emotional, and social factors.

It is important to remember, however, that in thinking about this definition of stress, we are *not* equating appraisal or cognition with conscious awareness or intentional decision making. In fact, most appraisals and reactions occur in an automatic, habitual, and preconscious manner. Stress is neither a stimulus nor a response. It is a dynamic *relationship*, which is constantly changing between the person and the environment. Individuals are not helpless victims of stress. How individuals appraise events (primary appraisal) and their coping resources and options (secondary appraisal) determine the nature of the stress they experience.

Personality Factors and Stress

How individuals and groups behave can inadvertently contribute to their level of stress. All too often, one unwittingly acts in ways that increase stress or provoke reactions in others that maintain inappropriate responses to stress. Consider the following example:

> *Mary was shy and fearful. She often avoided social gatherings, especially if strangers were present. As a result, other family members became overprotective of her. Because they often took the initiative and provided support, Mary did not pursue opportunities to test her fear of being rejected. The result was a further lack of self-confidence. A* **vicious cycle** *was set in motion as Mary's fears led others to be overprotective, which prevented Mary from developing social skills, which further eroded her self-confidence. Her behavior elicited reactions from others that perpetuated her problem.*

vicious cycle pattern of maladaptive behavior that elicits reactions from others that in turn strengthen the maladaptive behavior

This example illustrates the interpersonal nature of stress. How individuals behave and appraise events plays an important role in the nature and level of stress they feel.

A good example of how personality factors can affect the stress response is illustrated by the research on the personality dimension called locus of control. Julian Rotter (1966) noted that some people generally hold an *internal view of control*. They feel it is important to exert control over the environment, to feel as if they are captains of their fate. Such individuals experience stress if the sense of personal control is compromised or thwarted. As long as they exercise some mastery over the environment, believing that there is a relationship be-

Personality factors
can influence the
stress response.

tween their own efforts and resultant consequences, the stress level is low. Such internally oriented people are more likely to initiate change, seek information, mobilize others, and generally engage in active means of coping with stress.

In contrast, Rotter has identified individuals whom he characterizes as holding an *external view of control*. These people tend to feel that they are often victims of circumstances and that events are normally beyond their control. Such externally oriented people are more likely to deal with stress by being passive, waiting out events, and accepting negative events as part of life.

Neither the internal nor external style of coping is better by itself. Which one is used depends on the person and the demands of a particular situation. In some instances, when little can be done to change a situation, an external orientation may be the best way to cope with stress. In other situations, where direct action is called for, an internal orientation is more appropriate. The important point is that the match or fit between a person's preferred means of coping with stress and how the person appraises the demands of a situation will determine the nature and level of stress experienced.

SOURCES OF STRESSORS

Three major sources of stressors have been identified by researchers, namely, traumatic events, personal loss, and daily annoyances. In each instance, stress may affect an individual, a group, or society as a whole. Keep in mind that while the same event may affect a group of people at the same time, its effect on each of them may be radically different.

Traumatic Events

A major class of stressful events results from traumatic or cataclysmic events, such as natural disasters (earthquakes, tornados, floods) or human-initiated crises (accidents, fires, riots, wars, demonstrations). These events are usually sudden, unique, and powerful. They threaten nearly everyone in a group or community.

People's reactions to a number of disasters have been studied in some detail. These disasters include floods (Gleser, Green, & Winget, 1981), nuclear accidents (Baum, Fleming, & Singer, 1982), illnesses (Silver & Wortman, 1980), and terrorist attacks (Ayalon, 1983). A number of factors influence how people react to such events: (1) the scope or impact of the disaster (how large an area and how many people are involved), (2) the speed of its onset (sudden, gradual, chronic), (3) its duration (how long it took to occur), and (4) how prepared the community is to cope with it.

While many individuals accept and recover from such stressful life events, a sizable minority (between 20 percent and 40 percent) do *not* fully recover from the crisis despite the passage of time (Silver & Wortman, 1980). For example, research on rape victims indicated that 26 percent did not feel that they had recovered from the assault four to six years later.

Personal Loss

Another potent source of stress is loss—the death of a loved one, loss of a job, or loss of one's community when moving to another city, state, or country. When individuals were asked to rank all possible stressful life events, they rated the death of a loved one as the most stressful. Among the bereaved, Parkes (1972) found that 30 percent still experienced psychological distress and social and physical problems two to four years after the loss. However, even though a sizable minority of people evidence prolonged difficulties, most people recover fairly quickly from such losses and are able to become active and optimistic again. At this point, psychology cannot predict with any real certainty which people will have a harder time recovering and which will be able to bounce back.

Unemployment (getting fired or being laid off) also ranked high on the list of stressors. Once again, however, different people react to this stressor in

Natural disasters may
threaten nearly
everyone in a
community.

different ways. A fascinating example was reported by Baum and his colleagues (1981), who studied the employees of the space center at Cape Kennedy during the last years of the United States moon program. Employees were faced with a paradoxical and personally stressful problem. With each successful mission, culminating in putting a man on the moon, the workers knew that the space project was one step closer to being discontinued, which meant they would be out of a job. In addition, the workers faced extreme deadline pressures as they feverishly attempted to meet NASA's objectives.

The results of this double stress were startling. Some workers, as would be expected under such conditions, showed increased rates of alcoholism, divorce, and heart attack. Others, however, *thrived* under these stressful conditions, enjoying the increased group camaraderie and viewing their impending unemployment as an opportunity to develop other talents. The same stressful event was perceived differently by each group and led to quite different consequences.

Future Shock
Toffler's concept that rapidly accelerating technological and social changes impose new stresses

As Toffler (1970) noted in his popular book, **Future Shock,** rapidly accelerating technological and social change impose new stresses. How one appraises and copes with these events determines the quality of one's life. Perhaps this fact is most clearly indicated by research on **acculturation,** or the adoption of a culture different from one's own.

acculturation process by which one adapts to another culture

A number of communities and peoples have had to adjust to major social changes that accompany the exposure and adoption of the values and life-style of another culture. At the end of the Vietnam War, for example, thousands of Cambodians, Vietnamese, and Laotions came to the United States to live. They were faced with learning a new language, new customs, new skills, and new legal responsibilities. Many of them came from rural areas but found themselves transplanted into a bewildering urban environment. The result was a severe strain on family ties, an increase in physical and psychological problems, and a strong need for outside support. Those able to find the resources to help them through the transition tended to make the adjustment with fewer problems.

In the United States, the recent family farm bankruptcies have created another loss of a familiar way of life. Families who for generations have farmed the same piece of land are suddenly faced with the prospect of living in cities and working for other people. The reaction to such stress has ranged from severe depression and suicide for some farmers to a gradual acceptance of change and a search for a new way of life for others.

Daily Annoyances

A third class of stressful events are known as daily annoyances. Such situations are usually chronic, such as job dissatisfaction, financial problems, overcrowded living conditions, commuting, and conflicts in relationships. Interestingly enough, the gradual buildup of relatively insignificant events over time can prove more stressful than can a single traumatic event. The more one sees a stressor as attacking one's sense of self-worth, the more likely that stressor is to affect mental health. Recent studies have suggested that such situations have *five times* the impact on a person's psychological health as do stressors that may be catastrophic but appear only rarely (Lazarus, 1984a). The role of daily annoyances in causing stress is nicely illustrated in Charles Bukowski's (1972) poem, "the shoelace."

> *it's not the large things that send a*
> *man to the madhouse*
> *no, it's the continuing series of small tragedies*
> *that send a man to the madhouse*
> *not the death of his love*
> *but a shoelace that snaps*
> *with no time left.*

Stress derived from traumatic events, personal loss, and daily annoyances can take its toll psychologically and physically.

EFFECTS OF STRESS

When under considerable stress, one may feel that the pressures of living are too much to handle. Tolerance of daily annoyances may be lower than normal. One may feel restless, tense, irritable, anxious, angry, or depressed. One may suffer from loss of appetite, disturbed sleep or insomnia, repetitive night-mares, extensive fatigue, impaired concentration and memory, withdrawal from social contact, loss of sexual potency, and excessive use of alcohol and drugs. One may have physical complaints and symptoms. Lowered resistance to infections and diseases, heavy sweating, swollen ankles and feet, upset stomach, dry mouth, accelerated or uneven heart rate, and mounting blood pressure may be warning signs that one is under undue stress. These signs should be taken seriously. The longer one is exposed to chronic stressors and fails to adopt appropriate coping strategies, the more one puts mental and physical health at risk.

Not all reactions to stress are immediate. Some reactions to severe stress or trauma may be delayed for several days, months, or even years. This reaction, known as *posttraumatic stress disorder (PTSD)*, has been found in such diverse groups as combat soldiers, hostages, victims of catastrophic events, and vic-tims of childhood physical and sexual abuse. Symptoms of PTSD include the following:

1. Reexperiencing the traumatic event in the form of nightmares, flashbacks (in which the event seems to be recurring as it actually happened), painful moods, and emotional storms that seem to have only trivial causes.

2. A sense of isolation, alienation, depersonalization, or psychic numbing, in which the person feels cut off from others and either unable to feel emo-tion or unable to share what he or she is feeling.

Combat soldiers sometimes experience posttraumatic stress syndrome.

3. Emotional upheaval, in which the person experiences wild mood swings, or sudden losses of emotional control, or an intensifying of sadness, shame, anger, guilt, frustation, and the like. These emotions are often accompanied by poor self-concept, impaired social relationships, difficulty in concentrating, and memory lapses.

The symptoms may be intensified when an individual is exposed to situations or activities that resemble or symbolize the original trauma conditions.

Individuals who have trouble handling stress are less likely to develop the skills needed to cope with stressful events. For example, several long-term studies of soldiers indicated that persons who had a history of difficulty in coping with stressful events would have more problems adjusting to wartime stressors (Helzer, 1980; Robins, 1980). Such factors as duration of combat, number and rate of casualties, role conflicts, and group support also influenced how well the individual coped with traumatic events. Both the individual's predisposition to stress and the situation play a part in determining how the individual reacts in combat.

Stress and Disease

An individual's vulnerability or susceptibility to stress has important implications for the understanding of the complex relationship between stress and disease. In recent years, our concept of disease has changed. At the turn of the twentieth century, a *monocausal* concept of disease predominated. The work of such microbiologists as Ehrlich, Koch, and Pasteur led to a germ theory of disease, in which each disease had a single cause (one gets sick because germs invade the body).

However, it soon became evident that not all individuals exposed to germs actually contracted a disease. The monocausal view of disease soon gave way to a *multicausal* model, which recognized that diseases may have many interacting and contributing causes. Since not everyone infected with a **pathogen** (virus, bacteria) becomes ill, other factors play a role in determining who remains healthy and who succumbs to disease. An individual's susceptibility to disease and the condition of the body's immune responses are as important, perhaps even more so, than the presence of an invading microbe.

pathogen agent that causes disease

In addition, research on disease has indicated that the major causes of illness in Western society today are *avoidable*. Recent estimates are that half the deaths in the United States are linked to unhealthy behaviors or maladaptive lifestyles. For instance, at least seven of the ten leading causes of death could be reduced substantially if people at risk changed five habits: (1) improved their diets, (2) quit smoking, (3) exercised more, (4) cut back on or eliminated alcoholic drinks, and (5) learned to handle tension (United States Surgeon General, 1979). Behavior under stress strongly influences health.

Direct and Indirect Influences of Stress

The complex links between stress and disease may be direct (since stress affects the body's immune systems) or indirect (since many coping responses to stress can endanger one's health).

Direct influences. How one copes with stress can have a direct effect on the hormonal system, autonomic arousal system, and immune system. Research has demonstrated that just the thought of future stressful events (test, job interview, term paper) may produce stressful physical responses similar to those present during the actual event (Mason, 1971). Psychological factors may influence the secretion of stress-related hormones such as catecholamines, neurotransmitters in the brain that are involved in the regulation of blood pressure, heart rate, and blood glucose. If periods of high catecholamine secretion are prolonged or frequent, the cardiovascular system may be damaged, which can result in an increased chance of coronary heart disease (Frankenhaeuser, 1980; Glass, 1977). See Figure 5-1 for the endocrine glands and their functions.

immune system
complex system that protects the body by destroying foreign materials, such as bacteria, viruses, fungi, and tumors

Psychological stress may contribute to physiological changes in the immune system as well. The **immune system** plays a fundamental role in maintaining the body's internal balance (homeostasis) and resistance to disease. The immune system helps keep one healthy by destroying foreign materials (viruses, bacteria, tumors, irregular cells). Stress appears to have a suppressive effect on certain functions of the immune system, reducing its efficiency and its capacity to protect the body. A person under stress is less able to produce antibodies to specific invaders. Even slight changes in the immune system can dramatically increase a person's susceptibility to pathogens present in the body or environment. As a result, stress can also make an individual more vulnerable to other disorders, such as allergies and perhaps some forms of cancer. Figure 5-2 (p. 142) shows common physical reactions to stress.

How stress may affect one's health is illustrated in the study by Andrew Baum and his colleagues of residents of Three Mile Island (TMI), Pennsylvania. One year after the 1979 nuclear accident at TMI, residents were showing high levels of stress and an abnormally high incidence of illness (for example, high blood pressure, upper respiratory infections). Since these illnesses were not normally linked to radiation, Baum and his colleagues suspected that stress was affecting the residents' immune functions. The researchers found that compared with people who lived outside the area, the residents near the nuclear power plant had deficient immune systems (fewer T-cells, B-cells, and T-helper cells, which are important in fighting diseases). They also had higher levels of epinephrine and norepinephrine, which are chemicals released into the bloodstream when the body is under stress.

Although these preliminary findings are exciting in terms of discovering links between stress and disease, it is not yet possible to draw any hard and fast conclusions from the data. The immune system is highly complex, and so it is only partially understood. At this point, scientists have not worked out all the ways in which stress and coping affect the nervous, endocrine, and immune system functions.

However, the information we have gained in this exciting line of research has many implications for adjustment (Adler, 1981; Borysenko, 1984). For example, some investigators have suggested that positive emotions and a strong will to live trigger chemicals in the brain that can reduce pain and speed healing (Cousins, 1976). While these are only speculations, they underscore the intimate connections between stress, coping, and disease or health.

FIGURE 5-1   Endocrine Glands

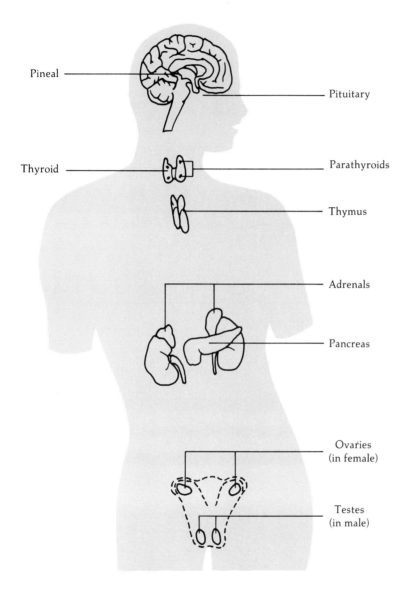

Gland and Function

Pituitary
Regulates ovaries and testes
Stimulates growth

Pineal
Affects activities of the ovaries

Thyroid
Regulates body metabolism
Causes storage of calcium in bone

Parathyroids
Balance calcium level in the
blood

Thymus
Enables the body to produce
antibodies

Adrenals
Regulate blood pressure, salt and
water balance in the blood, and
metabolism

Prepares the body for action in
times of emergency

Ovaries and testes
Influence male and female traits

Pancreas
Regulates blood sugar level

FIGURE 5-2   Common Physical Reactions to Stress

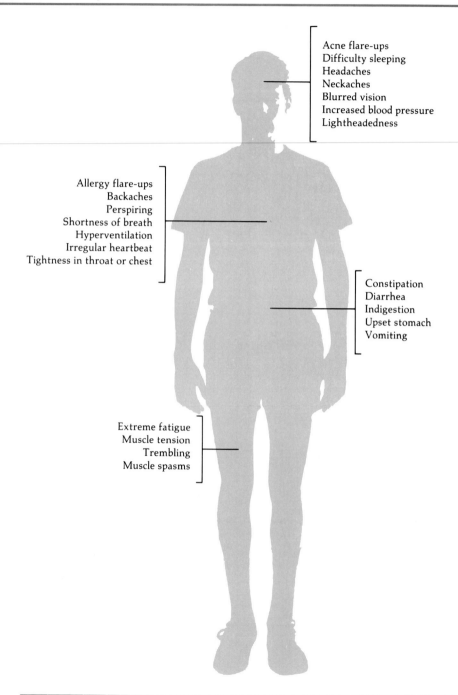

Acne flare-ups
Difficulty sleeping
Headaches
Neckaches
Blurred vision
Increased blood pressure
Lightheadedness

Allergy flare-ups
Backaches
Perspiring
Shortness of breath
Hyperventilation
Irregular heartbeat
Tightness in throat or chest

Constipation
Diarrhea
Indigestion
Upset stomach
Vomiting

Extreme fatigue
Muscle tension
Trembling
Muscle spasms

Indirect influences. Stress can also influence health by affecting how individuals cope, that is, how they perceive their symptoms, how they relate to health professionals, and what habits they adopt. People under stress may deny the significance of their symptoms, avoid seeking help, or engage in behaviors such as smoking that impair their health.

In the 1950s, two cardiologists found that life-style factors strongly influence the health of victims of coronary heart disease. Each year, over one million people in the United States alone die from this disease. The cardiologists, Meyer Friedman and Ray Rosenman, developed an assessment technique (a fifteen-minute structured interview) to determine if there is any relation between personality and life-style factors and the risk of heart disease. They identified **Type A behavior** pattern and Type B behavior pattern of coping style. Type A people tended to be hard driving; feel a sense of time urgency; and display aggressiveness, competitiveness, chronic impatience, and underlying hostility. In contrast, Type B people were easygoing and had few of the Type A characteristics.

It is not clear which of the several components of Type A behavior cause the most harm. In general, however, Type A behavior plus a family history of heart disease can put an individual more at risk of developing coronary heart disease than does Type B behavior. In fact, if an individual has had a heart attack, a Type A person is twice as likely to suffer a second heart attack than is a Type B person. These results indicate that one's life-style can significantly affect one's health. The mechanisms by which a stressful life event can make one more vulnerable to specific illnesses are not clearly understood, but considerable research on this topic is now under way, as described in "On the Research Frontier: Assessing Stressful Life Events and Their Relationship to Health" on pages 144–146.

Type A behavior behavior of hard-driving, competitive, hostile-aggressive individuals who have a great sense of time urgency.

THE PROCESS OF COPING

As Hans Selye (1978) noted, "stress is ever present" (p. 3). He even suggested that life would be boring without stress. There would be little productivity, few challenges, and less excitement. He observed that some people seek stress in the form of high-risk leisure activities (skydiving, investing in the stock market, mountain climbing), occupational choices, or personal relationships. Selye draws a distinction, however, between what he calls **eustress** (productive stress), which accompanies challenges and may be beneficial, and *distress*, which is harmful and accompanies failures and frustrations.

eustress Selye's term to describe productive or beneficial stress that individuals may actively seek

If stress is always present, what distinguishes individuals in their ability to cope? After all the vast majority of people exposed to stressful life events do *not* develop emotional or mental disorders. They are able to handle these events with style and grace, and they may even become stronger because of the experiences. Coping with stress is really the story of courage and resilience, as illustrated in the following true story from the *Kitchener-Waterloo Record* (November 23, 1985):

ON THE RESEARCH FRONTIER

ASSESSING STRESSFUL LIFE EVENTS
AND THEIR RELATIONSHIP TO HEALTH

Perhaps you have come across self-administered stress tests in magazines, newspapers, or even psychology textbooks. Such tests list a number of possible calamities. You are asked to check the ones you have encountered in recent months and then to determine the likelihood of your becoming ill. Those who score high are advised to avoid daily annoyances. What is the logic behind such tests, and are they indeed valid? Should one heed their warnings?

The assessment of stressful life events has a long tradition, going back to Greek physicians who noted that an individual's health may suffer following a wide variety of life stressors. In this tradition, two physicians, Thomas Holmes and David Rahe, developed a self-report questionnaire entitled *The Social Readjustment Scale* (SRS) in 1967. In developing this measure, they went through the life charts of five hundred medical patients to determine if stressful life events clustered at the time of disease onset. Then they asked judges to rate forty-three such events in terms of how much readjustment each required (that is, the intensity of the event and the length of time necessary to accommodate to it, regardless of the desirability of the event). For example, the death of a spouse scored 100 units, marriage 50 units, and vacation 13.

The assumption behind the scale is that life changes (either negative or positive) create a disequilibrium that imposes a period of readjustment. The readjustment period can leave the person more vulnerable to stress and its consequences.

According to Holmes and Rahe, significant life events strain adaptive capacities, accumulatively wear the body, and cause greater vulnerability to disease. The scale focuses on the occurrence of change, regardless of whether it was experienced as pleasant or unpleasant.

Extensive research has attempted to relate scores on life event scales to one's physical and mental well-being. The more one has been exposed to recent stressful events, the greater the likelihood of susceptibility to illness. However, it does *not* thus far appear that specific stressful events relate to specific disorders. While provocative, this line of research has been subjected to the following methodological and conceptual criticisms:

1. The reported relationships between scores on such scales and illness are quite small, usually of the order of less than 0.30. This means that only a weak relationship is evident between stressful life events and health outcomes. In a technical sense, researchers usually take the correlation and square it (times it by itself) in order to estimate the explanatory power of the relationship. In this case, the square of 0.30 is only 9 percent of the total relationship (or what is technically called variance). In other words, the relationship between health outcomes and stressful life events is quite meager.

2. A second major issue is the ambiguity of the association between stressful events and physical disorders. Some

prior emotional difficulties may bring about some events such as divorce or job loss. In addition, health problems can cause stressful life events just as readily as they can be caused by them.

3. Another source of criticism is the retrospective nature of such assessments. People are asked to report on the occurrence of stressful life events during the past several months. Not only may one's memory be faulty, but one's present mood (for example, being depressed) may color one's recall.

4. Others have challenged the basic assumption of equating negative and positive life events. More recent studies have noted that the desirability of events is an important factor in determining health outcome. Undesirable, or negative, events account primarily for the adverse consequences of life change.

5. Finally, stressful life event scales usually fail to consider the impact of important nonevents (that is, things that do not occur, such as not getting promoted) and the impact of daily annoyances.

Much research is now under way to improve the life event scales. It is clear that stressful events are multidimensional. Some improvement is realized by discriminating events in terms of their desirability, controllability, predictability, seriousness, and time clustering (Thoits, 1983). Whether stressful life events occur at a

stage of one's life when one expects them also may be critical in determining their impact and outcome. For example, if the death of one's parents occurs at an age-appropriate period, it can be anticipated and rehearsed. Whether the event occurs to many people or not is likely another important variable in determining the impact on one's health.

In response to such concerns, investigators have recently developed more sophisticated life event scales, daily hassle scales, and interview techniques. For example, Horowitz and his colleagues have developed an impact of events scale, in which they obtain subjects' ratings of the subjective distress currently experienced as a result of specific events (for example, death of a spouse, job loss). In this way, they determine the degree of intrusion and the nature of avoidance that follow such experiences (Horowitz, Wilner, & Alvarez, 1979; Horowitz & Wilner, 1980). Subjects' endorsement of such items as "I have strong feelings about it," "I thought about it when I didn't mean to," or "Pictures about it popped into my mind," reflect the degree of intrusion. Similarly, one can query individuals about the degree to which their feelings are still numbed by the event, or to which they felt they could not deal with their feelings. This approach not only identifies stressful events that occur but also attempts to assess the meaning such events hold for individuals.

A research approach related to the study of stressful life events takes a develop-

Continued

mental perspective, focusing on the various life hurdles that come with each life stage. Each period of maturity is linked with unique personal tasks (such as, seeking employment, marrying, rearing children, retiring). One can assess the degree to which individuals satisfactorily accomplish each task (see Levinson et al., 1978; Vaillant, 1977).

The research on life stress assessment has had a marked influence on the field of stress research. However, until the many methodological and conceptual problems have been worked out, one should take all such scales with a grain of salt. They are research instruments in an early developmental stage. The widespread popularization of such psychological tests is premature. Stressful life events have the potential of contributing to one's physical and psychological vulnerability, as illustrated in the recent findings that persistent marital and familial discord can contribute to a number of disorders, including depression, schizophrenia, and arthritis. On the other hand, stressful life events can have a steeling effect, inoculating individuals against the impact of future stressors. The exploration of the relationship between stressful life events and one's physical and psychological vulnerability and sense of well-being is on the research frontier.

Stressful Life Events Taken from the Holmes and Rahe (1967) Readjustment Scale

Death of a spouse	100
Divorce	73
Marital separation	65
Jail term	63
Death of a close family member	63
Personal injury or illness	53
Marriage	50
Fired at work	47
Marital reconciliation	45
Retirement	45
Change in health of family member	44
Pregnancy	40
Sex difficulties	39
Gain of new family member	39
Change in financial state	38
Death of close friend	37
Change to different line of work	36
Change in number of arguments with spouse	35
Mortgage over $10,000	31
Foreclosure of mortgage or loan	30
Change in responsibilities at work	29
Son or daughter leaving home	29
Trouble with in-laws	29
Outstanding personal achievement	28
Wife beginning or stopping work	26
Beginning or ending school	26
Revision of personal habits	24
Trouble with boss	23
Change in work hours or conditions	20
Change in residence	20
Change in schools	20
Change in recreation	19
Change in social activities	18
Mortgage or loan less than $10,000	17
Change in sleeping habits	16
Change in number of family get-togethers	15
Change in eating habits	15
Vacation	13
Minor violations of the law	11

Because congenital birth defects had left David's lower legs severely deformed, the doctors thought he would never walk. David spent the first three years of his life in a hospital, receiving hip realignments, bone grafts, amputations, and surgery to shape his legs to fit prosthetic devices. His family lived hundreds of miles from the hospital, so David saw them infrequently during this period.

The following years entailed over one hundred trips to the hospital for surgery, checkups, and fittings. Thus, the news that at the age of eighteen David had secured a part in his community's musical review captured the town's imagination. Throughout both the audition and the performance, David never commented on his disability. He not only danced his way into the hearts of the townsfolk, but he did it with style, grace, good humor, and courage.

There were few things that David would not try. He said, "I just have to constantly prove to myself that I'm normal. Anything I can't do, I have to do just because I can't." Thus, his talents were not limited to dancing. He was in his high school marching band and was a member of several entertainment groups.

David was popular and well liked. A positive attitude and a supportive family were at the root of his successful drive to undertake new projects. To quote David, "Without a positive attitude, you're history."

At the heart of the story of stress and coping is the ability to recognize and accept one's limitations, the courage to try, and the resilience to recover and maintain high self-esteem and self-confidence in the face of inevitable failures along the way. People have endured and overcome the most disabling physical handicaps, catastrophic losses, and severely stressful life events.

Coping Defined

Exactly how do individuals cope with stress? To answer this question, we must consider what is meant by coping with stress. The term *coping* refers to the responses made by an individual or group to a situation with a potentially harmful outcome. A more formal definition of coping has been offered by Cohen and Lazarus (1979). They defined coping as an "effort, both action oriented and intraphyschic [mental and emotional reactions], to manage (that is, master, tolerate, reduce, minimize) environmental and internal demands and conflicts which tax or exceed a person's resources."

Such coping efforts may focus on (1) altering the problem directly, (2) changing one's way of viewing the problem, or (3) managing the emotional and mental distress aroused by the problem. In many instances, individuals use all three types of coping efforts to handle stress. It is important to view coping efforts as a process involving a combination of acting, thinking, and feeling over a period of time.

Functions of Coping

Coping may serve two functions: (1) solving problems or (2) regulating emotions. *Problem-solving functions* involve dealing with the source of the stress by changing either your environment or your behavior through direct action.

Coping efforts may
focus on managing
emotional distress.

This may include leaving a job, talking things out with someone, trying to find
a compromise, relinquishing certain goals, and thinking of alternatives. Such
direct actions are particularly helpful in situations where it is possible to anticipate the stressor and act to prevent or lessen the threat to well-being.

Emotion-regulation functions involve efforts to modify the distress that accompanies a threatening situation, without necessary resolving the problem. Such
responses include remaining detached, adopting a philosophical attitude, ra-
tionalizing aspects of the situation (It can't be all that bad), and seeking support
from others. Some people choose to regulate their emotions by using tranquilizers or alcohol, by denying the problem, or by deceiving themselves. When
such coping techniques are used excessively, the coping response itself (such as
drinking or denial) becomes an additional problem or stressor.

Individuals and groups may use problem-solving and emotion-regulating
coping procedures in different combinations at different times. In fact, what
works best to reduce stress in one situation may not work at another time. For
that matter, what proves useful for one type of stressor or one population may
be irrelevant on other occasions. For example, Pearlin and Schooler (1978)

found that specific types of coping strategies vary in effectiveness, depending on the type of stress being faced. Coping strategies involving commitment and engagement with others were most effective in dealing with stressors that arose out of close, interpersonal relationships. In contrast, ways of thinking about the problem to make it seem more remote and impersonal were most effective for stressors in economics and occupational areas. For example, someone who had been laid off from work can rationalize the situation by saying, "If everyone is being laid off work at my plant, then it's not so bad that *I* lost my job, too."

The main point is that *different stressors call for different coping responses.* When victims of the nuclear accident at Three Mile Island were studied, researchers discovered an interesting pattern of coping among the victims. Individuals who used problem-focused coping strategies tended to report more stress than did those who relied on emotion-focused strategies (Baum, Fleming, & Singer, 1982). Since it was impossible for the individuals to control the continuing radiation danger at the power plant, those who favored the action-oriented problem-solving coping style met with repeated failures—which in turn increased their stress. The most adaptive coping style used emotion-regulation strategies, such as sharing one's feelings with others, providing mutual support, and seeking help from outside the community.

These and other studies show that individuals need to learn different strategies to cope with various situations. They must be willing to experiment to find what works best. The critical factor may not be *which* coping strategy one uses but rather *how many* are in one's repertoire and *how flexible* one is in employing the different coping responses. As Pearlin and Schooler (1978) note: "Having a particular weapon in one's arsenal is less important than having a variety."

The relationship between stress, coping, and well-being indicates that individuals are not mere victims of stress. Rather, how they appraise events and cope with stress can influence their psychological and physical health. Individuals have choices, as described in "Exploring Choices: Stress, Appraisal, and Coping—Taking Stock." The choices you make can determine the quality of your life.

EXPLORING CHOICES

STRESS, APPRAISAL, AND COPING—TAKING STOCK

It is one thing to read about such psychological concepts as stress, appraisal, and coping and another to consider how these concepts apply in everyday experience. Let's perform a small experiment to determine what causes our stress and how we cope.

Signs That Tell If You Are Stressed
To begin with, how do you know when you are stressed? Each of us seems to have a personal pattern of thoughts, bodily signs, feelings, and behaviors. What is yours?

In some instances, your response patterns vary across settings or over time. Do you experience specific signs of stress? Would you first notice certain feelings— anxiety, fear, anger, depression? Do you notice butterflies in your stomach, physical tenseness, headaches, more frequent visits to the bathroom? Are there specific thoughts about feeling threatened or overwhelmed? On a sheet of paper, list the physiological, emotional, bodily, and cognitive signs that you use to tell if you are stressed. Think about a friend, relative, or roommate. What clues do you use to tell if she or he is distressed?

Identifying the Signs and Patterns of Stress
One way to become aware of these signs is to close your eyes and imagine a stressful situation. Are you about to begin an examination? Do you have to give a speech before a group? Are you in a difficult social situation? Do you have too much to do in too little time? Have your plans been interrupted? What about the stress you experience in a positive situation, on a scary ride at the amusement park? Choose a scene that you can recall in some detail. Now play in your mind's eye, in slow motion, what happened before, during, and after the stressful event. What feelings, thoughts, images, and physical signs preceded, accompanied, and followed the situation?

Now choose another stressful incident to imagine. As you imagine several such stressful situations, do you notice any patterns? Do certain feelings, thoughts, behaviors, physical reactions, or reactions from others occur?

Some students have found it useful to record on a sheet of paper the specific feelings and thoughts they experience. They record the situation (for example, "With my girlfriend and we argued"), the accompanying feelings ("Becoming angry, uptight"), and the accompanying thoughts (" I should give in sometimes, but that is difficult when I feel I'm right").

Common Themes in Your Stressful Incidents

As you conduct this analysis across several stressful situations, begin to explore whether certain themes emerge. Do you have specific concerns about fairness, personal control, social acceptance, or achievement? In order to answer this question about personal themes, you may wish to increase your sample of stressful incidents. To supplement the imagery procedure, keep a daily diary of stressful events and the accompanying thoughts and feelings. Rate each stressful incident on a simple three-point scale from very stressful (3), to moderately stressful (2), to mildly stressful (1). How do the situations rated 3 differ from those rated 1? What are the common features among the situations rated 3? Were certain concerns raised in some situations and not others? How did your appraisal and coping processes differ in the various stressful situations? What do these various incidents say about you as a person?

How Others React When You Feel Stressed

In terms of the transactional nature of stress, can you use the reactions of those around you to tell how stressed you are? How do others respond? What is the impact of their reactions on you? Do you inadvertently contribute to your own stress level? Are you merely a victim of stress, or do you unwittingly engender the very stress you experience?

Managing the Stress You Experience

Is this stress productive and useful? Does it act as a warning? Does it help you mobilize your coping efforts? Is there a way to view the stressor as a problem to solve instead of a personal threat or provocation? What are the things you do, as well as those you can do, to cope with your stress? Are there ways you can use your stress productively? How would you know if these worked?

Taking Stock

The answers to these many questions illustrate that stress is influenced by how you appraise events as well as how you appraise your ability to cope. As you perform this personal experiment, playing Sherlock Holmes in order to understand your own stress, do not forget that the critical factor is not that you are stressed in itself, but rather how well you cope with the stress. Exactly how do you cope with stress? What direct-action problem-solving steps might you take? What emotion-regulation steps might you take? Attempting to answer such questions can help you explore the choices available.

How do you know
when you're stressed?

SUMMARY

1. Stress has been defined as a stimulus (external event) and as a response (psychological or physical reaction).

2. The nature and level of stress one experiences are determined in large part by one's appraisal system. In primary appraisal, one judges an event in terms of whether it is stressful, harmless, positive, or neutral. Secondary appraisal is one's evaluation of psychological, material, and social resources available for dealing with stress.

3. Stress is a process, in which appraisal and coping change to meet the demands of the situation. Stress is not always a negative state to be avoided; it can be stimulating and useful.

4. People are distinctly different in their abilities to cope with stressful situations. People are not mere victims of stress—they often create their own stresses through habits of thinking, feeling, and acting. Regardless of the situation, people experience stress if they perceive some threat to well-being and they judge their resources to be inadequate to deal with the situation.

5. The three major sources of stressors are traumatic events, personal loss, and daily annoyances.

6. The links between stress, coping, and disease are complex. Stress can exert a direct influence by affecting the body's nervous, endocrine, and immune systems, making the person more vulnerable to illness. Stress exerts an indirect influence by affecting one's appraisal processes and behavioral patterns. Type A behavior has been implicated in an increased risk for coronary heart disease.

7. How one copes with various stresses is critical in determining the quality of one's life. Problem-solving and emotion-regulating strategies are the two major forms of coping. People are generally more successful in dealing with stress if they develop a flexible, varied repertoire of coping strategies than if they have only a single coping strategy.

Chapter 6

WAYS OF COPING
WITH STRESS

As described in the last chapter, stress and coping are complex processes that are connected like the two sides of a coin. How we appraise events and how well we can handle them influence what we perceive as stressful and what, if anything, we do about it. How we cope, whether it be by taking direct action or by controlling our emotional reactions, influences the degree of stress we experience. This chapter considers the variety of ways to cope with stress. As previously noted, we are not mere victims of stress; rather, we have choices. Before considering these choices, we examine a few cautionary guidelines to ensure that the choices we make are fully informed by the research findings on stress and coping.

GUIDELINES

There is a need to be cautious in either accepting or giving advice about how to cope with stress. This is a particular concern these days. We are continually bombarded by people telling us how best to cope with stress. In fact, so-called stress reduction and prevention workshops, self-help books, and retreats (for example, take a cruise and learn how to cope with stress) are among the growth industries of North America. Everyone seems to have advice on how best to reduce or avoid stress. Workshop leaders and authors usually advocate a specific technique—such as relaxation, exercise, assertiveness, medication, or diet—or an eclectic hodgepodge—an array of techniques that may include meditation, cognitive restructuring (that is, learning to appraise stressors differently), time management, life-style changes, and value clarification (reassessing one's priorities).

The claims have not usually been matched by evaluation of their usefulness. Moreover, the proponents often convey the impression that there is a right way to cope. This chapter describes a variety of coping strategies and summarizes what the evaluative research says about specific coping techniques. The goals are to nurture a flexible coping repertoire and a critical attitude toward those who would offer advice. A critical attitude comes from a better understanding of some of the basic facts and persistent myths concerning coping.

Coping is a complex dynamic (ever-changing) process that involves a series of adaptational tasks. To illustrate this process, consider the epidemic problem of divorce in North America. The divorce rate is now approaching 35 percent, and by the year 2000, an estimated 1 in 3 children will come from a divorced family.

The losses children face in divorce can be quite stressful. Children of divorce must deal with such intense emotions as sadness, loneliness, fear of abandonment, guilt, anger, and worry. While some children benefit from the end of parental disputes and discord, many show a number of stress-related problems, such as depression, social and academic problems, and delays in development. A child's relationship with the custodial parent and the noncustodial parent and the child's vulnerabilities are factors related to the child's ability to adjust to the divorce experience. In trying to help children cope with the aftermath of divorce, it is important to appreciate that children's coping strategies vary with age. Younger children may withdraw and use wish-fulfilling fantasies; older children may adopt a more direct problem-solving approach. Younger children often have concerns and reactions to divorce growing out of anxiety and fear of abandonment. Older children may use humor and sarcasm, as well as alternative activities (such as school, sports, drugs), to cope with divorce. Efforts to help such children are complicated not only by age but also the adaptational tasks that they must deal with. Wallerstein (1983) has noted that children of divorce have six overlapping tasks:

1. Acknowledgement of the reality of the breakup of the marriage.
2. Disengagement from parental conflict and distress and a return to normal activities and relationships.
3. Coming to terms with the multiple losses associated with divorce.
4. Resolving feelings of self-blame and anger.
5. Acceptance of the permanence of the divorce.
6. Achieving realistic hope regarding future family relationships.

This list of adaptational tasks indicates the complex pattern of challenges and problems involved in coping with the stress accompanying divorce. Thus, no simple coping remedy will suffice. A complex set of interventions is likely required to help children of divorce and their families.

A similar analysis may be applied to many other stressors individuals face. Each adaptational task (such as illness, divorce, and going to college) calls for a variety of complex coping responses.

There is no right or only way to cope. One must be cautious in advocating any particular coping strategy or technique. For instance, many advocate that keeping one's emotional distress within manageable limits reflects good adjustment. Research has indicted that some victims of stress, (for example, patients suffering from tuberculosis, cancer, or spinal cord injuries, or mothers who gave birth to deformed infants) cope much better in the long run if they initially express their emotions rather than behaving in a restrained manner (Wortman, 1983). Similarly, individuals who showed the most extreme psychological distress initially when placed in old age homes made a better adjustment than those who initially showed passive acceptance (Wortman, 1983). Moreover, coping techniques that work in the short run may not work in the long run, as evident in the studies on denial by the parents of children suffering from leukemia (Chodoff, Freedman, & Hambarg, 1964).

One should not prejudge the potential usefulness of any particular coping strategy. In some instances, coping actions such as denial, intrusive thoughts, intense emotional expression, and social withdrawal may be most effective, but even this judgment must be qualified by the fact that often the various indices of coping (self-report, physiological indicators, behavioral adjustment) do not correlate highly with each other. Individuals may improve on one index but not on another. Thus, one should be leery of claims that someone is a good coper. Your immediate question should be, "As evidenced on what particular measure?"

Coping is a multidimensional concept, not a uniform concept. Individuals show marked variability in their emotional reactions to stressful life events. They do *not* go through a predictable, orderly set of emotional and behavioral stages, as some have suggested. There is currently a popular belief in so-called stages of reaction, partly advanced in the popular book *On Death and Dying* by the psychiatrist Kubler-Ross (1969). She suggested that individuals who face death go through a predictable sequence of reactions consisting of denial, anger, bargaining, depression, and acceptance. Silver and Wortman (1980) argue that individuals do *not* usually go through such a sequence. Instead, evidence indicates marked variability in emotional reactions for stressed individuals, multiple simultaneous emotional reactions, skipped emotional reactions (so-called stages), or failure to reach the final so-called stage of acceptance. It is important to recognize this marked variability so we do not come to expect a certain pattern of emotional reactions, and thus view negatively someone who has not experienced a certain emotional state.

Coping efforts vary cross-culturally. Cultures vary markedly in their preferred mode of coping. For instance, among some groups in South American countries the preferred mode of coping is to adopt a fatalistic, passive stance when confronting major stressful events ("It's God's will!"). In contrast, in North America the preferred mode of coping for many groups is a direct-action problem-solving style ("Let's roll up our sleeves and get to work!"). Thus, the understanding of coping must consider the individual in the context of his or her environment.

Moreover, there is also a need to appreciate that the evaluation of coping is often value-laden and not strictly scientific. Consider the case of a mother who devotes herself to her dying child at the expense of her family members versus the mother who does the reverse (Silver & Wortman, 1980). Which approach constitutes the better coping effort? This decision is not merely a matter for science.

Coping efforts should be multileveled and flexible. Given that stress often requires multiple adaptational challenges, coping efforts should address various levels. For instance, consider work by Gordon and his colleagues (1980), who surveyed 135 cancer patients. They were able to identify 122 medical and psychosocial problems, covering thirteen areas of life functioning (for example, physical discomfort, medical treatment, vocation, and finances). Some coping efforts focused on attempts to come to terms with the disease, reappraise priorities, and make plans. Other coping attempts involved social support agents (such as family and friends), peer groups (other cancer patients), and institutional practices (such as interacting with doctors and hospital staff).

Sometimes individuals can cope best by reappraising events or by learning new coping skills. At other times, coping efforts involve changing organizational rules. There is often a need to change environmental presses as well as bolster the individual or group. Each coping effort should be tailored to the needs of the specific population and the changing demands of the situation.

The cumulative impact of these observations on coping is to provide a warning to those who too readily offer advice to others as to how best to cope.

Coping efforts should
be flexible.

"YOU MEAN YOUR BIG SMILE IS BOTTLED-UP AGGRESSION? MINE IS BOTTLED-UP HOSTILITY."

behavior-analytic approach means of studying stressful experiences by conducting an analysis of the problem (problem identification), an identification of coping alternatives (response enumeration), and an evaluation of their relative usefulness (response evaluation)

Before giving advice or conducting a training package there is a need to perform a careful evaluation of what to train and how to evaluate it. Goldfried and D'Zurilla (1969) have offered a useful framework for conducting such a systematic analysis. They propose a **behavior-analytic approach.** This approach consists of three steps:

1. *Problem identification*—systematically assessing of the range of problems and challenges that confront the specific group of stressed (or potentially stressed) individuals. A number of inquiry techniques (such as questionnaires, interviews, diaries, observations, and role playing) can be used with the targeted group, and significant others (such as friends, relatives, coworkers, and health care providers) in order to compile a comprehensive list of the variety of stressful problems.

2. *Response enumeration*—identifying the range of responses that can be employed to deal with the stressful demands catalogued during the problem-identification stage. There is a need to specify the intrapersonal, familial, group, organizational, and societal changes necessary to deal with the stressors.

3. *Response evaluation*—determining the relative efficacy of different coping responses. As noted above, this is not always easy, given that different indices of coping often do not correlate and that some judgments about coping efficacy may be value-laden.

Now we address the array of choices available when we are called upon to cope. Table 6–1 summarizes researchers' attempts to categorize the plethora of coping options available. We examine a few of these coping strategies in more detail.

COPING STRATEGIES

Coping strategies include tension reduction, problem solving, denial, cognitive reappraisal, social support, and communication. We consider these strategies and the factors that influence their usefulness in reducing, avoiding, or constructively using stress.

Tension Reduction

Letting off steam, ventilating one's feelings, using humor, and relaxing are constructive means of unwinding and coping with stress. They are all forms of **tension reduction.** The value of being able to unwind is nicely illustrated in research conducted by Marianne Frankenhaeuser (1979) at the Stress Institute in Stockholm, Sweden. She found that the speed with which individuals can unwind after stressful situations influences the total wearing of the body. After stressful job experiences, workers who could quickly return to prestress physiological levels (as evident in biochemical changes) tended to report fewer psychological symptoms and more job satisfaction than workers who had difficulty unwinding. Workers have reported using a variety of different methods to unwind:

tension reduction variety of means to help individuals reduce the level and impact of stress

1. Taking a passive attitude to ride out the situation.

2. Ignoring the sources of stress for the time being.

TABLE 6-1   Category Systems of Coping Responses

Pearlin and Schooler (1978) categorized coping in the following ways:

1. Responses that modify the situation, such as direct action, negotiation, advice seeking.
2. Responses that control the meaning of the problem, such as engaging in positive comparisons, selectively ignoring, changing goals and values, devaluing objects, disengaging from others.
3. Responses that control stress after it has occurred, such as avoiding confrontations, using relaxation, engaging in denial or withdrawal, and maintaining hopefulness.

Billings and Moos (1981) categorized coping in the following ways:

1. Cognitive coping (active), whereby individuals attempt to manage their perceptions or appraisals of the problem.
2. Behavioral coping (active), whereby individuals engage in overt attempts to deal directly with the problem.
3. Avoidance, coping whereby individuals avoid the problem.

Stone and Neale (1984) enumerated the following list of coping techniques:

1. Distraction—diverting attention away from the problem.
2. Situation redefinition—seeing the problem in a different light.
3. Direct action—getting information or doing something about the problem.
4. Catharsis—expressing emotion to reduce anxiety and tension.
5. Acceptance—realizing that nothing can be done about the problem.
6. Seeking social support—finding emotional support from others.
7. Relaxation—doing something to relax.
8. Religion—seeking spiritual guidance.
9. Enduring—facing that which cannot be avoided.

Folkman et al. (1986) enumerated the following list of coping techniques:

1. Confrontative coping—standing one's ground, being firm.
2. Distancing—acting as if nothing happened.
3. Self-control—keeping one's feelings to oneself.
4. Seeking social support—talking to someone, accepting sympathy.
5. Accepting responsibility—criticizing and lecturing oneself.
6. Escape-avoidance—wishing that the situation would go away.
7. Positive reappraisal—finding new faith, rediscovering what is important in life.

3. Letting the feelings wear off.
4. Dropping what they were doing and taking up something totally unrelated.
5. Moving on to something else that gives them satisfaction.
6. Carrying on as usual.
7. Temporarily removing themselves from stressful situations.

8. Talking over the problem away from the stressful environment.
9. Engaging in outside activities, such as physical exercise, meditation, hobbies, and family life.
10. Seeing the humor in the situation.
11. Doing relaxation exercises.

As one stressed teacher reported, "In order to cope with stress I have learned to 'kiss the bricks goodbye.' I don't get paid enough to bring my problems home to my family."

The list illustrates that while many coping efforts are designed to reduce tension, they also serve additional functions, such as information gathering, distancing, distracting oneself from the stressor, and reframing the nature of the stressor and one's ability to cope. These diverse psychological functions indicate the difficulty in developing a specific classification system of coping techniques. Coping strategies often serve multiple functions, illustrated by relaxation at home.

Relaxation has been characterized as the aspirin of the stress reduction field. When people are tense and upset, the usual advice offered is to try to relax. This is often easier said than done. Specific training programs have been developed to help individuals learn to relax. A pioneer in this area was Edmund Jacobson, a physician who developed a progressive relaxation training procedure in 1938. The training lasted fifty to two hundred sessions, during which individuals learned to tense and release specific muscle groups (fingers, hands, arms, chest, stomach, legs, feet) and to control physiological arousal by means of slow deep breaths. Since Jacobson's work, much has been learned about relaxation. First, relaxation skills can be learned in significantly fewer sessions than Jacobson proposed. Several audiotapes that teach relaxation in four to eight sessions are now commercially available. In some clinics, the training is supplemented by biofeedback training, whereby individuals review information about the level of muscle tension, heart rate, or respiration rate. Such training should be supplemented by the client's conscientiously practicing relaxation.

A second important observation is that mental relaxation is a central feature in the physical relaxation process. Some people relax by engaging in strenuous exercise, such as jogging or swimming. Others relax by becoming absorbed in a task such as knitting or gardening. As Folkins and Sime (1981) noted, there is increasing evidence that exercise can help reduce a number of symptoms of stress (for example, anxiety, depression, and tension) and such coronary risk factors as obesity and hypertension. Exercise can also enhance feelings of well-being and self-satisfaction.

At this point, there is little evidence to suggest that one form of relaxation is superior. Whatever works best for the individual in a particular setting should be employed, since there is evidence that relaxation can reduce physiological arousal, tenseness, and level of stress (Woolfolk & Lehrer, 1984).

Meditation is a form of relaxation.

Relaxation such as taking slow deep breaths (see "Exploring Choices: Relaxation Exercises) should be viewed as active coping that can be employed in various stress-engendering situations, especially at the onset. In this way, individuals can reduce physiological arousal that might otherwise interfere with higher-level cognitive processes (for example, concentrating, recalling complex events, solving problems, and planning). Relaxation can also provide individuals with a sense of control. They can do something if stressed, namely, relax.

EXPLORING CHOICES

RELAXATION EXERCISES

A number of different procedures teach people how to relax. No one approach appears to be most beneficial. A common objective in each is to have people learn to recognize the differences between tension and relaxation by having them systematically tighten and then release various muscle groups. A second goal is to teach people how to lower the level of physiological arousal and to elicit a state of calmness. The use of slow, deep breathing can foster alertness and relaxation. The following protocol illustrates a relaxation exercise.

Begin by finding a relaxing chair in a quiet spot, where you can make yourself as comfortable as possible. Let the chair totally support your body. Loosen tight clothing. After reading the following protocol, remove your glasses (if appropriate), close your eyes, and take a moment to become as relaxed as possible. Breath evenly and easily. Good.

In order to note the differences between being tense and being relaxed, focus on

the muscles of your dominant hand. Make a fist with the muscles of the right hand (if right-handed). Feel the pull across the top and bottom of the hand. You can feel the bending of the fingers as they press into the palm of the hand. Hold, hold, now slowly, very slowly, let your fingers uncurl, slowly moving them away from the palm of your hand until they assume their normal positions, being supported by the arm of the chair. As you uncurl the fingers, you may notice a sense of calmness, warmth, and ease flowing into the muscles of the hand and fingers. Note that your hand is becoming more and more relaxed. Notice the changes that you are able to bring forth. Compare the present state of your hand with that when your hand was tense.

Once again tense, hold, and slowly release the muscles of the right hand. Go ahead, let the tension go and feel the muscles unwind. Notice the changes you are able to bring about. You can now do the same with other muscles of your body,

systematic desensitization treatment procedure developed by Wolpe, whereby individuals are taught to relax and then asked to imagine stressful scenes along a hierarchy from least to most distressing

ventilation of feelings expression and sharing of feelings with others

Because relaxation has both physiological and psychological effects, it has been incorporated into a number of stress management techniques, such as **systematic desensitization** and stress-inoculation training. In both of these procedures, stressed individuals are taught to systematically relax and then imagine various stress-engendering situations along a graduated hierarchy from low stressful to high stressful. By means of mental rehearsal (imagery practice), they can learn to anticipate and plan for future stressful events. Such relaxation and mental practice can facilitate their problem-solving abilities.

Another means of reducing tension is to express and share one's feelings with others one knows and trusts. The ability to blow off steam and relive stressful experiences in a safe, accepting, reassuring, environment can help people cope with stress. The **ventilation of feelings** (such as shock, confusion,

even those in which you may be particularly prone to experience tension.

This same process of tensing, slowly releasing, relaxing, and comparing tension and calmness can be undertaken in a systematic fashion for other portions of your body. Now that you have worked on the right hand, try the muscles of the left hand, the face, the chest, the stomach, the thighs, the legs and the feet.

A second major way people learn to relax is slow, deep breathing. Many different types of breathing exercises are used. You must find the one that is most comfortable for you. Each can prove helpful, since controlling respiration has a direct calming affect on one's heart rate and in turn on one's state of arousal. Consider the following exercise.

Focus on the muscles of the chest and back. Do this by filling your lungs slowly, with a deep breath. Hold it, and then part your lips slightly and slowly exhale. Slowly. Good. Repeat this manner of breathing several times. As you exhale,

note the sense of relaxation and warmth you are able to bring forth.

Slowly fill the muscles of the chest by inhaling fully and then exhaling slowly. In order to control how fast you exhale, imagine you are gently blowing across the top of a spoon of hot soup so that you don't spill it or that you are flickering a lit candle without blowing it out. You may instead wish to imagine a pleasant, calm, peaceful scene or say to yourself, "Relax," or "Calm" as you exhale. Note the differences between the state of tension and the state of relaxation that you are able to bring forth.

The use of slow, deep breathing is a fine way for you to short-circuit the negative effects of stress, interrupt the tension cycle, and bring forth a state of calmness. Keep in mind that learning to relax is a skill, and like any other skill, it requires practice. Additional information about relaxation procedures can be found in Benson (1976), Bernstein and Borkovec (1973), and Woolfolk and Lehrer (1984).

anger, depression, and fear) *at the individual's own pace* can facilitate the coping process. For example, Ayalon (1983) has described how such expressions were achieved by means of play and fantasy in the cases of children who had been victims of terrorist attacks. Group discussion, drawing pictures, role playing, puppets, and fantasy play were used to help the children cope.

In some instances, stressed individuals may benefit from medication (tranquilizing drugs) taken under a doctor's orders. While the drugs themselves do not solve problems, they may reduce emotional reactions and thus permit a more level-headed problem-solving coping approach. Like most modes of coping, if taking medication is overdone, then it can become a stressor. Sometimes individuals use maladaptive forms of coping, including excessive drinking, smoking, and acting out. Each can take its toll.

Problem Solving

As noted in the last chapter, how we view stressful events and how able we are to cope with them are critical in determining the stress we experience. If we can appraise events as problems to be solved instead of personal threats and provocations, we are more likely to reduce or avoid stress. When we can engage in anticipatory coping (selecting our environment, planning, choosing, avoiding, tolerating, and so on), we are more likely to reduce the negative effects of stress. A number of researchers have proposed that a step-by-step approach to **problem solving** can facilitate coping (D'Zurilla & Nezu, 1982; Goldfried & Davison, 1976). The following steps have been suggested for coping with stress:

problem solving
complex set of cognitive and behavioral skills that include problem identification, goal selection, generation of alternatives, consideration of consequences, decision making, implementation, and evaluation

1. Set realistic goals as concretely as possible. Indicate the situation. Then indicate how you would like it to be.
2. State the problem in simple operational behavioral terms. Instead of exclaiming that nothing works, that no one likes you, or that life has no purpose, try to specify the behaviors you would like to see increased or decreased in a situation. Pin down the source of trouble.
3. Generate a wide range of possible alternative courses of action and delineate the steps necessary to reach your goals.
4. Imagine and consider how others might respond if asked to deal with a similar stress problem. If you wish, seek input from others about the merits of alternative courses of action.
5. Evaluate the pros and cons of each proposed solution and order the solutions from least practical and desirable to most practical and desirable. Consider both the short-term and long-term consequences of your decision.
6. Try the most acceptable and feasible solution.
7. Expect some failures, but reward yourself for having tried.
8. Reconsider the original problem in light of the attempt at problem solving.

Wasik (1984) described problem-solving steps in terms of questions that one can ask oneself.

Steps	Questions
1. Problem identification.	What is the concern?
2. Goal selection.	What do I want?
3. Generation of alternatives.	What can I do?
4. Consideration of consequences.	What might happen?
5. Decision making.	What is my decision?
6. Implementation.	Now do it!
7. Evaluation.	Did it work?

By noting the discrepancy between what is and how one would like situations to be one can become aware of the potential usefulness of problem-solving efforts. Adopting such a problem-solving approach involves a variety of subroutines:

1. Checking how things are by asking oneself, "What caused or led up to this problem?" "How do I know I have a problem?" "Is it my problem or someone else's?"
2. Checking how things are by asking others for their perceptions and advice.
3. Specifying in precise terms how one would like things to be.
4. Noting skills needed and possible obstacles to achieve one's objectives.
5. Recalling what you have done before that required similar skills.
6. Dividing the stressful event into smaller, more manageable chunks.
7. Seeking information, guidance, and support from others.
8. Thinking of what lies ahead and making contingency plans.
9. Mentally rehearsing ways to handle each small stress.
10. Practicing by rehearsing skills.
11. Gradually exposing oneself to small amounts of stress before entering high-pressure situations.
12. Maintaining self-confidence and hope when trying.
13. Using coping skills but not catastrophizing if things don't work out. Failures and disappointments should be viewed as necessary feedback to fine-tune problem-solving and coping efforts.

decisional balance sheet means of making decisions that considers anticipated consequences for each course of action

Wheeler and Janis (1978) offer an example of how individuals have used such systematic problem solving and decision making. They suggest that individuals use a **decisional balance sheet** to itemize expected consequences in terms of tangible gains and losses for oneself and others, as well as to record the implications for oneself, including social approval and disapproval.

Figure 6–1 provides a decisional balance sheet of the pros and cons for Bob, who is trying to decide whether to stay at his job. Such a balance sheet analysis helped Bob weigh the pluses and minuses of each course of action. What other positive and negative consequences might Bob consider? Perhaps Bob could use his problem-solving skills in exploring how to decrease the negative features of his job and enhance the positive features?

To appreciate the potential usefulness of such a decisional balance sheet, identify an important decision that you will have to make in the near future. Set up your own personal balance sheet, specifying the expected consequences for each course of action you consider. In most instances, our decision-making processes are not systematic, and our problem-solving efforts are usually haphazard. The decisional balance sheet can thus prove helpful.

Such a problem-solving approach is designed to help individuals break seemingly overwhelming problems into smaller, potentially manageable chunks,

FIGURE 6-1   Decisional Balance Sheet

Expected Consequences	Positive Anticipations	Negative Anticipations
Tangible gains and losses for *self*	1. Satisfactory pay. 2. Plenty of opportunities to use my skills and competencies. 3. For the present, my status in the organization is okay (but it won't be for long if I am not promoted in the next year).	1. Long hours. 2. Constant time pressures, short deadlines. 3. Unpleasant paper work. 4. Poor prospects for advancement to a higher-level position. 5. Repeated reorganizations make my work chaotic.
Tangible gains and losses for *others*	1. Adequate income for family. 2. Wife and children get special privileges because of my position in the firm.	1. Not enough time free to spend with my family. 2. Wife often has to put up with my irritability when I come home after bad days at work.
Self-approval or self-disapproval	1. This position allows me to make full use of my potentialities. 2. Proud of my achievements. 3. Proud of the competent team I have shaped up. 4. Sense of meaningful accomplishment.	1. Sometimes feel I'm a fool to continue putting up with the unreasonable deadlines and other stupid demands made by the top managers.
Social approval or disapproval	1. Approval of men on my team, who look up to me as their leader and who are good friends. 2. Approval of my superior who is a friend and wants me to stay.	1. Very slight skeptical reaction of my wife she asks me if I might be better off in a different firm. 2. A friend who has been wanting to wangle a new job for me will be disappointed.

Source: Reprinted from D. D. Wheeler & I. L. Janis (1980). *A practical guide for making decisions.* New York: Free Press, 58.

draw on past experiences, mentally rehearse alternative actions, and acquire information about the nature of a stressful event (when it is likely to happen, how long it will last, preliminary signs of stress, and so forth). Such information can tell individuals what they are likely to experience. The more accurate people's expectations, the less likely they are to feel stressed. Stress is most likely to occur when no actions or thoughts are available to handle the situation.

People also need the social skills to implement their plans and to take concrete actions to deal directly with the source of stress. In some instances, additional help may be necessary to nurture such skills. For example, communicating more effectively, managing time, reappraising one's priorities and values, delegating authority, and sharing responsibilities may be areas for skill building.

Keep in mind however, that not all problems are solvable, as in the case of incurable illnesses and irreplaceable losses. In such circumstances, individuals need to better understand their responses. We may not be able to control the stressors, but we can influence how we respond. In coping with stressful events, it is worth keeping in mind the advice offered by Reinhold Nieburh, which has been adopted as a closing prayer by the Alcoholics Anonymous organization.

> *O God, give us the serenity to accept what cannot be changed, courage to change what should be changed, and wisdom to distinguish the one from the other.*

Denial

denial coping that involves not thinking about or not taking certain actions

In some stressful situations the most effective means of coping may be *not* engaging in reality testing or problem solving, but instead using some form of **denial**. Richard Lazarus (1984) has written thoughtfully about the potential adaptive value of denial, especially in circumstances where it is impossible to do anything. When the individual has nothing to lose by not attending to the stressor, then using denial may be beneficial. Denial may take many forms, such as detachment ("It's not my problem."), distraction ("I will do something else."), rationalization ("The chances it will affect me are 1,000 to 1."), minimizing the seriousness of a crisis ("It can't be all that bad."), or even self-deception ("Don't worry, I can handle anything.").

Denial can help individuals distract themselves or protect themselves from being overwhelmed, thus maintaining feelings of hope and well-being and a sense of self-worth. It can also let stressed individuals dose themselves, that is, deal with small amounts of stress at a time. For example, burn or accident patients may need to come to terms with their accidents gradually and may use denial (selective inattention, maintaining detachment, self-deception) to cope. In this way, individuals are less likely to become overwhelmed, thus providing the necessary time to marshal other coping resources. Subsequently, they use more direct means of coping. Lazarus noted that many authors, including Cervantes (*Don Quixote*), Eugene O'Neill (*The Iceman Cometh*), and Edward Albee (*Who's Afraid of Virginia Woolf*) have examined the use of denial (illusion) as a means of coping.

There are, however, occasions when denial is maladaptive (denial can result in people's not taking proper precautions). For instance, denial is maladaptive when a woman denies the significance of a lump in her breast or avoids self-examination or when a man who experiences a heart attack denies the significance of the pain and continues to perform strenuous exercise instead of seeking medical assistance (Katz et al., 1970; Hackett & Cassem, 1975). In both of these cases, denial as a coping strategy is maladaptive. It endangers people's lives. Once again, we have evidence that a coping process (in this case denial) can be adaptive under one set of conditions and maladaptive under different conditions. This finding underscores the need for caution in advocating or rejecting a specific coping strategy.

Cognitive Reappraisal

A major cause of stress is being victimized as a result of illness (such as cancer), circumstance (such as nuclear accident or natural disaster), or violence (such as rape). In each instance, being a victim can severely affect individuals' assumptions about themselves and the world. Life crises can severely shake individuals' beliefs in their invulnerability, views of the world as being meaningful and comprehensible, assumptions that other people can be trusted, and views of themselves as competent and worthwhile (Janoff-Bulman & Timko, 1987). Self-questioning; feelings of insecurity, unworthiness, and weakness; and perceptions of threat and danger are often manifested. The world may be viewed as threatening, with a high likelihood of future recurrences. Victims may feel that they can no longer control what happens in their lives.

In order to avoid or cope with such feelings, individuals may accept their basic circumstances but cognitively reappraise or restructure them to find something favorable. By **cognitive reappraisal**, they may try to think of something favorable to occur out of a crisis, consider that things could be worse, compare themselves to others who are worse off, or alter their values and priorities so the present situation does not appear to be so bad.

cognitive reappraisal means by which individuals restructure or reframe experiences as well as their ability to cope

In recent years, stress investigators have focused on social comparison as a means of coping with stress. For example, Taylor and her colleagues described several ways in which individuals try to redefine stressful events so that their views of themselves and the world are not challenged (Taylor, Wood, & Lichtman, 1983). To redefine the stress, victims may selectively refocus their attention by comparing themselves with less-fortunate others; create hypothetical worse-world scenarios of what might have happened, selectively focus on one aspect of the stressful event and view it in a more favorable light, or manufacture normative standards of adjustment (a scenario as to how most people would cope) in order to make their own adjustment appear exceptional. In some instances, victims may even speak of benefits that occurred because of the stressful event. For example, the individual who was paralyzed because of an automobile accident stated:

> I know this may seem odd, but in some ways this accident has worked out to be for the best. I was living in the 'fast lane' and the accident forced me to reevaluate my life. I'm now closer to my family and to God.

Some individuals come to terms with stressful situations by resigned acceptance. They may hold a fatalistic philosophy that life is basically unfair and view stressors as natural outcomes. They may mitigate distress by engaging in a conscious decision to accept or to avoid the situation. Others cope by viewing stressful events as a natural outgrowth of a coherent view of life that arises from religious, scientific, or philosophical beliefs (Antonovsky, 1979).

In some situations, stressed individuals turn to others in the same boat. Often, victimized individuals join self-help groups consisting of other, similarly stressed people. Examples include Alcoholics Anonymous, Weight Watchers, and Gamblers Anonymous. Such meetings can provide victims with normative information, a new framework for understanding their reactions, and social support. On some occasions, stressed individuals may require the services of mental health professionals (psychotherapists) to help them cope with stress.

Social Support

social support
personal contacts
available from others
that may provide
material and emotional
aid

buffering hypothesis
argument that social
support exerts
beneficial effects in the
presence of stress by
protecting people from
the negative effects of
such stress

Most people who encounter stressful life events do *not* turn to professional mental health providers. Rather they turn to family, friends, neighbors, clergy, and coworkers to provide social support. During the past decade, a great deal of research has been directed at the possible buffering effects of social support. **Social support** refers to personal contacts available from other individuals, groups, and the community, which presumably protect (buffer) people from the deleterious effects of stress. According to the **buffering hypothesis**, we use others in many ways—to express feelings; to identify with those who have had similar experiences; to obtain information about a crisis, alternate courses of action, and probable outcomes; to find meaning in crises with others; to receive assistance and feedback; to maintain hope; and to receive material aid. People with established social support networks (such as spouses, confidants, friends, and coworkers) tend to be in better mental and physical health and to cope better with stress than unsupported individuals. People who live alone and who are not involved with other people or social organizations are more vulnerable to a variety of chronic diseases, have more psychiatric complaints, and experience more physiological indices of stress (Heller, 1979). Being a member of a group or identifying with one can act as a protective device against stress.

Social support can help people with stress.

Not only the number of support systems but also the quality of the relation-ships influences how individuals react to stress. In some instances, social sup-ports may *not* be beneficial, as when they are critical, intrusive, and unwel-come. For example, there is increasing evidence that the nature of the family interaction that psychiatric patients experience upon discharge from mental hospitals plays an important role in influencing the likelihood of relapse (Fal-loon, Boyd, & McGill, 1984; Vaugh & Leff, 1976). Hostile feelings and intru-siveness on the part of a patient's family can make things worse and cause more distress. Under most conditions, social support can moderate the impact of stress. However, under certain conditions, social support can be intrusive, can be conflictual, or can lead to group pressure that interferes with efficient problem solving.

Researchers do not understand exactly what transpires in social contacts that reduce the detrimental effects of stress. One research strategy asks vic-tims what types of support they find most *unhelpful*. The following observa-tions by various victims have been offered (as described by Kessler, Price, & Wortman, 1985):

1. Victims find little comfort in so-called moving-on statements. For exam-ple, parents whose infants died are *not* comforted by suggestions that the mother is young and can have another child or that little attachment could have been established since the child was only an infant.

2. By telling a crisis victim to look on the bright side, the supporter may lead the victim to feel that his or her feelings and behavior are inappropriate. The helper may remind the person that things are not really as bad as they seem ("You could have lost both children in the accident. Be thankful you have another son."). Such attempts may subtly suggest to the crisis victim that it is wrong to be so distressed.

3. Telling stressed victims that you know how they feel or that they should not question God's will were also found to be unhelpful.

4. By offering advice or tangible aid, supporters may convey to the recipients that they are incapable of handling their own problems. The fact that oth-ers are repeatedly offering help may imply that the crisis victim is neither capable nor responsible enough to undertake such tasks. This is especially problematic for individuals who like to see themselves as self-reliant.

As Kessler and his colleagues (1985) note, people who provide support fre-quently underestimate the extent of distress experienced by persons in need, and they often find it difficult to tolerate the victim's distress. As a result, they often engage in behavior to minimize the victim's problems. For instance, a widower received a greeting card proclaiming "When life gives you a lemon, make lemonade" in response to the death of his wife. Would-be helpers often attempt to be cheerful, more often in order to reduce their own distress. How-ever, such effort (as sending the card) may make the victim feel worse. As social support agents, we should recognize that we have the potential to make things worse as well as better. We should be sensitive to the impact of our behavior on others, especially those most in need.

Then, how can we be of most help to those in need? In their study of the bereaved, Wortman and Silver (1987) have offered several suggestions:

1. Permit those who experience a life crisis to talk about feelings, but only if they wish to do so.

2. Provide contact with others who have experienced a similar crisis. Such individuals are less likely to become upset by signs of distress from stressed individuals and less likely to cut off discussions of feelings.

3. Don't push stressed individuals toward a quick resolution of feelings or encourage them to use reasoning to initially solve problems. As a result of using a more moderate, less-pressured form of social support, advice and suggestions are less likely to be viewed as judgmental.

Following these guidelines will help us to be better providers of social support. But providing such support may *not* always be without a toll. For instance, Kessler and his colleagues (1985) reported that women are more prone than men to take on the task of nurturing others who seek them out during times of crisis. Providing such support has been found to sometimes take a psychological and physical toll (distress and illness) on the caregiver.

In order to appreciate the nature of social support as a coping strategy, consider the following questions. To whom do you usually provide social support? What form does the social support take? Has providing such social support caused you to become distressed? On the other side of the coin, to whom can you turn for social support, especially in times of crisis? Do you have different support agents for different spheres of your life—work, family, school? Under what conditions will turning to others reduce stress? When may turning to others have the paradoxical effect of increasing your stress? Finally, what can you do to improve and nurture your already existing support systems and to develop new ones? A number of communication skills help in nurturing your social support system.

Communication

People are social. We are reared in families, dependent on others for survival, nurturance, and love. We are influenced by peer groups and cultural, economic, and religious forces. How well we convey our needs to others, assert ourselves, establish intimacy, and provide succor to others greatly influence the quality of our life. A number of specific social skills influence the nature of an individual's social support:

1. The ability to listen, relate, share feelings, and stand up for one's rights without being seen as pushy or aggressive.

2. The ability to state requests and communicate one's needs clearly. For example, one can use X-Y-Z communication, namely: "When you do X in

situation Y, it makes me feel Z. Did you realize that it made me feel that way? What can we do about that?"

3. The ability to take someone else's perspective or viewpoint toward a request for help. Question yourself about how you would feel if someone asked you for help in this particular manner at this particular time.

Even from this short list of social skills we can appreciate the complexity of communicating. As Linehan and Egan (1983) observe, social skills call for the following:

1. Sensitivity—the ability to pick up from people and settings fairly subtle cues that indicate exactly what is going on, but doing so in a way that one does not jump to premature conclusions.

2. Social judgment—the ability to think out a plan of action and imagine what effect it will have, being realistic when thinking through actions in advance and when implementing them.

3. Self-regulation—combining both external information (such as reactions of others) and internal information (such as assessment of one's abilities) when interacting. Emotions and the psychological responses that accompany them are linked with social effectiveness. Ability to control or self-regulate our emotions can influence how well we communicate.

The ways we communicate affect our coping repertoire. How we communicate influences the nature and quality of our social support. For many people, such naturally occurring support systems are not sufficient to reduce the deleterious effects of stress. In these cases, professional help may be required.

Researchers have begun to explore what common factors contribute to the usefulness of the various coping strategies. See "On the Research Frontier: Self-Efficacy—A Possible Common Factor Contributing to Successful Coping" for some of their discoveries.

In summary, we have available a variety of coping response alternatives, including tension reduction, problem solving, denial, cognitive reappraisal, social support, and communication. Since stressful life events typically require handling a number of adaptational tasks, individuals often use a variety of coping skills, as described in "On the Research Frontier: People's Resilience—An Expression of Choice."

TREATING STRESS DISORDERS

Much of what we know about the treatment of stress disorders comes from work with soldiers who have experienced the harshness of war. The treatment of soldiers suffering from what has been called shell shock, combat fatigue, and stress disorders has yielded valuable clinical guidelines. The first guideline is the need to provide treatment as early as possible. The earlier the detection that someone is undergoing undue stress and the more *immediate* the treat-

ON THE RESEARCH FRONTIER

SELF-EFFICACY—A POSSIBLE COMMON FACTOR CONTRIBUTING TO SUCCESSFUL COPING

What do the coping strategies described in this chapter have in common? Researchers have searched to identify a common element that contributes to their effectiveness. While the answer to this important question is not yet available, a description of the research effort is informative. One leader in this area is the psychologist Al Bandura, who with his colleagues at Stanford University has proposed that an individual's level of self-efficacy is an important determiner of coping ability. *Self-efficacy* refers to the degree of self-confidence an individual has in performing a specific task.

Using rating scales, Bandura (1986) has systematically assessed individuals' expectancies as to whether they feel they can perform a task and also whether they feel that doing so will make a difference. Those who have a high sense of self-confidence and a general high self-esteem tend to attempt more difficult tasks, expend more effort, persist longer at problem solutions in the face of adversity, and feel less self-blame when encountering failure. They tend to overestimate their capabilities and have an optimistic outlook. Often they view themselves as more adroit and capable than they are.

In contrast, those with low levels of perceived self-efficacy tend to mistrust their capabilities, shy away from difficult tasks, have lower levels of aspiration, and have a weak commitment to goals they choose to pursue. In taxing situations, individuals with low self-efficacy tend to dwell on personal deficiencies, the toughness of the challenge, and potential adverse consequences. They allow negative thoughts to divert their attention from how best to perform. Instead, they focus on personal deficiencies and possible calamities. Those with perceptions of low self-efficacy tend to reduce efforts, give up quickly, and recover slowly following failure. They fall easy prey to stress and depression.

Most exciting are recent findings that when challenged, those low in self-efficacy produce substantial increases in catecholamines (stress hormones), while those high in self-confidence have greater transmission of brain opioids—chemicals that seem to block or reduce pain transmission. If these initial findings on the biochemical changes that accompany personal expectancies hold up, then we will see the beginning of a new research frontier—the biology of hope. The degree of self-efficacy may prove to be an important ingredient in many diverse coping strategies.

EXPLORING CHOICES

PEOPLE'S RESILIENCE—AN EXPRESSION OF CHOICE

A central theme of this book is that people have choices. Perhaps this is most starkly illustrated when we consider how people under the most unmanageable stressful conditions maintain a sense of control, manifest courage and resilience, and express a choice. Consider the autobiography of Alexander Dolgun (1975), who survived the cruelty of the Soviet Gulag (imprisonment). He reported that as long as he believed that he could in some way affect or control the conditions of his incarceration, even if it meant having only one option—suicide— he could withstand the daily torment. He felt he could choose between giving in to the persecution of his jailers or maintaining a sense of personal control.

Another testimony to courage and the sense of choice comes from the postwar interview studies of the survivors of the Nazi concentration camps (Dimsdale, 1974, 1980). While chance or fate often dictated who lived and who died, many of those who survived the unbelievable brutalization and degradation of the camps described a variety of coping strategies they employed. These included the following:

1. *Differential focus on the good.* Many inmates focused their attention on small gratifications, such as getting through the food line without a beating. Thus, they attempted to ignore the larger tragedies of the camps. Viktor Frankl (1963) found escape from the unbearable reality of the concentration camps by focusing intensely on memories of better times. He saw himself taking a bus, unlocking his door, speaking to his wife, and hearing her saying encouraging words. Taking some small actions contributed to survival.

2. *Survival for some purpose.* Others felt a need to survive to help a relative, to bear witness, to show the world what had happened, or to seek revenge.

3. *Psychological removal.* This strategy involved insulating oneself from stress by developing ways of not feeling any emotion. One individual developed a delusion that the soldiers who raped and abused her were devils incarnate and that she was immune to their assaults.

4. *Concept of mastery.* Some individuals attempted to find one area in which they did not feel defeated by stress by engaging in some activity, such as keeping a diary. Humor also played an important role in the survival process.

5. *Group affiliation.* Social supports in the camps helped to reduce stress by providing information, advice, protection, and a source of identification.

6. *Hope.* The psychiatrist Karl Menninger (1959) described how a group of thin, hungry, weary, imprisoned doctors established a medical society within the concentration camp. They met regularly late at night to discuss cases,

prepared and presented papers, made plans for improving health conditions in the camp, and even secretly built an X-ray machine with stolen and smuggled materials. Their dedication to medicine and hope in the future reflected a commitment to cope, to survive.

Thus, in even the most dehumanizing conditions people were able to marshal the will to live and the ability to cope. In this way, they exerted a choice. In fact, we may take heart in the findings reported by the Israeli sociologist Aaron Antonovsky (1979) that more than 25 percent of concentration camp survivors, despite long years of suffering, the constant threat of annihilation, and other life-threatening stressors, have survived the ordeal without evidence of psychiatric disorder or chronic physical disease. They were able to lead productive lives and raise psychologically healthy children.

The Nazi concentration camps were dehumanizing.

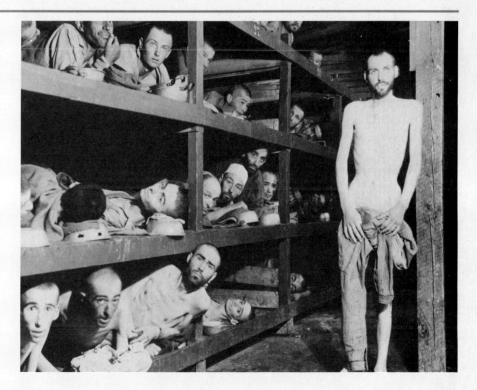

ment, the better the outcome. Second, insofar as treatment can be provided in close *proximity* to the stressful environment (for example, the combat zone), the better the outcome. In this way, stressed soldiers were reunited with their buddies as soon as possible. The third guideline involves the need to maintain an *expectancy* that the soldier will recover and return to his unit with a useful role to perform. Combat zone treatment of stress reactions based on the clinical guidelines of immediacy, proximity, and expectancy has generally proved successful, with approximately 80 percent to 90 percent of distressed soldiers returning to combat. Only about 10 percent of those who return to combat break down a second time.

A central feature of the treatment that the soldiers received was that of tension reduction. Treatment usually consisted of rest, sleep (perhaps assisted by a sedative), a warm meal, the chance to clean up, relaxation, and supportive psychotherapy to permit the stressed soldiers to discuss their experiences and ventilate their feelings. Blowing off steam and reliving stressful experiences in a safe, accepting, reassuring environment helped them cope with the stress.

In some cases, stressed individuals are given an injection of sodium pentathol, which helps them to remember or relive the stressful situation and allows a strong emotional discharge, or catharsis, to relieve tension. In a minority of cases, however, combat stress may have residual effects well after discharge. In such instances, more prolonged forms of psychotherapeutic intervention are offered, especially in the case of posttraumatic stress disorder. Table 6-2 provides a description of several forms of treatment for those suffering from posttraumatic stress disorder.

Individuals differ in susceptibility to stressful events such as combat. If we could identify such vulnerable individuals in not only military but also civilian life, then perhaps we could begin to develop programs to train or inoculate them against stress. The idea of bolstering an individual's defenses against the negative effects of stress is in some respects analogous to the notion of inoculation against disease. The underlying principle is that a person's resistance is enhanced by exposure to a stimulus strong enough to arouse defenses but not to overcome the individual.

For the past ten years, Don Meichenbaum and his colleagues at the University of Waterloo in Ontario, Canada, have been researching the potential usefulness of a psychological training program to help individuals improve their ability to cope with stress (Meichenbaum, 1985; Meichenbaum & Jaremko, 1983). **Stress inoculation training** (SIT) has been applied on preventative and treatment bases to a variety of populations. On a preventative basis, it has been used with such diverse groups as surgical patients, nurses, teachers, athletes, and Type A executives. On a treatment basis, it has been employed with victim populations, such as rape victims, pain and cancer patients, anxious students, and psychiatric patients who have severe problems with anger control.

SIT can last from as little as one hour (preparing patients about to undergo surgery), to as many as forty sessions (with psychiatric outpatients). The training has been conducted on both individual and group bases. The program usually involves three phases:

stress inoculation training treatment procedure developed by Meichenbaum, whereby individuals are taught a variety of affective, cognitive, physiological, and interpersonal coping skills

TABLE 6-2   Therapeutic Interventions Used in the Treatment of
Posttraumatic Stress Disorder (PTSD)

Type	Description
Family therapy	Since PTSD can take a toll on not only the victim but also family members, involvement of the family is seen as important.
Rap groups	PTSD victims may find it helpful to share their experiences with other victims. Such group meetings can provide needed social support.
Brief dynamic therapy	Since prestress levels of adjustment can often exert a marked influence on level of adjustment, one on one or small-group meetings can be useful in dealing with the issues that the traumatic stressor has exacerbated.
Crisis intervention	Therapeutic support immediately after the traumatic event can provide opportunities for communication, information, and ministration of physical and emotional needs.
Aerobic exercise training (such as jogging or swimming)	Such exercise has been found to be helpful in reducing the severity and duration of depressive reactions following severe life changes. Exercise may facilitate both physiological and psychological changes.
Relaxation training and biofeedback training	Since tension and related hyperarousal are critical symptoms, learning to relax and to develop a sense of bodily and personal control can be helpful.
Cognitive behavioral therapy	Individual and group sessions are used to help PTSD victims reappraise the stress experience; develop and nurture a flexible coping repertoire including problem solving, impulse and anger control, assertiveness and interpersonal skills; reestablish trust; and strengthen a sense of personal efficacy.

1. In the initial phase, or *educational phase*, information is provided about the ways distressing emotions are generated. The client is given a better understanding of his or her stress.

2. The second phase, or *rehearsal phase*, teaches a variety of coping skills and tries to ensure that the coping skills already in one's repertoire are used. The goal is to foster flexibility. Specific coping skills taught include relaxation, problem solving, and communication.

3. In the final phase, or *application phase*, the client tries what has been learned and practices in both the clinic and real life. The results of these personal experiments are then evaluated. A number of techniques, including behavioral and imagery rehearsal and role playing, are used to help clients practice their coping skills.

SIT helps clients to do the following things:

1. Discover that others often have similar problems and learn what they do to solve them.

2. Understand more about how thinking, feeling, and behaving are inter-related.

3. Learn to approach problems in a step-by-step manner in order to avoid feeling threatened or overwhelmed.

4. Ensure that they have adequate coping skills.

5. Experiment with and practice their coping skills systematically.

SIT training helps clients appreciate that they are not the mere victims of stress. How they appraise and cope with stress is critical in influencing their reactions. They are taught that stressful events may be broken down into a sequence of phases, which include the preparing for the stressor, confronting and handling the stress, coping with feeling overwhelmed, and finally, reflecting how the situation was handled. Together, the client and trainer generate a list of alternative coping strategies to handle each of the different phases of a stressful event. Since the coping strategies taught in SIT can help anyone who must face stressful encounters, they are enumerated in Table 6–3. The strategies are summarized in terms of possible self-statements that individuals may make before, during, and after confronting stressful events. The proposed purposes of the various coping strategies are also indicated.

The following case study of SIT illustrates the way stressed individuals may be treated. In reading this case, described by Novaco (1977), imagine how someone you know who is extremely stressed might benefit from such a treatment approach. The client was Tom, a 38-year-old credit manager for a national firm, who had been hospitalized because he was tense, depressed, feeling worthless and inadequate, and was even considering suicide. He had been under considerable job pressure and had developed headaches and chest pains. He was married and had six children, one of whom had been diagnosed as hyperactive.

Clinical interviews revealed that Tom had a great deal of anger and hostility toward his colleagues and supervisors, even though he bottled them up and reacted in an overcontrolled fashion. He would actively suppress his anger but then periodically explode in verbal fireworks. At home, he was intolerant and easily provoked. The children's fights frequently elicited anger, which he readily expressed both verbally and physically. As he stated, he was reacting out of proportion. He felt overwhelmed and helpless.

During hospitalization, stress-inoculation training was conducted three times a week for three and a half weeks. Follow-up sessions were conducted twice weekly for two months. The initial phase of treatment focused on making Tom aware of his personal anger pattern and the functions of anger (that is, what causes anger and how anger can be regulated). The discussion focused on such topics as (a) recognizing the first signs of tension and arousal, (b) identifying persons and situations that triggered stress and anger, (c) discriminating between justified and unnecessary anger, and (d) appreciating how sometimes he inadvertently exacerbated his stress (that is, lit his own fuse).

The second phase of treatment was devoted to learning and rehearsing coping skills. Tom was taught how to view situations in terms of problems to be

TABLE 6-3   Coping Self-Statements Used in Stress Inoculation Training

1. **Preparing for the stressor.**
   Purposes:
   • To focus on specific preparation for a task.
   • To combat negative thinking.
   • To emphasize planning and preparation.
   Examples:
   • What do I have to do?
   • Remember, stick to the issues and don't take it personally.
   • Stop worrying. Worrying won't help anything.
   • What are some of the helpful things I can do instead?
   • I'm feeling uptight—that's natural.
   • Maybe I'm just eager to confront the situation.

2. **Confronting and handling the stress.**
   Purposes:
   • To control the stress reaction.
   • To reassure that one can handle the situation.
   • To reinterpret stress as something that can be used constructively.
   • To use coping responses such as relaxation.
   • To remain focused on the task or situation.
   Examples:
   • I can meet this challenge.
   • I can convince myself to do it.
   • One step at a time.
   • Don't think about my stress, just about what I have to do.
   • This stress is what the trainer said I might feel.
   • This tenseness can be an ally, a cue to cope.
   • Relax, I'm in control. Take a slow deep breath. Ah, good.
   • Don't make more out of this than I have to.
   • Look for positives, don't jump to conclusions.
   • I have a lot of different coping techniques I can call upon.

3. **Coping with feeling overwhelmed (this stage does not always occur).**
   Purposes:
   • To set up contingency plans and prepare for the possibility of becoming extremely stressed.
   • To remain in the situation.
   • To stay focused on the present.
   • To accept feelings and wait for them to decrease.
   Examples:
   • When stress comes, just pause.
   • Keep my focus on the present. What is it I have to do?
   • Label my stress on a 0 to 10 scale and watch it change.
   • Don't try to eliminate stress totally; just keep it manageable.
   • Time to take a slow, deep breath.
   • Let's take the issue point by point.
   • My stress is a signal.
   • Time for problem solving.

4. **Evaluating coping efforts and self-rewards.**
   Purposes:
   • To evaluate the coping attempt. What helped and what didn't?
   • To look back over the experience to see what has been learned.
   • To recognize small gains and not belittle gradual progress.
   • To praise oneself for trying.
   Examples:
   • I made more out of stress than it was worth.
   • It's getting better each time I use this procedure.
   • It didn't work. That's okay. What can I learn from my try?

solved instead of as personal threats. Tom was encouraged to identify the result he wanted and then to list the best possible approaches to achieving the desired outcome. Tom also found it helpful to practice relaxation, maintaining a sense of humor, taking the other person's perspective, and communicating his feelings effectively without stridency.

During the final phase, Tom underwent graded doses of anger stimuli by means of imagery and role-playing. He was asked to imagine a series of scenes ranging from those least likely to provoke anger to those which, in the past, had driven him into fury and frustration. While imagining these scenes, Tom mentally rehearsed the various anger control skills he had already developed. Later, these scenes were actually played out, with Tom and the therapist taking opposing roles. Finally, Tom was encouraged to use his anger control coping skills in real life, initially in relatively safe situations and then, with practice, in more demanding social situations.

The treatment proved successful in helping Tom to deal with his anger and to reduce his accompanying depression. For example, he found it much easier to control his irritation with his children, even though there were many highly provocative incidents. At work, too, he was much better able to express his feelings in a constructive manner.

Although one must be careful in generalizing from a given case study, Novaco's report on the potential value of stress-inoculation training has now been repeated in many other cases, with people who work in stressful occupations (such as police officers and soldiers) and with students who must face the stress of evaluation, social acceptance, and the like. Much research is now under way to fully assess the relative efficacy of SIT in reducing and avoiding stressful reactions.

In considering these treatment approaches, keep in mind that in order to help people cope with stress it is important to sometimes go well beyond the targeted group. For example, consider the case of police officers, who are a high-risk group as evident in the high incidence of marital discord, alcoholism, and stress-related illnesses. Any intervention designed to help police officers must involve other levels of intervention, such as organizational structure, peer groups, and family members.

The difficulties in attempting to change entrenched organizational practices and attitudes should not be underestimated. In some cases, change can be brought about by providing feedback and constructive alternatives; in other instances, change can be achieved only by mobilizing group pressure. The important point is that efforts to reduce stress may be needed at the institutional or organizational level as well as at the level of the group and individual. Similarly, in work with stressed students, one can focus treatment interventions on the students, but one should also consider the way that institutional practices (such as administrative policies and professional demands), as well as student pressure, may inadvertently exacerbate the level of stress. It would be both shortsighted and damaging to limit the treatment to only the stressed population, for such an approach may be a further way of blaming the victim.

Surely, the stressed student has an active role to play in ameliorating his or her stressful situation, but similarly, the therapist also has a responsibility in assessing and, wherever possible, changing environmental pressures. The transactional model of stress offered in this book calls for interventions that are both multifaceted and multileveled.

We can help individuals reduce and avoid the negative effects of stress by teaching better coping skills, raising self-esteem, helping people identify and establish support groups, and reducing preventable and unnecessary forms of stress. Such efforts directed at the individual or group are not substitutes for social changes that would enhance the quality of life.

We can help individuals reduce the negative effects of stress by helping them identify support groups.

Relaxing can enhance
one's ability to cope.

SUMMARY

1. Coping is a multidimensional concept that is influenced by situational, contextual, and ethnic factors. Often, various indices of coping do not correlate, and the evaluation of coping efforts may sometimes be value-laden. Thus, much caution is required in proposing specific coping efforts, since people do *not* go through orderly patterns of emotional reactions (stages). Since coping requires dealing with multiple adaptational tasks, multileveled and flexible interventions are required.

2. Before embracing or espousing a specific coping technique, it is necessary to analyze the stressful challenges that must be handled. A behavior-analytic approach should be undertaken. Such an approach consists of problem identification, response enumeration, and response evaluation.

3. Coping efforts may take several forms, including tension reduction, problem solving, denial, cognitive reappraisal, social support, and communication. A flexible coping repertoire can enhance adaptational functioning.

4. Unwinding, releasing emotions, and relaxing can enhance one's ability to cope. Relaxation exercises should be viewed as active coping efforts that nurture a sense of personal control.

5. In certain stressful situations, where taking action may be useful, adopting a problem-solving, information-gathering, direct action approach can facilitate coping. Often, explicit skill training is used to supplement problem-solving efforts. In other situations, however, the opposite coping mode, denial, may prove most beneficial. When it is impossible to change things, denial may serve the adaptive functioning of self-dosing, thus permitting people to deal with a limited amount of stress at one time. When denial retards direct action, its use can prove injurious.

6. Stressed victims often cope by cognitively reappraising their situations by employing social comparison.

7. The deleterious effects of stress can be reduced by turning to others for social support in the form of emotional, psychological, and material aid. Like most coping efforts, social support is double-edged. The wrong type of social support can exacerbate stress. How we communicate plays a critical role in improving the quality and nature of our social support contacts.

8. The treatment of stress disorders of soldiers has revealed that the principles of immediacy, proximity, and expectation enhance therapeutic outcome. Because of developmental and personality factors, *some* individuals seem more vulnerable to stressful events and prove less responsive to treatment. A stress-inoculation treatment approach can be used with high-risk groups on a preventative basis, as well as with victims of stressful life events. While initial results are encouraging, much more systematic evaluation is needed. Any intervention, however, should be multileveled in order to improve the quality of life.

Chapter 7

MALADAPTIVE BEHAVIOR

MALADAPTIVE HEALTH BEHAVIOR

EATING AND THE CONTROL OF OBESITY

Eating Disorders
    Anorexia nervosa
    Causes and treatment of anorexia
    Bulimia
Diets and the Regulation of Obesity
Behavior Control of Obesity

SUBSTANCE USE

Smoking
Drug and Alcohol Dependence
Alcohol Abuse
    Health effects of alcohol abuse
    Causes of alcohol abuse and dependence
    Treatment
    Controlling drinking

PSYCHOLOGICAL DISORDERS

Defining Psychological Disorders
    Myths about psychological disorders
    Description and frequency
Anxiety Disorders
Affective Disorders: Depression
    Causes of depression
    Coping with depression
Suicide
    Common myths about suicide
    Campus suicide
Schizophrenia

SUMMARY

Coping with the challenges of life can affect both your physical and mental health. Maladaptive behaviors, such as smoking, drinking, anxiety, and depression, are likely to be a part of your own life or the life of someone you care about. In this chapter, we consider a number of maladaptive behaviors and the choices available for coping with them.

- Keith drinks too much, and some mornings he can't make it to class.
- Dorothy worries about her weight. Still she finds herself "pigging out" with some friends every week or so. Recently she has been going into the bathroom and forcing herself to vomit to make up for the eating binges.
- Julie has always wanted to go to medical school, but her grades are slipping and she is feeling depressed. Sometimes she has thoughts of suicide, but she hasn't told anyone about them yet.

Table 7–1 provides a brief list of the wide range of maladaptive patterns of behavior listed in the diagnostic and statistical manual (DSM-III) of the American Psychiatric Association (1980). You will notice that among this list are adjustment disorders. In this chapter, we consider important patterns of maladaptive behavior, including eating disorders that often develop in adolescents; substance use disorders, including smoking, alcohol, and drug abuse; and other major patterns of maladaptive behavior, including anxiety disorders, affective disorders, and schizophrenic disorders.

Most, if not all, of the maladaptive patterns of behavior that we discuss in this chapter are likely to be products of both biological factors and the social environment of the individual. In fact, most researchers agree that many maladaptive behaviors are best understood in terms of a diathesis-stress model (Zubin & Spring, 1977; Price & Lynn, 1986). This model suggests that some people possess higher levels of vulnerability to stress and that this vulnerability is at least in part determined by genetic or other biological factors. When vulnerable people are confronted by a stressful event such as the loss of a loved one or a personal failure, they are more likely to develop maladaptive patterns of behavior than are people who are not vulnerable. In the various forms of maladaptive behavior, both environmental and biological factors often play a part in the development of maladaptive behavior.

MALADAPTIVE HEALTH BEHAVIOR

We are becoming an increasingly health-conscious society. It seems as if everyone is dieting and jogging. At the same time, drinking too much, drug use, smoking, and obesity remain major health problems. In the first part of this chapter, we discuss what psychologists have discovered about changing health behavior and explore our choices in dealing with problems of health and life-style.

TABLE 7–1	Major Diagnostic Categories of DSM-III

1. *Disorders of infancy, childhood, and adolescence* include mental retardation, problems of attention and conduct, anxiety disorders, eating disorders, and problems of language development.
2. *Organic disorders* are psychological or behavioral abnormalities associated with temporary or permanent dysfunction of the brain. They may be due to diseases of aging, intoxication, or withdrawal from drugs or alcohol.
3. *Substance use disorders* are behavioral changes associated with more or less regular use of substances that affect the central nervous system. Behavioral changes include impairment in social or occupational functioning, inability to stop taking the substance, or withdrawal symptoms.
4. *Schizophrenic disorders* are severe disorders involving delusions, hallucinations, incoherent speech, deterioration in role functioning, social withdrawal, and markedly peculiar behavior.
5. *Affective disorders* are disturbances of mood or emotion that generally involve depression or elation. They may involve either bipolar disorders, with shifting cycles of depression and elation, or episodes of major depression.
6. *Anxiety disorders* are disorders in which anxiety is the predominant disturbance. They may occur as generalized anxiety or panic disorders or as fear of a specific object or situation.
7. *Somatoform disorders* involves physical symptoms such as pain, paralysis, or deafness that suggest physical disorders, but for which there are no demonstrable organic findings. There is strong evidence that psychological factors or conflicts are involved.
8. *Dissociative disorders* involve sudden temporary alteration of consciousness, identity, or motor behavior. Dissociative disorders include amnesia, assumption of a new identity, or the existence of more than one personality within an individual.
9. *Psychosexual disorders* include gender identity disorders, sexual arousal by nonnormative objects or situations, and sexual dysfunctions characterized by inhibitions in sexual desire or the sexual response cycle.
10. *Factitious disorders* involve physical or psychological symptoms that are under the voluntary control of the individual but with no obvious, immediate goal.
11. *Disorders of impulse control* involve failure to resist an impulse that is harmful to oneself or others. Included are pathological gambling, stealing, fire setting, or explosive aggression.
12. *Adjustment disorders* are maladaptions to an identifiable stressor such as business, school, or marital problems. The reaction to the stressor is in excess of what would be normally expected for that stressor.

EATING AND THE CONTROL OF OBESITY

A casual stroll through any bookstore will uncover several, and perhaps even dozens, of diet books offering apparently easy and effective ways to lose weight. The best-seller lists usually contain a couple of diet books at any given time.

Eating Disorders

The messages from our culture are very clear. Bathing suit ads, models for clothes, and athletes have a pencil-thin look that we seem to find desirable. Furthermore, the expectations seem more strongly directed at women than men. But when you combine these cultural norms with our ingrained eating habits and the body's own biological processes, eating disorders can result. Such disorders are not only personally distressing but also threatening to health.

Anorexia nervosa. The following case from Price and Lynn illustrates a relentless pursuit of thinness:

> *Denise, age 20, acknowledges that she is too thin but says she finds it hard to make herself eat. Everyone she knows diets, and she is afraid if she breaks her diet she will never stop eating. She reports that lately she has felt faint and that sometimes her*

Karen Carpenter (the singer) was a victim of anorexia.

heart flutters. She says, "If I could get back up to ninety pounds things would be better, I guess."

anorexia nervosa
eating disorder
involving fear of
obesity, distorted body
image, excessive
thinness, and refusal
to maintain body
weight

Denise has an eating disorder called **anorexia nervosa.** Typically anorexia nervosa is diagnosed when a person experiences an intense fear of becoming obese, a body image distorted so that the person feels fat even when extremely thin, and a loss of 25 percent or more of the original body weight. Sufferers of anorexia nervosa also refuse to maintain body weight. No known physical illness accounts for the weight loss.

Causes and treatment of anorexia. About one percent of women from twelve to eighteen years old are anorexic. The disorder is nine times more frequent in females than males. A variety of health complications of anorexia can develop. They include the stopping of menstruation, heart arrhythmias, and imbalances in electrolytes in the body.

While it is likely that our cultural preoccupation with thinness contributes to the development of anorexia, some theorists have suggested that psychological factors are important, too. For example, Bruch (1973) sees anorexia as a struggle for independence and self-respect. She believes that the parents of anorexics don't allow them to develop a sense of independence and competence, so the anorexic expresses the need for independence by controlling one of the few controllable things in his or her life, eating behavior. Special treatment for anorexic disorders usually involves hospitalization, individual or family therapy, and nutritional counseling. Since the disorder can be life threatening, stabilizing the physical condition of the anorexic is crucial, even if intravenous or tube feeding is required.

Bulimia. Another eating disorder has gained attention in recent years. It is bulimia. **Bulimia** is a disorder involving periods of extreme binge eating frequently followed by purging through either self-induced vomiting or the use of laxatives.

bulimia eating
disorder involving
periods of extreme
binge eating followed
by purging through
either self-induced
vomiting or the use of
laxatives

People with bulimic disorders are aware that their patterns of eating are not normal, and they frequently try to hide them. One young woman, for example, ate three separate meals at three restaurants during a binge so that no one would notice her actions (Price & Lynn, 1986). After a binge eating episode, most bulimics feel depressed and guilty and frightened by their loss of control.

We don't really know what proportion of women have bulimic problems. Estimates are hard to obtain because of the embarrassment associated with the disorder. Some estimates indicate as many as 7 percent to 20 percent of women have experienced the disorder (Price & Lynn, 1986), while the incidence is much lower for men.

Treatment of bulimia takes a variety of forms. Recently, Kirkley, Schneider, Agras, and Bachman (1985) showed that group therapy treatments that teach bulimics to make specific changes in their eating behaviors produced positive changes for approximately 38 percent of participants.

Diets and the Regulation of Obesity

Most people assume that overeating is the cause of obesity. They believe that through conscious control and diet they can regulate the intake of calories and, therefore, reach a desired weight.

Research is beginning to show that these cherished beliefs may be at least partly in error. A theory now emerging (Bennett & Gurin, 1982) argues that a physiological control system is built into each of us and that this physiological system determines how much fat we carry. This idea, called the **set point theory**, suggests that a physiological control mechanism, or thermostat, controls our weight. The theory says that different people have different set points, some higher than others. Going on a diet then is really an attempt to overpower the built-in set point. But the set point is a tireless opponent, and it may be difficult to change except perhaps through long-term programs of exercise.

Bennett and Gurin believe that real physiological pressures are at work to maintain a preset amount of fat on the body. The body's fat cells may send chemical messages to the brain, which regulates eating behavior through *glycerol* and blood levels of *insulin*. These chemical messengers moving from the fat cells to the brain may play an important role in the set point mechanism. Inner physiological regulators may be more important than we thought in controlling body weight.

In fact, new research (Polivy & Herman, 1985) goes further. It suggests a connection between dieting and binge eating, but not the sort we might suspect. The very act of dieting may encourage binge eating. Polivy and Herman have conducted experiments where people are placed on strict diets and then provided with different-sized preloading meals. After the preloading meal, they are free to eat additional food until satisfied. Giving dieters a large preload or alcoholic beverages produces a pattern of *counter-regulation*, where all restraint is lost and periods of binge eating may occur.

The counter-regulation effect may be partly psychological. People often experience a sense of losing control of their diets, which then leads to binge. For example, telling dieters that they have just eaten a high-calorie meal can lead them to lose control even if in reality the meal was low in calories.

This research suggests that dieting fads may actually be producing higher frequencies of binge eating and eating disorders. As pressures toward thinness have escalated, there has been a dramatic upsurge in the frequency of eating disorders. If this pressure for thinness continues, so may the increase in eating disorders.

Behavioral Control of Obesity

Can you learn how to eat appropriately without fad diets or engaging in extreme and dangerous eating patterns? Richard Stewart and Barbara Davis (1972) have developed a self-control method they call the **situational management of overeating**. Their strategy is designed to help people cope with

---

set point theory theory that weight is controlled by physiological mechanisms that increase eating behavior when weight is too low and decrease eating behavior when weight is too high

situational management of overeating behavior-control strategy to reduce cues in the environment that stimulate overeating and strengthen cues in the environment that signal alternatives to overeating

overeating problems that may lead to obesity. Their basic philosophy is based on the social learning approach. They argue that the environment rather than the person is the agent of control over eating behavior. Therefore, efforts to modify behavior should be to change the *environment* rather than the person. Stewart and Davis suggest that you eliminate or suppress cues that trigger overeating and strengthen cues in the environment that produce appropriate eating. For example, in eliminating undesirable cues, Stewart and Davis recommend the following:

- Do not engage in any other activity while eating, such as watching television or reading.
- Shop only from a list, and take to the store only enough money to cover the cost of necessary purchases.
- Have other people in your environment monitor your eating patterns.
- Serve foods on plates in small measured quantities.
- Leave the table soon after you finish a meal.
- Don't allow yourself to become overly hungry, which will lead to overeating.
- Take a number of steps to *strengthen appropriate eating behavior*, too.
- Provide yourself a reasonable array of acceptable food choices, such as low-calorie foods, fruit, and vegetables for snacks.
- Slow the pace of eating; take your time.
- Update eating, exercise, and weight change graphs daily.

Of course, while changing habits is important, regular exercise is a critical ingredient in weight control. It should be a critical part of your own health habits.

SUBSTANCE USE

Substance use and abuse, including smoking and drinking alcohol, confront us with choices every day. Following are some facts about both.

Smoking

This year, a third of the American population will continue to smoke. They will smoke over 593 billion cigarettes. Studies at the National Institute of Drug Abuse indicate that cigarette smoking is now the most serious and widespread addiction in the world (U.S. Department of Health and Human Services, 1982, 1983). Your life will be shortened by approximately fourteen minutes for every cigarette that you smoke. One in three smokers will die as a result of smoking.

We know that cigarette smoking affects the developing fetus. It also increases the risk of spontaneous abortions, still births, and early postpartum deaths of children. Smoking is a major factor each year in approximately 220,000 deaths from heart disease, 78,000 from lung cancer, and 22,000 from other forms of cancer (U.S. Department of Heath and Human Services, 1982, 1983). This means, as former secretary of Health, Education and Welfare James Califano observed, "[P]eople who smoke are committing slow motion suicide" (Blakeslee, 1984).

These facts about the relationship between smoking and health are widely known, and a substantial proportion of people who currently smoke have tried to quit. Why then is the smoking habit so difficult to break? Recent research into the pharmacology and psychology of smoking suggest a primary component of cigarette smoke, **nicotine,** helps explain the persistence of smoking (Barrett, 1983). Nicotine has the capacity to alter the availability of important brain chemicals that affect feelings of well-being. Nicotine is a stimulant that makes brain receptors more sensitive to neurotransmitters that increase heart rate, blood pressure, and digestive activity.

nicotine chemical in tobacco that has the capacity to alter brain chemicals and affect feelings of well-being

The stimulating feeling produced by nicotine is not the only reason people smoke. Smoking also fulfills psychological needs. Advertising makes smoking glamorous. For some young people, smoking enhances self-esteem, and it can even become part of their identity and self-definition. People who say, "I am a smoker," have made the idea of smoking a part of the definition of who they are.

By now, it should be clear that smoking is a persistent, maladaptive behavior with serious long-term health effects. It is a behavior that is maintained because of the biochemical effects of the stimulant nicotine and because it fulfills social and psychological needs.

Smoking was once considered a matter of private and personal decision that could affect only one's own health, but recent research (U.S. Department of Health and Human Services, 1983) has shown that other people exposed to an atmosphere of smoke can also experience negative health effects by passive smoking. Increasingly, employers are developing no-smoking policies in the workplace. Some companies give their employees incentives not to smoke. Others pay smokers to quit or limit the time and location of smoking. Still other employers refuse to hire or promote smokers.

While citizens' groups and employers are becoming increasingly vigorous in their objections to smoking, smokers themselves are finding it difficult to quit. Figure 7-1 shows that among both men and women, the number of former smokers has increased, but approximately a third of all adults still smoke even though most want to quit.

A variety of approaches to helping people stop smoking have been tried, including group pressure, behavior modification, hypnosis, and even nicotine chewing gum. So far, no single approach appears to be superior to all others. As we see, in "Exploring Choices: Changing Behavior That Threatens Your Health," however, there is evidence that, with persistence, smokers *can* succeed in giving up the habit.

FIGURE 7-1   Quitting Proves Hard

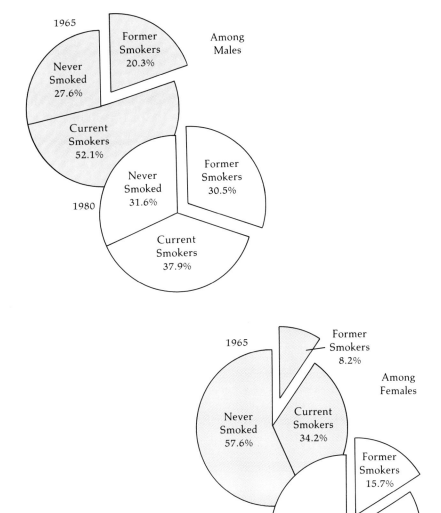

The percentage of adults able to stop smoking has risen since the Surgeon General's 1964 report linking cigarettes to health risks, but one third of all adults still smoke, even though most want to quit.

Sources: Public Health Service and *The New York Times* (1984, December 25).

EXPLORING CHOICES

CHANGING BEHAVIOR THAT THREATENS YOUR HEALTH

Several years ago, social psychologist Stanley Schachter came upon a puzzling inconsistency between the research literature and his own experience (Schachter, 1982). He observed that experts in weight loss and smoking cessation reported that most people who entered therapy to change their behavior tended to drop out. Even if they did not drop out, they tended to experience relapses. The experts concluded that these behaviors were indeed deeply ingrained and therefore extremely hard to change. Yet Schachter knew many friends and colleagues who had succeeded over long periods of time in giving up smoking and losing weight.

Schachter conducted a survey of his own of his colleagues at Columbia University and of the townspeople where he frequently spent his summers. From this survey, he concluded that over 60 percent of the people who tried to quit smoking eventually did succeed. A comparable proportion of people managed to keep off weight for relatively long periods of time. Schachter wondered, Why the disagreement between the experts and his survey?

Two explanations for these results are possible. First, perhaps people who go to therapists to change health behavior have more severe problems. If so, the relatively poor success rate for therapy really reflects the fact that only the most severe cases actually seek therapy. But an even more interesting explanation is possible. The usual estimates of therapeutic effectiveness are based on *single attempts* to change some habitual health behavior. Schachter's results were based on success rates for *multiple attempts over long periods of time.* In other words, if you keep trying, you have a better than even chance of eventually succeeding.

Other researchers have conducted studies of the psychology of relapse to understand how to maintain positive health-related behaviors. Alan Marlatt and Judith Gordon (1980) have conducted studies that attempt to understand any habit excess, including overeating, biting fingernails, or even impulsive use of credit cards. Marlatt began by trying to understand why people could not live up to their New Year's resolutions. Typically, he found people felt bad about themselves for breaking the resolution and afterward tended to downplay its importance. Later studies of people with alcohol problems showed that it was relatively easy for them to stop drinking but extremely difficult to prevent them from having relapses. Indeed, Marlatt and Gordon interviewed people in drug abuse programs and found that they relapsed when they had to cope with negative emotional experiences, such as anger, fear, loneliness, or depression.

From our point of view, Marlatt's most important finding is that a slip from abstinence typically is followed by a full-blown relapse because *the slip undermines the person's self-image as an abstainer.* This all-or-nothing attitude is often encouraged by treatment programs and communicates to patients that all relapses are total failures. Instead, Marlatt and his colleagues suggest a different approach to handle the risk of relapse and to minimize its effects.

- *Recognize high-risk situations.* These are situations in which relapses are most likely. If you are a dieter, you may recognize that you are most likely to overeat when alone and bored. If you wish to control your drinking, a bar may be a high-risk situation for you. Spend at least a week recording the circumstances surrounding the behaviors you want to change. Use the record to distinguish between the times you eat because you are hungry and the times you eat for other reasons, such as boredom or anxiety.

- *Eliminate the high-risk situations.* Use your week-long record to identify your own high-risk situations. Then eliminate as many of them as you can. You can eliminate these situations by avoiding them and seeking support from friends.

- *Give yourself an alternative activity.* The alternative is a key to maintaining new habits. Having choices helps! You should experiment with alternatives and as Schachter suggests, keep at it. Chew gum instead of smoking. Eat an apple instead of three cookies.

- *Imagine the benefits.* You can support yourself cognitively by thinking of the benefits of continuing with the health behavior. Imagining the benefits helps support your motivation.

- *Do not think of a slip as a full-blown relapse.* Everyone is bound to have a slip now and then. A slip is an opportunity to learn how to be more effective at maintaining your health behavior. Analyze the situation again and develop a specific strategy for avoiding the high-risk relapse situation in the future.

Schachter's and Marlatt's research suggests that altering maladaptive health behaviors is not an all-or-none short-term activity. It is one that requires persistence over long periods of time and has a very real chance of succeeding.

Drug and Alcohol Dependence

Every day medical research is producing new miracle drugs to treat serious diseases, reduce anxieties, and enhance performance. At the same time, people are becoming increasingly dependent on both legal and illegal drugs to cope with stress, boredom, and fatigue. Using drugs to cope can become maladaptive and have serious consequences for you. Not only can drug dependence interfere with your daily functioning but it can have long-term physical and mental health effects. It is not just the illegal drugs that can be dangerous. Alcohol and even nonprescription drugs can also pose serious health hazards.

substance abuse inability to stop using a drug, with impairment in work or social functioning

Current diagnostic practice distinguishes between substance abuse and substance dependence. **Substance abuse** is the inability to stop using a drug, with impairment in work or social functioning. **Substance dependence** is more severe. It involves the development of a tolerance to the drug and withdrawal symptoms if use of the drug is reduced or stopped (American Psychiatric Association, 1980).

substance dependence severe form of disorder, involving the developing of a physical tolerance of a drug and withdrawal symptoms if the drug is reduced or stopped

Drugs are divided into several major classes. *Sedatives* include alcohol and several types of tranquilizers. One type of sedative, **barbiturates**, is widely abused. At low levels, barbiturates can reduce anxiety and induce sleep; at higher levels, people develop a tolerance for barbiturates, and sudden withdrawal can cause convulsions and even death.

barbiturates sedatives that can reduce anxiety and induce sleep

A second major class of drugs includes the *opiates and narcotics*, by far the best known of which is *heroin*. Physical dependence on heroin can develop quickly, and addicts may become addicted to prevent withdrawal symptoms as much as for the pleasurable experience that the drug provides.

stimulants chemicals that activate the central nervous system and can produce feelings of euphoria, confidence, and increased alertness

Still another class of drugs are the **stimulants**, which include illegal stimulants such as *cocaine*. Central nervous system stimulants can provide feelings euphoria, confidence, and increased alertness. In the case of *amphetamines*, which are prescription drugs, a cycle of stimulation by taking the drug is sometimes counteracted with sedative drugs, such as barbiturates, producing a vicious cycle.

hallucinogens chemicals that produce profound changes in consciousness, including hallucinations, shifts in cognitive perspective, and shifts in sensory experiences

Finally, **hallucinogens**, such as LSD, marijuana, mescoline, and peyote, are much less widely used than they once were (Johnston, O'Malley, & Bachman, 1984). The primary characteristic of these drugs is the ability to produce profound changes in consciousness, including hallucinations, shifts in cognitive perspective, and shifts in sensory experiences.

Alcohol Abuse

Alcohol is a potent and potentially dangerous psychoactive drug. In our culture, alcohol is widely accepted for its recreational use. Approximately one person out of ten may develop a dependence on alcohol that may lead to even more destructive patterns of use (Jaffe, 1980).

What is the difference between occasional reactional alcohol use and dependence? Most commonly, the diagnosis of serious alcohol abuse involves continuous or episodic use for at least one month followed by social complications or work impairment. Typically, the person shows a strong psychological dependence on alcohol and feels a compelling desire to drink and an inability to cut down or stop drinking (Jaffe, 1980).

Health effects of alcohol abuse. What are the effects of alcohol on behavior, consciousness, and physiology? Intoxication depends on how rapidly alcohol is absorbed into the bloodstream through the stomach and intestines. Since alcohol is a central nervous depressant, it may reduce inhibitions in low doses. In higher doses, however, alcohol tends to affect the motor centers of the brain and to impair coordination, walking, and speech (Ritchie, 1980).

While the short-term effects of alcohol can be serious if people try to drive or engage in other tasks requiring motor control, the long-term health effects of alcohol are even more serious. The life expectancy of alcoholics is reduced by ten to twelve years. Furthermore, approximately 58 percent of successful suicides are people who were alcoholic in the past. Alcohol abuse is estimated to be a factor in nearly 55 percent of all automobile accidents (Jaffe, 1980).

Alcohol use constitutes the third leading cause of death in the United States after heart disease and cancer. **Cirrhosis** is a disease that produces liver tissue degeneration. It is the cause of most alcohol-related deaths. Some estimates suggest that alcohol is involved as a major cause in 40 percent to 90 percent of all cases of cirrhosis.

cirrhosis disease involving degeneration of liver tissue

Psychological impairment and brain damage are also common health effects. More than half of all alcoholics show evidence of psychological impairment, particularly in memory and vision. Of course, this psychological impairment can have serious effects on work and family life.

Causes of alcohol abuse and dependence. Researchers have offered several different explanations for the development of alcohol dependence and abuse. Some learning theorists (Holroyd, 1978) have suggested that alcohol reduces tension; therefore, it reinforces drinking and the likelihood of future drinking. Other learning theorists, such as Alan Marlatt (1976), qualify this explanation by arguing that drinking is used to reduce stress only when the situation is seen as stressful and the drinker believes that drinking alcohol is an appropriate response to the situation.

Different cultures hold very different orientations to the use of alcohol. Kinney and Leaton (1982) observe that in societies where total abstinence from alcohol is normal, alcoholism is infrequent. On the other hand, in societies where there are few controls on drinking, the highest rates of alcoholism tend to occur. Of course, even within any single culture, there is a wide range of variation in individual problem drinking, and differences among cultures are clearly not the whole explanation.

A number of researchers have identified biological and genetic clues to the causes of alcoholism. Goodwin (1979) reviewed studies that show that alcoholism is more likely to occur in identical twins, who have exactly the same genetic makeup, than in fraternal twins. This sort of evidence is usually taken to suggest that there is a genetic basis for the disorder in question.

Treatment. The evidence suggests that alcohol abuse is not necessarily irreversible. Some people change drinking behavior spontaneously without treatment, and heavy drinkers can sometimes change their patterns of drinking, moderating them to a substantial degree (Vaillant, 1983).

A variety of treatments for alcohol abuse problems are available. They include psychotherapy, behavioral therapy, medication, family therapy, and, in some cases, hospitalization to allow detoxification to occur. Perhaps one of the most famous forms of treatment for alcohol problems is **Alcoholics Anonymous**, a voluntary organization of alcoholics who support each other in maintaining sobriety.

There is considerable controversy about whether or not people with severe alcohol problems can learn to control their drinking or whether they must totally abstain from the use of alcohol in order to recover. The weight of evidence seems to suggest that for people whose drinking problems are not yet extremely severe, controlled drinking is a reasonable treatment goal (Miller & Munoz, 1982). However, for people with extremely severe alcohol problems, controlled drinking is probably not realistic.

Controlling drinking. William Miller and Ricardo Munoz (1982) have developed a method to help people control their drinking. Some people regard anyone who has a problem related to drinking as an alcoholic. You can often find checklists of symptoms in popular magazines. These checklists suggest that if you score above a certain number of points you are probably an alcoholic. Miller and Munoz point out that a more careful definition suggests that a number of people have problems with drinking, but only some of them qualify for the diagnosis of alcohol dependence, or alcoholism. They say, "[I]n our opinion what really matters is this: what effect is alcohol having in your life, and what do you need to do about it?" (p. XVIII).

Miller and Munoz focus their strategy for controlled drinking on three critical areas: (1) controlling your behavior *while you drink*, (2) focusing on the things that occur *before you drink*, and (3) identifying *alternatives to drinking*. If you are interested in the program outlined by Miller and Munoz, we recommend that you obtain their book and work on their self-change strategies in detail. To illustrate some of their strategies, we describe their recommendations for reducing alcohol intake while you drink.

First, set limits for yourself. Table 7–2 shows equivalent drinks in amounts of alcohol. It also shows the percentage of Americans who consume different numbers of drinks per week. Once you have estimated how many drinks you consume per week, set a reasonable limit for yourself to reduce the number of drinks that you take.

Second, count your drinks. Carry a daily record card with you to record the date, time, type of drink, amount, and situation in which you took each drink. You will find that simply taking the trouble to record each drink you may actually reduce the amount of drinking that you do. If someone asks you what you are doing? You can say things like, "I'm trying to cut down, and I want to keep

Sidebar:

Alcoholics Anonymous voluntary organization of people with drinking problems who support each other in maintaining sobriety

TABLE 7-2   Alcohol Consumption by Type and Number of Drinks

One Drink Equals

10 oz. (296 ml.) glass of beer (5% alcohol)
4 oz. (118 ml.) glass of table wine (12% alcohol)
2½ oz. (74 ml.) glass of fortified wine (20% alcohol)
1½ oz. (37 ml.) of 80 proof distilled spirits (40% alcohol)
1 oz. (30 ml.) of 100 proof distilled spirits (50% alcohol)

Number of Drinks	Percent of U.S. Adults Who Drink at Least This Amount of Alcohol
1 or 2 occasionally	68%
1 per week	53%
3 per week	38%
6 per week	27%
10 per week	18%
13 per week	16%
17 per week	12%
20 per week	11%
30 per week	8%
40 per week	6%
50 per week	5%
60 per week	4%
70 per week	3%
80 per week	2%
90 per week	1%
100 per week	0.25%

Source: Adapted from W. R. Miller & R. F. Munoz (1982). *How to control your drinking* (rev. ed.). Albuquerque, NM: University of New Mexico Press.

track of my drinks," or "I'm on a diet and I'm keeping track of everything I eat," or "I'm taking notes for the CIA," or "It's something I'm doing for a class."

Third, slow down. The idea here is to begin to reduce the amount of alcohol that you take in. One way is to substitute weaker drinks, such as beer and table wines, for stronger drinks, such as straight liquor. Another strategy is to space your drinks in time, attempting to increase the number of minutes that it takes to consume a drink. You should seriously consider refusing drinks that are offered to you. You can say, "Not right now, thanks. Maybe a little later," or "No thanks. I just finished one." What if someone persists? Then you should be more forceful in your refusal and say, "No, really, I'm fine," or "I'm really trying to cut down, so how about helping me, okay?" or "Hey, don't take it personally! I just don't want another one right now."

Fourth, reward yourself for successes. When you meet a goal for cutting down or when you successfully refuse a drink, reward yourself. Buy yourself a magazine or record album, go to a play or a museum, or just set aside some do-your-own-thing time. You also can reward yourself mentally. Remind yourself, "I handled that situation well," or "I'm in control, and I like myself better because of it." It is important to remember that not all problem drinking can be easily

ON THE RESEARCH FRONTIER

UNDERSTANDING SUBSTANCE USE AS A FORM OF COPING

In defining the concept of adjustment at the beginning of this book, we emphasize that *coping* is a crucial element of adjustment and that coping can be either adaptive or maladaptive. Recently, researchers have begun to view substance abuse as a *maladaptive form of coping*. As Shiffman and Wills (1985) observe:

> Research on drug use traditionally has tended to focus on biological factors, but in recent years there has been a shift toward viewing *substance use as a maladaptive attempt to deal with life stresses*. In this revised formulation of substance use, research on stress and coping has become increasingly relevant. From this perspective, persons are viewed as *active agents who try to cope with the stressors and temptations they experience*, rather than reacting passively to biological impulses or psychological temptations. (p. XXI, italics added)

Michael Perri (1985) has used this framework to develop a better understanding of the coping behaviors that people use in trying to control or reduce substance use without any outside help. Perri reasoned that since some naturally occurring episodes of self-change are dramatically successful, studying both successful and unsuccessful attempts at self-regulation may tell a great deal about strategies for successful self-management. Perri and his colleagues studied a number of people who attempted to stop smoking or to control their drinking on their own by interviewing them in detail about their self-change efforts. In one study of problem drinking, Perri contrasted people who were successful with those who were unsuccessful in controlling problem drinking. He found the following:

controlled. Seeking professional help is a choice that anyone with patterns of problem drinking should consider. See "On the Research Frontier: Understanding Substance Use as a Form of Coping" for additional information on substance use.

PSYCHOLOGICAL DISORDERS

Consider the following case study:

> *Ralph was sinking swiftly into what he called a "blue funk." Nothing much had happened worth getting upset about but Ralph knew he was going to feel bad the moment he got out of bed. He woke up thinking, "something is missing; something is wrong." He opened his eyes and sensed a great emptiness. . . . He had made a mess of his life and had failed everyone who had ever had confidence in him. He had failed them miserably, and it was all his own fault. . . . Ralph was both sad and ashamed because*

- When commitment to change is truly *self-initiated,* instead of prompted by others, success is more likely.
- People who have *plans for self-change* at the outset of their efforts are more likely to succeed than those who do not.
- People who use a greater *array of strategies* for self-change are more likely to be successful than those who use fewer strategies.
- People who use *stimulus control,* particularly the removal of alcohol or cigarettes from immediate availability, are more successful.
- People who develop *alternative behaviors* to take the place of drinking or smoking are more successful than those who do not.

What about the long haul? Are certain self-control strategies more effective for people in the long run? Perri found that people who find *alternative sources of satisfaction,* such as hobbies, work, or eating, have the best chance for long-term abstinence. Finally, people who report a higher degree of *support* or approval for their efforts from family and friends also tend to be more successful in the long run.

Perri's results point to a number of important differences between successful and unsuccessful attempts to cope with problematic patterns of substance abuse. The stress and coping framework promises to provide a way of understanding both the development of subtance abuse and other maladaptive coping patterns and ways of changing those behaviors.

he knew it was happening again. He recognized how grim he was feeling and that it was worse today than yesterday. He had felt it coming, and he dreaded it, but it was like the bad dreams he had regularly in which a building was toppling down on him while he was able to run only in slow, slow motion. . . .

Alone in the early hours of the morning, he began to brood about his life, the kind of person he was, his weaknesses and many failures, and the generally miserable condition of the world. By the time he got to class, he was deeply depressed. (Adapted from McNeil, 1967)

Defining Psychological Disorders

Every year, more than 7 million Americans receive treatment for some form of psychological disorder. The social and economic costs of psychological disorders are enormous. They include not only losses of productivity and creativity but also the personal cost of extreme emotional distress.

What is abnormal? There is no single definition of psychological disorder, but several different criteria are typically used to define abnormality. First, many definitions of abnormal behavior emphasize the idea that abnormal behavior is frequently *disturbing to other people*. These definitions focus heavily on the idea that abnormal behavior may violate cultural norms and expectations.

A second major way of defining psychological disorder emphasizes *subjective distress*. This definition assumes that a disorder must involve at least some degree of psychological discomfort in the form of fear, sadness, or a sense of loss of control.

Still another approach to defining psychological disorder focuses on the idea that it is *psychologically handicapping*. The behavior may interfere with the person's ability to cope with the demands of everyday life. Certainly, some of the forms of psychological disorder that we describe can be extremely disabling.

It is not easy to establish a sharp dividing line between what is considered normal and abnormal. Instead, behavior ranges along a continuum, with most people falling somewhere in the middle. Of course, from time to time, major changes or stresses (such as school failure, divorce, or a loss of a loved one) can produce feelings of hopelessness, depression, or panic. The vast majority of people recover from these emotional upsets and temporary setbacks, but for some people, getting professional help is an important alternative. In what follows, we describe several forms of psychological disorder, ranging from relatively common and mild forms to more severe and handicapping forms.

Myths about psychological disorders. Our ideas about psychological disorders have been rooted in myth and superstition since before the beginning of recorded history. Hoping to release evil spirits, early humans drilled holes in the skulls of people who acted oddly. In the Middle Ages, people who behaved oddly were often thought of as witches and were tortured or killed because of their odd behavior (Price & Lynn, 1986). Still, myths about psychological disorders persist. Consider the following myths (Kazdin, 1980):

1. *Psychological disorders are incurable. False.* People who spontaneously recover from psychological disorders or who recover through threatment greatly outnumber the people for whom treatment is ineffective. Both psychological and biological treatments can be effective for even the most severe forms of psychological disorder.

2. *People with psychological disorders are often dangerous and violent. False.* While occasional incidents of violence involving people suffering from psychological disorders get a great deal of attention in the newspapers and television, the facts are that people with psychological disorders are rarely prone to violence. In fact, they may be no more so than the rest of the population.

3. *People with psychological disorders act in very strange ways and are very different from the rest of us. False.* Only a very small portion of all people with psychological disorders behave in ways that are strikingly different from the general population. Most people experiencing psychological disorders are no different in behavior from the rest of us. The distinctions between suspicion

and paranoia, feeling blue and feeling depressed, and being a heavy drinker and being an alcoholic are often far from clear.

4. *A psychological disorder should be a source of shame. False.* Some people see a psychological disorder as a source of shame or stigma. Others see it as a source of personal weakness. But psychological disorders can strike anyone from any background. Senators, artists, and entertainers have made outstanding contributions despite their experiences with psychological disorder.

Description and frequency. Table 7–3 lists four major types of psychological disorder that we describe in this chapter. We have already discussed substance use disorders; we now consider anxiety disorders, affective (or mood) disorders, and schizophrenia. A major survey has provided us with important new information on the extent of psychological disorder in the United States population (Regier et al., 1984). These studies indicate that about 19 percent of adults over age eighteen suffered from at least one psychological disorder. Furthermore, from 28 percent to 38 percent of those surveyed reported a psychological disorder at some point in life.

TABLE 7–3   Major Forms of Psychological Disorder

Psychological Disorder	Age and Sex Differences	Estimated Percent of Americans	Estimated Number of Americans
1. *Substance use disorder.* Behavior changes are associated with more or less regular use of substances that affect the central nervous system, including impairment in social or occupational functioning or inability to stop taking the substance.	More common in men. More common in people younger than forty-five.	Alcohol—6.4 percent Drugs—2.0 percent	10 million 3.1 million
2. *Anxiety disorders.* Anxiety is the predominant disturbance when confronting a specific feared object or situation or in a more generalized anxiety or panic disorder.	More common in women. More common in people under forty-five.	8.2 percent	13.1 million
3. *Affective disorders.* These disturbances of mood or emotion generally involve depression or elation. A disorder may involve shifting cycles of depression and elation or episodes of major depression.	More common in women.	6.0 percent	9.4 million
4. *Schizophrenic disorders.* These severe disorders involve delusions, hallucinations, incoherent speech, deterioration in role functioning, social withdrawal, and markedly peculiar behavior.	Equally common in men and women.	1 percent	1.5 million

Table 7-3 summarizes information about the frequency of the most common forms of psychological disorder. Earlier studies had led researchers to believe that psychological disorders were more common in women than men. But as Table 7-3 indicates, recent findings present a more balanced picture. Substance use disorders are more common in men, while anxiety and affective disorders are more common in women.

Anxiety Disorders

The woman described in the following case history was experiencing a severe form of **anxiety disorder.** She not only experienced serious distress but found that her fears were interfering with her ability to function in her daily life. Between 2 and 4 percent of the general population will experience some form of anxiety disorder during their lifetime.

> *A twenty-eight year old housewife complained that she was afraid that she would no longer be able to care for her three young children. Over the past year, she had recurrent episodes of 'nervousness,' lightheadedness, rapid breathing, trembling, and dizziness, during which things around her suddenly felt strange and unreal.*
>
> *Formerly active and outgoing, over the past six months she has become afraid to leave home unless in the company of her husband or mother. She now avoids supermarkets and department stores and states that any crowded place makes her uneasy. When unable to avoid such situations, she tries to get near the doorways and always checks for windows and exits. Last summer, the family did not go on their usual country vacation because the patient told her husband, 'I wouldn't feel safe so far away; it would make me a nervous wreck.' Neither she nor her family can understand what is happening to her. (Spitzer et al., 1981, pp. 268–269)*

Anxiety disorders are divided into two large groups: **phobias** and **anxiety states.** Phobic disorders are characterized by a persistent and irrational fear of some specific situation, object, or activity. Typically, the fear leads the person to avoid the feared object or situation. The fear is excessive in proportion to any actual dangerousness.

Simple phobias are common and familiar to us all. Many people are frightened of harmless spiders or snakes, and others experience an irrational fear of heights or closed places. In most cases, these commonplace phobias do not pose major problems for functioning in social or work roles. On the other hand, some phobias can be crippling to work or social life.

The case study at the beginning of this section is an example of **agoraphobia.** People experiencing agoraphobia frequently fear being alone or being in public places where escape might be difficult. Often, normal activities become more and more difficult as fear and various kinds of avoidance behavior start to dominate the person's life. People experiencing agoraphobia may avoid being in crowds, tunnels, or bridges or on public transportation. Frequently, a person experiencing agoraphobia feels a strong need to be accompanied by a friend or a relative.

anxiety disorder psychological disorder characterized by extreme fear either attached to a particular object or as a continuous state

phobias persistent and irrational fears of some specific situation, object, or activity

anxiety states generalized feelings of anxiety occurring either periodically or on a continuing basis

simple phobias fears of specific commonplace objects or situations, such as heights or spiders

agoraphobia fear of being alone or in public places that may result in considerable restriction of physical and social activity

Social phobias involve a persistent irrational fear of situations where the person may be exposed to the scrutiny of other people. People experiencing social phobias are often frightened that they will be humiliated or embarrassed. Social phobics may be frightened of eating in public, writing in the presence of others, speaking or performing in public, or even using public washroom facilities.

panic attack
unpredictable attack of intense fear, often characterized by sweating, trembling, a sense of unreality, and heart palpitations

Another anxiety disorder is the **panic attack,** which can happen unpredictably. A panic attack may involve heart palpitations, a feeling of choking, a sense of unreality, sweating, trembling, and dizziness. Needless to say, panic attacks are extremely distressing. They may represent the early stages in some forms of agoraphobia.

Panic disorders often begin in late adolescence or early adult life, but they can occur initially in midlife. They are diagnosed much more commonly in women than men. In some cases, a panic disorder may be limited to a single brief period lasting several weeks or months, or it may recur several times.

Recent studies suggest that oversensitive chemical receptors in the brain may be responsible for some panic attacks. Some researchers (Fishman & Sheehan, 1985) speculate that panic disorders may result when a hormone or neurotransmitter in the brain that normally regulates anxiety is missing or deficient. While this explanation for panic attacks is speculative, research on the biological aspects of panic attacks is increasing rapidly.

obsessive-compulsive disorder condition in which persistent ideas, thoughts, or images senselessly invade one's consciousness and are often coupled with persistent, repetitive behaviors or desires

Another common form of anxiety disorder is called **obsessive-compulsive disorder.** Obsessions are persistent ideas, thoughts, and images that senselessly invade one's consciousness. Often people attempt to ignore or suppress these thoughts or impulses. Typical obsessions include repetitive thoughts of violence, fear of contamination, or doubt. Compulsions are persistent repetitive behaviors that may include a desire to touch, check, or count things or to wash one's hands. In the case of compulsions, the person generally recognizes the behavior is senseless but experiences a release of tension from performing the ritualized act.

Many people experience obsessions and compulsions without having them interfere with everyday life. For example, you may wonder whether you locked the door or turned off the stove when you left home. However, in the most severe cases, obsessive-compulsive disorders can be major handicaps in social and work roles. A compulsion is a major handicap for a person who spends six to ten hours preparing for work, rising in the middle of the night and arriving at work late and exhausted (Price & Lynn, 1986).

Affective Disorders: Depression

depression
predominantly sad and hopeless mood often associated with changes in appetite, changes in sleep patterns, agitation, and feelings of worthlessness and fatigue

The blues. The blahs. The pits. Down in the dumps. Under the weather. Lower than a snake's belly. Just about everybody has a favorite phrase to describe a depressed mood. For the most part, people regard depression as a feeling, a mood, or an emotion. As such, **depression** is a normal human experience, an unavoidable part of existence. Sadness, grief, frustration, and discouragement are dark threads interwoven in life.

Depression affects all kinds of people, rich and poor, old and young. Abraham Lincoln suffered from severe bouts of depression, and Winston Churchill called his periodic depression, with chilling accuracy, "the black dog." One of our astronauts, Edwin Aldren, suffered from episodes of depression, as did Senator Thomas Eagleton (Lobel & Hirschfeld, 1984).

Recent surveys (Regier et al., 1984) indicate that in general, depression is twice as common in women as in men, that younger as well as older people get depressed, and that depression even occurs in infants and children, as well as adolescents and adults. Between 4 and 10 percent of the American public suffers from an identifiable depressive disorder today. In a course of a lifetime, 25 percent of the population will experience a major depressive episode. In fact, clinical depression is so common that it is likely that you have a friend or relative who is suffering from a depressive episode now or has suffered from one in the past.

Major depressive episodes are indicated by a number of critical signs, including those shown in Table 7–4. These signs reflect changes in mood, eating patterns, sleep patterns, and feelings about oneself.

Causes of depression. Explanations for depression vary considerably. Some researchers have focused on the experience of separation, loss, and change as major triggers for depression. The death of a loved one or the loss of a job, for example, are major life events thought to trigger depression. Dynamically oriented theorists have argued that the experience of loss during childhood can make one especially vulnerable to depression in later life, particularly if this vulnerability is triggered by some current life crisis.

Learning theorists, including Martin Seligman (1975), have argued that depression is actually a learned feeling of helplessness. Learned helplessness involves the belief that you cannot control the aspects of life that relieve suffering or bring gratification. The person has come to believe that he or she is helpless to control his or her own life circumstances.

Still other researchers, such as Beck et al. (1979), have argued that the most striking aspects of the depressed person's behavior are negative expectations and thoughts. These habitual aspects of depressing thinking are actually cog-

TABLE   7–4   Signs of Major Depression

- Sad and hopeless depressed mood.
- Decreases or increases in appetite.
- Changes in sleep patterns, with increases in sleep or insomnia.
- Increased agitation.
- A loss of interest in usual activities.
- Feelings of chronic fatigue.
- Feelings of worthlessness.
- Recurrent thoughts of death or suicide.

Source: American Psychiatric Association. *DSM-III: Diagnostic and statistical manual of mental disorders* (3rd ed.). Washington, DC: American Psychiatric Association.

EXPLORING CHOICES

EXAMPLES OF DEPRESSIVE THINKING

Depressed people often exhibit habitual patterns of thinking. Such patterns probably reflect both a depressed mood and further shape their experience, making them even more depressed. Consider the following examples:

- When Jon received a parking ticket, he took one look at it and said, "Life really is hopeless."
- Becky received a notice that she had just won $50 in a lottery. Her first feelings were those of guilt because someone more worthy had not won.

- Ron just received a notice from the bank that he had bounced a check. By midafternoon, he was referring to it as "my bankruptcy."
- Her college intramural squad lost a softball game. Jane spent the rest of the day stewing that she alone was responsible for the loss.

While all of us engage in thoughts of this sort from time to time, Beck et al. (1979) believe they occur much more frequently in depressed people.

nitive schemas that shape the depressed person's experience. From Beck's point of view, changing these negative thoughts is the key to treating depressed people. See also "Exploring Choices: Examples of Depressive Thinking."

Biological researchers, on the other hand, have noted that certain chemicals, such as lithium carbonate, can have powerful effects on mood disorders. This finding suggests that brain biochemistry plays an important role in depression (Toteson, 1981). It is very likely, however, that both prior life experience and biological factors contribute to depression.

Coping with depression. Everybody has feelings of depression. Sometimes you just lack enthusiasm and feel down without knowing why. In other cases, a specific loss or disappointment depresses you. Can you do anything about your feelings of depression? Peter Lewinsohn and his colleagues (1978) have written a book titled *Control Your Depression*, which explains how your level of activity, your interactions with others, and your thoughts affect your mood. They describe three important steps you can take to deal with feelings of depression.

First, don't worry too much if you feel down. Some people begin to worry about why they aren't happier and wonder if something is wrong with them. Remember, depression is a very common feeling. It is unpleasant, but in most cases, it doesn't need to interfere with your daily life. You *can* cope.

Second, changing the way you think about things can affect how you feel about them. Consider the following examples from Miller and Munoz (1982):

- Peter invites Martha for dinner. Martha obviously does not like what he has cooked. Peter says to himself, "Wow, I must be a terrible cook and a useless person. I can't do anything right!" He is depressed about the whole thing for several days.

- John invites Mary to dinner. Mary obviously does not like what he has cooked. John says to himself, "She must have pretty limited tastes." He decides to try a simpler dish next time. After dinner, they have a pleasant evening together.

John and Peter experienced the same events but reacted to them in different ways. Peter took the situation personally and ended up feeling worthless. John, on the other hand, observed what had happened but began to think about how it might work out better next time. There are many ways to see any situation, and some approaches make you feel better and will help you cope more effectively the next time.

Third, change your pattern of activities and reward yourself. Make a long list of things that you like to do, things you can do with people and alone, physical activities, and restful activities. Then schedule some times in your life to do them. Having rewarding leisure time is critical to mental health. But don't get in a rut. Use variety in scheduling your leisure. Remind yourself that it is okay to have fun.

Of course, not all depression can be handled on your own. If you are having continued trouble with sleeping, eating, or feeling down, you should consider seeking help from a competent mental health professional. We discuss getting help in Chapter 8.

Suicide

Suicide is one of the ten leading causes of death in the United States (Lobel & Hirschfeld, 1984). Among people between twenty and forty, it is the third leading cause. Furthermore, the figures may substantially underestimate the real rate of suicide because many deaths in automobile accidents and as a result of drug overdoses may actually be suicides, even if they are not classified that way.

Many different theories about the causes of suicide have been offered. The sociologist Durkheim (1952) proposed that societies with higher levels of anonymity would produce higher rates of suicide because of weakened social ties. Psychoanalysts, on the other hand, argue that the inability of some people to express anger leads them to turn it inward. The inwardly turned anger is experienced as depression that may be expressed in suicidal attempts. Whatever the reason for the depression, we do know that a high proportion of people who commit suicide feel extremely depressed and hopeless (Lobel & Hirschfeld, 1984).

Yet, under some circumstances, suicide may not be just an expression of hopelessness and despair. For example, a chronically ill person with a painful terminal disease may consider suicide as a viable alternative to burdening his or her family. In other cultures, too, suicide may be regarded as an honorable act, as was the case in traditional Japanese society.

Common myths about suicide. There are numerous myths about suicidal behavior. Consider the following:

- *Myth: Discussing suicide with someone who is contemplating it will increase the chances that the person will commit suicide.* On the contrary, talking it out and getting help for the person can actually reduce the danger.
- *Myth: People who make suicide threats are just seeking attention.* It is well known that successful suicide attempts are very frequently preceded by some kind of warning or cry for help.
- *Myth: People who have suicidal thoughts will act on them.* Many people briefly contemplate suicide, especially when they are under considerable stress.
- *Myth: Thinking about suicide is a sign of insanity.* Actually, only a relatively small proportion of people who successfully complete a suicide attempt are severely disturbed.
- *Myth: Suicide attempts that fail are just attention-seeking devices.* Research has shown that nearly three quarters of the people who commit suicide have made previous attempts.

Campus suicide. College life is a potent mixture of challenges, demands, and changes that produce intense pressure for many college students. Current estimates are that one college student in eight has contemplated suicide. The suicide rate for young people and college students has more than tripled over the past two decades from 8 in 100,000 to the current rate of nearly 27 in 100,000.

The sheer accumulation of life challenges that go along with living away from home creates major stresses for some students. Especially at first, the feelings of loneliness that go with moving from home to campus are very real. For some students, family pressures and high expectations from home can also be major sources of stress. Some students may feel guilt and responsibility for family sacrifices, and still others may be worried about family conflict or marital disruptions at home.

College is a time that can produce disappointment in love relationships or new sexual pressures. Sometimes it will seem as if it is hard to find a way out of your troubles. Uncertainty about the future, especially a future career can be still another source of stress. All of these pressures may feel like too much to some students, and they may contemplate suicide. If you suspect that someone you know is contemplating suicide, what can you do?

First of all, *listen to the person's feelings.* The feelings of the person you are talking to are very real to that person. It helps for you to be able to listen to the feelings with empathy. Let the person know that you hear what he or she is saying. Above all, don't dismiss the feelings as crazy or silly.

College life can
produce intense
pressures.

As you hear more about the problems that the person is experiencing, *suggest some alternatives and explore them together*. There may be options that the person is unable to consider because of the way he or she feels. Don't be disappointed if the person doesn't see these alternatives as an automatic solution to the problems, but you will find that exploring choices does help.

Try to assess how serious the person's intentions are. There are several things that you should try to find out. Does the person have a plan? Does the person have a clear idea of the method? Is the intended method a particularly lethal one, such as a gun?

Take the person to seek help. It is important that you go with the person to a dorm counselor or the college or university counseling center or that you and the person call a community mental health hot line. Stay with the person, rather than just recommending that the person seek help. You can make a difference.

Finally, *if the person refuses to go with you, get help anyway.* Don't hesitate, even if you promised not to tell anyone about the person's suicidal intentions.

Schizophrenia

Listen as Rodgers (1982) describes a young schizophrenic named Franz.

> *Franz, 23, says he is a riddle of bones. He hears buzzing noises, penetrating squeals, and voices with messages he sometimes understands but cannot remember. He sees flashes of light and shadows in the middle of the room. Strangers, he says, can send their shadows to visit him in bed. He tastes soap in his mouth and absorbs poison from the bedpost. He chews his tie, hoards garbage, sits in a stupor for weeks, and hits his nurses. Occasionally he clowns around and walks on his hands. (p. 85)*

schizophrenia severe psychological disorder involving a tendency to withdraw from social involvement, disjointed language and thought processes, and inappropriate emotional responses

delusions strongly held false beliefs

hallucinations seeing, hearing, or smelling things that do not actually exist but seem very real

This description is of a severe psychological disorder, **schizophrenia**, that affects approximately one percent of the population. More than half of the patients in mental institutions in the United States are diagnosed as schizophrenic. Many more live in society and experience periodic hospitalization. Approximately one third of all schizophrenics improve, a third deteriorate, and a third remain approximately the same throughout their lives (Price & Lynn, 1986).

Some of the key characteristics of schizophrenia are a tendency to withdraw from involvement in the external world, disjointed language reflecting disturbed thought processes, and inappropriate emotional responses. Some schizophrenics also experience **delusions**, which are strongly held false beliefs. They may also experience **hallucinations**, which involve seeing, hearing, or smelling things that do not actually exist but nevertheless seem very real. See "On the Research Frontier: Schizophrenia—Clinical Symptoms" on page 214 for further description of schizophrenia.

Schizophrenics often have difficulty controlling their own thoughts. They may say for example, "I can't keep the thoughts out. It comes on automatically. It happens at the most peculiar times, not just when I am talking, but when I am listening as well. I lose control in conversation, then I sweat and shake all over" (Chapman, 1966).

Clearly, schizophrenia is a severe disorder of perception and thought, but what are the likely causes? In searching for genetic causes of schizophrenia, researchers study families where schizophrenia occurs with high frequency. Of course, children of schizophrenic parents may be schizophrenic either because of the experience of living in the schizophrenic family or because of genetic factors. Consequently, most genetic researchers study identical and fraternal twins. Identical twins have identical genetic makeups, while fraternal twins are no more similar than any other sibling pair. If there is an important genetic factor in schizophrenia, both members of a pair of identical twins should be more likely to develop the disorder than both members of a pair of fraternal twins. Many studies have shown that if one member of an identical twin pair develops schizophrenia, the other will be more likely to do so than is the case with fraternal twins. Kendler (1983) suggests that genetic factors are

ON THE RESEARCH FRONTIER

SCHIZOPHRENIA—CLINICAL SYMPTOMS

The word *schizophrenia* was coined by the Swiss psychiatrist Eugen Bleuler (1911/1950) from the Greek words *schizen* (to split) and *phren* (mind). Bleuler meant to emphasize the idea that the mind became split to chaos in schizophrenia. Unfortunately, this derivation of the term has led to widespread confusion between schizophrenia and multiple personality. Multiple personality is considered a kind of dissociative disorder that in actuality bears little resemblance to schizophrenia.

After observing his schizophrenic patients, Bleuler suggested the following key characteristics of the disorder.

- *Autism* is the tendency to withdraw from involvement in the external world and to become preoccupied with private fantasies. In autistic fantasies, perceptions frequently become distorted.

- *Associative disturbance* (also called loose associations or thought disorder) often takes the form of language that wanders and skips from topic to topic in a vague, disjointed way. A graphic example of this can be seen in the reply of a man who was asked whether he felt that people imitated him (Mayer-Gross, Slater, & Roth, 1969).

Yes. . . . I don't quite gather. I know one right and one left use both hands, but I can't follow the system that's working. The idea is meant in a kind way, but it's not the way I understand life.

It seems to be people taking sides, as I understand it. . . . To say things are all wrong means right in turn, but I don't appreciate it that way.

- *Ambivalence* was Bleuler's way of describing the frequent juxtaposition of opposing emotions or impulses. For example, schizophrenics frequently report that they simultaneously experience love and hate for the same person.

- *Affective disturbance* refers to inappropriate emotional responses. Situations or stimuli that elicit joy or sadness in most of us may bring little response. Conversely, some schizophrenics may burst into laughter when told a friend or relative has died.

- *Delusions* are strongly held beliefs not shared by others in our culture.

- *Hallucinations* are sensations not experienced by others—seeing, hearing, or smelling things that do not actually exist but are perceived as being real.

Bleuler had a singular aptness for describing precisely the behavior he observed among his schizophrenic patients, and his descriptions remain useful when dealing with this disorder today.

Source: Adapted from R. H. Price, M. Glickstein, & D. L. Horton (1987). *Principles of psychology* (2nd ed.). Glenview, IL: Scott, Foresman & Company.

dopamine chemical
that affects the
transmission of nerve
impulses in the brain

probably as important in schizophrenia as in such medical conditions as hypertension or diabetes.

Recent studies have also shown that the chemistry of the brain may be affected. One chemical, called **dopamine**, is thought to play an important role. Dopamine affects the transmission of nerve impulses in the brian. It may be that an excess of dopamine is responsible for some of the symptoms of schizophrenia.

Other researchers (Seidman, 1983) believe that abnormalities in the actual physical structure of the brain may be responsible for some aspects of schizophrenic behavior. Modern methods for studying brain structure and blood flow including the *PET scan* allow scientists to study the brain using radioactive tracers. These new research techniques are uncovering physical abnormalities that may be important in schizophrenia and give new hope for better understanding and possibly preventing or curing this severe disorder.

SUMMARY

1. Coping with the challenges of life can affect both physical and mental health. Some ways of coping are maladaptive, such as smoking, drinking, anxiety, and feelings of depression.

2. Maladaptive patterns of eating can be responses to life stressors. Recent research has produced the set point theory, which suggests that eating is partly controlled by internal physiological mechanisms. However, eating is also under the control of external situations and stimuli. Eating disorders such as anorexia nervosa and bulimia can result when preoccupations with weight or eating are inappropriately managed.

3. The use of chemical substances such as tobacco, particularly in the form of cigarette smoking, is maladaptive. It can produce severe health consequences, including heart disease, and mouth, lung, and throat cancer in both the smoker and persons in the smoker's immediate environment.

4. A variety of chemical substances, including sedatives, stimulants, and hallucinogens, can have serious health effects and can produce either drug abuse or drug dependence.

5. Alcohol is one of the most widely abused substances. A wide variety of health effects are associated with it. However, recent research suggests that controlled drinking is possible for some people who are not yet dependent on alcohol use.

6. An emerging body of evidence suggests that maintaining healthy behaviors and preventing relapses into maladaptive health behaviors are possible by recognizing and avoiding high-risk situations, producing alternative rewarding activities, and persisting in the face of occasional relapses.

7. Psychological disorders are difficult to define, but most definitions include behaviors that are disturbing to other people, that are psychologically handicapping, and that cause personal and subjective distress.

8. Anxiety disorders, including phobias and panic attacks, are characterized by intense feelings of fear or nervousness that are difficult to control and that sometimes occur unpredictably.

9. Depression is one of the most common psychological disorders. It is characterized by feelings of sadness and hopelessness, changes in appetite and sleep patterns, as well as increases in feelings of fatigue and worthlessness. Occasionally there are thoughts of suicide and death.

10. While severe forms of depression should be treated by a professional, more commonplace episodes of depression can be improved by efforts to change your activity patterns, to avoid major preoccupations with the feelings of depression, and to change your perspective on the problem.

11. Suicide is one of the ten leading causes of death in the United States. It is increasing rapidly among adolescents and young adults. If you encounter someone expressing suicidal intent, you should listen to and not dismiss the person's feelings. Alternative courses of action should be explored, and some assessment of the seriousness of the person's intentions should be made. Above all, the person should be brought into contact with a mental health professional.

12. Schizophrenia is a severe psychological disorder affecting approximately one percent of the population. It is characterized by disturbed thought processes, disjointed speech, social withdrawal, and inappropriate emotional responses. Recent research has identified major chemical and physical changes in the brain that may help us to understand this severe form of psychological disorder.

Chapter 8

GETTING HELP

PSYCHOTHERAPY

What Goes On in Psychotherapy
Common Factors in Psychotherapy

PSYCHOTHERAPEUTIC APPROACHES

Psychoanalytic Therapy
Behavior Therapy
  Illustrative behavior therapy procedures
  Manipulating consequences
  Training behaviors
  Changing the impact of antecedents
Humanistic Approaches

DIFFERENT FORMS OF PSYCHOTHERAPY

Individual Psychotherapy
Couples Psychotherapy
Family Therapy
Group Psychotherapy
Community-Based Interventions

THE VALUE OF PSYCHOTHERAPY

SUMMARY

In some instances, individuals seek professional help in order to cope with stress more effectively. This chapter describes various types of psychotherapy and then considers their effectiveness. Psychotherapy, or psychological interventions designed to change clients' emotional and behavioral problems, may take many different forms, including individual, couple, family, group, and community-based approaches. These forms of psychotherapy vary, depending upon the theoretical orientation of the therapist, the nature of client or clients, and the length and goals of intervention. For example, Henrink (1980) has described over fifty different treatment approaches. While space does not permit a description of each, we consider the major commonalities across psychotherapeutic approaches and describe a few of the major approaches (namely, psychoanalytic, behavior, and humanistic). We also consider the overall effectiveness or value of psychotherapy. However, before we consider the various treatment approaches, let us consider the following general questions: What is psychotherapy? What goes on in psychotherapy? and What are the common factors in psychotherapy?

PSYCHOTHERAPY

psychotherapy
therapy process to
help clients modify
feelings, thoughts, and
behaviors

Psychotherapy has been described as "an interpersonal process designed to modify feelings, cognitions, attitudes and behaviors that have proven troublesome to the person seeking help from a trained clinician" (Hartley & Strupp, 1980, p. 421). The clinician may be a psychiatrist, clinical psychologist, social worker, or psychiatric nurse, as described in Table 8–1. The actual formal structure of therapy varies greatly. According to Hartley and Strupp (1980):

> The therapy may include only a therapist and a patient, or may include cotherapy teams working with groups or families. Sessions are usually 50–60 minutes in length, but may include marathon sessions lasting many hours. A patient may be seen four or five times a week, or only once a month; and treatment may last a few weeks or several years. (p. 438)

This quote illustrates many ways psychotherapy may differ. In addition, psychotherapists may differ in their conceptual systems, therapeutic goals, personal styles, and treatment procedures. They may employ a variety of techniques, including empathic listening, reassurance, questioning, clarification, interpretation, explanation, skill training, and suggestion, to help the client make desired changes. In most instances, psychotherapists establish a collaborative working relationship to help clients assume greater responsibility for the changes required. In this sense, the psychotherapist may be seen as a coach or teacher who helps clients learn to cope with stress more adequately and to actualize their potentials (foster personality growth). The goals of treatment are most often self-examination and self-help.

Many clients enter treatment because they are troubled or dissatisfied. They may feel helpless about changing, hopeless about future improvement, or demoralized. They may experience a sense of victimization about external

TABLE 8-1　　　Mental Health Professionals

1. **Psychiatrist**—requires an M.D. degree and typically a four-year postdoctoral residency in psychiatry. Psychiatrists have legal responsibility for managing patients and are licensed to administer medication and other physical treatments, such as electric shock treatment. Psychiatrists frequently provide psychotherapy, as well.

2. **Clinical psychologist**—requires a Ph.D. in psychology and a one-year clinical internship. Clinical psychologists specialize in assessment and research and are skilled in conducting a number of psychotherapies.

3. **Social worker**—usually trained at the master's level, with an MSW degree plus supervised experience in social service agencies and clinics. Social workers usually provide contact with patients' families and help with community relations (contact with various social agencies). Besides providing valuable input in the form of a social history detailing patients' background, family, and work history, social workers often provide counseling.

4. **Psychiatric nurse**—requires a Registered Nurses' (RN) degree and has specialized in psychiatric services. The psychiatric nurse (and a subprofessional staff of aides) provide front-line continued care for hospitalized patients. The nursing staff administers medication and helps to oversee the treatment schedule. Given the continued contact with patients, the psychiatric nurses can provide ongoing counseling.

events or internal events ("These thoughts, feelings, just overwhelm me."). They may not understand what factors have contributed to and help maintain their difficulties. Moreover, they may be unaware of how they inadvertently and unknowlingly contribute to their own problems. In order to understand how such clients may be helped, let us consider what goes on in psychotherapy.

What Goes On in Psychotherapy

Psychotherapy may take many different forms; however, some common features emerge across approaches. For example, psychotherapists usually begin treatment by interviewing the client (and in some instances, significant others in the client's life, such as family members) in order to obtain a history and a description of the presenting problem. In some approaches, the couple or family may be viewed as the client. Table 8-2 (on page 222) describes the types of questions that may be covered during an initial session. From such discussions, and in some instances from additional testing and observation, the client and therapist develop a working formulation of the client's problems and specify treatment goals.

As the therapy progresses, clients are encouraged to discuss any areas of difficulty and to explore specific troubling incidents in order to determine how they felt, thought, and acted. The therapist may help clients search for common themes, which cut across stressful situations, in order for the clients to appreciate the **transactional** nature of the stress, namely, how the client may inadvertently and unknowingly contribute to his or her own stress. Are there any particular issues or concerns that elicit stress across situations? Are there any particular patterns (thoughts, feelings, reactions of others) that co-occur with the client's distressed reactions?

transactional referring to the fact that not only do environmental events affect individuals but individuals affect others

TABLE 8-2   The Clinical Interview

I. Definition of problem behavior.

A. *Nature of the problem as defined by client.* "As I understand it, you came here because. . . ." (Discuss reasons for contact as stated by referral agency or other source of information.) "I would like you to tell me more about this. What is the problem as you see it?" (Probe as needed to determine client's view of the problem behavior, that is, what he or she is doing, or failing to do, that the client or somebody else defines as a problem.)

B. *Severity of the problem.*

1. "How serious a problem is this as far as you are concerned?" (Probe to determine client's view of the problem behavior, that is what he or she is doing, or failing to do, or that somebody else defines as a problem.)

2. "How often do you (exhibit problem behavior, if a disorder of commission, or have occasion to exhibit desired behavior, if a problem of omission)?" (The goal is to obtain information regarding frequency of response.)

C. *Generality of the problem.*

1. *Duration.* "How long has this been going on?"

2. *Extent.* "Where does the problem usually come up?" (Probe to determine situations in which problem behavior occurs, for example, "Do you feel that way at work? How about at home?")

II. Determinants of problem behavior.

A. *Conditions that intensify problem behavior.* "Now I want you to think about the times when the problem is worst. What sorts of things are going on then?"

B. *Conditions that alleviate problem behavior.* "What about the times when (the problem) gets better? What sorts of things are going on then?"

C. *Perceived origins.* "What do you think is causing (the problem)?"

D. *Specific antecedents.* "Think back to the last time (the problem) occurred. What was going on at that time?" As needed:

1. *Social influences.* "Were any other people around? Who? What were they doing?"

2. *Personal influences.* "What were you thinking about at the time? How did you feel?"

E. *Specific consequences.* "What happened after (the problem occurred)?" As needed:

1. *Social consequences.* "What did (significant others identified above) do?"

2. *Personal consequences.* "How did that make you feel?"

F. *Suggested changes.* "You have thought a lot about (the problem). What do you think might be done to improve the situation?"

G. *Suggested leads for further inquiry.* "What else do you think I should find out about to help you with this problem?"

Source: Reprinted from D. Peterson (1968). *The clinical study of social behavior.* Englewood Cliffs, NJ: Prentice-Hall, 121–122.

In some instances, therapists may have clients look back on their lives in order to determine how such patterns have emerged. Such insight of developmental antecedents can often help clients become aware of how they tend to repeat self-destructive patterns of behavior. Such understanding can act as a catalyst in developing more constructive means of thinking, feeling, and behaving.

In some forms of psychotherapy, clients are given explicit training in developing alternative adaptive ways of coping. The objective of such training is to help clients find and implement their own solutions to problems. Clients can learn, initially in therapy and then in their everyday experiences, to recognize and interrupt maladaptive patterns of thoughts, feelings, and actions and to choose different adaptive alternatives. In this way, clients can learn a general process of self-examination and problem solving.

Psychotherapists use many different strategies to achieve these goals. Some focus on here-and-now experiences, while others emphasize more distant events (some use childhood memories, and experiences), as well as clients' fantasies and dreams. Psychotherapists also differ in whether treatment is limited to the office setting or is extended into the client's environment (the therapist may visit and work with clients in their natural settings, called *in vivo*). In some instances, follow-up sessions may be arranged.

No matter the exact form of psychotherapy, a critical feature is the *nature of the relationship* that develops between the client and the therapist. The establishment of a constructive therapeutic relationship can greatly facilitate the process of change. The psychotherapist's warmth, genuineness, degree of accurate empathy, trustworthiness, attractiveness, confidence, enthusiasm, and clinical skill have been implicated in facilitating the development of a constructive working relationship (Arnkoff, 1983). In other words, the therapist's respect for and acceptance of the client and his or her ability to understand the client's problems and perceptions of the world can influence both the client's motivation to change and the client's susceptibility to social influence.

Moreover, there is a need for the therapist to assess the client's expectations about therapy and to ensure that they are in agreement with the therapist's expectations. Clients who receive treatment that does not match their expectations are most prone to drop out of psychotherapy. Such individuals are more likely to be from lower social classes, less educated, less integrated into society, less verbal, less self-disclosing, and less psychologically minded. Psychotherapists often take a more action-oriented approach with such clients. There is a need to individually tailor treatment to the needs and style of the client, taking into consideration personal, ethnic, and cultural factors. As Hartley and Strupp (1980) note:

> The secret of good therapy seems to be in the unique match between a therapist and a patient who are compatible, communicate effectively with each other, and who are able to commit themselves to the collaborative task of overcoming the obstacles to the patient's growth. (p. 438)

Common Factors in Psychotherapy

In a fine book, entitled *Persuasion and Healing,* the psychiatrist, Jerome Frank (1973) described common factors that cut across the many different forms of psychotherapy. He also argued that these same principles apply to many other behavior change approaches (for example, religious healing, brainwashing, and treatment by witch doctors). The common features include the following:

1. The psychotherapist or change agent is given a certain degree of official authority, which helps him or her inspire faith in clients. The healer (therapist, shaman, or religious healer) is viewed as a potent figure in his or her own right. This authority may be created through special systems of training, elaborate symbolic paraphernalia (such as degrees or special equip-

ment), the use of special treatment settings, social expectations, and the payment of fees.

2. A second common feature is the healer's wish to help the client. Among other techniques, therapists use direct and indirect suggestions to encourage the client to change. The treatment process is not routine or perfunctory; it implies a definite personal commitment to aid the client.

3. The therapist acts as a mediator between the suffering individual and the larger society. In part, the healer protects the client from the effects of society by creating a situation in which freedom of expression is encouraged without concomitant punishment. The therapist becomes a representative of society in an attempt to lead the client back to a mode of expected bahavior. The therapist or healer is charged by society to normalize any deviant behavior of the client.

4. Usually, there is some self-disclosure, discussion, or confession by the client of past errors and current difficulties that the healer listens to in an empathic, understanding, and forgiving manner. By means of listening and talking, the therapist helps the client release emotions, rethink problems, and restore morale. The helper usually accepts whatever the person has done in the past.

5. The healer offers a theoretical system or explanatory scheme to help explain why the client is suffering. Such a rationale makes the client's problems more understandable and provides a framework for change. In some forms of therapy, the rationale may be described explicitly, while in other forms of therapy it may be more implicit, so that clients have to piece it together on their own. Frank indicates that the validity of the particular theoretical system is less important than its impressiveness, consistency, and ability to engender belief on the part of both the client and the helper. The rationale constitutes the articles of faith for fostering change. It helps clients make sense of their problems and the processes of change. In other words, inherent in every form of psychotherapy is an attempt by the therapist to help clients reconceptualize or translate their problems into more hopeful and less demoralizing terms. In this way, the rationale gives clients more confidence that they can solve their problems and nurtures hope.

6. Finally, a central feature of various forms of psychotherapy is the active involvement of both the therapist and the client in the process of change, usually over a number of sessions.

Other scholars have also highlighted common features of diverse psychotherapeutic interventions. A useful summary has been offered by Gottman and Markman (1978), as described in Table 8–3. This list of components of psychotherapy illustrates that the therapist often acts as a coach, helping clients undertake personal experiments in the real-life environment. Therapists differ in how directive they are in implementing each of these compo-

TABLE 8-3   Components of Psychotherapy

1. The therapist conveys his expectations that change is possible and likely to occur.
2. The therapist conveys a faith that every problem has a solution.
3. The therapist helps the client elaborate and specify the problems presented.
4. The therapist provides a new language system for organizing behavior and events. This may include a relabelling of what is "pathological," what is "healthy," (problems and goals), and perhaps etiology.
5. The therapist gives client normative data for client's experiences in therapy (e.g., "It is common to feel panicky at this point. We expect people to feel that way.").
6. The therapist provides ground rules (e.g., about fees, coming to sessions, number of sessions, calling if unable to come, homework, practice).
7. The therapist describes goals and methods for attaining goals.
8. The therapist structures situations that require approach instead of avoidance; therapist may also restructure situations so that it is more likely that approach behaviors will be rewarded naturally.
9. The therapist conveys the belief that positive consequences follow approach and negative consequences follow avoidance.
10. The therapist conveys an "experimental" norm:
    a. First try it.
    b. Then evaluate it.
    c. Then modify it.
    d. Then try it again.
11. The therapist conveys the message that he cares about the client (he is listening, empathetic, supportive).
12. The therapist teaches alternative ways of behaving and thinking with consideration of step size (small enough to maximize likelihood of success), pacing (mostly at client's own pace), and feedback (specific).
13. The therapist restructures norms of social interaction in behaviors setting of importance (e.g., changes consequences of specific behavior exchanges, and changes eliciting stimuli).
14. The therapist reinforces client for trying new behaviors, for sticking to programmed interventions, and for personalizing change within client's own style.
15. The therapist fades self out and ensures that the client attributes change to self, not to therapist, and provides for transfer of training.

Source: Reprinted from J. Gottman & H. Markman (1978). In S. Garfield & A. Bergin (Eds.), *Handbook of psychotherapy and behavior change: An empirical analysis*. New York: Wiley, 36.

nents. In some instances, psychotherapists are explicit in the ways they teach, direct, and encourage clients to change. In other forms of psychotherapy, the therapist places more responsibility on clients in order to develop self-awareness and insight. A description of some of the major approaches to psychotherapy highlights these differences.

PSYCHOTHERAPEUTIC APPROACHES

We consider three major psychotherapeutic approaches—psychoanalytic, behavioral, and humanistic. Each has played a central role in the development of psychological interventions and has laid the groundwork for current efforts at developing an integrative therapeutic approach.

psychoanalysis psychotherapeutic approach
that helps clients
develop insight into
self-destructive
(defensive) behavior
and to make
unconscious influences
conscious and subject
to change

free association
psychoanalytic
procedure of having
clients say whatever
comes to mind without
censoring it

dream analysis
analysis of a client's
dreams in order to
appreciate deeper
meaning underlying
the surface features of
the dreams

latent meaning basic
conflicts, wishes, or
needs such as appear
in dreams, and their
blocked expressions
underlying overt
behavior

manifest content
surface features of
one's dreams that one
can recall or
reconstruct for a
therapist

transference process
by which clients
transfer important
feelings and behavioral
reactions usually
expressed toward
others toward the
therapist

countertransference
distorted feelings and
thoughts that a
therapist transfers to a
client

Psychoanalytic Therapy

At the turn of the century, Sigmund Freud and his followers introduced a form of treatment called **psychoanalysis,** which was based on the notion that human behavior is motivated by unconscious needs and conflicts that arise in childhood. The objective of treatment is to help the patient make the unconscious conscious and develop insight into how his or her defensive behavior interferes with daily functioning. As developed initially by Sigmund Freud, psychoanalysis entailed daily sessions for nine to twelve months, although Freud's followers lengthened the psychoanalysis to three to four years. As it evolved, classical psychoanalysis became an intensive, long-term procedure (normally, several sessions a week for several years). The psychoanalyst uses the clinicial tools of free association, dream analysis, and the interpretation of transference and resistance to help the patient change.

While reclining on a couch, the patient is asked to say whatever comes to mind without censoring it (**free association**), no matter how personal, painful, or trivial the thought. With the analyst's guidance the expression of one's stream of consciousness permits unconscious (repressed) impulses to emerge. As this procedure continues, the patient usually begins to avoid certain topics and show other forms of resistance to treatment. The analyst interprets and helps the patient become aware of his or her characteristic ways of reacting.

The analyst may also use **dream analysis,** focusing on the **latent meaning** of the dream, going beyond the symbolism or **manifest content** (surface material) of the dream. Freud believed that dreams are the "royal road to the unconscious," since people's defenses are lowered during sleep. Thus, the analyst may have patients free-associate to aspects of the manifest content of their dreams in order to search for the underlying, latent meaning.

During the course of analysis, patients transfer important feelings that had been previously directed at significant others toward the analyst. By means of interpretation, the analyst helps patients gain insight into the ways in which their distorted ideas and unconscious impulses and feelings lead to self-defeating behavior. The use of the couch, the frequent sessions, and the distant analytical style of the analyst are designed to foster such **transference.** The analyst may also experience somewhat distorted thoughts and feelings toward the patient. This is known as **countertransference,** and it can interfere with treatment.

The increased insight into how the patient relates to the analyst, as well as to significant others, provides the basis for behavior changes. By a working-through process, the patient can implement on a trial and error basis the insights that have emerged. The combination of insight and working through nurture the patient's personal growth.

The following vignette offered by Baker (1985) illustrates the way in which the therapist uses observation, reflection, and interpretation to help the patient gain insight into the relationships between angry feelings and a behavioral pattern of withdrawal.

This is a caricature of
Sigmund Freud
analyzing himself.

Patient: You know, I really didn't want to come today. I just don't seem to
have very much to talk about. (Long silence) I'm just not really sure what to
say; maybe you can suggest a topic.

Therapist: You'd like for me to tell you what to talk about, to give you some
structure?

Patient: Sure, after all, that's what I'm paying you for. (Pause) It seems that you just sit there all the time not saying anything. I'm not really sure this is helping very much.

Therapist: Perhaps we should talk about your feeling that I'm not giving you what you want.

Patient: It's not so much want; it's what I need. You always just sit there; you never give me advice; you never tell me what to do. I thought therapy would be different from this.

Therapist: You expected more?

Patient: I expected something. You know, it's a little irritating to pay out good money and feel like you're not getting your money's worth.

Therapist: So it feels as if I'm cheating or depriving you in some way. Perhaps that is why you're feeling so angry today.

Patient: I'm not feeling angry. (Pause) Well, . . . I guess I am a little. In fact, I really didn't even want to come.

Therapist: Perhaps there's a relationship between those feelings . . . feeling angry and then wanting to withdraw.

Patient: You know, I think I do that a lot. I feel uncomfortable being angry at you. It doesn't seem justified somehow and yet I do feel angry and feel like I just want to not come and not talk; or not pay my bill or do something to get even. I guess I do that a lot. I mean, when I get angry, I get quiet and I just don't talk.

Therapist: Perhaps that is why you were so quiet at the beginning of the hour. It was a way of indirectly letting me know that you were angry, while at the same time protecting yourself and me from that anger and your fears of what it might do.

Patient: I guess you are right. I am afraid of anger and I have a lot of difficulty letting people know directly when I feel they have done something bad or hurt me in some way. I typically just . . . withdraw.

Therapist: It somehow feels safer that way.

Patient: Safer and . . . like I have more power and control. (pp. 41–42)

In turn, the patient can then apply this knowledge to everyday experiences during the working-through phase. During the last fifty years, such psychoanalytic theory and techniques have had a profound influence on psychotherapy. Freud's approach, however, has been both challenged and refined. Such theorists as Carl Jung, Alfred Adler, Karen Horney, and Harry Stack Sullivan have highlighted the interpersonal and cultural aspects that must be taken into consideration in understanding psychopathology and in formulating treatment.

In recent years, formal classic psychoanalysis has given way to shorter, less intensive, briefer forms of psychodynamic therapy (Malan, 1979; Sifneos, 1972; Strupp & Binder, 1984). In the newer forms of psychodynamic treatment, therapeutic sessions are more likely to occur only once or twice a week. The couch has been replaced by a comfortable chair. Interpersonal problems, as compared with intrapsychic conflicts, are emphasized, and the working-through phase has taken on greater importance.

Behavior Therapy

In contrast to the psychoanalytic focus on unconscious conflicts as the cause of emotional and behavioral disorders, behavior therapists emphasize the role of observable environmental factors. Based on the work of learning theorists such as Pavlov, Watson, Hull, and Skinner, behavior therapists believe that many behaviors that society labels abnormal result from the client's inadequate learning experiences. According to behavior therapy, maladaptive thoughts, emotions, and behaviors are learned for a variety of reasons:

1. They lead to some reinforcement or payoff, such as getting people's attention.
2. They avoid unpleasant activites.
3. They result in the termination or avoidance of some discomforting emotional state, such as anxiety.

Behavior therapists have developed a number of procedures to teach clients adaptive behaviors to replace their learned inappropriate behaviors. Each of the interventions begins with a careful assessment to identify problematic behavioral patterns and the relationships of those patterns to environmental consequences. Kanfer and Saslow (1969) have suggested two ways to view clients' behaviors:

1. *Behavioral excesses.* They occur too often, are too intense, last too long, or occur in the wrong situation.
2. *Behavioral deficits.* They fail to occur with sufficient frequency, with adequate intensity, in appropriate form, or when socially expected.

In addition, clients may evidence *behavioral assets*, or nonproblematic behaviors, that can be used productively in the process of change. Behavior therapists systematically assess clients' behavioral excesses, deficits, and assets by means of interview, observation, role playing, and psychological testing. Major objectives are to determine the parameters of the maladaptive behaviors and to strengthen adaptive behaviors. The questions to be addressed are, What? How? When? Where? Under what conditions? and What consequences follow the client's behavior? (See Table 8–2.) The answers to these questions suggest specific forms of intervention.

Illustrative behavior therapy procedures. A number of behavior therapy techniques affect the relationship between antecedents, behaviors, and consequences. *Antecedents* are events that precede a given behavior, such as feelings (being depressed) or things someone else does or says. *Consequents* follow a given behavior, such as receiving attention from others or reducing one's anxiety level. Some techniques focus on manipulating the consequences that follow behavior; others focus on training new behavioral skills; and still others focus on influencing the eliciting value of antecedents (that is, changing the meaning of stimuli). Often, behavior therapists use combinations of the three approaches.

Manipulating consequences. Operant principles, as espoused by B. F. Skinner, have had a major impact on the treatment of behavioral disorders. Stated most simply, an operant framework argues that we tend to engage in and repeat behaviors that lead to payoffs and avoid or reduce behaviors that lead to punishment or the loss of reinforcement (extinction). This simple principle has been applied in a creative manner to a variety of clinical populations ranging from autistic children to adult schizophrenics and from classroom disorders to neurotic behaviors. Such operant procedures are best employed under environmental control.

For example, Paul and Lentz (1978) established a token economy in which chronic hospitalized schizophrenics could earn various goodies (for example, praise, privileges, and money) contingent upon socially appropriate behaviors (such as communicating with others, keeping tidy, or attending recreational activities). In order to achieve these objectives, the staff would use the behavioral principle of successive approximation, or shaping, to develop more complex integrated responses. **Successive approximation** is the principle of making reinforcement contingent upon increasingly more demanding behaviors—the client must do more and more to earn payoffs. The notion of shaping is illustrated most clearly in the teaching of language to nonverbal children, where the trainer slowly and methodically shapes the child's verbalizations. At first, the autistic child has a very limited verbal repertoire. The trainer tries to build up the child's speech by making the reinforcement (M and M's candies) contingent upon the child's verbalizaiton of single syllables and then contingent upon the production of simple words, then simple command sentences, and so forth. In this way, the trainer systematically shapes the desirable behavior.

A similar application of the principle of successive approximation has been used in education. Teaching machines illustrate the principles of shaping, as the curriculum slowly and systematically builds and reinforces increasingly complex components of desirable behavior.

Another powerful operant technique is *extinction*, using removal of reinforcement or time out from reward. **Time-out procedures** place the individual in a setting that removes reinforcement for a time. Sending a child to a quiet room, removing attention, or ignoring may influence the expression of behavior. There are many other nuances and intricacies to the operant approach. The interested reading should see Kazdin (1975).

In terms of our own adjustment, it is worthwhile to identify a set of specific behaviors we might wish to change (for example, smoking, overeating, lack of exercise, improving study habits, or reducing emotional outbursts). We can

successive approximation making reinforcement contingent upon increasingly more demanding behaviors

time-out procedures procedures used in behavior therapy to place the individual in a setting that removes reinforcement for a time

B. F. Skinner's theories have had a major impact on the treatment of behavioral disorders.

begin by trying to answer the questions listed in Table 8–2. What are the payoffs, both immediate and long term, for specific maladaptive behaviors? What incompatible behaviors should be shaped up? How can rewards be built into maintaining these more adaptive behaviors? What stimuli trigger the maladaptive behaviors? What behavior change procedures can be used to break the chain? If we are creatures of habit, can we change such habits? Answering such questions is consistent with recent efforts by behavior therapists to have clients become their own personal scientists so they can implement their own self-control programs.

self-control procedures keeping track of one's behavior by self-monitoring, learning to set realistic goals, and reinforcing oneself

Self-control procedures entail the extension of operant procedures to oneself by having clients self-monitor, self-evaluate, and self-reinforce their own behaviors. In recent years, an interesting extension has been the development of **biofeedback** procedures, whereby clients receive information (feedback) about their physiological responses (for example, the level of muscle tension, heart rate, or body temperature) and are taught to alter these reactions. Although there is much interest in biofeedback, the therapeutic usefulness of this procedure is yet to be fully demonstrated. Biofeedback is still in the experimental stage—clearly an experiment worth keeping a close eye on.

biofeedback extension of self-control procedures using informational cues of the body to alter one's reactions

Training behaviors. Behavior therapy has been particularly helpful in generating behavioral skills training programs. Some clients who evidence deficits can benefit from coaching procedures (for example, in communication skills, anger control, or assertiveness). The coaching efforts usually include modeling, or exposure to live or videotape models who demonstrate the desirable behaviors. Modeling may be followed by the client's behaviorally rehearsing the demonstrated behavior initially in the clinic and then **in vivo** (in the natural environment). The client may receive feedback in the form of a videotape. The training may be offered individually or in groups.

in vivo in natural environment

Changing the impact of antecedents. Behavior therapists are also concerned with how individuals react to both internal and external events. This is most clearly indicated in the treatment of phobic clients, who engage in avoidance behavior in response to specific stimuli (such as fear of dogs or crowds). In 1958, Joseph Wolpe, a South African psychiatrist, was instrumental in developing an innovative therapeutic procedure called *systematic desensitization* for the treatment of phobics. Desensitization involves teaching clients to (1) systematically relax (2) generate a hierarchy of scenes from least fear-engendering to most fear-engendering, and (3) imagine the scenes in graded sequence while relaxed. The aim is to have clients maintain a relaxed state while imagining the anxiety-engendering scenes. In this way, clients can become aware of anticipatory anxiety cues that can come to trigger the use of coping relaxation responses. Wolpe viewed this process as a form of **counterconditioning**, whereby antecedent stimuli (phobic objects) are neutralized and elicit anxiety-reducing responses. For example, instead of feeling anxiety at the sight of a phobic object, a client emits a coping relaxation response.

counterconditioning process by which a new, more adaptive relationship is established between a stimulus (triggering event) and a response

A related and somewhat more effective treatment with phobics is to replace the imagery portion of desensitization with graded *in vivo* exposure. By requiring phobic clients to return to situations that they have avoided, one can help them overcome their fears. For example, such programmed practice is the treatment of choice with agoraphobics (those suffering from fears of leaving home; see Mathews, Gelder, & Johnston, 1981). The phobic client's spouse or friend may be enlisted to aid in the practice routine. The training involves daily practice in situations that elicit moderate anxiety, so the client can learn how to handle such feelings and develop a sense of competence or efficacy. Prior to treatment, internal and external events may signal the occasion for panic attacks and avoidant behaviors. The behavior therapy techniques are designed to change the impact and eliciting value of such events.

In recent years, behavior therapists have paid increasing attention to mediating cognitive events as a focus of treatment. A number of cognitive behavior modification procedures are designed to alter the client's thinking style (Kendall & Bemis, 1983; Mahoney & Arnkoff, 1977; Meichenbaum, 1977). Two prominent contributors to the shift to a more cognitive perspective are Albert Ellis and Aaron Beck.

Albert Ellis's (1962) rational-emotive therapy (RET) approach proposes that much emotional suffering is due to the irrational ways people construe the world and the implicit assumptions they hold. The ways in which individuals evaluate and interpret events and the irrational beliefs they hold can exert adverse effects on behavior and cause emotional disturbances. For example, the belief that your self-worth depends upon what others think of you or the belief that there is or should be a right or perfect solution to each problem can lead to preoccupation about self-worth or concerns about perfectionism, with resultant feelings of worthlessness. Ellis highlighted Karen Horney's (1950) concept of the tyranny of the shoulds—"I should do this" or "I must do that." Ellis has even gone so far as to suggest that people can overindulge in what he calls **musturbation** (too many *musts*) and **awfulizing**, which can lead to striving for unattainable goals (see the quote in Table 8–4).

The RET therapist attempts to help clients become aware of the habitual nature of their expectations or beliefs and of the self-fulfilling aspects of their thinking processes. The therapist uses a combination of clarification, interpretation, explanation, and *in vivo* behavioral exercises (or personal experiments) to help clients develop more adaptive behavioral patterns. In some instances, systematic problem solving or skills training may be undertaken.

A related cognitive therapy approach used primarily with depressed patients is cognitive therapy, as described by Aaron Beck and his colleagues (Beck et al., 1979). Cognitive therapy involves the following:

1. Eliciting the client's thoughts, feelings, and interpretation of events.
2. Gathering evidence with the client for or against such interpretations.

musturbation Ellis's term to describe an individual's feeling of need to accomplish internally established goals

awfulizing Ellis's term to reflect an individual's feeling that it is awful if a failure or frustration occurs

---

TABLE 8–4   Ellis's Rational-Emotive Therapy

Cognitively, RET teaches clients the ABC's of personality formation and disturbance-creation. Thus, it shows people that their emotional Consequences (at point C) do *not* directly stem from the Activating events (at point A) in their lives, but from their Belief Systems (at point B) *about* these Activating events. Their Belief systems, when they feel disturbed, consist of, first, a set of empirically based, rational Beliefs (rB's). For example, when they fail at a job or are rejected by a love partner (at point A), they rationally convince themselves, "How unfortunate it is for me to fail! I would much rather succeed or be accepted." If they stick rigorously to these rational Beliefs, they feel appropriately sorry, regretful, frustrated, or irritated (at point C); but they do *not* feel emotionally upset or destroyed. To make themselves feel inappropriately or neurotically, they add the nonempirically based, irrational Beliefs (iB's): "How *awful* it is for me to fail! I *must* succeed. I am a thoroughly *worthless person* for failing or for being rejected!" Then they feel anxious, depressed, or worthless.

In RET, the therapist or teacher shows people how to vigorously challenge, question, and Dispute (at point D) their irrational Beliefs. *Thus, they are shown* how to ask themselves: "*Why* is it awful that I failed? *Who* says I *must* succeed? *Where* is the evidence that I am a *worthless person* if I fail or get rejected?" If people persistently and forcefully Dispute their insane ideas, they acquire a new cognitive Effect (at point E), namely, the Beliefs that (1) "It is not awful but only very inconvenient if I fail," (2) "I don't *have* to succeed, though there are several good reasons why I'd *like* to," and (3) "I am never a *worthless person* for failing or being rejected. I am merely a person who has done poorly, for the present, in these areas, but who probably can do better later. And if I never succeed or get accepted, I can *still* enjoy myself in *some* ways and refrain from downing myself."

Source: Reprinted from A. Ellis (1971). Emotional education in the classroom: The living school. *Journal of Clinical Child Psychology, 1*, 19.

3. Setting up personal experiments (homework) to test the validity of the interpretations and gathering more data for discussion.

collaborative empiricism joint effort by a client and psychotherapist to test the validity of the client's beliefs and expectations

This joint effort by the client and therapist is called **collaborative empiricism.** It tries to frame the client's automatic thoughts, interpretations, and conclusions as hypotheses worthy of testing. By asking probing questions, the therapist helps clients become more aware of their thinking processes. The therapist's questions may include the following:

- What do you think will happen in that situation?
- What do you picture happening?
- What are you saying to yourself in that situation?
- Then what?
- How do you know that will indeed happen?
- What is the evidence of that's being a threat?
- How serious is it?
- What do you think you can do about that?

The cognitive therapist also helps clients become aware of their thinking styles (cognitive errors) and the impact on their feelings and behaviors. Table 8–5 describes some of the major cognitive errors. The trainer tries to make the client aware of absolutistic thinking, such as equating one mistake with total failure or employing overgeneralized labels, in order to replace them with more relative terms. For instance, one may change one's expressions:

- *Always* may be more appropriately viewed as *often.*
- *Never,* as *rarely.*
- "I must," as "I want."
- "I need," as "I prefer" or "I would like."
- "I can't," as "I would find it difficult."
- "I can never," as "In the past, I have been unable to."

This shift is not a simple matter of semantics or a lesson in logic; it is a collaborative effort to help clients appreciate how thinking styles can influence feelings and behavior.

It is worth noting, however, that one's feelings can also affect one's thoughts. For example, when people are depressed, they tend to focus on negative events in the present, past, and future. Similarly, behavior and its consequences can affect feelings and thoughts. Thus, the various processes of emotion, cognition, and behavior are ongoing, highly interdependent streams that can mutually affect one another.

The cognitive therapist helps clients become aware of this interconnectedness and influence it by becoming a personal scientist (Mahoney, 1974) or personal problem solver (Meichenbaum, 1977). The questions the therapist asks act as models for the client's own self-interrogation. Several examples follow:

TABLE 8-5	Examples of Cognitive Errors

1. *Dichotomous reasoning* is the tendency to divide into opposites or to think solely in terms of extremes. The patient has a proclivity to see events in absolutes, either black or white, good or bad, right or wrong. This is often exemplified by remarks such as "I must do my job perfectly," or "Everyone is against me."

2. *Overgeneralization* is a tendency to make far-reaching conclusions on the basis of little data. Often, a patient makes an unjustified generalization on the basis of a single incident. Illustrative of this is the patient who thinks, "I'll never succeed at anything!" when he has a single, isolated failure. As Arnold Lazarus (1972) has pointed out, the dichotomous reasoner usually tends to overgeneralize—for example, "My girlfriend Betty let me down again; I'll never trust another woman as long as I live."

3. *Magnification* is the tendency to view things as much more important, fearful, or catastrophic than they are objectively. The patient exaggerates the significance of a particular event. Beck et al. (1979) give the example of a person with a fear of dying who interprets every unpleasant sensation or pain in his body as a sign of some fatal disease. Ellis (1962) terms this kind of thinking catastrophizing.

4. *Arbitrary inference* is the process of drawing conclusions when evidence is lacking or is actually contrary to the conclusions. A depressed patient may observe a frown on the face of someone and think, "That person is disgusted with me," or a person who is not greeted upon arrival at a party may think, "What's the use of my coming—no one wants to talk to me. I'm just worthless." The patient tends to take certain features out of context and emphasize them to the exclusion of others.

- What exactly is at stake?
- Does this situation reflect a threat of potential harm or a challenge for opportunity?
- Do I have the resources to handle the situation?
- How do I know that this will indeed happen?
- Are there other ways of looking at the situation?
- There are times when I don't do as well as I would like, but at other times I do. What are the differences?
- Have I had only failures in the past, or were there times I did okay?
- What am I saying (or imaging) to myself when I get uptight?
- What is the evidence for this conclusion?
- Is there evidence that contradicts this conclusion?
- Are there alternative explanations for how I am feeling?

Cognitive therapy has been used with a variety of populations. While the initial results are encouraging, research is continuing to evaluate its efficacy.

Humanistic Approaches

A third major approach to behavior change is designed to nurture the client's already existing abilities and potential. Although there are many different variants of humanistic psychotherapy (for example, Fritz Perls' Gestalt therapy, encounter and sensitivity group experiences, and related existential approaches), we focus on the client-centered approach of Carl Rogers. Rogers (1951) developed a nondirective form of therapy in contrast to the interpretative approach of psychoanalytic therapy and the prescriptive-educational approach of behavior therapy. In this humanistic approach, the therapist attempts to create therapeutic conditions that will foster the client's self-acceptance and personal growth. In order to remove the client's inhibitions, an accepting, genuine, empathic, therapeutic relationship is nurtured. As therapy progresses, the client takes on greater responsibility for developing and implementing treatment plans. The accepting, empathic therapeutic environment permits clients to explore feelings and to develop greater **congruence** between their feelings and their behaviors. In the main clinical technique, **reflection**, the therapist helps clients put into words their feelings and attitudes.

As Raskin (1985) has noted "[T]he therapist aims to capture exactly what the client is consciously feeling and wishing to communicate, evoking in the client a reaction of 'yes, that's exactly it!' which then facilitates exploration and expression of feeling" (p. 165). In this way, the therapist can catch the subtle meanings of the client's statements and reflect them in ways that permit personal awareness and growth. The following example illustrates ways in which a therapist used empathy to help a 40-year-old client better understand his personal relationship (Raskin, 1985).

congruence
consistency between one's feelings and behaviors

reflection
psychotherapist's putting a client's feelings into words

> **Client:** In my relationships with people I find the same thing. I'm no longer blowing off steam in the office. I haven't done this for quite some time. But I do find myself getting angry, as I think everybody does, but holding it inside. And I seem to release it—well, I don't know how I release it, to tell you the truth.
>
> **Therapist:** You're not sure what happens to that anger.
>
> **Client:** I'm not sure what happens to it. I know one thing, when I come home I don't release it there. Occasionally I have, and I really feel this is normal. I really feel that anyone can come home and release their anger at one time or another about certain things that happen at work. And this is accepted because it's not such a big thing. I'm not making a big furor over it at home, but they see that I'm tired and I'm irritable, and so they cooperate and they just leave me alone, and it passes. Under these same conditions I'm not blowing my top. And some time or another it just thwarts itelf.
>
> **Therapist:** M-hm. So you find you're having many of the same reactions as far as getting angry, but there's a difference in your control of the anger, your handling of it and how much you take home with you. It seems to be more easily resolved one way or another. . . .
>
> **Client:** . . . than it has in the past. So I begin to see a lot of things, and, as I conclude it, it's all in my anger against my mother, I believe.
>
> **Therapist:** More than anything, that seems to be the heart of it.

Carl Rogers
developed a
humanistic approach
to therapy.

Client: More than anything, that is the heart of it, I really believe this. Because families are important. I know how important it is to my family. I didn't have the same relationships that my children have.

Therapist: M-hm.

Client: Therefore, if my brothers and sisters react to each other the same way because they are a product of the same parents, we have this anger at each other. We know nothing but anger and hostility.

Therapist: M-hm.

Client: Just to give you an example—did you want to say something?

Therapist: Well, you seem to be saying that the feelings you exhibited toward each other you got from your parents—all of you.

Client: I would think so. (p. 165)

The therapist then helped the client explore how his style of interacting affected his relationships and how he had the potential to overcome such an inhibiting style. Such a humanistic approach holds the most potential for individuals who are functioning relatively well but who wish to further develop their interpersonal relationships and to actualize their potential. These therapeutic goals have been incorporated in group sensitivity training and encounter groups where normal individuals meet to promote personal growth.

DIFFERENT FORMS OF PSYCHOTHERAPY

We now consider a variety of ways psychotherapy may be conducted. Treatment interventions may be at the level of the individual, the family, the group, or even the community.

Individual Psychotherapy

While most forms of individual intervention are brief and limited in time, some forms are long-term, as in the case of psychoanalysis. Brief forms of individual psychotherapy, ranging from four to twenty sessions conducted on a weekly basis are usually applied to clients experiencing difficulties in personal relationships or reactions to situational crises. In fact, a form of problem-oriented *crisis intervention* therapy has been developed to let clients seek help at mental health drop-in centers and psychiatric facilities. The longer-term interventions are usually reserved for clients who suffer from more serious forms of psychopathology or who manifest long-standing, habitual personality disorders. In terms of outcome, there is *little data* to suggest that the more demanding long-term interventions are more effective than short-term interventions (Smith & Glass, 1977). The style and content of individual psychotherapy varies, depending in part on the therapist's conceptual orientation and the treatment goals, as noted previously.

Couples Psychotherapy

In recent years, there has been increasing interest in broadening who is seen in psychotherapy. In many instances, psychotherapists see both the husband and wife (or common-law inhabitants whether of the opposite or same sex). The central notion behind this decision is that the presenting clinical problems are viewed as arising from the social interaction between the client and significant others in his or her life. The need to involve spouses in therapy is indicated by the finding that half of the patients who request psychotherapy do so because of marital discord and that 30 percent of marital problems involve at least one spouse who is clinically depressed. These numbers take on additional significance when we consider that 20 percent of the total population of married couples are maritally distressed (Rush, Khatami, & Beck, 1986). The object of couples treatment is to examine and improve communication by focusing on the interpersonal conflicts, the role expectations, and in some instances, the sexual problems that occur.

Family Therapy

A natural extension of the couples approach is that of family therapy, whereby the therapist (and sometimes a cotherapist) involves other family members. Most often, the therapist includes the children, especially in the case of adolescent-related problems. However, family therapists have seen extended families, including grandparents and other relatives, sometimes covering several generations. Such writers as Jay Haley (1971), Salvador Minuchin (1974) and Virginia Satir (1967) have emphasized the importance of viewing clients' problems as part of an overall family system that contributes to the etiology and maintenance of maladaptive behavior.

Family processes, however, can also be mobilized to foster change. By help-ing the family members make their expectations and rules explicit and become aware of the potential destructive impact of their interactional style, the ther-apist can nurture change. Some family therapists are quite directive in teach-ing family members to communicate more effectively. One can help clients by focusing on significant family members, or in many cases, by involving the client and his or her family members.

Group Psychotherapy

While the use of groups as a forum for change goes back to the turn of this century, it was only after World War II, when clinical services were in high demand, that group psychotherapy was given its greatest impetus. Like indi-vidual psychotherapy, group psychotherapy may take many different forms. Whatever the exact form, common factors seem to mediate behavior change. These factors include a sense of belonging or cohesiveness (we-ness); recogni-tion of the shared universality of one's problems; opportunity for interper-sonal learning resulting from advice giving, feedback, modeling, and perspec-tive taking; the mustering of hope arising from the sense of being valued and helped; and the opportunities to help others, share experience, ventilate feel-ings, and make public commitments to change.

Psychotherapeutic groups usually include six to ten members, and sessions usually last from 1½ to 2 hours. The group members may be homogeneous (sharing a similar clinical problem) or heterogeneous (quite diverse). Some groups are open (members who drop out can be subsequently replaced), while other groups are closed (membership is limited to only those who started in the group).

Yalom (1975) has described the variety of different formats groups may take. These include **sensitivity groups**, or T-groups, where the object is to fos-ter personal awareness and growth, and *encounter groups*, where clients focus on understanding and changing patterns of feeling and thinking. Some group therapists use a procedure called **psychodrama**, introduced by Moreno (1968), in which group members act out various scenes that derive from their own situations (such as family conflicts). Such role-playing can act as a catalyst for increased self-analysis and group discussion.

Group therapy is not limited to professional services. There is a substantial movement toward self-help groups, where individuals who share similar prob-lems come together on a weekly basis to provide support and guidance. The most famous of these are Alcoholics Anonymous and Weight Watchers, but similar groups have emerged for psychiatric patients or (ex)patients, gamblers, parents who abuse children, different types of medical patients, and so forth. These groups usually are run by the members themselves without the pres-ence of professional mental health workers, although such professionals may act as backups or as consultants. Such self-help groups are gaining increasing attention since most people do *not* present their mental health problems to

sensitivity groups form of psychotherapy where groups are used to nurture personal awareness and growth

psychodrama form of group therapy where members act out scenes that depict personal concerns and conflicts

professionally trained healers. Instead, they turn to family members, friends, neighbors, and nonprofessional mutual help groups.

While systematic evaluations of the efficacy of the many forms of group therapy are quite limited, two important observations have been made. First, group psychotherapy is better than no treatment, and moreover, group therapy appears to be as effective as individual therapy. Second, some caution should be followed in entering certain forms of group therapy, especially when the leader tends to be confrontational and inexperienced (Yalom, 1975). A minority of participants who have taken part in encounter groups have experienced adverse personal effects. This is particularly true for those who have had a history of prior emotional difficulties. Each form of psychotherapy has the potential to make clients better or worse (Bergin & Lambert, 1978).

Community-Based Interventions

As part of the movement in community mental health, psychotherapeutic efforts have been directed at the prevention, as well as the treatment, of mental disorders. Programs such as the detection and treatment of school children who are at high risk for developing emotional problems (Zax & Cowen, 1967) and treatment services with widows (Silverman, 1972) illustrate community-based interventions. The reduction of social stressors, the opening of drop-in centers, telephone hot lines, suicide prevention services, mass media educational programs, the training of **paraprofessionals**, and the support of community agencies also indicate the current interest in community-based interventions (Bloom, 1973; Rappaport, 1977).

Clearly, there is a need to embrace a broad definition of treatment, given the tremendous need and the limited professional resources available. Psychotherapy is more than a one-on-one talking cure, or what one of Sigmund Freud's patients called "chimney sweeping." Our changing environment and social demands require a combination of innovation, critical thinking, and new ways of helping while maintaining the highest standards of program evaluation.

paraprofessionals
individuals employed or working as volunteers who have been trained by professional staff to perform therapeutic activities

THE VALUE OF PSYCHOTHERAPY

There are much controversy and heated debate concerning the efficacy of various forms of psychotherapy. In part, this controversy grows out of a realization that many factors influence the outcome of psychotherapy. For example, various indices of change (such as patient self-report; therapist ratings; and behavioral, social, and physiological measures) do not intercorrelate highly. Thus, improvement in one domain may not be evident in another domain. A second complicating factor is that improvement may often occur without formal treatment. People often get better without formal professional interven-

There is much controversy over the effectiveness of psychotherapy.

"MY ASTROLOGER SAYS ONE THING, MY GURU SAYS ANOTHER, MY PSYCHIATRIST SAYS SOMETHING ELSE— I DON'T KNOW WHO TO TURN TO ANYMORE."

tion. Third, the psychotherapeutic treatments offered are so complex that it is difficult to identify the ingredients that lead to change.

These issues were highlighted in an important assessment of the relative efficacy of different forms of the psychotherapy conducted by the English psychologist, Hans Eysenck (1952). Eysenck concluded that psychotherapy (especially, psychoanalytically oriented therapy) was no more effective than no treatment and that behavioral therapy procedures were more effective than psychoanalytically oriented treatment or no treatment. In drawing these conclusions, he also considered the likelihood of patient improvement that would occur due to spontaneous remission (improvement that would occur without formal treatment, as in the case of wound healing). He also considered the degree of change that would occur when patients were placed in placebo or attentional control groups (in which treatments were seen as essentially inert, or as not including active treatment ingredients). In medicine, a placebo is a sugar pill included in studies in order to control for such factors as social expectations of improvement, patient faith, and treatment demand characteristics. In psychotherapy, investigators attempt to create a comparable placebo effect by including treatments that are seen as controlling for suggestion and faith factors (simple discussion groups that do not focus on the client's specific problems).

Eysenck's review drew a storm of criticism, and the subsequent debate underscored the complexities in evaluating psychotherapy. Eysenck was justifiably faulted on several grounds, including his tendency to collapse different types of clients and different types of treatments into single outcome groups when judging the value of psychotherapy. For example, in assessing the usefulness of a particular psychotherapy approach, he did not differentiate or divide the clients into different subtypes, nor was he sensitive to the different indices of outcome. In short, he imposed a **uniformity myth** on clients, treatment, and outcome (Kieslar, 1966). It is as if we asked physicians, "Does surgery work?" The doctor would readily reply, "Which type of surgery? With which patients? Conducted when? By whom? As evident on which measures?" One can raise similar concerns when trying to answer the question Eysenck posed, "Does psychotherapy work?" Instead of such a broad question, there is a need for a more precise question: Which treatment, offered by which therapists, to which clients, and when, as assessed on which measures, and relative to which comparison groups is most effective? Each of these factors influences the judgment about the value of psychotherapy.

In order to consider these multiple factors, many attempts are now under way to carefully analyze the nature of each client's problems and to individually tailor specific forms of intervention. For example, patients suffering from certain forms of depression seem to be most responsive to cognitive therapy; individuals suffering from phobias and obsessions seem to be most responsive to certain forms of behavior therapy; and marital and sex therapy have been offered with some success to distressed couples. However, efforts to develop the precision of matching clients and treatment are still at a preliminary stage, and much research is still needed to assess the relative efficacy of different forms of psychotherapy for different groups of patients. Moreover, some types of patients seem better candidates for psychotherapy—for example, clients who are less severely disturbed and who are motivated for treatment (as evident in the client's seeking treatment of his or her own accord) and are willing to actively participate and follow the therapist's suggestions. The de-

uniformity myth
dubious practice of collapsing clients with different problems, treatments, or outcome measures into one group and overlooking differences

gree to which the client can establish a trusting relationship, the client's psychological mindedness, and his or her ability to self-disclose seem to be important in certain forms of psychodynamic or insight-oriented therapies. Much more research is needed to further identify patient, therapist, and setting characteristics that facilitate the change process.

While we await the results of such research, a legitimate concern is that of the overall general value of psychotherapy. In spite of the many methodological problems, some progress has been made in addressing the issue of psychotherapy effectiveness. Part of the solution has arisen from the use of sophisticated statistical analyses of the outcomes of many psychotherapy studies, which yield composite estimates of the degree of patient change. A procedure called **meta-analysis** permits investigators to compare the outcomes of various psychotherapeutic treatments with those of untreated control groups, taking into consideration several factors, such as the severity of the client's condition. While some controversy surrounds the use of meta-analysis, in terms of collapsing different forms of treatment, the general conclusions from these analyses are worth noting. Smith and Glass (1977) combined the results of 375 psychotherapy outcome studies and concluded, "[T]he average client receiving psychotherapy was better off than 75% of the untreated controls" (p. 754). The effectiveness of psychotherapy varies with the severity of the initial clinical problem, that is, the more disturbed the patient initially, the less effective the treatment. Thus, on the basis of meta-analysis, we can conclude that psychotherapy does work relative to no treatment, especially in cases when the client is not severely or chronically disturbed.

Yet, is one form of psychotherapy better than another, as Eysenck intimated in his review? Once again, heated debate is tempered partly by research. In order to address the question of the relative efficacy of different therapies, researchers use a comparative outcome research design. For example, Sloane and his colleagues (1975) compared behavior therapy with psychoanalytically oriented therapy and a waiting list (minimal contact) control group in the treatment of neurotic outpatients. Six therapists treated ten clinical patients in each treatment group. The results indicated that the two therapy groups were more effective than the control group, but they were not distinguishable from each other. This result is consistent with other studies, in which it was generally found that psychotherapy is better than no treatment but that the results of various forms of psychotherapy are not different from one another. The search for matching specific treatments with specific populations continues. For instance, the National Institute of Mental Health in Washington, DC, has recently sponsored a $3 million multisite psychotherapy study comparing cognitive therapy, interpersonal therapy, and medication for the treatment of depression. The field eagerly awaits the results of such studies, since they will prove helpful in matching specific psychotherapeutic procedures to specific patient groups.

In the interim, it is still not clear that one approach is better than any other treatment approach. In fact, the field of psychotherapy is trying to integrate

meta-analysis
statistical procedure for assessing the aggregate or cumulative efficacy of a procedure such as psychotherapy by combining results across studies

the various forms of psychotherapy. Each school of psychotherapy has been humbled by the results of its efforts, and a dialogue is emerging, whereby psychotherapists are mutually searching for mechanisms common across psychotherapeutic approaches that contribute to change. Thus, we see two important trends in the field of psychotherapy. On the one hand, there are increasing dialogue and searching for common mechanisms that underlie behavior change. On the other hand, there is a continuing search to discover

ON THE RESEARCH FRONTIER

MEDICATION AS A FORM OF HELP

One of the major research topics in the mental health field is the proper role of medication in helping people cope with stress and overcome various forms of psychopathology. The importance of this issue is heightened by the widespread use of psychotropic medication for behavioral and emotional problems. Approximately 10 percent to 15 percent of the adult population in North America take tranquilizers to combat restlessness, anxiety, and related signs of emotional disturbance. Moreover, women consume two thirds to three quarters of all psychotropic medication, and they tend to take such medication for longer periods of time. Most of the prescriptions for tranquilizers and antidepressant medication are offered by general practitioners, not psychiatrists. Although these drugs have beneficial effects on a short-term basis, they may lead to dependence when taken for long periods of time. In some cases, dangerous side effects occur. Clearly, caution and medical supervision are required.

Counterbalancing these concerns is the increasing evidence that pharmacological

agents can play a beneficial role in the treatment of a number of mental disorders. We consider the evidence for three major classes of medication, namely, antianxiety drugs, antidepressant drugs, and antipsychotic drugs. The relevant data are summarized in the following drug fact sheet. As you read the summary research findings on psychotropic medication, keep in mind that medication does *not* cure mental disorders, because a relapse may occur if one stops taking the medication. In some cases, relapses occur even if patients continue to take the medication.

On the positive side, research indicates that psychotropic drugs do have beneficial effects in reducing debilitating symptoms, often making the patient more amenable to other forms of treatment. Research is now under way to determine if there is a synergistic effect, whereby a combination of medication and psychotherapy are more effective than either one alone. For instance, Falloon and his colleagues (1985) have found that the combination of antipsychotic medication and family-based intervention, rather than either alone, is most beneficial in treating schizophrenic

which specific treatment procedures are most applicable to which specific client group. The answer to both of these lines of investigation will help improve the value of psychotherapy. Moreover, as "On the Research Frontier: Medication as a Form of Help" notes, the effectiveness of psychotherapy may be enhanced when it is combined with the use of medication (called psychotropics) to treat individuals with mental disorders. Now that you have read the chapter, consider your own attitudes toward seeking help by reading "Exploring Choices: Attitudes Toward Psychotherapy" on page 246.

patients. Similar studies are now under way with other mentally disturbed patients. While we await the results of these studies, it is important to remember that well-controlled studies convincingly demonstrate that under proper medical supervision, clients suffering from mental disorders benefit from taking medication. The passions surrounding the use of medications should not blind us to their potential benefits.

Drug Fact Sheet

1. **Antianxiety drugs.** There are more than forty different types (for example, muscle relaxants and hypnotics). The most popular is Valium, which combats restlessness, anxiety, and related signs of emotional disturbance. When taken in concert with other drugs, such as alcohol, or even tobacco, the effectiveness of antianxiety drugs may be lessened and side effects may occur.

2. **Antidepressant drugs.** Several different types are available (for example, imipramine for depression and lithium for manic-depression). Such symptoms as self-blame, suicidal ideation, indecision, and mental distraction are reduced and mood improves. The medication can reduce the likelihood of relapse if taken for a sufficiently long time (six to twelve months), even when symptoms of depression are gone. In some instances, there may be a time lag of several weeks between drug intake and signs of symptomatic relief.

3. **Antipsychotic drugs.** The major class of this medication is the phenothiazines (brand names include Thorazine and Stelazine). They reduce thought disorders, withdrawal, and hallucinations, especially in psychiatric patients with a diagnosis of schizophrenia. Their prolonged use, especially in the elderly, can lead to such side effects as psychomotor disturbances (for example, Parkinsonian-like shaking symptoms of the arms known as tardive dyskinesia).

EXPLORING CHOICES

ATTITUDES TOWARD PSYCHOTHERAPY

Imagine that you need psychological help. Would you seek the services of a professional mental health worker? Would you consider entering psychotherapy? What exactly is your attitude toward someone who is in psychotherapy? If you undertook psychotherapy, would you try to hide this fact from your spouse, relatives, friends, neighbors, employer? Does being in psychotherapy carry a stigma in your social circle, does it represent a badge of courage, or does it reflect how much you are with it? If you are not sure, consider asking significant others in your life what they would think about someone who goes into psychotherapy. Their answers may surprise you.

If your psychotherapy appointment interfered with work or with a social engagement what would you tell your employer or friend? Would you make up some excuse, "Oh, I have to visit my doctor," or would you be honest and indicate that you have to visit your psychotherapist, or jokingly, your shrink?

One reason for these questions is the fact that in some cultures, psychotherapists have an office arrangement with a separate entrance and exit. In this way, the client in the waiting room does not see the client who is exiting from the psychotherapy session. This ensures the client's anonymity, but it also reflects the pejorative attitude toward visiting a psychotherapist. The fear in this particular setting is that clients will be penalized at work or in social circles because they are in psychotherapy.

Importantly, the negative attitude toward seeking mental health is changing in North America. Individuals, employers, insurance companies, and government agencies are now recognizing the potential benefits from participation in psychotherapy. The attitudes of society toward psychotherapy are changing. What is your attitude toward psychotherapy? Whether to seek such professional help or some other mode of social support is a choice each of us may have to make.

SUMMARY

1. Psychotherapy has been defined as a therapy process designed to help clients modify their feelings, thoughts, and behaviors. The exact form of psychotherapy varies widely, depending upon the therapist's theoretical orientation, the client characteristics, and the goals of treatment.

2. Although the procedures of psychotherapy vary, the nature of the therapist-client relationship provides an important medium for behavior change. In addition, a number of common factors cut across the diverse procedures. These factors include suggestion, faith, expectation of improvement, explanatory scheme, and features under the heading placebo effect.

3. The three major psychotherapeutic approaches include psychoanalytic, behavioral, and humanistic. Each approach has developed its own specific clinical techniques. The psychoanalytic approach focuses on making the unconscious conscious and on the working-through process. The behavioral approach focuses on the antecedents and consequences of behavior and emphasizes skill training. The humanistic approach focuses on nurturing a therapeutic relationship, whereby personal growth can be achieved. In recent years, the three approaches have become more similar, as the behavioral approach has become more cognitive and the psychoanalytic approach more limited in time.

4. Psychotherapy can take many different forms, including individual, couple, family, group, and community-based. Thus, one should *not* view psychotherapy as limited to a one-on-one talking cure.

5. The evaluation of psychotherapy is complex and difficult. Nevertheless, the treatment outcome literature suggests that psychotherapy is better than no treatment, but at this point, no one approach has proven most effective. In some instances, psychotropic drugs enhance the efficacy of psychotherapy.

6. Much research tries to match the treatment form with the client's specific clinical problems. A second movement in the field of psychotherapy is the attempt to integrate the various therapeutic approaches. This organization should help break down barriers that exist between diverse psychotherapeutic approaches and nurture a more thoughtful integrative treatment approach.

Part 3

RELATIONSHIPS AND SEXUALITY

Chapter 9

SEX ROLES AND RELATIONSHIPS

UNDERSTANDING SEX ROLES

GROWING UP FEMININE AND MASCULINE

The Biological Perspective
Genetic factors
Sex hormones
Brain differences
Differences in physical maturation
Critique of the biological perspective
The Psychoanalytic Perspective
Masculinity and femininity
Critique of the psychoanalytic perspective
The Learning Perspective
Sex-role acquisition
Ethnic, racial, and economic issues
Critique of the social learning perspective
The Cognitive-Developmental Perspective
Cognitive influences on sex-role development
Gender schema theory
Moral development
Critique of the cognitive-developmental perspective

ACTUAL SEX DIFFERENCES

Intellectual Sex Differences
Intellectual abilities
Success and achievement motivation
Behavioral Sex Differences
Verbal communication
Nonverbal communication
Sex differences in dominance
Sex differences in adjustment

SEX-ROLE STEREOTYPES

Myths That Ignore Individual Differences
Harmful Effects of Sex-Role Stereotypes
Overcoming Sex-Role Stereotypes and Sexism

SUMMARY

Imagine for a moment that you wake up to a world without sex differences. In such a world, people would differ in height, skin color, and physical features, but these differences would not say anything about their reproductive or social roles. It would be a world of parents but not of mothers and fathers. Individuals would have different abilities, behaviors, beliefs, and places in the economy, but the differences would not be linked to sex roles. Ursula K. LeGuin (1969) wrote of such a world in her science fiction book, *The Left Hand of Darkness.* Her description of an Earth visitor's reaction to a unisex world is thought provoking.

> *Extraven had conversed amiably at table; now sitting across the hearth from me, he was quiet. Though I had been nearly two years on Winter I was still far from being able to see the people of the planet through their own eyes. I tried to, but my efforts took the form of self-consciously seeing a Gethenian first as a man, then as a woman, forcing him into those categories so irrelevant to his nature and so essential to my own. Thus as I sipped my smoking sour beer I thought that at table Estraven's performance had been womanly, all charm and tact and lack of substance, specious and adroit. Was it in fact perhaps this soft supple feminity that I disliked and distrusted in him? For it was impossible to think of him as a woman, that dark, ironic, powerful presence near me in the firelit darkness, and yet whenever I thought of him as a man I felt a sense of falseness, or imposture; in him, or in my own attitude towards him? His voice was soft and rather resonant but not deep, scarcely a man's voice, but scarcely a woman's voice either . . . but what was it saying? (pp. 17–18)*

Like Earth's ambassador to the planet Winter, we would be confused to find ourselves in a world without sex differences. Throughout our lives, sex is central to our self-image, our relations with others, and our expectations for the future. Sex roles (cultural prescriptions for masculinity and femininity) are intimately entwined with psychological adjustment.

This chapter examines sex roles in our society and describes their relationship to psychological adjustment. It introduces key concepts for understanding sex and sex roles, and discusses four theories about the development of sex differences in children: the (1) biological, (2) psychoanalytic, (3) social learning, and (4) cognitive-developmental perspectives. Finally, the chapter compares actual sex differences with stereotypes about them. Many researchers have been unable to find evidence for popular beliefs about the differences between boys and girls and men and women. Nevertheless, expected and actual differences between males and females have an impact on your mental health, the way you influence others, and how you are treated in society. Throughout, the chapter suggests ways to use your understanding of sex roles to improve your psychological adjustment and personal relationships.

UNDERSTANDING SEX ROLES

Before undertaking the major task of examining the relationship between sex roles and adjustment, it is important to learn new terms. We can start by imagining all the concepts that a Gethenian from Winter would need to learn to understand the importance of sex differences to human beings on Earth.

We might take our Gethenian visitor first to a hospital to witness the birth of twins—one a girl and the other a boy. We would point out how **sex** is distinguished for each: The little girl has a vagina or inwardly folding genitals, whereas the little boy has a penis or outwardly projected genitals. These physical differences reflect an underlying genetic one; the baby girl has XX chromosomes and her baby brother has XY chromosomes. Each twin is destined for different reproductive roles. Only the male twin will be able to impregnate; only the female twin has the potential of bearing children and giving birth.

Lessons continue as we take the Gethenian to a nursery school. We interview several children there, interrupting their play with the question, Are you a girl or a boy? All of the children answer correctly. They have learned to label themselves according to their correct biological sex, **sex identity**, by the time they are two or three years old. As children learn to talk, they gain a permanent sense of who they are.

A party would be an excellent place to point out **sex differences** in physical appearance, clothing, and social behaviors. Here, we could explain that many of the differences in guests' appearances, abilities, and personality characteristics are dictated by **sex roles**, approved ways of demonstrating that one is a girl or boy, or a man or woman. **Sex-role behaviors** are actions orchestrated by the dictates of traditional sex roles.

If the Gethenian asked, "Do the biological differences between the sexes account for sex roles?" we would have to answer no. Most differences between males and females are learned. It would be important to teach the Gethenian about **sex-role development**, the process through which humans acquire culturally approved sex roles. This process is a result of their observations of and experiences with peers, parents, teachers, other adults, and the society at large. To demonstrate this, we could point out a parent or teacher admonishing a girl for pushing another child with the remark, "Girls don't fight," while playmates yell, "Cry baby, sissy, cry baby," in response to a little boy's tearful tantrum.

Our Gethenian guest is likely to wonder if we humans make too much of sex differences. Such an objective outsider is apt to notice that many children and adults behave in ways that are supposed to characterize the opposite sex. To help the Gethenian discriminate real from illusory sex differences, we would have to explain **sex-role stereotypes**. Sex-role stereotypes are beliefs, correct or incorrect, about the qualities that differentiate males and females. Stereotype beliefs help people think about themselves and others in an organized way. Unfortunately, they also may be used to justify prejudices against males or females.

"How do sex-role stereotypes influence the way people feel about themselves?" our alien friend asks.

"That's a good question!" we exclaim. Regardless of whether people recognize themselves as male or female, they may label their actions, beliefs, and feelings, as masculine, feminine, or androgynous. **Sex-role identification** is an

---

sex biological sex of an individual (male versus female), which is assigned at birth

sex identity labeling oneself as a male or female

sex differences differences between males and females in appearance, abilities, behavior, and personality

sex roles culturally approved ways of being a girl or boy, man or woman

sex-role behaviors actions orchestrated by the dictates of expected sex roles

sex-role development process by which children and adolescents learn culturally approved sex roles

sex-role stereotypes correct or incorrect beliefs about the qualities that characterize males and females

sex-role identification self-description of psychological sex, regardless of biological sex and sex identity

individual's self-described personality or psychological sex, regardless of biological sex and sex identity. Hence either men or women might describe themselves as **masculine** (like the typical boy or man), **feminine** (like the typical girl or woman), or **androgynous** (exhibiting characteristics of both males and females).

masculine like the typical boy or man

feminine like the typical girl or woman

androgynous exhibiting personality characteristics that typify both males and females

Attempts to educate our Gethenian guest would be incomplete without an explanation of the sexual division of labor and sex-role attitudes. The **sexual division of labor** refers to the fact that men and women are often assigned different economic and family responsibilities. In our society, men are expected to work outside the home, providing for most or all of their families' economic needs. Women, on the other hand, are expected to provide most of the child care and homemaking services whether or not they are employed outside the home. Because women are regarded as less career-oriented and tend to enter sex-segregated occupations (such as food service and clerical work), their jobs generally pay less than men's jobs and are viewed—often quite erroneously—as less critical to their own and their family's economic survival (Tavris & Wade, 1984).

sexual division of labor economic and family responsibilities that are assigned to each sex

Sex-role attitudes are beliefs about the rightness or wrongness of society's current sexual division of labor. **Egalitarian** people have more liberal sex-role attitudes; they believe that men and women should be equal under the law and in the economy. **Traditional** people have conservative sex-role attitudes; they uphold a sexual division of labor that assigns different responsibilities and rights to men and women strictly on the basis of sex.

sex-role attitudes beliefs about the rightness or wrongness of society's sexual division of labor

GROWING UP FEMININE AND MASCULINE

egalitarian favoring positions regarding equal rights and responsibilities for men and women

traditional believing women should be homemakers and mothers, whereas men should be the economic and political leaders

Now that you understand the key concepts, it is appropriate to ask how sex roles become established. Researchers have been asking the same question and have developed four theories for the development of sex differences in children: the biological, psychoanalytic, social learning, and cognitive-developmental perspectives. According to the biological perspective, males and females differ because genetic, hormone, and structural differences program them to take separate developmental paths. The psychoanalytic perspective, based in part on the biological perspective, argues that physical differences between girls' and boys' genitals destine them for radically different sex roles in adulthood. The social learning perspective depicts the acquisition of sex-role behaviors and sex-role identification as quite flexible. Depending on what an individual child observes and experiences, he or she is likely to acquire any number of masculine, feminine, or androgynous characteristics. The cognitive-developmental perspective emphasizes how the various stages of maturation shape ideas about masculinity and femininity and associated behaviors.

The Biological Perspective

The biological perspective examines the impact of physical differences between males and females on sex-role development and sex-role behaviors.

Four different
theories attempt to
explain the
development of sex
differences in
children.

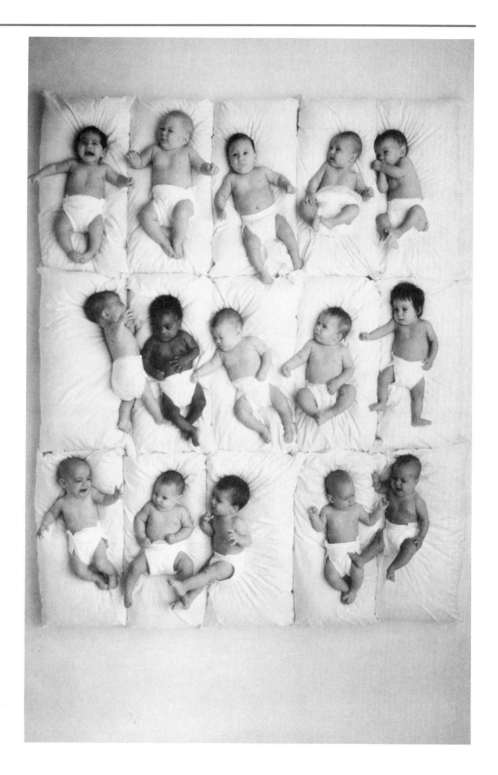

Four biological factors are relevant to the study of sex differences: (1) genetic factors, (2) sex hormones, (3) brain differences, and (4) developmental differences.

Genetic factors. Only one pair of the total of forty-six chromosomes determines an infant's sex, an X chromosome from the mother and either an X or a Y chromosome from the father. The XX sex chromosomes program a fertilized egg to become a girl, and the XY chromosomes program a fertilized egg to become a boy. The single cell of the fertilized egg soon multiplies rapidly to form an embryo. The embryo's rudimentary organs are truly unisex; it contains growth buds that might form into either male or female sex organs. After the first six weeks of life, the sex chromosomes begin to send mesages that cause the embryo to develop either male or female sex organs and manufacture hormones that contribute further to the physical differences between the sexes. Sex hormones may also be involved in establishing a predisposition for different behaviors for girls and boys.

In contrast with the sex-role stereotype of the strong male and the weak female, research suggests that females may be genetically superior to males. Females have a pair of genes controlling every sex-linked trait, while males, with their single X chromosome, have only one gene for each trait. As a result, females are less likely than males to exhibit a bad trait inherited from one parent. They are less susceptible than males to sex-linked genetic diseases and learning disabilities, including reading problems (Seward & Seward, 1980). In addition, males have a higher death rate than females throughout the life span (Gersh & Gersh, 1981).

sex hormones powerful chemicals produced by the endocrine glands that influence physical appearance and reproduction

Sex hormones. The bodies of females and males manufacture different proportions of **sex hormones,** powerful chemicals produced by the endocrine glands (Hyde, 1985). **Estrogens**, a group of hormones that feminize physical appearance and facilitate **ovulation** (the release of a mature egg from a woman's ovary) are produced at higher levels in women's bodies (Allgeier & Allgeier, 1984). Males produce higher levels of **androgens,** a group of hormones that increase sexual desire and masculinize physical appearance.

estrogens hormones that feminize physical appearance and facilitate ovulation

Most people realize that sex hormones play an important role during adolescence, the period between childhood and adulthood, during which young people achieve sexual and reproductive maturity. However, different levels of sex hormones are also critical to human development **prenatally**, in the time between conception and birth (Hyde, 1985).

ovulation release of a mature egg from a woman's ovary

Research with laboratory animals suggests that some behavioral sex differences may be triggered by hormones, especially the presence or absence of the so-called male sex hormone androgen (Gersh & Gersh, 1981; Money & Tucker, 1975). Regardless of sex, animals with a lot of androgen in their bodies are aggressive, mount others during mating, actively explore their environment, and are slow to respond to a baby animal's distress. Conversely, animals with low levels of androgen are passive, allow themselves to be mounted, lack curiosity about their environment, and are quick to assist a baby animal. In

androgens group of hormones that increase sexual desire and masculinize physical appearance

prenatally in the time between conception and birth

lower animals, it seems that male dominance and female passivity are triggered by hormones.

In some studies, children exposed to abnormal prenatal levels of androgen reveal sex differences in behavior consistent with animal research. For example, girls exposed to too much androgen are likely to be tomboys and to embrace career over marriage and family goals (Money & Tucker, 1975). In contrast, boys exposed to abnormally low amounts of androgen are quieter and less interested in competitive sports than other boys are. However, these findings do not prove that prenatal hormones alone cause children to reject or accept expected sex roles. Parental expectations probably play a role that is equally important or even more important.

Hormones are less important in determining behavior for human beings than they are for lower animals. Thanks to our highly developed brains, environment, experience, learning, and individual preferences are probably more important in accounting for sex differences in our society and the sexual division of labor.

hemisphere half of
the brain

lateralized having
specific kinds of
thinking and behavior
controlled by each
hemisphere of the
brain

Brain differences. Numerous studies comparing the mental abilities of males and females suggest that females are superior in verbal tasks throughout the life span and that beginning with adolescence, males have superior mathematical and spatial abilities (Seward & Seward, 1980). Some scientists have speculated that the brains of men and women are organized differently. For most individuals, each **hemisphere** (half of the brain) assumes different functions. The left hemisphere often controls speech and language, abilities in which females excel. In contrast, the right hemisphere specializes in spatial and nonverbal concept formation, abilities that are stronger in males (Gersh & Gersh, 1981). People vary according to how much their brains are **lateralized**, or have specific intellectual functions controlled by only one hemisphere. Is it possible that male-female differences in lateralization account for some of the supposed sex differences in mental abilities?

Despite the excitement this area of research has stirred in the popular press, the results of research are inconclusive (Hyde, 1985). At this time, it's unclear whether either sex is more likely to have a dominant hemisphere or to use both hemispheres equally to solve problems. It may be that girls' superiority in intellectual tasks during childhood and boys' superiority in mathematical and spatial tasks beginning with adolescence are accounted for by the way the brain develops as children mature. Girls may be more lateralized in the early years and boys may be more lateralized later on.

colicky having an
upset stomach because
of the infant's
immature digestive
system

Differences in physical maturation. In contrast with the confusing results regarding brain lateralization, research is quite clear regarding sex differences in physical maturation. During both infancy and adolescence, girls mature earlier than boys. These physical differences may influence the adults who play major roles in children's sex-role development. For example, parents may talk to baby girls more because baby boys are more likely to be **colicky** (have immature digestive systems) and therefore may be less receptive to soothing parental banter (Parsons, 1980). Exposed to more parental speech, girls then might learn to speak earlier and better than boys.

Genetic and hormonal differences also program the sexes to have different physical strengths, which in turn have an impact on sex-role development. Infant boys are slightly larger at birth than infant girls (Gersh & Gersh, 1981). During adolescence, boys develop deeper voices, denser bones and skulls, and greater muscle strength than girls. These physical differences could contribute to expectations from others that males be more physically active and aggressive than females.

Critique of the biological perspective. The biological perspective is an overly simplistic explanation for human sex differences. In contrast with lower animals (whose actions are more automatic), learning and cognition play key roles in determining masculine and feminine behavior in human beings. For example, the higher death rate for boys and men compared with that for women and girls is probably not the result of genetic factors alone. Instead, there appears to be a complex interaction between biology and learning. Consistent with traditional sex roles, which dictate that males should be highly active and willing to take risks, boys may be more likely than girls to have accidents. The stressful life-style of middle-aged men, combined with their tendencies to consume more tobacco and alcohol than women, probably puts them at higher risk for developing heart disease.

The more advanced the organism, the less important sex hormones are in determining characteristic behaviors. Environment, experience, and individual preferences appear to be more critical to a child's interests and characteristic behaviors than the balance of prenatal androgens. The belief that the brain is organized differently in males and females is still largely unsubstantiated. The only clear impact that biology has is maturational; girls mature socially earlier than boys and are treated differently as a result.

The Psychoanalytic Perspective

phallic stage according to psychoanalysts, the ages of three to six, when children are supposed to be in love with their opposite-sexed parent and begin masturbation

clitoris female's most sexually responsive genital tissues

Chapter 2 provides an excellent summary of the psychoanalytic perspective espoused by Freud, the father of modern psychotherapy. Essentially, this perspective maintains that human development occurs in particular stages, each organized according to the zone of the body that provides the most sexual pleasure. The psychoanalytic perspective argues that sex roles and the roots of the traditional sexual division of labor begin during the **phallic stage** in childhood, ages three to six (Freud, 1940/1969).

According to Freud, children realize that males and females have different genitals during the phallic stage. Freud considered the **clitoris**, the female's most sexually responsive genital tissues, to be an inferior sort of penis (Freud, 1933/1965). Freud believed that women's inferior role in society was based on their inferior genitals.

castration complex
according to
psychoanalysts, a small
boy's fear of losing his
penis for being in love
with his mother

Masculinity and femininity. Orthodox psychoanalysts believe that boys develop a **castration complex**, anxiety that their fathers will cut off their penises upon discovering that they have a crush on their mothers, during the phallic stage. To handle this anxiety, boys begin identifying with their fathers instead of their mothers and take on masculine sex roles. The psychoanalytic perspective does not consider the possibilities of androgynous sex-role identification and considers men with feminine interests to be disturbed.

After an initial attachment to their mothers, psychoanalysts believe that girls develop a crush on their fathers, which will be the basis for later hetero-sexual attachments. However, when girls begin to examine and play with their genitals, they develop **penis envy**, concluding that they are inferior to males because the clitoris is much smaller than the penis. Normal female sex-role identification is difficult. Girls and women must continue to have positive feelings about their fathers and other males while establishing a positive identification with their mothers, who like them, have the allegedly inferior sex organs. Penis envy is resolved only by identifying closely with the mother, desiring to be a homemaker, and eventually having children, especially sons.

penis envy according
to psychoanalysts, a
small girl's conclusion
that her clitoris is
inferior to a boy's
penis

masculinity complex
according to
psychoanalysts, a
female's behaving like
a male to compensate
for a sense of
inferiority

The psychoanalytic perspective assumes that many girls and women never adjust to the absence of a penis, developing a **masculinity complex**, or behaving like a stereotypical male instead. Freud could not accept tomboy girls, career women, women who chose to remain childless, and **lesbians** (women who prefer other women as lovers) as normal. He saw them as suffering from a masculinity complex, because he equated traditional sex roles and the acceptance of sex-role stereotypes with mental health.

lesbians women who
prefer other women as
lovers

Critique of the psychoanalytic perspective. Freud's beliefs about women were very much a product of the prevailing medical and philosophical ideologies of his times. It is not surprising, then, that his ideas have been criticized by modern psychoanalytic thinkers such as psychiatrist Karen Horney (1967), who argued that penis envy and the masculinity complex were shaped by male-dominated society, not biological destiny. Instead of suffering from penis envy, Horney believed women were envious of the superior privileges available to men in a society that does not treat men and women equally.

Researchers criticized orthodox psychoanalytic ideas for other reasons. First, the psychoanalytic perspective consists of a set of vague, untestable speculations based on a few therapists' experiences with a few clients. Concepts such as the unconscious, castration anxiety, and penis envy do not lend themselves to well-designed experiments or survey research. Second, the psychoanalytic perspective explains sex-role development in an overly complex and confusing manner. Finally, some recent research challenges Freud's assumptions that recognition of genital differences during the preschool years has a significant impact on sex-role development and identification. A study by Goldman and Goldman (1982) found that most children in our culture don't fully understand the genital differences between males and females until age nine. Their findings make it difficult to accept Freud's beliefs that sex-role development is a reaction to genital differences noticed by youngsters ages three to six.

The Learning Perspective

The learning perspective assumes that life experiences play a major role in the development and maintenance of sex differences. Children learn about sex roles much the way they learn in general, through rewards and punishments. They are more likely to repeat behaviors that are praised and avoid behaviors that bring negative consequences. Often, girls are perceived as better behaved than boys. One of the major reasons is that girls are more praised than boys for good behavior and are more likely to be scolded for bad behavior (Mischel, 1970).

Children don't need rewards and punishments to learn about sex roles; they also learn about sex roles by watching others. Observational learning takes place when children imitate **models**, that is, other children and adults they know and those they see in books, in movies, and on television.

models people others imitate during observational learning

Sex roles are acquired in part because children and adolescents are more likely to imitate models of the same sex (Mischel, 1970). The little boy who mows the grass dutifully—with his plastic lawn mower—alongside his father, the little girl dressed in her mother's stockings and high heels, and the junior-high student who insists on buying the same brand of jeans as his or her friends at school exemplify the power of observational learning.

Expectations about which behaviors will be rewarded and which will be ignored or punished are also critical. Children may want to imitate a behavior they observe but fail to act it out because of the consequences. For example, even after watching an aggressive model, girls are often less physically aggressive than boys. In part, this occurs because girls realize that people have less tolerance for physically aggressive girls than for physically aggressive boys. However, psychologists have found that when girls are rewarded for being physically aggressive, they are just as rambunctious as boys.

Sex-role acquisition. Although children learn about sex roles from many sources, the messages are tempered by their unique ethnic, racial, and economic backgrounds. Families teach children a great deal about sex roles, especially during the first six years of life. Parents and siblings of the same sex serve as models for appropriate sex-role behavior. In addition, parents do not treat sons and daughters alike, which tends to increase sex differences.

Mothers are more likely to touch, talk to, and handle infant daughters than infant sons (Mischel & Mischel, 1971). These maternal behaviors may be responsible in part for the tendencies of girls to touch, talk to, and be more dependent on their mothers than boys. Female dependency is strengthened by the fact that many parents are overprotective of their daughters. Typically, girls enjoy less freedom than boys to take physical risks, select their own activities and companions, be away from home, and come home late.

Parents of the same sex serve as models for children.

On the other hand, parents may subject their sons to harsher sex-role train-ing than their daughters. Fathers in particular react more negatively when a preschool boy acts like a "sissy" or chooses a girl's activity than when a girl plays roughly or acts like a tomboy. Children learn their lessons well. By age five, children know that their parents prefer boys to engage in typically mascu-line activities and girls to engage in typically feminine activities (Mischel & Mischel, 1971).

Boys usually are spanked and scolded more than girls (Brooks-Gunn & Mat-thews, 1979). Boys may comply less easily than girls to adult demands as a result of both a biological predisposition to be more physically aggressive and parental expectations. After beginning school, boys get less warmth and phys-ical affection from parents than do girls. Colder treatment from parents may interfere with the development of the capacities of boys and men for nur-turance and intimacy.

Brothers and sisters also serve as models of sex-appropriate behavior (Brooks-Gunn & Matthews, 1979). Boys with older brothers prefer masculine games, like baseball, more than boys with older sisters, who like feminine and androgynous games, such as jacks and farmer-in-the-dell. In fact, siblings may encourage more rigid sex roles than parents do. Weis and Sacalis (1982) found that children from a suburban day-care center were more likely to provide nonstereotyped descriptions of the ideal family's sexual division of labor if they had few or no brothers and sisters.

Children imitate others who are more like themselves (Mischel, 1970). For this reason, friends and classmates of the same sex can be very influential. From elementary school through high school, the sexes are relatively segre-gated in cliques of boys or girls. These friendship groups teach sex-role appro-priate behavior as understood by the group leaders. In this manner, young people's preferred activities and values may be relatively independent of those taught by their parents.

Compared with girls, boys have more academic and behavioral problems during the early years of school, when female teachers predominate. There is no research support for the accusation that female teachers cause boys' school problems by favoring girls. Instead, boys mature somewhat more slowly, catching up with girls in the higher grades (Pleck, 1981).

More than teachers, children's textbooks may play a critical role in sex-role development by defining social realities. Children's first schoolbooks discuss boys more than girls and associate boys with actions such as answering, shout-ing, thinking, working, and playing (Freebody & Baker, 1985). Girls, in turn, are more likely to be described as little and to be associated with dependency on others through concepts like love, holding on to someone else, and kissing.

Illustrations in elementary school textbooks depict substantially fewer fe-males than males and show boys interacting in a world of action and energy while girls passively watch and wait for boys (Weiner, 1980). Throughout these books, girls focus their time on increasing their attractiveness and are allowed the full gamut of emotions, while boys are shown being skillful, ad-venturous, and emotionally controlled. Illustrations of adult men and women follow the same rigid sex-role stereotypes. Men are shown in over a hundred occupational roles, whereas women are either ignored or depicted disproportionately as mothers and homemakers. Despite the clamor against sexist books in recent years, numerous children's books retain sex-role stereotypes.

Popular culture in the form of newspapers, magazines, music, radio, film, and especially television plays a tremendous part in sex-role development. In printed and televised advertisements, women continue to be depicted largely in the home, dependent upon men, and unable to make important and independent decisions (Courtney & Whipple, 1983). Today, as in the past, men more than women are portrayed as having the option of becoming economically and personally successful through their own achievements.

Television probably has the greatest impact on sex-role development for young children, whose family set is turned on about six hours every day (Richmond-Abbott, 1983). Prime-time television is more likely to depict men as economic providers and leaders than women. Female characters are even more underrepresented and passive in children's cartoon shows than in general audience programming (Williams, LaRose, & Frost, 1981). Not surprisingly, preschool children who have little exposure to television develop less stereotyped ideas about sex roles and the sexual division of labor than frequent viewers do (Weis & Sacalis, 1982). To raise your consciousness about the sex-role choices depicted in television, work through the exercise in "Exploring Choices: Sex Roles in Children's Television" on page 264.

Ethnic, racial, and economic issues. Most of the research presented on sex-role development is based on children in the **middle class** from white families. But the United States is not a homogeneous society. Many children are from ethnic and racial minorities, and many children live in families from the **lower class** or the **working class**.

Working- and lower-class families may teach more rigid sex roles than middle- and upper-class families do (Weitzman, 1979). Youngsters from less affluent families often can distinguish between male and female sex roles at earlier ages. In addition, they hold more traditional sex-role attitudes than do affluent children. Often working-class and lower-class families are organized in more sex-segregated ways than are middle-class families (Rubin, 1976). Instead of the husband-wife togetherness that characterizes the middle class, working-class men tend to socialize with other men more than with their wives, and working-class women tend to spend more time with female relatives and friends than with their husbands.

Working-class boys often adhere to more masculine sex roles than do middle-class boys (Weitzman, 1979). In the working-class world, there are more severe sanctions for acting feminine or crying. Because of limited family income, boys may be obliged to act like little men and assume part-time work at an early age to help the family financially. Working-class girls are given a consistent message: Be nurturant and relationship oriented; being a mother and homemaker is more important than paid employment during adulthood. In

middle class unwealthy but relatively educated white-collar people whose incomes match or exceed the national average

lower class uneducated, unemployed or underemployed people who struggle with poverty, live in substandard housing, and may require public welfare funds to survive

working class people with limited formal education earning average or below-average income, usually employed in skilled or semiskilled blue-collar occupations

EXPLORING CHOICES

SEX ROLES IN CHILDREN'S TELEVISION

Spend between one and three hours watching children's television programs and advertisements on a commercial station Saturday morning or after school. As you watch these programs, perhaps with children you know or your own, take notes on the kinds of sex-role messages that are being provided. Give examples from particular programs or advertisements in answering the following questions:

1. What ideas about sex roles, sex-role stereotypes, sex-role identification, and the expected sexual division of labor are presented?
2. How do programs and advertisements communicate these sex roles?

3. What happens if a male or female fails to adhere to expected or traditional roles?

4. If you are fortunate enough to have children present while you do this exercise, ask them to tell you in their own words what they have learned about the differences between boys and girls and men and women from watching television.

5. How, if at all, would you like to rewrite these programs and advertisements? Could television be changed to provide youngsters with an expanded view of the sex-role choices that are open to them?

contrast, the middle-class girl receives a mixed message: Be feminine but also achievement oriented.

Ironically, rigid expectations about the ideal sexual division of labor are difficult to maintain among the very poor. Lower-class women, particularly poor minority women, have always had to work outside the home *and* take care of their families.

In low-income groups, black men experience high rates of unemployment, and many single-parent families are headed by the mother. Poorly designed studies, which ignored cultural differences and harsh economic realities, have falsely concluded that black men are belittled and undervalued in the lower-class black family while girls and women are given preferential treatment (Pleck, 1981). Careful consideration of the research shows such a conclusion to be simplistic and negative. Black men are just as masculine as white men; however, they are particularly likely to lack educational and economic opportunities. Black women do not enjoy any special advantages compared with black men and white women (Smith, 1982). At college, black women are very much like white women; and both these groups have lower educational and career aspirations than men do.

Critique of the social learning perspective. Despite its appeal, the learning perspective has limitations in explaining human sex differences. First, every individual has a unique learning history that may or may not determine the general pattern of sex-role behaviors. Each ethnic group, social group, and even family presents somewhat different models for appropriate masculine and feminine behavior and varying consequences for conforming to those models. Second, the learning perspective is overly simplistic, ignoring the impact of maturation and biological influences on human behavior. Finally, learning theorists sometimes disregard the fact that individuals may react to the same stimulus differently. For example, one girl may imitate a male television character's independent and assertive behavior because she sees herself more like the male hero than like the subordinate, female characters in the program. Another girl may consider being a male hero unappealing and identify with the passive female who is rescued.

The social learning perspective has not been as effective as researchers had hoped in challenging children's sex-role stereotypes by teacher modeling, changing the home environment, and presenting nonstereotyped behavior in television commercials (Katz, 1986). In general, girls are more receptive than boys in learning new sex-role behaviors and attitudes. However, social learning efforts, when they work at all, are more effective with children ages four to ten than with younger or older individuals. In fact, attempts to change young adolescent boys' sex-role stereotypes have sometimes backfired. In one study, junior high school boys appeared to be more rigidly masculine after being exposed to nontraditional sex roles than before. The sensitive male figures depicted in the program probably contrasted too strongly with the boys' self-image and the more traditional ideal of masculinity reinforced by others.

The Cognitive-Developmental Perspective

According to the cognitive-developmental perspective, maturation and reasoning are not learned but are triggered by innate processes in the developing individual (Katz, 1986).

Cognitive influences on sex-role development. After they learn to talk, children teach themselves about sex roles by actively searching for information about how boys and girls are supposed to act (Parsons, 1983). Unfortunately, the learning experience is hampered by their limited intellectual abilities. Preschool children engage in **concrete thinking**, basing their ideas only on what they have seen or heard. They also **overgeneralize**, or apply a handful of ideas to too many situations. As a result, preschool children generally have very rigid sex-role stereotypes. To the amusement and sometimes despair of their parents, these stereotypes persist even when their families advocate nontraditional family roles. Children believe that mothers do all the housework and child care, while fathers work outside the home even when the mothers have jobs and the fathers cook, clean, and help take care of them (Carlson, 1984). Most sex-role stereotyped gifts like dolls for girls and footballs for boys are

concrete thinking ideas based only on what is seen or heard

overgeneralize to apply a handful of ideas to too many situations

requested by young children rather than being selected by parents (Robinson & Morris, 1986).

Young children may not be capable of understanding that the world can be looked at from many perspectives. They sort experiences into rigid either-or categories, such as things that mommies do and things that daddies do. It is only with greater intellectual maturity that they recognize that mommies and daddies, men and women, can and often do the same things (Allgeier & McCormick, 1983).

Gender schema theory. Cognitive theorists have been concerned with the fact that beliefs about differences and sex-role stereotypes are widespread in the culture. The many differences people believe exist between males and females cannot be explained by biological principles and learning alone. One researcher, Bem (1981), theorized that children learn far more than simply which behaviors and qualities are linked with which sex. They also learn to process all new information in terms of **gender schema**, that is, rigid categories about what boys and girls, men and women, can be and do.

According to Bem, gender schema are so structured that children and adults come to think about the two sexes as "not only different in degree but different in kind" (p. 355). For example, children think categorically that boys are strong and girls are nurturing. Because of gender schema, they are unable to consider the possibility at any level that girls could be strong or boys could be nurturant. Bem believes that gender schema blind people to the similarities between males and females, actively encouraging children and adults to evaluate themselves and interpret almost all experience in terms of the differences between masculinity and feminity.

Moral development. For many years, cognitive theorists have been concerned with **moral development**, children's understanding of and adherance to rules that define the right way to treat others. According to Kohlberg, children progress through a predetermined sequence of moral stages (Dacey, 1979). Kohlberg's research suggested that females are less morally developed than are males because most conform to please others instead of understanding the rules governing appropriate conduct. Gilligan (1977) argued that Kohlberg's theory reflected a male bias and concluded that females progress through a different set of moral stages than males do. In her research, Gilligan found that girls and women were less judgmental, more self-sacrificing, and more concerned about not hurting others than were boys and men.

Critique of the cognitive-developmental perspective. The newest of all theoretical models explaining sex differences, the cognitive-developmental perspective is beset by a number of problems. Like psychoanalytic theory, cognitive theory is difficult to test in experiments and survey research. Concepts like gender schema and stage of moral development do not lend themselves to direct observation. More importantly, researchers have failed to do enough research across the life span to support their cognitive-developmental ideas. For the

---

gender schema
cognitive structures that organize how people perceive males and females and determine personal sex-role identification

moral development
sequence of stages based on cognitive maturity, which determine understanding of and adherence to rules defining the right way to treat others

most part, researchers have used adolescent and young adult subjects, and they have largely ignored middle-aged and elderly persons. Finally, many studies suggest that what people think and believe does not always determine how they act. For example, ideas about sex and sex roles become increasingly flexible during late childhood and adolescence—the very time when children often adhere to rigid sex-role stereotypes (Katz, 1986). Peer group pressure may influence young people to act like traditional females or males even when the young people accept the possibility of androgynous traits and the merit of equality in relationships.

While the cognitive-developmental perspective compensates for some of the deficits in learning theorists' explanations of sex-role development, neither theory has been completely corroborated by research. As a result, the most useful way to think about sex-role development is to consider a combination of biological, learning, and cognitive issues.

ACTUAL SEX DIFFERENCES

It may come as a surprise that relatively few differences between males and females have been confirmed. However, even these should be regarded with a critical eye. Within any group—of girls and boys, men and women—a substantial minority always excel at some skill or engage in some behavior that is supposedly characteristic of the opposite sex. Moreover, these differences may change or even fade as our society continues to change.

Intellectual Sex Differences

Intelligence is the ability to adapt the new situations and make sense out of experiences. Which sex is more intelligent? In this section, we take a look at the running controversy and see what science has to say about it.

Intellectual abilities. In their comprehensive review of numerous studies, Maccoby and Jacklin (1974) report no differences between males and females in general intellectual ability and the capacity to study, learn, and memorize information. However, as mentioned earlier, males and females show different levels of skill in some areas. Females perform better than males on verbal tasks throughout the life span. They are better readers, have greater vocabularies, and are able to use verbal concepts more abstractly. Males are more likely than females to excel in quantitative skills.

The early difficulties of males with verbal skills and later difficulties of females with quantitative skills may be self-fulfilling prophecies. While there are no sex differences in young children's quantitative abilities, males begin to outshine females by late childhood and early adolescence, when visual-spatial skills become critical (Maccoby & Jacklin, 1974). Then, males are more likely to pursue technical careers than are females. Hyde (1985) has proposed two reasons for this: (1) the subject matter is usually easier for them and (2) they are willing to take a greater number of math and science courses to improve their quantitative abilities (Hyde, 1985). When individuals believe that they can't do well at something, they develop a sense of helplessness and stop trying. As Hyde (1981) has pointed out, sex differences in verbal and quantitative-spatial abilities are too small to explain the sex segregation that characterizes some occupations. Perhaps many capable women avoid training for careers in which they see little chance of success in overcoming sexual stereotypes.

Success and achievement motivation. The differences between men and women in the work force are far greater than any differences in verbal and quantitative abilities. Few women are found in top management positions, nor are most women paid as much as most men. Researchers have tried to explain these discrepancies psychologically. Perhaps, they argue, women are less motivated to succeed than men. Or given their unique learning experiences, women may direct their efforts toward social and interpersonal achievements and devalue success in the competitive academic and work worlds. For example, when asked to respond to ambiguous pictures, women are less likely than men to make up stories emphasizing achievement themes after completing a task that supposedly measured their intelligence and organizational abilities (Maccoby & Jacklin, 1974). However, after they have been told that their previous contributions to a discussion group predict social acceptability and overall popularity, women tell more achievement-related stories than men given the same ambiguous pictures.

As described in Chapter 3, Horner (1972) in the late 1960s and early 1970s tried to cast some light on motivational problems that contribute to women's functioning more poorly than men in achievement situations. She asked college students to complete a story that describes an individual of the same sex, Anne or John, reaching the top of the medical school class. Horner found that women were much more likely than men to describe the successful medical student as a social reject, as anxious about self-worth and sex role, or as clearly fictitious. When such negative imagery was present in a story, Horner concluded that the students suffered from fear of success, a motive to avoid success.

Horner's work seemed like a promising way to explain women's failure to achieve as much as men in academic circles and business. However, some recent studies have found that about the same number of men as women tell fear of success stories (Romer, 1977). Research has also challenged Horner's contention that women fail to achieve only because they believe that success will make them unpopular or masculine. For example, Peplau (1976a, 1976b) failed to find a relationship between female college students' fear of success and the women's own sex-role attitudes, career aspirations, college grades, scores on the Scholastic Aptitude Test (SAT), and self-ratings of intelligence. Peplau reported that women who were high in fear of success performed just as well when they competed against their steady boyfriends as they did when their boyfriends were teammates.

Both men and
women may suffer
from fear of success.

"DON'T YOU SEE RICK — YOUR SLUMP IS JUST
A SUCCESS NEUROSIS. You FOUND YOUR
.394 AVERAGE DANGEROUS, BECAUSE YOU
FANTASIED THAT IT WOULD BRING ABOUT
RESENTMENT..."

Peplau believes that traditional sex-role attitudes are a better predictor of women's difficulties in achievement situations than is fear of success. In contrast with egalitarian women, who performed better when competing against their boyfriends, traditional women performed significantly better when on their boyfriends' teams than when in individual competition against them.

Also, traditional college women had substantially lower career aspirations, SAT verbal scores, and self-rated intelligence than egalitarian women.

As the research shows, men and women seem to suffer from different kinds of success anxiety. Females who are high in fear of success worry that personal achievements may be made at the expense of interpersonal relationships (Romer, 1977). In contrast, males with the same fear devalue success itself. To these males, "[T]he drive for success makes life one-sided and therefore unfulfilling; where success takes priority over humanitarian concerns, life is seen as unrewarding" (Schnitzer, 1977, p. 280).

Perhaps it is time to reevaluate whether it is worthwhile to sacrifice intimate relationships in order to be a success. Increasing numbers of men share women's serious doubts about competitive achievement. Instead of trying to cure women of the fear of success, it may be more fruitful to help men and women make better choices. Ideally, people should be free to have satisfying interpersonal relationships and opportunity for individual achievement.

Behavioral Sex Differences

In our society, men and women have characteristic ways of communicating with others. These communication patterns are important in understanding the relationships between sex roles and dominance, that is, how men and women influence others and are influenced in turn. Sex differences in verbal and nonverbal communication and the exercise of power are discussed next.

status respect due to an individual by virtue of his or her place in society

Verbal communication. Generally, people who have high **status** or importance in our culture are addressed formally by their last names and titles (President Reagan, Prime Minister Thatcher). People with lower status usually are called by their first names. By virtue of the traditional sexual division of labor, men are more likely than women to have titles, be addressed by their last names, and address subordinates by their first names. For example, a physician (who is usually male) must be addressed as Dr. Jones but is free to call a nurse (who is usually female) by her first name.

The manner in which individuals address others, and their characteristic speech patterns and phrases, convey much about a person's status. In a study of people with high and low status, Henley (1977) found that when people with high status talk, they do not hedge, hesitate, or use a questioning tone of voice the way their subordinates do. Some authors have suggested that women use less powerful patterns of speech. However, their hedging, hesitating, and questioning speech is more a reflection of their place in the work force; being female alone does not create low status. As Henley (1977) commented, "[W]hen status differences are controlled, sex differences do not necessarily appear" (p. 101).

Another common misconception is that women talk more than men and interrupt conversations more frequently. Study after study has shown just the opposite: Men speak more often and at greater length than women and interrupt other speakers more than women do (Henley, 1977). When individuals of the same sex are talking, overlapping speech and interruptions are distributed fairly evenly among the speakers. However, in conversations among men and women, virtually all interruptions and overlaps are made by male speakers (Lips, 1981). In addition, men are more successful than women in introducing new topics of conversation. Taken as a whole, these findings suggest that men exert more power over conversation than do women and that such control may be a sign of the greater prestige associated with the male sex role.

Women also have the reputation of being more willing to self-disclose than men. In fact, some researchers, such as Jourard (1964), have claimed that low **self-disclosure** is partly responsible for men's psychological and physical problems. Recent studies, however, have failed to find expected sex differences in self-disclosure (Pleck, 1981). On the other hand, there is evidence that men disclose about less sensitive topics than do women and restrict their most intimate self-disclosures to a single relationship, such as their wives or lovers. In contrast, women have several close relationships that involve high levels of self-disclosure (Komarovsky, 1976). Because men reserve their most intimate disclosures for one individual, often their wife or lover, they seem to be more vulnerable when a relationship ends.

self-disclosure
sharing personal information with others

Nonverbal communication. Nonverbal communication consists of the subtle cues or body language people use, sometimes unconsciously, to convey how they feel (Mehrabian, 1980). Cues such as the use of physical space, posture, gestures, body position, touching, eye contact, and facial expressions are more difficult to interpret than speech. Words can be looked up in the dictionary; body language cannot. In addition, the meaning conveyed by nonverbal communication can vary from one culture to another. Latin Americans, for example, often stand close to one another when talking. North Americans feel crowded by such closeness and tend to label someone who stands so near as pushy or aggressive.

Despite such drawbacks, nonverbal communication remains one of the most important ways people relate to and understand others. When words and actions do not match, people tend to rely more on nonverbal communication in drawing conclusions about someone's emotional state and control over a situation.

Some research suggests that men and women give off different messages nonverbally. Affection or attraction is conveyed by gestures like smiling, leaning forward, and facing a partner. Dominance is suggested by assuming a relaxed posture and neutral facial expression. By posture and gestures, women may be more likely than men to signal their attraction to someone. Women look and smile at others more and are better at understanding the meaning of nonverbal behavior (LaFrance & Mayo, 1979). Men may be more likely than women to signal dominance or the desire to control the interaction (Mehrabian, 1971). Generally, dominant people (such as bosses and adults) touch subordinates (such as employees and children) more than subordinates touch dominant people. Echoing their subordinate status, women touch men less than they are touched in return in public places (Henley, 1977). Also, they are less likely to use dominant body language than men. When walking, the woman links arms with her partner as if requesting guidance, whereas the man places his arm around her shoulders, conveying both intimacy and control (Morris, 1977). Women also control less physical space than men. They move out of the way earlier than men when being approached by a stranger on the sidewalk, select postures that take up a minimum of space, and in the family are less likely to have a special room or chair than the man of the house (Lips, 1981).

Sex differences in dominance. What does all this mean? Research on both verbal and nonverbal communication suggests that sex roles are associated with **dominance**, that is, high status and the potential to influence others. In their typical communications, men seem to convey that they are the dominant ones and women seem to acknowledge their subordinant status. Aggressiveness is one indication of a feeling of dominance.

dominance high status and the potential to influence others

Aggressive people may attack others, in either words or actions. Throughout the life span, but especially in childhood, males are seen as more aggressive than females (Mischel, 1970). Such aggressiveness may be the result of both a biological predisposition and learning. While high levels of androgen hormones are associated with aggression, boys and men are also taught to act forcefully in many cultures. In the United States, for example, boys who avoid physical confrontations are labeled as sissies or queers.

In actual fact, boys are more aggressive than girls in only one type of behavior, *physical aggressiveness* (Feshbach, 1970). When more subtle forms of aggression (such as hostile words or social ostracizing) are considered, girls are equally aggressive and sometimes more aggressive than boys. Recent studies such as those by Hyde (1984) point out that individual differences, and not sex roles, account for almost all the variation observed in aggressive behavior among boys and girls.

Power is the ability to change another person's behavior or beliefs (Raven, 1965) or to achieve particular goals. Aggressive behavior may be used to exert power, but it tends to be regarded by others as a sign of immaturity and poor self-control. For this reason, well-adjusted men and women do not resort to aggression on a regular basis. Instead, they rely on many other strategies for exerting power.

Do men and women use different strategies to get their way? Are these strategies consistent with expected sex roles? While some strategies are more likely to be used by men and others are more often used by women, there is considerable variation because of personality differences (Falbo, 1977, 1982). Most men and women who see themselves as strong and independent influence others by using *masculine* strategies, such as demonstrating their superior knowledge. Conversely, most women and men who see themselves as sensitive and nurturant influence others with *feminine* strategies, such as manipulating or changing the topic of conversation when it is clear that the other person is becoming upset.

The various masculine and feminine strategies are summarized in Table 9-1. Look them over and see which ones you may have used when dealing with employers, teachers, casual acquaintances, friends, and important family members. One of the masculine strategies and all three of the feminine strategies can pose problems for good psychological adjustment. For example, those who use the masculine strategy, anger, often strike out with hostile words and actions before they think. While those who use anger get their way in the short run, their relationships with loved ones and coworkers suffer in the long term. In addition, chronic anger can be harmful to health and mental well-being.

Those who use feminine strategies to get their way may be no better off. For instance, people who act helpless are programming themselves to be incompetent. As long as helplessness works, there is little reason to acquire the competencies that will enable them to solve future problems. Although helpless people get what they want for a time, their clinging dependency eventually drives many people away. Well-adjusted people get tired of relating to individuals who put themselves down and are unwilling to learn how to solve their own problems.

Depression, a second feminine strategy, shares some of the same negative consequences as anger. The sulking, pouting, tearful individual may get his or her way at first, but if the individual uses this strategy too often, close relationships may suffer and the person may end up alone. Such individuals will not have the psychological resources to learn how to cope with their problems and grow in the absence of a current intimate relationship.

TABLE 9-1	Differences in Power Strategies

Masculine Strategies	**Feminine Strategies**
1. **Expertise**—influence another person through demonstration of one's superior knowledge, skills, or ability.[1]	1. **Helplessness**—point out dependency and inability to solve one's own problems. Appeal to the other person's responsibility to provide aid.[1]
2. **Anger**—protest against the other person's undesirable behavior by getting mad.[2]	2. **Depression**—sulk, pout, and cry in the attempt to get one's way.[2&3]
3. **Assertiveness**—be direct and straightforward in indicating what one wants. Remain open to a possible compromise given awareness of the other person's position.[4]	3. **Manipulation**—withdraw or take independent action without regard for the other person's position. One may be indirect or subtle in the attempt to get one's own way.[3&4]

Note: Most people expect men to use masculine strategies and women to use feminine strategies. However, many men and women use either masculine or feminine strategies to get their way. Assertiveness is popular with androgynous people of both sexes.

Sources: This table summarizes information from different studies.
[1]Johnson, 1974
[2]Johnson & Goodchilds, 1976
[3]Falbo, 1977
[4]Falbo, 1982.

Relationships flourish when both individuals have some say regarding decisions that affect both parties. For this reason, an assertive strategy is usually more effective than manipulation. Manipulative people get what they want secretly, revealing a lack of real power. The hidden nature of the influence creates a vicious cycle. Without credible power, people are forced to continue using manipulation to influence others.

Assertive people are able to act in their own best interests by standing up for themselves and expressing their feelings honestly. Both men and women can have difficulties learning **assertiveness**. Consistent with traditional sex roles, women are often passive or helpless instead of assertive. In contrast, men may act aggressive and angry when assertive behavior would be more appropriate. Mental health professionals who do assertiveness training attempt to help women and men use power effectively but respectfully, in a manner that neither apologizes nor attempts to dominate others (Lange & Jakubowski, 1976).

Although in general an assertive strategy is best, there are times when a gentle form of manipulation can be effective. For example, one can encourage a friend to share intimate feelings by moving from a public to a private setting and being the first to divulge a secret. Subtle or manipulative approaches can be appropriate in flirtation and courtship, particularly at the beginning. No one wants to be hit over the head by a partner's demand for intimacy. The well-adjusted individual uses power in a flexible way. He or she is assertive when appropriate and benignly manipulative when interpersonal sensitivity and gentleness are called for by the situation.

Sex differences in adjustment. The tendencies of men to dominate and women to assume a subordinate status in communicative and power relationships have implications for mental health. When individuals become emotionally disturbed, their behavior is often an exaggeration of expected sex roles. Most male psychopathology is an extension of the sex-role expectation of male activity and aggressiveness. Most female psychopathology is an extension of the sex-role expectation of female passivity and dependency.

Parents do not perceive sons as having more problems than daughters. Rather, disturbed boys and girls are viewed as having different kinds of problems. Using the **Child Behavior Checklist**, Achenbach and Edelbrock (1981) reported significant sex differences in parents' perceptions of their youngsters' behavior problems (a sample of the checklist is provided in Table 9–2). Boys were much more likely than girls to be classified as having **externalizing** problems (for example, displaying immaturity; getting into trouble with other children; and being destructive, disobedient, and hyperactive). Girls were much more likely than boys to be classified as having **internalizing** problems (for example, displaying excessive dependency, depression, loneliness, fear, anxiety, and excessive self-consciousness, and suffering from aches and pains).

Equally consistent with expected sex roles, girls and boys were perceived as having different kinds of social competencies on the Child Behavior Checklist.

---

assertiveness taking care of one's own interests without anxiety or hostility

Child Behavior Checklist psychological assessment tool that examines children's behavior problems and competencies

externalizing displaying poor adjustment by getting into trouble with other people

internalizing displaying poor adjustment by inner suffering

TABLE 9-2   Sample Items from the Child Behavior Checklist

Problems More Characteristic of Girls	Problems More Characteristic of Boys
• Too dependent	• Showing off
• Lonely	• Bragging
• Cries a lot	• Can't concentrate
• Fears	• Destroys own things
• Feels unloved	• Destroys others' things
• Bites fingernails	• Disobedient at school
• Nightmares	• Sets fires
• Overeating	• Teases a lot
• Aches or pains	• Cruel to animals and others
• Headaches	• Fighting
• Skin problems	• Hangs around with children who get in
• Stomach aches, cramps	trouble
• Self-conscious	• Steals outside home
• Shy or timid	• Poor school work
• Moody	• Swearing
• Unhappy, sad, or depressed	• Hyperactive
• Worrying	• Temper tantrums

Source: This table is condensed from T. M. Achenbach & C. Edelbrock (1981), Table 1 of The Child Behavior Checklist, *Monographs of the Society for Research in Child Development*, 46 (1, serial no. 188), 37–39. The Child Behavior Checklist asks parents to describe how much their child has displayed various social competencies and behavior problems during the past six months. Behavior problems and competencies were reported by parents of normal and disturbed children ages four through sixteen.

Girls were viewed by parents as more competent at school and in nonathletic activities; boys were viewed as more competent at sports.

Maturing later and starting off with poorer verbal skills, boys may not be able to please parents and teachers as well as girls. Boys are more likely than girls to suffer from learning disabilities. Less equipped to do well at school or conform to adult expectations for controlled behavior, some boys react by becoming more aggressive. Yet, aggressive behavior is more likely to cause adults to refer to child for treatment than dependency and withdrawal, which is more characteristic of girls (Al-Issa, 1982b). As a result, boys are much more likely to receive psychological treatment in childhood years until adolescence, when girls are equally likely to get professional help with their problems.

In her well-known book, *Women and Madness*, Phyllis Chesler (1972) showed that women were more commonly treated for mental illness than were men, either as inmates of hospitals or as outpatients in psychotherapy. We might conclude from such work that either the mental health establishment aims to keep women in a dependent and passive place or that women are less well adjusted than men.

More careful studies revealed a third and probably more realistic explanation. Women apparently are more willing to report psychological problems than are men, and as a result, women may utilize mental health facilities more often (Russo & Sobel, 1981). There are consistent differences in the kinds of emotional disturbances that men and women tend to experience. Not surprisingly, these differences parallel those found for children. In general, women are more likely to have internalized problems, and men are more likely to have externalized problems, as summarized in Table 9–3. It is important not to take these categories too literally, however, nor interpret them too simplistically.

conversion disorders
forms of poor adjustment that convert emotional problems into body dysfunctions

Sex roles seem to affect the ways in which an individual's problems are viewed by others, including family and mental health professionals. For example, **conversion disorders**, an allegedly feminine reaction, are common among men during war, yet men are rarely labeled as hysterical. Depression, too, may not be an especially female psychiatric disorder. Although women make more suicide attempts than men do, men are more than three times as likely to die as a result of their attempts (Walden, 1982). Men tend to end their lives using such means as guns, while women use less effective methods, such as drugs or poison. It may well be that contrary to the widely accepted view that women are more depressed than men, depression affects both sexes equally, as shown in "On the Research Frontier: Are Women More Depressed Than Men?" As you have just learned, men and women may feel equally depressed, but women are more likely to be treated for depression than are men. What do men do with all those sad feelings? Perhaps they attempt to treat themselves by using alcohol or drugs or making others unhappy through antisocial behavior.

TABLE 9–3   Sex Differences in Mental Illness

Female Disorders

1. **Depression**—intensely dependent, passive, helpless, tearful, exhausted, poor self-confidence, hopeless. May be suicidal.[1]
2. **Phobias**—debilitating fears, especially fear of going outside, fear of being alone, leaving home, or being incapacitated in a public place.[1]
3. **Conversion disorders**—formerly known as hysteria. Emotional problems are converted to body dysfunctions in absence of known organic illness.[1]
4. **Eating disorders**—includes obesity (excessive body weight), and disorders associated with insufficient calorie intake (anorexia and bulimia).[2]

Male Disorders

1. **Alcohol addiction**—excessive consumption of and dependence on alcohol.[3]
2. **Drug addiction**—dependence on illicit drugs such as marijuana, hashish, heroin, cocaine, hallucinogens, and inhalants.[4]
3. **Antisocial personality/criminal activities**—violates the rights of others on a continuous basis. Irritable and aggressive. Impulsive and unable to maintain intimate relationships.[5]

Note: Diagnoses most commonly given to women are female disorders and those most commonly given to men are male disorders.

Sources: Information is from various sources.
[1]Al-Isaa, 1980
[2]Wooley & Wooley, 1980
[3]Leland, 1982
[4]Fidell, 1982
[5]Campbell, 1982

ON THE RESEARCH FRONTIER

ARE WOMEN MORE DEPRESSED THAN MEN?

Women may not be more depressed than men. Rather, expected sex roles encourage women but discourage men from expressing depressive symptoms. Instead of being less depressed, men may either hide their underlying despair or express it in a more masculine manner. Hammen cites research she did with Padesky that supports this position. According to Hammen (1982):

> [Male] and female college students did not differ in degree of depressive symptomatology . . . but displayed somewhat different patterns. For instance, moderately depressed men were especially likely to report . . . an inability to cry, various somatic concerns, social withdrawal, and a sense of failure. It was speculated that whereas women's more affectively expressive presentation of depression might be defined by self and others as depression, men's experiences could be seen as based on overwork or physical ailments. (p. 141)

Why may men mask their depressed feelings? According to Hammen, the depressed man is viewed as less socially desirable and less capable than the depressed woman. By looking tearful, helpless, dependent, and lacking in self-confidence, he compromises his manhood. The depressed woman, in contrast, may be regarded as unpleasant to be with but not as unfeminine. As a result, there is more social pressure on men to act as if they are in control of their lives, regardless of how out of control they really feel.

Asking who is more depressed may not be useful. Instead, it seems more fruitful to inquire, Do men and women cope with depression in different ways? According to Kleinke and his colleagues, the answer is yes (Kleinke, Staneski, & Mason, 1982). Studying college students on both the East and West coasts, these researchers found that men and women use different strategies when depressed:

1. Women are more likely than men to blame themselves for their problems.

2. Women are more likely to cope by smoking cigarettes, eating, and drinking coffee or tea.

3. Women are more emotionally expressive when depressed. They cry more readily and become irritable and short-tempered, yet they are also willing to confront their feelings.

4. Men are more likely to handle depression by becoming aggressive.

5. Men use sex more often to forget being depressed.

6. Men make greater use of marijuana to relieve depression.

7. Men are more likely to cope with depressed feelings by daydreaming, meditating, relaxing, or going for walks.

Now, take a second look at "On the Research Frontier: Are Women More Depressed Than Men?" What do you and people you know do when feeling depressed? Is your behavior or theirs consistent with sex-role stereotypes? What are the costs and benefits of the characteristic ways of coping with depression? How, if at all, would you like to change the ways you or people you care about handle depression?

SEX-ROLE STEREOTYPES

Although some genuine sex differences exist between men and women, they are far less rigid than most people believe. The presence of influential, quantitatively gifted women and sensitive, verbally articulate men indicates that such qualities are possible for all of us, not just members of a particular sex. Nonetheless, society continues to perpetuate numerous sex-role stereotypes, beliefs that simplify and exaggerate the differences between males and females. This is true for two basic reasons. First, it is hard work to study and learn about each individual's unique personality in order to predict how he or she may behave in the future. Stereotypes enable us to operate on automatic pilot, providing crude but useful guidelines for predicting other people's behavior. Second, stereotypes may become self-fulfilling prophecies. For example, a woman who expects men to fix flat tires and lift heavy packages won't learn how to do these things for herself. Her helplessness is likely to convince the men she meets that women truly are unable to take care of themselves.

Sex-role stereotypes persist. Some are myths that ignore the similarities between men and women. Others are based on actual sex differences but overgeneralize and ignore individual differences.

Myths That Ignore Individual Differences

Despite their differences, men and women share many of the same desires, traits, and beliefs. Yet all of us have been oppressed by sex-role stereotypes, myths that exaggerate sex differences. Table 9–4 lists some of the sex-role stereotypes upheld by college students (Broverman et al., 1972). What do you think about these stereotypes? Are men really less emotional than women and never gentle or tender? Are women always submissive, talkative, and indecisive? Do you and the people you know fit these stereotypes?

It is probably safe to bet that individual differences in people's personalities and values strike you as more important than supposed sex differences. When asked to describe yourself, you would probably list traits from both the masculine and feminine sides of Table 9–4. Yet you may have had experiences in which others failed to appreciate you because of harmful or erroneous sex-role stereotypes. Too many girls and women have been told that they are too emotional to be authorities or leaders. Too many boys and men have been discouraged from sharing their feelings and from nurturing others.

TABLE 9–4   Stereotypic Sex-Role Items

Masculine characteristics are more desirable

Feminine

- Not at all aggressive
- Not at all independent
- Very emotional
- Very subjective
- Very submissive
- Not at all competitive
- Not at all adventurous
- Has difficulty making decisions
- Not at all ambitious

Masculine

- Very aggressive
- Very independent
- Not at all emotional
- Very objective
- Very dominant
- Very competitive
- Very adventurous
- Can make decisions easily
- Very ambitious

Feminine characteristics are more desirable

Feminine

- Doesn't use harsh language at all
- Very talkative
- Very tactful
- Very gentle
- Very aware of feelings of others
- Very neat in habits
- Very quiet
- Enjoys art and literature
- Easily expresses tender feelings

Masculine

- Uses very harsh language
- Not at all talkative
- Very blunt
- Very rough
- Not at all aware of feelings of others
- Very sloppy in habits
- Very loud
- Does not enjoy art and literature
- Does not express tender feelings at all easily

Source: Adapted from I. K. Broverman et al., Table 1 in Sex-role stereotypes: A current appraisal, *Journal of Social Issues, 28*, 63.

Personality differences may be more important than sex differences. Which has played the strongest role in determining your choices—your unique personality or sex-role socialization? To what extent have you or would you like to challenge sex-role stereotypes?

Eagly and Steffen (1984) have a creative solution to the problem of sex-role stereotypes. They have done away with concepts of masculine and feminine entirely. According to these researchers, people will not be free to live up to potential as long as they think a particular trait makes them socially undesirable or like someone of the opposite sex. The term *masculine* has been replaced with the word **agentic**, which means assertive, sensible, willing to tackle problems, and achieving. The term *feminine* has been replaced with the word **communal**, which means appreciative, sensitive, tactful, and concerned about others. According to Eagly (1983), the positions people hold in society, not their sex, make us see them as agentic or communal. Both women and men are seen as agentic when they hold down powerful positions, such as business executives or elected government officials. Regardless of sex, subordinates in the workplace, such as secretaries and nurses, are seen as communal.

agentic having personality traits that emphasize achievement, self-assertion, and competence in overcoming difficulties and controlling the environment

communal having personality traits that emphasize sensitivity, tact, and appreciation of other people

Harmful Effects of Sex-Role Stereotypes

Sex-role stereotypes have many harmful effects. First, stereotypes can trap people into making life-style or occupational choices that are wrong for them as individuals. There is no inherent reason why a bright woman who is interested in business should be prevented from becoming an executive. Why should she be told that a secretarial career is more appropriate? Similarly, natural law does not prevent men from desiring to stay home and care for their small children. Yet, people let sex-role stereotypes limit their choices in both careers and intimate relationships with partners and children.

Second, sex-role stereotypes diminish the skills and pleasures that are open to people because they believe that men aren't supposed to enjoy certain things or women aren't supposed to be good at certain things. For instance, Canter and Meyerowitz (1984) found that college students' sex-role stereotypes predicted which activities they tried and which they enjoyed. The pleasure we take in doing things is often associated with our competence at them. But competence cannot be achieved without practice. One positive choice everyone can make is to try new activities even if they are inconsistent with sex-role stereotypes.

Third, sex-role stereotypes foster **sexism**, that is, prejudices against men or women that harm self-esteem and restrict opportunities no less than racial or religious prejudices do. For example, some vocational counselors and mental health professionals are biased against women and falsely believe that all well-adjusted people conform to expected sex roles (Schaffer, 1980). Because of sex-role stereotypes, a qualified woman may be denied an administrative position and a divorced man's request for custody of his children may not be given a fair hearing. Have you ever had an experience in which someone else unwittingly limited your choices because that individual had sexist beliefs?

Finally, people who choose to conform to sex-role stereotypes live unnecessarily restricted lives. The rigidly masculine man is denied warm, emotionally expressive relationships. The stereotypically feminine woman is obliged to live her life through her husband and children, constantly fretting about her attractiveness and ability to please others.

Overcoming Sex-Role Stereotypes and Sexism

We are not obliged to conform to rigid rules of being men and women and deny ourselves opportunities to be fully functioning human beings. We can choose to explore our abilities and preferences and adopt more equal roles in our work and relationships.

Slowly but surely, people are making progress toward achieving more egalitarian sex roles. In the United States, recent legislation and judicial decisions give job security to women who take leaves of absence as a result of health and child-care needs when they have babies. Progressive corporations and governmental agencies are providing good child-care services for employees who

sexism prejudices against men or women that harm self-esteem and opportunities for advancement or growth

People in the United States are making progress toward achieving more egalitarian sex roles.

are part of the growing number of dual-career and single-parent families. Although women are still paid less than men and are less likely to be in positions of authority in the work force, affirmative action programs are working to correct these inequalities. A courageous group of men are asking for flexible hours at work or are experimenting with being full-time homemakers to provide better care for their small children and more enriching experiences for themselves.

Couples are beginning to explore more egalitarian relationships as well. As discussed in the next two chapters, it is no longer taken for granted that the woman will do the housework and have less independence than the man. The women's movement, which encourages women to be powerful and to feel good about themselves, is being joined by the men's movement, which gives men greater permission to share feelings and express affection openly. It is an exciting time to be alive.

When asked to describe their personality traits, people acknowledge numerous individual differences. Both men and women may describe themselves as feminine, masculine, or androgynous on the popular scales known as the **Bem Sex-Role Inventory (BSRI)** and the **Personal Attributes Questionnaire (PAQ)** (Bem, 1974; Spence, Helmreich, & Stapp, 1974). *Feminine* people describe themselves as having numerous communal traits, such as sensitivity to others. *Masculine* people ascribe numerous agentic traits to themselves, such as independence and competitiveness. *Androgynous* people describe themselves as having many communal and agentic traits. Researchers report that compared with feminine people of either sex, both masculine and androgynous people feel better about themselves and are more likely to be well adjusted (Burchart & Serbin, 1982; Kimlicka, Cross, & Tarnai, 1983).

It is easy to speculate why androgynous people may be well adjusted. Their openness to experience and flexible behavioral repertoire enable them to solve problems and relate to others in manners less open to those who conform to sex-role stereotypes. The superior psychological adjustment of masculine men and women is not so easy to understand. Appreciation for the social context in which we live explains why it is so adaptive to have a masculine personality. North American society continues to emphasize competitive achievement and independence. As long as this is true, regardless of actual sex, the masculine person may have better coping strategies than the feminine one, who is dependent on close relationships for good feelings. In some cases, the masculine person may be better adapted to our society than the androgynous person, as the latter may be more ambivalent about defeating others.

Does this mean that people must be masculine or androgynous to be happy? Not quite. There are costs and benefits for each type of individual. Feminine men and women are likely to enjoy richly intimate relationships with others but are at a disadvantage when socially isolated or thrust into competitive situations. Masculine persons are likely to achieve in school, sports, and the workplace, but they may find it difficult to share their feelings or put sufficient energy into friend, family, and love relationships. Androgynous people have

Bem Sex-Role Inventory (BSRI) popular psychological measure of sex-role identification

Personal Attributes Questionnaire (PAQ) popular psychological measure of sex-role identification

the advantages and disadvantages of both feminine and masculine individuals. Both independent and affectionate, their main problem is deciding which traits are most adaptive for a given situation. Others may find it hard to deal with the androgynous person's multifaceted personality, preferring the company of the more predictable masculine or feminine individual.

How would you describe your own personality? Feminine? Masculine? Androgynous? How, if at all, would you like to change, and why? Remember, each of us has the right to make choices about personal qualities we would like to develop. There are no right or wrong answers.

SUMMARY

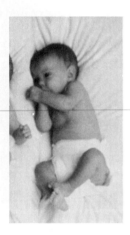

1. Many differences between males and females are learned. Sex roles are approved ways of demonstrating that one is male or female.

2. Biological factors contribute to some sex differences. Females mature earlier, live longer, and are less susceptible than males to sex-linked genetic problems. Androgen, a hormone more common in males than females, may contribute to active, aggressive behavior.

3. The psychoanalytic perspective concludes identification with the same-sex parent in preschool youngsters is based on the boy's anxiety and girl's envy experienced after noticing differences between their genitals and those of members of the opposite sex.

4. The social learning perspective concludes that children learn how to behave like typical girls and boys by being rewarded for conforming and punished for failing to conform to expected sex roles. More importantly, children learn a great deal about how to be masculine or feminine by observing family members and other children and by absorbing information from schoolbooks and the mass media.

5. The cognitive-developmental perspective emphasizes that sex-role acquisition takes place as a result of changing thought processes triggered by maturation. Young children hold more rigid ideas about the dichotomy between the sexes than do older persons.

6. Each of the four major perspectives for explaining sex-role development has theoretical flaws and is not fully supported by research. A combination of these perspectives is best when attempting to understand sex differences.

7. Most research on sex-role development (how children acquire culturally approved sex roles) is based on middle-class children from white families. These children may differ from working-class, lower-class, and minority children in important ways.

8. Both sexes are equally intelligent. However, females tend to have better verbal skills, and males tend to have better quantitative abilities. These sex differences are much too small to explain the sex segregation that characterizes some occupations.

9. Initially, it was thought that women were less likely than men to do well in competitive situations because they suffered from fear of success. This idea has been challenged because adherence to traditional sex-role attitudes may play a larger part in keeping women out of the competition and because men may fear success as much as women.

10. Men convey their dominant status and women demonstrate a more passive role in society through verbal and nonverbal communication.

11. All children are aggressive but boys are more physically aggressive than girls. Depending on whether they are masculine, feminine, or androgynous, adult men and women may use power in different ways, too. Being an expert and getting angry are masculine strategies for getting one's way. Both masculine and androgynous people use assertiveness. Helplessness, getting depressed, and trying to manipulate someone else are feminine strategies.

12. There are some stable sex differences in psychological adjustment that are consistent with expected sex roles. Sex differences in psychological adjustment are relative, not absolute, however.

13. Sex-role stereotypes depict males as agentic, or achievement oriented, and females as communal, or concerned about getting along with others. The sexual division of labor, in which men are expected to be breadwinners and women are expected to be homemakers and mothers, contributes to the persistence of these stereotypes.

14. People who question sex-role stereotypes are likely to make better choices for their lives. However, masculine and androgynous people may be better adjusted than feminine people, because gentleness and interpersonal sensitivity are less valued in our society than are competitive achievement and independence.

Chapter 10

Intimate Relationships

Developing close relationships is very important. Yet intimacy is not easy. The challenge is to learn how to balance our own needs with those of a partner and friends. Good relationships require reaching out without overwhelming others with our demands. At the same time, we shouldn't sacrifice personal identity and independence for the sake of intimacy.

Beginning with a consideration of cultural influences, this chapter explores how people make and deepen friendships and love relationships. Researchers have documented some differences in the ways in which men and women handle intimacy. Building on information presented in the previous chapter, this chapter also looks at the impact of sex roles on intimate relationships. It takes considerable skill to achieve and maintain intimacy.

UNDERSTANDING INTIMATE RELATIONSHIPS

friendship
relationship that typically excludes sexual intimacy and is based on two or more individuals' enjoyment of one another's company

love deeply involved relationship in which sexual intimacy is common

culture customs and civilization of a particular people or group

pluralistic society in which the members of minority groups and individuals from different social classes maintain independent traditions

People are drawn together for a variety of reasons. Typically, they seek each other out because of mutual attraction and stay together because they enjoy the sharing, nurturance, trust, tolerance, and caring that an intimate relationship provides. There are two basic kinds of intimate relationships—**friendship** and **love**. Friends enjoy each other's company and typically do not have a sexual relationship. Lovers are more deeply involved in each other's lives than are friends, and often, but not always, have a sexually intimate relationship.

There is no single set of guidelines for establishing and maintaining friendships and love relationships. Depending on cultural group, family background, and sex, we may develop widely different expectations about intimacy.

Culture and Intimacy

Most of the psychological research on intimacy has been done with middle-class Westerners. As a result, this chapter is more relevant to these groups than to others. However, no discussion of friendship and love is complete without some consideration of how **culture**, the customs and civilization of a particular people or group, influences the choice of an intimate partner and how we form that intimacy. This is particularly important because we live in a **pluralistic** society, where members of minority groups and individuals from different social classes maintain independent traditions. As anthropologist James Armstrong argues, culture may limit our choices of friends and love relationships more than we would like to admit.

In some minority and cultural groups, for example, such considerations as economics and social station, including the approval of other family members, may be more critical in establishing friendships and sexual relationships than affection is. Also, how we develop intimacy often depends on the sex roles prescribed by a particular culture, minority group, or social class. For instance, men from the Middle East and Mediterranean Europe have far more intimate friendships than do North American men. On the other hand, women from the same region are unlikely to form close friendships with women outside their extended families. Though they may be very close to female relatives, traditional women from Middle Eastern and Mediterranean cultures seldom have the opportunity to cultivate friendships in the larger community.

Cultural prescriptions for intimacy are quite different for North Americans and northern European people. Here, sex roles encourage women but inhibit men from the open expression of feelings. As a result, we tend to misunderstand people who come from cultures with different values. For example, it is perfectly normal for men from Arab, Latin American, and southern European cultures to stand very close to one another and touch, hold hands, and embrace as they converse (Watson, 1970). Although most heterosexual men from these cultures act this way with male friends, North Americans and northern Europeans are quick to draw the false conclusion that men who touch other men must be homosexual. Our prejudice against men touching other men restricts the expression of affection in male friendships. In a study of United States college students' experiences with touching, most **affectionate touching** (such as hugs, kisses, and warm pats) occurred in male-female friendships (Jones & Yarbrough, 1985). Next in frequency were female-female affectionate touches. In contrast, male-male affectionate touches were rare.

Does this mean that North American and northern European men never touch each other? Hardly! Rather, they have to be careful to look "masculine" when they do. When college men touch their male friends in our culture, they are likely to do so in playful or aggressive ways. Instead of being able to express physical affection directly for a friend, North American and northern European men give each other mixed messages by wrestling, tickling, punching, pinching, bumping, grabbing, and slapping each other. Among United States college students, between 20 percent and 40 percent of **playful affectionate touches** and **playful aggressive touches** are between men.

How is the expression of intimacy established by a culture? Anthropologists who study **proxemic behavior**, the distance between people during their interactions, have provided some answers.

Rules for interacting with others. There is nothing natural about how close people get to others physically. Instead, the rules for closeness and distance are carefully defined by each culture. As Edward Hall (1966) first noted, there are four different categories of interpersonal distance. Each culture has its own set of rules or **physical guidelines** (approximate distance in inches and feet) for various social relationships. Table 10-1 (p. 290) defines the four categories of interpersonal distance that have been established in our society and describes the physical guidelines for each. As you can see from information provided in the table, people remain at a considerable distance when interacting with strangers and business associates but move closer when conversing with friends and lovers.

Depending on the culture they grow up in, people feel comfort or discomfort in relating to others in particular ways. Essentially, there are two types of culture—high-contact and low-contact cultures (Watson, 1970). **High-contact cultures**, such as Arab, Latin American, and southern European nations, are

---

affectionate touching touching that expresses generalized positive or warm feelings

playful affectionate touches touches that lighten an interaction and express warm feelings with qualifications and a lack of seriousness

playful aggressive touches touches that combine mock physical aggressiveness with the expression of warm feelings

proxemic behavior distance between people during their interactions

physical guidelines cultural expectations regarding how close (in inches or feet) people will be for different kinds of social interactions

high-contact cultures cultures where people get physically close, face others, talk loudly, and establish much eye contact while conversing

TABLE   10-1   Categories of Interpersonal Distance

1. *Intimate distance*—the distance between lovers, individuals who are wrestling or fighting, and those who are comforting and protecting others. Touching is likely, and sensory input is intense. Individuals may be so close that visual impressions are distorted. In the closest phase, individuals can hear the softest speech, smell the other person, and feel the person's breath. The close phase is under six inches. The far phase is six to eighteen inches.

2. *Personal Distance*—the distance for close but not deeply intimate social and work relationships. Individuals have a small, protective space bubble between themselves and others. Touching is not inevitable, but it is relatively easy. Details of the other person's face and body are easily seen. This is the ideal distance for looking another person in the eyes. The close phase is 1.5–2.5 feet. The far phase is 2.5–4 feet.

3. *Social distance*—the distance for conversing with strangers, new acquaintances, and business or work associates of substantially different status (such as a secretary and an executive). Touching is unlikely, and intimate visual detail is lost. Most impersonal business and social discourse are conducted at this distance. The close phase is four to seven feet. The far phase is seven to twelve feet.

4. *Public distance*—the distance used by public figures or anyone addressing a group in a formal way. The role of people as strangers is emphasized, and individuals can take evasive action to protect themselves from unwanted intrusions. People have to talk loud and appear flat or two-dimensional to others. The close phase is twelve to twenty-five feet. The far phase is twenty-five feet or more.

Source: E. T. Hall (1966). *The hidden dimension*. Garden City, NY: Doubleday & Co., 109–120.

low-contact cultures cultures where people maintain distance between one another, engage in little touching, avoid intense eye contact, and prefer the shoulder-to-shoulder position for conversing

those in which people are likely to get physically close, face others, talk loudly, and establish much eye contact while conversing. In contrast, people in **low-contact cultures**, such as northern European, North American, and Southeast Asian, prefer to maintain distance between one another, engage in little touching, avoid intense eye contact, and converse from the shoulder-to-shoulder position.

When people from these two different types of cultures meet, they are likely to misunderstand each other. Typically, the individual from the high-contact culture moves closer and talks louder while the individual from the low-contact culture backs away and tries to avoid being touched and looked at. If people aren't sensitive to cultural differences, they may not give the other person a chance. Instead, the high-contact person falsely concludes that the other person is cold and rejecting, whereas the low-contact person falsely concludes that the other person is pushy and intrusive.

Research is unclear as to the extent to which culture influences intimacy in nations such as the United States, Canada, and Australia, which are composed largely of immigrants. Ethnic and racial differences in how close people stand are often overriden by socioeconomic and regional differences (Henley, 1977). Whether they come from a high-contact or low-contact culture, working- and lower-class people stand much closer to each other than do middle- and upper-class people. Similarly, people in big cities allow less space between themselves and others than do those who live in suburban and rural areas.

In determining interpersonal distance, culture per se is not critical, but perceived cultural and racial differences are critical. Sadly enough, people from different races stand farther apart than do those of the same race (Henley, 1977). In interracial schools, black and white children stand farther from each other in the upper grades than they did in the primary grades. Apparently, some people learn that they should keep those who are different from them at arm's length. This lesson does more than foster racism and prejudice. It also keeps people from forming intimate relationships that may be personally enriching.

Defining the purpose of close relationships. The purposes, advantages, and disadvantages of intimacy are also culturally defined. The larger social groups teach us what to expect from friends and family. Affluent people from low-contact cultures learn that intimacy is to foster each individual's psychological growth, and they learn to reject relationships that limit their autonomy. In contrast, those from high-contact cultures and lower economic status are taught to value group goals over individual goals and to emphasize mutual dependence in intimate relationships with friends and kin.

support group close network of family and friends who provide dependable economic and emotional support

Community psychologists and psychotherapists have observed that having a **support group**, family and friends who provide dependable economic and emotional support, can do much to facilitate individual adjustment. Support groups are particularly important to minority groups and to lower- and working-class people. Middle-class and wealthy white people may be able to buy their way out of trouble, and they have greater access to the best mental health services. In contrast, members of some minority groups and all economically deprived persons have fewer financial resources and face greater life obstacles. Physical survival and emotional well-being may depend on the availability of informal support groups.

fictive kin people who are unrelated but close enough to be regarded as honorary family members

Some people triumph over the most difficult of circumstances by sticking together in mutually supportive ways. In a study of black mothers living in the Washington, DC, area, McAdoo (1980) noted that the majority took delight in an extended family support network that included both blood relatives and **fictive kin**, people who were unrelated but close enough to be regarded as honorary family members. Most mothers indicated that they could count on a support group in times of emotional upheaval and for help with child care and finances. Both married and single mothers described their support systems as providing as much or more help than they gave in exchange. Family and friends were especially helpful to single-parent families, responding to this group's greater economic and social needs. Frequently, single mothers lent each other money in times of financial crisis. Single mothers were much more likely than married mothers to keep in close contact with relatives through numerous visits, telephone conversations, and letters.

Liking and Loving

liking feeling good about someone in general

We tend to like people who are similar to ourselves and who posses qualities we admire. In **liking** (that is, feeling good about someone in general), we look forward to spending our time with friends and are disappointed when unable to be around those we like. In contrast, our feelings are more intense for the people we love. In loving, attachment is more emotionally involving and enduring, and our lives become more intertwined. In place of the disappointment accompanying separation from those we like, loneliness or emptiness is often associated with prolonged separation from those we love. Both liking and loving require sacrifice and compromise. Well-adjusted people get as much pleasure from giving to friends and loved ones as they do from receiving affection and favors.

Zick Rubin (1973) has contributed much to the understanding of intimate relationships by developing useful scales to measure liking and love. His scales also can help us understand the differences between these two kinds of emotional attachment. Sample items from his liking and love scales, originally designed for college students, are reproduced in Table 10-2. Items on the liking scale emphasize **respect** (looking up to someone) and **similarity** (shared qualities, interests, and attitudes). In contrast, the love scale measures more intense feelings—attachment, caring, and intimacy. **Attachment** refers to how strongly people feel they need another person in order to be happy. **Caring** is the extent to which people want to give of themselves or sacrifice for the other. **Intimacy** is closeness in which people feel that their lives are linked together.

Sex roles contribute to the ability to like and love. In our culture, women are more likely to report loving their friends of the same sex than men are (Rubin, 1973). If two women embrace or say they love each other; outsiders are not as quick to assume that they are homosexual as they would be if two men did the same. There are sex differences, too, in the way young lovers feel about each other. Rubin asked heterosexual dating couples to describe how they felt about their partner on the liking and love scales, using a nine-point rating system in which one equalled not at all true and nine equalled definitely true. Men and women loved each other equally. However, women liked their male dating partners somewhat more than they were liked in return. It is possible that Rubin's liking scale is biased against women. Because of sex-role stereotypes and the traditional sexual division of labor, women may be less likely than men to be regarded as intelligent, responsible, and confidence inspiring.

In the best of intimate relationships, we like and love the same person simultaneously. Sternberg and Grajek (1984) found a strong positive relationship between people's love and liking scores on the Rubin scales. In fact, this same recent study found that to predict how successful a relationship would be on a long-term basis, you would be better off looking at people's scores on the liking scale than asking them how much they loved each other. One important type of love (friendly love) is based more on liking than on the passionate attachment people associate with romantic love.

How Friends and Lovers Are Selected

Psychotherapists are often consulted by intelligent, charming, and sensitive clients who describe themselves as lonely despite their obvious assets. Some may find they are not close to anyone, but most report they are trapped in

---

respect looking up to someone

similarity shared qualities, interests, or attitudes

attachment extent to which people feel they need another in order to be happy

caring extent to which people want to give of themselves or make sacrifices

intimacy close relationship in which people feel that their lives are linked together

TABLE 10–2   Sample Items from Liking and Love Scales

Liking Scale

- I would highly recommend _____ for a responsible job.
- I think that _____ and I are quite similar to one another.
- I would vote for _____ in a class or group election.
- I feel that _____ is an extremely intelligent person.

Love Scale

- I feel that I can confide in _____ about virtually everything.
- I would do almost anything for _____.
- If I could never be with _____ I would feel miserable.
- If I were lonely, my first thought would be to seek _____ out.

Source: Z. Rubin (1973). Table 10–1. *Liking and loving: An invitation to social psychology.* New York: Holt, Rinehart & Winston, 216.

unsatisfactory relationships. For example, a client's friends may be demanding and shallow, and have little in common with the person while the primary love relationship is dull or draining. It may be worth the client's time to work on improving ongoing relationships. However, it is often better for clients to reach out to new people. Yet many are reluctant to do so. Why are they afraid of reaching out?

People may avoid reaching out to others simply because they don't know what to do. Forming close relationships takes time, effort, and considerable skill. Yet, with the exception of a few colleges and mental health agencies, no one offers formal classes on how to meet prospective friends and lovers. Fortunately, we can turn to a considerable body of research on this topic. This information can be used to help establish realistic guidelines for forming and maintaining close relationships.

Physical attractiveness. Although people may not judge a book by its cover, they certainly judge others by their looks. In our youth and beauty oriented society, people who are homely, fat, disabled, disfigured, and elderly are presumed to be undesirable as friends and lovers (Berscheid & Walster, 1974). Numerous studies indicate that regardless of age, most of us think that physical attractiveness is more important in a potential dating partner than intelligence, a pleasant personality, or shared values. For example, Riggio and Woll (1984) found that young and middle-aged adults belonging to a videodating organization had a strong preference for potential dates who were physically attractive and smiled a lot during their television interviews. Consistent with traditional sex roles, men found quieter, less-outgoing women more attractive while women preferred outgoing, animated men.

The belief that the beautiful are better may be a self-fulfilling prophecy. Unattractive people are treated badly, and rejection may have a negative impact on both psychological adjustment and interpersonal skills. When talking to someone they never met on the telephone, men were less sociable and charming when they believed they were talking to unattractive as opposed to beautiful women (Synder, Tanke, & Berscheid, 1977). Researchers found that women were deflated by such ill treatment. Regardless of their actual appearance, women who were believed to be unattractive came across as less friendly, poised, and socially adept than those who the men had been led to believe were blessed with good looks.

In singles bars, at assorted social events, and in long-term relationships, people generally end up with partners who are equally attractive (Hatfield, 1985). Hence, those who wish to have greater success in beginning close relationships—especially those who would prefer attractive friends and lovers—are well advised to spend money, time, and energy on improving their appearance. It is not fair that others place such great stock in appearance, but it is an unavoidable reality. The trick for those who wish to be well adjusted is to consider just what proportion of their lives should be devoted to diet, dress, exercise, and cosmetic treatment and what proportion is better left for devotion to work, hobbies, personal enrichment, and the intimate relationships that their appearance elicits.

Similarity and complementary needs. Besides external appearance, people are attracted because they share similar interests (like reading science fiction) or can do things for each other (such as fixing an appliance for someone who lacks mechanical skills). Related to this, psychologists have asked whether similarity (shared qualities, interests, or attitudes) or **complementary needs** (having a quality a partner lacks) are most important in the establishment of friendship and love relationships. As folk wisdom puts it, do "birds of a feather flock together" or do "opposites attract"?

complementary needs situation in which each partner in a relationship has qualities that the other lacks

Numerous studies indicate that similarity of values and attitudes are critical in the formation and maintenance of friendships and love relationships (Byrne, 1971). People in intimate relationships spend a lot of time together. It makes sense that they would prefer to spend this time pursuing interests that are mutually enjoyable. In addition, similar people are attracted because it is easier to trust someone who shares one's opinions than an individual who sees the world in a very different way.

People are attracted to similar individuals and become even more alike as their relationships deepen. New friends like each other because they have superficial things in common. For example, both may enjoy running or may belong to the same organization. Old friends are similar in more important ways. They may actually think alike and experience the world in the same way (Duck, 1977). Going out to dinner together, established friends and lovers need not talk to communicate how they feel. As they watch the social actions unfolding before them, one may catch the other's eye as if to say, "Yes, I know just what you're thinking." Shared experiences intensify the similarity between friends and lovers.

What are the implications of the research on similarity? It may be difficult to become close to those with whom we have little in common; there would be

People generally end up with partners who are equally attractive.

very little on which to base the relationship. Nonetheless, it is good to pick as friends and partners those who are both similar and somewhat different. Our similarity to intimates is fertile soil for relationship development and self-expansion. The differences between intimates challenge people to become more sensitive, tolerant, and wise. It would be hard to grow as people if our friends and lovers had nothing to teach us.

Observing that opposites do attract at times, some social scientists have asserted that intimate relationships may be based on a pair's complementary needs. Complementary needs are the basis for friendship and love when people prefer partners who have qualities they lack or who lack certain abilities or characteristics they possess. (Seyfried & Hendrick, 1977). For example, a warm, nurturant individual might seek a dependent person to care for. A shy but socially interested individual might choose an extroverted friend who will make sure that the pair attends parties and meets new people.

Seyfried (1977) notes that complementary needs can be the basis of intimate relationships in two different ways. First, two people might have very different needs of equal intensity and find their relationship can satisfy both their needs at the same time. Picture a married couple in which one partner is neat and the other is messy. Their relationship will work only if the neat partner enjoys picking up after others and the messy partner appreciates being helped.

In another type of complementary relationship, both people have the same need or dislike but one feels more intensely about it than does the other. The two individuals negotiate so that the partner who agrees to meet the need or take on an obligation is compensated by having one of his or her needs met in exchange. For example, you and your roommate may dislike cooking but you hate it more than your roommate does. You can work out an exchange of services so that your roommate agrees to prepare meals and, in exchange, you do all the shopping and cleaning up.

Complementary needs theory has much less research support than does the theory which states that close relationships are fostered by similarity (Levinger, 1983). There are two reasons for this. First, people change as they mature. A relationship that began because a couple had complementary needs may deteriorate if the partners develop skills and qualities they used to lack. For example, a formerly shy husband will resent an overly protective wife if he becomes more self-confident in social situations. Second, the complementary needs theory may be better explained by the sexual division of labor. A woman might be nurturant and family oriented while her male partner is emotionally distant but achievement oriented because that is the way the sexes are socialized, not because of complementary needs. With androgyny, it is possible for people to take care of themselves and others more fully. Partners can be chosen because their company gives pleasure, not because they make up for a missing half.

Proximity. Attraction, similarity, and in some cases, complementary needs are the bases for the development of intimate relationships. But we can only become friends and lovers with those we meet. Few relationships can develop in the absence of **proximity,** or physical accessibility.

proximity physical
accessibility to others

The closer people live and work together, the more likely they are to develop friendships and love relationships (Berscheid & Hatfield-Walster, 1969). Neighbors, people who sit next to each other in class, and those who are in contact frequently at work are much more likely to become friends, fall in love, or get married than are those who see each other less frequently.

Knowing others who introduce potential friends and lovers is just as important as physical proximity. Gay men are more likely to have a current lover if they are involved with a circle of gay friends (Harry, 1984). For homosexuals and heterosexuals alike, social isolation is a vicious cycle. The more cut off a person is from others, the greater the barrier to forming meaningful new relationships.

To develop close relationships, it is important to be around others as much as possible. Prince Charming and Sleeping Beauty don't make house calls. It is important to go to new places, approach others, and risk making the first move in a relationship. This is frightening for some people, because they are shy and afraid of being rejected. Women in particular are socialized to think that it is wrong to start a relationship, especially one with a man. The best antidote to such fear is for people to remind themselves that being rejected by one individual is no reflection of their value as persons.

Looking for new relationships can be viewed as akin to putting coins in a slot machine. Eventually, after many trials, it is bound to pay off. If the rejections and losses can be accepted as disappointing but not devastating, people are free to work at improving their social skills. With persistence, their chances of meeting similar individuals with whom to develop meaningful, close relationships increase greatly. In contrast with popular folklore, hard-to-get people are not especially liked. In fact, people prefer partners who present themselves as selectively hard to get, that is, easy for them to get to know but more reserved with others (Berscheid & Walster, 1974).

Self-Disclosure

Our closest relationships are characterized by high levels of sharing. Intimacy cannot occur in the absence of self-disclosure, or sharing personal information. Open expression of feelings, talking about feelings and being able to exhibit good and bad emotions, is critical in the development and maintenance of friendships and love relationships.

Other people tend to be less mysterious and frightening when they disclose their experiences fully, honestly, and spontaneously (Jourard, 1971). As Kelvin (1977) puts it, "[T]o be able to love requires the ability to tolerate and accept the vulnerability which follows from disclosures of privacy" (p. 372). There are no safety nets for intimate relationships. In sharing feelings and disclosing personal information, individuals open themselves up to the possibility of being hurt or exploited. But if they fail to take emotional risks, intimacy itself is impossible.

We live in a world of extremes. On the one hand, many of us are immersed in relationships characterized by pseudocloseness. Countless people socialize with, live with, and even marry individuals who remain strangers to them. On the other hand, some of us give up all our autonomy when entering a close relationship, burdening our partners with too many of our demands and feelings. It is possible to share so much of ourselves that we literally forget that there is a boundary between us and the other person. In *close relationships,* each of us has choices regarding how much to reveal, when to share, and whom to reveal ourselves to. We hope the research cited below will help you make the best choices in your relationships.

Self-disclosure in new relationships. People can disclose many things. Sidney Jourard (1971) designed a particularly well-known questionnaire to examine the extent to which individuals have shared their true beliefs and feelings in a variety of areas. Not surprisingly, Jourard (1971) found that people were more willing to share information about their work, tastes, hobbies, interests, and attitudes toward politics and religion than the details of their sexual lives, their feelings about their bodies and personalities, and their financial statuses. Superficial as opposed to intimate details may be easier to share in a new relationship. However, intimacy is not based on such superficialities. Deeper self-disclosures are necessary if true intimacy is to be achieved.

It is important to take risks in relationships. In study after study, re-searchers find that the best way of increasing a partner's self-disclosures is to be willing to be vulnerable oneself. Self-disclosures are like the exchange of gifts. The more one is willing to reveal about oneself, the more a partner will reveal in return (Jourard, 1971). This happens for two reasons (Rubin, 1973). First, open and honest people model self-disclosures for others to imitate. Sec-ond, trust is increased in relationships as a result of mutual self-disclosures. People feel less vulnerable for having exchanged their deeper thoughts and feelings.

Sometimes, people can disclose too much at first. Although sharing per-sonal information can deepen a new relationship, saying too much too soon can drive the other person away. Perhaps you have met strangers on a bus, train, or plane who strike up a conversation and then immediately begin re-vealing intimate facts about their personal, family, and sexual lives. It is un-likely you would want to share on an equally intimate basis in return. It is difficult to trust someone who discloses the most revealing things before a relationship has time to develop.

Just as the Trojans should have been wary of their Greek enemies bearing gifts, it is wise to be wary of people who say too much too soon. Such people lack the ability to judge when the amount of what they share is inappropriate. Their actions suggest social insensitivity at best and poor psychological ad-justment at worst. Consistent with this point of view, researchers have re-ported that lonely college students may contribute to their own isolation by sharing too much with others in their initial conversations. Compared with their well-adjusted peers, lonely individuals relate to new acquaintances with "less awareness of or concern for others, with less responsiveness, and in a more self-focused or self-absorbed manner" (Jones, Hobbs, & Hockenbury, 1982).

Self-disclosure in long-term relationships. Self-disclosures are important in not only the establishment of new relationships but also the maintenance of inti-macy in old ones. In an international study of friendship rules, Argyle & Henderson (1984) found that regardless of culture, most people regarded self-disclosure as critical to the survival of close relationships with peers of the same sex. People, particularly Westerners, believed that friends should dis-close their feelings and personal problems, ask each other for advice, avoid discussing what was said in confidence with outsiders, share news of success, maintain eye contact during conversations, be emotionally supportive, and trust and confide in each other. If enough of these friendship rules are broken over a period of time, friendships are discarded. In the friendships that survive, individuals are willing to disclose personal feelings and problems and discuss controversial issues like religion, politics, sex, and death within a context of caring. Lasting friendships and love relationships are nurtured by interper-sonal sharing and trust.

Sex Differences in Self-Disclosure

Sex differences in self-disclosure are relative and not absolute. As discussed earlier, some cultures foster male friendships and inhibit female ones. The opposite pattern holds true in our culture. Therefore, men depend on women for intimacy more than women depend on men.

Same-sex friendships. North American women appear to have more intimate friendships with others of their sex than do men. After analyzing lengthy, in-depth interviews with 300 adults, Lillian Rubin (1985) concluded, "At every life stage between twenty-five and fifty-five, women have more friendships, as distinct from collegial relationships or workmates, than men, and the differences in the content and quality of their friendships are marked and unmistakable" (pp. 60–61).

Women are more likely than men to discuss personal topics with friends, such as feelings and problems, and to bring up other people in their conversations (Caldwell & Peplau, 1982). Women friends are more likely than men friends to get together just to talk. As a middle-aged secretary put it, "There are a lot of people I can play with but . . . my real friends are the ones I can talk to. . . . [T]hey're the people I can share *myself* with, not just my time" (Rubin, 1985, p. 61). Men, in contrast, focus their relationships on mutual activities, such as sporting events and social drinking. As Rubin put it, men "tend to *do* rather than *be* together" (p. 61). In describing interactions with friends, a young, working-class man told her, "We go to the pool hall and shoot pool, maybe hit a bar or two and drink and tell stories" (p. 61). Similarly, a middle-class man of the same age indicated, "I play tennis with one of my friends every week. Every now and then I'll go to a ball game with a couple of friends, or we'll get together to watch some big game on the tube" (pp. 61-62).

Women put more time into their friendships with persons of the same sex than do men. They are less likely to let work and family responsibilities interfere with these important relationships. At the same time, it is more difficult for men to reach out to each other and show vulnerabilities in friendship. Because of traditional, sex-role socialization, women express feelings and provide emotional support to one another more readily than men do (Caldwell & Peplau, 1982). They are more likely to ask how a friend feels and take responsibility for their own feelings.

Women, as opposed to men, are quick to reveal information about their experiences with friends, sexual partners, and relatives. When role playing how they would tell a friend about the ending of a dating relationship, men are more likely than women to dismiss the emotional impact of such an event with comments like, "It's springtime, and there are lots of other dames out," or, "I'd rather play the field" (p. 730). Women are more apt to express affection toward their friends (Hays, 1984). The female sex role seems to lend itself to such sensitive gestures as praising a friend's good qualities, sending a card or calling when a visit would be difficult, and celebrating the friendship through rituals such as a meal out or a party.

Men explain their reluctance to share personal matters with friends as originating from both unwillingness to allow another man to see their vulnerability and a sense of privacy, which dictates they should not reveal what goes on in their love relationships and marriages (Rubin, 1985). At the same time, men can develop deep emotional **bonds** with other men under the right circumstances. The shared experience of maleness and especially the hardships and dangers brought on by war bond men together. Observations of combat soldiers reveal deep loyalties between individuals who have little in common except separation from women and the need to depend upon others for survival. Yet, oddly enough, self-disclosure or emotional sharing are not characteristic of even such close male relationships. Few wartime friendships are continued or intensified when life returns to normal.

> **bonds** deep, nonverbalized attachments to other persons, characterized by dependency and identification

Rubin acknowledges the almost mystical quality that men give their bondings with other men. At the same time, she believes that traditional, or macho, men miss out on true intimacy, which unlike mere bonding, requires a willingness to reveal one's inner life to someone else. Perhaps friendships are more difficult to form and maintain for traditionally masculine men than they are for androgynous men and for women in general. This is unfortunate, as men are just as likely as women to value intimate friendships (Caldwell & Peplau, 1982).

Friendships between women and men. In part because of the frustrations of attempting to have intimate friendships with other men, single men are more likely than single women to name a woman as a best friend (Rubin, 1985). As some of the men put it, "I can be more open with a woman"; "I've tried reaching out to men, . . . but they don't reciprocate, and I begin to feel like the friendship stands or falls on my initiative"; and "Women have a special way of being friends. They're more emotionally open and expressive than men" (pp. 63–64). Women, in comparison, may have close friendships with persons of either sex.

When people marry, they sometimes feel pressured to give up friends of the opposite sex. Men expect their wives to be their best friend, while women rely on both other women and their husbands for intimacy and steady companionship. In general, single men and women enjoy more friendships with people of the opposite sex than couples in committed relationships. However, middle-class and college-educated professionals tend to continue or seek out cross-sex friendships after marriage more often than do working-class people (Rubin, 1985).

Friendships between women and men are rewarding but fraught with difficulties because of the common expectation that such relationships are potentially sexual. Some of the mature adults interviewed by Rubin said that they had to get sex out of the way before becoming friends. Others avoided having sex with friends, stating it could complicate the relationship by giving rise to possessiveness and jealousy on both sides.

Relating to a lover. The reluctance of men to share feelings and vulnerabilities shows up in love relationships as well. In herterosexual love relationships, men disclose as often as their partners but are less revealing in what they disclose. Men tend to share more about their political views and strengths, while women tend to share about such intimate issues as their feelings toward people and their fears (Rubin et al., 1980).

In sexual and love relationships, as in friendships, the traditionally masculine man is less free to reveal his weaknesses and ask for support. Jourard (1971) interprets this as a lethal tendency. He speculates that men's difficulties with self-disclosure impair their ability to gain insight into themselves, develop empathy for others, have more than one intimate relationship, lead healthy and well-balanced lives, and love their partners fully. Jourard argues that this deficit in self-disclosure makes it more difficult for many men to love and be loved. One of the negative effects of this situation is that men, particularly North American and northern European men, have a harder time than women when a love relationship ends. They simply have fewer people to turn to. It may be helpful for men to take more interpersonal risks, self-disclosing their vulnerabilities to both a lover and other good friends. Such disclosures could be an insurance policy against despair should the primary relationship become shaky or end.

Sexual Attraction and Interest

The sexual relationship is an important aspect of intimacy. Some sexual relationships are fleeting, one-night stands while others grow and withstand the ravages of time. Typically, a sexual encounter is set in motion when people find each other physically attractive, one or both individuals experiences physical arousal (or "feels turned on"), and they can convince themselves that a sexual relationship is justified.

Reasons for Wanting a Sexual Relationship

People have many reasons for engaging in sexual relationships. Sex in a marriage serves a double purpose—pleasure and procreation. In more casual relationships, sex is a way of showing how much you love someone or in some cases, like the person. Sex can be an enjoyable means of passing time, like watching television or bowling. For some, sex is a form of relaxation after a stressful day or a way of playing after being overly engrossed in work. Other people use sex to gain money or prestige or to increase their power over others. For example, some traditional women hold off having sex until they are certain that a man will want to take care of them economically or marry them. For a few traditional men, the opportunity to brag about sexual conquests may be more valued than the sexual relationship itself.

Unfortunately, many people feel uncomfortable about discussing with a partner why they want to have sex. Some individuals don't want to appear unsophisticated, while others believe the partner can read their mind or must feel the same way they do. Such hesitancy arises partly from the fact that people feel extremely vulnerable when contemplating whether or not to have sex. However, this vulnerability may be an opportunity for greater intimacy if both individuals are willing to share their feelings or their purpose for having sex. It is important to remember that lovers or spouses often experience their sexuality in different ways. Good communication is an important part of good sexual relationships.

Communicating Sexual Attraction and Interest

The communication of sexual attraction and interest works like a dramatic production in which each partner's moves are determined in part by what the other says and does (McCormick, 1987). Relationships work when people are sensitive to the messages their partner sends them. Like a bad play, relationships fail when people do not listen to each other, use the wrong lines, and step on each other's toes. Whether a new sexual relationship in which two people meet at a bar or an old one in which a couple talk about whether they have time to make love before the children awake, the expression of attraction and love requires lines, flirtation, and strategies. **Lines** are the words used to convey attraction and interest, usually to a new partner. **Flirtation** is the nonverbal communication and touching through which a courting couple indicates sexual interest. Once the sexual possibilities of a relationship are established by lines and flirtation, **sexual strategies** are used by each partner to have or avoid sexual intercourse.

lines words used to convey attraction and interest in a potential intimate partner

flirtation nonverbal communication and touching characteristic of courtship or the communication of sexual interest

sexual strategies moves taken to influence a partner to have increased physical intimacy or to avoid it

Lines. One of the best ways to meet someone you find attractive is to start a conversation. Unfortunately, sex-role stereotypes inhibit both sexes from using opening lines to advantage. According to these historically accepted stereotypes, women aren't supposed to start a conversation with new men or ask them out. At the same time, men are supposed to be experts, who are always ready with a clever line.

The reluctance of women to use opening lines is understandable. Women are perceived more negatively than men when they are the first to ask someone out (Green & Sandos, 1983). At the same time, it is understandable why gentle and sensitive men sometimes get tongue-tied when approaching attractive women. How can they present themselves as the self-confident seducers that men are supposed to be in our culture?

Recent studies may provide some reassurance for those who are perplexed about the use of opening lines. Studies of college students indicate that women who approach men with lines such as, "I have been noticing you around campus. I find you very attractive," do interest men in dating and visiting them (Clark & Hatfield, 1981). Sensitive, nontraditional men may feel reassured to learn that the lines that women like best are innocuous lines, such as, "I feel embarrassed by this, but I'd like to meet you" (p. 591), and that most women are turned off by cute-flippant lines, such as, "I'm easy. Are you?" (p. 593). (Kleinke, Meeker, & Staneski, 1986). See "Exploring Choices: Lines and the Singles Scene" for further information about lines.

After listening to singles bar patrons for nearly five hundred hours, Murray (1985) describes three basic kinds of opening lines. Examples of each are presented in Table 10–3 on page 304. The most popular opening line is the question, the attempt to exchange information with someone else. Advertisements/declarations, announcing oneself as available and to some extent noting one's credentials as a lover are second in popularity. Due perhaps to the implications that only a desperate single person would use them, compliments or praise for the other person's assets are least popular.

Murray's research is intriguing from the standpoint of its implications for modern relationships. Are the complexities of close relationships and urban life so great that people seek solace in encounters with no strings attached? What do people want from sexual encounters—physical pleasure only or an understanding of one's inner nature and that of another person? Apparently, the physical pleasure of sex is more highly valued by singles bar clientele than

EXPLORING CHOICES

LINES AND THE SINGLES SCENE

The places that people frequent in search of romantic encounters vary greatly in our society. Each environment has its own traditions, and one of the most unique of these is the singles bar. The singles bar, also known as a cruise (or dating) bar, is a place where unattached people (or those who want to pass as unattached) go to meet each other. In his delightful study of the slang used by St. Louis, Missouri, bar partrons, Murray (1985) points out that the singles bar is definitely not a place for shy persons or anyone looking for a committed relationship. Using their own witty argot, people introduce themselves to others in their favorite "ballroom," an establishment noted for the sexual availability of its patrons (p. 18). Their

opening lines are as streamlined as their sexual goals: "AWOL," amour without love; "ONE," a one-night experience; and "McQ," a meaningful quickie (pp. 17–18).

As you might expect, men are more active than women in being the first to give an opening line (Murray, 1985). However, there were no substantial sex differences in the types of lines used, women being just as humorous and raunchy as the men. As Murray suggests, ". . . [T]he singles bar atmosphere—providing, as it does, the opportunity for the . . . satisfaction of primitive needs—succeeds in toppling several bastions of chauvinism that have stood for so long and remained comparatively impervious to the forces of other social institutions" (p. 21).

TABLE 10-3   Some Opening Lines in Single Bars

1. **Questions**
   • What's your name?
   • Want a date?
   • Looking for some fun?
   • Come here often?
   • Can I toot your horn?
2. **Advertisements/Declarations**
   • I'm hot . . .
   • I want you.
   • I'm a sextech [person skilled in lovemaking].
   • I'm a retread [recently divorced person].
   • I want to play.
3. **Compliments**
   • I like your (article of clothing).
   • You have good taste in drinks.
   • Nice bod.
   • I like what I can see.
   • You look like you could go all night.

Source: T. E. Murray (1985). The language of singles bars. *American Speech, 60,* 20-26.

an emotional bond or the possiblity of a long-term relationship. Obviously, this preference is not shared by everyone. In addition, it increases the risk of contracting a sexually transmitted disease.

courtship sequence of behaviors in humans and other animals initiated with the goal of terminating in mating or copulation

Flirtation. Many animals, and humans are no exception, engage in **courtship**, a complex sequence of behaviors with the ultimate goal of achieving sexual union. The courtship rituals of insects, fish, birds, and lower mammals are wired into the animals' genetic makeup. Human courtship is more varied; it is dependent on learning. However, the cross-cultural similarity of some courtship behaviors, such as looking deeply into a partner's eyes, suggests an evolutionary origin (Perper, 1985). Flirtation, as introduced earlier, consists of all nonverbal communication and touching that takes place during human courtship. Whether or not lines are exchanged or conversation takes place, courting couples define and increase intimacy through an established sequence of nonverbal gestures followed by physical contact. Flirtation can take place anywhere—in singles bars, at school, at work, in public, or in private. Body language is often more subtle or ambiguous than words (opening lines). As a result, people sometimes flirt without being aware that they are.

Cross-cultural research indicates that people have similar patterns of flirtation regardless of where they live (Rosenblatt, 1974). However, individuals, and women in particular, are restricted from flirting openly in many societies. Fortunately, women and men are relatively free to flirt in our society. This enables us to make sexual choices that may be unavailable to people in other parts of the world.

Flirting is an effective way to show someone you are interested. It is also fun with a long-term partner. Both heterosexuals and homosexuals flirt. Just as a dancing couple works together, neither partner dominates a flirtation. Instead, each individual uses facial expression, body language, and touching to signal whether or not he or she would welcome further advances (McCormick & Jesser, 1983). There are six different types of flirtation behavior: (1) establishing eye contact, (2) moving closer to a partner, (3) shifting to an open body posture, (4) maintaining a pleasant facial expression, (5) touching, and (6) grooming. Examples and definitions of each are provided in Table 10–4.

In contrast with sex-role stereotypes, women often take the sexual initiative during flirtation (Perper, 1985). Although neither sex dominates entirely, women often understand what goes on during flirtations better than men do. Moore's (1985) well-designed observational research suggests that women actually control the frequency of male approaches by soliciting men's interest by facial and head movements (such as lip licking), gestures (like hiking up their skirts), and postures (including accidently-on-purpose brushing against an attractive man). In Moore's research, the more different flirtation behaviors a woman used and the more frequently she signalled, the more often she was approached by a man.

A growing number of observational studies challenge the sex-role stereotype that only men should start a sexual interaction. The tendencies of women to touch their flirting partners also contradict the finding reported in the last chapter that men touch women more than they are touched in return. Monica

---

TABLE 10–4   Flirtation Behaviors

Type and Definition	Example
1. Establishing *eye contact*—gazing toward a partner. The glance is soft and liquid, and quite unlike a stare.	Her pupils widening, a woman looks into her lover's eyes. He returns her longing gaze.
2. *Moving closer*—positioning one's body in order to be closer to a partner.	A man walks up to an attractive woman at a bar to be close enough to be noticed by her.
3. Shifting to an *open body posture*—sitting, standing, or reclining without any tension. Avoiding crossing legs and arms or holding limbs tightly against body.	Two attracted gay men talk with each in a relaxed manner. One man's arms are open. Seated, the other man's legs are parted widely.
4. Maintaining a *pleasant facial expression*—face displays positive feelings.	A woman smiles at someone she just met. Her expression is warm and friendly.
5. *Touching*—placing part of one's own body on or next to the partner's. Touch may be *brief* (fleeting physical contact), *continuous* (ongoing or done for longer than a few seconds), or *intimate* (aimed at conveying ownership of partner or attempting to increase arousal).	• *Brief Touching*—woman smooths out another woman's collar. • *Continuous Touching*—man puts his arm around the back of a woman's chair. • *Intimate Touching*—two individuals kiss and hug each other; their bodies touch in several places as they do so.
6. *Grooming*—Any public attempt to improve personal appearance.	Woman sucks in her stomach and runs her fingers through her long hair.

Source: Adapted from N. B. McCormick, T. Perper, & A. J. Jones (1983, April). *Bar hopping as science: Results and methodological issues related to naturalistic observation research in bars.* Philadelphia: Paper presented at the Eastern Region Conference of the Society for the Scientific Study of Sex.

Moore (1975), for example, documented women caressing a man's face and neck, stroking the man's thigh and inner leg, patting him on the buttocks while standing, making sure that her knees or feet touched his, and even taking the man's hand and placing it on her body.

Flirtation involves more than a random combination of selective nonverbal behaviors and touching. Instead, most flirtation sequences follow a general pattern. Spending more than nine hundred hours observing North American adults flirt in bars and other public places, Perper (1985) points out that successful flirtation is a five-step process:

1. *Approach*—one individual moves toward another and this approach is acknowledged by positive nonverbal signals (such as a smile).
2. *Talk*—a conversation begins typically on superficial topics like the setting or employment.
3. *Turn*—the individuals change from the shoulder-to-shoulder position to a face-to-face position. This gradual change in direction can take anywhere from a few minutes to hours.
4. *Touching*—one or both individuals touch each other often, fleetingly at first. Touching becomes more continuous and intimate as courtship escalates.
5. *Synchronization*—each partner mirrors the other's body movements and postures. In full-body synchronization, people look at each other nearly continuously, touch each other frequently, and talk face to face.

A number of interesting things may occur during full-body synchronization (Perper, 1985). Being in a public place inhibits some couples, but others kiss and embrace openly. Activities around the couple are ignored. It is as if the couple has "built an enclave of privacy around them into which the external world only rarely penetrates" (p. 79).

Flirtation and relationship skills. As you think about what you have just read, consider your own style of relating to a new or long-term partner. Depending on your preferences, you can communicate your desires for intimacy either delicately (through flirtation) or directly (through lines). Paying attention to your partner's responses to your own actions will increase your social sensitivity. Do not believe that if a particular person isn't interested in pursuing a relationship, you are a loser and should give up pursuing relationships entirely. The more people you try to meet, the more likely that you will be successful.

Strategies for having or avoiding sex. Flirtation and opening lines establish the intimate potential of a relationship. An individual's next move depends in part on cultural expectations (Hall, 1959). Latin American culture, unlike our own, emphasizes external control over sexuality. It is assumed that people have no willpower when it comes to sex. Therefore, if a man and woman are alone, Latin American people are certain that they will be unable to resist having sex.

In contrast, North American culture presents a complex model of sexual behavior (McCormick & Jesser, 1983). On the one hand, sexual urges are supposed to be hard to control, especially for men. On the other hand, women are expected to set limits on the attempts of men to seduce them.

North Americans believe that people have choices as to whether or not to have sex. These choices are made through the use of sexual strategies (power or influence attempts that are directed toward the goal of having or avoiding sex with a partner). College students' expectations and use of strategies in sexual encounters are discussed in "On the Research Frontier: Strategies for Having or Avoiding Sex" on pages 308 and 309.

Regardless of sex roles, people in our culture are free to take risks or experiment with unstereotyped behavior in close relationships. This process of risk taking may help people make better sexual choices. Men have every right to refuse sex. Men are not sex machines, and a lack of interest in sex at a given moment or with a particular partner is hardly proof of a lack of sexiness or failing manhood. On the other hand, women don't have to be passive. Sexually assertive women increase their chances of having pleasurable sex.

LOVE RELATIONSHIPS

authentic love
relationship based on the ability to care deeply for someone else without losing a sense of self

romantic love type of authentic love based on intense passion for and identification with a beloved

friendly love type of authentic love that is similar to the affectionate relationship between two best friends

Sometimes, the declaration "I love you" is greeted by the question "Exactly what kind of love do you feel?" This question is more reasonable than it may appear. Love is hard to define in general because each of us experiences it differently. To make matters more confusing, any given individual can have more than one type of love for each significant person in his or her life. It is helpful to realize that love, like colors, can be broken down into basic types from which the vast variety are blended. Just as a spectacular rainbow is created from three primary colors, there are six basic types of love that in combination can describe just about any deeply intimate relationship accurately (Hendrick et al., 1984). Focusing on the love relationships heterosexual and homosexual adults may have with a sexual partner, these six types of love follow.

Authentic love relationships are based on the ability to care deeply for other persons without losing oneself in the relationship. Authentic lovers balance accurate understanding of the beloved's needs with an appreciation of the importance of continued individual development. The three types of authentic love are (1) romantic love, (2) friendly love, and (3) altruistic love.

- **Romantic love** is compelling and passionate. For an intense but brief moment in their lives, romantic lovers identify with each other completely, always have the beloved in mind, and find separations exceptionally painful.

- **Friendly love,** in contrast, is the affection shared between two best friends. Enriched by years of intimacy, friendly lovers treat each other as equals and encourage the partner's independence. Unlike romantic lovers, friendly lov-

ON THE RESEARCH FRONTIER

STRATEGIES FOR HAVING OR AVOIDING SEX

Happy sexual relationships facilitate good psychological adjustment. Yet such relationships are impossible unless people communicate effectively whether or not they desire sex. For more than a decade, my colleagues and I have studied college students' expectations and strategies for influencing sexual encounters with dating partners. While our results are most pertinent to young, single heterosexuals attempting to influence new partners, they may interest more mature individuals, those in long-term relationships, and gay men and lesbians.

Regardless of their sex-role attitudes or personalities, men and women hold powerful stereotypes about intimate sexual relationships. Traditional and egalitarian students usually report that men are likely to use any strategy in the book to have sex whereas women are most likely to try to get out of having sexual intercourse (McCormick, 1979). Whether or not they feel in charge of their own lives or have strong needs to please others, college students expect men to push for sex and women to be coy or resist (LaPlante,

McCormick, & Brannigan, 1980; McCormick, Brannigan, & LaPlante, 1984).

When faced with sexual choices, to what extent do college students live up to the belief that sex is a tug-of-war between a lusting man and a reluctant woman? The answer is unclear. It all depends on what you ask them. When we list numerous techniques for having or avoiding sexual intercourse and ask students to indicate which strategies they have used and which were used on them, just about everyone agrees that men push for sex and women resist. However, when we ask these same young people to write an essay describing how they might influence an attractive dating partner, many sex differences disappear. Both women and men write about subtle or indirect strategies, for example, "I would test my limits by holding hands, sitting closer to this person, . . . doing more listening and minimal talking" (McCormick, 1979, p. 199). Seduction (setting the stage for a romantic atmosphere and touching the partner in increasingly intimate ways to heighten arousal) was popular with both sexes.

altruistic love type of authentic love that is based on giving

false love relationships that are passed off as loving but in actuality are attempts to use or live through others

ers do not think about each other constantly and are comfortable with brief separations.

- **Altruistic love** is the love of giving. Altruistic lovers are forgiving, supportive, and empathic. Putting the beloved before oneself, the altruistic lover is even willing to sacrifice the relationship if it appears that this is in the partner's best interests.

All that glitters is not gold; all that passes for love is not. **False love**, the fool's gold of intimate relationships, exists when people use the beloved to

In contrast with the elaborate seductive plans and indirect approach for influencing a partner to have sex, men and women said they would use obvious, or direct, strategies to avoid sex. When asked how they would convey that they didn't want sex to an obviously aroused partner, a common approach was something like this: "If (----) still insists on making love, I'd remind (----) that it's my apartment and (----) can just leave" (p. 199).

The implications of our research are interesting. Apparently, men and women have the potential for behaving much the same when faced with sexual choices. It makes sense to be manipulative or indirect if you want to convince someone to have sex. Subtle body language, arousing touches, and creating a romantic atmosphere lend themselves to this.

On the other hand, it is important to be very clear and direct if you don't want to have sex. Otherwise, there is a greater risk that a partner will misread your actions and think that you are playing hard to get but really want sex anyway. Unfortunately, some aggressive, traditional men assume that women always want sex, regardless of what they say or do. The most common form of sexual assault, acquaintance rape, frequently takes place because of the man's failure to attend to the woman's verbal and nonverbal signals that she does not want to have sex, even though she may have liked or felt some attraction to her partner.

Despite their potential to assume either the active or resistant role in a sexual encounter, young single heterosexuals usually conform to the sex-role stereotypes. Why might this be the case? The answer seems to be that men and women face different rewards and costs in a sexual relationship. First, our culture's sexual double standard (the belief that premarital and extramarital sex are more permissible for men than for women) makes having sex costly for women and avoiding sex costly for men. Women who have had many sexual partners and sexually inactive men are targets for gossip and hostile humor. Second, women, but not men, face the possibility of an unwanted pregnancy or acquaintance rape.

compensate for poor self-esteem and provide themselves with a purpose or prestige. Often, the false lover expects to be taken care of as if he or she were a helpless child.

Most of people's love problems concern false relationships. There are three types of false love relationships: (1) self-centered love, (2) practical love, and (3) addicted love.

self-centered love
type of false love based on exploitation and game playing

- **Self-centered love** is expressed by those who play at love affairs as if they were games, are frightened by commitment, and like to keep more than one lover on a string. Self-centered lovers view other people as objects that can be replaced easily.

practical love type of false love in which loyalty exists as long as the relationship serves one's best interests

- **Practical love** occurs when people treat intimacy as if it were a business deal. Loyal as long as the relationship is in their best interests, practical lovers are in love with good looks, money, and family background.

addicted love type of false love in which the individual sacrifices independence, outside interests, and all other relationships for the sake of the relationship

- **Addicted love,** the most pernicious of false love relationships, is hard to detect because it resembles romantic love. Addicted lovers sacrifice independence, outside interests, and other relationships on the altar of love. In exchange, they expect the beloved to be at constant beck and call. Prone to irrational jealously, addicted lovers are extremely anxious when away from the beloved.

Many films, television programs, magazine articles, and songs present false love, especially addicted love, as if it were the real thing. To raise your consciousness about this, you may wish to do the exercise in "Exploring Choices: Popular Songs Define Love."

As you may see from the exercise, addictive love is frequently passed off as romantic love in popular culture. In addition, romantic love receives more attention than the other two types of authentic love. Yet romantic love, by its very nature, cannot last long (Hatfield 1983). Once you have nursed a partner through stomach flu, heard all of his or her favorite stories several times, run out of ideas for thoughtful surprise gifts for birthdays and holidays, and made love so many times that you know his or her body by heart, it is not easy to view the person through the gossamer of romance. If you think that romantic love is the only real love, it is easy to grow impatient with long-term partners. Popular culture generally devalues friendly and altruistic love, the kinds of love that nurture lasting relationships. While the well-adjusted person leaves a relationship that causes more pain than pleasure, he or she doesn't drop a partner just because the flame of romance has been extinguished.

Sex Differences in Handling Love Relationships

Consistent with the sex roles they learn throughout their lives, men and women sometimes respond to love relationships in different ways. However, not all the sex differences that characterize North American love relationships are consistent with our stereotypes. Love is important to both sexes. The scientific literature often contradicts the popular view of the strong silent man, unwilling to make a commitment, and the clinging woman who is desperate for love. In fact, both sexes value such traditional aspects of close relationships as spending time together and knowing that the relationship will endure (Cochran & Peplau, 1985). **Sexual exclusivity,** the expectation that partners will not have sex outside the primary relationship, is highly valued by many couples. Traditionally, heterosexuals placed greater importance on sexual exclusivity than lesbians and gay men (Peplau & Gordon, 1983). However, the recent increase in the number of individuals contracting sexually transmitted

sexual exclusivity expectation that a partner or spouse will not have sex outside the primary relationship

EXPLORING CHOICES

POPULAR SONGS DEFINE LOVE

Spend some time listening to popular songs about love on the radio, television, or stereo. Select a song on the following bases: (1) it is currently popular, (2) it is a love song, and (3) there are enough lyrics to analyze. Answer the following questions about the song(s) you considered:

1. To what extent do the lyrics describe authentic or false ways of loving? Support your conclusions by citing specific lines from the song.
2. What messages does this song give about the choices or lack of choices for women and men in love relationships? If you believed these messages, how might you behave in your own intimate relationships? Why might such behavior be beneficial or problematic?

3. Argue against any of the messages from the song that you think would inhibit people from making healthy choices in intimate relationships. How, if at all, should this song be rewritten to minimize harmful sex-role stereotypes and reflect a more realistic depiction of love relationships?

diseases, such as herpes and AIDS, has contributed to a renewed emphasis on sexual exclusivity in couples regardless of sexual preference.

Men are sometimes more vulnerable in love relationships than women are. Among college students, women are more likely than men to initiate a breakup in a serious dating relationship even when they are the more highly involved (Hill, Rubin, & Peplau, 1976). Women, in contrast to men, tend to be more aware of problems in the relationship and to consider alternatives to the present involvement.

When the relationship terminates, men frequently are hit harder than women. Men describe themselves as being more depressed, unhappy, lonely, and helpless when a love affair dies than women do. It may be harder for men to accept that they are no longer loved, because in our culture they feel less free to self-disclose. The only individual that some men share their intimate secrets with is the lover. When she is gone, there may be no one else to turn to, even to discuss his feelings about the ending of the relationship.

There seem to be some sex differences in the ways that people express love. In authentic love relationships, men are more likely to be romantic lovers and women are more likely to be friendly lovers (Hatfield, 1983). In false love relationships, women are more likely to be practical and addicted lovers, whereas men are more likely to be self-centered lovers (Hendrick et al., 1984).

Sex differences aside, the experience of loving and being loved is usually similar for women and men. Both men and women may feel the passion of romantic love and the tenderness of friendly love. Altruistic love is rare for either sex. Some women exploit others in self-centered love affairs as much or more than men do. Similarly, men may select partners for practical reasons (such as how the partners' attractiveness will improve their status with other men) or be addicted lovers in a self-destructive relationship. Regarding addictive love, men are more likely than women to commit suicide after a disastrous addictive love affair (Hatfield, 1983).

Clearly, there is no evidence that one sex is more capable of intimacy than the other. Similarly, research suggests that whether a relationship is heterosexual or homosexual, both partners tend to like as well as love the other a great deal. Peplau and Cochran (1980) noted no differences between heterosexual and homosexual men and women in the extent to which partners felt close to each other, felt satisfied with the love relationship, felt committed, and were interested in seeing each other frequently. When asked to describe the best and worst aspects of their relationships, lesbians, gay men, and heterosexuals report the same joys and difficulties (Peplau & Gordon, 1983). The best thing about most relationships was that they provided people with affection, opportunities for personal development, companionship, and good sex. The worst things included interfering relatives and having a partner who was either too emotionally dependent or had difficulty sharing feelings.

Although men and women are similar in their capacity to care for each other, there are some sex differences in what they would like out of love relationships. Interestingly enough, these sex differences cut across sexual orientations. Women, both heterosexual and lesbian, are more likely than men to emphasize the importance of emotional sharing and equal power in a love relationship (Peplau & Gordon, 1983). Men, in contrast, are more likely to view sex as one of the major advantages of having a close relationship (Peplau, Rubin, & Hill, 1977).

Love and Good Adjustment

The capacity to love and the opportunity to receive love are aspects of the good life. As the warm sun and gentle rain nurture plants, liking and loving facilitate healthy development and good psychological adjustment. It is important, nonetheless, to place intimacy in its proper perspective. Individuals should learn to discriminate between authentic friendships and love affairs on the one hand, and false, exploitative, or addictive relationships on the other. Unlike false love relationships, partners in authentic intimate relationships value autonomy and have interests and close relationships aside from the primary ones. The authentic lover takes pleasure in the company of the beloved but can be satisfied or happy when alone as well. Largely free of possessiveness and jealousy, the authentic lover encourages the beloved to maintain serious interests in other people and pursuits, to function independently as well as in the relationship. Most importantly, the authentic lover recognizes that he or she is not the center of the universe, including the beloved's life. With warmth and objectivity, the authentic lover can tolerate the fact that the beloved sees things differently and may have different objectives at times.

In authentic love relationships, there is an appreciation for what the beloved can teach about life. This appreciation contrasts with the false lover's demands that those she or he cares for conform to expectations like dogs obeying a master. The authentic lover cares for another person for who he or she is, not just for what this individual can do to enhance the lover's ego. Exploitive lovers, however, are unsure about their value as people outside their relationships. For them, self-esteem is generated by the responses of those who are significant in their lives. Practical lovers overemphasize how others regard them as well. They become obsessed with whether or not their relationship is a bargain. In constantly weighing the costs and advantages of being in love, they can become inflexible when a partner desires change, thereby failing to take the emotional risks that encourage meaningful personal growth.

It is important, too, to remember there is more to life than loving and being loved. Without this perspective, the ending or threatened ending of an intimate relationship can be devastating. To be sure, life lacks some of its pleasure or charm if we lose a close friend or lover. However, we can continue to value ourselves, focus on doing what makes us happy as individuals, and recognize that rejection by one individual hardly means that we can never have a satisfactory love relationship in the future (Ellis, 1977). People are always free to make choices, even if they have been trapped in false love relationships before.

A number of self-help books and tapes provide helpful advice for people who find themselves trapped in a network of false and unrewarding love relationships. Some of the favorite books include *Why Do I Think I Am Nothing Without a Man?* by Penelope Russianoff (1981) and *Love and Addiction* by Stanton Peele and Archie Brodsky (1975). For those who prefer listening to tapes, a tape of Albert Ellis's (1978) dynamic lecture "Conquering the Dire Need for Love," is available from the Institute for Rational-Emotive Therapy in New York.

When considering intimacy, the difficulties of even the best of authentic friendships and love affairs should be recognized by partners. Friendship and love relationships may become strained because these might be the only places in which people feel free to remove their social masks and allow themselves to share feelings and experience vulnerability. Wear and tear from frequent interactions over time take their toll as well. Sometimes, the battle scars of these close relationships are proof of their value as well. The recognition that two people have struggled through previous conflicts successfully is reassuring during the next challenging period in the relationship. It is difficult to balance one's own needs and desires with those of a partner. Individuals may experience inner conflict regarding how close or how autonomous to be. Growth occurs as people recognize the capacity to choose whom to be close to, how close to be, and how to maintain individuality in the context of intimacy. Growth is especially fostered when people recognize that healthy, intimate relationships change over time and that people can make choices about what they want from them throughout their lives.

SUMMARY

1. Intimate relationships are important but difficult. The two basic kinds of intimate relationships are friendship and love.

2. Culture and sex roles influence the choices available to people in intimate relationships. In North America, women are freer to touch each other and develop intimate friendships than men are. The opposite holds true in the Middle East and in Mediterranean Europe.

3. Cultures prescribe how close people should stand, how much touching they should engage in, and how free they are to look into one another's eyes. For this reason, it is sometimes uncomfortable to interact with someone from another culture.

4. Support groups of family and friends can help people solve financial, emotional, and child care-problems. Such groups may be especially important to the poor and minorities.

5. Liking is based on respect and similarity. Loving is based on attachment, caring, and intimacy. The most successful, long-term relationships are those in which partners both like and love each other.

6. Sex roles contribute to the ability to like and love. In our culture, women love their friends of the same sex and like their lovers of the opposite sex more than men do.

7. Both physical attractiveness and similarity in values and interests play roles in the selection of friends and lovers. People may become both more similar and more tolerant of differences as relationships mature.

8. The belief that opposites attract enjoys little research support. Instead, spouses and lovers who appear to have complementary needs may simply be demonstrating the sexual division of labor.

9. The closer people are geographically, the more likely they are to become friends or fall in love. To achieve intimacy, it is important to be around other people as much as possible.

10. In new and long-term relationships, intimacy is fostered by openness, the willingness to discuss controversial issues, appropriate levels of self-disclosure, and respect for confidentiality.

11. Women have more intimate friendships with others of their sex than men do. Men may feel strong bonds with other men, but they are reluctant to show vulnerability. Friendships between men and women are more common among singles and middle-class married people than among working-class married people.

12. Men and women disclose about the same amount of material to lovers, but women share more intimate experiences than men do. Both lesbians and

heterosexual women value self-disclosure and emotional expressiveness in love relationships more than do gay and heterosexual men.

13. Women are less likely than men to use opening lines. However, they may be more likely than men to make the first move in a flirtation or to touch a partner while flirting. Flirtation takes place in the following steps: (1) approaching someone else, (2) talking, (3) turning to face the partner, (4) touching, and (5) synchronization of the couple's movements and postures.

14. Relationships and relationship skills are built through practice and refusal to condemn oneself in the face of rejection.

15. College students believe that men use any and all strategies to have sexual intercourse and women do the same to avoid it. However, when considering the same choices, male and female students influence a potential sexual partner in much the same way.

16. There are six types of love that may be experienced with a particular partner. The three types of authentic love are romantic, friendly, and altruistic love. The three types of false love are self-centered, practical, and addicted love. Romantic love receives too much emphasis and is often confused with addicted love in our society.

17. All people experience love relationships in similar ways. However, emotional sharing and equal power with a lover are more important to women than to men. Men are more likely to be romantic lovers, and women are more likely to be friendly lovers. In sharp contrast with sex-role stereotypes, men feel more vulnerable than do women when a relationship ends.

18. Authentic love relationships are largely free of possessiveness and jealousy. False love, in contrast, is characterized by escalating demands and a lack of trust. Numerous self-help materials are available to help people make better choices in love relationships.

Chapter 11

Marriage and Other Committed Relationships

The maiden, lonely and suffering, worthy but unappreciated, at last meets her knight in shining armor. Struggling against incredible odds, fighting off dragons and a host of enemies, the couple fall in love and escape together. Once and forever with the beloved, there are no self-doubts, no difficult decisions, no irritations. Predictably, the couple, a match made in heaven, marry and have children. Then maiden, knight, and the children live happily and prosperously ever after—or so the fairy tale goes.

Is everyone happily married? Does every couple have children? What happens to adults and children when committed relationships mature or end? Aside from marriage, what kinds of intimate relationship are possible? How does family life vary for those from different social classes and ethnic groups? This chapter replaces the fairy tale with reality and attempts to answer these and other questions about committed relationships.

WHY PEOPLE WANT COMMITTED RELATIONSHIPS

Most people desire the same things from committed relationships. When asked what they want from a partner, men and women, both heterosexual and homosexual, indicate that they are looking for someone with whom to share affection, intimate secrets, and companionship (Peplau & Gordon, 1983). Few people prefer hit-and-run intimacy. Both hetereosexuals and homosexuals strive to obtain and maintain secure, lasting relationships that endure in bad as well as good times.

social facade front, or image, people present to others in order to look good

It is exhausting to have to keep putting one's best foot forward to impress a new partner. The deepest intimacy is possible only between those who relax their **social facade**, the good front they present to others. Yet, if partners relax their social graces too much, it can hurt the relationship over time. It may feel good to be irritable, overlook a birthday or anniversary because of fatigue or overwork, and be somewhat careless about one's appearance. At the same time, these qualities can contribute to a long-term partner's dissatisfaction with the relationship, rooted in the belief that he or she is taken for granted.

single living independently from a sexual partner

cohabitation living with a sexual partner of the same or the opposite gender

Although may people strive for and work hard at maintaining committed relationships, well-adjusted people vary in their preferences. Some couples love to do everything together. Others try to balance companionship with devotion to a career, time alone to pursue interests, and a social life with personal friends. Women among the educated, young adult groups are more likely than men to define a good relationship as one that does not infringe too much on their personal independence (Peplau, 1983).

marriage legal and sometimes religiously binding relationship between a man and woman

There are many possible life-styles to choose from—being **single** and living independently, **cohabitation** (living with a partner of the same or opposite sex in the absence of a formal legal contract), and **marriage** (a legal and sometimes religiously binding relationship). Although these choices may be limited by cultural and economic constraints, each of us has choices about whether to have a committed relationship, raise children, or work on improving marital and family interactions.

UNMARRIED ADULT LIFE-STYLES

Unmarried people vary greatly. Some have never been married, some have been married once before, and others have had several previous marriages. They also live in different types of households. Single people may live alone or with friends and relatives. Cohabiting people live with a sexual partner. Both single and cohabiting people may take care of their own or a partner's children as well.

Single People

Well over one third of adults in the United States are unmarried, and the largest proportion of these have never been married (Phillis & Stein, 1983). Separated, divorced, and widowed persons make up the rest of the unmarried population. Homosexuals are single in part because they are not allowed to marry legally. Heterosexuals may remain single throughout their lives for numerous reasons. Some people delay marriage until they feel emotionally and economically ready to bear the burders of such an important commitment. Others have little choice.

For example, a disproportionately large number of households among impoverished, black American families are headed by women for several reasons (Darity & Myers, 1984). Initially crushed by slavery in the United States, the black family continues to be vulnerable. Denied access to education and jobs, poor black men find it difficult to support a family. Worse still, economic hardship and political oppression create hopelessness in many young men who reside in urban slums, contributing to an excessively high male death rate due to illness, alcohol or drug addiction, suicide, and homicide. As a result, many lower-class black women cannot get married—whether they want to or not—because fewer eligible men are available to them.

The large numbers of single people argue against the stereotype that only disturbed people and losers make up the ranks of the unmarried. All kinds of people remain single. In fact, single life seems to agree with women more than marriage. Single women describe themselves as happier than single men, and they are less likely to be treated for psychological problems than are married women (Stevens-Long, 1984). Ironically, men and women with little education and highly educated women are more likely never to marry than others groups (Phillis & Stein, 1983). It is possible that some highly educated women prefer to remain single because they see marriage as a threat to their careers and personal development. On the other hand, traditional and insecure men may avoid such women because they find them too competent or powerful.

In contrast with the fairy tale of falling in love and living happily ever after, there are positive reasons for being single. Traditional marriage, founded on conventional sex roles, may diminish one's chances of realizing one's full human potential. Single people may enjoy greater opportunities to develop in an androgynous way. The single woman, more than her married counterpart, may take pleasure in becoming competent in a career or at household repairs.

The single man, more than his married counterpart, may take pleasure in developing his career and entertaining friends. In addition, being single does not preclude the possibility of having committed and close relationships, one or more of which is sexually intimate. Living alone and being lonely are not the same things.

In addition, many single people live with others—family members, friends, and roommates. Finally, numerous single people are parents. The children they tend may or may not be the products of previous marriages. Because many homosexuals have had partners of the opposite sex at some point in their lives, lesbian women and gay men are often parents, too (Miller, 1979). Like other separated and divorced persons, they may struggle with the challenges of raising a child alone or with the agony of being separated from a youngster who lives with the other parent.

Cohabitation

The decision to live with a sexual partner has important implications for both partners, their respective social networks, and the larger community. To function effectively, previously autonomous partners must learn to compromise and to share economic and housekeeping responsibilities. Family and friends are pressured to accept the new partner as a permanent member of their intimate group. Faced with the possibility of social disapproval, the cohabiting couple has to decide whether or not to be open about the status of their relationship with significant others, neighbors, coworkers, and casual acquaintances.

Heterosexual couples. In the past quarter of a century, increasing numbers of heterosexuals are living together outside of marriage (Spanier, 1983). Although most cohabiting couples are in their twenties and thirties, a substantial minority are older. Approximately half of these couples have never been married, while the other half are either previously married or officially married to a partner they are not living with. In some cases, the children of one or both of the partners live with them. However, the vast majority either do not have children or are not living with their children.

All together, nearly four million persons in the United States live in a household that includes a man and woman who are not married to each other. Cohabiting couples differ from married ones in some important ways. Both partners in a cohabiting relationship are more likely to be in the labor force. Cohabiting couples may have more liberal values. Interracial couples and couples in which both partners are highly educated are more prevalent among cohabiting than among conventionally married people (Glick & Spanier, 1980).

When a man and woman decide to live together on an informal basis, friends, family members, and the individuals themselves may wonder whether they should get married. There are a number of reasons for choosing cohabitation over marriage. First, the couple may desire greater intimacy but not feel enough commitment to bind the relationship legally and perhaps religiously

(Newcomb, 1981). Some couples view cohabitation as a temporary relationship; others view it as preparation for marriage. Second, individuals may be opposed to the institution of marriage itself, believing that a truly intimate relationship between a man and woman should be entirely voluntary and not controlled or sanctioned by society as a whole.

Whatever their reasons are for living together, cohabiting couples tend to be as satisfied with their relationships as married couples (Newcomb, 1981). Consistent with their liberal values, cohabiting couples tend to have more androgynous personalities. Cohabiting women, in particular, are likely to state a strong preference for egalitarian relationships between men and women (Newcomb, 1981). Despite androgynous and egalitarian tendencies, traditional sex roles are alive and well among cohabiting couples. Heterosexuals who live together divide household tasks according to sex and not necessarily personal preference or ability. Both married and cohabiting women do most of the housework. However, cohabiting individuals are more likely to perform cross-sex traditional chores as well (such as men doing the dishes and women mowing the grass).

Cohabiting individuals tend to be more liberal about sex than other heterosexuals. Studies comparing married couples who had cohabited with those who had not generally reveal that cohabitors are more likely to have had sex with partners outside of the primary relationship and to have engaged in greater sexual experimentation prior to marriage (Newcomb, 1981). Related to their liberal sexual values, cohabiting individuals are less religious and are more likely to be attracted to alternative life-styles than noncohabitors.

Many cohabiting couples marry eventually. When they do, they are less likely than other couples to participate in elaborate marital rituals, such as a big wedding and honeymoon (Risman et al., 1981). In addition, they are less likely than other couples to bear children during the first four years of marriage, refuting the popular belief that the pull toward parenthood motivates couples to formalize the relationship with marital vows (Newcomb & Bentler, 1980). In fact, married couples who have cohabitated plan to have smaller families than noncohabitors.

It is difficult to say how living together before marriage affects marital adjustment. Each couple is unique, and the research literature is not consistent. Some researchers (Jacques & Chason, 1979) find no differences in marital satisfaction between cohabitators and nocohabitators who are well educated and religious. Others, such as DeMaris and Leslie (1984) find that compared with noncohabitors, cohabitors are much less satisfied with married life. It may be that educated and religious people in general are more likely to be satisfied with their marriages than less-educated and religious people.

Related to the advocacy of alternative life-styles, those who live together before marriage may have greater difficulty coping with a partner's outside interests and friends, alcohol or drug abuse, and interest in extramarital relationships than do noncohabitors (Newcomb, 1981). In contrast, they are less susceptible than noncohabitors to such marital problems as career conflicts and constant bickering. Cohabitors seem to have higher standards for mar-

It is difficult to say
how living together
before marriage
affects marital
adjustment.

"NOT COUNTING THE YEARS WE LIVED TOGETHER BEFORE WE WERE MARRIED, THE TRIAL SEPARATIONS AND THE TIMES WE WORKED ON OPPOSITE COASTS, THIS IS OUR FIRST ANNIVERSARY."

riage than noncohabitors; they are more likely to divorce given fewer marital difficulties than are married couples who have not lived together prior to marriage. This does not imply that all cohabitors lack a strong commitment to marriage. Overall, those who cohabited in the past are no more likely than other married people to seek divorce.

Homosexual couples. Couples of the same sex also live together on a long-term basis. However, unlike either cohabiting or married heterosexuals, most homosexual couples actively reject traditional husband-wife roles. Instead, most gay and lesbian couples model their relationships after close friendships (Peplau & Gordon, 1983). The majority studied by researchers report that both partners share in housekeeping, outside employment, decision making, and an active role in sex. This is especially the case with highly educated, middle- and upper-class couples.

In the typical gay or lesbian couple, both partners are employed outside the home. Sometimes, wide income discrepancies are a source of conflict between partners (McWhirter & Mattison, 1984). However, as relationships mature, individuals gradually merge their finances and support each other willingly during times of unemployment. Household chores are handled according to the stage of a couple's relationship. In new relationships, both partners may do everything together, taking pleasure in the intimacy that such teamwork fosters. Later, individuals assume responsibility for particular chores according to each partner's abilities and interests. The person who cooks is the one who enjoys cooking most or is best at it and is not, as some would assume, the subordinate or more feminine partner.

Regardless of their sexual preference, men and women are socialized in different ways. Therefore, it should not be surprising that there are some differences between the intimate relationships of lesbians and gay men. Peplau's (1982) review of the research suggests that lesbians are more likely than gay men to desire sexual exclusivity, live with the partner, and value emotional intimacy and equality. Like their heterosexual counterparts, lesbian women value emotional expressiveness more than do men (Peplau, 1979). Sex differences in close relationships, however, should not blind people to individual differences. Like their heterosexual counterparts, homosexual couples vary greatly in the extent to which they prefer togetherness or independence and social and political involvement in the outside community (Peplau et al., 1978).

Homosexual couples have a lot in common with cohabiting and married couples; the majority in all three groups are highly satisfied with their partners and have good relationships (Peplau, Cochran, & Mays, 1986). A study of nearly three hundred black lesbians who currently had lovers revealed that most of the women described the relationships as both happy and likely to last for years to come.

MARRIAGE AND THE FAMILY

social class division in society based on income and rank

ethnic group distinctive racial, cultural, or language group

Most North Americans get married one or more times. By the time they are in their early thirties, over 90 percent of the adults living in the United States have been married (Stevens-Long, 1984). Singlehood and cohabitation appear to be stages in the lives of the majority of heterosexuals and not permanent life-styles. However, opportunities to marry are influenced greatly by **social class** and **ethnic group.** Lower-class people, for example, marry at a younger age than do their middle-class counterparts (Rubin, 1976). Black American women have fewer opportunities to marry, and they stand a greater chance of experiencing a breakup of the marriage than do white women (Heiss, 1975).

A Multicultural and Realistic Perspective

intact, nuclear families families in which children and both biological parents live together in an independent household

extended families families including all relatives by blood or marriage (parents, sons, daughters, siblings, uncles, aunts, cousins, grandparents, great grandparents, and in-laws of various types)

upper middle class affluent businesspeople and professionals whose status and educational advantages are surpassed only by the wealthiest members of society

lower middle class white-collar, or office, workers and those who have skilled blue-collar jobs in industry, construction, and agriculture

upper lower class semiskilled workers who are less highly paid than members of the lower middle class

lower lower class impoverished and uneducated persons who are either chronically unemployed or engaged in menial jobs

What is the North American family like? Popular television programs present an unrealistic picture. According to those who write situation comedies, the typical family—white or minority—is affluent, happy, and rarely childless. Almost always, children are portrayed as living in **intact, nuclear families**, with both biological parents. Problems are minor and hardly ever interfere with the quality of family relationships. Outside of the parents, family members play at most a minor role. Mom and Dad never think about ending their relationship; theirs is a marriage characterized by sharing and equality. Free from marital stress and liberated from time-consuming jobs, both adults are readily the happy targets of the children's wisecracks. There is plenty of leisure time for family members to pursue enjoyable interactions, and children—even adolescents—want to interact with their parents.

In contrast with television's idealized portrait, communal life can be stressful, and there are many alternative kinds of marriage and family. Few families are as affluent as those portrayed on television. In most intact, nuclear families, both husband and wife find it necessary to work outside the home (Pleck, 1985). As a result, both partners have three full-time jobs: worker, caretaker of home, and parent. It is not always easy for couples to balance such a heavy work load. At times, marital and parental relationships suffer as a result.

Real American families differ from television families in important ways. Many have major problems, as opposed to minor ones. Numerous children grow up in single-parent or **extended families** (which include relatives other than the parents, such as uncles, aunts, cousins, and grandparents); the nuclear family is more common in middle-class homes than in the homes of the less affluent. Few parents, especially among the poor, have limitless free time for family interactions. Definitions of good marital and family relationships vary as a function of social class and culture.

Social class and family life. Most North Americans belong to one of four social classes. The **upper middle class** consists of affluent businesspeople and professionals whose status and educational advantages are surpassed only by the wealthiest members of society. The **lower middle class** consists of white-collar, or office, workers and those who have skilled blue-collar jobs in industry, construction, and agriculture. Below these two classes are the **upper lower class** (semiskilled and less highly paid blue-collar workers) and the **lower lower class** (those who are impoverished and uneducated and are either chronically unemployed or engaged in menial jobs).

The division of labor in the family—how economic, homemaking, and child care responsibilities are shared—varies greatly according to social class. Even when women work outside the home, they are often expected to assume primary responsibility for housecleaning, meal preparation, and parental duties. In defining these duties as women's work, lower-class husbands are less likely to help out around the house than are middle-class husbands (Rubin, 1976). In contrast, the middle-class husbands of highly paid, professional women and feminists in particular are expected to do more housework and child care than the typical man (Beckman & Bosak-Houser, 1979).

The balance of power in the family also varies for members of different social classes. **Family power** is the ability to influence the attitudes or behavior of one's spouse and children. Middle-class families tend to be egalitarian; husbands and wives wield equal power (Rainwater, 1965). However, the spouse who earns a higher salary and holds down a more prestigious job, typically the middle-class husband, has a good chance of becoming the dominant family member (Scanzoni, 1972). Egalitarian marriages are less common among the poor. Husbands tend to be more powerful than wives in families in the upper lower class (Rainwater, 1965). Wives from such marriages are likely to complain that their husbands won't let them do what they want. In contrast, wives are more likely than husbands to dominate lower lower-class families. In part, this occurs because lower lower-class husbands may not be the primary breadwinners and are likely to spend little time at home.

Expectations for marital intimacy also vary for members of different social classes (Rainwater, 1965). Middle-class people are more likely than their lower-class counterparts to have a **joint marital role relationship**. In such relationships, the spouse is expected to be the best friend, a companion with whom to share interests, feelings, and confidences. Poor people, especially those from the lower class, as opposed to middle class, tend to have a **segregated marital role relationship**. Spouses spend little time together and have very different duties. The relationship between social class and marital intimacy is illustrated in "Exploring Choices: Expectations for Marital Intimacy" on pages 326 and 327.

As suggested in this "Exploring Choices," each pattern of marital intimacy has advantages and disadvantages. Middle-class couples may enjoy marital sex and the company of their spouses more; lower-class couples may feel less dependent on their spouses and have a deeper sense of belonging in their extended families and communities. Clearly, there is more than one path to marital happiness; lower-class and middle-class people can be equally pleased with their marital relationships. In addition, social class influences but does not determine completely the course a marriage will take. To some extent, a couple are free to choose the intimate relationship that suits them the best. Their marital relationship may vary somewhat from the pattern that characterizes other couples from the same class.

The black family. Numerous ethnic groups reside in North America, each with its own characteristic set of expectations for marital and family life. In comparison with the typical white, middle-class family, minority families place higher value on living with or relating to members of the extended family. Households that include aunts, uncles, cousins, and grandparents are more common than among whites. Depending on income and cultural heritage, the families of minority groups differ in other ways. This section focuses on the largest minority group—black Americans.

family power ability to influence the attitudes or behavior of one's spouse and children

joint marital role relationship relationship in which spouses expect each other to be best friends and constant companions

segregated marital role relationship relationship in which spouses spend little time together and have very different duties

EXPLORING CHOICES

EXPECTATIONS FOR MARITAL INTIMACY

A Joint Marital Role Relationship in a Middle-Class Couple

Sue and Bob, a couple in their late forties, have been married for over twenty years and have two children attending prestigious colleges away from home. Sue and Bob are both employed full-time. Sue manages her own interior decorating business, and Bob is a corporate lawyer. Both Sue and Bob think of theirs as a good marriage and describe their partner as "my best friend." They see themselves as different from many of their friends, who are divorced, because they "share the same interests and aren't tempted to prove their sexual attractiveness by having an affair." The couple take lavish vacations in Europe and the United States, enjoy gourmet cooking, and share athletic interests. Before work, they jog together every day, and both like to take ski trips and to play tennis.

Proud of their children, who are doing well at school, Sue is able to admit, "[I]t has been kind of a relief to have the house and our lives to ourselves again." Bob says that he is just as enthusiastic about sex as ever and "if anything, Sue seems more relaxed about lovemaking than when she was younger." When asked about their difficulties, the couple say their only major concern is for their aging parents, who live in a distant city. "I think they are doing adequately financially, but we worry about their health and whether or not they will need our care in the future," Sue remarked.

With the exception of occasional involvement in a civic or charitable organization, the couple spend their leisure time together. Favorite activities include "eating out, attending the theatre, organizing and attending parties, and fixing up the house or just plain relaxing."

Generally, black families differ from white families in four ways (Heiss, 1975). First, black people are more likely than white people to live in multigenerational households, spanning three or four generations. Intimate relationships with the extended family are more common for members of minority groups as a whole. Second, marital role segregation is more common among blacks than among whites. This lack of marital togetherness is in part related to social class. Lower-class people are more likely to uphold segregated family roles than more affluent people are. A disproportionate number of black people are poor. A third difference between black and white people, the higher frequency of failed marriages among blacks, is also related to social class. Regardless of race, poorer and less educated people are more likely to experience marriage breakups than are middle-class individuals (Udry, 1970). The fourth difference, the disproportionate number of households headed by women

A Segregated Marital Role Relationship in a Lower-Class Couple

Sandy and Jack are a young, struggling couple. Jack is in his early twenties and Sandy is nineteen. As Sandy put it, "We had to get married when I was still a high school junior because I was pregnant." Sandy stays home with their two preschool children, and Jack works full-time as a dishwasher in a nearby restaurant. According to Jack, the biggest struggle is "keeping ahead of the bills." Frequently, Jack is away from home, fishing or bowling with friends or just "shooting the breeze" at a favorite bar. He wishes that Sandy would be more understanding about his need to "get away from it all with the boys."

Sandy describes her husband as a "good provider" and is grateful that he "doesn't have a bad temper, drink, or run around on her" like some of her friends' husbands.

She just wishes that they were "closer." As Sandy puts it, "About the only time we're together is when we're watching TV or when Jack wants sex. I wish he'd hug me and show me more attention the rest of the time." Sandy also complains about "being stuck in the house with the kids," but Jack is opposed to her working or having anyone besides her sisters and the grandparents take care of the children.

Jack praises Sandy for being a "great mother and homemaker" but complains about her intense involvement with her family. "I've really got mother-in-law problems. The two of them are on the phone or visiting each other daily. The women are always nagging me about what to do. Sandy's sisters are a pain, too. They and their kids are always underfoot here. Sometimes, I just don't feel welcome in my own home."

among black families, as opposed to white ones, is the result of both economic oppression and historical forces. Seventeen percent of American families as a whole but more than 40 percent of black families are headed by women (Darity & Myers, 1984).

Lower-class children in general, and not just poor black children, have a high probability of growing up in a single-parent household headed by the mother. In all advanced, industrialized countries, single-parent, female-headed families earn less income than male-dominated and two-parent families. They also have the worst chance of breaking out of grinding poverty (Kamerman, 1984). Political and economic oppression and a declining pool of eligible men to head black families increase the chances that black women will fail to find husbands and that their children will grow up without fathers (Darity & Myers, 1984). Many lower-class black women face an impossible dilemma. Either they work outside the home at dead-end, poorly paying jobs, delegating child rearing to female relatives, or they stay home with the children and collect welfare. Poverty for these women and their children may seem inevitable, regardless of the choice made.

Sadly, our society seems to have lost momentum in the war against poverty. There is a relative absence of social programs designed to increase the choices available to low-income, single-parent families in general and black families in particular. To their credit, poor black people have adjusted as well as anyone might. In some urban housing projects, the female-headed family may include a **quasi-father**, a man who although not the biological parent provides financial help and child care and is regarded by relatives as a legitimate family member (Schulz, 1970). Rising above their difficulties, many poor, black, single mothers raise emotionally secure, hardworking, happy children. Nurturance from other members of the extended family—grandparents, aunts, uncles, and cousins—plays an important role in the lives of many poor black children.

Finally, it must be remembered that not all black children grow up in poor, fatherless families. There is a growing black middle class. Children from black middle-class families are likely to have the same advantages and close relationships with both parents that are available to white middle-class children. Educated, middle-class black adults have the same egalitarian values—including a preference for joint marital roles (sharing decisions and feelings with a spouse)—as do middle-class whites (Middleton & Putney, 1970).

quasi-father man who is not the biological parent but who takes on a father's role and responsibilities

Changes in Marriage over Time

With life expectancies rising, the couple who remain in their initial marriage can expect many changes in themselves and in their relationship over time. First, sex becomes a less significant part of a couple's relationship. The majority of married couples experience a decline in the frequency of sexual intercourse over time, especially after the birth of the first child (James, 1981). This is not to say that married couples do not enjoy sex after many years together. Rather, their time is challenged by many competing activities. In addition, not everyone works hard at keeping an exciting sex life. Some couples fail to vary the sexual routine, and the monotony of the relationship may impair their passion for each other needlessly.

Sex isn't the only part of married life that changes over time. Couples who have children and stay together until old age can expect to pass through the following developmental stages: (1) the spouses become more familiar, (2) children are born and have to be cared for during infancy and the preschool years, (3) the children are in school and are slightly less dependent on parents, (4) the children enter adolescence and begin to challenge their parents for increasing independence, (5) the children enter young adulthood and begin to leave home, (6) the spouses adjust to "the empty nest" until retirement, and (7) one or both spouses retires (Spanier, Lewis, & Cole, 1975).

Each developmental task challenges marital adjustment in different ways. However, research cannot provide guidelines for what a given couple can ex-

Couples can expect many changes in their relationships over time.

pect. The evidence is strong that marital adjustment suffers following the birth of the first child and continues to be poorer through the early childhood years. Beyond that point, couples differ in how happy they are about the relationship. In some studies, couples seem to experience improved marital adjustment after their children become independent young adults and leave home. However, this may be true in part because couples who remain married for such a long time are likely to be more satisfied with the relationship than those who divorce (Spanier, Lewis & Cole, 1975).

Sexual Choices for Married Couples

sexually compatible partners who enjoy and desire sex equally

When a married couple enjoy the sexual component of the relationship and both partners desire sex about the same amount, they are **sexually compatible.** Sexual compatibility can enhance good marital adjustment; however, a pleasurable sex life in and of itself does not guarantee a happy marriage. Psychotherapists treat happily married couples who are dissatisfied with the sexual relationship and distressed couples who enjoy making love to each other but take pleasure in little else in the relationship. In any event, the demands of married life can wear away at a couple's sexuality no matter how good the relationship was in the beginning. Work, children, and the day-to-day frictions of life can interfere with the time available for sex.

Maintaining an exciting sex life during marriage challenges couples in two ways. First, husbands and wives have to overcome unrealistic expectations that keep them from working on improving the sexual relationship as the years go by. **Low frustration tolerance**, the unrealistic belief that intimacy and sex should be effortless and free of difficulties, can gnaw away at the close relationships of normal adults (Jordan & McCormick, 1988). The second challenge is to accept the cold fact that romantic love, a major reason most people get married in the first place, does not last forever. As suggested in the previous chapter, long-term relationships flourish when there is friendly love, the kind of love that grows between old friends who know each other's strengths and flaws. In a recent study of couples married for fifteen years or more, the most frequently mentioned reason for having an enduring and happy marriage was considering the spouse a best friend (Lauer & Lauer, 1985). Friendly love does not destroy good sex. Rather, it changes its nature. Sex may become more of a partnership and less a dramatic performance. As a result, the sexual relationship may become more meaningful and satisfying.

Continued work on the relationship helps some couples keep marital sexuality pleasurable and meaningful. Others spice things up by making love to other partners, or having **extramarital sex.** Whatever sexual choices people make, **monogamy** (the belief that the legal spouse is the only legitimate sexual partner) continues to be the prevailing sexual standard in our culture (McMurty, 1977). The Sexual Revolution of the 1960s and 1970s created greater tolerance toward premarital sex, but in general, extramarital relationships are still considered immoral and improper (Glenn & Weaver, 1979). Almost 75 percent of the United States adult population agrees that extramarital sexual relations are always wrong.

Certainly, the majority of North Americans strongly believe that they and their partners should practice monogamy. For them, the knowledge that people are sexually faithful is the cornerstone of a loving, trusting relationship. Nonetheless, people don't always live up to the values they espouse.

Although most people say that they are opposed to extramarital sex, a conservative estimate is that at least 50 percent of married men and women have one or more affairs by the time they reach their forties (Thompson, 1983). Of these, most have a **secret affair**, an extramarital liaison that occurs without the awareness of the spouse. Others, in contrast, tell the spouse about the other sexual partners or even expect the spouse to participate in extramarital sex along with them. Some couples have a **sexually open marriage**, in which the husband and wife accept the possibility that the partner will have affairs and show little or no jealousy (Knapp & Whitehurst, 1977). About 2 percent of the married population try **swinging**, having recreational sex with others they know only slightly to add excitement to the primary relationship (Weis, 1983).

low frustration tolerance belief that intimacy and sex should be effortless and free of difficulties

extramarital sex sex involving a married person and a person other than the legal spouse

monogamy belief that the legal spouse is the only legitimate sexual partner

secret affair extramarital liaison that occurs without the awareness of the other spouse

sexually open marriage marriage in which the spouses agree to permit each partner to have sexual relationships with other partners

swinging situation in which married couples exchange partners and in some cases have group sex with other married individuals whom they know only slightly

group marriage
highly open and
committed form of
extramarital sex in
which married couples
may live with one
another and share
spouses sexually

Even more remarkable are those who express their intimacy with others symbolically by making love to one or two close friends as a couple or even living together in a **group marriage**, in which household duties, child care, and sexual expression are shared among all partners freely and equally.

Why do people rebel against monogamy, one of the most popular values in our society? What benefits and costs occur as a result of the rebellion? Every person who has extramarital sex does so for different reasons, and experiences marriage in a different way. Some people have affairs because they are unhappy in marriage. Others are happily married but wish to be close to more than one person at a time. For some, an extramarital involvement helps them feel more sexy and interested in the primary partner. For others, an extramarital relationship can destroy a marriage either because a jealous partner resents the other's behavior or because the extramarital relationship turns out to be stronger than the original marriage.

Regardless of motives, extramarital relationships present potential benefits and costs that cannot be predicted at the onset of a relationship. Increased self-knowledge and sensitivity as a result of the new relationship and successful management of jealousy may bring the original spouses closer together. However, for others, knowledge of extramarital relationships can be the proverbial straw that breaks the camel's back. Relatively good relationships can crumble as a result of sexual exploration by one or both partners.

No single sexual life-style, be it monogamy or nonmonogamy, can guarantee everyone permanent happiness. Like the next difficult set of choices to make—whether or not to have children and how to raise a family—each of us is obliged to assess the possible costs or benefits of our sexual decisions.

Parenthood

Well-adjusted adults are concerned with the welfare of the next generation, not just themselves. Teaching and nurturing the young, especially as a parent, has been revered by people throughout history and in all cultures.

Deciding whether or not to become a parent. Unlike single people who have children but receive little social support, married couples are expected to have and raise children. The first decision facing a married couple is whether or not to have children. If the answer is yes, the second decision is how many children to have. Decisions about parenthood are complex. They may be made on an individual, couple, or community level (Beckman, 1982). On an individual level, one partner (usually the woman) can use or fail to use contraceptives with or without the partner's knowledge or consent. On a couple level, a husband and wife may have very different values and thus negotiate about having children, a decision that profoundly affects each partner's economic responsibilities and physical and emotional well-being. On a community level, the opinions of friends, other family members, neighbors, and opinion leaders may play a major role in whether a couple decide to have children.

Some people have children without consciously planning to become parents. Most others have children because they want to nurture a new generation and believe that the experience will enrich their lives. A minority may become parents to please others or to conform. We live in a society that pays tribute to parents at religious holidays and especially during Mother's Day and Father's Day. Married women who decide to remain childless are stereotyped as materialistic, overly ambitious, and self-centered individuals who will regret the decision during lonely older years (Callan, 1983). Despite the social pressures that oppose the life-style, the benefits of being childless—considerable personal and financial freedom—are recognized by parents and nonparents alike.

The decision whether or not to have children should not be taken lightly. Raising healthy and happy children can be one of the richest experiences of marital life. Parenthood may be the single most important and fulfilling adult responsibility. However, parenthood is not the only way to make a significant contribution to society, and it cannot guarantee marital stability or bliss. Research is unclear as to whether or not having children improves marital adjustment. Children may be the only source of marital satisfaction for some couples (Spanier & Lewis, 1980). On the other hand, mothers of preschool children, especially sons, are likely to find more fault with their marriages than are childless women (Abbot & Brody, 1985).

Before deciding to become a parent, it is valuable to accept the fact that children will be dependent, both economically and emotionally, for at least eighteen to twenty-two years. To be sure, parents may delight in their intimate interactions with youngsters and teenagers, but these pleasures are fleeting and are sometimes outweighed by the problems and conflicts of family life. Parents of young children make many economic, physical, and emotional sacrifices. As a result, they may not have enough time, energy, or emotional sensitivity to meet the spouse's needs.

Adjustment is particularly difficult for working parents, who are trying to balance commitment to a career with the needs of their children. The results of one survey indicated that over half of the married professional women who had children "stated that they had ambivalent feelings when someone else took care of their children" (Dreyfus-Gray, 1983, pp. 238–239). For many dual-career couples, the difficulty of juggling personal, career, and parenting goals creates **role strain**, psychological distress from trying to do too much at once. Rearing children is a calculated risk. Many of the pleasures and costs cannot be known until the couple become parents.

role strain
psychological distress from trying to do too much or fulfill too many contradictory responsibilities at once

Merle Bombardieri (1981), who counsels couples agonizing over the decision whether or not to have children, provides some useful advise. She recommends that prospective parents give themselves adequate time to consider the positive and negative consequences of each choice open to them. It is important, too, to recognize there is no absolutely right or wrong decision. Whatever people decide, there will be regrets and pleasures, all of which can be managed by well-adjusted individuals. Perhaps you are already a parent but wonder if you would like additional children. Perhaps you are wondering whether or not you would like to have children at all. Whatever your life circumstances are, you may enjoy participating in "Exploring Choices: Inner Dialogue—Deciding Whether or Not to Become a Parent."

Deciding when to become a parent. Most married people want to have children. The issue for them, then, is timing. When should they have the first baby? How many children? How closely spaced should their births be? Unlike men, women are fertile for only a limited period of life. Children change a couple's relationship dramatically. Therefore, it is reasonable to ask how old the

EXPLORING CHOICES

INNER DIALOGUE—DECIDING WHETHER OR NOT TO BECOME A PARENT

Merle Bombardiere (1981) advises that when you are torn between conflicting desires (for example, whether or not to have your first child or another child), "a conversation between these two parts of you can help you better understand the nature of your conflict" (p. 28).

Begin by setting up two chairs facing each other. Label the first the parent chair and the other the child-free, or do-not-want-a-baby, chair. Sitting on the parent chair, tell the child-free part why you want a baby. Switching to the other chair, tell the parent part why you do not want a baby. Continuing the dialogue, change chairs for each side of the argument. To ensure that you express your feelings honestly, do this exercise alone. Following is an example of one young woman's dialogue. PC is the parent chair, and CC is the child-free chair:

PC: I think I would miss something if I never had a child.

CC: But I don't think I'm willing to make the sacrifices I'd have to make for a child.

PC: But wouldn't it be worth it for the pleasure of seeing a child grow and change?

CC: It looks to me like 90% pain for 10% pleasure. I don't think it's worth it.

PC: Aren't you just being selfish?

CC: No! I'm looking out for what's best for all of us. My career as a systems analyst doesn't leave much time for a child. I don't want to give up my work, and I don't want to be overburdened either. I don't think I would enjoy being a mother. . . .

If you try this exercise more than once, you may discover that your feelings change from time to time. Using this technique can help keep you in touch with your real feelings.

Source: M. Bombardieri (1981). *The baby decision: How to make the most important choice of your life.* New York: Rawson, Wade, 28–30.

mother should be and now long a couple should be together before considering parenthood. To some extent, modern contraceptive technology helps people make these choices. However, reproductive biology is not always under control. Many children are conceived despite the use of an effective birth control method or the mother's belief that she was too old to have any more children.

There are no perfect answers regarding when to have children, how many children to have, and how many years apart the birth of each child should be. Ideally, these choices should be the result of a thoughtful dialogue between spouses, in which both partners' values and aspirations are carefully considered. There is no absolutely right time to have children; each decision about parenting has particular costs and benefits.

Young couples who decide to have children early in marriage can benefit in a number of ways. They have a lot of energy to devote to child rearing and can look forward to seeing the children develop into responsible adults. Perhaps they can have grandchildren while they are still relatively young. On the other hand, this parenting choice is likely to interrupt the education or career of one or both parents and present financial burdens that make it difficult to send the children to college or to afford the type of life-style they would like. Also, some couples who have had children early in the marriage have difficulty being just a couple when their children grow up and leave home. As one parent put it, "We're like strangers. We put everything into the children and enjoyed them so much. Now, we hardly know what to say to each other and are not sure we have that much in common."

Couples who wait until midlife or later in marriage to have children benefit because both the husband and wife have had a chance to complete their educations and advance in their careers. Greater financial security enables them to provide a better life-style for the children than struggling younger parents can. Another advantage to delaying child rearing is that older couples may be more confident about their relationship. They have had many years to get to know each other without being distracted by the needs of a growing family.

The psychological maturity of older parents may be an asset, although such parents may not have the physical energy they would like to devote to raising children. In addition, it may feel odd to have small children later in life than most couples. It helps to be nonconformist. One woman in her late forties, the mother of small children, put it this way: "I'm the oldest mother at the daycare center, and one of the young mothers thought I was Tammy's grandmother when I picked her up. That's okay; I enjoy Tammy and I don't have to prove anything to a sweet but inexperienced young girl." Older parents also worry that they will be too old to have many years watching their children mature as adults and to enjoy their grandchildren.

Adjustment issues for childless couples. Increasing numbers of couples are choosing not to have children. There are many advantages to this life-style. First, both partners, can devote themselves to their educations and careers without worrying about child care. Second, such couples usually enjoy greater financial affluence than people who have children. They can often afford a more affluent life-style and set aside more money for retirement. They also have greater time for adult-oriented leisure and fitness programs. Finally, there are other ways of giving to and enjoying the younger generation. Child-free couples can still nurture the young by spending time with other people's children, teaching, and doing volunteer work. Just because one is good with kids or likes young people hardly means that one must become a parent. At the same time, people have a right to decide not to have children if they don't think they would enjoy parenthood.

Those who decide not to have children face some social costs. Friends with children, the couple's parents, and work acquaintances may put pressure on them to do the "right" thing and have children. Some couples describe feeling especially uncomfortable at particular social events, like baby showers, when everyone is talking about children and child-rearing experiences they have not shared. It takes courage, a sense of humor, and creativity to adjust to being childless in a society that continues to equate marriage with parenthood.

infertility biological inability to conceive children

It is important to remember that some married people want to have families but cannot. **Infertility** is the inability to conceive children for biological reasons. Some couples wait to have children only to discover they are unable to conceive. Infertility affects all age groups, but it is a greater problem for older couples. Moreover, adoption has become increasingly more difficult and time-consuming. Unless a couple is willing to raise a handicapped youngster, a baby from a minority group, or an orphan from overseas, legal adoption may not be a practical option for a childless couple.

In other instances, partners may not agree about whether to have children. A husband or wife may want children desperately, while the spouse is deeply opposed. Conflicts about parenthood can take place even among couples who are otherwise happily married. It is not easy to resolve such conflicts, especially since it is unwise to conceive a child who may be unwanted by one parent. In some cases, people are able to persuade spouses that they, too, want to have a baby or to remain childless. In other cases, marriages are destroyed as a result of the conflict.

The individual or couple obliged to give up the hope of having children faces important challenges. Besides parenthood, what meaning or joy can life provide? Childless couples need to give up bitter feelings that might poison the marriage and take away pleasure in life. Professional counseling or psychotherapy may help in this regard. However a satisfactory adjustment is achieved, there are many alternatives open to those who are childless involuntarily. They can put more energy into careers, hobbies, friendships, and family relationships. In addition, being childless doesn't condemn people to a life devoid of children. Childless people can foster mutually satisfying relationships with the young, including nephews and nieces, neighbors, foster children, and the children of close friends. Teachers and adults who lead youth groups, like the Girl Scouts and 4-H Club, can enjoy being with children and participating in their lives.

Improving Marital Relationships

The quality of marriage varies widely among couples and over time. Some marriages or periods of time within a given marriage bring happiness and fulfillment; others are characterized by unhappiness, conflict, and in some cases, violence. Not every marriage is worth saving. However, there are a number of choices open to those who are committed to improving their marriage.

Conflict. Nothing is more challenging than living with someone in a long-term, committed relationship. Over the years, marital partners may make unreasonable demands upon each other and dig in their heels as each argues a different point of view. To some extent, **conflict**, or disagreement about an issue important to both spouses, is inevitable in marriage. Even mature, sensitive individuals find it difficult to compromise when their partner fails to share particular goals and desires. For this reason, couples contemplating marriage should become well acquainted with the partner's values on important issues. They also should practice negotiating when their goals are incompatible (Ross, 1985). Marital conflict can take place because of disagreement about values, sexuality, sex roles, marital roles, money, children, interests, and how to spend leisure time. Couples also argue about how committed each spouse is to the marriage, ties to the extended family, how independent each one should be, and personality traits they find irritating in each other. Table 11–1 lists some of the common areas of marital conflict.

conflict disagreement about issues

Disturbed relationships. There is nothing wrong with experiencing conflict in marriage. Marital conflict is healthy when it opens up communication, allowing unjust or inequitable situations to be discussed, negotiated, and resolved (Scanzoni, 1972). Conflict contributes to greater intimacy when spouses convey mutual respect and willingness to compromise throughout the negotiation process.

Conflict is unhealthy when partners are intolerant of each other's differences, avoid conflict situations, and blame themselves when their partners fail to agree with them (Dryden, 1985). Unresolved arguments, whether verbal attacks or the silent treatment, harm relationships. Studies have found that sarcasm and hostile body language and tone of voice characterize disturbed marriages (Gottman, 1979). In contrast with the happily married, unhappy spouses are much more likely to be inattentive, frown, sneer, smirk, look angry, speak in a cold or tense voice, whine, and throw up their hands in disgust during conflict. An abundance of expression of such negative feelings leads to a vicious cycle of mutual hostility and withdrawal.

Often, marital therapists try to intervene by urging the couple to do something positive together. For example, a constantly bickering couple may be asked to start the day on a positive note instead—the wife giving her spouse a hug, the husband bringing his wife her morning coffee in bed. Successful com-

TABLE 11-1   Common Areas of Marital Conflict

Conflict Areas	Discussion of Related Issues
1. **Commitment**	• How hard is each spouse willing to work at the marriage? • To what extent is divorce seen as a way out of problems?
2. **Values**	• Do the couple agree on religion, politics, and other social values? • How well do they handle disagreement?
3. **Sexuality**	• How frequently does each partner want to have sex and what sexual activities are disliked or liked? • How does each feel about monogamy versus extramarital sex?
4. **Sex roles and marital roles**	• What roles should the wife and husband assume in outside employment and housekeeping? • To what extent will the couple adhere to traditional versus egalitarian (shared and interchangeable) roles?
5. **Ties to extended family**	• How close does each partner expect to remain with the family of origin (parents and siblings)? • How comfortable is each in relating to in-laws?
6. **Independence**	• To what extent does each partner anticipate activities outside the marital relationship, such as pursuing hobbies, investing heavily in work and organizational responsibilities, and enjoying separate friendships?
7. **Money**	• How freely should money be spent and on what goods and services? • Should partners consult with each other on purchases? • To what extent should the couple stick to a predetermined budget?
8. **Children**	• How many children, if any, should the couple have and when? • What child-rearing values does each spouse have, especially when it comes to disciplining children and showing parental affection?
9. **Personality**	• To what extent are a partner's personality traits and habits found endearing or irritating? • Can spouses anticipate tolerating difficult traits and cherishing good ones in the years to come?
10. **Interests and leisure**	• Do the couple share the same interests and leisure pursuits? • How much do partners enjoy or dislike doing particular activities together or just talking?

pliance with this simple suggestion may be a first step toward reducing hostility and increasing the frequency of other pleasurable times together.

Unfortunately, some marriages have such a long history of hostile, destructive conflict that partners are no longer willing to try to change. Then, separation and divorce may be the best recourse.

Violent marriages. The women's movement has sensitized the public to a particular type of disturbed relationship, the **violent marriage**. Large national studies suggest that about one in four married couples has had at least one experience in which an angry spouse physically assaulted the partner (Doyle, 1985). A smaller number of marriages are characterized by chronic domestic violence, a situation in which the household is a war zone and the victimized partner (typically the wife) lives in a state of constant fear and physical danger. When women are violent, they throw things like kitchen utensils at their husbands.

violent marriage
marriage characterized by physical assaults on a spouse (usually the wife)

When men are violent, they are apt to use more direct physical force—hitting, choking, or throwing their wives.

On average, battered husbands are attacked less forcefully and sustain less injury than do battered wives (Frieze et al., 1979). Children who see their parents hitting each other, especially those who are also beaten by the parents, are at high risk for becoming either batterers themselves or victims of marital violence when they grow up and marry (Kalmuss, 1984).

Why do battered wives, at risk of losing their emotional and physical well-being, remain in violent marriages? There are many reasons, foremost of which may be a rigid adherence to traditional sex roles. The violent marriage may be the extreme of a family in which the man dominates and the woman submits. There are also practical reasons for remaining in such a relationship. Battered women may have several children to support and at the same time lack education, income, and job skills to live away from their husbands (Frieze et al., 1979).

Until recently, battered women had few choices. They had to either tolerate a violent marriage or break away on their own. Often, they received little or no support from family members or the community. Today, there is greater understanding and awareness of the plight of battered women. Several community and mental health agencies, such as the YWCA (the Young Women's Christian Association), offer shelter, counseling, and legal services.

Minimizing conflict and maximizing marital satisfaction. In contrast with the fairy-tale depiction of a couple living happily ever after, good marriages require hard work. Essentially, partners are faced with three challenges: (1) establishing good communication, (2) balancing intimacy with individuality, and (3) establishing an equitable relationship. Good communication requires open expression of feelings, not using the partner as a garbage dump for negative feelings. An atmosphere of safety and trust is critical. No one will be honest if he or she fears being attacked physically or verbally or rejected as a result. Generally, spouses take risks and open up the communication process when they are assured that they are accepted and cared for despite their differences and mistakes.

The second important challenge to marital partners is the ability to balance intimacy with individuality. Too frequently, couples get caught in the cult of togetherness, spending all their free time together and losing any sense of self in the process. On the other hand, some couples become so immersed in their careers and personal interests that they spend little quality time with their spouses. Good relationships require compromises. Nena and George O'Neill (1972), the authors of *Open Marriage: A New Life Style for Couples*, address this issue with wisdom and sensitivity. They define open marriage as a relationship that nurtures the growth of both the individual and the couple. As partners change, they can renegotiate their marital goals.

Unfortunately, readers have often misinterpreted the O'Neills' book and assumed that an open marriage is synonymous with an agreement that both partners can have extramarital sex. Certainly, some open marriages have sexual freedom as a component; however, couples can have an open marriage even if they remain sexually monogamous. There are as many types of open marriages as there are couples who wish to have an intimate and lasting relationship that is flexible, trusting, honest, open, and realistic.

In contrast with those who have a closed relationship, partners in an open marriage recognize that it is unlikely that one human being (the spouse) will be able to fulfill all of the other's needs. Hence, individuals who have an open marriage enjoy both a shared life and a personal life. The couple have friends they see together, but each person also has individual friends. They share interests, but each partner pursues personal hobbies and career goals as well.

If a couple desire, they can conform to traditional sex roles—the man supports the family and the woman does the bulk of the housework and child care. Alternatively, a couple can model their relationship after friendship and divide tasks according to what each does best or enjoys.

equitable relationship relationship in which both partners feel they are treated fairly

The third important challenge of marriage is the establishment of an **equitable relationship**. Marriages are equitable when both husband and wife believe that they are getting as much out of the marriage as they put into it. Elaine Hatfield and her colleagues (1982) have presented some strong evidence in favor of equitable marriages. They found that couples in equitable relationships enjoy marital sex more and describe happier marriages and lives than do other couples.

How do a couple minimize conflict and enhance marital satisfaction? What helpful hints can help couples communicate well, nurture both intimacy and individuality, and develop and maintain an equitable relationship? Increasingly, marital researchers and therapists are saying that the answer to these questions is "to think." Individuals who have rational or reasonable beliefs about committed relationships may manage them better than those who subscribe to fairy tales. Roy Eidelson and Norman Epstein (1982) are pioneers in the study of how irrational beliefs about committed relationships can interfere with marital adjustment. Their contributions are reviewed in "On the Research Frontier: Irrational Beliefs About Marriage" on page 340.

Other myths, not investigated by Epstein and Eidelson, also are harmful to marriage. Albert Ellis (1986), the founder of rational-emotive therapy, has identified three of these myths:

1. I need to be assured of my partner's constant love and approval or else I must be a rotten failure.

2. My partner must treat me considerately and fairly. Failure to meet this demand even once proves that my spouse is no good and deserves my hatred.

3. My marriage should be just the way I want it to be and require little or no effort on my part to work. Otherwise, this relationship is unbearable.

One woman who believed these myths considered divorcing her husband because he bought her cheap gifts while she spent a fortune buying him pres-

ON THE RESEARCH FRONTIER

IRRATIONAL BELIEFS ABOUT MARRIAGE

In an unhappy marriage, one or both partners behave in self-defeating ways. Partners may feel depressed, angry, and resentful much of the time. Particular irrational beliefs about committed relationships, which in mild forms are common in our culture, may contribute to marital unhappiness (Epstein & Williams, 1981). Eidelson and Epstein (1982) have developed and validated a questionnaire, *The Relationship Belief Inventory*, which assesses five irrational beliefs about marriage. These irrational beliefs follow:

1. *Disagreement is destructive.* It is irrational to believe that in a good relationship, spouses never disagree about anything or that any disagreement means a lack of love or is a sign that the relationship is ending.

2. *Mind reading is necessary.* It is irrational to believe that if partners really love each other they should know what the other wants, needs, and feels in the absence of overt communication.

3. *Partners cannot change.* It is irrational to believe that trying to improve an unhappy relationship or alter behavior is useless.

4. *Sex must be perfect.* It is irrational to believe that one must be a perfect sexual partner or that it is never

normal to have difficulty with arousal or performance.

5. *The sexes are different.* It is irrational to believe that the sex role stereotypes are always true or that men and women differ so dramatically that husbands and wives can never really understand each other.

The more irrational beliefs that individuals hold on *The Relationship Belief Inventory,* the more likely the individuals are to score in the maladjusted range on Locke and Wallace's (1959) *Marital-Adjustment Test,* a popular instrument for measuring marital happiness. Clients in marital therapy are more likely than untreated individuals to demonstrate emotional disturbance on both *The Relationship Belief Inventory* and the *Marital-Adjustment Test.* Clients who have very rigid and irrational beliefs about close relationships are more pessimistic than other clients. They would rather have individual psychotherapy than be seen as a couple because they think that marital therapy cannot save their marriages (Epstein & Eidelson, 1981). In addition, such irrational individuals have less desire to work on a relationship and are more motivated to separate. Compared with marital therapy clients who subscribe to more rational beliefs about committed relationships, irrational clients are less satisfied with their marriages.

ents and taking him out on holidays. She believed that the inexpensive gifts proved that her husband didn't love or respect her. Through marital therapy, the woman learned that her husband did love her, even if his tastes were not as expensive as hers. She also used the sessions to identify other good qualities he had (like his excellence as a father and his warm trust in her) that made up for his lack of sensitivity regarding gifts. It is important to develop reasonable expectations for close relationships. Marriages are nurtured by partners who are not excessively demanding and can accept each other as fallible human beings. Good relationships require hard work and tolerance. The more positive time and energy invested by both spouses in a relationship, the more each will feel understood, helped, and supported by the partner.

WHEN MARRIAGE ENDS

Love and commitment not withstanding, every marriage ends at some point—through separation, divorce, or the death of a partner. Good psychological adjustment is based in part on the ability to anticipate and cope with the tragedies of everyday life.

Divorce and Separation

There are about 1.2 million divorces in the United States each year, greatly altering the lives of 2.4 million adults and more than 1 million children (Furstenberg & Spanier, 1984). Over one third of those marrying for the first time are likely to file for divorce, and an additional third or more of those who divorced and remarried are likely to apply for additional divorces (Spanier & Anderson, 1979). Conservatively speaking, only half of all married people are able to live up to the marriage vows, "until death do us part." The other half are likely to end up separated or divorced.

People separate and divorce for many reasons. One of the most important is realizing that they are not ready or able to handle the complex economic and emotional demands of a long-term relationship. Those who marry when they are teenagers, especially the uneducated and poor, have greater marital instability than the population as a whole (Spanier & Glick, 1981). Sometimes people are unhappily married but stay together because they believe that their alternatives are worse. The more children a couple have, the less likely they are to divorce. This may be for good or bad reasons. The parents of big families may stay together for the sake of the children, because they believe remarriage would be difficult, or for financial reasons. Women may be particularly vulnerable in a divorce, since many lack the skills and work experience necessary to support their children as single parents. The economic well-being of divorced women and their children is weakened further because a substantial number of former husbands fail to keep up with legally required child-support payments.

Sometimes, marriages fail because one or both partners have psychological difficulties. Psychologically disturbed, rigid, or intensely competitive individuals are not likely to be happily married, no matter who their partners are (Newcomb & Bentler, 1981). Not all bad marriages can be blamed on a problematic individual, however. Well-adjusted individuals can and do have unsuccessful marriages because they lack common interests, values, or goals; communicate poorly; or avoid or exaggerate conflict. A couple's strategies for handling conflict are particularly important. Couples who are willing to disclose feelings, listen to each other with empathy, and compromise are most likely to be happily married. On the other hand, both the dead relationship (in which disagreement is felt but never discussed) and the explosive one (in which even the smallest issue becomes fuel for a major battle) are not likely to survive.

The role of extramarital sex in marital separation and divorce is not clear. Divorced people who had affairs say the extramarital sex was the result rather than the cause of marital problems (Spanier & Margolis, 1983). In contrast, those who claimed that the spouse had been unfaithful believed that extramarital sex was a major cause of the marital failure. However, extramarital sex does not seem to affect how couples adjust to life after the divorce. Both those who had extramarital sex and those who felt victimized by the spouses' affairs were as likely to be well adjusted after divorce as were people who left a monogamous marriage.

Regardless of why relationships fail, their breakup can take different forms. Some people elect to formalize the end of the relationship by using lawyers to work out a **separation agreement** and eventually go through a legal **divorce**. Others present themselves as separated or divorced but are in fact still legally married. People may avoid the legal process of divorce because they are ambivalent about a relationship, too poor to afford the help of an attorney, unassertive, or confused about their rights and responsibilities. Failure to seek a legal divorce can be a problem if an individual wishes to remarry or to establish control over joint financial resources and decisions affecting children.

Couples who elect to pursue an official divorce face challenging choices. In some states, especially if no children are involved, couples can save money and minimize conflict by initiating a do-it-yourself or no-fault divorce. In most instances, it is wise to consult an attorney or legal service. The divorce makes the end of a marriage legal, enabling the spouses to remarry. It may also stipulate how the couple's financial resources are to be divided and whether or not one partner should supply the other with **alimony** (income for an economically disadvantaged spouse) and **child support** (income to help support children who live with the other spouse).

Parents who divorce are also faced with a series of choices regarding **custody**, legal guardianship of the children, which can be discussed informally or with lawyers' assistance. Homes and courtrooms are the sites in which people decide which parent(s) should have legal custody or guardianship of each child. The traditional pattern of automatically awarding custody to mothers has been changing in recent years. Fathers frequently are given custody when their ex-wives either don't want the children or are inadequate parents (Greif,

separation agreement legal contract describing financial and other rights and responsibilities of a married couple that are no longer living together

divorce ending of a marriage by an accepted legal process

alimony income for an economically disadvantaged spouse after a legal separation or divorce

child support income to help support children who live with the spouse after a legal separation or divorce

custody legal guardianship of children

A marriage may fail
because a couple
exaggerate conflict.

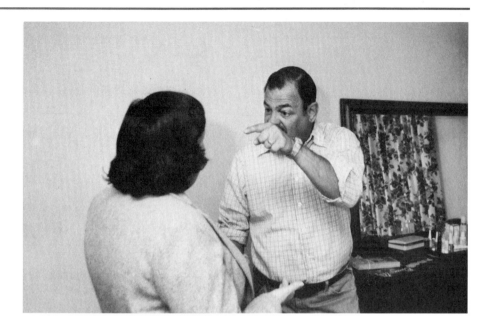

1985). Fathers are also likely to be awarded custody when their children prefer to live with them and when they battle for custody in the courtroom.

Courtroom proceedings can increase the hostility between former spouses (Spanier & Anderson, 1979). Nonetheless, divorce does not always turn former lovers into combatants. Some couples continue to be friends after the divorce. They usually feel they left the marriage because they grew in different ways and not because there was any reason to dislike the partner (Blood & Blood, 1979). The majority do not part on such amicable terms, however. Intense negative emotions, such as grief, depression, anxiety, and rage, are common, especially shortly after a couple has separated (Hunt & Hunt, 1977). These negative emotions dissipate as the divorced person adjusts to single life or, perhaps, remarries.

In the beginning, about 10 percent of divorced people experience periods of ambivalence and even elation as they develop new intimate relationships, discover their strengths, and remind themselves of the advantages of having ended a difficult relationship. On the other hand, 20 percent of separated and divorced people continue to feel discontent and suffer troublesome health problems on a long-term basis (Spanier & Thompson, 1984). However, these people may not be suffering as a result of marital disruption alone. In a recent study, Erbes and Hedderson (1984) found that most divorced and separated men had been just as unhappy years before their marriages terminated.

The end of a marriage is a period of great emotional pain for many persons. Each separated individual has to adjust to loneliness and grief at the good things lost when the marriage ended. Only the rare few are completely certain that ending the marriage was the best choice. In the difficult period of adjusting to being single again, people may torture themselves with questions like, Did I do the right thing? and What if we could have worked things out given a little more time and hard work? As it is unlikely that the marriage was completely bad or that the former marital partner had no good qualities, there is often some self-blaming. People may tell themselves, "Maybe it was my fault; perhaps I couldn't have a good relationship with anyone."

The separation and divorce crisis does not last forever. If a person was relatively well adjusted before the marriage ended, it is likely that she or he will return to good psychological functioning in a relatively short time. Psychotherapy and the help of friends and the extended family help people adjust during the crisis period and beyond.

Marital disruption hurts men and women in different ways. Emotionally, men are hit harder by divorce than women are (Allgeier, 1983). As suggested in the previous chapter, men may be more vulnerable when a love relationship ends because traditional sex roles prohibit intimacy with anyone but a primary partner. Women suffer more than men from the financial strain caused by divorce. Corcoran, Duncan, and Hill (1984) discuss the reasons and repercussions:

> Alimony and child support payments from an ex-husband are rare and, even if paid, usually do not represent more than a fraction of the lost income. Although most divorced women enter or remain in the labor force, their low level of earnings and part-time work arrangements result in a dramatically lower income level for the family. Private transfer payments from other relatives or friends are rare. Roughly one-fifth of ex-wives receive public transfer payments in the year following a divorce, but they do not replace much of the lost income. (p. 241)

Financial security contributes to the psychological well-being of both sexes after a divorce. Good adjustment is also more likely when the divorced person is able to accept the end of the marriage and to reach out to others (Spanier & Thompson, 1984). In the case of men, sexual activity with new partners has an especially healing effect. For women, it is helpful to reject traditional sex roles. Consistent with the research discussed in Chapter 3, women with more masculine personalities adjust to divorce better than highly feminine women (Hansson et al., 1984).

Widowhood

Marriages do not always end in divorce; sometimes they end in the death of a beloved spouse. Widowhood is especially difficult for a young person or when the death of a partner comes suddenly; people do not have enough time to prepare for the loss. When people we love die, there is a tendency to idealize their good qualities and minimize their bad qualities. We recall a perfect, loving partner instead of the human being who actually existed. This can pose problems for adjustment, since widowed persons may find it difficult to begin relationships with new people who differ from the idealized image of the deceased spouse. Psychotherapy and membership in a support group for widowed persons can help.

widowed having lost a marital partner through death

In the United States, 52 percent of women and 19 percent of men are **widowed** before they reach age sixty (Stevens-Long, 1984). By the time people are in their eighties, 30 percent of the men and over 70 percent of the women are widowed. Widowhood is difficult for both men and women. Like divorce, the death of a spouse is usually more psychologically traumatic for men and more economically traumatic for women (Allgeier, 1983).

bereavement physical distress and emotional despair associated with the loss or death of a loved one

Bereavement, physical distress and emotional despair experienced in response to the loss of a loved one, may contribute to the deterioration of one's physical health and psychological adjustment. As for divorced persons, it is helpful for widowed people to accept the loss of the loved one, establish a support system, and expand their social contacts and interests.

Widowed people, especially women, have a much lower chance of remarrying than divorced people (Spanier & Glick, 1980). It is possible that grief for a departed spouse and social pressure from close relatives play active roles in inhibiting remarriage. However, the strongest reasons for widows remaining single is age. Compared with divorced people, widowed people tend to be substantially older (middle-aged or elderly) when they lose their spouses. Those with little education or few financial advantages are especially unlikely to remarry after the death of a spouse.

Harsh social realities make life very difficult for many widows. Good psychological adjustment depends in part on developing close ties with friends of the same sex and the extended family. Compared with their contemporaries whose husbands are still living, elderly widows rely on a greater variety of kin for emotional and social support. Widows "are more likely to feel a close emotional attachment to and to confide in siblings or distant relatives than are their married counterparts" (Anderson, 1984, p. 113).

The Impact of Family Disruption on Children

Unhappy marriages and the family disruption that results when a parent dies or parents separate and divorce has a tremendous impact on children. This section takes a look at the relationship between interparental conflict and the psychological adjustment of children. It includes the choices facing single parents and blended families. **Single-parent families** are those headed by one parent, usually the mother, after separation, divorce, or widowhood. **Blended families** are created by remarriage or cohabitation following marital disruption. In the blended family, a child has one new parent figure (a stepparent) and the possibility of new siblings, either a stepparent's own children or new children from the new marriage.

single-parent families families headed by only one parent, usually the mother

blended families families created by remarriage

Parents in troubled marriages generally love their children regardless of how poorly they themselves get along. Such parents are faced with a difficult choice: Should they stay together for the sake of the children? According to current research, the answer is usually no. Interparental conflict, not divorce per se, is associated with children's behavior problems (Emery, 1982). It doesn't matter to children whether the constant parental conflict occurs in an intact marriage, before a divorce, or after a divorce. What matters is that it is difficult to feel secure in a relationship with either parent when domestic life is a constant battleground. Parents who decide to separate can help their children adjust to the loss by reassuring them that their parental love is intact and by refusing to use the children as pawns in their conflicts with each other.

In a study of the children of divorce, Wallerstein (1984) noted that half of the young people continued to fantasize that their biological parents would get back together even though most of their lives had been spent in the divorced or remarried family. At first, children, particularly boys, were greatly upset about the divorce. Later, time and conscientious parenting had healing effects. Five years after divorce, the majority of children from single-parent or blended families showed good psychological adjustment, especially if they had been very young at the time of the marital breakup. However, divorce has a lasting negative effect on some young people. About one third of the children from divorced families were still depressed years after their parents had separated.

To minimize the negative impact of divorce, both biological and stepparents should work hard at setting consistent standards and creating a rich, emotionally gratifying life for their children. When this is not possible, a good relationship with one parent can protect the children from some of the negative effects of marital turmoil (Emery, 1982).

Nearly two out of every five children in the United States experience some kind of family disruption by the time they are teenagers (Furstenberg et al., 1983). Only a small fraction of these lost a parent through death; nearly 90 percent come from separated and divorced families. Living arrangements, not just parental conflict, influence children's psychological adjustment. The single-parent family, for example, may be better than an intact, nuclear family in which the parents could never agree on how to raise the children. Children may be exposed to a more consistent set of parental values. As one single father put it, "I don't need to deal with varying child-rearing philosophies where my wife says, 'We must take a rigid stand,' and I say, 'There is no need; this is a time for understanding' " (Greenberg, 1979, p. 315) Another advantage is that single parents may enrich their children's lives and their own happiness by exposing them to a network of friends of the same sex as well as to caring dating partners.

Single-parent families also have disadvantages. Foremost of these, loneliness and isolation may contribute to parental resentment or the psychological exploitation of children, such as demanding that children nurture a parent. Other problems include strain from financial hardships, especially for female heads of households (Spanier & Glick, 1981) and feeling worn out and exhausted by parental responsibilities (Furstenberg & Spanier, 1984). Posing an even greater adjustment hazard is the fact that most children from disrupted families have little contact with the outside parent (Furstenberg et al., 1983). This is particularly the case in the typical single-parent family, where the children live with their mother apart from their father. Only a third of the children in one study saw their father once a month or more and just one sixth saw their father every week.

Yet the outside parent is not always to blame. Sometimes, the parent who has custody actively prevents the outside parent from seeing the children. In addition, visits with the outside parent may be awkward and stressful for the children, who must adjust to a new setting and parental style. Whatever the cause, children suffer when the parent-child relationship is ruptured. Most children experience the departure of one of their parents from their household as terrifying (Wallerstein & Kelly, 1980). Children's psychological adjustment is greatly enhanced when they are permitted frequent visits, especially in the absence of family conflict, with the absent parent.

Four out of five divorced people remarry, half of these within three years of the divorce (Spanier & Glick, 1980). At present, nearly 10 million children under age eighteen (one out of every six) live with a biological parent and a stepparent. These remarriages create blended families. Blended families present many challenges to children, including the tasks of establishing intimacy and avoiding conflict with a stepparent and possibly stepsisters and stepbrothers. As divorce rates are higher among the remarried than among the first married, some children face the challenge of getting used to a new family configuration more than once.

How does remarriage affect parents and children? Most parents feel that the new relationship helps them to be better parents (Furstenberg & Spanier, 1984). However, these same parents often describe themselves as being more worn out by the burdens of raising a family than those who head single-parent households. On the positive side, parents in blended families feel less fearful than single parents that they may lose control over their feelings when children and adolescents misbehave. In general, the advantages of remarriage are balanced by the complexities of managing a blended family. Occasionally, remarried individuals feel less adequate as parents because of the strains of managing two families. At the same time, the presence of an additional parent at home may compensate for the added difficulties of rearing a parent's own children and stepchildren.

The best advice to parents and children in blended families is to accept the fact that it will take hard work for the family to function smoothly (Turkington, 1984). Children's adjustment to a blended family may be facilitated by taking one or more of the following steps. First, adults should help the child understand that a stepparent will not be just like the biological parent. The child should realize that this new adult is likely to have a different and equally legitimate way of relating to the child. Second, both biological and stepparents can work together to provide firm, loving consistency in child-rearing practices.

SUMMARY

1. There is no single model for a committed relationship. People may have committed relationships while remaining single, cohabitating with a partner of the same or opposite gender, or by getting married. Everyone wants the same things from committed relationships—a partner with whom to share affection, intimate secrets, and companionship.

2. Well over one third of adults in the United States are single, and these people may enjoy greater opportunities to develop in an androgynous way.

3. Increasing numbers of heterosexuals, nearly four million people, live together outside marriage. Cohabiting people are as satisfied with their relationships as married couples are, but they espouse more liberal values. Couples who cohabited previously are likely to divorce given fewer marital difficulties than other married couples are.

4. Typically, lesbian and gay couples reject the roles of husband and wife. Instead, their committed relationships are modeled after close friendships, both partners initiating sex, working outside the home, and contributing to housekeeping equally.

5. Most people marry one or more times. Opportunities to marry and experiences within marriage are influenced greatly by social class and ethnicity. Middle-class couples tend to interact predominantly with their spouses. Lower-class couples often have a segregated marital role relationship, in which spouses spend little time together and have very different duties. Poor children, especially poor black children, are likely to grow up in a single-parent household headed by a woman.

6. Marriages change over time. Marital adjustment is most difficult when couples have to care for preschool children.

7. Marital happiness is most likely when spouses consider each other a best friend and don't expect romantic love to last forever. Most adults believe in monogamy, but it is likely that half of the married population has had extramarital sex.

8. Two of the most important decisions a couple can make are whether or not to have children and when to begin having children. Although they are aware of the advantages of not having children, most people view childless, married women negatively. Raising children can be pleasurable, but it is difficult when both spouses are employed outside the home.

9. Marital conflict is inevitable about such issues as commitment, values, sex, roles, money, family relationships, independence, personality traits of a spouse, and how to spend free time.

10. Marital conflict may either enhance or destroy relationships. Conflict is particularly destructive in violent marriages, in which wives are usually the victims and husbands are usually the perpetrators. Good marriages require partners to (1) establish good communication, (2) balance intimacy with individuality, and (3) achieve an equitable relationship. Rational beliefs about committed relationships are associated with improved marital adjustment.

11. About half of all recent American marriages will terminate in separation and divorce. Those who marry young and the poor have more unstable marriages than others. Although some marriages fail because one or both partners are psychologically disturbed, well-adjusted people can also have unsuccessful marriages. Egalitarian marriages are particularly stable and happy. The relationship between extramarital sex and marital disruption is unclear.

12. Most people adjust well to marital disruption over time. However, some divorced and separated people continue to feel discontent and suffer from health problems years after their marriages failed. Divorce hits men harder emotionally and women harder financially. Acceptance of the end of marriage and the avoidance of loneliness contribute to good adjustment.

13. Widowed people, mostly women, suffer economically and emotionally and are less likely to remarry than the divorced. Good psychological adjustment depends on forming closer ties with friends of the same sex and the extended family.

14. Nearly two out of every five children experience family disruption by the time they are teenagers. Children suffer more from interparental conflict than from divorce or separation per se, and most children make adequate adjustment to new living situations, especially if the marital disruption took place when they were very young. However, half of the children of divorce continue to fantasize about a reconciliation between their biological parents and a third are depressed years after their parents separated. Raising children alone or in blended families presents special challenges to parents.

Chapter 12

SEXUALITY

In the Victorian era (1837–1901), it was thought that boys were poorly adjusted if they masturbated and that women who experienced sexual desire or orgasm were sinful or abnormal. Today, many in our culture think that women should have multiple orgasms, that both men and women should experience sexual desire, and that there is something wrong with their adjustment if they don't. Despite the greatly different attitudes toward sex between Victorians of the 1800s and Americans of the 1980s, one fact remains constant: Sexuality is viewed as an important aspect of adjustment. This chapter presents basic information about biological, psychological, and social aspects of sexuality.

THE SEXUAL BODY

A first step in this chapter on sexuality is to discuss the parts of male and female sexual anatomy, shown in Figures 12–1 and 12–2. Many people have only vague ideas of the nature of the male and female reproductive organs and how they function.

vulva external genitals of the female

vagina tubular organ in the female in which the penis is inserted during intercourse and through which a baby passes during birth

uterus organ in the female in which the fetus develops

cervix lower third of the uterus

fallopian tubes tubes in the female through which an egg passes on its way from an ovary to the uterus

ovary organ in the female that produces the female sex hormones and releases eggs

progesterone sex hormone secreted by the ovaries in the female

The Female Sexual Body

The external genitals of the female are known collectively as the **vulva**. The most important external organ is the clitoris (pronounced KLIT-or-is), the most sexually sensitive part of a woman's body. For many women, stroking or massaging it is the best way to produce arousal and orgasm. Behind the clitoris is the opening to the urethra, through which urine passes. Behind that is the opening to the vagina. Running along the side of the vaginal opening are the *inner lips* and *outer lips,* which are also sexually sensitive. The third opening is the anus.

One other external structure in some women is the *hymen,* a thin membrane stretching across the vaginal entrance. Because it is torn or stretched during sexual intercourse, women who have had intercourse do not have a hymen. However, women who have never had intercourse (virgins) may or may not have a hymen. Some girls are born without one.

Internally, the **vagina** is a tubular organ that serves two functions: It is the birth canal (through which a baby passes during childbirth) and it is the sexual organ into which the penis is inserted during sexual intercourse. It is sexually sensitive, although not so sensitive as the clitoris.

The **uterus** is an organ about the size and shape of an upside-down pear, located just above the vagina. Its inner lining is prepared to nurture a fertilized egg as it grows into a fetus. This same inner lining, when the woman is not pregnant, is sloughed off each month as the menstrual flow. The lower third of the uterus, the part that connects to the vagina, is called the **cervix**. Extending from each side of the uterus are the **fallopian tubes**, and at the end of each fallopian tube is an **ovary**. The ovaries serve two purposes: They secrete the female sex hormones (estrogen and **progesterone**) and they release eggs. An

FIGURE 12-1   Female Reproductive System

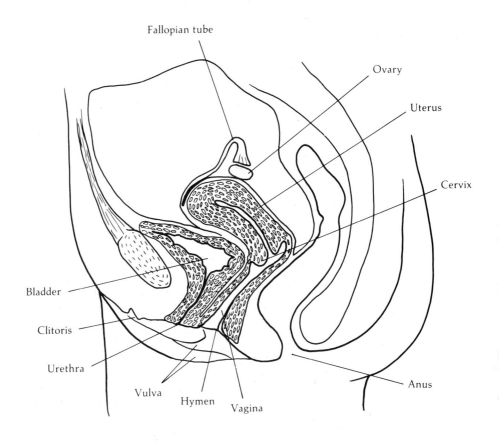

Fallopian tube

Ovary

Uterus

Cervix

Bladder

Clitoris

Urethra

Vulva

Hymen

Vagina

Anus

egg travels down the fallopian tube. If sperm from a man are present, the egg may be fertilized in the fallopian tube and then travel to the uterus, where it attaches to the lining and develops. Otherwise, it disintegrates.

The Male Sexual Body

penis male sexual organ through which urine or semen passes

Externally, the important parts of male sexual anatomy are the penis, scrotum, and testes. The **penis** is a tubular-shaped organ that consists of a tip portion called the glans, a main portion called the shaft, and a ridge separating the two called the corona. The penis serves several functions. First, urine passes out through the urethra that runs the length of it. Second, it is the organ inserted into the vagina during sexual intercourse. Finally, semen containing sperm passes out through it during orgasm and ejaculation. It is the most sexually sensitive part of a man's body. Internally, three tubes run the length of it. Each has a structure rather like a sponge. *Erection,* the enlarging and hardening of the penis, occurs when these spongy structures become engorged with blood. Erection may occur as a result of direct physical stimulation (such as stroking the penis or thighs) or from psychological stimulation (such as an arousing fantasy).

scrotum pouch of skin containing the testes

The **scrotum** is a pouch of skin hanging down behind the penis. It contains the **testes,** which serve functions analogous to the ovaries in women. The testes manufacture the male sex hormone (**testosterone**) and they manufacture *sperm* (tiny cells that are contained in the ejaculate, or semen, that is emitted during orgasm). Millions of these tiny, tadpole-like cells engage in a swimming marathon up into the uterus and fallopian tubes in search of an egg to fertilize.

testes sex glands in the male (located in the scrotum)

testosterone hormone secreted by the testes in the male

The **prostate** is a gland located below the urinary bladder. It produces most of the fluid in semen, secreting the fluid into the urethra. Cancer of the prostate is the second most common form of cancer in men (lung cancer is the most common). However, it is not a major cause of death because it generally affects older men, and the tumors tend to be small and to spread slowly. Treatments such as hormone therapy and surgery are usually effective, and it is recommended that all men over fifty have an annual rectal exam for prostate tumors.

prostate gland that produces most of the fluid of the semen

The Sexual Response Cycle

Masters and Johnson (1966) conducted a major investigation of the physiology of the body's response during sexual arousal and orgasm. From 1954 to 1966, they collected data on 382 women and 312 men observed in over 10,000 cycles of sexual response.

vasocongestion engorgement of blood in the vessels of a region, such as the genitals

They found that two basic physiological processes occur during arousal: vasocongestion and myotonia. **Vasocongestion** occurs when a great deal of blood flows into the blood vessels in a region, in this case the genitals, as a result of dilation of blood vessels in that region of the body. **Myotonia** is muscular contraction, including contractions of muscles in the genitals and other parts of the body.

myotonia muscular contractions

Masters and Johnson describe the sexual response cycle as occurring in four stages: (1) excitement, (2) plateau, (3) orgasm, and (4) resolution. During the first stage, *excitement,* the major physiological process is vasocongestion— a great deal of blood flows into the genitals. This produces the obvious arousal response in males, erection of the penis. The corresponding response in females is vaginal lubrication. Although this may seem a much different response from the male's, the physiological basis is actually the same—vasocongestion. Masters and Johnson discovered that vaginal lubrication results when fluids seep through the semipermeable membranes of the vaginal walls, producing lubrication as a result of vasocongestion in the tissues surrounding the vagina. Other changes during the excitement phase include erection of the nipples, swelling and opening up of the inner lips, and expansion of the upper two thirds of the vagina. In men, the testes and scrotum pull up closer to the body.

FIGURE 12-2   Male Reproductive System

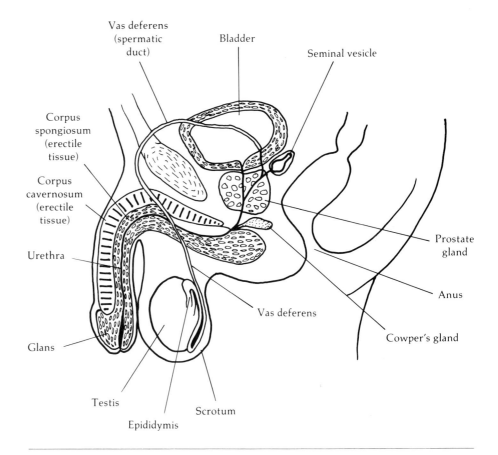

During the *plateau* phase, vasocongestion reaches its peak. In men, the penis is completely erect and the testes are enlarged by the vasocongestion. In women, the orgasmic platform appears—a thickening and swelling of the walls of the vagina at its entrance.

The third stage of sexual response, *orgasm*, consists of a series of rhythmic contractions of the pelvic organs. Actually, male orgasm occurs in two phases. In the first, the vas, seminal vesicles, and prostate contract, forcing the ejaculate into a bulb at the base of the urethra. Masters and Johnson call the sensation in this stage ejaculatory inevitability (coming). In the second phase, the urethral bulb and the penis itself contract, forcing out the semen.

For females, the process is basically similar. The orgasm consists of a series of rhythmic muscular contractions of the orgasmic platform. In both males and females there are sharp increases in pulse rate, blood pressure, and breathing rate, and there are contractions of muscles throughout the body.

In the fourth stage, *resolution*, the physiological processes that built up to orgasm reverse themselves and the body returns to the unaroused state. Orgasm triggers a massive release of muscular tension and of blood from the engorged blood vessels. During the resolution stage, men experience a refractory period, during which they cannot be restimulated to orgasm. The length of the refractory period varies considerably and depends on a number of factors, such as age, alcohol consumption, and general health. For some men, it may last only a few minutes, whereas an elderly man may have to wait twenty-four hours. Women, in contrast, do not experience a refractory period. This fact enables them to have multiple orgasms (several orgasms within a short period of time).

CONTRACEPTION

Today's college students have grown up in the era of the pill, a technological advance that has had an enormous impact on people. For the first time in human history, women have been able to control, with considerable reliability, when and if they have children. This development, in turn, has had a significant impact on men's and women's roles. Certainly the current liberation of gender roles and the commitment of many women to their careers could not have occurred if women had frequent, unplanned pregnancies.

This section provides basic information about some of the most important methods of contraception, as well as a discussion of the psychological aspects of contraceptive use (and nonuse). This information should help you as you make choices about contraception.

Table 12–1 provides a summary of contraceptive methods, with their failure rates and costs. The second column of that table, actual failure rate, refers to the following: If one hundred women actually use that method of contraception for one year, the number who still become pregnant by the end of the year is the actual failure rate. Thus, the actual failure rate results from both failures of the method and failures of individuals to use it properly (such as, forgetting to take pills or neglecting to use a condom).

The Pill

birth control pill pill that contains sex hormones (usually estrogen and progesterone) and prevents ovulation

The most common type of **birth control pill** contains the two female sex hormones (estrogen and progesterone) at higher levels than normally occur in the body. The pills stop the woman from ovulating (releasing an egg) so that conception cannot occur. They also change the mucus in the cervix so that it is difficult for sperm to get through.

Many people express concern about the health risks associated with the use of the pill. The most serious side effect associated with use of the pill is an increased risk of blood-clotting problems (Hatcher et al., 1986). These can be serious if the blood clot moves to the lungs or brain, where it can cause death or a stroke. However, such incidents seem to occur mainly in women who have a

TABLE 12-1   A Comparison of Various Methods of Contraception

Method	Actual Failure Rate (percent)	Death Rate (per 100,000 women)	Yearly Costs[1]
1. Birth control pill	2	0.3-3.0	$ 26-$130
2. IUD	5	1.0	$125
3. Condom	10	1.7[2]	$ 52
4. Diaphragm with jelly	19	2.0[2]	$100
5. Sponge	17	2.0	$150
6. Rhythm	24	2.5[2]	None
7. Vaginal foam	22	2.0[2]	$ 75
8. Withdrawal	20-25	2.0	None
9. Unprotected intercourse	90	10.0[3]	None
10. Sterilization, male	less than 1	—	$250[4]
11. Sterilization, female	less than 1	—	$850[4]

[1]Based on an assumption of 150 acts of intercourse.
[2]Based on the death rate for pregnancies resulting from failures of the method.
[3]Deaths from pregnancy or childbirth.
[4]These are one-time only costs.
Sources: R. E. Hatcher et al. (1986), *Contraceptive technology, 1986-1987*, New York: Irvington. J. S. Hyde (1989), *Understanding human sexuality* (4th ed.), New York: McGraw-Hill.

personal or family history of blood-clotting problems. Women over forty, particularly smokers, are at high risk and are advised not to take the pill. There is no evidence that the pill causes cancer of the cervix or breasts, and it actually seems to protect against cancer of the ovaries. Many experts believe that the pill is a relatively safe method of contraception (Hyde, 1989). Notice in Table 12-1 that the death rate associated with the pill is at most 3 per 100,000 women, considerably lower than the death rate resulting from pregnancy and childbirth.

The IUD

IUD (intrauterine device) small piece of plastic (perhaps also containing copper or hormones) that is inserted into the uterus to prevent implantation of the fertilized egg

The **IUD**, or **intrauterine device**, is a small piece of plastic that may also contain metal or hormones. It is inserted by a physician into the woman's uterus and may stay there for several years. No one is exactly certain how the IUD works. The leading theory is that because it is a foreign object inside the uterus, it creates a constant, slight inflammation in the lining of the uterus. Thus a fertilized egg cannot successfully implant itself in the lining to grow and develop, and pregnancy cannot occur. As you can see in Table 12-1 the IUD is highly effective, coming in close to the pill and sterilization.

There are two possible serious side effects of using the IUD. One is perforation of the uterus, which can cause death, although uterine perforation is rare and is usually caused by improper insertion by the physician. The other is an increased risk of pelvic inflammatory disease (PID)—an inflammation of the uterus or fallopian tubes or other pelvic organs. There is no evidence that the IUD causes cancer. Notice in Table 12–1 that, on balance, the IUD has approximately the same death rate as the pill. Because of lawsuits, many manufacturers have withdrawn IUDs from the market, making them less available than they once were.

The Diaphragm

diaphragm dome-shaped piece of thin rubber that fits over the cervix inside the woman's vagina and acts as a contraceptive

The **diaphragm** is a dome-shaped piece of thin rubber with a rubber-covered rim of flexible metal, as shown in Figure 12–3. It is inserted into the vagina, and when placed properly, it covers the cervix. Diaphragms come in different sizes and thus must be individually fitted by a physician. In order to use one properly, a contraceptive cream or jelly must be spread on the rim and the inside surface. The diaphragm works in two ways. First, it provides a mechanical barrier to sperm, preventing them from swimming through the opening in the cervix and into the uterus. Second, the contraceptive cream or jelly kills any sperm that happen to sneak past the barrier of the diaphragm.

Notice in Table 12–2 that the diaphragm has a considerably higher failure rate than the pill or IUD. Most of those failures, however, are the result of people's not using the diaphragm every time they have intercourse or using it improperly (for example, not using a contraceptive cream or jelly on it). If the diaphragm is used properly, it can have a failure rate as low as 3 percent. There are essentially no health risks associated with use of the diaphragm.

The Condom

condom male contraceptive sheath that fits over the penis

The **condom** is a thin sheath of latex ("rubber") or intestinal tissue of lambs ("skins") that fits snugly over the penis. It must be unrolled onto the penis as soon as the man has a firm erection; it is left in place during intercourse and ejaculation. The man then holds it tightly against the base of the penis as he withdraws. The condom works by catching the semen and thus preventing any sperm from entering the vagina. As you can see in Table 12–1, it has a somewhat higher failure rate than the pill and IUD. As in the case of the diaphragm, most of those failures result from a failure to use the condom (they are not at all effective when left in a pocket or a drawer). If the condom is used perfectly, the failure rate can be as low as 2 percent, making it more effective than most people think.

There are no health risks associated with use of the condom, and it has the advantage of allowing the man to share in the responsibility for contraception. It also provides some protection against sexually transmitted diseases, such as herpes and AIDS.

rhythm method of birth control that involves abstaining from sexual intercourse during the fertile days of the woman's menstrual cycle

Rhythm

There are actually several versions of the **rhythm** method of birth control. They attempt to determine when the woman is fertile—that is, when she ovu-

FIGURE 12–3   Contraceptive Methods

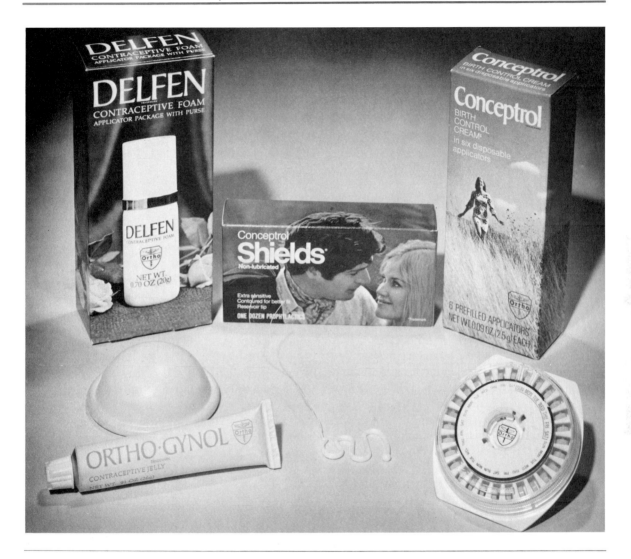

lates. The couple then refrain from having intercourse around the time of ovulation. With the calendar method, the woman keeps track of her menstrual cycles for a year to find out how long they typically are. She then makes use of the fact that women ovulate about fourteen days before they menstruate. Thus if she has a regular 28-day cycle, she will ovulate around day fourteen (counting day one as the first day of menstruation). If she has a 34-day cycle, she will ovulate around day twenty. She then abstains from intercourse for about two days before and two days after the estimated day of ovulation. The basal body temperature method is similar, except that the woman determines when she ovulates by taking her temperature every morning. Her temperature should fall on the day of ovulation and then rise on the day after. With the cervical mucus method, the woman monitors the mucus discharged by her cervix every day. She learns the precise change in its texture that occurs around the time of ovulation. Again, she abstains from intercourse for several days before and after that time.

The rhythm method is not very effective, whether one looks at the actual failure rate or even failure rates calculated for perfect use (that's why some people call it "rhythm and blues"—baby blues, that is). The other side of the coin is that the methods for determining ovulation that are used in rhythm can also be used by couples who are trying to conceive a child. Ironically, the calendar and temperature methods are probably more effective in producing conceptions than in preventing them!

Other Methods

Contraceptive vaginal foams (for example, Delfen) are spermicides, that is, they contain chemicals that kill sperm. They have a failure rate that is unacceptably high for many people. On the other hand, it is possible to combine two less-than-perfect methods—such as foam and the condom—and achieve nearly 100 percent effectiveness. Foam also provides some protection against AIDS. In fact, it seems to be more effective at killing the AIDS virus than at killing sperms.

The contraceptive sponge, newly introduced in the 1980s, also deserves mention. The sponge is made of polyurethane and soaked with a spermicide. It is inserted into the vagina and fits over the cervix. It has the advantage that, like foam, it can be purchased without prescription in a drugstore. On the other hand, it has a failure rate about as high as foam, and thus it cannot be recommended for those who definitely want to prevent pregnancy.

Abstinence—not engaging in sexual intercourse—is another alternative. It may be particularly appropriate for the unmarried, but it is largely a matter of personal preference.

Sterilization

Sterilization is a surgical procedure whereby a person is made permanently sterile, that is, unable to reproduce. The previous methods considered are reversible—that is, the person can stop using them and become fertile again. Sterilization, however, is usually irreversible. A few surgeons report success in reversing the surgery, but the rates are low. When deciding whether to have sterilization surgery, one should assume that the effects are irreversible.

vasectomy surgical method of male sterilization involving severing of the vas deferens

The male sterilization operation is called a **vasectomy**, named for the vas deferens (see Figure 12–2), which is tied off or cut. This prevents sperm from leaving the testes and becoming part of the ejaculate. Thus, the man has a normal ejaculation except that it contains no sperm. The female sterilization

tubal ligation surgical method of female sterilization involving severing of the fallopian tubes

surgery is often called a **tubal ligation** because the fallopian tubes are cut and tied off. This prevents the egg from traveling down the fallopian tube and being fertilized.

Both male sterilization and female sterilization are close to 100 percent effective. Neither has any serious health risks except those associated with the surgery itself. The vasectomy is especially simple and can be done in a physician's office.

Readers who want more detailed information on sterilization or any other method of contraception should consult *Contraceptive Technology* (1986) by Hatcher et al. A new edition is published every two years and gives excellent, up-to-date information. Your local Planned Parenthood clinic has a great deal of free information available, and professionals there are happy to have discussions with anyone seeking information on birth control.

Psychology and Contraceptive Use

As indicated in the preceding sections, the actual failure rates of most contraceptives would be considerably lower if the methods were used perfectly. The best contraceptive technology is useless if a person does not obtain a contraceptive or has one and fails to use it. To give some idea of the magnitude of this problem, each year in the United States, one million teenagers (mostly unmarried) become pregnant; 30,000 of those pregnant teenagers are girls fifteen years of age or younger (Byrne, 1983). Therefore psychologists are devoting a great deal of attention to what is involved psychologically in using contraceptives effectively and why some people fail to do so.

According to social psychologist Donn Byrne (1983), there are five steps involved in effective contraception:

1. The person must acquire accurate information about contraception and remember it.
2. The person must acknowledge that there is a likelihood that intercourse will occur. Being prepared, of course, makes sense only if one has some expectation of having intercourse. Gender-role socialization has made it particularly difficult for women to be honest with themselves about this topic.
3. The person must obtain the contraceptive, whether by visiting a doctor, a drugstore, or a Planned Parenthood clinic.
4. The person must communicate with his or her partner about contraception. Otherwise, both may assume the other is taking care of things.
5. The person must actually use the contraceptive.

erotophobia guilty, fearful attitudes toward sex

erotophilia positive, nonguilty attitudes toward sex

According to Byrne's analysis, a number of psychological factors can short-circuit the process at any one of the five steps. These factors include attitudes, emotions, and expectations. To study these attitudes and emotions, Byrne devised a scale to measure where a person stands on a dimension ranging from **erotophobia** (guilty, fearful attitudes toward sex) to **erotophilia** (pleasant attitudes toward sex and having little guilt about it). Research shows that eroto-philes are more likely to be consistent, effective contraceptive users.

Erotophobes, on the other hand, are more likely to fail at every one of the five steps of contraceptive use. They have less information about sex. Because of their fearfulness, they are less likely to acknowledge realistically that intercourse may occur. It is hard for them to go to a doctor, drugstore, or clinic to obtain contraceptives. They have trouble discussing sex with their partner. Finally, erotophobes have difficulty with the final step—actually using the contraceptive. An erotophobic man isn't likely to feel cool as he pulls out his condom and rolls it on. So he doesn't, and he risks causing a pregnancy.

If you are committed to preventing pregnancy in yourself or your partner, you should consider where you might fall on the erotophobia-erotophilia scale. This fact may have an impact on how well you follow through with the five steps of effective contraception.

PREMARITAL SEX

In the 1940s, Kinsey found that 71 percent of the men he interviewed but only 33 percent of the women engaged in premarital sexual intercourse (Kinsey et al., 1953). In contrast, a carefully conducted survey of the 1970s found that 75 percent of male college students and 60 percent of female college students had engaged in premarital intercourse (DeLamater & MacCorquodale, 1979). The shift in patterns of premarital sexuality that has occurred over those decades has been called the Sexual Revolution. The trend has been toward an increased incidence of premarital intercourse, particularly among women. The formerly large gap between men's and women's experience has narrowed considerably. Premarital intercourse is now the experience of a majority of both men and women.

An increased incidence of premarital intercourse has not been the only phenomenon in the Sexual Revolution; a dramatic increase in the *variety* of sexual techniques has also occurred. Perhaps most striking is the increased use of mouth-genital techniques (oral sex). In the Kinsey data from the 1940s, 33 percent of males had experienced **fellatio** premaritally and 14 percent had engaged in **cunnilingus**. In a 1970s survey, 61 percent of male college students had experienced fellatio and 60 percent had performed cunnilingus (DeLamater & MacCorquodale, 1979). Today, too, people increasingly experiment with different positions during sexual intercourse.

fellatio mouth stimulation of the penis

cunnilingus mouth stimulation of the vulva

Is the Revolution Over?

In the 1980s, the media have carried many articles focusing on the idea that the Sexual Revolution is over and that there is a trend toward sexual conservatism, both in behavior and in attitudes, accompanied by an emphasis on intimacy and long-term, committed relationships. There is some evidence to support these contentions. For example, in one study, students at Ohio State

Is the Sexual
Revolution over?

University were surveyed every year from 1968 to 1980 (Clatworthy, 1980).
For females, there was an increase in the incidence of premarital intercourse
from 21 percent in 1968 to 80 percent in 1975; but then the incidence fell back
to 50 percent in 1980. For males, the trends were less dramatic, with the incidence being around 75 percent for many years. Nonetheless, there was a peak
in incidence of 87 percent in 1972 and a decline to 73 percent in 1980. In sum,
there may be a trend away from engaging in premarital intercourse, at least for
women.

A number of factors may be contributing to this trend toward conservatism. Certainly, one is the emergence of two presently incurable sexually

transmitted diseases, herpes and AIDS. Another may be the realization that casual sex is not so much fun as it was expected to be by the 1960s generation, for whom it was largely forbidden.

Values and Choices

Sexuality, and particularly premarital sexuality, is an area in which values often play a strong role. We can either behave according to the values we have learned or disregard them partially or completely. It has been said that the dominant attitude toward premarital sex in our culture in the 1960s and 1970s was one of permissiveness with affection. That is, premarital intercourse was viewed as acceptable if it occurred in the context of a stable relationship that involved love and commitment. Another possible approach is to be accepting of casual sex (intercourse occurring in a relationship that involves no love or commitment). Still others hold to a standard of abstinence, maintaining that intercourse is legitimate only when there is a marriage license. In our culture, then, values about premarital sex vary widely. Your values about sex are the result of many factors—values instilled by parents and other relatives, religious beliefs, the values of your peers, and the sexual experiences you have had.

People tend to feel best about themselves when their behavior is consistent with their values and attitudes. What are your own values about premarital sex? Do you approve of casual sex? Do you think sexual intercourse is appropriate when the couple are involved in a loving, committed relationship, even though they are not married? Or do you believe that intercourse is acceptable only in marriage? If you are making decisions about whether to engage in sexual activity, you need to examine your values and then consider what behaviors are consistent with them.

SEXUAL ORIENTATION

The gay liberation movement began in 1969, when in response to police harassment, gays rioted outside a gay bar in Greenwich Village, New York. Since then, there has been a great deal of discussion of the issue of homosexuality— whether gay men and lesbian women should have the same civil rights as straights, whether homosexuality is a normal form of adjustment, and why some people become gay and others become straight.

homosexual person who is sexually attracted mainly to members of his or her own gender

A **homosexual** is a person who is sexually attracted to members of his or her own gender. Gay activists prefer the term *gay* to *homosexual*. Usually the terms *gay* and *homosexual* are used for males and the term *lesbian* is used for female homosexuals.

More people are gay or lesbian than you may think. Kinsey found that 37 percent of all men had had a homosexual experience to orgasm sometime in adulthood, as had 13 percent of all women (Kinsey et al., 1953). These figures caused much of the controversy over the Kinsey report. Most experts now

More people are gay
or lesbian than you
may think.

believe that because Kinsey did not have a random sample, these figures are a bit high, and that 25 percent of males and 15 percent of females may be more accurate (Hyde, 1989). These statistics, of course, include some people who experiment with homosexuality only once. Exclusive homosexuality is less common. The estimate from the Kinsey report and other studies is that around 2 percent to 4 percent of males and 1 percent to 2 percent of females are exclusively homosexual throughout their lives (Kinsey et al., 1953).

Although some people view homosexuality as unnatural, the scientific data indicate that homosexuality is found in all human societies and in many other species as well (Beach, 1976; Whitam, 1983). Read "Exploring Choices: What Are Your Attitudes Toward Homosexuals?" and see how you score on the attitude scale.

Implications for Adjustment

Research indicates that the majority of Americans believe homosexuality is a form of sickness (Levitt & Klassen, 1974). Yet in 1973, the American Psychiatric Association (APA) removed homosexuality as a category of mental disorder from its *Diagnostic and Statistical Manual*, stating that homosexuality is not in itself a mental or emotional illness. Thus, a rather large gap exists between what ordinary people think on the subject and what professionals think. Opinions aside, what does the research evidence say?

The latest research tends to find no differences in adjustment between heterosexuals and homosexuals. This finding supports the position of the APA but flies in the face of the stereotypes most people have about homosexuals. Kinsey Institute researchers Alan Bell and Martin Weinberg (1978) studied various types of heterosexual and homosexual relationships. They found that homosexual men and women were as well adjusted as heterosexual men and women. Gay men, for example, involved in long-term gay relationships had the same scores as heterosexual men on adjustment measures—and actually scored higher on happiness. On the other hand, gay men who were involved in only casual sex or who had trouble finding partners were less well adjusted, as were the heterosexual men in the same situation.

Such studies point to the importance of recognizing that homosexual people are not one type—they have many different life-styles, just as heterosexuals do. In general, research evidence and professional opinion reveal no important differences in adjustment between heterosexuals and homosexuals.

Reasons for Sexual Orientation

How and why people develop their sexual orientation are fascinating questions that researchers are still trying to answer. In the early years of investigation, it was assumed that heterosexuality was the only natural orientation. More recently, however, psychologists seek to explain sexual orientation in general, including why people become heterosexual.

EXPLORING CHOICES

WHAT ARE YOUR ATTITUDES TOWARD HOMOSEXUALS?

It is important to be aware of your own attitudes toward homosexuality. These attitudes may or may not agree with your values. Many students, for example, say that while they feel negative or anxious about gays, they wish they felt differently. They want to work to build more positive attitudes. *Homophobia* is the term used by psychologists to describe an excessive fear of homosexuality. To get an objective assessment of your attitudes, answer the following items as honestly as possible. They are taken from a homophobia scale (Hudson & Rickettes, 1980). For each item, rate your attitude using the following scale: (1) Strongly agree, (2) Agree, (3) Neither agree nor disagree, (4) Disagree, or (5) Strongly disagree.

_____ 1. I would feel comfortable working closely with a male homosexual.

_____ 2. I would enjoy attending social functions at which homosexuals were present.

_____ 3. I would feel disappointed if I learned that my child was homosexual.

_____ 4. I would feel comfortable knowing that my clergyman was homosexual.

_____ 5. If I saw two men holding hands in public, I would feel disgusted.

In order to score yourself, you must first reverse your score on the positively worded items (items 1, 2, and 4) so that high scores on these items will indicate more homophobia as with the other items; that is, if you put 5 for that item, change it to 1, if you put 4, change it to 2, if you put 1, change it to 5, and so on. Then add up your ratings on the five items. Scores can range from 5 to 25. The highest scores indicate the most homophobia. If your score was between 20 and 25, you score as highly homophobic. If your score is between 15 and 19, you are somewhat homophobic. If your score is 14 or below, you are nonhomophobic. Does your score agree with your own personal values and ideals? For example, if you scored as highly homophobic, is that the way you want to be?

Another way to explore your own attitudes toward homosexuality is to imagine that one of your good friends has just come out (revealed his or her homosexuality) to you. Write down on a sheet of paper what you would say and how you would respond to your friend. After you complete that exercise, write out at least two other possible responses you could make to your friend. Which of these responses do you think is the best one? Why?

Some psychologists believe homosexuality is the result of an imbalance in hormones. Others believe the answer lies in disturbed relationships between the child and the parents. The child may receive insufficient love from the parent of the same sex or learn to fear relationships with members of the opposite sex. When these disturbances are unresolved, the child continues to be sexually attracted to members of the same sex as an adult. Still others claim that we are born neither heterosexual nor homosexual; we learn to be one or the other by the pleasant or unpleasant sexual experiences we have as we grow up.

One of the more recent theories suggests that the age at which the individual matures sexually is the critical factor in determining sexual orientation (Storms, 1981). Most children before the age of twelve play almost exclusively with children of the same sex. If the sex drive matures during this time, they will be attracted to others of the same sex and have a greater chance of becoming homosexual. If the sex drive matures after age twelve, when they are more involved in heterosexual groups, they have a greater chance of becoming heterosexual.

Which of these theories is best? With all the studies that have been done on this topic, the answer is that no one really knows what causes people to be either homosexual or heterosexual. Little or no evidence has been found to support the theories that sexual orientation is the result of an imbalance in hormones (Gartrell, 1982), disturbed relationships with parents, or learned behavior (Bell, Weinberg, & Hammersmith, 1981). There is general agreement only on the fact that sexual orientation seems to be established relatively early in life, either in early childhood or by adolescence (Bell, Weinberg, & Hammersmith, 1981). The truth is that a person's sexual orientation is complex and probably determined by a number of factors, some of them yet to be discovered.

Sexual Reorientation

Over the years, researchers have studied whether a person's sexual orientation, once established, can be changed. The studies have focused primarily on psychologists' efforts at turning homosexuals into heterosexuals. Traditionally, these efforts have not been very successful, achieving changes of only 10 percent to 20 percent. Masters and Johnson (1979), however, reported a change rate of 78 percent among the homosexuals they treated who expressed dissatisfaction with their sexual orientation.

Closer examination of the Masters and Johnson research, however, revealed an important flaw. Many of their clients could be described more accurately as **bisexual,** that is, people who are sexually attracted to both men and women. Thus, the therapy may have achieved only a slight change in sexual orientation rather than a radical change from homosexual to heterosexual. In general, it seems that sexual orientation, once set, is not easy to alter. Like other factors in our personality, our sexual identity as homosexual, heterosexual, or bisexual appears to remain stable through life.

bisexual person who is sexually attracted to both males and females

SEXUAL DYSFUNCTION AND SEX THERAPY

sexual dysfunctions
problems with sexual
responding that cause
mental distress,
including erection
problems in men and
orgasm problems in
women

Sexual dysfunctions are various disturbances of sexual functioning, such as premature ejaculation in men and difficulty in having orgasm in women. These problems can create mental anguish in the sufferers. As it turns out, however, many cases can be treated simply and effectively by a sex therapist. There are also some steps one can take to avoid such problems . This section reviews some of the most common sexual dysfunctions, what causes them, what is involved in sex therapy, and what one can do to avoid having a sexual dysfunction.

Sexual Dysfunctions

**premature
ejaculation** sexual
dysfunction in which
the man has an
orgasm and ejaculates
too soon

Premature ejaculation occurs when a man ejaculates too soon or is not able to control when he has his orgasm. In extreme cases, ejaculation can occur so soon after erection that there is not even time to insert the penis into the vagina. Although it is easy to define premature ejaculation as ejaculating too soon, when is too soon? Should the man be able to hold back for at least thirty seconds after getting a complete erection or for at least ten thrusts in the vagina? The possibilities are endless. Two definitions are particularly good. Sex therapist Helen Singer Kaplan (1974) believes that the key is the man's sense that he lacks voluntary control over when he ejaculates. Self-definition is also legitimate: If a man finds that he has become very concerned over his lack of ejaculatory control, then he can reasonably say a problem exists.

Premature ejaculation is common particularly among college-aged men. Most men gain more ejaculatory control with age.

**erectile
dysfunction** inability
to get or maintain an
erection

Erectile dysfunction is the inability to get an erection or to maintain one. The more common term is *impotence*, but sex therapists such as Masters and Johnson (1970) have rejected that term because it carries so many negative connotations.

anorgasmia inability
to have an orgasm

Anorgasmia in women (also called orgasmic dysfunction) is the condition of being unable to have an orgasm. In some cases, a woman may have never had an orgasm in her life. In others, the woman has had orgasms and then develops difficulty in having them. In still other cases, the woman is able to have an orgasm in some situations—say when masturbating—but not in other situations, such as during sexual intercourse. Statistics from many surveys indicate that this last pattern is quite common and may be typical of the majority of women (Hite, 1976). For most women, it is far easier to have an orgasm when masturbating or from hand-genital or mouth-genital stimulation from a partner than it is to have an orgasm from sexual intercourse. Thus, women who have this difficulty should not consider themselves inadequate. Nonetheless, our society prizes sexual technique and orgasms—indeed, multiple orgasms—in women, so it is understandable that women may be distressed if they find it difficult or impossible to have an orgasm during sexual intercourse.

Problems of sexual desire may occur in women or men. Sexual desire, or libido, refers to feelings that lead a person to be interested in engaging in sexual activity. If a person is not interested in sexual activity, the dysfunction is termed inhibited sexual desire or low sexual desire (LoPiccolo, 1980). People with low sexual desire try to avoid situations that evoke sexual feelings, or they experience a loss of desire if they are in an arousing situation. A related problem is a *discrepancy of sexual desire,* in which one partner wants to engage in sexual activity considerably more frequently than the other partner does.

Causes of Sexual Dysfunction

There are two broad categories of causes of sexual dysfunctions: organic factors and psychological factors. Organic, or physical, factors may cause some cases of sexual dysfunction. For example, diabetes or an injury to the spinal cord can create erectile dysfunction in a man. A vaginal infection may cause painful intercourse and a loss of sexual desire in a woman. However, it is estimated that only about 10 percent to 20 percent of cases of sexual dysfunction are caused by organic factors. The remaining cases are caused by psychological factors.

A number of psychological factors can create sexual dysfunction. One of these is prior learning, particularly the things learned in childhood. For example, a woman who has difficulty having orgasms from masturbating or from intercourse may have been taught, as a child, that sex is dirty and wrong and that it is evil to touch one's genitals, or she may have been the victim of incest or rape. Her difficulties in adulthood would not be surprising.

Psychological factors during sexual activity itself can also contribute to dysfunctions. At the head of the list is anxiety. Anxiety may be caused by fear of failure, that is, a fear that one will not perform well (for example, not get an impressive erection or not have an ecstatic orgasm). Unfortunately, high levels of anxiety can create sexual dysfunction, resulting in a vicious cycle—fear of failure produces anxiety, which produces dysfunction, which produces more fear of failure (dysfunction), which produces more anxiety, and so on.

Other causes of sexual dysfunction are rooted in the couple and their relationship. Some couples have great difficulty communicating about sex, so neither partner knows what pleases the other. Thus, neither is getting the best kind of stimulation, and dysfunction results. A high degree of conflict in the relationship can also lead to sex problems; it is hard to have great sex when you are angry with or dislike the other person.

Sex Therapy

There are two basic approaches to sex therapy—the psychoanalytic (psychodynamic) approach and the behavioral approach. They stem from very different understandings of the causes of a sexual dysfunction, and they lead to substantially different kinds of treatment.

Psychoanalytic theory assumes that sex problems are the result of conflicts in the unconscious, which are often the result of early childhood experiences.

Following from this assumption, sex problems can be cured only by long-term, intensive psychotherapy designed to uncover and resolve the unconscious conflicts. The person's sex problem then should disappear.

In contrast, the behavioral approach is rooted in learning theory. It does not concern itself with the unconscious. Rather, it focuses on the problem behavior (such as not getting an erection) and how the behavior can be changed by applying the principles of learning theory. According to this view, sexual dysfunction may be seen as excessive anxiety about sex. Behavior therapists use the method of systematic desensitization, which gradually lowers the person's anxiety and fears until they no longer interfere with sexual enjoyment. Treatment using behavior therapy is often quite rapid, perhaps requiring only six to ten visits, once per week.

William Masters and Virginia Johnson ushered in sex therapy as we know it today with the publication of their book, *Human Sexual Inadequacy* (1970). Their form of therapy can basically be seen as behavior therapy. They conduct therapy in an intensive, two-week treatment period at their research and therapy center in St. Louis, the Masters and Johnson Institute. In order to treat an individual, they require that the person's partner also participate. They argue that there is no such thing as an uninvolved partner in a case of sexual dysfunction. For example, if a wife has problems having orgasm during intercourse, it is likely that her husband also feels inadequate and distressed about the situation.

William Masters and Virginia Johnson ushered in sex therapy as we know it today.

At the beginning of therapy, the therapist forbids the couple to have intercourse until they are instructed to do so. This has the effect of immediately reducing some anxiety, removing the fear of failure, and decreasing pressure to perform. Then, the therapist assigns homework exercises for each day. The basic exercises are called **sensate focus.** In the first sensate focus exercise, one partner takes the role of the giving partner and the other takes the role of the getting partner. The giving partner is instructed to stroke, massage, or fondle the getting partner while the two are in bed together, except that the genitals and breasts are off limits. The responsibility of the getting partner is to communicate to the giving partner which kinds of touch are most pleasing and arousing.

This exercise has the effect of removing performance demands and fear of failure, thereby reducing anxiety. It fosters couple communication and a focus on sensuous pleasure; too often people's sexual response is dulled because they are distracted by other thoughts ("I should have gotten more done at work today" or "Should I take Johnny to the doctor with his terrible cough?"). With the sensate focus exercises, sexy thoughts and feelings become the focus. Gradually the sensate focus assignments become more advanced: The genitals and breasts can be stroked; then the penis can be in the vagina but no thrusting is allowed; and finally intercourse is permitted. Generally, at this point the couple are having successful sex, and the dysfunction has disappeared.

Specific treatments for specific dysfunctions are also used. For example, the *stop-start technique* is used in treating premature ejaculation. The man's partner arouses him until he feels close to orgasm. The stimulation is then stopped, and his level of arousal subsides. Over time, the man learns control; he can be highly aroused without having an orgasm. A treatment often used with women who have anorgasmia is **masturbation** (LoPiccolo & Lobitz, 1972). In a set of guided exercises, the woman explores her own genitals, gradually begins masturbating, and eventually can give herself an orgasm. Because it is so much easier for most women to have orgasms through masturbation than through sexual intercourse, this is a good first step in therapy for women who wish to be able to have an orgasm during intercourse.

sensate focus
exercises prescribed by sex therapists to increase sexual response

masturbation self-stimulation of the genitals to produce sexual arousal and orgasm

Some Practical Suggestions

Suppose you feel you have a sex problem. What should you do about it? First, ask yourself, Is this a real sexual dysfunction? One episode of premature ejaculation, one time of trouble getting an erection, or once not having an orgasm is not really a sexual dysfunction. The problem is one of definition; that is, if a persistent problem with sexual functioning is distressing you, then it is reasonable to call it a sexual dysfunction and to seek therapy.

Before seeking therapy from a qualified professional, you may want to consider reading and working through some of the excellent self-help books that are available. Lonnie Garfield Barbach's *For Yourself: The Fulfillment of Female Sexuality* (1975) for women and Bernie Zilbergeld's *Male Sexuality* (1978) for men are particularly recommended. Both contain excellent personal growth exercises that may help you get over your problem yourself. These books are also excellent for individuals who do not have problems with sexual dysfunction but who want to enrich their capacity for sexual expression.

If you decide that you want to see a sex therapist, you should use some thought and care in choosing a well-qualified professional. You should look into your state's licensing policy and find someone who is licensed, or if your state does not do licensing, find someone who has the appropriate training as a psychiatrist or psychologist, with special work in sex therapy. Often a referral from a physician, a psychologist, a helping professional you trust, a local mental health agency, a medical bureau, or your campus counseling center is a good way to find someone. There are also professional organizations (such as The American Association of Sex Educators, Counselors, and Therapists in Washington, DC) that certify sex therapists.

Positive Steps to Avoid Sexual Dysfunction

Beyond all of these considerations, it is important for everyone to practice positive mental health by engaging in healthy sexuality that helps to avoid sexual dysfunctions in the first place. Here are some practical suggestions:

1. *Communicate with your partner.* Don't expect him or her to be a mind reader about what is sexually pleasing to you and then be disappointed when the ESP fails. If you communicate with your partner, you'll have a better chance of getting what you like and giving what he or she likes.

2. *Don't be a spectator when you have sex.* Avoid mentally stepping outside your sexual interactions to evaluate your performance. Instead, concentrate on the giving and receiving of sensual pleasures.

3. *Don't set up goals for sexual performance.* If you have your heart set on multiple orgasms or simultaneous orgasm or something else, it might not happen; you may feel like a failure or experience considerable anxiety. Relax and enjoy yourself.

4. *Failures do occur, as they do in anything else.* The important point is how you and your partner deal with them. Learn to view the occasional failure positively, saying, "How can we make this turn out well anyway?"

SEXUALLY TRANSMITTED DISEASES

What do you think are the two most common sexually transmitted diseases (STDs, or venereal diseases) in the United States today? Most students generally say gonorrhea and syphilis, or herpes and gonorrhea. Actually, both answers are only partially correct. The two most common STDs today are chlamydia and gonorrhea, with herpes coming in third. Many readers may not even have heard of chlamydia. This points out the need for better information on this topic.

Chlamydia and NGU

chlamydia organism that causes a sexually transmitted disease in both men and women, with symptoms rather similar to those of gonorrhea

Chlamydia (pronounced klah-MIH-dee-uh) is an organism that is spread by sexual contact and infects the genital organs of both males and females. In the female, the disease is called a chlamydia infection; in the male, because the organism invades the urethra in the penis, the disease is often labeled NGU (for nongonococcal urethritis).

In the male, the symptoms include a thin, usually clear discharge from the tip of the penis and mild discomfort when urinating. These symptoms are rather similar to those of gonorrhea (with gonorrhea, the discharge is thicker and the pain is more intense). It is important to have a physician make a careful diagnosis because NGU is treated with the drug tetracycline, whereas gonorrhea is treated with penicillin.

In women, the disease usually produces no obvious symptoms. As a result, the woman may unknowingly pass the disease on to other partners. In addition, if the disease goes untreated the consequences can be serious, including damage to the cervix, pelvic inflammatory disease, and even infertility if the fallopian tubes become scarred. In men, leaving the disease untreated may result in damage to the urethra. Anyone who discovers he or she has the disease *must* inform the sexual partner or partners immediately. Otherwise, the partner(s) may suffer serious health consequences and spread the disease even further.

Gonorrhea

gonorrhea common sexually transmitted disease, producing a penile discharge and burning sensation when urinating for males but often asymptomatic in females

Gonorrhea is a disease transmitted primarily by sexual intercourse. In the male, the bacteria invade the urethra, producing a thick, creamy discharge from the penis and a painful, burning sensation when urinating. In some men and most women, however, gonorrhea, like chlamydia, produces no symptoms. The disease, untreated, may cause pelvic inflammatory disease in women, including infection of the fallopian tubes, which may result in sterility.

There are other possible sites for a gonorrhea infection: the mouth or throat (the disease can be spread by mouth-genital sex); the rectum (in cases of anal intercourse in either homosexuals or heterosexuals); and the eyes (in babies born to a mother who has gonorrhea).

Treatment consists of a large dose of penicillin. Again, because of the possibility of asymptomatic cases, it is essential for infected persons to inform their partners.

Herpes

genital herpes sexually transmitted disease producing painful bumps on the genitals

Time magazine splashed a large red H (for herpes) across its cover, calling it today's scarlet letter. Herpes is surely one of the most publicized diseases of this decade, and some even argue that it is one of several forces creating a return to sexual conservatism and monogamous relationships.

Genital herpes is caused by the herpes simplex virus Type II (cold sores on the lips are caused by herpes Type I). The symptoms are small, painful bumps or blisters on the genitals, as shown in Figure 12–4. In women, they are usually found on the vaginal lips. In men, they usually occur on the penis. The blisters burst and are painful. They heal on their own, usually within about three weeks for the first episode. The disease can then remain inactive in the person's body for life or it can flare up in unpredictable espisodes.

The chief problem with herpes is that there is no known cure. Anyone infected has it for life. Researchers are currently pursuing two solutions: (1) drugs to cure the painful symptoms and (2) a vaccination to prevent herpes. Acyclovir is a new drug that has been successful in relieving the symptoms when applied to the genitals in ointment form. Progress is also being made on the vaccine, and it seems likely that it will be available within the next ten years.

The disease also has implications for people's mental health. Because herpes is incurable and contagious, some patients report serious emotional consequences, and difficulty in establishing new relationships. Surely these are reasons to pursue vigorous research on the disease. In the meantime, psychologists are developing therapies that emphasize relaxation to control tension.

Pubic Lice

Pubic lice (crabs) are tiny lice, about the size of a pinhead, that attach themselves to the base of pubic hairs. Though not a disease, they are usually transmitted by sexual contact; however, they can live for a short while off a human host and thus can be picked up from sheets or toilet seats. The major symptom is itching in the region of pubic hair. They do not pose any serious long-term health risk, but the itching is generally intolerable, so that the person seeks treatment. The drug Kwell, in lotion or shampoo, is available by prescription; A-200 Pyrinate is also effective and is available without prescription.

FIGURE   12–4   Genital Herpes

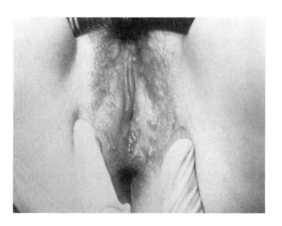 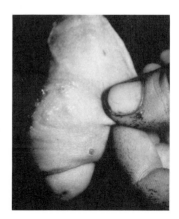

AIDS

In 1981, a physician in Los Angeles reported a mysterious and frightening new disease identified in several gay men. By the late 1980s, more than 30,000 Americans had been diagnosed as having the disease and more than 15,000 had died from it.

AIDS (acquired immune deficiency syndrome) incurable disease that attacks a person's immune system and leaves the person vulnerable to infections that can lead to death

The disease was called **acquired immune deficiency syndrome**, or **AIDS**. Caused by a virus named HIV, the disease destroys the body's natural immune system. Once the immune system is destroyed, opportunistic diseases may take over the body, and the person usually dies within a few months to a few years. The two most common of these diseases found in AIDS patients are a form of pneumonia (pneumocystis carinii pneumonia) and a rare form of cancer (Kaposi's sarcoma, which produces purplish lesions on the skin).

Although the disease has most often been found in gay or bisexual men, they are not its only victims. Of those diagnosed as having AIDS, 65 percent are gay or bisexual men, 17 percent are men or women who abuse intravenous drugs (usually heroin addicts), 7 percent are heterosexual partners of people with AIDS, and 2 percent are persons with hemophilia or others receiving blood transfusions (Liskin & Blackburn, 1986).

Some have termed AIDS the gay plague, ignoring the fact that there are many documented cases of exclusive heterosexuals contracting it. At a time when gay activists have put so much effort into changing public opinion about homosexuality, AIDS seems to be adding new fuel to the fire of prejudice against homosexuals. Gays complain that they are experiencing heightened discrimination (people assuming that they must have AIDS because they are gay). Victims of AIDS complain especially of discrimination; many people seem to think that AIDS can be spread by casual contact, as when two children sit next to each other in school. Based on this belief, such people argue that AIDS patients should be segregated. Some children with AIDS have been barred from attending school on this basis, and court suits charging discrimination have been filed. It is important to know that AIDS cannot be spread by casual contact. It is spread only by sexual contact, by contaminated hypodermic needles, or through contaminated blood used in transfusions.

Medical research is progressing rapidly, and there is hope that a vaccine against the disease, as well as a drug to halt the virus, will be developed within the next ten years. In the meantime, health professionals are advising people to use condoms when having sex, to avoid anal intercourse, and to limit themselves to a single sexual partner.

SEXUAL VICTIMIZATION

This section considers four cases in which sexual behavior produces a victim: (1) rape, (2) child molestation, (3) incest, and (4) sexual harassment.

Rape

rape forcible sexual contact with an individual without that person's consent

Based on interviews with a random sample of San Francisco women, researchers concluded—after adjusting for age—that there is a 26 percent chance that a woman will be the victim of a completed **rape** (forcible sexual contact) at some time in her life (Russell & Howell, 1983). Rape is not just a rare crime committed by a psychopathic man. It is common, and it may affect any woman. It is important to understand the typical psychological responses of the rape victim, as well as what can be done by her and for her.

Researchers use the term *rape trauma syndrome* for the emotional responses of some rape victims (Burgess & Holmstrom, 1974). Immediately after the rape, most women experience a variety of emotional responses—crying, fear, anger, anxiety, self-blame—but some women are subdued and express little or no emotion. The next phase begins several weeks after the attack. The rape typically causes a major disruption in a woman's life, and women adopt different strategies for dealing with it. Fearing that the rapist will strike again, some move to a different apartment or home. Others develop phobias, such as a sexual phobia or a fear of being outdoors if the rape occurred outdoors.

Research indicates that rape victims are significantly more depressed than nonvictims, but the research also indicates that most victims have restabilized from the incident by about four months after the rape (Atkeson et al., 1982). It is important to understand the trauma of rape; however, it is also important to understand the strengths people have in coping with the experience.

If you have been or ever become a rape victim, here are some suggestions for dealing with the situation. If you are a man, these suggestions are still worth reading because they may enable you to help a woman in this situation. Also, research shows that men are occasionally victims of rape and experience responses similar to those of women victims (Sarrel & Masters, 1982).

1. Immediately after the rape, it is important for you to decide whether you want to report it to the police. If you do, you should report it immediately. Do not wait until you have gone home, had a shower, and changed clothes, because you will destroy a great deal of evidence.

2. If you do not report it to the police, you should talk to someone, rather than keeping your feelings bottled up inside you. You might talk to a psychologist, dial a telephone crisis line or a Planned Parenthood clinic (many provide rape counseling), or simply talk to an understanding friend.

3. Do not blame yourself. Our society has a history of blaming the victim of rape, resulting from the myth that women secretly desire to be raped and bring on rape by seductive behavior. If a bank teller were shot in the middle of a robbery, would you wonder what he had done to bring on the shooting?

4. Allow yourself to feel anger toward your assailant. Because of sex-role socialization, many women have difficulty recognizing their own anger and expressing it. It is *very* appropriate to feel anger toward a man who has raped you.

Although the above represent ways of dealing with the situation after the rape has occurred, it would be far better to prevent rape. Many experts recommend self-defense training for women. Statistics indicate that women who resist an attack do not increase the risk that they will be seriously harmed, and many manage to escape (Bart, 1980). Many theorists also believe that traditional gender-role socialization plays a role in creating rapists and rape vitims (Russell, 1975). Males are socialized to be aggressive and hypersexual, while women are socialized to be passive. If rape is the outcome, new patterns of socializing children are necessary to liberate them from these stereotypes.

Child Molestation

pedophilia sexual contact by an adult with a child (child molestation)

Pedophilia (child molestation) refers to an adult's engaging in some kind of sexual activity with a child. It is generally considered a despicable crime because the adult misuses power and authority, because a child cannot make a true informed choice about the activity, and because there is the potential for serious psychological and physical damage to the child.

In recent years, the increased publicity given to child molestation has revealed that it is not a rare crime. In a survey of university students, 30 percent of the men and 35 percent of the women reported having had childhood experiences with sexual deviants (Landis, cited by McCaghy, 1971).

How traumatic is the experience for the child? Clearly, it depends on the individual case, the extent of violence or coercion, and the number of times the activity is repeated. Many authorities believe that often the experience itself is relatively untraumatic for the child and that much of the trauma is caused by overly emotional reactions from parents (McCaghy, 1971). Nonetheless, individual cases can be extremely traumatic, leaving serious emotional scars and requiring extensive psychotherapy in either childhood or adulthood. Parents need to encourage patterns of open communication with their children, so that the children will feel free to report such an event if it occurs. Parents also need to keep their own emotions in check if a child should report an incident, so that they do not make it more traumatic for the child than necessary.

Police in many areas conduct prevention and reporting programs in the schools. They make sure that children understand inappropriate behavior from an adult and that they should report it. A police officer in one town stated that elementary school children now come to him with a license plate number if a stranger asks them to take a ride.

Incest

incest sexual contact between relatives

Incest is defined as sexual contact between relatives. Like child molestation, it is a topic that has come out of the closet in recent years, and researchers are discovering that it is far more common than they once believed. Studies of *reported* cases of incest (reported to the police) indicate that father-daughter incest is the most common pattern (Weinberg, 1955). However, surveys of the general population indicate that brother-sister, or sibling, incest is actually the most common form. In one survey of college students, 15 percent of the females and 10 percent of the males said they had had a sexual experience with a sibling (Finkelhor, 1980). It seems likely that most of these cases are never reported to the police. The children probably do not even realize at the time that they are engaging in incest.

Most research has focused on father-daughter incest, because it accounts for the majority of reported cases and because it appears to be more damaging psychologically than sibling incest is. What kind of man commits incest with his daughter? Research indicates that he is a very controlling, authoritarian person who rules the family (Herman, 1981). The division of male-female roles is traditional, and the mother is typically a full-time housewife. The activity may satisfy his needs for love and being nurtured. Doubtless he experiences a sense of power in the incestuous act, because he can control the situation, something he could not do if an adult woman were his partner. Also, he need not fear the rejection that might come from an adult woman.

What are the psychological consequences for the incest victim? As with child molestation, it depends. Father-daughter incest is likely more damaging than sibling incest is. Indeed, in one survey of sibling incest, the participants were evenly divided, half saying the experience had been negative for them and half saying it had been positive (Finkelhor, 1980). Other facts are doubtless important, too, regarding the effects on the victim—the extent of coercion or violence used, how often and over how long a period the activity occurred, and the extent to which the family is disrupted (such as by daddy's being put in jail).

If you have been a victim of incest or if you are aware of incestuous activity, consider the following options:

1. Is it best for you to talk with a psychologist, or make a report to the police, or simply forgive and forget? if you are an adult and have moved away but other children still remain in the home, it may be important for you to make a report to the police or other authorities. The father who commits incest with one daughter is likely to repeat it with other daughters. Some women feel they can overcome the whole experience and make a more complete recovery by working with a psychologist. Others are able to put the matter behind them and forget it. Consider what is best for you.

2. Would it be helpful to confront the person who initiated the contact? In some cases, this allows the victim to experience a feeling of triumph over the situation. The relative involved may come to recognize how wrong his behavior was, acknowledge that it occurred, and apologize—all of which can be healing. In other cases, however, the incestuous relative may end up accusing the victim of having caused or encouraged the incest, and the confrontation becomes damaging instead of helpful.

One final point emerges in the current discussion and the research on incest. If you are a parent and your child reports an incestuous incident to you, take him or her seriously. The language may be vague ("Uncle Bob was touching me funny"), but some calm questioning can usually provide the necessary clarification. In addition, children need to be taught what kind of physical contact is appropriate with adults and what kind is not. They also need to know that they have a right to refuse contact that makes them feel uncomfortable.

Sexual Harassment

MacKinnon (1979) defined **sexual harassment** as "the unwanted imposition of sexual requirements in the context of a relationship of unequal power" (p. 1). This relationship of unequal power may involve a boss and an employee at work, a professor and a student at a university, or a psychotherapist and client.

In a well-sampled study of 20,000 people working for the federal government, 42 percent of the women and 15 percent of the men reported having been sexually harassed at work within the preceding two years (Tangri, Burt, & Johnson, 1982). The great majority of the harassers (78 percent) were men. Both women and men victims reported that the harassment had negative effects on their emotional and physical well-being.

A survey of a random sample of undergraduate women at the University of California, Berkeley, found that 30 percent had received unwanted sexual attention from at least one male professor during their four years at college (Benson & Thomson, 1982). The women gave the following as examples of harassment: explicit sexual propositions, invitations for dates or invitations to the professor's apartment, kissing or fondling, standing too close, and a high grade offered in exchange for an affair. Some women coped with the situation by avoiding further courses with the same professor. Others reported that the experience had devastating effects on them; they doubted their own judgment, lost confidence in their academic ability, and became disillusioned with male faculty in general.

If you are a victim of sexual harassment, note the following possible courses of action:

1. You can file a lawsuit against the offender. In many cases, sexual harassment is considered a violation of civil rights.

2. You can confront the harasser and try to make him or her stop the behavior. You might do this by writing a letter or having an attorney send one.

3. Keep a careful diary of the incidents, recording specific dates, what occurred, and names of witnesses if there were any. This will be useful if you decide to go to court or pursue a grievance procedure at your college or workplace.

4. You can file a grievance with an appropriate authority, for example a dean or affirmative action officer at your college, or a union official if you are a unionized worker.

5. If other methods fail, you can file a grievance with the Equal Employment Opportunity Commission. If you have been fired, you may be entitled to back pay in addition to damages.

6. Don't blame yourself. As with rape victims, there is a tendency to blame the victim. Remember that it is the harasser who is to blame.

RAISING SEXUALLY HEALTHY CHILDREN

Often, when students are asked to evaluate how they were taught about sex, the majority comment that their parents did a poor job of sex education. Today, we have a new generation of parents emerging, many of whom are far better informed about sex—perhaps as a result of taking a college human sexuality course—than were previous generations. This section offers some suggestions for raising sexually healthy children, based on the experiences and research of sex educators.

Your first step as a parent is to inform yourself. That may involve taking a course in human sexuality or getting a copy of one of the available textbooks (for example, Hyde, 1986) to read and have on hand when questions come up. One of the important things to learn from a course or a textbook is the normal (common) sexual behavior of children at various ages.

The next message is, Don't wait! Many parents think that all sex education can take place in an hour-long conversation with a fifth-grade daughter who they fear may begin menstruating any time. With boys, there is no similar compelling deadline, so the one-hour conversation may never occur. Sex educators agree that sex education should take place every year of a child's life, beginning when the child is two or three. The concepts you talk about with a teenager must build on concepts that were acquired earlier. If those earlier concepts are missing, later talks about sex can be rough going. "On the Research Frontier: Children's Sexual Thinking" (pages 382 and 383) presents some startling results of a study conducted by two researchers who wanted to find out about children's understanding of sex.

If sex education occurs every year, the parent needs to be sensitive to the child's intellectual level, emotional development, and interests when choosing what to discuss. Two- and three-year-olds can learn terms for their sexual organs—*penis, testes, vulva*—just as they are learning words like *elbow* and *shoulder*. Sex educators recommend that children learn proper scientific terms from the beginning rather than confusing euphemisms, such as *peter*. Four- and five-year-olds are interested in and notice the odd shapes of pregnant women, and they can learn how babies are made and how they are born.

One good guide to the appropriate material for children at a particular age is simply to notice what interests them. This means that you must be a good listener when they ask questions. According to an old joke, five-year-old Billy walked into the kitchen one day and asked Mom, "Where did I come from?" Knowing that the dreaded moment had arrived, Mom sat Jimmy down and launched into a twenty-minute discussion of male and female sexual anatomy, sexual intercourse, fertilization, pregnancy, and childbirth. After all that, Billy strolled away with a puzzled look on his face, mumbling, "That's funny, Bobby said he was from Illinois." The point is that parents need to be sensitive to what the child wants to know and the appropriate explanation, given the child's intellectual level and previous knowledge.

Social learning theory states that imitation and modeling effects are very strong. Surely, this is the case with sexuality as well. Parents who want to raise

ON THE RESEARCH FRONTIER

CHILDREN'S SEXUAL THINKING

Our scientific knowledge of human sexual behavior lags far behind our knowledge of most other aspects of human activity. Sex has been a taboo topic in our culture, and researchers have been unwilling to tackle this subject. Even more restricted and sensitive is the area of children's sexuality.

Psychologists Ronald and Juliette Goldman (1982) took a daring step forward with their massive study of children's understanding of sexuality. They conducted face-to-face interviews with a total of 838 children, aged five, seven, nine, eleven, thirteen, and fifteen. The samples were drawn from four different cultures: Australian, English, North American, and Swedish. The Swedish sample is particularly interesting because Swedish children receive compulsory sex education beginning at age eight. This situation is in distinct contrast to the haphazard and inadequate sex education most American children receive. Indeed, the American sample originally was to be limited to the United States. However, school officials in the United States proved so uncooperative that the sample had to be stretched to include Canada (where there was more cooperation) to get enough subjects.

The Goldmans were careful to avoid controversial topics, such as homosexuality, in the interview. They questioned children only about their understanding of sexual concepts, not about their actual sexual behavior—this last topic is important, but it will have to await the next generation of even more daring researchers.

A comparison of the results from the North American children with those from children in the other three cultures led the Goldmans to conclude that American children are sexual illiterates. They are strikingly lacking in sexual information and understanding. Some of the results are shown in Table 12-2. Notice, for example, that only 23 percent of the North American nine-year-olds, but 60 percent of the Australian nine-year-olds, know the genital differences between newborn baby boys and girls. The Swedish children were consistently more knowledgeable than the North Americans, indicating the positive effects of the Swedish program of sex education.

Other researchers have documented that children go through stages in understanding sexual concepts, progressing to more and more accurate, scientific ideas

TABLE 12-2   Understanding of Sexual Concepts by Nine-Year-Olds in Four Cultures

	Percent of Correct Answers			
Concept	Australians	British	N. Americans	Swedish
1. Knowing physical sex differences of newborns	60	35	23	40
2. Knowing correct terms for the genitals	50	33	20	*
3. Knowing length of gestation is eight to ten months	35	32	30	67

*Owing to the difficulties of translating from the Swedish language, this percentage is not available.

Source: R. Goldman & J. Goldman (1982). *Children's sexual thinking.* London: Routledge & Kegan Paul, 194, 213, & 240.

and terms (Bernstein & Cowan, 1975). Some sex concepts are abstract and apparently difficult to understand, as indicated by these amusing responses about contraception:

- The pill goes down the stomach and dissolves the baby and it goes out in the bowels. You should take three pills a day. (American boy, seven years old)
- If you don't want to start one, you don't get married. There's no other way. (English girl, seven years old)
- The tubes are tied, the vocal cords. (Australian girl, fifteen years old)

The Goldmans' study is a major contribution to the field because it provides a wealth of information about what children think about sex and because it compares children across four cultures. It gives valuable information for designing sex education programs, and the motivation to do so when we see how far behind the American children are.

sexually healthy children must consider whether they are modeling sexually healthy attitudes. For example, how is nudity treated in the household? Are bodies kept carefully covered at all times, or are people more at ease with their bodies? Do children see parents openly expressing affection for each other, is affection shown only behind closed doors, or is affection not shown at all? Are the parents anxious and tense about sex—for example, how do they react when they discover their children and the neighbor children playing doctor? Children can pick up anxieties quickly if parents overreact to harmless situations.

One final suggestion—one of the most difficult things for many parents—is just beginning the conversation with your child. An easy, relaxed way to do this is simply to read a sex education book together. *Where Did I Come From?* (Mayle, Robins, & Walter, 1973) is a good one for preschool and elementary school children. Mary Calderone is one of the leading sex educators in the country. Her book *Talking With Your Child About Sex* (Calderone & Ramey, 1983) provides a wealth of useful ideas and information.

Why is it important for parents to educate their children about sex? Masters and Johnson (1970) hold the opinion that many cases of sexual dysfunction are a result of simple ignorance about sex. These dysfunctions have caused mental anguish—not to mention conflict in marriages and other relationships—in millions of people. Many cases of teenage pregnancy and sexually transmitted diseases also result from ignorance. In short, good sex education is a way of nurturing your child's mental and physical health.

SUMMARY

1. You should know the following anatomical terms: *vulva, clitoris, vagina, uterus, fallopian tubes, ovary, penis, scrotum, testes, prostate.* You also should know the terms *vasocongestion* and *myotonia* and the four stages of sexual response.

2. The birth control pill contains estrogen and progesterone. It is a highly effective method of contraception. The IUD is a device inserted into the uterus, and it is nearly as effective as the pill. The diaphragm and condom are other effective methods. Sterilization is a surgical method for achieving permanent birth control.

3. A majority of males and females in the United States engage in premarital sexual intercourse; the rates are higher than they were earlier in this century, but there seems to be a trend toward conservatism in the 1980s.

4. Psychologists have not yet determined what factors are important in influencing a person's sexual orientation—whether heterosexual or homosexual. Research indicates no differences in adjustment between heterosexuals and homosexuals.

5. Sexual dysfunctions include premature ejaculation, erectile dysfunction, anorgasmia, and problems of sexual desire. Most sexual dysfunctions are caused by psychological rather than physical factors and respond well to sex therapy.

6. The two most common sexually transmitted diseases in the United States today are chlamydia and gonorrhea, with herpes coming in third. AIDS is less common but more devastating in its effects.

7. Rape, child molestation, incest, and sexual harassment are situations in which sexuality becomes distorted by an abuse of power, so that there is a sexual victim.

8. Suggestions for raising sexually healthy children include beginning sex education early, providing it frequently, being well informed, and being aware of the attitudes and behaviors modeled in the home.

Part 4

WORK AND SOCIAL INFLUENCES

Chapter 13

WORK IN TODAY'S WORLD

Listen to Grace Clements. For her, work is an *affliction* (Kahn, 1981). She makes the molded linings of suitcases. She stands at a tank every day and repeatedly takes wet felt out of the tank. She says,

> [P]ut the wet piece on the dry die, push this button that lets the dry press down, inspect the piece we just took off, the hot piece, stack it and count it—when you get a stack of ten, you push it over and start another stack of ten—then go back and put our blanket on the wet piece coming up from the tank . . . and start all over again. Forty seconds. We also have to weigh every third piece in that time, it has to be within so many grams. We are constantly standing and moving. If you talk during working, you get a reprimand, because it is easy to make a reject if you are talking. . . .
>
>   All day long is the same thing over and over. That's about ten steps every forty seconds about 800 times a day. . . . (Terkel, 1974, pp. 384–385)

For Grace Clements, work is physically demanding and montonous. She dreams of starting a small hamburger place with her husband some day.

Ward Quaal, president of a large broadcasting corporation, sees his work not as affliction but as *addiction*.

> My day starts at 4:30 and 5:00 in the morning, at home in Winnetka. I dictate in my library until about 7:30. Then I have breakfast. The driver gets there about 8:00 and often times I continue dictating in the car on the way to the office. . . .
>
>   I talk into a dictaphone. I will probably have as many as 150 letters dictated by 7:30 in the morning. I have five full-time secretaries who do nothing but work for Ward Quaal. I have several swing girls, who work for me part-time. This does not include my secretaries in New York, Los Angeles, Washington, and San Francisco. . . .
>
>   Although I don't go to the office on Saturday or Sunday, I do have mail brought out to my home for the weekend. I dictate on Saturday and Sunday. When I do this on holidays, like Christmas, New Year's, and Thanksgiving I have to sneak a little bit, so the family doesn't know what I'm doing. . . . (Terkel, 1974, pp. 511–512)

Clearly, Ward Quaal's work life is driven. He resembles a workaholic, and yet he says, "I am in a seven day-a-week job and I love it!"

Yet for some, Robert Kahn (1981) observes that work life need neither be an affliction or addiction. Work can have qualities described by Kay Stepkin, a director of a small bakery that produces and sells about 250 loaves of bread a day. For Kay Stepkin, work is *fulfillment*, it is characterized by a sense of belonging, a sharing with coworkers, and a wholeness that we seldom hear described so well.

> We try to have a compromise between doing things efficiently and doing them in a human way. Our bread has to taste the same way every day, but you don't have to be machines. On a good day it's beautiful to be here. We have a good time and work hard and we're laughing. . . . I think a person can work as hard as he's capable, not only for others but for his own satisfaction. . . .
>
>   Work is an essential part of being alive. Your work is your identity. It tells you who you are. . . . There is such a joy in doing work well. (Terkel, 1974, p. 612)

The experience of work and the choices that we make about working are central to our psychological well-being. Yet, the world of work today is changing rapidly and confronts us with more choices than ever before. To understand working life today, we look at what psychologists know about the meaning of work in life, about changing trends in working life, and how those changes may affect our choices about work and the rest of life. We look at how to make career decisions and to cope on the job. Work is not an isolated aspect of life. Instead, working life mingles with other aspects in ways that affect us and those around us.

work human activity that produces something of acknowledged value

Robert Kahn (1981) defines **work** as "human activity that produces something of acknowledged value." He reminds us that in organized, industrial societies work is available in ready-made packages—jobs for paid employment. Furthermore, jobs have important characteristics that affect psychological well-being. These characteristics include the degree to which one is autonomous, the degree to which one has control over the work itself, and the degree to which the job itself offers variety.

Why do people work? It is clear that people work for more than money. At the University of Michigan's Institute for Social Research, researchers have surveyed nationwide samples of workers over the past twenty-five years. In these surveys, workers were asked, "If you were to get enough money to live as comfortably as you'd like for the rest of your life, would you continue to work?"

Kahn (1981) reports that almost three quarters of employed men and the majority of employed women report that they would prefer to work even if they had no financial needs. There are good reasons for this. Seventy percent of the workers surveyed say they had met some of their best friends at work. Even those who say they would quit if they had enough money still agree that they would miss some of their coworkers if they were not working. People also report that not working would be boring and that continuing to work gives direction to their lives. Work is central to psychological well-being even though not all jobs are equally desirable or equally well suited to one's individual interests and talents.

CHANGING TRENDS IN WORK LIFE

A number of important changes are transforming the world of work. Women are entering the work force in unprecedented numbers. Two decades ago, 23,000,000 American women worked. Today there are 48,000,000. Since 1960, there has been a 109 percent increase in the female work force while the male work force has increased only 36 percent. Even more important, in 1960, only 19 percent of women with children younger than six worked outside the home. But in 1983, 50 percent of women with children under six worked full-time outside the home (Robey & Russell, 1984). The entrance of women into the paid labor force is changing not only the workplace but also family life and the roles of men and women at both work and home.

industrial economy
economy that depends on the manufacture and sale of goods to sustain it

information economy
economy that depends on communication and the exchange of information to sustain it

technological change
change in the workplace resulting from a technological process or the use of machinery and automation in industry

Economic changes are also transforming the world of work. The country is shifting from an **industrial economy** to an **information economy**. Information skills are replacing manual skills. At the same time, work is being transformed by **technological change**. For example, last year, about one million computers joined the four million already in offices throughout the United States. The number of computers is expected to increase approximately 25 percent each year for the next ten years.

These rapid technological changes are changing the nature of jobs. Workers already on the job are feeling the pressure. Technological change creates opportunities for some while it reduces opportunities for others. Manual skills are rapidly being replaced in the increasingly automated workplaces. Those who are trained to use new technological tools find themselves in demand while others must make career changes.

The *organizational culture* of work is changing as well. There is increasing emphasis on worker participation and worker control over the planning and conduct of work (Lawler, 1982). Where offices and factories were once organized in a hierarchical pyramid, with the president at the top of the corporation, managers in the center, and workers at the bottom, many companies are replacing these hierarchical relationships with work teams that have considerable freedom to innovate and control their own work. Both technological and organizational changes are reflected in the shift of work organizations from the traditional pyramid to the diamond-shaped organization. See Figure 13–1 for examples of these organizational forms.

Finally, we are coming to recognize that work life and family and community life are not separate domains. Instead they penetrate each other and stand in a complex relationship. The experiences, pressures, and satisfactions of each life sphere spill over into the other, weaving a complex web of influences and demands for each of us.

Because work is so important for your psychological well-being, and because it is changing so rapidly, you are confronted with important choices about your work life. You face decisions about what career to pursue. And once you are launched in a career, you must make numerous choices in coping with the demands and opportunities of the workplace. Finally, you may be faced more than once with an opportunity or need to change career. The rest of this chapter examines each of these choices in more detail.

OCCUPATION AND CAREER CHOICE

career professional occupation for which one trains and which one pursues as a life's work

You have probably already given some thought to choosing a **career**. Perhaps you have made some important choices about your future work. Certainly career opportunities and pay are important in anyone's career choice. But psychologists have found that personality can also be a critical factor in which job you choose and in how satisfied you will be with your job.

Perhaps the best-known work on this problem has been conducted by John Holland (1985), who has conducted research on vocational choice for nearly

FIGURE   13-1   Changing Technology in Work Organizations

Traditional Work Organization

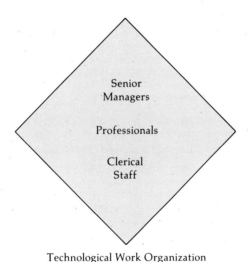

Technological Work Organization

Source: Based on D. Goleman (1983). The electronic Rorschach. *Psychology Today*, 35–43.

two decades. Holland's basic theory suggests that the selection of a career is in part an expression of personality. Holland makes fundamental assumptions about (1) various types of personalities, (2) various types of working environments, (3) how people actually search for jobs, and (4) what the outcome of those searches may be.

First, Holland assumes that people can be classified according to six major personality types. In this scheme, people are classified as conventional, enterprising, artistic, realistic, investigative, or social in their orientation. Table 13-1 describes each of these types and shows the kinds of jobs for which each type is thought to be best suited. Holland's idea is not to pigeonhole individuals into a single type but to suggest that everyone possesses at least some of the

TABLE 13-1   Personal Orientations and Related Work Environments

Themes	Personal Orientations	Work Environments
Realistic	Values concrete and physical tasks; perceives self as having mechanical skills and lacking social skills.	Setting involves concrete, physical tasks requiring mechanical skills, persistence, and physical movement. Careers include machine operator, aircraft mechanic, truck driver, service station worker, draftsperson, barber, and bricklayer.
Investigative	Wants to solve intellectual, scientific, and mathematical problems. Sees self as scholarly, analytical, critical, curious, introspective, and methodical.	Typical settings are research laboratory, diagnostic medical case conference, work group of scientists or medical researchers. Careers include marine biologist, computer programmer, clinical psychologist, architect, dentist, mathematician, and physical scientist.
Artistic	Prefers unsystematic tasks or artistic projects in the form of painting, writing, or drama. Perceives self as imaginative, expressive, original, independent.	Setting involves theater, concert hall, library, radio or television studios. Careers include painter, sculptor, actor or actress, designer, musician, music teacher, symphony conductor, author, editor, reviewer, and radio or television announcer.
Social	Prefers educational, helping, and religious careers. Enjoys such activities as social involvement, church, music, reading, and dramatics. Perceives self as having understanding, liking to help others, and having teaching ability. Values social or ethical activities and is cooperative, friendly, helpful, insightful, persuasive, responsible, and sociable.	Typical settings are school and college classrooms, psychiatrist's office, religious meetings, mental institutions, community and recreational centers. Careers are counselor, nurse, teacher, social worker, judge, missionary, minister, and sociologist.
Enterprising	Values political and economic achievements, supervision, and leadership. Enjoys activities that satisfy personal need for control, verbal expression, recognition, and power. Perceives self as extroverted, sociable, happy, assertive, popular, self-confident, having leadership and persuasive abilities.	Setting involves courtroom, political rally, new car sales room, real-estate firm, and advertising company. Careers include realtor, politician, attorney, professional orator, salesperson, manager.
Conventional	Prefers orderly, systematic, concrete tasks involving verbal and mathematic data. Sees self as orderly, conformist, and having clerical and numerical skills.	Setting involves financial institution (bank), accounting firm, post office, file room, business office, and Internal Revenue office. Careers include banker, accountant, tax expert, timekeeper, financial counselor, key punch operator, secretary, and receptionist.

Source: Adapted from J. L. Holland, *Making vocational choices: A Theory of Careers* (2nd ed). Englewood Cliffs, NJ: Prentice-Hall, 19-23, 36-40.

Your career may be
an expression of your
personality.

personality orientation described in each type. Nevertheless, each of us can be classified fairly accurately by choosing the three types we most resemble.

A second major assumption that Holland makes is that there are six types of working environments, which are similar to the personality types just described. These environments are the way they are because they tend to have many people displaying a particular personality type. For example, a research laboratory has a great many people with investigative personality orientations or a manufacturing firm is dominated by people with realistic personalities. Similarly, a sales firm has many social and enterprising individuals in it.

Third, Holland believes that people go through life searching for work environments that fit their personality type. They do so because these environments encourage and reward their skills and abilities and allow them to express attitudes and values. According to Holland's view, vocational choices are attempts to find environments that produce a better and better match with one's personality. Finally, Holland believes that the degree of match between the work environment and personality is critical in determining work happiness and effectiveness and whether or not one changes jobs.

Vocational Preference Inventory scale developed by Holland to assess personal interest in different types of occupations

Holland (1977) has developed a scale called the **Vocational Preference Inventory**, which lists eighty-four occupational titles and asks the degree to which you are interested in each occupation. The scores are determined by the degree to which you express interest in jobs matching a particular personality type. Another instrument, the *Self-Directed Search* (Holland, 1979), not only provides scores in these six domains but also allows you to assess your own competencies and activities and to identify your occupational preferences.

Even without taking Holland's inventory, you can gain some insight into your own orientation to different job possibilities by reading Table 13–1 and reflecting on your feelings and preferences. Most people don't feel they fit neatly into a single type. They see themselves as a combination of two or perhaps three types. Can you identify one or two orientations that seem to fit your personality? Take a look at the work environments where these orientations are most common. Do they sound interesting to you? Making a career choice takes times and research, but a brief look at these preferences and work environments can give you a start.

Holland's approach to characterizing both personalities and occupational groups seems to make sense, but how correct is his assumption about the importance of fit between personality and job? A large number of studies provide some support for the idea. For example, Wiggins et al. (1983) studied the fit between personality preferences and work environments for a large sample of teachers. They found that the match between personality and work setting predicted satisfaction in the job much better than other personal characteristics, such as one's sex, age, or length of time in the job. See "Exploring Choices: Using the Decisional Balance Sheet in Career Choice" for more information.

In thinking about a career, remember that your interests, abilities, and personality can have important effects on your choice and your happiness in the job. Your university or college may have a career counseling office that can

EXPLORING CHOICES

USING THE DECISIONAL BALANCE SHEET IN CAREER CHOICE

While Holland's work on personality and career choice can help you identify good matches between your own personality and various work environments, many other considerations enter into career choice. Irving Janis (1982) has developed a decisional balance sheet effective in helping to make complex career decisions. Table 13-2 (pages 398 and 399) provides an example of the balance sheet procedure that Janis used in interviewing Yale college seniors about their job plans.

The balance sheet asks you to list the positive and negative aspects of each career choice considered in terms of four categories: (1) gains or losses for yourself, (2) gains or losses for significant others in your life, (3) feelings of self-approval or disapproval, and (4) how you think others would feel about your choice. You can search through your feelings and attitudes about alternatives and issues in each of these areas. When Janis used this strategy with graduating seniors, he found that some people identified aspects of career choices they had not considered earlier.

If you are considering several career alternatives, it is well worth the time and effort to fill out a decisional balance sheet to see where you really stand. To help you along the way, a sample list of considerations that may affect your career choice is also given in Table 13-2. Exploring career choices in this way is a real exercise in self-exploration. It will take some time and effort on your part as well as some emotional energy.

You may want to do the exercise in several steps. First, if you have some career alternatives in mind, write them down and try to narrow them to several choices. Second, look through the list of considerations on the right side of Table 13-2. Mark the ones that are most compelling for you. Third, list your considerations under each career alternative. As you continue, you will find the choices getting clearer and clearer, and you may learn something about yourself in the process.

Continued

Exploring Choices: Using the Decisional Balance Sheet in Career Choice, Continued

TABLE 13-2   A Schematic Balance Sheet Grid for Conceptualizing Decisional Conflict (based on Janis, 1959)

Types of Anticipation with examples from research on career conflicts of lawyers	Alternative Courses of Action					
	Alternative 1 (e.g., job with Department of Justice)		Alternative 2 (e.g., job with a Wall Street firm)		Alternative 3 (e.g., private practice in a small town)	
	+	−	+	−	+	−
A. Utilitarian gains or losses for self						
1. Personal income	___	___	___	___	___	___
2. Interest value of daily work	___	___	___	___	___	___
3. Opportunity to live in a preferred city	___	___	___	___	___	___
•	___	___	___	___	___	___
•	___	___	___	___	___	___
B. Utilitarian gains or losses for significant others						
1. Social status for family	___	___	___	___	___	___
2. Reducing political corruption in community	___	___	___	___	___	___
3. Advancing civil rights for nation	___	___	___	___	___	___
•	___	___	___	___	___	___
•	___	___	___	___	___	___
C. Self-approval or -disapproval						
1. Moral considerations pertaining to ethical legal practices	___	___	___	___	___	___
2. "Ego ideal" of being an independent thinker	___	___	___	___	___	___
3. Self-image as defender of innocent people	___	___	___	___	___	___
•	___	___	___	___	___	___
•	___	___	___	___	___	___
D. Social approval or disapproval						
1. From wife (or husband)	___	___	___	___	___	___
2. From close friends	___	___	___	___	___	___
3. From a national professional organization	___	___	___	___	___	___
•	___	___	___	___	___	___
•	___	___	___	___	___	___

The cells in this schematic grid should be visualized as being filled with positive (+) and negative (−) entries of varying magnitude depicting the strength of the incentives to accept or reject each alternative.

List of considerations that might affect career choice, used in the balance sheet procedure as tested with college seniors facing a decision about what to do after graduation.

1. Utilitarian considerations: gains and losses for self
    a. income
    b. difficulty of the work
    c. interest level of the work
    d. freedom to select work tasks
    e. chances of advancement
    f. security
    g. time available for personal interests—e.g., recreation
    h. other (e.g., special restrictions or opportunities with respect to social life; effect of the career or job demands on marriage; type of people you will come in contact with)

2. Utilitarian considerations: gains and losses for others
    a. income for family
    b. status for family
    c. time available for family
    d. kind of environment for family—e.g., stimulating, dull: safe, unsafe
    e. being in a position to help an organization or group (e.g., social, political, or religious)
    f. other (e.g., fringe benefits for family)

3. Self-approval or -disapproval
    a. self-esteem from contributions to society or to good causes
    b. extent to which work tasks are ethically justifiable
    c. extent to which work will involve compromising oneself
    d. creativeness or originality of work
    e. extent to which job will involve a way of life that meets one's moral or ethical standards
    f. opportunity to fulfill long-range life goals
    g. other (e.g., extent to which work is "more than just a job")

4. Approval or disapproval from others (includes being criticized or being excluded from a group as well as being praised or obtaining prestige, admiration, and respect)
    a. parents
    b. college friends
    c. wife (or husband)
    d. colleagues
    e. community at large
    f. others (e.g., social, political, or religious groups)

Source: I. L. Janis, "Pilot Studies on New Procedures for Improving the Quality of Decision Making," mimeo., Yale Studies in Attitudes and Decisions, 1968.

help with your career choice. Take advantage of this resource. You will probably find the time well spent.

FULFILLING JOBS AND THE IMPACT OF TECHNOLOGY

In modern society, jobs are pretty much ready-made packages of responsibilities, hours, rewards, coworkers, and places to work. But do all jobs have underlying characteristics that affect well-being? If they do, how is technology
changing those characteristics?

Characteristics of Fulfilling Jobs

Think for a moment of the jobs described by Kay Stepkin (the bakery owner),
Ward Quaal (the broadcast executive), and Grace Clements (the factory
worker). Are there characteristics that make some jobs more fulfilling than
others? Recently, researchers (Quinn, 1974, 1977) asked 2,000 workers in a
wide variety of jobs a number of questions about their work. Quinn and his
coworkers hoped to discover the underlying properties of jobs. A summary of
what they found can be seen in Table 13–3. How can these dimensions help us
understand what a good job is to most people? Robert Kahn summarizes the
profile description of a good job in the following way:

> A good job is one in which the work is interesting, I have a chance to develop my own
> special abilities, and I can see the results of my work. It is a job where I have enough
> information, enough help and equipment, and enough authority to get the job done. It
> is a job where the supervisor is competent and my responsibilities are clearly defined.
> The people I work with are friendly and helpful; the pay is good and so is the job
> security. (p. 48)

Reflect on each of the characteristics of fulfilling jobs and ask yourself how
important each one is to you. Of course, these dimensions represent the average response for 2,000 workers in a very wide range of occupations. Your own
preferences may differ, and some of the dimensions may be much more important to you than others. In considering your future job, these dimensions can
help you to evaluate the possibilities.

However, there is another even more intriguing meaning to these findings.
Imagine for a moment that you are a supervisor of several other workers and
believe that your employees will be happiest and do their best if you design
their jobs to improve on some of these dimensions. What would you do?

The Impact of Technology

Earlier, we said that computers are entering the workplace at the rate of approximately one million terminals a year and that the number will increase by
25 percent each year for the next decade. How will the introduction of this new
technology change jobs? Will computers provide new ways of coping or create

TABLE 13–3   Fulfilling Jobs

- *Task content*. What is actually done on the job—Is it interesting?
- *Autonomy and control*. Is there a choice about how to do the work?
- *Supervision*. Is the supervision competent? Do you have the resources you need to do the job?
- *Relationship with coworkers*. How well do you get along with the other workers? Is the relationship positive?
- *Wages*. Is the pay adequate both materially and symbolically?
- *Promotion*. Do you have a chance to advance?
- *Physical working conditions*. How are the noise, heat, space, freedom to move around? Does the job allow reasonable comfort and safety?

Source: Adapted from R. L. Kahn. *Work and health*. New York: Wiley, 46–47.

still more demands and stresses? While the entrance of computers into the workplace will unquestionably make some jobs easier and allow some tasks to be performed more quickly and efficiently, we are only beginning to anticipate the advantages and the consequences of the entrance of new technologies.

Researchers such as Argote, Goodman, and Schkade (1983, 1984) have been studying the impact of the computer revolution on work, and their preliminary findings provide hints about the future impact. There is little question that the impact of the computer on jobs will depend on the job. Blue-collar workers and professionals may be affected differently, and so may different industries and different organizations. Nevertheless, it is intriguing to look at some of the early findings on the impact of computer technology on each of the key characteristics of jobs we described earlier.

Consider first the impact of computers on the *content of work*. When Zuboff (1988) interviewed a pilot who had spent many years flying jetliners, she found that his job had been changed so that now he was primarily involved in monitoring a set of computerized controls. Many of the critical decisions that he once had to make on a minute by minute basis were now made for him. Some of the challenges and attractions of his job seemed gone. Similarly, a data analyst whose calculations were important for future company decisions now may find the calculations made by a computer program. Clearly, the content of many jobs will change with the introduction of computers and other forms of information processing technology.

autonomy freedom to pursue one's course

What about **autonomy** (freedom to pursue one's course) and *control*? Zuboff and her colleagues found that professionals are particularly affected, especially those who use their professional training to make complex decisions and diagnoses. When the decision rules for a diagnosis are built right into a computer program, the diagnostic reliability improves, but the computer seems to control the decision instead of the professional. Some of the sense of autonomy and control, as well as the creativity of finding a unique solution, is lost.

Surely, the introduction of computers and robots in the workplace should make many jobs less exhausting and safer. This is precisely what Linda Argote and her colleagues (1983, 1984) found in studying the impact of installing a robot in a factory. While workers found that much of the physical fatigue had been eliminated from their work, they also discovered they had to concentrate for long periods of time to monitor controls and performance. Although it had been possible to talk and joke with coworkers while performing the task in the past, to do so now meant that the worker's concentration would be broken. Interestingly, this means that the attention required by computer-aided work also may affect relationships with other workers, reducing the opportunity for spontaneous interaction. Of course, new opportunities for interaction may arise as coworkers help each other with the new task of taking on an electronic coworker.

supervisor-worker relationships
relationships between a supervisor and worker, including support, provision of information, and encouragement on the part of the supervisor and task performance on the part of the worker

What about **supervisor-worker relationships?** Does receiving instructions from your boss through a computer terminal change the way you respond? Lee Sproull and her colleagues (1984) found that when students tried to solve a problem together by communicating through computer terminals they showed much less courtesy and were much more likely to have emotional outbursts. It is as if the safety of the computer terminal allowed them to say things that they would not say in a face-to-face context. In addition, people who would normally dominate a group discussion had less opportunity to do so. In a sense, computer-based interaction was more democratic because everyone had a greater opportunity to participate in the problem-solving session.

The *organizational context* of work is likely to be changed with the introduction of more computer technology into the workplace. As we have already suggested, it may be that in the future, the organizational shape will change from the classic organizational pyramid to something resembling a diamond. Fewer workers will do clerical work, and many more technical and professional people will make up the technologically driven work organization of the future.

WORK STRESS AND COPING

Do particular aspects of jobs make them stressful? A long tradition of research on stressful aspects of work provides some hints. For example, one early line of research that studied various specialties within professions such as medicine, law, and dentistry (Russek, 1962) found that important differences existed among specialties. The most stressful specialties required continuous work under time pressure where direct responsibility for the well-being of other people was involved. In medicine, general practitioners experience the most stress. In law, general practitioners and trial lawyers were most stressed, while in dentistry, general practitioners experienced the heaviest demands and showed the highest rates of hypertension and coronary heart disease.

Sidney Cobb (Cobb & Rose, 1973) studied a profession that clearly appears to be stressful, air traffic control. Cobb and his colleagues compared over 4,000 air traffic controllers with second class airmen whose education and other background factors appeared quite similar. The results were fascinating. Air traffic controllers were four times as likely to show symptoms of hypertension and twice as likely to show symptoms of ulcers or diabetes. Futhermore, the controllers who worked at the airports with the heaviest traffic were more likely to show symptoms of ulcers and high blood pressure. Thus, it appears that work load as well as responsibility for the well-being of others are critical dimensions that cut across jobs and make them stressful.

Karasek (1979) has studied an extremely wide array of occupations to identify the job characteristics that are most stressful. As Figure 13–2 suggests, jobs that are high in demand and allow little *control* are most likely to be stressful. These findings suggest that some jobs may have specific characteristics that make them more stressful. It may be possible to redesign these jobs to increase control in ways that reduce stress without necessarily reducing effectiveness. See "On the Research Frontier: Stress in Women Managers" on page 404 for a special form of stress.

Beginning a new job or a career, you may wonder about the degree to which you are expected to make it on your own. Most of us think first of help from coworkers with similar experiences who are confronting similar challenges. House (1981) reports that coworkers can be important sources of support, advice, and tangible help in coping with the challenges of work.

Another source of support exists in the relationship between a junior worker and some more senior person in the organization (Kram, 1980). These **mentor relationships** can be important to both the young person entering a

mentor relationships relationships between junior workers and senior workers that provide support and encouragement for the younger worker and satisfaction for the more senior member

FIGURE   13–2   Job Demands and Control

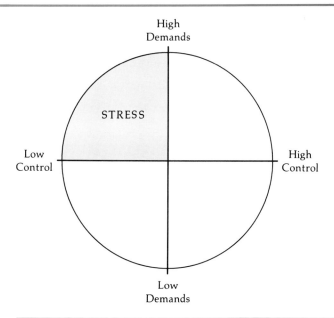

Source: Based on R. A. Karasek (1979). Job demands, job decision latitude and mental strain: Implications for job redesign. *Administrative Science Quarterly, 24,* 285–301.

ON THE RESEARCH FRONTIER

STRESS IN WOMEN MANAGERS

Women are entering managerial positions in increasing numbers, and many management positions can be quite stressful. Does this mean that we will observe higher levels of stress and related problems among women?

Marilyn Davidson and Cary Cooper (1983) have reported their extensive study of the stresses experienced by managers in England. Davidson and Cooper conducted a detailed survey of almost 700 female managers and an additional group of nearly 200 male managers in companies throughout England. In their survey, they asked about a wide range of potential stressors for both men and women and also studied health and productivity problems in both groups.

Their results make it clear that women executives do experience certain kinds of stressors much more than men do. For example, women often feel disadvantaged about promotions, stereotyped by others, and pressured to outperform the opposite sex. They also feel prejudice from *both* men and women in their organizations.

Davidson and Cooper went further, analyzing which groups of stressors were particularly acute for men and for women. They found, for example, that experiencing a lack of power and influence was a major stressor for female executives and only a minor stressor for male executives. The experience of sex discrimination was also an important stressor for women but irrelevant to men.

These findings clearly reflect different experiences in the working lives of men and women as managers. Davidson and Cooper also tried to discover whether these sources of stress actually had important effects on health, job satisfaction, and cigarette and alcohol consumption. What they found was surprising, and it adds complexity to the emerging picture. The stressors experienced by men actually had a bigger impact on their health and well-being. Even though women managers experienced a unique pattern of stresses in work life, the stressors had less impact on health and well-being for women than for men.

career and the senior member of the relationship, who may derive satisfaction in observing the development of a young worker. Kram's research points to a critical source of social support in the workplace that is often overlooked. Mentor relationships can be a source of instruction and support early in one's work life, when the going is most uncertain and difficult.

Kram has recently reported her research on the study of junior managers and their mentors. She interviewed both the junior managers and their mentors and found that the relationship went through a number of predictable stages. Early in the relationship, an initiation phase developed, in which the younger member admired the work of the senior partner. Later, initiation deepened into a phase of cultivation, in which the senior mentor made sure that visible projects were assigned to the young person and advice and guidance were provided. Still later, the younger person became more independent and mutual acknowledgment and appreciation characterized the relationship.

SEX AND THE WORKPLACE

Gutek (1985) cites the following case studies concerning sex in the workplace:

- Mary was hired as a secretary at a large insurance company. To her dismay, she found that her boss asked her to work late with him on several projects. He spent much of his time telling her about his personal problems including his unsatisfactory relationship with his wife. He usually apologized for keeping her at work so late and offered to take her to dinner. Mary refused each time but still felt uncomfortable. After three weeks, although she did not have another job offer, she quit. (p. 1)

- When Jennie applied for the job as an operator of a fork-lift truck, the personnel manager said the job was no place for a "lady" because workers used crude language and pin-ups were posted throughout the plant. Jennie said she didn't mind. After she started the job, she felt uncomfortable and unwanted. Her male colleagues never used crude language with her; they ignored her completely. The pin-ups bothered her more than she thought. After a month, resentful towards her male peers and disappointed in herself, Jennie quit her job. (p. 2)

The expression of sexuality at work can take many forms. In extreme cases, an initiator who has power over another person may require that person to engage in sexual activities in order to retain a job or be promoted. In other cases, sexuality at work can involve sexual jokes and comments, whistles, staring, or sexual touching.

Until recently, sexuality at work has been relatively invisible. MacKinnon (1979) contended that sexual harassment is primarily a problem for women and that it should be considered a form of sex discrimination. Recently, the Equal Employment Opportunity Commission (EEOC), an agency of the federal government concerned with insuring equality of opportunity, has established guidelines that are consistent with this idea. Although the precise definition of sexual harassment is difficult, Gutek (1985) points out that in recent years, a number of different points of view on the meaning of sexual harassment have emerged. Several of them are shown in Table 13-4 on page 406.

Notice in Table 13-4 that the feminist perspective views sexual harassment as a product of social circumstances, while the legal perspective seeks solutions through changes in the workplace. In addition, Table 13-4 makes it clear that work organizations may differ in their views of sexual harassment. Some organizations condone sexual harassment and others explicity condemn it.

Barbara Gutek (1985) conducted a survey of working women and men asking them about their experiences of social and sexual behavior in the work-

TABLE   13-4   Sexual Harassment from Different Perspectives

1. **Sexual harassment from a feminist perspective.**
   - Reflects a power relationship, male over female
   - Constitutes economic coercion
   - Threatens women's economic livelihood
   - Reflects the status of women in society
   - Asserts the woman's sex role over her work role
   - Parallels rape

2. **Sexual harassment from a legal perspective.**
   - Reflects an unequal power relationship that is exploitative
   - Involves both implicit and explicit terms of employment
   - Is used as a basis for employment decisions
   - Produces consequences from submission to, or refusal of, advances
   - Promotes an intimidating, hostile, or offensive work environment

3. **Sexual harassment from an organizational perspective—one view.**
   - Is interpersonal
   - Consists of misperception or misunderstanding of a person's intentions
   - Is a result of a "love affair gone sour"
   - Is personal and therefore not the organization's business
   - May be considered normal behavior at work
   - Can hurt the reputation of the accused

4. **Sexual harassment from an organizational perspective—another view.**
   - Is interpersonal
   - Is the improper use of power to extort sexual gratification
   - Treats women as sex objects
   - Is coercive, exploitative, improper
   - Asserts the women's sex role over work role
   - Is aberrant behavior

Source: B. A. Gutek (1985). The issues. *Sex and the workplace.* San Francisco: Jossey-Bass, 8–9.

place. Some of her results are summarized in Table 13-5. In particular, she asked people in the survey about a wide range of behaviors that could be viewed as sexual harassment, ranging from the offering of compliments through expected sexual activity. Interestingly, both men and women had experienced relatively similar rates of these social/sexual behaviors. For example, approximately one third of both men and women had experienced an episode of sexual touching in the workplace. However, men and women differed in their interpretation of these behaviors. Women tended to experience them as sexual harassment nearly twice as often as men did. These results suggest that not only the behavior but also the sense of vulnerability that one experiences may be important in the experience of sexual harassment.

Gutek (1985) makes a number of recommendations to top management in work organizations for policies to reduce the likelihood of sexual harassment. They include the following:

1. Work organizations should establish a policy on sexual harassment and establish a set of procedures to implement the policy.

TABLE   13-5   Workers Reports of Social Sexual Behaviors and
                      Sexual Harassment at Work

	Males (N = 405)	Females (N = 827)
• *Ever experienced on any job.*		
Complimentary comments	60.7%	68.1%
Insulting comments	19.3	23.3
Complimentary looks, gestures	56.3	66.6
Insulting looks, gestures	19.3	20.3
Nonsexual touching	78.0	74.4
Sexual touching	33.3	33.1
Expected socializing	8.4	12.0
Expected sexual activity	3.5	7.7
• *Ever experienced and labeled it sexual harassment.*		
Complimentary comments	10.4%	18.9%
Insulting comments	12.1	19.8
Complimentary looks, gestures	8.1	16.2
Insulting looks, gestures	9.6	15.4
Nonsexual touching	3.5	3.6
Sexual touching	12.3	24.2
Expected socializing	7.4	10.9
Expected sexual activity	3.2	7.6
• *Have you ever experienced sexual harassment?*	37.3%	53.1%

Source: Adapted from B. A. Gutek (1985). *Sex and the workplace.* San Francisco: Jossey-Bass, 46.

2. Work organizations should vigorously pursue allegations of sexual harassment and act on the bases of evidence found in the investigations.

3. Management policies should include sexual harassment and other unprofessional conduct in performance appraisals and act on the results.

4. Managers should promote professional behavior and a professional atmosphere throughout the organization. (p. 174)

Gutek's suggestions for organizational change in policies about sexual harassment imply that the problem is an organizational one, not just an individual one. Responsible leadership from management that promotes respect for women and men and does not condone exploitation is the best preventive measure, she believes.

WORK AND FAMILY LIFE

There has been a dramatic increase in the number of women in the paid work force. With that change, new attention is being paid to the stresses encountered by women and their families as their work and family roles change. How does the emergence of dual-earner families change marital relationships or patterns child care? What are the sources of strain and satisfaction for women in this new role?

Dual-Earner Families

Today, over half of the husband-wife families include an employed wife, and less than a third have only a male wage earner. This is a relatively new phenomenon in American society, and it involves two physically separated and socially distinct work roles for women. Unlike traditional families, these working families have two workers and three jobs—the wage earner jobs *and* the jobs of housework and child care. What does the research tell us about the three-job family?

dual-earner families families in which both adult members are engaged in paid employment

Piotrkowski and Repetti (1984) have carefully reviewed the research literature on **dual-earner families**. Their review reveals interesting changes in family life and even in the way researchers have thought about the problem. The focus of earlier research was on the possible harmful effects of maternal employment. Very little attention was paid to the possible positive effects.

The findings are fairly clear for school-aged children. Most school-aged children appeared not to be affected at all. On the other hand, infants did show some reaction. Thompson, Lamb, and Estes (1982) found that a mother's return to work changed the way a baby attached itself to the mother, but it did not necessarily produce greater insecurity.

The research showed few differences in the quality of marital relationships for dual-earner families, with the exception of some lower-income families, where employed wives, but not husbands, reported poorer marital relations. What about the division of household labor? Researchers have found little evidence that employed women play a greater role in decision making except in some financial decisions, where they seem to play a greater role once they are employed. The results also suggest that when women enter the paid labor force, husbands take up only a very small portion of the housework (Nickols & Metzen, 1982).

All of this suggests that much of the extra work is being taken on by the woman in dual-earner families. It appears that dual-earner families have not yet reallocated the work at home to accommodate the demands built into a family with two people and three jobs.

Spillover

spillover influences flowing from work to family life and from family life back to work

Some of the most exciting research on the relationship between work and family life recognizes the importance of influences flowing between work and family **(spillover)**. For example, in some pioneering research Piotrkowski (1979) found that boring, nondemanding work with little opportunity for control led husbands in blue-collar families to withdraw from family participation. When work was filled with conflict, a tense pattern of family interaction emerged.

But positive influences flow from work to family too. Crouter (1984a) found that work settings that emphasized participation in decision making spilled over with positive effects in the family and community. A machine operator in a plant where participative management had been initiated observed, "I say things to my eight-year-old daughter that I know are a result of the way we do things at work. I ask her, What do you think about that? Or, How would you handle this problem? I deal with her the way I deal with people at work, the logic is the same" (pp. 81–82).

Crouter (1984b) has also shown that influences can flow from family to work as well. Men and women experience very different amounts of negative spillover from the family to work life. When children are ill or other problems emerge in the family, men tend to experience little difference in the work role, but mothers with small children experience considerable stress.

These findings make it clear that influences flow from family to work and back again. Furthermore, not all the influences are negative. Some work experiences appear to have positive effects on family interaction. Finally, there are important role differences in the influences for men and women. Fathers appear to experience little negative spillover of family problems into work, while mothers experience considerably more.

A fascinating recent study by Kraus and Geyer-Pestello (1985) adds understanding of some of these influences in dual-earner families. Kraus and Geyer-Pestello interviewed a number of women with families who were in the active work force and asked them about their satisfaction with pay, commitment to the work role, and general sex-role orientation. Two interesting findings emerged. Women who said they were deeply committed to their work experienced considerably more satisfaction from their work and were less depressed than women whose commitment to work was lower. Having young children in the home was a stressor for only women with a traditional sex-role orientation. These more traditional women engaged in more solitary child-care activities and shared the task of child care less with others. Apparently, for these mothers, the combined demands of the job role and the mother role increased dissatisfaction and were experienced as stressful.

CAREER CHANGES

Most people today can expect to change jobs and even careers several times throughout their working lives. The pace of change in the world of work is actually accelerating and will present challenges in coping with career transitions for many of us. People change careers for a variety of reasons. Economic changes can eliminate whole groups of jobs. People in midlife may want new challenges or opportunities for growth. An initial career choice, appealing at the time, may not satisfy some personal or financial needs. On the other hand, a woman may enter the work force for the first time in midlife or reenter the work force after having launched a family. Whatever the case, career changes are going to continue to be the norm instead of the exception in the world of work. Knowing how to cope with career changes and what the choices are is critical for developing a sense of control.

Strategies for Career Change

If you already have a full-time job but are thinking about a career change, you need information and an opportunity to reflect on your goals and choices. You may need to find out what your abilities really are and what other fields are appropriate to your own abilities and interests (Dillard, 1985). Since you are already employed, you have a valuable resource already available. You have the time to explore your options.

As the labor market continues to expand and change, career choices require considerable thought and knowledge about yourself. You may want to consider the possibility of **career counseling**. During career counseling, you should have an opportunity to explore your life and clarify your basic goals as well as to find out how your skills can fit with those goals. Many career counseling services will ask you to complete a battery of interest and ability tests and will interview you in detail about your past career and your future aspirations. The end of a series of career counseling sessions should provide you with an integrated picture of your interests and goals as well as information about alternative careers and occupations.

Using a career counseling service requires you to be a careful consumer. The first place to look for career counseling is in your college or university. You may discover that your campus counseling service provides career counseling for students for a small fee. In addition, many community agencies, including YMCAs and community employment and training agencies, provide career counseling services. If you are unable to find career counseling services through your college or a local community agency, check the credentials of any private firm you consider. Before agreeing to pay any fees or signing a contract, ask about the credentials of the professionals involved in the service you are considering. See "Exploring Choices: Resources to Help with Career Transitions" for more information.

career counseling services provided to clarify career choices, including interest and ability testing, examination of alternative career opportunities, and in some cases, counseling in the process of job search

Unemployment and Job Search

If you don't already have a job, you face a double challenge. You have to not only think through the choices available to you but you also manage your feelings because the experience of unemployment can be stressful. Part of dealing effectively with the experience of unemployment involves knowing what it can be like. Kaufman (1982), Jahoda (1979), and other researchers have reported several distinctive stages in the unemployment experience. People who are about to lose their jobs may experience anxiety, disbelief, and denial. Typically, people who have lost their jobs experience a period of brief relief and relaxation when the time of uncertainty is past.

If the job search takes longer than anticipated, you may find yourself feeling moody, anxious, angry, self-doubting, and even depressed. Researchers have found that family conflict and strained parent-child relations can become more serious during prolonged unemployment (Leim & Raymon, 1982). This is a time when reaching out to others for help and having a plan can make an

EXPLORING CHOICES

RESOURCES TO HELP WITH CAREER TRANSITIONS

Assessing your interests and abilities is not a casual undertaking. Career counseling is only one approach to self-assessment. John Holland has identified different personality patterns that appear to be linked to certain types of occupations. You can obtain a series of exercises to match your interests with specific occupations in *Self-Directed Search*, written by John Holland.

Identifying your personal goals and opportunities to meet those goals is a second major stage in exploring career choices. A practical manual for career changers is *What Color Is Your Parachute*, by Richard Bolles, from Ten Speed Press. This entertaining book helps you think through your options and identify opportunities in the work environment. The United States Department of Labor publishes the *Guide for Occupational Exploration* and *The Occupational Outlook Handbook*, each of which can help you consider your options.

important difference. In the following job search strategy, you will find a number of suggestions that can help in this difficult period.

Commit yourself. Finding a job is, in itself, a full-time job. You need to commit yourself to the idea that job finding is an active, not a passive, process. It may require hard work over a long period of time. Your job search is your temporary full-time job.

Mobilize your support system of friends and family to help you with your job search. Ask friends and family to help with household tasks that divert you from the job search. Get them to help you with the tasks of typing and copying. If they have a car and you do not, consider borrowing it. If you have a friend or a relative who can take telephone messages, enlist that person in taking messages from prospective employers.

Set up shop. If you can, establish a work area for yourself. It should include a typewriter, a phone, writing materials, a list of prospective employers to contact, and a schedule of when to contact them. Start each day in your work area, plan your day carefully, and be there at the end of the day to record the results of your day's efforts.

Find job leads. There are more ways to find job leads than you may imagine. Look through the yellow pages of your telephone book and contact all the places in your field where you would like to work. Ask family and friends if they know of job openings in your field. Use your connections. Too often, we forget that our family and friends are also employers or know employers with real possibilities. After having an interview with a prospective employer, ask about other job openings in your field. Record any such leads and follow up on them. Respond to want ads in the newspaper. Also consider the possibility of advertising yourself. Put an ad in the paper, emphasizing your personal characteristics. You are more than just job skills. Prospective employers want to know what you are like as a person.

Organize your credentials. You should have open letters of reference available when you go to a job interview. If possible, obtain them from a previous employer, teachers, or leaders of religious groups or community organizations that are respected. You can use these open letters of reference as letters of introduction. Prepare a resume that includes not just your previous work experiences but also information that communicates your uniqueness. List your hobbies and interests and the organizations to which you belong. Emphasize the skills that you have acquired in previous volunteer experiences or work.

Present yourself effectively in the interview. When calling on a potential employer, do not ask directly about an opening. Instead, indicate that you want to talk about the possibility of future openings. Come prepared; have your questions ready about job possibilities. Present yourself in a positive way, and emphasize your personal attributes. Even if an opening is not available, make it clear that you are interested in future possibilities.

Follow up the interview by arranging a time to call back. This shows your seriousness and commitment. It also reminds the prospective employer that you are really interested. Using these strategies should help make the job search process more effective and interesting, and it should increase your choices.

Even if you carry out all these approaches to job search, you still may find that getting the right job is difficult. Other options to consider include moving to search where jobs are more plentiful and entering a training program to increase specific skills in demand.

SUMMARY

1. Work can be an affliction, an addiction, or a source of fulfillment. Research indicates that most people find friendships and meaning in working life and would continue to work even if they had no financial need.

2. There are a number of changing trends in work, including rapid increases in the number of women entering the work force, rapid technological change, and increased expectation for participation in the workplace. All of these changes are producing new choices and challenges for the work force.

3. Your personality can be a critical factor in career choice. People tend to search for—and be happier in—jobs that fit their orientations. A decisional balance sheet can help you think through your career choices.

4. Researchers have found that the more fulfilling jobs have interesting task content, provide autonomy and control, have high-quality supervision and positive relationships with coworkers, provide adequate pay, provide opportunities for promotion, and have safe physical working conditions.

5. While technological innovations such as the computer may make work more efficient, they can also have negative effects. In some cases, they reduce worker control or the opportunity for personal relationships at work.

6. Stressful jobs tend to be those in which demands are high and worker control over choices is low. Social support from coworkers and mentors can help reduce work stress.

7. Sexual harassment is a form of exploitation at work. In sexual harassment, the victim receives unwanted sexual attentions or demands from someone in a position of relative power. Sexual harassment can take a wide variety of forms and can be a form of sex discrimination. It is the responsibility of work organizations to develop policies and practices to virgorously discourage harassment in any form.

8. As women enter the work force in increasing numbers, working families must balance the demands of housework, child care, and two full-time jobs. Research suggests that the burdens of housework and child care are not yet equally distributed among two-job couples.

9. A career change during your work life is likely to occur more than once. Career counseling, which involves learning about your interests and abilities as well as alternative careers choices, is an option you may want to consider.

10. Even more stressful than career change is the experience of unemployment. You can increase your choices for a new job, however, if you commit yourself to the job search. Use your social support system, actively pursue job leads, and follow up on each lead systematically.

Chapter 14

SOCIAL INFLUENCE AND INDIVIDUAL CHOICE

COPING WITH SOCIAL INFLUENCE ATTEMPTS

Reciprocation
Consistency and Commitment
Conformity and Social Proof
The Power of Attraction
Deference to Authority
Scarcity

COPING WITH PREJUDICE

Theories to Explain Prejudice
Social Impact of Prejudice
Strategies for Reducing Prejudice

HELPING AND ALTRUISM

DILEMMAS OF COOPERATION

SUMMARY

Here is what Robert Cialdini (1984) found when he went to learn how some real estate agents use psychological principles to influence customer choices.

'To learn the ropes' I was accompanying a company realty salesman on a weekend of showing houses to prospective home buyers. The salesman—we can call him Phil— was to give me tips to help me through my break-in period. One thing I noticed was that whenever Phil began showing a new set of customers potential buys, he would start with a couple of undesirable houses. I asked him about it, and he laughed. They were what he called 'set-up' properties. The company maintained a rundown house or two on its list at inflated prices. The houses were not intended to be sold to customers, but to be shown to them, so that the genuine properties in the company's inventory would benefit from the comparison. Not all the sales staff made use of the set-up houses, but Phil did. He said he liked to watch his prospects' 'eyes light up' when he showed the place he really wanted to sell them after they had seen the rundown houses. 'The house I got them spotted for looks really great after they've first looked at a couple of dumps.' (pp. 26–27)

Now let us look at a very different situation in which you might have to make a choice. This is an example that John Platt (1973) calls "the case of the missing hero."

Consider this situation, a summer Sunday evening, when thousands of cars are coming back from a Cape Cod weekend on a two lane road and a mattress falls unnoticed from the top of a stationwagon and lies in the northbound lane. All of the cars behind, being uncertain, go around the mattress, waiting for the cars in the southbound lane to go by, and the result is a traffic jam that backs up for miles.

Now who moves the mattress? The answer, is generally, no one. People far back in the line do not know what the trouble is and cannot help, and the drivers close to the mattress are thinking only of how to get around it quickly—and after they have spent so long in line, they are damned if they will spend another several minutes, perhaps endangering themselves, to stop to move the thing. Those who have gone past, of course, no longer have any incentive for moving it. (p. 644)

Here, clearly, is another kind of social choice. It involves a choice between short-term risk for the individual and long-term gain for the group. While the details may differ, it resembles a great many social situations. As different as these two examples are, they both involve social choices, and they require that we understand some of the underlying psychological principles affecting our behavior if we are to make informed choices.

We live in a social world that both shapes us and that we can shape. That social world consists of groups and institutions in which we live, work, learn, and play. Each group or institution communicates **norms** (expectations) and values about what is fair or appropriate. For example, your college or university communicates its own norms about academic honesty. The interesting thing about that norm is that it both supports and constrains individual behavior. A norm about academic honesty supports and rewards hard work, and of course at the same time, it constrains you from taking shortcuts.

norms implied or specifically stated expectations about behavior that exist in social groups, organizations, and societies

But we are not just passive members of the social world; we can shape it through our choices and behavior. In fact, we are constantly confronted with choices offered by various groups and institutions. These choices are also critical to our social and psychological adjustment. We can choose to repay a favor or not, to question an authoritative opinion, to give blood, to help a stranger in apparent distress, or to join a community group. Each of these choices can be made more thoughtfully if we understand the underlying psychological principles of social influence and choice and how they work in everyday life. The choices we make affect not only our own adjustment but that of others as well.

This chapter explores a number of different principles of social influence and how they affect our behavior. To better understand how we may benefit or lose as individuals and a society, it also explores situations that require choices.

COPING WITH SOCIAL INFLUENCE ATTEMPTS

compliance professionals
salespeople or other professionals who make their livings by persuading others

A social psychologist named Robert Cialdini in Tempe, Arizona, had a bright idea. Having already embarked on a scholarly research career aimed at understanding the principles of social influence, he decided to go out into the world and see how the professionals do it. Cialdini developed a program of observing **compliance practitioners** (people who make their livings persuading others) at their trade in sales training programs. He observed real estate agents, vacuum cleaner salespeople, and police bunko squad officers at their work to fully under the psychology of compliance. He wanted to understand how people think when their livelihoods depend on skill in making others do what they want.

This section explores some of Cialdini's findings and the social psychological principles that underlie his observations. By examining the various tactics of compliance professionals and understanding the principles that underlie those tactics, we can better understand and make our own social choices.

Early in his discussion, Cialdini makes the interesting point that each of the tools of influence he describes has developed in our social behavior because it is *actually adaptive*. That is, each of the responses to social stimuli and situations simplifies our social choices in a complex world, reduces our decision burden, or promotes our adaptation as individuals or groups. It is only when these principles are used by influence professionals in unethical ways that we ought to recognize them and take countermeasures.

Another interesting feature of these tools of social influence is that they trigger responses in us in a relatively automatic way. This means that often we are unaware that we are being influenced. Finally, while Cialdini provides numerous examples of the real-world application of these principles of influence in his book, all of them have been documented by social psychologists in surveys and experiments, and all are included in our fundamental social psychological knowledge about attitude and behavior change. "Exploring Choices:

Understanding Social Influence" summarizes the six rules discussed and provides examples and suggestions of ways to make ourselves aware of our choices in the face of social influence attempts.

Reciprocation

One of the strongest social norms in all cultures is the expectation that we repay a debt, gift, or favor if we receive one. Anthropologists tell us that the norm of reciprocity exists in all cultures. **Reciprocation** allows us to exchange various forms of goods and services, divide labor, and organize ourselves in efficient, cooperative units. But what happens when the norm of reciprocation is used to influence behavior?

In the field of sales and merchandising, one of the commonest examples is the use of free samples in supermarkets or the mail. This strategy exposes

reciprocation norm that one is obliged to repay a debt, gift, or favor

EXPLORING CHOICES

UNDERSTANDING SOCIAL INFLUENCE

The following list indicates six tools of influence, gives examples of each, and provides hints to help you say no.

1. *Rules of reciprocation.* The norm is to repay a debt, gift, or favor or to return a concession if given one. Examples include free samples and gifts designed to instill a feeling of indebtedness and increase the tendency to make a purchase or contribution to repay the debt. To say no, you have the following choices:
   - Reject the initial favor or concession.
   - Recognize the obligation that you incur for the future.
2. *Consistency and commitment.* The desire to be consistent with past behavior is a central motivator. Requests for commitment can activate a desire for consistency. Examples include contests

that ask you to endorse a product in twenty-five words or less and automobile dealers' low-ball techniques. To say no, you have the following choices:
   - Recognize you have been trapped into a request you don't want to comply with.
   - Point out the dangers of foolish consistency.
   - Review your earlier decision: Would you do it again?
3. *Conformity and social proof.* We view behavior as more correct when we see others performing it. Examples include claims of "largest selling, fastest, growing," laugh tracks on television, and salting tip jars with big bills. To say no, you have the following choices:
   - Look for rigged social proof where the basis for the claim may be false or misleading.

potential buyers to the qualities of a product. It may be used to create uninvited debts that people feel they must repay. Cialdini notes that the soliciting technique of the Hare Krishna Society frequently uses this strategy to solicit contributions in airports or other public places. A traveler may be given a flower or a book as a gift only to be solicited for a contribution a few minutes later. Many people dimly recognize that they are being influenced by the rule of reciprocation, but they find it difficult to resist.

What then should we do to increase our choices when the rule of reciprocation is used to manipulate our behavior? Cialdini suggests that we reject the initial favor or concession, or at the very least, that we recognize we have been placed under an obligation by accepting the favor and that it is an obligation we have implicitly at least agreed to repay. This does not mean that we should actually repay the "favor" when we have been manipulated.

- Check the objective facts in the situation.

4. *Liking: attraction by association.* We prefer to comply with requests of someone we know and like. Examples include Tupperware and other sales schemes built on acquaintance, referral of influences by a friend, use of compliments, and physical attractiveness. To say no, you have the following choices:
    - Notice the attraction you feel. Be attuned to your reaction.
    - Mentally separate the salesperson from the product, and unchain the association.

5. *Deference to authority.* We are likely to be influenced by and comply with someone in authority. Examples include titles that imply authority, clothes,

uniforms, or use of authoritative references. To say no, you have the following choices:
    - Check the evidence for authority on the issue at hand.
    - Ask, How truthful can the expert be expected to be here?

6. *Scarcity.* Opportunities and things seem more valuable when their availability is limited. Examples include the last model available, sale ends soon, competing customer on the scene, or get them while they last. To say no, you have the following choices:
    - Recognize the automatic arousal response to apparent scarcity.
    - Ask, What exactly do I want from this item or experience?

Source: Based on R. B. Cialdini (1984). *Influence: How and why people agree to things.* New York: William Morrow & Co.

Consistency and Commitment

Perhaps one of the most important developments in social psychology in the last three decades has been the identification of consistency and commitment as major forces that influence behavior. Leon Festinger (1957) and Theodore Newcomb (1961), in particular, have developed theories and conducted experiments to demonstrate the power of this principle. The principle of **consistency** suggests that the desire to be consistent with one's past behavior is a central motivator of behavior. Furthermore, requests for **commitment** to some future course of action can activate the desire for consistency.

consistency principle that asserts that people desire to behave in ways that follow or agree with their past behavior

commitment personal intention to take a particular course of action in the future

This important principle is not a mere scientific curiosity, however. It is used by influence professionals all of the time. We are familiar with examples of the consistency principle, especially when salespeople have managed to trigger it by getting us to make a commitment. Frequently, the goal of small transactions is not a profit but a commitment to future behavior.

> When a person has signed an order for your merchandise, even though profit is so small it hardly compensates for the time and effort of making the call, he is no longer a prospect—he is a customer. (American Salesman *as cited in Cialdini*)

A similar strategy is to conduct a contest in which each entrant must write a statement in twenty-five words or less explaining the virtues of a product. By formulating the statement and writing it down, the entrant has managed to make a commitment to the product and may be more likely to purchase it in the future. Hell week initiation into fraternities and sororities has the commitment principle underlying it as well.

Like other rules of social influence, commitment and consistency are actually socially adaptive in most situations. Consistency offers a shortcut in the complexities of modern life. It simplifies complex decisions. After all, being personally consistent is valued in our culture.

How then can you provide yourself with choices in the face of strong pressures to remain consistent even when consistency is not in your interests? One strategy is to recognize that you have been trapped into a request you do not want to perform. In the face of a persistent influence, you can point out the dangers of foolish consistency and review your earlier decision. Would you really do it again knowing what you know now?

Conformity and Social Proof

In many situations, we look at the behavior of others in order to judge the appropriateness of our own behavior. That is, we engage in social comparison. This is not just mindless conformity, because in many situations conforming to the behavior of others can be adaptive. As a general rule, we are likely to make fewer errors by conforming with social evidence, as opposed to behaving in ways that are contrary to it. **Conformity** is a convenient way of simplifying a complex world.

conformity tendency to act, dress, or think like others

But like most adaptive patterns of social behavior, the pressure for conformity can be used to influence our behavior without our being fully aware of it. Evidence that other people are engaging in a particular act can influence us in surprising ways. For example, frequently we hear ads suggesting that a product is the best selling. Ushers taking collections in churches may salt the collection plate or bartenders may salt a tip receptacle with bills in order to provide social "evidence" that bills, rather than change, are the appropriate contribution. It even seems that laugh tracks on television make material seem funnier whether we are aware that they are laugh tracks or not.

Albert Bandura and his colleagues (1963), psychologists interested in the power of examples and modeling, has shown that social evidence can be put to important and even therapeutic uses. Children who are frightened of a dog are much more likely to climb into a playpen and pet and scratch the dog after having observed other children playing happily with it.

If the pressures for conformity can influence our choices, we can increase our choices by recognizing the power of social conformity to shape our behavior. Cialdini suggests two strategies. First, look for rigged social proof, where the basis for a particular claim may be false or misleading. A related strategy is to check the objective facts in the situation. When someone tells you "everybody's doing it," you may well ask, Who is everybody?

The Power of Attraction

attraction principle of influence that states that people prefer to comply with requests made by others they know and like

Still another tool of influence, **attraction,** is based on the fact we prefer to comply with requests made by someone we know and like. Everyone would rather do a favor for a friend than a stranger. Furthermore, like the rest of our principles of social influence, this principle works on a relatively automatic basis. In most cases, it is appropriate and adaptive. Only when others use the principle of attraction to unscrupulously manipulate our willingness to comply should we be concerned. Perhaps more than for any other psychologial principle of social influence, numerous methods are used for producing influence by increasing attraction. One of the most fascinating examples is Joe Girard, a Chevrolet dealer in Detroit, who set a Guinness world record as the greatest car salesman by using the attraction principle. While offering customers a fair price, he also got them to like him through the simple tactic of sending a card in the mail every month that said, "I like you," and signing his name, Joe Girard. This message came to each customer twelve times a year, and the flattery implied in this message, even though it was printed, presumably increased customer liking and sales.

Standard sales devices that use the attraction principle include ads with physically attractive models and Razran's (1940) luncheon technique, in which the pleasant experience of having lunch with others makes it more likely that you will comply with their requests. If the liking principle is so powerful in increasing our tendency to comply with requests, how do we say no? Cialdini suggests that we begin by noticing the attraction we feel in a particular circumstance. Being aware of our reactions may be the first line of defense. Second, he suggests that we mentally separate the influencer from the product or action advocated. Ask, Is it the product that interests me or is it the salesperson? This sort of separation should help defuse unscrupluous applications of the principle of attraction.

Deference to Authority

deference to authority tendency to be influenced by or comply with someone who is in authority or shows signs of authority

Another important principle of social influence is **deference to authority**, the idea that we are likely to be influenced by and comply with someone who is in authority. Perhaps one of the most famous experiments in the history of social psychology demonstrated how powerful authority can be in influencing behavior. Stanley Milgram (1974) set up a study described to participants as a study of memory. Volunteers served as teachers for learners, who were actually accomplices. They were described to the teacher as attached to electrical shock equipment. The teacher was told to administer shocks if memory errors occurred in the task.

By using a laboratory coat and other symbols of authority, Milgram and his colleagues were able to persuade teachers to deliver what they thought were painful and even nearly fatal shocks to learners in response to their errors. Although distressed, most of the teachers complied. In addition to demonstrating the power of authority to cause compliance with behavior that we normally would avoid, this study has raised important questions about the degree to which we are vulnerable to manipulation by authority figures.

Of course, compliance to authority makes adaptive sense from the point of view of social organization. Cooperation in response to leaders can produce important and socially useful results. But unthinking responses to authority can create real problems. A number of different ways of communicating authority can trigger an unthinking response of compliance. In a series of experiments, Leonard Bickman (1974) demonstrated that simply wearing the uniform of a security guard was enough to get passersby to comply with a variety of requests, provide people with change for other people's parking meters, and engage in other acts of compliance that could be elicited only at a lower rate without the uniform.

We tend to respond automatically to authority, but how do we say no? Cialdini suggests that we check the evidence of authority on the issue at hand. Is the person actually an authority in this particular case? A second question, even for people with legitimate authority, is how truthful can the expert be expected to be in this particular situation? Is there a personal reason for the expert to want you to comply? If you think there is, you should be cautious in your response.

Scarcity

scarcity principle
principle that things limited in supply are more valuable and desirable

Still another potent principle of social influence is the **scarcity principle.** Opportunities and objects seem more valuable when their availability is limited. We almost automatically respond to items that appear scarce by seeing them as more valuable and more desirable. It is no surprise that compliance professionals advertise that the sale ends soon or that a salesperson may tell you that this is the last model in the warehouse. A number of carefully controlled experiments demonstrate the power of the scarcity principle. Even identical cookies in a cookie jar appear more desirable to naive judges when there are fewer of them than when there are more.

Perhaps the most amusing example of the use of the scarcity principle is recounted in a story by Cialdini (1984) about his brother who worked his way through school by buying and reselling cars on weekends. Customers who called for an appointment to see the car were scheduled at roughly the same time so that soon after the first customer arrived, a second would arrive to look at the same car. Being in competition for the same resource made it more scarce. Therefore, it became more valuable. Car sales boomed.

Cialdini (1984) suggests that saying no to the scarcity response begins with recognizing the automatic and powerful arousal response to apparent scarcity. When we feel this urgency in ourselves, we ought to recognize it for what it is and be cautious. A second strategy is cognitive. We should ask ourselves, What exactly do I want from this item or experience? Is it something about the item itself, or is it merely its scarcity that is making it desirable?

Like all other tools of influence, the scarcity principle is an adaptive shortcut in the complexity of life in most circumstances. Most of the time, things that are in short supply are more valuable. But when the scarcity principle is used to manipulate behavior, we should be cautious, recognize the initial response, and separate the scarcity from the value of the item itself.

COPING WITH PREJUDICE

prejudice inflexible attitudes toward others based on incorrect or incomplete information

Whether you are a man or woman, a member of an ethnic minority group or not, or differ from most people in your sexual preference, you will confront **prejudice** in a variety of forms throughout your adult life. If you are a member of a minority group, you already know that discrimination is a social reality with which you have to cope. If you are a woman, you have probably experienced sexual discrimination. If, on the other hand, you are not a member of an ethnic minority or a woman, you may have encountered prejudice from another perspective. Perhaps you have heard a friend casually dismiss members of an ethnic or minority group or a woman.

Prejudice reflects inflexible attitudes toward others based on incorrect or incomplete information. It is a critical aspect of intergroup relations. Prejudice is very hard to change. Social psychologists have been concerned with the relationships between not just individuals but also groups. They have studied the causes and consequences of prejudice, as well as strategies for reducing it in our society. Thinking about prejudice as an intergroup problem adds to our understanding of the nature of the problem.

stereotypes rigidly held misconceptions about individuals or groups, particularly minority groups

Some aspects of prejudice are clearly rooted in the psychology of individuals. For example, Nisbett and Ross (1980), have shown that we tend to hold misconceptions and **stereotypes** because we selectively recall events about individuals and groups. We tend to recall information that fits our preconceptions and to forget or ignore information that doesn't fit our preconceived notions.

At the same time, Deaux (1976b) has shown that we use judgment biases to explain exceptions to our stereotyped views. If, for example, a woman succeeds in a traditionally male-dominated profession, we are inclined to attribute her success to extraordinary ability. This makes her an exception to the rule, or bias, that we hold.

It is important to recognize that prejudice is not merely a product of individual psychological biases. The very nature of relationships between groups also makes prejudice persistent. Since no individual is absolutely essential to the group, prejudice and bias persist. A second important thing to remember is that when groups are in conflict, cohesiveness within the group increases as people unite against a common enemy. This, in turn, reinforces biased perceptions and increases the chances that the group will maintain a hostile attitude toward other out-group members. These last two aspects of behavior between groups help make it clear why prejudice, whether it be in the form of racism or sexism, is so hard to change. Even if individuals change their own attitudes, the dynamics of the group make prejudice especially resistant to change.

Prejudice reflects
inflexible attitudes
toward others.

Theories to Explain Prejudice

Social psychologists have developed a number of different theories to account
for the nature of prejudice and discrimination. The theories range from accounts that locate the cause of prejudice in individual personality to theories
that focus primarily on the nature of behavior that occurs between groups.

    Perhaps one of the most famous early theories of prejudice suggested that
some people possess an **authoritarian personality** (Adorno et al., 1950), which
reflects a preference for strong antidemocratic leaders and rigid adherence to
conventional values. Authoritarian persons were assumed to be particularly
fearful and negative about anyone different from themselves and inclined to
follow the orders of those in authority in an unquestioning way. These early
researchers assumed that the authoritarian personality develops in families
with dominant fathers, who are rigid and punish any disobedience harshly.
The explanation that prejudices are due entirely to personality characteristics
has been largely discredited.

    A second hypothesis about the development of prejudice focuses on the
experience of socialization within the family. Ashmore and Del Boca (1976),
observe substantial correspondence between children's racial attitudes and
those of their parents. It appears that a good deal of prejudice is transmitted in

**authoritarian
personality**
personality pattern
reflecting a preference
for antidemocratic
leaders and rigid
adherence to
conventional values

the family through cultural learning and that racial prejudice becomes a cultural norm in some groups. As the song goes, "You have to be carefully taught."

Children tend to learn prevailing racial biases, partly because they receive social approval within the family and group for doing so and partly because this early learning encourages children to interact only with those that are like themselves. As a result, children learning early racial stereotypes find little opportunity to have them discomfirmed in the group, where they are likely to interact only with those who like themselves.

Still another major theory about the development of prejudice suggests that prejudice is a result of competition for scarce resources among groups. This **theory of economic competition** is partly supported by historical accounts of immigration into the United States. Typically, newly arrived immigrants were lower in socioeconomic status and represented a threat to other recently arrived groups, who saw them as presenting economic competition. Stereotypes and negative attitudes about the immigrants prevailed. As immigrant groups began slowly to improve social and economic status despite these stereotypes, prejudice and discrimination were reduced to some degree.

theory of economic competition theory that prejudice arises against some groups because they represent a threat for economic resources

Social Impact of Prejudice

Whether against a particular ethnic or cultural group or against women, prejudice takes an enormous toll in self-esteem and productivity. Because prejudice can lead to discrimination, barring equal opportunities to jobs and education, the courts have been active in establishing the civil rights of individual citizens. The Civil Rights Act of 1964 sought to eliminate biases based on race, ethnic background, or sex in employment and education. It is important to recognize that the government's attempt to compensate for years of discrimination through affirmative action do not require that businesses or schools accept unqualified candidates. Instead, affirmative action requires good faith efforts to offer minority groups and women equal opportunity.

Strategies for Reducing Prejudice

While legal attempts to deal with prejudice and discrimination are important, how do social psychologists analyze the situation? Under what conditions can relationships between groups be changed to reduce prejudice and discrimination? Psychologists have come up with a number of informative and potentially useful answers. Cook (1979) has described a number of conditions where relationships between racial groups can produce positive attitude change. These include conditions under which the status of the two groups is not very different, opportunity to interact with the other group, norms and expectations for courtesy and friendliness, and opportunities to observe people who do not conform to the stereotypes held by the group.

Perhaps the most important and most interesting condition for the elimination of prejudice and discrimination is the opportunity for members of differ-

interdependence
conditions in which
individuals or groups
must depend on one
another to achieve
some larger goal

ent groups to work together *interdependently* to achieve some larger goal. In **interdependence**, each group must depend on the other to achieve some larger goal it cannot achieve alone. Under such conditions, prejudice and discrimination tend to be rapidly reduced. Two fascinating experiments, one a classic in the field of social psychology and one more recent, demonstrate this principle.

The most famous study of intergroup conflict and prejudice was conducted thirty-five years ago by social psychologist Muzafer Sherif (Sherif & Sherif, 1953). Sherif and his colleagues set up a series of summer camps for eleven- and twelve-year-old boys. His idea was to create social conditions in which hostility and prejudice could be generated between different groups. If he then could change the conditions in which the campers interacted, perhaps the prejudice could be eliminated. Sherif began by segregating the boys into two separate residential groups and building cohesion within the groups by involving them in cooperative tasks, overnight hikes, and other activities. The two groups were given different names, the Rattlers and the Eagles, and were pitted against each other in competitive tournaments, games, and contests. It was not long before the Rattlers and the Eagles were exchanging insults, vandalizing the possessions of the other group, and raiding the enemy camp. Each group began to develop biased perceptions of the characteristics of the other group, downplaying the other group's achievements and overestimating their own. It seems clear that many of the conditions of intergroup conflict and prejudice had emerged in this situation.

Then Sherif and his colleagues decided to see if they could discover ways to reduce the conflict and tensions. At first, educational methods were tried, using lectures on the necessity for friendly camp relations and increases in social contact, but these only increased the tension. Next, Sherif thought that a series of circumstances in which the two groups worked together toward larger common goals might promote harmony. Cleverly, Sherif and his colleagues began to create a series of emergencies. First, the camp water supply was disrupted, and the two groups had to search together to find the cause—a plugged faucet. The food truck stalled, and the groups literally pulled together, using the same rope they had used before in fierce tug-of-war competitions. As time went on, hostility between the two groups began to diminish, friendships developed, and each group began to see the other in a more positive light.

A recent series of studies by Elliott Aronson and his colleagues (1980) demonstrates in still another setting how interdependence can be a critical ingredient in reducing hostility and prejudice—in this case, in desegregated classrooms. Aronson developed a method of cooperative learning that required students to work together to learn the material for an examination. Because each student had only part of the information, the jigsaw puzzle they had to put together was the total body of information needed to master the test. Classrooms that used the jigsaw method, which required cooperation, produced children with higher levels of self-esteem and friendship, as well as reductions in prejudice. Students reported that they liked school better in the jigsaw classes, and minority students' test scores improved.

Working together to solve problems that require interdependence appears to be critical for the reduction of intergroup hostility and prejudice, but is that all it takes? It may also be that individuals and groups must succeed in these cooperative adventures if intergroup antagonisms are to be reduced. Researcher Stephen Worchel and his colleagues (1977) demonstrated that competitive groups of college students who then were asked to cooperate on a series of superordinate tasks felt better about each other only when they succeeded in the task. Students who cooperated but who were told that they failed the task actually showed a slight increase in hostility and tended to blame others in the group for not contributing their share. Thus, we see the reduction of intergroup conflict and prejudice is not a simple matter; it appears that working together interdependently to achieve larger goals is crucial, but some measure of success is also important if hostility is to be reduced.

HELPING AND ALTRUISM

You are faced with choices about helping others every day. A classmate may ask to borrow your notes, you may pass a person in a wheelchair trying to ascend an icy ramp or sight a stranded motorist at the side of the road. While each of these experiences may lead you to pause momentarily, some events are serious and dramatic. Nearly twenty years ago, Catherine Genovise was murdered in a savage, late-night attack as she returned to her home from work. While murders are not uncommon in New York, what was unusual was that the attack continued over a period of nearly thirty-five minutes, and thirty-eight of her neighbors either heard her cries or observed aspects of the incident. Yet, no one called the police.

When interviewed after the event, the witnesses offered a number of confused excuses for the inaction. Psychologists Bibb Latane and John Darley (1968) decided to conduct a series of studies to try to understand why not even an anonymous telephone call was placed to police in an attempt to save Catherine Genovise. Their research consisted of staging a series of emergencies in circumstances in which the number of bystanders and the ambiguity of the event varied.

Latane and Darley staged epileptic seizures on the street, sent smoke underneath the door of waiting rooms, and staged accident scenes. Invariably, when a large crowd or even several bystanders observed an emergency event they were much less likely to go to the aid of the victim than when only one bystander was present. It was almost as if everyone was waiting for someone else to do something, particularly when the event was ambiguous. When the investigators varied the ambiguity of the event, ambiguous events were also much less likely to spur intervention. It appears that the specific circumstances surrounding the emergency influence helpful behavior. Ambiguous circumstances or the presence of others diffuses responsibility and actually makes people less likely to help.

altruism unselfish concern for others and the unselfish giving of aid or help to others

Psychologists have also studied **altruism**, the unselfish concern for others. Melvin Lerner (1974) examined people's attitudes toward justice in the world and tried to measure the degree to which each of us believe that good will be rewarded and that wrongdoing will be punished in the long run. This **just world hypothesis** can have important effects on the inclination to help others. Lerner believes that people who believe strongly in a just world may try to restore justice when innocent people suffer. In one study, Zuckerman (1975) found that students who scored high on a scale measuring a belief in social justice were more willing to help a person in a research task or read for the blind immediately before an exam than those who did not hold a strong belief in a just world. Presumably, students who believed in a just world may have thought that the altruism would be repaid with a better exam score when the exam loomed on the horizon.

just world hypothesis belief that good behavior will be rewarded and wrongdoing will be punished in the long run

But a strong belief in a just world can also operate in the opposite fashion. Lerner argues that people with a belief in a just world may view victims of misfortune as deserving the misfortune and even think less of them as a result. In laboratory experiments, Lerner and his coworkers have shown that people experiencing painful shocks are seen as having less desirable qualities.

It is clear then that a number of important components are involved in the tendency to behave altruistically or to help others. Some aspects of helping clearly are consequences of our own beliefs, as Lerner's research on the just world suggests. Still other aspects are the specific circumstances in which we are asked to help. The degree to which others seem to be available to help seems to diffuse the feeling of responsibility to help. Each of us will need help at one time or another, and each of us will be in a position to help others. The choices that we each make will affect the quality of our lives and those of others as well.

DILEMMAS OF COOPERATION

cooperation dilemma situation in which an individual must choose between individual short-term interests on the one hand and the long-term interests of the group on the other

Effective coping in the social world involves more than recognizing social influence attempts, understanding the dynamics of prejudice, or even understanding what leads us to help others. Recall for a moment the case of the missing hero at the beginning of the chapter. The dilemma for anyone considering moving the mattress from the middle of the road is really one of social cooperation, a **cooperation dilemma**. It raises questions of individual versus collective interests, cooperation versus competition, and the rights and responsibilities of individuals and of communities.

Social scientists have used three general approaches to understanding this set of social dilemmas. Each approach focuses on the conflict between short-term individual interests on the one hand and long-term group interests on the other. Perhaps the most famous approach to these dilemmas was introduced by Garrett Hardin (1968) in an article called "Tragedy of the Commons." In explaining this social dilemma, Hardin used an ecological example.

In colonial times, a common grazing ground existed in New England villages, where farmers could graze their cows. This arrangement worked reasonably well until individual farmers realized that enlarging their herds would increase their own profits. But as each individual farmer increased his herd, the total number of cattle increased and the grass became increasingly scarce. Finally, the common grazing ground was destroyed entirely. Each individual farmer was seeking individual gains but ultimately found himself experiencing a loss rather than a gain. Individuals engaged in activity to their advantage in the short term but damaging to the group and ultimately themselves as well.

We are faced with many such dilemmas in our society today, ranging from decisions about water and air pollution to decisions about whether or not to join and support a political party or union or to work for a voluntary or neighborhood organization. In every case, we are confronted with a short-term decision to either maximize our gain or minimize our personal cost. That decision may have long-term implications for both the group to which we belong and ultimately ourselves.

John Platt (1973) described this type of situation as a *social trap* and used a learning theory formulation to help understand it. From this point of view, the social trap depends on the differences between personal short-term rewards for a given action and the long-term consequences of behavior. The social trap occurs when the rewards for short-term individual behavior lead us to act in ways that punish the group as a whole in the long run.

Still other researchers use game theory to understand these dilemmas. In dilemma games, each player makes one of two choices, either to act cooperatively or to act competitively. If a player decides to act competitively, he or she will be in a position to take advantage of players who have decided to act cooperatively. This works in the short term, but in the long term, everyone begins to act competitively, resulting in losses for all the players. While each of these theoretical approaches helps us understand different aspects of the cooperation dilemma, it is truly a dilemma, because there is no easy or automatic solution to solve the problem of social cooperation. See "On the Research Frontier: Can Cooperation Emerge in a Selfish World?" for more on this subject.

Economists have developed theories about problems of collective action. They have even given a name to an individual who decides not to make the effort to contribute money or time to some common cause. They call such a person a **free rider** (someone who will ultimately benefit from a common good but who does not contribute to it thus gets a free ride). For example, people who do not pay all of their taxes are free riding, since they benefit from a variety of public goods such as parks and state roads that are supported by tax revenues.

In any instance where scarce resources are held in common by the group and each individual has a choice involving a cooperative or competitive response common dilemmas emerge. Coping in the social world involves recognizing the common dilemmas before they occur and having the courage to act. As Lewis Thomas (1981) observed,

free rider person who benefits from a commonly held good or resource but does not contribute to the common good

ON THE RESEARCH FRONTIER

CAN COOPERATION EMERGE IN A SELFISH WORLD?

In a world where everyone seems to be pursuing self-interest, is it possible for cooperative behavior to emerge? If so, are there particular behavioral strategies that will help encourage cooperation? In an important book, *The Evolution of Cooperation* (1984), Robert Axelrod examines this age-old question in a new way. Because actual social situations involving cooperation and competition are complicated, scientists have used formal simplified games of cooperation and competition to understand the underlying principles that encourage cooperation. One of the best-known of those games is Prisoners' Dilemma. The story behind this game is that the two prisoners have committed a crime together and are being questioned separately by the police. Each has a choice to confess or remain silent.

You can see that if both players in the prisoners' dilemma game cooperate, each wins. But if one player decides not to cooperate, that player may actually benefit at the other player's expense. Thus, the temptation to behave competitively is real.

Axelrod decided to use a computer simulation involving the prisoners' dilemma game to discover strategies that would produce cooperation in the long run, but he did something that was quite unusual. He invited numerous experts, including behavioral scientists, mathematicians, and game theorists, to submit various computer programs that specified different strategies to a tournament. Each of the strategies would compete against the other to see which ones would gain the most points in the

long run. Thus, Axelrod cleverly combined the computational power of the computer with the intuition of experts from all over the world to discover which strategies would survive against all others.

What Axelrod found was deceptively simple and yet very important. A strategy he called tit for tat was able to survive against all other strategies in several different tournaments. The tit-for-tat strategy simply mirrors the other player's response, cooperating when the other player cooperates and competing when the other player competes. This strategy reflects the general social norm of reciprocity discussed earlier in considering social influence attempts. The strategy is simple, it can be provoked, and it is forgiving.

If Axelrod has discovered a simple strategy for cooperation, why is there not more cooperation in the world? The answer, he says, is that two conditions are necessary for the evolution of cooperation. First, there must be an opportunity to cooperate. Second, there must be anticipated opportunities to cooperate with the same individual in the future. That is, in order to have an incentive to cooperate, people must not only see the rewards of cooperation but also anticipate the payoff of cooperative encounters with the same individual in the future. While Axelrod's findings involve a computer simulation of a simplified situation, the principles he has uncovered have important implications for understanding how cooperation can develop in a world in which self-interest is compelling.

Oil spills create
pollution and
cooperation
dilemmas.

We live today in a world densely populated by human beings living in close communi-
cation with each other all over the surface of the planet. Viewed from a certain dis-
tance, the earth has the look of a single society, a community, the swarming of an in-
tensely social species trying to figure out ways to become successfully interdependent.
(p. 3)

SUMMARY

1. We are faced with social influence attempts and individual choices throughout life. Some of these situations require that we recognize the attempt to influence us and resist it. In other cases, we are faced with choices to cooperate or compete or to discriminate or exercise tolerance.

2. Social influence attempts can be powerful. They often trigger automatic reactions in us. Automatic reactions are often adaptive and simplify our lives, but when influence attempts are unethical, we must be able to recognize them and take countermeasures.

3. A number of psychological principles underlie influence attempts, including reciprocation, consistency, conformity, attraction, deference to authority, and scarcity.

4. Coping with influence attempts requires learning how to say no. This begins by recognizing that you are in an influence situation. You can resist manipulation by gathering more information, examining your feelings and reactions, and deliberating carefully.

5. Prejudice and discrimination continue to be part of our everyday social lives. While a number of theories account for the presence of prejudice, circumstances requiring an interdependence among groups often help reduce prejudice.

6. Helping others is a choice that we face almost every day. Researchers have found that bystanders help others when they are alone (and feel a personal responsibility) and when the circumstances are not ambiguous.

7. Dilemmas of cooperation arise whenever we must choose between our own short-term interests on the one hand and the long-term interests of the group on the other.

GLOSSARY

A

accommodation according to Piaget, a process by which the person interprets elements of the environment in terms of his or her current understandings of the world

acculturation process by which one adapts to another culture

addicted love type of false love in which the individual sacrifices independence, outside interests, and all other relationships for the sake of the relationship

adjustment the active process of coping and making choices that affects an individual's well-being and personal growth

affectionate touching touching that expresses generalized positive or warm feelings

agentic having personality traits that emphasize achievement, self-assertion, and competence in overcoming difficulties and controlling the environment

agoraphobia fear of being alone or in public places that may result in considerable restriction of physical and social activity

AIDS (acquired immune deficiency syndrome) incurable disease that attacks a person's immune system and leaves the person vulnerable to infections that can lead to death

Alcoholics Anonymous voluntary organization of people with drinking problems who support each other in maintaining sobriety

alimony income for an economically disadvantaged spouse after a legal separation or divorce

altruism unselfish concern for others and the unselfish giving of aid or help to others

altruistic love type of authentic love that is based on giving

androgens group of hormones that increase sexual desire and masculinize physical appearance

androgynous exhibiting personality characteristics that typify both males and females

anorexia nervosa eating disorder involving fear of obesity, distorted body image, excessive thinness, and refusal to maintain body weight

anorgasmia inability to have an orgasm

anxiety disorder psychological disorder characterized by extreme fear either attached to a particular object or as a continuous state

anxiety states generalized feelings of anxiety occurring either periodically or on a continuing basis

appraisal one's judgment of the situational demands and one's assessment of the ability to meet them

assertiveness taking care of one's own interests without anxiety or hostility

assimilation according to Piaget, a process by which a person's understandings of the world are modified by new information from the environment

attachment extent to which people feel they need another in order to be happy

attachment process process by which the infant becomes bonded to the mother

attraction principle of influence that states that people prefer to comply with requests made by others they know and like

authentic love relationship based on the ability to care deeply for someone else without losing a sense of self

authoritarian personality personality pattern reflecting a preference for antidemocratic leaders and rigid adherence to conventional values

authoritarian style parenting style characterized by parental strictness, demands for maturity, and poor communication

authoritative style parenting style characterized by parental control carried out in a democratic, nurturant way

autonomy   freedom to pursue one's course

awfulizing   Ellis's term to reflect an individual's feeling that it is awful if a failure or frustration occurs

B

barbiturates   sedatives that can reduce anxiety and induce sleep

behavior-analytic approach   means of studying stressful experiences by conducting an analysis of the problem (problem identification), an identification of coping alternatives (response enumeration), and an evaluation of their relative usefulness (response evaluation)

Bem Sex-Role Inventory (BSRI)   popular psychological measure of sex-role identification

bereavement   physical distress and emotional despair associated with the loss or death of a loved one

biofeedback   extension of self-control procedures using informational cues of the body to alter one's reactions

birth control pill   pill that contains sex hormones (usually estrogen and progesterone) and prevents ovulation

bisexual   person who is sexually attracted to both males and females

blended families   families created by remarriage

bonds   deep, nonverbalized attachments to other persons, characterized by dependency and identification

buffering hypothesis   argument that social support exerts beneficial effects in the presence of stress by protecting people from the negative effects of such stress

bulimia   eating disorder involving periods of extreme binge eating followed by purging through either self-induced vomiting or the use of laxatives

C

career   professional occupation for which one trains and which one pursues as a life's work

career counseling   services provided to clarify career choices, including interest and ability testing, examination of alternative career opportunities, and in some cases, counseling in the process of job search

caring   extent to which people want to give of themselves or make sacrifices

castration complex   according to psychoanalysts, a small boy's fear of losing his penis for being in love with his mother

cervix   lower third of the uterus

Child Behavior Checklist   psychological assessment tool that examines children's behavior problems and competencies

child support   income to help support children who live with the spouse after a legal separation or divorce

chlamydia   organism that causes a sexually transmitted disease in both men and women, with symptoms rather similar to those of gonorrhea

cirrhosis   disease involving degeneration of liver tissue

classical conditioning   process in which a previously neutral stimulus repeatedly paired with another stimulus that normally produces a given response produces the latter response

clitoris   female's most sexually responsive genital tissues

cognitive behaviorism   psychological approach that emphasizes that how people think about themselves is a powerful determinant of their behavior

cognitive reappraisal   means by which individuals restructure or reframe experiences as well as their ability to cope

cohabitation   living with a sexual partner of the same or the opposite gender

colicky   having an upset stomach because of the infant's immature digestive system

collaborative empiricism   joint effort by a client and psychotherapist to test the validity of the client's beliefs and expectations

commitment   personal intention to take a particular course of action in the future

communal   having personality traits that emphasize sensitivity, tact, and appreciation of other people

complementary needs   situation in which each partner in a relationship has qualities that the other lacks

compliance professionals   salespeople or other professionals who make their livings by persuading others

conceived values   ideals as emphasized by the culture, religion, or philosophers

concrete operational stage   second Piagetian stage of thinking

concrete thinking   ideas based on what is seen or heard

conditions of worth   For Rogers, the bases upon which approval, attention, and rewards are given

condom   male contraceptive sheath that fits over the penis

conflict   disagreement about issues

conformity   tendency to act, dress, or think like others

congruence   consistency between one's feelings and behaviors

consistency   principle that asserts that people desire to behave in ways that follow or agree with their past behavior

continuous development   development that occurs gradually, without any clearly delineated stages

control   the ability to influence events or behaviors

conversion disorders   forms of poor adjustment that convert emotional problems into body dysfunctions

cooperation dilemma   situation in which an individual must choose between individual short-term interests on the one hand and the long-term interests of the group on the other

coping   action or thought that responds to the demands of the environment

counterconditioning   process by which a new, more adaptive relationship is established between a stimulus (triggering event) and a response

countertransference   distorted feelings and thoughts that a therapist transfers to a client

courtship   sequence of behaviors in humans and other animals initiated with the goal of terminating in mating or copulation

cross-sectional research   research in which subjects of different ages are tested at about the same time

culture   customs and civilization of a particular people or group

cunnilingus   mouth stimulation of the vulva

custody   legal guardianship of children

D

death instincts   in psychoanalytic theory, the instincts responsible for the destructive aspects of human behavior (referred to as Thanatos by Freud)

decisional balance sheet   means of making decisions that considers anticipated consequences for each course of action

deference to authority   tendency to be influenced by or comply with someone who is in authority or shows signs of authority

delusions   strongly held false beliefs

denial   coping that involves not thinking about or not taking certain actions

depression   predominantly sad and hopeless mood often associated with changes in appetite, changes in sleep patterns, agitation, and feelings of worthlessness and fatigue

determinists   people who believe that all events have causes, even if the causes are not yet known

diaphragm   dome-shaped piece of thin rubber that fits over the cervix inside the woman's vagina and acts as a contraceptive

differentiation   process by which a child achieves an identity separate from the cultural group

discontinuous development   development that occurs in discrete stages

discriminative stimuli   in operant conditioning, characteristic or specific stimuli that come to signal the proper occasion for a given response

diseases of adaptation   illnesses such as ulcers or increased susceptibility to infection that result from chronic exposure to stress

disengagement   process of mutual withdrawal of the person and society, often said to begin in late middle age but especially prominent as one retires from work

divorce   ending of a marriage by an accepted legal process

dominance   high status and the potential to influence others

dopamine   chemical that affects the transmission of nerve impulses in the brain

dream analysis   analysis of a client's dreams in order to appreciate deeper meaning underlying the surface features of the dreams

drives   biological needs created by bodily deficits

dual-earner families   families in which both adult members are engaged in paid employment

E

egalitarian   favoring positions regarding equal rights and responsibilities for men and women

ego   in psychoanalytic theory, the reality-oriented portion of the personality, which utilizes learning and reasoning to satisfy id impulses in the light of real-world constraints

ego defenses   methods employed by the ego that distort experience to protect the person against threats from the id

Electra complex   in psychoanalytic theory, the counterpart in girls of the Oedipus complex in boys

endocrinologist   medical specialist of the endocrine system, which controls hormones and related bodily processes

equitable relationship   relationship in which both partners feel they are treated fairly

erectile dysfunction   inability to get or maintain an erection

erotophilia positive, nonguilty attitudes toward sex

erotophobia guilty, fearful attitudes toward sex

estrogens hormones that feminize physical appearance and facilitate ovulation

ethnic group distinctive racial, cultural, or language group

eustress Selye's term to describe productive or beneficial stress that individuals may actively seek

euthanasia painlessly putting to death someone who is suffering from an incurable illness

extended families families including all relatives by blood or marriage (parents, sons, daughters, siblings, uncles, aunts, cousins, grandparents, great grandparents, and in-laws of various types)

externalizing displaying poor adjustment by getting into trouble with other people

extramarital sex sex involving a married person and a person other than the legal spouse

F

fallopian tubes tubes in the female through which an egg passes on its way from an ovary to the uterus

false love relationships that are passed off as loving but in actuality are attempts to use or live through others

family power ability to influence the attitudes or behavior of one's spouse and children

fear of failure fear that in combination with the desire for success determines achievement-oriented behavior

fear of success fear said to occur in women who anticipate social disapproval or feel they will not be seen as feminine if they behave in achievement-oriented ways

fellatio mouth stimulation of the penis

feminine like the typical girl or woman

fictive kin people who are unrelated but close enough to be regarded as honorary family members

flirtation nonverbal communication and touching characteristic of courtship or the communication of sexual interest

formal operational stage third Piagetian stage of thinking

free association psychoanalytic procedure of having clients say whatever comes to mind without censoring it

friendly love type of authentic love that is similar to the affectionate relationship between two best friends

free rider person who benefits from a commonly held good or resource but does not contribute to the common good

friendship relationship that typically excludes sexual intimacy and is based on two or more individuals' enjoyment of one another's company

Future Shock Toffler's concept that rapidly accelerating technological and social changes impose new stresses

G

gender schema cognitive structures that organize how people perceive males and females and determine personal sex-role identification

general adaptation syndrome pattern of nonspecific physical reactions to a variety of stressors, as proposed by Selye

generativity in Erikson's theory, the developing concern in middle age for the well-being of the next generation

genital herpes sexually transmitted disease producing painful bumps on the genitals

gonorrhea common sexually transmitted disease, producing a penile discharge and burning sensation when urinating for males but often asymptomatic in females

group marriage highly open and committed form of extramarital sex in which married couples may live with one another and share spouses sexually

H

hallucinations seeing, hearing, or smelling things that do not actually exist but seem very real

hallucinogens chemicals that produce profound changes in consciousness, including hallucinations, shifts in cognitive perspective, and shifts in sensory experiences

hemisphere half of the brain

high-contact cultures cultures where people get physically close, face others, talk loudly, and establish much eye contact while conversing

homosexual person who is sexually attracted mainly to members of his or her own gender

hospice care system in which emotional and physical support as well as relief from pain are provided to the terminally ill

humanistic-existential approach psychological approach that emphasizes the positive aspects of people and focuses on their abilities to freely choose among alternatives

humanistic-existential theory a theory that views each person as an integrated whole and that takes an optimistic view of the human potential for growth and choice

hypotheses propositions tested in an experiment and denied or supported by empirical results but never proved conclusively

I

id in psychoanalytic theory, the deep, unconscious part of the personality composed of the biological, instinctual drives, which seek immediate gratification

identity crisis according to Erikson, a period in life in which the person struggles to define the "real me"

immune system complex system that protects the body by destroying foreign materials, such as bacteria, viruses, fungi, and tumors

implicit personality theory theory used by laypersons to account for the way another person's traits are seen as fitting together to form the personality

incest sexual contact between relatives

industrial economy economy that depends on the manufacture and sale of goods to sustain it

infertility biological inability to conceive children

information economy economy that depends on communication and the exchange of information to sustain it

instrumental values values that refer to the means by which goals are attained

intact, nuclear families families in which children and both biological parents live together in an independent household

integrity for Erikson, a period of contentment resulting from the acceptance of the worth of one's life in the past as well as the value of the present

interdependence conditions in which individuals or groups must depend on one another to achieve some larger goal

internalizing displaying poor adjustment by inner suffering

intimacy close relationship in which people feel that their lives are linked together

in vivo in natural environment

IUD (intrauterine device) small piece of plastic (perhaps also containing copper or hormones) that is inserted into the uterus to prevent implantation of the fertilized egg

J

joint marital role relationship relationship in which spouses expect each other to be best friends and constant companions

just world hypothesis belief that good behavior will be rewarded and wrongdoing will be punished in the long run

L

latent meaning basic conflicts, wishes, or needs such as appear in dreams, and their blocked expressions underlying overt behavior

lateralized having specific kinds of thinking and behavior controlled by each hemisphere of the brain

lesbians women who prefer other women as lovers

life instincts in psychoanalytic theory, the instincts responsible for the positive, constructive aspects of behavior (referred to as Eros by Freud)

liking feeling good about someone in general

lines words used to convey attraction and interest in a potential intimate partner

logotherapy Frankl's existential approach to therapy, which is often referred to as the therapy of meaning

longitudinal research research in which subjects are tested and retested over intervals during their lives

love deeply involved relationship in which sexual intimacy is common

low-contact cultures cultures where people maintain distance between one another, engage in little touching, avoid intense eye contact, and prefer the shoulder-to-shoulder position for conversing

lower class uneducated, unemployed, or underemployed people who struggle with poverty, live in substandard housing, and may require public welfare funds to survive

lower lower class impoverished and uneducated persons who are either chronically unemployed or engaged in menial jobs

lower middle class white-collar, or office, workers and those who have skilled blue-collar jobs in industry, construction, and agriculture

low frustration tolerance belief that intimacy and sex should be effortless and free of difficulties

M

manifest content surface features of one's dreams that one can recall or reconstruct for a therapist

marriage   legal and sometimes religiously binding relationship between a man and woman

masculine   like the typical boy or man

masculinity complex   according to psychoanalysts, a female's behaving like a male to compensate for a sense of inferiority

masturbation   self-stimulation of the genitals to produce sexual arousal and orgasm

maturation   developmental changes that are regular, preprogrammed, and relatively unaffected by environmental conditions

menopause   in women who are in their late forties or early fifties, cessation of ovulation and menstruation sometimes accompanied by physical changes such as hot flashes and mood swings

mentor relationships   relationships between junior workers and senior workers that provide support and encouragement for the young worker and satisfaction for the more senior member

meta-analysis   statistical procedure for assessing the aggregate or cumulative efficacy of a procedure such as psychotherapy by combining results across studies

middle class   unwealthy but relatively educated white-collar people whose incomes match or exceed the national average

midlife crisis   popular term used to describe a stressful period of identity crisis thought to commonly occur in middle-aged males

models   people others imitate during observational learning

monogamy   belief that the legal spouse is the only legitimate sexual partner

moral anxiety   in psychoanalytic theory, an emotional state experienced as guilt, stemming from the threat of punishment by the superego

moral development   sequence of stages based on cognitive maturity, which determine understanding of and adherence to rules defining the right way to treat others

motivation   forces or factors that energize behavior and give it direction

musturbation   Ellis's term to describe an individual's feeling of need to accomplish internally established goals

myotonia   muscular contractions

N

narcissism   psychoanalytic term for extreme absorption with oneself

need for achievement   learned desire to perform well and strive for excellence

need for affiliation   desire to seek the company of others, to value being with others, and to care for others

neurotic anxiety   in psychoanalytic theory, a fear that unconscious id impulses will find expression

nicotine   chemical in tobacco that has the capacity to alter brain chemicals and effect feelings of well-being

norms   implied or specifically stated expectations about behavior that exist in social groups, organizations, and societies

O

observational learning   learning by means of observing a live or symbolic model (sometimes referred to as modeling)

obsessive-compulsive disorder   condition in which persistent ideas, thoughts, or images senselessly invade one's consciousness and are often coupled with persistent, repetitive behaviors or desires

Oedipus complex   in psychoanalytic theory, sexual longing by a boy for the mother, which occurs during the phallic stage

operant conditioning   process by which responses become more likely when followed by desirable consequences and less likely when followed by negative ones

operative values   values that influence behavior in the immediate, concrete situation

ovary   organ in the female that produces the female sex hormones and releases eggs

overgeneralize   to apply a handful of ideas to too many situations

ovulation   release of a mature egg from a woman's ovary

P

panic attack   unpredictable attack of intense fear, often characterized by sweating, trembling, a sense of unreality, and heart palpitations

paraprofessionals   individuals employed or working as volunteers who have been trained by professional staff to perform therapeutic activities

pathogen   agent that causes disease

pedophilia   sexual contact by an adult with a child (child molestation)

penis   male sexual organ through which urine or semen passes

penis envy according to psychoanalysts, a small girl's conclusion that her clitoris is inferior to a boy's penis

permissive style parenting style characterized by considerable communication on the part of the parents in the context of little discipline and few demands on the child

Personal Attributes Questionnaire (PAQ) popular psychological measure of sex-role identification

personal growth increasing personal capacities in terms of skill, insight, or wisdom

personality pattern of characteristic thoughts, feelings, and behaviors that persists over time and situations and distinguishes one person from another

personal self-concept part of the self containing physical, behavioral, and psychological characteristics

phallic stage according to psychoanalysts, the ages of three to six, when children are supposed to be in love with their opposite-sexed parent and begin masturbation

phenomenological approach the humanistic-existential approach, which emphasizes the importance of one's perceptions

phobias persistent and irrational fears of some specific situation, object, or activity

physical guidelines cultural expectations regarding how close (in inches or feet) people will be for different kinds of social interactions

physical health a state of physical well-being and absence of illness

playful affectionate touches touches that lighten an interaction and express warm feelings with qualifications and a lack of seriousness

playful aggressive touches touches that combine mock physical aggressiveness with the expression of warm feelings

pleasure principle in psychoanalytic theory, the operational principle by which the id seeks to avoid pain and obtain pleasure

pluralistic society in which the members of minority groups and individuals from different social classes maintain independent traditions

power motivation desire to exert control over the events that occur in one's life

practical love type of false love in which loyalty exists as long as the relationship serves one's best interests

prediction the foretelling of future events or behaviors based on current knowledge

prejudice inflexible attitudes toward others based on incorrect or incomplete information

premature ejaculation sexual dysfunction in which the man has an orgasm and ejaculates too soon

prenatally in the time between conception and birth

preoperational stage first Piagetian stage of thinking

primary appraisal evaluation of the significance of an event as stressful, harmless, positive, or neutral

primary drives basic, innate drives such as hunger and thirst

problem solving complex set of cognitive and behavioral skills that include problem identification, goal selection, generation of alternatives, consideration of consequences, decision making, implementation, and evaluation

problem-solving expectancies in Rotter's approach, beliefs about how best to categorize situations in order to solve the problems presented by them

progesterone sex hormone secreted by the ovaries in the female

prostate gland that produces most of the fluid of the semen

proxemic behavior distance between people during their interactions

proximity physical accessibility to others

psychic determinism psychoanalytic notion that a person's every behavior, thought, and emotion have meaning and purpose

psychoanalysis psychotherapeutic approach that helps clients develop insight into self-destructive (defensive) behavior and to make unconscious influences conscious and subject to change

psychoanalytic theory school of psychology based on the work of Sigmund Freud that looks beyond conscious awareness to unconscious desires and impulses

psychodrama form of group therapy where members act out scenes that depict personal concerns and conflicts

psychological stress dynamic concept that reflects the discrepancy between individuals' perceptions of the demands of the environment and their perceptions of their resources when they believe their well-being is endangered

psychological well-being a subjective sense of happiness, optimism, or control that is a result of effective coping

psychology the scientific study of behavior, the goal of which is to predict, understand, and control behavior

psychosexual stages   in Freudian theory, a universal course of sexual development with a different body area serving as a focus in each stage

psychosocial stages   Erikson's term for development over the life span, which incorporates psychosexual factors but emphasizes interaction with the social environment and the resolution of crises at each stage

psychotherapy   therapy process to help clients modify feelings, thoughts, and behaviors

punishment   event that decreases the likelihood that a behavior will occur, since the latter is seen as leading to an aversive outcome

Q

quasi-father   man who is not the biological parent but who takes on a father's role and responsibilities

R

rape   forcible sexual contact with an individual without that person's consent

reality principle   in psychoanalytic theory, the operational ego principle whereby gratification is postponed until an appropriate situation is identified

reappraisal   process by which one reevaluates one's primary and secondary appraisals

reciprocation   norm that one is obliged to repay a debt, gift, or favor

reflected appraisals   self-esteem as determined by one's views of how others evaluate or react to one

reflection   psychotherapist's putting a client's feelings into words

reflexes   automatic, involuntary reactions

reliability   the extent to which a test or observation method is consistent in measuring

reminiscence   process in which review and recall of the past can hasten the stage of integrity (sometimes referred to as life review)

repression   in psychoanalytic theory, an unconscious ego defense in which threatening impulses or thoughts are involuntarily banished to the unconscious

research   systematic collection of observations to test their consistency with a hypothesis or theory

respect   looking up to someone

rhythm   method of birth control that involves abstaining from sexual intercourse during the fertile days of the woman's menstrual cycle

role strain   psychological distress from trying to do too much or fulfill too many contradictory responsibilities at once

romantic love   type of authentic love based on intense passion for and identification with a beloved

S

scarcity principle   principle that things limited in supply are more valuable and desirable

schema   according to Piaget, internal psychological structures or organizations

schizophrenia   severe psychological disorder involving a tendency to withdraw from social involvement, disjointed language and thought processes, and inappropriate emotional responses

scrotum   pouch of skin containing the testes

secondary appraisal   evaluation of a person's coping resources and options

secondary drives   learned drives, such as fear, guilt, and need for approval

secret affair   extramarital liaison that occurs without the awareness of the other spouse

segregated marital role relationship   relationship in which spouses spend little time together and have very different duties

self   perception of oneself and its associated values; the I or the me

self-actualization   tendency or desire to become all that one is capable of becoming

self-centered love   type of false love based on exploitation and game playing

self-control-procedures   keeping track of one's behavior by self-monitoring, learning to set realistic goals, and reinforcing oneself

self-disclosure   sharing personal information with others

self-efficacy   belief that one can successfully execute the behaviors required in a given situation

self-esteem   one's overall level of self-evaluation, self-regard, or self-confidence

self-ideals   self as one would like it to be

selfism   excessive preoccupation with oneself

self-schemata   broad generalizations people make about themselves that then affect such things as information processing

self-system   Sullivan's term to describe the self as consisting of the good-me, the bad-me, and the not-me.

sensate focus   exercises prescribed by sex therapists to increase sexual response

sensitivity groups form of psychotherapy where groups are used to nurture personal awareness and growth

sensorimotor stage Piagetian stage for the individual from birth to two years of age

separation agreement legal contract describing financial and other rights and responsibilities of a married couple that are no longer living together

set point theory theory that weight is controlled by physiological mechanisms that increase eating behavior when weight is too low and decrease eating behavior when weight is too high

sex biological sex of an individual (male versus female), which is assigned at birth

sex differences differences between males and females in appearance, abilities, behavior, and personality

sex hormones powerful chemicals produced by the endocrine glands that influence physical appearance and reproduction

sex identity labeling oneself as a male or female

sexism prejudices against men or women that harm self-esteem and opportunities for advancement or growth

sex role(s) culturally approved way(s) of being a girl or boy, man or woman

sex-role attitudes beliefs about the rightness or wrongness of society's sexual division of labor

sex-role behaviors actions orchestrated by the dictates of expected sex roles

sex-role development process by which children and adolescents learn culturally approved sex roles

sex-role identification self-description of psychological sex, regardless of biological sex and sex identity

sex-role stereotypes correct or incorrect beliefs about the qualities that characterize males and females

sexual division of labor economic and family responsibilities that are assigned to each sex

sex dysfunctions problems with sexual responding that cause mental distress, including erection problems in men and orgasm problems in women

sexual exclusivity expectation that a partner or spouse will not have sex outside the primary relationship

sexual harassment unwanted imposition of sexual requirements in the context of a relationship of unequal power, such as boss/employee or professor/student

sexually compatible partners who enjoy and desire sex equally

sexually open marriage marriage in which the spouses agree to permit each partner to have sexual relationships with other partners

sexual strategies moves taken to influence a partner to have increased physical intimacy or to avoid it

shaping in operant conditioning, the gradual molding of behaviors into the final desired behavior through reward

similarity shared qualities, interests, or attitudes

simple phobias fears of specific commonplace objects or situations, such as heights or spiders

single living independently from a sexual partner

single-parent families families headed by only one parent, usually the mother

situational management of overeating behavior-control strategy to reduce cues in the environment that stimulate overeating and strengthen cues in the environment that signal alternatives to overeating

social class division in society based on income and rank

social comparison comparing oneself to others, which in turn, affects one's level of self-esteem

social discrimination lesser treatment of others based on their race, religion, sex, or ethnic background

social facade front, or image, people present to others in order to look good

social interest according to Adler, a predisposition nurtured by experience to contribute to society

socialization process by which a child comes to resemble the other members of the cultural group

social learning theory learning theory of personality that describes the two-way interaction between the individual and the environment

social self-concepts self as one believes others view it

social support personal contacts available from others that may provide material and emotional aid

spillover influences flowing from work to family life and from family life back to work

stage period in life in which a particular behavior or psychological characteristic asserts itself

status respect due to an individual by virtue of his or her place in society

stereotypes rigidly held misconceptions about individuals or groups, particularly minority groups

stimulants chemicals that activate the central nervous system and can produce feelings of euphoria, confidence, and increased alertness

stress inoculation training   treatment procedure developed by Meichenbaum, whereby individuals are taught a variety of affective, cognitive, physiological, and interpersonal coping skills

substance abuse   inability to stop using a drug, with impairment in work or social functioning

substance dependence   severe form of disorder, involving the development of a physical tolerance of a drug and withdrawal symptoms if the drug is reduced or stopped

successive approximation   making reinforcement contingent upon increasingly more demanding behaviors

superego   in psychoanalytic theory, the conscience, representing the ideals, values, and standards of society as acquired from the parents or parent figures

supervisor-worker relationships   relationships between a supervisor and worker, including support, provision of information, and encouragement on the part of the supervisor and task performance on the part of the worker

support group   close network of family and friends who provide dependable economic and emotional support

swinging   situation in which married couples exchange partners and in some cases have group sex with other married individuals whom they know only slightly

systematic desensitization   treatment procedure developed by Wolpe, whereby individuals are taught to relax and then asked to imagine stressful scenes along a hierarchy from least to most distressing

T

technological change   change in the workplace resulting from a technological process or the use of machinery and automation in industry

tension reduction   variety of means to help individuals reduce the level and impact of stress

terminal values   values that refer to ultimate goals or ends

testes   sex glands in the male (located in the scrotum)

testosterone   hormone secreted by the testes in the male

third force   Maslow's emphasis on experience, choice, creativity, and self-actualization

theory of economic competition   theory that prejudice arises against some groups because they represent a threat for economic resources

time-out procedures   procedures used in behavior therapy to place the individual in a setting that removes reinforcement for a time

traditional   believing women should be homemakers and mothers, whereas men should be the economic and political leaders

transactional   referring to the fact that not only do environmental events affect individuals but individuals affect others

transference   process by which clients transfer important feelings and behavioral reactions usually expressed toward others toward the therapist

tubal ligation   surgical method of female sterilization involving severing of the fallopian tubes

Type A behavior   behavior of hard-driving, competitive, hostile-aggressive individuals who have a great sense of time urgency

U

unconditional positive regard   For Rogers, total and genuine love and respect for the individual

unconscious motivation   term describing the notion that much of what people do, think, and feel is motivated by unconscious forces

understanding   the ability to see the relationships between behaviors and events in terms of some larger scheme or idea

uniformity myth   dubious practice of collapsing clients with different problems, treatments, or outcome measures into one group and overlooking differences

upper lower class   semiskilled workers who are less highly paid than members of the lower middle class

upper middle class   affluent businesspeople and professionals whose status and educational advantages are surpassed only by the wealthiest members of society

uterus   organ in the female in which the fetus develops

V

vagina   tubular organ in the female in which the penis is inserted during intercourse and through which a baby passes during birth

values   things regarded by a person as good, desirable, or preferred

vasectomy   surgical method of male sterilization involving severing of the vas deferens

vasocongestion engorgement of blood in the vessels of a region, such as the genitals

ventilation of feelings expression and sharing of feelings with others

vicarious reinforcement achievement of reinforcement by observing a model's being reinforced

vicious cycle pattern of maladaptive behavior that elicits reactions from others that in turn strengthen the maladaptive behavior

violent marriage marriage characterized by physical assaults on a spouse (usually the wife)

Vocational Preference Inventory scale developed by Holland to assess personal interest in different types of occupations

vulva external genitals of the female

W

widowed having lost a marital partner through death

work human activity that produces something of acknowledged value

working class people with limited formal education earning average or below-average income, usually employed in skilled or semiskilled blue-collar occupations

REFERENCES

A

Abbot, D., & G. W. Brody (1985). The relation of child age, gender, and number of children to the marital adjustment of wives. *Journal of Marriage and the Family, 47,* 77–84.

Achenbach, T. M., & C. S. Edelbrock (1981). Behavioral problems and competencies reported by parents of normal and disturbed children aged four through sixteen. *Monographs of the Society for Research in Child Development, 46*(1, Serial No. 188).

Achenbach, T. M., & C. S. Edelbrock (1983). *Manual for the Child Behavior Checklist and Revised Child Behavior Profile.* Burlington, VT: Queen City Printers.

Adler, A. (1939). *Social interest: A challenge to mankind.* New York: Putnam.

Adler, R. (1981). *Psychoneuroimmunology.* New York: Academic Press.

Adorno, T. W., E. Frenkel-Brunswick, D. J. Levinson, & R. N. Sanford (1950). *The authoritarian personality.* New York: Harper & Row.

Aiken, L. R. (1982). *Later life* (2nd ed.). New York: Holt, Rinehart & Winston.

Ainsworth, M. D. S., & S. M. Bell (1970). Attachment, exploitation and separation: Illustrated by the behavior of one year olds in strange situations. *Child Development, 41,* 49–67.

Al-Issa, I. (1980). *The psychopathology of women.* Englewood Cliffs, NJ: Prentice-Hall/Spectrum.

Al-Issa, I. (1982a). Gender and adult psychopathology. In I. Al-Issa (Ed.), *Gender and psychopathology.* New York: Academic Press, 83–101..

Al-Issa, I. (1982b). Gender and child psychopathology. In I. Al-Issa (Ed.), *Gender and psychopathology.* New York: Academic Press, 53–81.

Allgeier, A. R. (1983). Sexuality and gender roles in the second half of life. In E. R. Allgeier & N. B. McCormick (Eds.), *Changing boundaries: Gender roles and sexual behavior.* Palo Alto, CA: Mayfield, 135–157.

Allgeier, E. R., & A. R. Allgeier (1984). *Sexual interactions.* Lexington, MA: Heath.

Allgeier, E. R., & N. B. McCormick (Eds.) (1983). *Changing boundaries: Gender roles and sexual behavior.* Palo Alto, CA: Mayfield.

Allport, G. W. (1961). *Patterns and growth in personality.* New York: Harcourt, Brace & World.

Allport, G. W., P. E. Vernon, & G. Lindzey (1960). *A study of values* (3rd ed.). Boston: Houghton Mifflin..

Alston, W. P. (1971). Comments on Kohlberg's "From is to ought." In T. Mischel (Ed.), *Cognitive development and genetic epistomology.* New York: Academic Press.

American Psychiatric Association (1980). *DSM-III: Diagnostic and statistical manual of mental disorders* (3rd ed.). Washington, DC: American Psychiatric Association.

Anderson, T. B. (1984). Widowhood as a life transition: Its impact on kinship ties. *Journal of Marriage and the Family, 46,* 105–114.

Antonovsky, A. (1979). *Health, stress and coping.* San Francisco, Jossey-Bass.

Argote, L., & P. S. Goodman (1984). *Human dimensions of robotics.* Proceedings of the World Congress on the Human Aspects of Automation, MM84-640. Dearborn, MI: Society of Manufacturing Engineers.

Argote, L., & P. S. Goodman, & D. Schkade (1983). The human side of robotics: How workers react to a robot. *Sloan Management Review, 24,* 31–41.

Argyle, M., & M. Henderson (1984). The rules of friendship. *Journal of Social and Personal Relationships, 1,* 211–237.

Arnkoff, D. (1983). Common specific factors in cognitive therapy. In M. Lambert (Ed.), *Psychotherapy and patient relationships.* Homewood, IL: Dorsey Press.

Aronson, E., & N. Osherow (1980). Cooperation, prosocial behavior, and academic performance: Experiments in the desegrated classroom. In L. Bickman (Ed.), *Applied Social Psychology Annual* (Vol. 1). Beverly Hills, CA: Sage.

Ashmore, R. D., & F. K. Del Boca (1976). Psychological approaches to understanding intergroups conflicts. In P. A. Katz (Ed.), *Towards the elimination of racism.* Elmsford, NY: Pergamon Press.

Atchley, R. C. (1976). *The sociology of retirement.* Cambridge, MA: Shenkman.

Atkeson, B. M., et al. (1982). Victims of rape: Repeated assessment of depressive symptoms. *Journal of Consulting and Clinical Psychology, 50,* 96–102.

Atkinson, J. W. (1984). *An introduction to motivation.* Princeton, NJ: Van Nostrand Reinhold.

Atkinson, J., & T. L. Huston (1984). Sex role orientation and division of labor early in marriage. *Journal of Personality and Social Psychology, 46,* 330–345.

Ayalon, D. (1983). Coping with terrorism: The Israeli case. In D. Meichenbaum & M. Jaremko (Eds.), *Stress reduction and prevention.* New York: Plenum Press.

Axelrod, R. (1984). *The evolution of cooperation.* New York: Basic Books.

B

Babladelis, G. (1984). *The study of personality.* New York: Holt, Rinehart & Winston.

Baker, E. L. (1985). Psychoanalysis and psychoanalytic psychotherapy. In S. J. Lynn & J. P. Garske (Eds.), *Contemporary psychotherapies: Models and methods.* Columbus, OH: Merrill Publishing Co..

Balswick, J. O., & C. W. Peek (1975). The inexpressive male: A tragedy of American society. In J. W. Petras (Ed.), *Sex: Male; Gender: Masculine.* Port Washington, NY: Alfred Publishing Co., 120–128.

Bandura, A. (1974). Behavior theories and models of man. *American Psychologist, 29,* 859–869.

Bandura, A. (1977). *Social learning theory.* Englewood Cliffs, NJ: Prentice-Hall.

Bandura, A. (1982). Self-efficacy mechanism in human agency. *American Psychologist, 33,* 344–358.

Bandura, A. (1986). From thought to action: Mechanisms of personal agency. *New Zealand Journal of Psychology, 15,* 1–17.

Bandura, A., E. B. Blanchard, & B. Ritter (1963). The relative efficacy of desensitization and modeling approaches for inducing behavioral, affective, and attitudinal changes. *Journal of Personality and Social Psychology, 13,* 173–199.

Bandura, A., & R. Walters (1963). *Social learning and personality development.* New York: Holt, Rinehart & Winston.

Barbach, L. G. (1975). *For yourself: The fulfillment of female sexuality.* New York: Anchor Press/Doubleday.

Bardwick, J. M. (1979). *In transition: How feminism, sexual liberation, and the search for self-fulfillment have altered our lives.* New York: Holt, Rinehart & Winston.

Barrett, J. E. (1983). Interrelationships between behavior and pharmacology as factors determining the effects of nicotine. *Pharmacology, Biochemistry and Behavior, 19,* 1027–1029.

Bart, P. (1980). Avoiding rape: A study of victims and avoiders. Final report to the National Institute of Mental Health, MH29311, Rockville, MD.

Bateson, G., D. Jackson, J. Haley, & J. Weakland (1956). Towards a theory of schizophrenia. *Behavioral Science, 1,* 251–264.

Baum, A., R. Fleming, & J. Singer (1982). Stress at Three Mile Island: Applying psychological impact analysis. In C. Beckman (Ed.), *Applied social psychology annual* (Vol. 3). Beverly Hills, CA: Sage.

Baum, A., J. Singer, & C. Baum (1981). Stress and the environment. *Journal of Social Issues, 37,* 4–35.

Baumrind, D. (1968). Authoritarian vs. authoritative control. *Adolescence, 3,* 255–272.

Beach, F. A. (1976). Cross-species comparisons and the human heritage. *Archives of Sexual Behavior, 5,* 469–485.

Beck, A. T. (1976). *Cognitive therapy and the emotional disorders.* New York: International Universities Press.

Beck, A. T., A. J. Rush, B. F. Shaw, & G. Emery (1979). *Cognitive therapy of depression: A treatment manual.* New York: Guilford Press.

Beckman, L. J. (1982). Communication, power, and the influence of social networks in couple decisions on fertility. In R. A. Bulato & R. D. Lee (Eds.), *Determinants of fertility in developing countries* (Vol. 2). New York: Academic Press, 856–878.

Beckman, L. J., & B. Bosak-Houser (1979). The more you have, the more you do: The relationship between wife's employment, sex-role attitudes, and household behavior. *Psychology of Women Quarterly, 4,* 160–174.

Bell, A. P., & M. S. Weinberg (1978). *Homosexualities.* New York: Simon & Schuster.

Bell, A. P., M. S. Weinberg, & S. K. Hammersmith (1981). *Sexual preference.* Bloomington: Indiana University Press.

Bell, R. R. (1983). *Marriage and family interaction* (5th ed.). Homewood, IL: Dorsey Press.

Bem, S. L. (1974). The measurement of psychological androgyny. *Journal of Consulting and Clinical Psychology, 42,* 155–162.

Bem, S. L. (1981). Gender schema theory: A cognitive account of sex typing. *Psychological Review, 88,* 354–364.

Bennett, W., & J. Guron (1982). *The dieter's dilemma.* New York: Basic Books.

Benson, D. J., & G. E. Thomson (1982). Sexual harassment on a university campus: The confluence of authority relations, sexual interest, and gender stratification. *Social Problems, 29,* 236–251.

Benson, H. (1976). *The relaxation response.* New York: Avon.

Bergin, A., & M. Lambert (1978). The evaluation of therapeutic outcomes. In S. Garfield & A. Bergin (Eds.), *Handbook of psychotherapy and behavior change.* New York: Wiley.

Bernstein, A. C., & P. A. Cowan (1975). Children's concepts of how people get babies. *Child Development, 46,* 77–92.

Bernstein, D., & T. Borkovec (1973). *Progressive relaxation training: A manual for the helping professions.* Champaign, IL: Research Press.

Berscheid, E., & E. Hatfield-Walster (1969). *Interpersonal attraction.* Reading, MA: Addison-Wesley.

Berscheid, E., & E. Walster (1974). A little bit about love. In T. L. Huston (Ed.), *Foundations of interpersonal attraction.* New York: Academic Press, 355–381.

Bickman, L. (1974). The social power of a uniform. *Journal of Applied Social Psychology, 4,* 47–61.

Bieber, I., et al. (1962). *Homosexuality: A psychoanalytic study of male homosexuals.* New York: Basic Books.

Billings, A. G., & R. H. Moos (1981). The role of coping responses and social resources in altering the impact of stressful life events. *Journal of Behavioral Medicine, 4,* 139–157.

Blakeslee, S. (1984, December 25). Smoking depicted as an addiction with many lures. *The New York Times*, 33–34.

Bleuler, E. (1950). *Dementia praecox, or the group of schizophrenias.* Translated by J. Zinkin. New York: International Universities Press. Originally published in 1911.

Blood, R. O., Jr., & M. C. Blood (1979). Amicable divorce: A new lifestyle. *Alternative Lifestyles, 2,* 483–498.

Bloom, B. (1973). *Community mental health: A historical and critical analysis.* Morristown, NJ: General Corporation Press.

Bombardiere, M. (1981). *The baby decision: How to make the most important choice of your life.* New York: Rawson, Wade.

Borysenko, J. (1984). Stress, coping, and the immune system. In J. Matarazzo, S. Weiss, J. Herd, N. Miller, & S. Weiss (Eds.), *Behavioral health: A handbook of health enhancement and disease prevention.* New York: Wiley.

Boss, M. (1963). *Psychoanalysis and Daseinsanalysis.* New York: Basic Books.

Botwinick, J. (1984). *Aging and behavior* (3rd ed.). New York: Springer.

Bourne, L. E., Jr., & B. R. Ekstrand (1982). *Psychology: Its principles and meanings* (4th ed.). New York: Holt, Rinehart & Winston.

Brooks-Gunn, J., & W. S. Matthews (1979). *He and she: How children develop their sex-role identity.* Englewood Cliffs, NJ: Prentice-Hall/Spectrum..

Broverman, I. K., D. M. Broverman, F. E. Clarkson, P. S. Rosenkrantz, & S. R. Vogel (1970). Sex-role stereotypes and clinical judgments of mental health. *Journal of Consulting and Clinical Psychology, 34,* 1–7.

Broverman, I. K., S. R. Vogel, D. M. Broverman, F. E. Clarkson, & P. S. Rosenkrantz (1972). Sex-role stereotypes: A current appraisal. *Journal of Social Issues, 28,* 59–78.

Bruch, H. (1973). *Eating disorders.* New York: Basic Books.

Bruner, J. S., & R. Tagiuri (1954). The perception of people. In G. Lindzey (Ed.), *Handbook of social psychology* (2 vols.). Cambridge, MA: Addison-Wesley.

Bukowski, C. (1972). "The shoelace." *Mockingbird, wish me luck.* Los Angeles: Black Sparrow Press, 114–117.

Burchardt, C. J., & L. A. Serbin (1982). Psychological androgyny and personality adjustment in college and psychiatric populations. *Sex Roles, 8,* 835–851.

Burgess, A. W., & L. L. Holmstrom (1974). *Rape: Victims of crisis.* Bowie, MD: Robert J. Brady.

Burke, D. M., & L. L. Light (1981). Memory and aging: The role of retrieval processes. *Psychological Bulletin, 90,* 513–546.

Butler, R. N. (1961). Re-awakening interest. *Nursing Homes, 10,* 8–19.

Butler, R. N., & M. I. Lewis (1982). *Aging and mental health* (3rd ed.). St. Louis: Mosby.

Byrne, D. (1971). *The attraction paradigm.* New York: Academic Press.

Byrne, D. (1983). Sex without contraception. In D. Byrne & W. A. Fisher (Eds.), *Adolescents, sex, and contraception.* Hillsdale, NJ: Lawrence Erlbaum.

Byrne, D., & K. Kelley (1981). *An introduction to personality* (3rd ed.). Englewood Cliffs, NJ: Prentice-Hall.

C

Calderone, M. S., & J. W. Ramey (1983). *Talking with your child about sex: Questions and answers for children from birth to puberty.* New York: Random House.

Caldwell, M. A., & L. A. Peplau (1982). Sex differences in same-sex friendship. *Sex Roles, 8,* 721–732.

Callan, V. J. (1983). Perceptions of parenthood and childlessness: A comparison of mothers and voluntarily childless wives. *Population and Environment, 6,* 179–189.

Campbell, A. (1982). Gender and crime. In I. Al-Issa (Ed.), *Gender and psychopathology.* New York: Academic Press, 237–254.

Cann, A., & A. K. Garrett (1984). Sex stereotype impacts on competence ratings by children. *Sex Roles, 11,* 333–343.

Canter, R. J., & B. E. Meyerowitz (1984). Sex-role stereotypes: Self-reports of behavior. *Sex Roles, 10,* 293–306.

Carlson, B. E. (1984). The father's contribution to child care: Effects on children's perceptions of parental roles. *American Journal of Orthopsychiatry, 54,* 123–136.

Chapman, J. (1966). The early symptoms of schizophrenia. *British Journal of Psychiatry, 112,* 225–251.

Chesler, P. (1972). *Women and madness.* Garden City, NY: Doubleday.

Chodoff, P., S. Freedman, & D. Hamburg (1964). Stress, defenses, and coping behavior: Observations in parents of children with malignant disease. *American Journal of Psychiatry, 120,* 743–749.

Cialdini, R. B. (1984). *Influence: How and why people agree to things.* New York: Morrow.

Clark, R. D., III, & E. Hatfield (1981). *Gender differences in receptivity to sexual offers.* Available from Dr. Elaine Hatfield, Psychology Department, 2430 Campus Road, Honolulu, HI 96822.

Clarke-Stewart, A., S. Friedman, & J. Koch (1985). *Child development: A topical approach.* New York: Wiley.

Clatworthy, N. (1980). *Morals and the ever-changing college student.* Paper presented at the North Central Sociological Meetings, Dayton, OH.

Cobb, S., & R. M. Rose (1973). Hypertension, diabetes and peptic ulcer in air traffic controllers. *Journal of the American Medical Association, 224,* 489–492.

Cochran, S. D., & L. A. Peplau (1985). Value orientations in heterosexual relationships. *Psychology of Women Quarterly,* 477–488.

Cohen, F., & R. Lazarus (1979). Coping with stress of illness. In G. Stone, F. Cohen, N. Adler & Associates (Eds.), *Health psychology: A handbook.* San Francisco: Jossey-Bass.

Cohen, L. (1968). *Selected poems 1956–1968.* New York: Viking.

Cook, S. (1979). *Social science and school desegregation: Did we mislead the Supreme Court?* Boulder, CO: Institute of Behavioral Science, University of Colorado.

Cooley, C. H. (1902). *Human nature and the social order*. New York: Scribner's.

Coopersmith, S. (1967). *The antecedents of self-esteem*. San Francisco: W. H. Freeman.

Corcoran, M., G. J. Duncan, & M. S. Hill (1984). The economic fortunes of women and children: Lessons from the panel study of income dynamics. *Signs: Journal of Women in Culture and Society, 10*, 232–248.

Costa, P. T., Jr., & R. R. McCrae (1985). Hypochondriasis, neuroticism, and aging: When are somatic complaints unfounded? *American Psychologist, 40*, 19–28.

Courtney, A. E., & T. W. Whipple (1983). *Sex stereotyping in advertising*. Lexington, MA: Heath.

Cousins, N. (1976). Anatomy of an illness (as perceived by the patient). *New England Journal of Medicine, 195*, 1458–1463.

Crouter, A. C. (1984a). Participative work as an influence on human development. *Journal of Applied Developmental Psychology, 5*, 71–91.

Crouter, A. C. (1984b). Spillover from family to work: The neglected side of the work-family interface. *Human Relations, 37*(6), 425–442.

D

Dacey, J. S. (1979). *Adolescents today*. Santa Monica, CA: Goodyear Publishing Company.

Damon, W. (1983). *Social and personality development*. New York: Norton.

Darity, W. A., Jr., & S. L. Myers, Jr. (1984). Does welfare dependency cause female headship? The case of the black family. *Journal of Marriage and the Family, 46*, 765–779.

Davidson, M., & C. Cooper (1983). *Stress and the woman manager*. New York: St. Martin's Press.

Deaux, K. (1976a). *The behavior of men and women*. Monterey, CA: Brooks/Cole.

Deaux, K. (1976b). Sex: A perspective on the attribution process. In J. H. Harvey, W. J. Ickes, & R. F. Kidd (Eds.), *New directions in attribution research* (Vol. 1). Hillsdale, NJ: Lawrence Erlbaum.

DeLamater, J., & P. MacCorquodale (1979). *Premarital sexuality: Attitudes, relationships, and behavior*. Madison: University of Wisconsin Press.

DeMaris, A., & G. R. Lesie (1984). Cohabitation with the future spouse: Its influence upon marital satisfaction and communication. *Journal of Marriage and the Family, 46*, 77–84.

Dillard, J. M. (1985). *Lifelong career planning*. Columbus, OH: Merrill Publishing Co.

Dimsdale, J. (1974). The coping behavior of Nazi camp survivors. *American Journal of Psychiatry, 131*, 792–797.

Dimsdale, J. (1980). *The holocaust: A multidisciplinary study*. Washington, DC: Hemispheric Press.

Dolgun, A. (1975). *Alexander Dolgun's story: An American in the Gulag*. New York: Knopf.

Doyle, J. A. (1985). *Sex and gender: The human experience*. Dubuque, IA: Wm. C. Brown.

Dreyfus-Gray, J. (1983). The married professional woman: An examination of her role conflicts and coping strategies. *Psychology of Women Quarterly, 4*, 235–243.

Dryden, W. (1985). Marital therapy: The rational-emotive approach. In W. Dryden (Ed.), *Marital therapy in Britain: Context and therapeutic approaches* (Vol. 1). London: Harper & Row, 195–221.

Duck, S. W. (1977). Personality similarity and friendship choice: Similarity of what, when? In S. Duck (Ed.), *Theory and practice in interpersonal attraction*. London: Academic Press, 301–316.

Durkheim, E. (1952). *Suicide*. Translated by J. A. Spaulding & G. Simpson. London: Routledge & Kegan Paul.

D'Zurilla, P., & A. Nezu (1982). Social problem-solving in adults. In P. Kendall (Ed.), *Advances in cognitive-behavioral research and therapy* (Vol. 1). New York: Academic Press.

E

Eagly, A. H. (1983). Gender and social influence: A social psychological analysis. *American Psychologist, 38*, 971–981.

Eagly, A. H., & V. J. Steffen (1984). Gender stereotypes stem from the distribution of women and men into social roles. *Journal of Personality and Social Psychology, 46*, 735–754.

Eidelson, R. J., & N. Epstein (1982). Cognition and relationship maladjustment: Development of a measure of dysfunctional relationship beliefs. *Journal of Consulting and Clinical Psychology, 50*, 715–720.

Ellis, A. (1962). *Reason and emotion in psychotherapy*. New York: Lyle Stuart Press.

Ellis, A. (1971). Emotional education in the classroom: The Living School. *Journal of Clinical Child Psychology, 1*, 19–22.

Ellis, A. (1977). Sex and love problems in women. In A. Ellis & R. Grieger (Eds.), *Handbook of rational-emotive therapy*. New York: Academic Press, 153–169.

Ellis, A. (1978). Speaker on cassette recording. *Conquering the dire need for love*. New York: Institute for Rational-Emotive Therapy, 45 East 65th Street, New York, NY 10021.

Ellis, A. (1986). Rational-emotive therapy (RET) applied to relationship therapy. *Journal of Rational-Emotive Therapy, 4*, 4–21.

Elpern, S., & S. A. Karp (1984). Sex-role orientation and depressive symptomatology. *Sex Roles, 10*, 987–992.

Emery, R. E. (1982). Interparental conflict and the children of discord and divorce. *Psychological Bulletin, 92*, 310–330.

Epstein, N., & R. J. Eidelson (1981). Unrealistic beliefs of clinical couples: Their relationship to expectations, goals and satisfaction. *American Journal of Family Therapy, 9*, 13–22.

Epstein, N., & A. M. Williams (1981). Behavioral approaches to the treatment of marital discord. In G. P. Sholevar (Ed.), *The handbook of marriage and marital therapy*. New York: Spectrum, 219–286.

Epstein, S. (1980). The self-concept: A review and the proposal of an integrated theory of personality. In E. Staub (3rd ed.), *Personality: Basic aspects and current research*. Englewood Cliffs, NJ: Prentice-Hall.

Erbes, J. A., & J. J. C. Hedderson (1984). A longitudinal examination of the separation/divorce process. *Journal of Marriage and the Family, 46*, 937–941.

Erikson, E. H. (1963). *Childhood and society* (2nd ed.). New York: Norton.

Erikson, E. H. (1964). *Insight and responsibility*. New York: Norton.

Eysenck, H. (1952). The effects of psychotherapy: An evaluation. *Journal of Consulting Psychology, 16*, 319–324.

F

Falbo, T. (1977). Relationships between sex, sex role, and social influence. *Psychology of Women Quarterly, 2*, 62–72.

Falbo, T. (1982). PAQ types and power strategies used in intimate relationships. *Psychology of Women Quarterly, 6*, 399–405.

Falloon, I. R. H., J. L. Boyd, C. W. McGill, M. Williamson, & J. Razani (1985). Family management in the prevention of morbidity of schizophrenia: Clinical outline of a two-year longitudinal study. *Archives of General Psychiatry, 42*, 887–896.

Fenigstein, A. (1984). Self-consciousness and the overprotection of self as a target. *Journal of Personality and Social Psychology, 47*, 860–870.

Feshbach, S. (1970). Aggression. In P. H. Mussen (Ed.), *Carmichael's manual of child psychology* (3rd ed., Vol. 2). New York: Wiley, 159–259.

Festinger, L. (1957). *A theory of cognitive dissonance*. Stanford, CA: Stanford University Press.

Fidell, L. S. (1982). Gender and drug use and abuse. In I. Al-Issa (Ed.), *Gender and psychopathology*. New York: Academic Press, 221–236.

Finkelhor, D. (1980). Sex among siblings: A survey on prevalence, variety and effects. *Archives of Sexual Behavior, 9*, 171–194.

Fishman, S. M., & D. V. Sheehan (1985, April). Anxiety and panic: Their cause and treatment. *Psychology Today*, 26–32.

Folkins, C. H., & W. E. Sime (1981). Physical fitness training and mental and health. *American Psychologist, 36*, 373–389.

Folkman, S. (1984). Personal control and stress and coping processes: A theoretical analysis. *Journal of Personality and Social Psychology, 46*, 839–852.

Folkman, S., R. S. Lazarus, R. J. Gruen, & A. DeLongis (1986). Appraisal, coping, health status and psychological symptoms. *Journal of Personality and Social Psychology, 50*, 571–579.

Fox, M., & H. L. Lipton (1983). AIDS—Two years later. *New England Journal of Medicine, 309*, 609–610.

Frank, J. (1973). *Persuasion and healing*. New York: Schocken Books.

Frankenhaeuser, M. (1979). Psychoneuroendocrine ap-

proaches to the study of emotion as related to stress and coping. In R. Dienstbier (Ed.), *1978 Nebraska Symposium on motivation*. Lincoln, NE: University of Nebraska Press.

Frankenhaeuser, M. (1980). Psychobiological aspects of life stress. In S. Levine & H. Ursin (Eds.), *Coping and health*. New York: Plenum Press.

Frankl, V. E. (1963). *Man's search for meaning*. New York: Washington Square Press.

Fredrich, L. K., & A. H. Stein (1975). Prosocial television and young children: The effects of verbal labeling and role playing on learning and behavior. *Child Development, 46*, 27–38.

Freebody, P., & C. D. Baker (1985). Children's first schoolbooks: Introduction to the culture of literacy. *Harvard Educational Review, 55*, 381–393.

French, E. G. (1956). Motivation as a variable in work partner selection. *Journal of Abnormal and Social Psychology, 53*, 96–99.

Freud, A. (1946). *Ego and the mechanisms of defense*. New York: International Universities Press.

Freud, S. (1959a). Civilized sexual morality and modern nervous illness. In the *Standard edition of the complete works of Sigmund Freud* (Vol. 12). London: Hogarth Press (1908).

Freud, S. (1959b). Some psychological consequences of the anatomical distinction between the sexes. In J. Strachey (Ed. & Trans.), *Collected papers of Sigmund Freud* (Vol. 5). New York: Basic Books, 186–197. Original work published in 1925.

Freud, S. (1964). New introductory lectures. In the *Standard edition of the complete works of Sigmund Freud* (Vol. 12). London: Hogarth Press (1933).

Freud, S. (1965). Femininity. In J. Strachey (Ed. & Trans.), *New introductory lectures on psychoanalysis*. New York: Norton, 99–119. Original work published in 1933.

Freud, S. (1969). *An outline of psychoanalysis*. Translated by J. Strachey. New York: Norton. Original work published in 1940.

Friedman, M., & R. Rosenman (1974). *Type A behavior and your heart*. Greenwich, CT: Fawcett Publications.

Frieze, I. H., J. Knoble, C. Washburn, & G. Zomnir (1979, November). *Psychological factors in violent marriages*. NIMH Grant No. 1, R01 MH 30193. Pittsburgh: University of Pittsburgh, Department of Psychology.

Furstenberg, F. F., Jr., J. L. Peterson, C. Winquist-Nord, & N. Zill (1983). The life course of children of divorce: Marital disruption and parental contact. *American Sociological Review, 48*, 656–668.

Furstenberg, F. F., Jr., & G. B. Spanier (1984). *Recycling the family: Remarriage after divorce*. Beverly Hills, CA: Sage.

G

Gartrell, N. K. (1982). Hormones and homosexuality. In W. Paul et al. (Eds.), *Homosexuality: Social, psychological and biological issues*. Beverly Hills, CA: Sage.

Geiwitz, J., & J. Moursund (1979). *Approaches to personality: An introduction to people.* Monterey, CA: Brooks/Cole.

Gerbner, G. (1972). Violence in television drama: Trends and symbolic functions. In G. Comstock, A. Rubenstein, & J. Murray (Eds.), *Television and social behavior* (Vol. 2). Washington, DC: U.S. Government Printing Office.

Gersh, E. S., & I. Gersh (1981). *Biology of women.* Baltimore: University Park Press.

Gilligan, C. (1977). In a different voice: Women's conceptions of self and of morality. *Harvard Educational Review, 47,* 481–517.

Glass, D. (1977). *Behavior patterns, stress and coronary disease.* Hillsdale: NJ: Lawrence Erlbaum Associates.

Glass, D., & J. Singer (1972). *Urban stress: Experiments in noise and social stressors.* New York: Academic Press.

Glenn, N. D. (1975). Psychological well-being in the postparental stage: Some evidence from national surveys. *Journal of Marriage and the Family, 37,* 105–110.

Glenn, N. D. (1985, June). Children of divorce. *Psychology Today,* 68–69.

Glenn, N. D., & C. N. Weaver (1979). Attitudes toward premarital, extramarital, and homosexual relations in the U.S. in the 1970s. *Journal of Sex Research, 15,* 108–118.

Glesner, G., B. Green, & C. Winget (1981). *Prolonged effects of disaster: A study of Buffalo Street.* New York: Academic Press.

Glick, P. C., & G. B. Spanier (1980). Married and unmarried cohabitation in the United States. *Journal of Marriage and the Family, 42,* 19–30.

Gold, D., & D. Andres (1978). Relations between maternal employment and development of nursery school children. *Canadian Journal of Behavioural Science, 10,* 116–129.

Goldfried, M., & G. Davison (1976). *Clinical behavior therapy.* New York: Holt, Rinehart & Winston.

Goldfried, M., & T. D'Zurilla (1969). A behavior-analytic model for assessment of competence. In S. Spielberger (Ed.), *Current topics in clinical and community psychology.* New York: Academic Press.

Goldman, R., & J. Goldman (1982). *Children's sexual thinking: A comparative study of children aged 5 to 15 years in Australia, North America, Britain and Sweden.* London: Routledge & Kegan Paul.

Goleman, D. (1983). The electronic Rorschach. *Psychology Today,* 35–43.

Goodwin, D. W. (1979). Alcoholism and heredity. *Archives of General Psychiatry, 36,* 57–64.

Gordon, W., I. Freidenbergs, L. Diller, M. Hibbard, C. Wolf, L. Levine, R. Lipkins, O. Ezrachi, & D. Lucido (1980). Efficacy of psychosocial intervention with cancer patients. *Journal of Consulting and Clinical Psychology, 48,* 743–759.

Gottman, J. M. (1979). *Marital interaction: Experimental investigations.* New York: Academic Press.

Gottman, J., & H. Markman (1978). Experimental designs in psychotherapy research. In S. Garfield & A. Bergin (Eds.), *Handbook of psychotherapy and behavior change: An empirical analysis.* New York: Wiley.

Gould, R. L. (1972). *Transformations: Growth and change in adult life.* New York: Simon & Schuster.

Green, S. K., & P. Sandos (1983). Perceptions of male and female initiators of relationships. *Sex Roles, 9,* 849–852.

Greenberg, J. B. (1979). Single parenting and intimacy: A comparison of mothers and fathers. *Alternative Lifestyles, 2,* 308–330.

Greene, J. G., & D. J. Cooke (1980). Life stress and symptoms at the climacterium. *British Journal of Psychiatry, 136,* 486–491.

Greif, G. L. (1985). Single fathers rearing children. *Journal of Marriage and the Family, 47,* 185–191.

Gruson, L. (1985). New laws and potential savings move employers to cut smoking on the job. *The New York Times,* 17.

Guntern, G. 1979). *Social change, stress and mental health in the Pearl of the Alps.* New York: Springer.

Gurin, G., J. Veroff, and S. Feld (1960). *Americans view their mental health.* New York: Basic Books.

Gutek, B. A. (1985). *Sex and the workplace.* San Francisco: Jossey-Bass.

H

Hackett, T., & N. Cassem (1975). Psychological management of the myocardial infarction patient. *Journal of Human Stress, 1,* 25–38.

Haley, J. (1971). *Changing families: A family therapy reader.* New York: Grune & Stratton.

Hall, C. S., G. Lindzey, J. C. Loehlin, & M. Manosevitz (1985). *Introduction to theories of personality.* New York: Wiley.

Hall, E. T. (1959). *The silent language.* Garden City, NY: Doubleday.

Hall, E. T. (1966). *The hidden dimension.* Garden City, NY: Doubleday.

Hammen, C. L. (1982). Gender and depression. In I. Al-Issa (Ed.), *Gender and psychopathology.* New York: Academic Press, 133–152.

Hansson, R. O., M. F. Knopf, E. A. Downs, P. R. Monroe, S. E. Stegman, & D. S. Wadley (1984). Femininity, masculinity, and adjustment to divorce among women. *Psychology of Women Quarterly, 8,* 248–260.

Hardin, G. (1968). The tragedy of the commons. *Science, 162,* 1243–1248.

Harlow, H. F., & M. K. Harlow (1966). Learning to love. *American Scientist, 54,* 244–272.

Harry, J. (1984). *Gay couples.* New York: Praeger.

Harter, S. (1982). The perceived competence scale for children. *Child Development, 53,* 87–97.

Hartley, D., & H. Strupp (1980). Verbal psychotherapies. In A. Kazdin, A. Bellack, & M. Hersen (Eds.), *New perspectives in abnormal psychology.* New York: Oxford University Press.

Hatcher, R. A., et al. (1986). *Contraceptive Technology, 1986–1987.* New York: Irvington Publ.

Hatfield, E. (1983). What do women and men want from love and sex? In E. R. Allgeier & N. B. McCormick (Eds.), *Changing boundaries: Gender roles and sexual behavior.* Palo Alto, CA: Mayfield, 106–134.

Hatfield, E. (1985). Physical attractiveness in social interaction. In J. A. Graham & A. M. Kligman (Eds.), *The psychology of cosmetic treatments.* New York: Praeger, 77–92.

Hatfield, E., D. Greenberger, J. Traupmann, & P. Lambert (1982). Equity and sexual satisfaction in recently married couples. *Journal of Sex Research, 18,* 18–32.

Hays, R. B. (1984). The development and maintenance of friendship. *Journal of Social and Personal Relationships, 1,* 75–98.

Heilbrun, A. B. (1981). *Human sex-role behavior.* New York: Pergamon Press.

Heiss, J. (1975). *The case of the black family: A sociological inquiry.* New York: Columbia University Press.

Heller, K. (1979). The effects of social support: Prevention and treatment implications. In A. Goldstein & F. Kanfer (Eds.), *Maximizing treatment gains.* New York: Academic Press.

Helzer, J. (1980). Methodological issues in the interpretations of the consequences of extreme situations. In B. Dohrewend & B. Dohrewend (Eds.), *Stressful life events and their contexts.* New York: Prodist.

Hendrick, C., S. Hendrick, F. H. Foote, & M. J. Slapion-Foote (1984). Do men and women love differently? *Journal of Social and Personal Relationships, 1,* 177–195.

Henley, N. M. (1977). *Body politics: Power, sex, and nonverbal communication.* Englewood Cliffs, NJ: Prentice-Hall/Spectrum.

Henrink, R. (1980). *The psychotherapy handbook.* New York: New American Library.

Hergenhahn, B. R. (1972). *Shaping your child's personality.* Englewood Cliffs, NJ: Prentice-Hall.

Herman, J. L. (1981). *Father-daughter incest.* Cambridge: Harvard University Press.

Hill, C. T., Z. Rubin, & L. A. Peplau (1976). Breakups before marriage: The end of 103 affairs. *Journal of Social Issues, 32,* 147–168.

Hill, J. P. (1980). The family. In M. Johnson (Ed), *Toward adolescence: The middle school years.* Chicago: University of Chicago Press.

Hite, S. (1976). *The Hite report.* New York: Macmillan.

Holland, J. L. (1977). *Manual for the Vocational Preference Inventory.* Palo Alto, CA: Consulting Psychologists Press.

Holland, J. L. (1979). *Professional manual for the self-directed search.* Palo Alto, CA: Consulting Psychologists Press.

Holland, J. L. (1984a). *Self-directed search: A Guide to educational and vocational planning.* Palo Alto, CA: Consulting Psychologists Press.

Holland, J. L. (1984b). *The occupation finder.* Palo Alto, CA: Consulting Psychologists Press.

Holland, J. L. (1985). *Making vocational choices: A theory of careers* (2nd ed.). Englewood Cliffs, NJ: Prentice-Hall.

Holmes, T., & R. Rahe (1967). *The social readjustment rating scale. Journal of Psychosomatic Research, 11,* 213–218.

Holroyd, K. A. (1978). Effects of social anxiety and social evaluation of beer consumption and social interaction. *Journal of Studies on Alcohol, 39,* 737–744.

Horner, M. (1969). Woman's will to fail. *Psychology Today, 3,* 36.

Horner, M. S. (1972). Toward an understanding of achievement-related conflicts in women. *Journal of Social Issues, 28,* 157–176.

Horney, K. (1950). *Neurosis and human growth: The struggle toward self-realization.* New York: Norton.

Horney, K. (1967). *Feminine psychology.* New York: Norton.

Horowitz, M. J., N. Wilner, & W. Alvarez (1979). Impact of event scales: A measure of subjective stress. *Psychosomatic Medicine, 41,* 209–218.

House, J. S. (1981). *Work stress and social support.* Reading, MA: Addison-Wesley.

Hudson, W. W., & W. A. Ricketts (1980). A strategy for the measurement of homophobia. *Journal of Homosexuality, 5,* 357–372.

Huesman, L. R., K. Lagerspetz, & L. D. Eron (1984). Intervening variables in the TV violence-aggression relation: Evidence from two countries. *Developmental Psychology, 20,* 746–775.

Hunt, M., & B. Hunt (1977). *The divorce experience.* New York: McGraw-Hill.

Hyde, J. S. (1981). How large are cognitive gender differences? A meta-analysis using w^2 and d. *American Psychology, 36,* 892–901.

Hyde, J. S. (1984). How large are gender differences in aggression? A developmental meta-analysis. *Developmental Psychology, 20,* 722–736.

Hyde, J. S. (1985). *Half the human experience* (3rd ed.). Lexington, MA: Heath.

Hyde, J. S. (1989). *Understanding human sexuality* (4th ed.). New York: McGraw-Hill.

I

Isaacs, W., J. Thomas, & I. Goldiamond (1960). Application of operant conditioning to reinstate verbal behavior in psychotics. *Journal of Speech and Hearing Disorders, 25,* 8–12.

J

Jacobson, E. (1938). *Progressive relaxation.* Chicago: University of Chicago Press.

Jacques, J. M., & K. J. Chason (1979). Cohabitation: Its impact on marital success. *Family Coordinator, 28,* 35–39.

Jaffe, J. H. (1980). Drug addiction and drug abuse. In A. G. Gilman, L. S. Goodman, & A. Gilman (Eds.), *The pharmacological basis of therapeutics* (6th ed.). New York: Macmillan.

Jahoda, M. (1979, August). The impact of unemployment in the 1930's and the 1970's. *Bulletin of the British Psychological Society, 32,* 309–314.

James, W. (1890). *The principles of psychology* (Vol. 1). New York: Holt.

James, W. H. (1981). The honeymoon effect on marital coitus. *Journal of Sex Research, 17,* 114–123.

Janis, I. L. (1982). *Counseling on personal decisions: Theory and research on short-term helping relationships.* New Haven, CT: Yale University Press.

Janis, I. L. (1983, February). The role of social support in adherence to stressful decisions. *American Psychologist, 38,* 143–160.

Janis, I. L., & L. Mann (1977). *Decision making: A psychological analysis of conflict, choice, and commitment.* New York: The Free Press.

Janoff-Bulman, R., & C. Timko (1987). Coping with traumatic events: The role of denial in light of people's assumptive world. In C. R. Snyder and C. E. Ford (Eds.), *Coping with negative life events.* New York: Plenum Press.

Johnson, P. (1974, May). *Social power and sex role stereotypes.* Paper presented at the meeting of the Western Psychological Association, San Francisco.

Johnson, P. (1976). Women and power: Toward a theory of effectiveness. *Journal of Social Issues, 32,* 99–109.

Johnson, P. B., & J. D. Goodchilds (1976, October). How women get their way. *Psychology Today,* 69–70.

Johnston, L. D., P. M. O'Malley, & J. G. Bachman (1984). *Highlights from drugs and American high school students: 1975–1983.* Washington, DC: National Institute on Drug Abuse.

Jones, M. C. (1924). The elimination of children's fears. *Child Development, 7,* 383–390.

Jones, S. E., & E. Yarbrough (1985). A naturalistic study of the meanings of touch. *Communication Monographs, 52,* 19–56.

Jones, W. H., S. A. Hobbs, & D. Hockenbury (1982). Loneliness and social skill deficits. *Journal of Personality and Social Psychology, 42,* 682–689.

Jordan, T. J., & N. B. McCormick (1988). The sexual irrationality questionnaire. In C. M. Davis, W. L. Yarber, & S. D. Davis (Eds.), *Sexuality-related measures: A compendium.* Lake Mills, IA: Graphic Publishing Co., 46–49.

Jourard, S. (1964). *The transparent self: Self-disclosure and well-being.* Princeton: Van Nostrand.

Jourard, S. M. (1971). *The transparent self* (Rev. ed.). New York: Van Nostrand Reinhold.

Jourard, S. M., & T. Landsman (1980). *Healthy personality: An approach from the viewpoint of humanistic psychology* (4th ed.). New York: Macmillan.

K

Kahn, R. L. (1981). *Work and health.* New York: Wiley.

Kalish, R., & D. K. Reynolds (1976). *Death and ethnicity: A psychocultural study.* Los Angeles: University of Southern California Press.

Kalmuss, D. (1984). The intergenerational transmission of marital aggression. *Journal of Marriage and the Family, 46,* 11–19.

Kamerman, S. B. (1984). Women, children, and poverty: Public policies and female-headed families in industrialized countries. *Signs: Journal of Women in Culture and Society, 10,* 249–271.

Kanfer, F., & C. Saslow (1969). Behavioral diagnosis. In C. Franks (Ed.), *Behavior therapy: Appraisal and status.* New York: McGraw-Hill.

Kaplan, H. S. (1974). *The new sex therapy.* New York: Brunner/Mazel.

Karasek, R. A. (1979). Job demands, job decision latitude and mental strain: Implications for job redesign. *Administrative Science Quarterly, 24,* 285–301.

Kastenbaum, R., & A. D. Weisman (1972). The psychological autopsy as a research procedure in gerontology. In D. P. Dent, R. Kastenbaum, & S. Sherwood (Eds.), *Research planning and action.* New York: Behavioral Publications.

Katz, P. A. (1986). Modification of children's gender-stereotyped behavior: General issues and research considerations. *Sex Roles, 14,* 591–602.

Katz, J., H. Weiner, T. Gallagher, & C. Hellman (1970). Stress, distress, and ego defenses. *Archives of General Psychiatry, 23,* 131–142.

Kaufman, H. G. (1982). *Professionals in search of work: Coping with the stress of job loss and underemployment.* New York: Wiley.

Kazdin, A. (1975). *Behavior modification in applied settings.* Homewood, IL: Dorsey Press.

Kazdin, A. E. (1980). Basic concepts and models of abnormal behavior. In A. E. Kazdin, A. S. Bellack, & M. Hersen (Eds.), *New perspectives in abnormal psychology.* New York: Oxford University Press.

Kelley, H. H. (1983). Love and commitment. In H. H. Kelley et al., *Close relationships.* New York: W. H. Freeman, 265–314.

Kelvin, P. (1977). Predictability, power, and vulnerability in interpersonal attraction. In S. Duck (Ed.), *Theory and practice in interpersonal attraction.* London: Academic Press, 355–378.

Kendler, K. S. (1983, November). Overview: A current perspective on twin studies of schizophrenia. *American Journal of Psychiatry, 140*(1), 1413–1425.

Keniston, K. (1975). Prologue: Youth as a stage of life. In R. Havinghurst & P. H. Dreyer (Eds.), *Youth.* Chicago: University of Chicago Press.

Kermis, M. D. (1984). *The psychology of human aging: Theory, research, and practice.* Boston: Allyn & Bacon.

Kessler, R., R. Price, & C. Wortman (1985). Social and cultural influences on psychopathology. *Annual Review of Psychology* (Vol. 36). Palo Alto, CA: Annual Review.

Kendall, P. (1983). Stressful medical procedures: Cognitive-behavioral strategies for stress management and prevention. In D. Meichenbaum & M. Jaremko (Eds.), *Stress reduction and prevention*. New York: Plenum Press.

Kendall, P., & K. Bemis (1983). Thought and action in psychotherapy: The cognitive-behavioral approaches. In M. Hersen, A. Kazdin, & A. Sellack (Eds.), *The clinical psychology handbook*. New York: Pergamon Press.

Kieslar, D. (1966). Some myths of psychotherapy research and the search for a paradigm. *Psychological Bulletin, 65*, 110–136.

Kimlicka, T., H. Cross, & J. Tarnai (1983). A comparison of androgynous, feminine, masculine, and undifferentiated women on self-esteem, body satisfaction, and sexual satisfaction. *Psychology of Women Quarterly, 7*, 291–294.

Kinney, J., & G. Leaton (1982). *Loosening the grip: A handbook of alcohol information* (3rd ed.). St. Louis: Mosby.

Kinsey, A. C., W. B. Pomeroy, C. E. Martin, & P. H. Gebhard (1953). *Sexual behavior in the human female*. Philadelphia: Saunders.

Kirkley, B. G., J. A. Schneider, W. S. Agras, & J. A. Bachman (1985). Comparison of two group treatments for bulimia. *Journal of Counseling and Clinical Psychology, 53*(1), 43–48.

Kivnick, H. Q. (1982). Grandparenthood: An overview of meaning and mental health. *Gerontologist, 22*, 59–66.

Kleinke, C. L., F. B. Meeker, & R. A. Staneski (1986). Preference for opening lines: Comparing ratings by men and women. *Sex Roles, 15*, 585–600.

Kleinke, C. L., R. A Staneski, & J. K. Mason (1982). Sex differences in coping with depression. *Sex Roles, 8*, 877–889.

Knapp, J. J., & R. N. Whitehurst (1977). Sexually open marriage and relationships: Issues and prospects. In R. W. Libby & R. N. Whitehurst (Eds.), *Marriage and alternatives: Exploring intimate relationships*. Glenview, IL: Scott, Foresman, 147–160.

Kohnberg, L. (1969). Stage and sequence: The cognitive-developmental approach to socialization. In D. Goslin (Ed.), *Handbook of socialization theory and research*. Chicago: Rand McNally.

Komarovsky, M. (1976). *Dilemmas of masculinity: A study of college youth*. New York: Norton.

Kram, K. E. (1983). Phases of the mentor relationship. *Academy of Management Journal, 26*(4), 608–625.

Kraus, N., & H. F. Geyer-Pestello (1985). Depressive symptoms among women employed outside the home. *American Journal of Community Psychology, 13*(1), 49–67.

Kubler-Ross, E. (1969). *On death and dying*. New York: Macmillan.

L

LaFrance, M., & C. Mayo (1979). A review of nonverbal behavior of women and men. *The Western Journal of Speech Communication, 43*, 96–107.

Lange, A. J., & P. Jakubowski (1976). *Responsible assertive behavior: Cognitive/behavioral procedures for trainers*. Champaign, IL: Research Press.

Langer, E. J., & J. Rodin (1976). The effects of choice and enhanced personal responsibility for the aged. A field experiment in an institutional setting. *Journal of Personality and Social Psychology, 34*, 191–198.

LaPlante, M. N., N. B. McCormick, & G. G. Brannigan (1980). Living the sexual script: College students' views of influence in sexual encounters. *Journal of Sexual Research, 16*, 338–355.

Larwood, L. (1985). Tracking stress in women managers. *Contemporary Psychology, 30*(2), 118–119.

Lasch, C. (1979). *The culture of narcissism*. New York: Norton.

Latane, B., & J. M. Darley (1968). Group inhibition of bystander intervention in emergencies. *Journal of Personality and Social Psychology, 10*, 215–221.

Lauer, J., & R. Lauer (1985, June). Marriages made to last. *Psychology Today*, 22–26.

Lawler, E. E. (1982). Strategies for improving the quality of work life. *American Psychologist, 37*, 486–493.

Lazarus, R. (1966). *Psychological stress and the coping process*. New York: McGraw-Hill.

Lazarus, R. (1972). *Behavior therapy and beyond*. New York: McGraw-Hill.

Lazarus, R. (1984a). Puzzles in the study of daily hassles. *Journal of Behavioral Medicine, 7*, 375–389.

Lazarus, R. (1984b). The costs and benefits of denial. In S. Breznitz (Ed.), *Denial of stress*. New York: International Universities Press.

Lazarus, R., & S. Folkman (1984). *Stress, appraisal, and coping*. New York: Springer.

LeGuin, U. K. (1969). *The left hand of darkness*. New York: Ace Books.

Leim, R., & P. Raymon (1982). Health and the social costs of unemployment. *American Psychologist, 37*, 1116–1124.

Leland, J. (1982). Gender, drinking, and alcohol abuse. In I. Al-Issa (Ed.), *Gender and psychopathology*. New York: Academic Press, 201–220.

Learner, M. J. (1974). Social psychology of justice and interpersonal attraction. In T. Huston (Ed.), *Foundations of interpersonal attraction*. New York: Academic Press.

Levinger, G. (1983). Development and change. In H. H. Kelley et al., *Close relationships*. New York: W. H. Freeman, 315–359.

Levinson, D., C. Darrow, E. Klein, M. Levinson, & B. McKee (1978). *The seasons of a man's life*. New York: Knopf.

Levitt, E. E., & A. D. Klassen (1974). Public attitudes toward homosexuality. *Journal of Homosexuality, 1*, 29–43.

Levy, L., & L. Rowitz (1973). *The ecology of mental disorder*. New York: Behavioral Publications.

Lewinsohn, P. M., R. F. Munoz, M. A. Youngren, & A. M. Zeiss (1978). *Control your depression*. Englewood Cliffs, NJ: Prentice-Hall.

Lewis, M., & J. Brooks (1975). Infants' social perceptions: A constructivist view. In L. B. Cohen and P. Salapatek (Eds.), *Infant perception: From sensation to cognition* (Vol. 2). New York: Academic Press.

Licht, B. B., & C. S. Dweck (1984). Determinants of academic-achievement: The interaction of children's achievement orientations with skill area. *Developmental Psychology, 20,* 628–636.

Liebert, R. M., J. M. Neale, & E. S. Davidson (1973). *The early window: Effects of television on children and youth.* New York: Pergamon Press.

Linehan, M., & K. Egan (1983). *Asserting yourself.* Toronto, Wiley.

Lips, H. M. (1981). *Women, men, and the psychology of power.* Englewood Cliffs, NJ: Prentice-Hall/Spectrum.

Liskin, L., & R. Blackburn (1986, July–August). AIDS—A public health crisis. *Population Reports,* Series L, No. 6, L193–L228.

Livson, F. B. (1976). Patterns of personality development in middle-aged women: A longitudinal study. *International Journal of Aging and Human Development, 7,* 107–115.

Lobel, B., & R. M. A. Hirschfeld (1984). *Depression: What we know.* DHHS Publication No. ADM 85–1318. Rockville, MD: National Institute of Mental Health.

Locke, H. J., & K. M. Wallace (1959). Short marital-adjustment and prediction tests: Their reliability and validity. *Marriage and Family Living, 21,* 251–255.

LoPiccolo, L. (1980). Low sexual desire. In S. R. Leiblum & L. A. Pervin (Eds.), *Principles and practice of sex therapy.* New York: Guilford Press.

LoPiccolo, J., & C. Lobitz (1972). The role of masturbation in the treatment of sexual dysfunction. *Archives of Sexual Behavior, 2,* 163–171.

M

Maccoby, E. E., & C. N. Jacklin (1974). *The psychology of sex differences.* Stanford, CA: Stanford University Press.

MacKinnon, C. A. (1979). *Sexual harassment of working women: A case of sex discrimination.* New Haven, CT: Yale University Press.

Mahoney, M. (1974). *Cognition and behavior modification.* Cambridge, MA: Ballinger.

Mahoney, M., & D. Arnkoff (1977). Cognitive and self-control therapies. In S. Garfield & A. Bergin (Eds.), *Handbook of psychotherapy and behavior change.* New York: Wiley.

Malan, D. (1979). *Individual psychotherapy and the science of psychodynamics.* London: Butterworth.

Marcia, J. E. (1980). Identity in adolescence. In J. Adelson (Ed.), *Handbook of adolescent psychology.* New York: Wiley.

Marin, P. (1975, October). The new narcissism. *Harper's.*

Markus, H. (1977). Self-schemata and processing information about the self. *Journal of Personality and Social Psychology, 35,* 63–78.

Markus, H., M. Crane, S. Bernstein, & M. Siladi (1982). Self-schemas and gender. *Journal of Personality and Social Psychology, 42,* 38–50.

Marlatt, G. A. (1976). Alcohol, stress, and cognitive control.

In C. D. Spielberger & G. Sarason (Eds.), *Stress and anxiety* (Vol. 3). Washington, DC: Hemisphere Publishing.

Marlatt, G. A., & J. R. Gordon (1980). Determinants of relapse: Implications for the maintenance of behavior change. In P. O. Davidson (Ed.), *Behavioral medicine: changing health lifestyles.* New York: Brunner/Mazel.

Marlatt, G. A., & J. R. Gordon (1985). *Relapse prevention: Maintenance strategies for addictive behavior change.* New York: Guilford Press.

Marshall, V. W. (1980). *Last chapters: A sociology of aging and dying.* Monterey, CA: Brooks/Cole.

Maslow, A. H. (1970). *Motivation and personality* (2nd ed.). New York: Harper.

Mason, J. (1971). A re-evaluation of the concept of "nonspecificity" in stress theory. *Journal of Psychiatric Research, 8,* 323–333.

Mason, J. (1975). A historical view of the stress field. *Journal of Human Stress, 1,* 6–12.

Masson, J. (1984). *The assault on truth: Freud's suppression of the seduction theory.* New York: Farrar, Straus & Giroux.

Masters, W. H., & V. Johnson (1966). *Human sexual response.* Boston: Little, Brown.

Masters, W. H., & V. Johnson (1970). *Human sexual inadequacy.* Boston: Little, Brown.

Masters, W. H., & V. Johnson (1979). *Homosexuality in perspective.* Boston: Little, Brown.

Mathews, A., M. Gelder, & D. Johnston (1981). *Agoraphobia: Nature and treatment.* London: Tavistock Press.

Mayer-Gross, W., E. Slater, & M. Roth (1969). *Clinical psychiatry* (3rd ed.). Baltimore: Williams & Wilkens. Revised and reprinted (1977), Bailliere, Tindall, London.

Mayle, P., A. Robins, & P. Walter (1973). *Where did I come from?* Secaucus, NJ: Lyle Stuart.

McAdoo, H. P. (1980). Black mothers and the extended family support network. In L. Rodgers-Rose (Ed.), *The black woman.* Beverly Hills, CA: Sage, 125–144.

McCaghy, C. H. (1971). Child molesting. *Sexual Behavior, 1,* 16–24.

McClelland, D. C. (1975). *Power: The inner experience.* New York: Irvington Publ.

McClelland, D. C. (1982). The need for power, sympathetic activation, and illness. *Motivation and Emotion, 6,* 31–41.

McClelland, D. C., J. W. Atkinson, R. A. Clark, & E. L. Lowell (1953). *The achievement motive.* New York: Appleton-Century-Crofts.

McCormick, N. B. (1979). Come-ons and put-offs: Unmarried students' strategies for having and avoiding sexual intercourse. *Psychology of Women Quarterly, 4,* 194–211.

McCormick, N. B. (1987). Sexual scripts: Social and therapeutic implications. *Sexual and Marital Therapy, 2,* 3–27.

McCormick, N. B., G. G. Brannigan, & M. N. LaPlante (1984). Social desirability in the bedroom: Role of approval motivation in sexual relationships. *Sex Roles, 11,* 303–314.

McCormick, N. B., & C. J. Jesser (1983). The courtship game:

Power in the sexual encounter. In E. R. Allgeier & N. B. McCormick (Eds.), *Changing boundaries: Gender roles and sexual behavior.* Palo Alto, CA: Mayfield, 64–86.

McCormick, N. B., T. Perper, & A. J. Jones (1983, April). *Bar hopping as science: Results and methodological issues related to naturalistic observational research in bars.* Paper presented at the Eastern Region conference of the Society for the Scientific Study of Sex, Philadelphia.

McMurty, J. (1977). Monogamy: A critique. In R. W. Libby & R. N. Whitehurst (Eds.), *Marriages and alternatives: Exploring intimate relationships.* Glenview, IL: Scott, Foresman, 1–13.

McNeil, E. B. (1967). *The quiet furies: Man and disorder.* Englewood Cliffs, NJ: Prentice-Hall.

McWhirter, D. P., & A. M. Mattison (1984). *The male couple: How relationships develop.* Englewood Cliffs, NJ: Prentice-Hall.

Mehrabian, A. (1971). *Silent messages.* Belmont, CA: Wadsworth.

Mehrabian, A. (1980). *Basic dimensions for a general psychological theory: Implications for personality, social, environmental, and developmental studies.* Cambridge, MA: Oelgeschlager, Gunn, & Hain.

Mehrabian, A., & S. Ksionzky (1974). *A theory of affiliation.* Lexington, MA: Heath.

Meichenbaum, D. (1977). *Cognitive behavior modification: An integrative approach.* New York: Plenum Press.

Meichenbaum, D. (1985). *Stress inoculation training: A clinical guidebook.* New York: Pergamon Press.

Meichenbaum, D., & M. Jaremko (1983). *Stress reduction and prevention.* New York: Plenum Press.

Menninger, K. (1959). Hope. *American Journal of Psychiatry, 116,* 481–491.

Middleton, R., & S. Putney (1970). Dominance in decisions in the family: Race and class differences. In C. V. Willie (Ed.), *The family life of black people.* Columbus, OH: Merrill Publishing Co., 16–22.

Milgram, S. (1974). *Obedience to authority.* New York: Harper & Row.

Miller, B. (1979). Gay fathers and their children. *Family Coordinator, 28,* 544–552.

Miller, W. R., & R. F. Munoz (1982). *How to control your drinking* (Rev. ed.). Albuquerque, NM: University of New Mexico Press.

Millon, T. (1981). *Disorders of personality.* New York: Wiley.

Minuchin, S. (1974). *Families and family therapy.* Cambridge: MA: Harvard University Press.

Mischel, W. (1968). *Personality and assessment.* New York: Holt, Rinehart & Winston.

Mischel, W. (1970). Sex-typing and socialization. In P. H. Mussen (Ed.), *Carmichael's manual of child psychology* (3rd ed., Vol. 2). New York: Wiley, 3–72.

Mischel, W. (1977). Self-control and the self. In T. Mischel (Ed.), *The self: Psychological and philosophical issues.* Towata, NJ: Rowman & Littlefield.

Mischel, W. (1986). *Introduction to personality* (4th ed.). New York: Holt, Rinehart & Winston.

Mischel, W., & H. Mischel (1971). The nature and development of psychological sex differences. In G. Lesser (Ed.), *Psychology and educational practice.* Glenview, IL: Scott, Foresman, 357–379.

Money, J., & P. Tucker (1975). *Sexual signatures: On being a man or a woman.* Boston: Little, Brown.

Moore, M. M. (1985). Nonverbal courtship patterns in women: context and consequences. *Ethology and Sociobiology, 6,* 237–247.

Moreno, J. (1968). Group psychodrama and community-centered counseling. In G. Gazda (Ed.), *Basic approaches in group psychotherapy and group counseling.* Springfield, IL: Charles C. Thomas.

Morris, D. (1977). *Man watching: A field guide to human behavior.* New York: Harry N. Abrams.

Murray, T. E. (1985). The language of singles bars. *American Speech, 60,* 17–30.

Mussen, P. H., J. J. Conger, J. Kagan, & A. Huston (1984). *Child development and personality* (6th ed.). New York: Harper & Row.

N

Naisbett, J. (1984). *Megatrends: Ten new directions transforming our lives.* New York: Warner Books.

Neugarten, B. L. (1976). *The psychology of aging: An overview.* Master lectures on developmental psychology. Washington, DC: American Psychological Association.

Neugarten, B. L., B. Wood, F. J. Kraines, & B. Loomis (1963). Women's attitudes toward the menopause. *Vita Humana, 6,* 140–151.

Neuhaus, R., & R. Neuhaus (1982). *Successful aging.* New York: Wiley.

Newcomb, M. D. (1981). Heterosexual cohabitation relationships. In S. Duck & R. Gilmour (Eds.), *Personal relationships 1: Studying personal relationships.* London: Academic Press, 131–164.

Newcomb, M. D., & P. M. Bentler (1980). Assessment of personality and demographic aspects of cohabitation and marital success. *Journal of Personality Assessment, 44,* 11–24.

Newcomb, M. D., & P. M. Bentler (1981). Marital breakdown. In S. Duck & R. Gilmour (Eds.), *Personal relationships 3: Personal relationships in disorder.* London: Academic Press, 57–94.

Newcomb, T. M. (1961). *The acquaintance process.* New York: Holt, Rinehart & Winston.

Newman, B. M., & P. R. Newman (1984). *Development through life: A psychosocial approach* (3rd ed.). Homewood, IL: Dorsey Press.

Nickols, S. Y., & E. J. Metzen (1983). Impact of wives' employment upon husbands' housework. *Journal of Family Issues, 3,* 199–216.

Nicol, S. E., & I. I. Gottesman (1983). Clues to the genetics and neurobiology of schizophrenia. *American Scientist, 71,* 398–404.

Nisbett, R. E., & L. D. Ross (1980). *Human inference: Strategies* *and shortcomings of social judgment.* Englewood Cliffs, NJ: Prentice-Hall.

Novaco, B. (1977). Stress inoculation: A cognitive therapy for anger and its application to a case of depression. *Journal of Consulting and Clinical Psychology, 45,* 600-608.

O

O'Neill, N., & G. O'Neill (1972). *Open marriage: A new life style for couples.* New York: M. Evans & Company.

Orlofsky, J. L., J. E. Marcia, & I. M. Lesser (1973). Ego identity status and intimacy versus isolation crisis of young adulthood. *Journal of Personality and Social Psychology, 27,* 211-219.

P

Parkes, C. (1972). *Bereavement.* New York: International Universities Press.

Parsons, J. E. (1980). Psychosexual neutrality: Is anatomy destiny? In J. E. Parsons (Ed.), *The psychology of sex differences and sex roles.* New York: Hemisphere/McGraw-Hill, 3-29.

Parsons, J. E. (1983). Sexual socialization and gender roles in childhood. In E. R. Allegeier, & N. B. McCormick (Eds.), *Changing boundaries: Gender roles and sexual behavior.* Palo Alto, CA: Mayfield, 19-48.

Paul, G., & R. Lentz (1977). *Psychosocial treatment of chronic mental patients: Milieu versus social learning programs.* Cambridge, MA: Harvard University Press.

Pearlin, L., & C. Schooler (1978). The structure of coping. *Journal of Health and Social Behavior, 19,* 2-21.

Peele, S., & A. Brodsky (1975). *Love and addiction.* New York: New American Library/Signet.

Peplau, L. A. (1976a). Fear of success in dating couples. *Sex Roles, 2,* 249-258.

Peplau, L. A. (1976b). Impact of fear of success and sex-role attitudes on women's competitive achievement. *Journal of Personality and Social Psychology, 34,* 561-568.

Peplau, L. A. (1979, April). *Homosexual love relationships: A comparison of men and women.* Paper presented at the meeting of the Pacific Sociological Association, Anaheim, CA.

Peplau, L. A. (1982). Research on homosexual couples: An overview. *Journal of Homosexuality, 8,* 3-7.

Peplau, L. A. (1983). Roles and gender. In H. H. Kelley et al., *Close relationships.* New York: W. H. Freeman, 220-264.

Peplau, L. A., & S. D. Cochran (1980, September). *Sex differences in values concerning love relationships.* Paper presented at the meeting of the American Psychological Association, Montreal.

Peplau, L. A., S. D. Cochran, & V. Mays (1986, August). *Satisfaction in the intimate relationships of black lesbians.* Paper presented at the annual meeting of the American Psychological Association, Washington, DC.

Peplau, L. A., S. Cochran, K. Rook, & C. Padesky (1978). Loving women: Attachment and autonomy in lesbian relationships. *Journal of Social Issues, 34,* 7-27.

Peplau, L. A., & S. L. Gordon (1983). The intimate relation-ships of lesbians and gay men. In E. R. Allgeier & N. B. McCormick (Eds.), *Changing boundaries: Gender roles and sexual behavior.* Palo Alto, CA: Mayfield, 226-244.

Peplau, L. A., & S. L. Gordon (1985). Women and men in love: Sex differences in close heterosexual relationships. In V. E. O'Leary, R. K. Unger, & B. S. Wallston (Eds.), *Women, gender, and social psychology.* Hillsdale, NJ: Lawrence Erlbaum, 257-292.

Peplau, L. A., Z. Rubin, & C. T. Hill (1977). Sexual intimacy in dating relationships. *Journal of Social Issues, 33,* 86-109.

Perlmutter, M., & E. Hall (1985). *Adult development and aging.* New York: Wiley.

Perper, T. (1985). *Sex signals: The biology of love.* Philadelphia: ISI Press.

Perri, M. G. (1985). Self-change strategies for the control of addictive behaviors. In S. Shiffman & T. A. Wills (Eds.), *Coping and substance use.* Orlando, FL: Academic Press.

Peterson, D. (1968). *The clinical study of social behavior.* Englewood Cliffs, NJ: Prentice-Hall.

Pettigrew, T. F. (1964). *A profile of the Negro American.* Princeton, NJ: Van Nostrand.

Phares, E. J. (1978). Locus of control. In H. London & J. E. Exner (Eds.), *Dimensions of personality.* New York: Wiley-Interscience.

Phares, E. J. (1988). *Introduction to personality* (2nd ed.). Glenview, IL: Scott, Foresman.

Phares, E. J., & N. Erskine (1984). The measurement of selfism. *Educational and Psychological Measurement, 44,* 597-608.

Phillis, D. E., & P. J. Stein (1983). Sink or swing? The lifestyles of single adults. In E. R. Allgeier & N. B. McCormick (Eds.), *Changing boundaries: Gender roles and sexual behavior.* Palo Alto, CA: Mayfield, 202-225.

Piaget, J. (1970). Piaget's theory. In P. Mussen (Ed.), *Carmichael's manual of child psychology.* New York: Wiley.

Piaget, J. (1977). *The development of thought: Equilibrium of cognitive structures.* New York: Viking Press.

Piotrkowski, C. S. (1979). *Work and the family system.* New York: Macmillan.

Piotrkowski, C. S., & R. L. Repetti (1984). Dual-earner families. In C. S. Piotrkowski & R. L Repetti (Eds.), *Women and the family: Two decades of change.* New York: The Haworth Press.

Platt, J. (1973). Social traps. *American Psychologist, 28,* 641-651.

Pleck, J. H. (1981). *The myth of masculinity.* Cambridge, MA: MIT Press.

Pleck, J. H. (1985). *Working wives/Working husbands.* Beverly Hills, CA: Sage.

Polivy, J., & C. P. Herman (1985). Dieting and binging: A causal analysis. *American Psychologist, 40*(2), 193-201.

Price, R. H. (1985). Work and community. *American Journal of Community Psychology, 13*(1), 1-12.

Price, R. H., M. Glickstein, & D. L. Horton (1987). *Principles of psychology* (2nd ed.). Glenview, IL: Scott, Foresman.

Price, R. H., & S. J. Lynn (1986). *Abnormal psychology in the human context* (2nd ed.). Homewood, IL: The Dorsey Press.

Q

Quinn, R. P., & T. W. Mangione (1973). *The 1967–1970 quality of employment study.* Ann Arbor, MI: Survey Research Center, University of Michigan.

Quinn, R. P., & G. L. Staines (1979). *The 1977 quality of employment survey.* Ann Arbor, MI: Institute for Social Research, University of Michigan.

Quinn, R. P., T. Walsh, & D. L. K. Hahn (1977). *The 1972–1973 quality of employment survey: Continuing chronicles of an unfinished enterprise.* Ann Arbor, MI: Survey Research Center, University of Michigan.

R

Rainwater, L. (1965). *Family design: Marital sexuality, family size and contraception.* Chicago: Aldine.

Rappaport, J. (1977). *Community psychology: Values, research and action.* New York: Holt, Rinehart & Winston.

Raskin, N. J. (1985). Client-centered therapy. In S. J. Lynn & J. P. Garske (Eds.), *Contemporary psychotherapies: Models and methods.* Columbus, OH: Merrill Publishing Co.

Raths, L. E., M. Harmin, & S. B. Simon (1978). *Values and teaching* (2nd ed.). Columbus, OH: Merrill Publishing Co.

Raven, B. H. (1965). Social influence and power. In I. D. Steiner & M. Fishbein (Eds.), *Current studies in social psychology.* New York: Holt, 371–382.

Razran, G. H. S (1940). Conditioned response changes in rating and appraising sociopolitical slogans. *Psychological Bulletin, 37,* 481.

Regier, D. A., J. K. Meyers, M. Kramer, L. N. Robins, D. G. Blazer, R. L. Hough, W. W. Eaton, & B. Z. Locke (1984). The NIMH epidemiologic catchment area program. *Archives of General Psychiatry, 41*(10), 934–941.

Rice, F. P. (1986). *Adult development and aging.* Boston: Allyn & Bacon.

Richmond-Abbott, M. (1983). *Masculine and feminine: Sex roles over the life cycle.* Reading, MA: Addison-Wesley.

Riggio, R. E., & S. B. Woll (1984). The role of nonverbal cues and physical attractiveness in the selection of dating partners. *Journal of Social and Personal Relationships, 1,* 347–359.

Risman, B. J., C. T. Hill, Z. Rubin, & L. A. Peplau (1981). Living together in college: Implications for courtship. *Journal of Marriage and the Family, 43,* 77–83.

Ritchie, J. M. (1980). The aliphatic alcohols. In A. G. Gilman, L. S. Goodman, & A. Gilman (Eds.), *The pharmacological basis of therapeutics* (6th ed.). New York: Macmillan.

Robey, B., & C. Russell (1984, March). A portrait of the American worker. *American Demographics,* 17–21.

Robins, L. (1980). Sturdy childhood predictors of adult outcomes: Replications from longitudinal studies. In J. Barrett (Ed.), *Stress and mental disorder.* New York: Raven Press.

Robinson, C. C., & J. T. Morris (1986). The gender-stereotyped nature of Christmas toys received by 36-, 48-, and 60-month-old children: A comparison between nonrequested vs. requested toys. *Sex Roles, 15,* 21–32.

Rodgers, J. E. (1982). Roots of madness: The schizophrenics's reality is not ours. *Science, 82,* 85–91.

Rodgers-Rose, L. (1980). Dialects of black male-female relationships. In L. Rodgers-Ross (Ed.), *The black woman.* Beverly Hills, CA: Sage, 251–263.

Rodin, J., & E. J. Langer (1977). Long-term effects of a control-relevant intervention with the institutionalized aged. *Journal of Personality and Social Psychology, 35,* 897–902.

Rogers, C. R. (1947). Some observations on the organization of personality. *American Psychologist, 2,* 358–368.

Rogers, C. R. (1951). *Client-centered therapy.* Boston: Houghton Mifflin.

Rogers, C. R. (1959). A theory of therapy, personality, and interpersonal relationships as developed in the client-centered framework. In S. Koch (3rd ed.), *Psychology: A study of a science* (Vol. 3). New York: McGraw-Hill.

Rogers, C. R. (1963). The actualizing tendency in relation to "motives"; and to consciousness. In M. Jones (Ed.), *Nebraska symposium on motivation* (Vol. 2). Lincoln, NE: University of Nebraska Press.

Rogers, C. R. (1980). *A way of being.* Boston: Houghton Mifflin.

Rogers, D. (1985). *Adolescents and youth* (5th ed.). Englewood Cliffs, NJ: Prentice-Hall.

Rokeach, M. (1973). *The nature of human values.* New York: Free Press.

Romer, N. (1977). Sex-related differences in the development of the motive to avoid success, sex role identity, and performance in competitive and noncompetitive conditions. *Psychology of Women Quarterly, 1,* 260–272.

Rosenblatt, P. C. (1974). Cross-cultural perspective on attraction. In T. L. Huston (Ed.), *Foundations of interpersonal attraction.* New York: Academic Press, 79–95.

Ross, J. (1985). Marriage preparation. In W. Dryden (Ed.), *Marital therapy in Britain: Special areas* (Vol. 2). London: Harper & Row, 149–171.

Rotter, J. B. (1954). *Social learning and clinical psychology.* Englewood Cliffs, NJ: Prentice-Hall.

Rotter, J. B. (1966). Generalized expectancies for internal versus external control of reinforcement. *Psychological Monographs, 80*(1, whole No. 609).

Rotter, J. B. (1971). Generalized expectancies for interpersonal trust. *American Psychologist, 26,* 443–452.

Rotter, J. B., J. E. Chance, & J. E. Phares (Eds.) (1972). *Applications of a social learning theory of personality.* New York: Holt, Rinehart & Winston.

Rubin, L. B. (1976). *Worlds of pain: Life in the working class family.* New York: Basic Books.

Rubin, L. B. (1985). *Just friends: The role of friendship in our lives.* New York: Harper & Row.

Rubin, Z. (1973). *Liking and loving: An invitation to social psychology.* New York: Holt.

Rubin, Z. (1974). From liking to loving: Patterns of attraction in dating relationships. In T. L. Huston (Ed.), *Foundations of interpersonal attraction.* New York: Academic Press, 383–402.

Rubin, Z., C. T. Hill, L. A. Peplau, & C. Dunkel-Schetter (1980). Self-disclosure in dating couples: Sex roles and the ethic of openness. *Journal of Marriage and the Family, 42,* 305–318.

Rush, A. J., M. Khatami, & A. J. Beck (1975). Cognitive and behavior therapy in chronic depression. *Behavior Therapy, 6,* 398–404.

Russek, H. I. (1962). Emotional stress and coronary heart disease in American physicians, dentists and lawyers. *American Journal of Medical Science, 243*(Part 6), 716–725.

Russell, D. (1975). *The politics of rape: The victim's perspective.* New York: Stein & Day.

Russell, D. E. H., & N. Howell (1983). The prevalence of rape in the United States revisited. *Signs, 8,* 688–695.

Russianoff, P. (1981). *Why do I think I am nothing without a man?* New York: Bantam.

Russo, N. F., & S. B. Sobel (1981). Sex differences in the utilization of mental health facilities. *Professional Psychology, 12,* 7–19.

S

Saghir, M., & E. Robins (1973). *Male and female homosexuality.* Baltimore: Williams & Wilkins.

Samelson, F. (1980). J. B. Watson's Little Albert, Cyril Burt's twins, and the need for a critical science. *American Psychologist, 35,* 619–625.

Sarrel, P., & W. Masters (1982). Sexual molestation of men by women. *Archives of Sexual Behavior, 11,* 117–132.

Satir, V. (1967). *Conjoint family therapy.* Palo Alto, CA: Science & Behavior Books.

Scanzoni, J. (1972). *Sexual bargaining: Power politics in the American marriage.* Englewood Cliffs, NJ: Prentice-Hall/Spectrum.

Schachter, S. (1959). *The psychology of affiliation.* Stanford, CA: Stanford University Press.

Schachter, S. (1982a). Don't sell habit-breakers short. *Psychology Today,* 27–33.

Schachter, S. (1982b). Recidivism and self-cure of smoking and obesity. *American Psychology, 37,* 436–444.

Schaffer, K. F. (1980). *Sex-role issues in mental health.* Reading, MA: Addison-Wesley.

Scheier, M. F., & C. S. Carver (1981). Private and public aspects of self. In L. Wheeler (Ed.), *Review of personality and social psychology* (Vol. 2). Beverly Hills, CA: Sage.

Schnitzer, P. K. (1977). The motive to avoid success: Exploring the nature of the fear. *Psychology of Women Quarterly, 1,* 273–282.

Schulz, D. A. (1970). The role of the boyfriend in lower-class Negro life. In C. V. Willie (Ed.), *The family life of black people.* Columbus, OH: Merrill Publishing Co., 231–243.

Schulz, R. (1976). Effects of control and predictability on the physical and psychological well-being of the institutionalized aged. *Journal of Personality and Social Psychology, 33,* 563–567.

Schulz, R., & B. Hanusa (1978). Long-term effects of control

and predictability-enhancing interventions: Findings and ethical issues. *Journal of Personality and Social Psychology, 36,* 1194–1201.

Seidman, L. J. (1983). Schizophrenia, and brain dysfunction: An integration of recent neurological findings. *Psychological Bulletin, 94*(2), 195–238.

Seligman, M. E. P. (1975). *Helplessness: On depression, development and death.* San Francisco: W. H. Freeman.

Selye, H. (1978). *The stress of life* (2nd ed.). New York: McGraw-Hill.

Seward, J. P., & G. H. Seward (1980). *Sex differences: Mental and temperamental.* Lexington, MA: Lexington Books/Heath.

Seyfried, B. A. (1977). Complementarity in interpersonal attraction. In S. Duck (Ed.), *Theory and practice in interpersonal attraction.* London: Academic Press, 165–184.

Seyfried, B. A., & C. Hendrick (1977). Need similarity and complementarity in interpersonal attraction. In S. Duck (Ed.), *Theory and practice in interpersonal attraction.* London: Academic Press, 271–283.

Sherif, M., & C. W. Sherif (1953). *Groups in harmony and tension.* New York: Harper & Row.

Sherman, J. A. (1980). Therapist attitudes and sex-role stereotyping. In A. M. Brodsky and R. T. Hare-Mustin (Eds.), *Women and psychotherapy: An assessment of research and practice.* New York: Guilford Press, 35–66.

Shiffman, S., & T. A. Wills (Eds.) (1985). *Coping and substance use.* Orlando, FL: Academic Press.

Sifneos, D. (1972). *Short-term psychotherapy and emotional crisis.* Cambridge, MA: Harvard University Press.

Silver, R. L., & C. B. Wortman (1980). Coping with undesirable life events. In J. Garber & M. E. P. Seligman (Eds.), *Human Helplessness: Theory and application.* New York: Academic Press.

Silverman, P. (1972). Widowhood and preventive intervention. *The Family Coordinator, 21,* 95–102.

Skinner, B. F. (1938). *The behavior of organisms.* New York: Appleton-Century-Crofts.

Sloane, R., P. Staples, A. Cristol, N. Yorkston, & K. Whipple (1975). *Psychotherapy versus behavior therapy.* Cambridge, MA: Harvard University Press.

Smith, E. J. (1982). The black female adolescent: A review of the educational career, and psychological literature. *Psychology of Women Quarterly, 6,* 261–288.

Smith, M., & G. Glass (1977). Meta-analysis of psychotherapy outcome studies. *American Psychologist, 32,* 752–760.

Snyder, C. R., & H. L. Fromkin (1980). *Uniqueness: The human pursuit of difference.* New York: Plenum Press.

Snyder, C. R., & G. R. Larson (1972). A further look at student acceptance of general personality interpretations. *Journal of Consulting and Clinical Psychology, 38,* 384–388.

Snyder, M., E. D. Tanke, & E. Berscheid (1977). Social perception and interpersonal behavior: On the self-fulfilling nature of social stereotypes. *Journal of Personality and Social Psychology, 35,* 656–666.

Spanier, G. B. (1983). Married and unmarried cohabitation in the United States: 1980. *Journal of Marriage and the Family, 45*, 277–288.

Spanier, G. B., & E. A. Anderson (1979). The impact of the legal system on adjustment to marital separation. *Journal of Marriage and the Family, 41*, 605–613.

Spanier, G. B., & P. C. Glick (1980). Paths to remarriage. *Journal of Divorce, 3*, 283–298.

Spanier, G. B., & P. C. Glick (1981). Marital instability in the United States: Some correlates and recent changes. *Family Relations, 31*, 329–338.

Spanier, G. B., & R. A. Lewis (1980). Marital quality: A review of the seventies. *Journal of Marriage and the Family, 42*, 825–839.

Spanier, G. B., R. A. Lewis, & C. L. Cole (1975). Marital adjustment over the family life cycle: The issue of curvilinearity. *Journal of Marriage and the Family, 37*, 263–275.

Spanier, G. B., & R. L. Margolis (1983). Marital separation and extramarital sexual behavior. *The Journal of Sex Research, 19*, 23–48.

Spanier, G. B., & L. Thompson (1984). *Parting: The aftermath of separation and divorce.* Beverly Hills, CA: Sage.

Spence, J. T., & R. L. Helmreich (1978). *Masculinity and femininity: Their psychological dimensions, correlates, and antecedents.* Austin, TX: University of Texas Press.

Spence, J. T., R. L. Helmreich, & J. Stapp (1974). The Personal Attributes Questionnaire: A measure of sex role stereotypes and masculinity-femininity. *JSAS Catalogue of Selected Documents in Psychology, 4*, 127.

Spitzer, R. L., A. E. Skodol, M. Gibbon, & J. B. W. Williams (1981). *DSM-III case book: A learning companion to the diagnostic and statistical manual of mental disorders* (3rd ed.). Washington, DC: The American Psychiatric Association.

Spranger, E. (1928). *Types of men.* Translated by P. Pigors. Halle, Germany: Niemyer.

Sproull, L. S., S. Kiesler, & D. Zubrow (1984). Encountering an alien culture. *Journal of Social Issues, 40*(3), 31–48.

Sternberg, R. J., & S. Grajek (1984). The nature of love. *Journal of Personality and Social Psychology, 47*, 312–329.

Stevens-Long, J. (1984). *Adult life: Developmental processes* (2nd ed.). Palo Alto, CA: Mayfield.

Stewart, R. B., & B. Davis (1972). *Slim chance in a fat world: Behavioral control of obesity.* Champaign, IL: Research Press.

Stone, A. A., & J. M. Neale (1984). New measure of daily coping: Development and preliminary results. *Journal of Personality and Social Psychology, 46*, 892–906.

Storms, M. D. (1981). A theory of erotic orientation development. *Psychological Review, 88*, 340–353.

Stricker, G. (1977). Implications of research for psychotherapeutic treatment of women. *American Psychologist, 32*, 14–22.

Streib, G. F., & C. J. Schneider (1971). *Retirement in American society.* Ithaca, NY: Cornell University Press.

Strupp, H. H., & J. L. Binder (1984). *Psychotherapy in a new key: A guide to time-limited dynamic psychotherapy.* New York: Basic Books.

Sullivan, H. S. (1953). *The interpersonal theory of psychiatry.* New York: Norton.

Swann, W. B., Jr., & C. A. Hill (1982). When our identities are mistaken: Reaffirming self-conceptions through social interaction. *Journal of Personality and Social Psychology, 43*, 59–66.

T

Tangri, S., M. R. Burt, & L. B. Johnson (1982). Sexual harassment at work: Three explanatory models. *Journal of Social Issues, 38*(4), 35–54.

Tarvis, C., & C. Wade (1984). *The longest war: Sex differences in perspective* (2nd ed.). New York: Harcourt Brace Jovanovich.

Taylor, S., J. Wood, & R. Lichtman (1983). It could be worse: Selective evaluation vs. a response to victimization. *Journal of Social Issues, 39*, 19–40.

Terkel, S. (1974). *Working* (Rev. ed.). New York: Avon Books.

Thoits, P. (1983). Dimensions of life events as influences upon the genesis of psychological distress and associated conditions: An evaluation and synthesis of the literature. In H. Kaplan (Ed.), *Psychological stress: Trends in theory and research.* New York: Academic Press.

Thomas, A., & S. Chess (1977). *Temperament and development.* New York: Bruner/Mazel.

Thomas, L. (1981, September 24). Unacceptable damage. *New York Review of Books, 3*.

Thompson, A. P. (1983). Extramarital sex: A review of the research literature. *Journal of Sex Research, 19*, 1–22.

Thompson, R. A., M. E. Lamb, & D. Estes (1982). Stability of infant-mother attachment and its relationship to changing life circumstances in a representative middle-class sample. *Child Development, 53*, 144–148.

Toffler, A. (1970). *Future shock.* New York: Random House.

Toffler, A. (1980). *The third wave.* New York: Morrow.

Toteson, D. C. (1981). Lithium and mania. *Scientific American, 244*, 164.

Turkington, C. (1984, October). Stepfamilies: Changes in the family tree can be for better or worse. *APA Monitor*, 8–9.

U

Udry, J. R. (1970). Marital instability by race, sex, education, occupation and income. In C. V. Willie (Ed.), *The family life of black people.* Columbus, OH: Merrill Publishing Co., 143–155.

United States Department of Commerce, Bureau of the Census (1983). *Statistical Abstract of the United States: 1984* (104th ed.). Washington, DC: U.S. Government Printing Office.

United States Department of Health & Human Services (1982). *The health consequences of smoking: Cancer.* Rockville, MD: U.S. Public Health Service.

United States Department of Health & Human Services (1983). *The health consequences of smoking: Cardiovascular disease.* Rockville, MD: U.S. Public Health Service.

United States Surgeon General (1979). *Healthy people: The surgeon general's report on health promotion and disease prevention.* U.S. Department of Health & Welfare, PHS Publication No. 79-55071. Washington, DC: U.S. Government Printing Office.

V

Vaillant, G. E. (1944). *Adaptation to life.* Boston: Little, Brown.

Vaillant, G. E. (1977). *Adaptation to life.* Boston: Little, Brown.

Vaillant, G. E. (1983). *The natural history of alcoholism: Causes, patterns, and paths to recovery.* Cambridge, MA: Harvard University Press.

Vaugh, C., & J. Leff (1976). The influence of family and social failure on the course of psychiatric illness: A comparison of schizophrenia and depressed neurotic patients. *British Journal of Psychiatry, 129,* 125-137.

Veroff, J., E. Douvan, & R. A. Kulka (1981). *The inner American: A self-portrait from 1957 to 1976.* New York: Basic Books.

Visotsky, H., M. Gross, & B. Lebovits (1961). Coping behavior under extreme stress. *Archives of General Psychiatry, 5,* 432-448.

W

Wagner, K. D., R. P. Lorion, & T. E. Shipley (1983). Insomnia and psychosocial crisis: Two studies of Erikson's developmental theory. *Journal of Consulting and Clinical Psychology, 51,* 595-603.

Waldron, I. (1982). Gender, psychological disorders, and morality. In I. Al-Issa (Ed.), *Gender and psychopathology.* New York: Academic Press, 321-335.

Walker, J. W., D. C. Kimmel, & K. F. Price (1980-81). Retirement style and retirement satisfaction: Retirees aren't all alike. *International Journal of Aging and Human Development, 12,* 267-281.

Wallach, M. A., and L. Wallach (1983). *Psychology's sanction for selfishness: The error of egoism in theory and therapy.* San Francisco: W. H. Freeman.

Wallerstein, J. S. (1983). Children of divorce: The psychological tasks of the child. *American Journal of Orthopsychiatry, 53,* 230-243.

Wallerstein, J. S. (1984). Children of divorce: Preliminary report of a ten-year follow-up of young children. *American Journal of Orthopsychiatry, 54,* 444-458.

Wallerstein, J. S., & J. B. Kelly (1980). Effects of divorce on the visiting father-child relationship. *American Journal of Psychiatry, 137,* 1534-1539.

Wasik, B. (1984). *Teaching parents effective problem-solving. A handbook for professionals.* Unpublished manuscript. Chapel Hill, NC: University of North Carolina.

Waterman, A. S., P. S. Geary, C. K. Waterman (1974). Longitudinal study of changes in ego identity status from the freshman to the senior year at college. *Developmental Psychology, 10,* 387-392.

Waters, H. F., & P. Malamud (1975, March 10). Drop that gun, Captain Video. *Newsweek, 85*(10), 81-82.

Watson, J. B. (1930). *Behaviorism* (2nd ed.). Chicago: University of Chicago Press.

Watson, J. B., & R. Rayner (1920). Conditioned emotional reactions. *Journal of Experimental Psychology, 3,* 1-14.

Watson, O. M. (1970). *Proxemic behavior: A cross-cultural study.* The Hague, Netherlands: Mouton & Co. N.V.

Weinberg, S. K. (1955). *Incest behavior.* New York: Citadel Press.

Weiner, E. H. (1980). *Sex role stereotyping in the schools.* Washington, DC: National Education Association.

Weis, D. L. (1983). "Open" marriage and multilateral relationships: The emergence of nonexclusive models of the marital relationship. In E. Macklin & R. Rubin (Eds.), *Contemporary families and alternative lifestyles: Handbook on research and theory.* Beverly Hills, CA: Sage, 194-215.

Weis, D. L., & J. Sacalis (1982). *The marriage and family scripts of young children.* Baltimore, MD: Johns Hopkins University, Center for Social Organization of Schools. ERIC Document Reproduction Service No. ED 217992.

Weitzman, L. J. (1979). *Sex role socialization: A focus on women.* Palo Alto, CA: Mayfield.

Wheeler, D. D., & I. L. Janis (1980). *A practical guide for making decisions.* New York: Free Press.

Whitam, F. L. (1983). Culturally invariable properties of the male homosexuality: Tentative conclusions from cross-cultural research. *Archives of Sexual Behavior, 12,* 207-226.

Whitbourne, S. K., & C. S. Weinstock (1979). *Adult development: The differentiation of experience.* New York: Holt, Rinehart & Winston.

White, R. W. (1976). *The enterprise of living: A view of personal growth* (2nd ed.). New York: Holt, Rinehart & Winston.

Wiggins, J. D., D. A. Lederer, A. Salkowe, & G. S. Rys (1983). Job satisfaction related to tested congruence and differentiation. *Journal of Vocational Behavior, 23,* 112-121.

Williams, F., R. LaRose, & F. Frost (1981). *Children, television, and sex-role stereotyping.* New York: Praeger.

Winter, D. G. (1973). *The power motive.* New York: Free Press.

Winter, D. G., & A. J. Stewart (1978). The power motive. In H. London & J. E. Exner (Eds.), *Dimensions of personality.* New York: Wiley-Interscience.

Wolpe, J. (1958). *Psychotherapy by reciprocal inhibition.* Stanford, CA: Stanford University Press.

Wooley, S. C., & O. W. Wooley (1980). Eating disorders: Obesity and anorexia. In A. M. Brodsky & R. T. Hare-Mustin (Eds.), *Women and psychotherapy: An assessment of research and practice.* New York: Guilford Press, 135-158.

Woolfolk, R., & F. Lehrer (1984). *Principles and practice of stress management.* New York: Guilford Press.

Worchel, S., V. A. Andreoli, & R. Folger, (1977). Intergroup cooperation and intergroup attraction: The effect of previous interaction and outcome of combined effort. *Journal of Experimental Social Psychology, 13,* 131–140.

Wortman, C. (1983). *Coping with victimization: Conclusions and implications for future research. Journal of Social Issues, 39,* 195–221.

Wortman, C. B., & R. C. Silver (1987). Coping with irrevocable loss. In G. R. VanderBos & B. K. Bryant (Eds.), *Cataclysms, crises, and catastrophes: Psychology in action.* Master Lecture Series (Vol. 6). Washington, DC: American Psychological Association, 185–235.

Wylie, R. (1984). Self-concept. In R. Gorsini (Ed.), *Encyclopedia of psychology* (Vol. 3). New York: Wiley-Interscience.

Y

Yalom, I. (1975). *The theory and practice of group psychotherapy.* New York: Basic Books.

Z

Zax, M., & E. Cowen (1967). Early identification and prevention of emotional disturbances in a public school. In E. Cowen, E. Gardner, & M. Zax (Eds.), *Emergent approaches to mental health problems.* New York: Appleton-Century-Crofts.

Zigler, E. F., & M. Finn-Stevenson (1987). *Children: Development and social issues.* Lexington, MA: Heath.

Zilbergeld, B. (1978). *Male sexuality.* Boston: Little, Brown.

Zubin, J., & B. Spring (1977). Vulnerability: A new view of schizophrenia. *Journal of Abnormal Psychology,* 103–126.

Zuboff, S. (1982). New world of computer-mediated work. *Harvard Business Review, 60*(5), 142–152.

Zuckerman, M. (1975). Belief in a just world and altruistic behavior. *Journal of Personality and Social Psychology, 31,* 972–976.

Acknowledgments

Credits for the illustrations and photographs not given on the page where they appear are listed below or in the References. All photographs not credited are the property of Scott, Foresman and Company.

Cover   Scott A. MacNeill for Scott, Foresman and Company.

PHOTO CREDITS

Chapter 1

5   Jean-Claude Lejeune
9   Marcia Weinstein
11   © Joel Gordon
13   Allan Tannenbaum/Sygma
15   Michael Weisbrot & Family
17   Jean-Claude Lejeune

Part 1 Opener

19   Jean-Claude Lejeune

Chapter 2

24   Bettmann Archive
32   © Universal Press Syndicate. Reprinted with permission. All rights reserved.
44   Michael Weisbrot & Family
48   Michael Weisbrot & Family
53   © 1988 Universal Press Syndicate. Reprinted with permission. All rights reserved.

Chapter 3

55   © Sidney Harris
65   © Universal Press Syndicate. Reprinted with permission. All rights reserved.
67   Marilyn Hamilton/Motion Designs Inc.
73   Jean-Claude Lejeune
77   Bruce Davidson/Magnum
82   Reprinted by permission of United Feature Syndicate
84   Marilyn Hamilton/Motion Designs Inc.

Chapter 4

99   Joseph A. DiChello
105   © Joel Gordon
109   © Sidney Harris
117   Comstock Inc./Tom Grill
119   Karen R. Preuss/Taurus

Part 2 Opener

123   Jean-Claude Lejeune

Chapter 5

127   © Sidney Harris
131   © King Features Syndicate. Reprinted with permission. All rights reserved.
133   © Joel Gordon
135   UPI/Bettmann Newsphoto
138   UPI/Bettmann Newsphoto
148   © Universal Press Syndicate. Reprinted with permission. All rights reserved.
152   © Sidney Harris
153   UPI/Bettmann Newsphoto

Chapter 6

159   © Sidney Harris
163   Janice Fullman/Picture Cube
171   Joan Liftin/Archive
177   Wide World Photo
184   © Sidney Harris
185   Janice Fullman/Picture Cube

Chapter 7

190   Bonnie Schiffman/Gamma Liaison
212   Paul Conklin
216   Paul Conklin

Chapter 8

227   Bettmann Archive
231   Joe McNally/Wheeler

237   Bettmann Archive
241   © Sidney Harris
247   Joe McNally/Wheeler

Part 3 Opener

249   Paul Conklin

Chapter 9

255   Michel Tcherevkoff/Image Bank
261   © Joel Gordon
269   © Sidney Harris
281   © Joel Gordon
284   Michel Tcherevkoff/Image Bank

Chapter 10

295   Barbara Pfeffer/Peter Arnold
314   Barbara Pfeffer/Peter Arnold

Chapter 11

322   © Sidney Harris

329   Comstock Inc./Tom Grill
343   © Michael O'Brien/Archive
348   Comstock Inc./Tom Grill

Chapter 12

359   Courtesy of Planned Parenthood Association,
      Chicago Area
363   © Sidney Harris
365   © Joel Gordon (both)
371   Tom Ebenhoh/Black Star
375   Centers for Disease Control, Atlanta
385   Tom Ebenhoh/Black Star

Chapter 14

421   Feiffer © 1982. Universal Press Syndicate.
      Reprinted with permission. All rights reserved.
425   Hal Franklin
432   UPI/Bettmann Newsphoto
433   Hal Franklin

Name Index

SUBJECT INDEX